MW00844219

VM/CMS
Concepts and Facilities

Ranade IBM Series

H. MURPHY • *Assembler for Cobol Programmers: MVS, VM,* 0-07-044129-4
H. BOOKMAN • *Cobol II,* 0-07-006533-0
J. RANADE • *DB2: Concepts, Programming, and Design,* 0-07-051265-5
J. SANCHEZ • *IBM Microcomputers Handbook,* 0-07-054594-4
M. CARATHANASSIS • *Expert MVS/XA JCL: A Complete Guide to Advanced Techniques,* 0-07-009816-6
P. DONOFRIO • *CICS: Debugging, Dump Reading and Problem Determination,* 0-07-017606-X
T. EDDOLLS • *VM Performance Management,* 0-07-018966-8
P. KAVANAGH • *VS Cobol II for Cobol Programmers,* 0-07-033571-0
T. MARTYN • *DB2/SQL: A Professional Programmer's Guide,* 0-07-040666-9
S. PIGGOTT • *CICS: A Practical Guide to System Fine Tuning,* 0-07-050054-1
N. PRASAD • *IBM Mainframes: Architecture and Design,* 0-07-050686-8
J. RANADE • *Introduction to SNA Networking: A Guide to VTAM/NCP,* 0-07-051144-6
J. RANADE • *Advanced SNA Networking: A Professional's Guide for Using VTAM/NCP,* 0-07-051143-8
S. SAMSON • *MVS: Performance Management,* 0-07-054528-6
B. JOHNSON • *MVS Concepts and Facilities,* 0-07-032673-8
A. WIPFLER • *Distributed Processing in the CICS Environment,* 0-07-071136-4
A. WIPFLER • *CICS Application Development Programming,* 0-07-071139-9
J. RANADE • *VSAM: Concepts, Programming, and Design,* Second Edition, 0-07-051244-2
J. RANADE • *VSAM: Performance, Design, and Fine Tuning,* Second Edition, 0-07-051245-0
J. SANCHEZ • *Programming Solutions Handbook for IBM Microcomputers,* 0-07-054597-9
P. DONOFRIO • *CICS Programmer's Reference,* 0-07-017607-8
M. CARATHANASSIS • *Expert MVS/ESA JCL: A Guide to Advanced Techniques* 0-07-009820-4
J. RANADE • *DOS to OS/2: Conversion, Migration, and Application Design,* 0-07-051264-7
K. BRATHWAITE • *Relational Databases: Concepts, Design and Administration* 0-07-007252-3
R.H. JOHNSON, R.D. JOHNSON • *DASD: IBM's Direct Access Storage Devices,* 0-07-032674-6
M. MARX, P. DAVIS • *MVS Power Programming,* 0-07-040763-0
G. HOUTEKAMER, P. ARTIS • *MVS I/O Subsystems: Configuration Management and Performance Analysis,* 0-07-002553-3
A. KAPOOR • *SNA: Architecture, Protocols, and Implementation,* 0-07-033727-6
D. SILVERBERG • *DB2: Performance, Design, and Implementation,* 0-07-057553-3
R. CROWNHART • *IBM's Workstation CICS,* 0-07-014770-1
C. DANEY • *Programming in REXX,* 0-07-015305-1
G. GOLDBERG, P. SMITH • *The REXX Handbook,* 0-07-028682-8
A. WERMAN • *DB2 Handbook for DBAS,* 0-07-069460-5
R. LEFKON, J. KNEILING, P. SOMERS • *Understanding CICS Internals,* 0-07-037040-0
A. FRIEND • *COBOL Application Debugging under MVS: COBOL and COBOL II,* 0-07-022453-6
L. BRUMBAUGH • *VSAM: Architecture, Theory, and Applications,* 0-07-008606-6

VM/CMS

Concepts and Facilities

Jeffrey Savit

McGraw-Hill, Inc.

New York San Francisco Washington, D.C. Auckland Bogotá
Caracas Lisbon London Madrid Mexico City Milan
Montreal New Delhi San Juan Singapore
Sydney Tokyo Toronto

This book is dedicated to Simcha Druck, for many years the president and guiding spirit of the Metropolitan VM Users Association. His efforts have made a lasting contribution to VM.

Library of Congress Cataloging-in-Publication Data

Savit, Jeffrey
VM/CMS: concepts and facilities / by Jeffrey Savit
p. cm.
Includes bibliographical references and index.
ISBN 0-07-054977-X
1. Operating Systems. 2. VM/CMS. I. Title.
QA76.76.063S357 1992
005.4'429—dc20 92-33744
CIP

1 2 3 4 5 6 7 8 9 0 DOC/DOC 9 9 8 7 6 5 4 3

ISBN 0-07-054977-X

The sponsoring editor for this book was Gerald T. Papke. Production supervisor was Katherine G. Brown. New York production supervisor was Suzanne Babeuf. This book was set in ITC Century Light.

Printed and bound by R.R. Donnelley & Sons Company

Contents

Acknowledgments

This section of the book gives me the opportunity to publicly thank members of the VM community. This community helped make VM/CMS become the valuable and important system it is today. I've benefited from the enhancements and information shared by members of the international "VM family," who interact continuously on the VMSHARE electronic conferencing system and meet at SHARE, the VM Workshop, and local groups like the Metropolitan VM Users Association (MVMUA).

I would like to acknowledge the past and continuing contributions, advice, and good company provided by the following individuals, most of whom I first "met" through VMSHARE or at MVMUA: Alan Ackerman, Bill Bitner, Ira and Pam Bland, Bob Bolch, Dave Boloker, Peter Carrier, Larry Chase, Robert Cowles, Mike Cowlishaw, Deborah Donovan, Simcha Druck, Arthur Ecock, Neale Ferguson, Jeff Fox, Janet Gobeille, Gabriel Goldberg, Serge Goldstein, Jonathan Goodblatt, Jeff Gribbin, John Hartmann, Sandra Hassenplug, Ted Johnston, Steve Jones, John Kinne Tom Klensk, Peter Koeppel, Jay Koonz, Barry Leiba, Charles Lickel, Paul Loftus, Anne-Marie Marcoux, Martha McConaghy, Chuck Morse, Bill Munson, Scott Nettleship, Dick Newson, Ross Patterson, Paul Russell, Barton Robinson, Sudhir Shah, Phil Smith III, Kent Taylor, Bill Temps, Eric Thomas, Joyce Tomaselli, Rick Troth, Melinda and Lee Varian, Brick Verser, John Wagner, Donna Walker, Harry Williams, and Romney White, Marty Zimelis.

I would also like to thank the reviewers of this book: Peter Fiore, Daniel Friedman, Gabriel Goldberg, Keith Landovitz, and Julie Tan, for their helpful comments. I also thank Hal Lorin for teaching me, at an impressionable age, how to appreciate system principles.

Finally, I would like to thank the "Renaissance Man of Merrill Lynch", series editor Jay Ranade, for his advice and encouragement.

Preface

This book explains the virtual machine (VM) computing environment. It discusses how VM is organized and operates, the functions and programming interfaces it provides, and programming and application design in the virtual machine environment. VM/ESA, the latest version of VM, is emphasized, although all versions of VM are discussed to illustrate the evolution of design.

VM's Significance in Computing

VM has a unique capability that sets it apart from other operating systems: it creates virtual machines for each of its clients, providing each VM user the image of a personal mainframe. Client applications under VM's Control Program (CP) run operating systems, rather than user processes run by other systems. Virtual machines on the same VM system can run any of IBM's mainframe operating systems: MVS, DOS/VSE, AIX, or VM itself. Therefore, the same computer system can be used for a wider variety of computing tasks than computers running a single operating system. Virtual machines are also called "guest" systems, because they are allocated computer resources by the CP "host".

Most VM users run the Conversational Monitor System (CMS), a single-user operating system designed to run in a virtual machine. CMS invented the personal computer style of computing, years before the advent of the desktop computer, by providing an easy-to-use, friendly, interactive, single-user environment that is flexible, easily programmed, and highly customizable. Because CMS runs in its own virtual machine, its users control their personal computing environments without interference from other users.

The virtual machine concept makes it possible to compartmentalize VM into different functional components, providing an elegant basis for computing innovation and simplicity. The Control Program manages real machine resources, while CMS and other operating systems provide file systems, editors, communications protocols, and other application interfaces needed in a computing environment. Because many operating system functions are implemented in virtual machines, rather than in CP, each component is more efficient, simple, and more easily understood than other operating systems. A well-designed, formal interface between CP and virtual machines fosters innovation by making it easy to change or replace system components.

Over the years VM has grown from a sparse but highly efficient vehicle for guest systems and interactive timesharing, to a richly functional, yet still efficient computing environment. VM pioneered key operating system concepts that are now widely accepted for modern operating systems, for example: virtualization of hardware resources and client-server style computing. VM continues to be the source of computing innovations: VM leads the mainframe world in supporting "open systems" and interoperability with workstations, and in implementing IBM's System Application Architecture (SAA).

VM is popular for end-user computing, client-server applications, and for allowing multiple system images to run on the same hardware, on systems ranging from desktop and departmental systems to supercomputers. More than 20,000 mainframe systems run VM, far more than MVS, the operating system most commonly associated with mainframes. Even in IBM's own computing sites, there are several times as many VM systems as MVS.

Intended Audience for this Book

When I started this book, I intended it for VM users and programmers who want to learn how VM works and how best to apply it. The book still retains that purpose. It is also a guide to VM/CMS that explains VM and how to exploit it.

However, as I worked on the book, I repeatedly returned to principles of operating systems, computing, and computer architecture that were crucial to VM's development or pioneered by VM. Gradually, the book took on a second purpose: to discuss the evolution of operating system principles from the VM perspective.

Consequently, this book also can be used in college-level courses on operating systems to provide an in-depth look at operating system and architectural concepts. It discusses operating system principles, including resource administration, virtual storage and virtual machine computing, storage management, resource management, file systems, communications methods, client-server applications, and other system-related topics.

The reader is not assumed to have prior knowledge of VM concepts and terminology. A working knowledge of VM is helpful to make the examples and concepts more "live," as is inevitable with any description of a computing environment, but VM-specific terms are explained as they are introduced.

What Is Included

Manuals from IBM and other vendors often list programming interfaces without structure or organization. If you know which command or subroutine to use, you can find excruciating detail on how to code the command or call, but not guidance in selecting the right command for the job. Product manuals rarely provide insight into how the system works, at least not at the level you need to best exploit or appreciate a system's capabilities.

VM/CMS Concepts and Facilities is a guide to key VM functions and programming interfaces. The book explains and expands on the technical information that appears in IBM manuals and source code. The goal is to provide context (and in a number of cases, history) to illustrate how VM works and to help the reader understand and use its facilities.

At the same time, concepts are explained in sufficient detail, and in vendor-independent language, to show the student of operating systems how a mature, commercially used operating system implements operating system concepts, explain the reasons for choices made by its developers.

A certain degree of selectivity, perhaps even favoritism, was involved in choosing subjects covered in detail. An operating system that has matured for years cannot be comprehensively covered in a single volume, regardless of its complexity. I've concentrated on subjects that have practical utility or help illustrate operating system or architectural concepts. These topics are discussed further and covered in deeper detail than subjects that I feel are mundane and generic to all systems.

Software Discussed

Unless further specified, "VM" refers to all VM versions used in 1992: the Virtual Machine/System Product (VM/SP), the Virtual Machine/System Product High Performance Option (VM/HPO), Virtual Machine/Extended Architecture System Product (VM/XA-SP), and Virtual Machine/Enterprise System Architecture (VM/ESA). VM/SP and HPO will sometimes be referred to as "370-mode" VM, since they use the System/370 architecture; VM/XA and VM/ESA will sometimes be referred to as "XA-mode" since they are based on System/370 extended architecture.

This book emphasizes VM/ESA, which consolidates and replaces previous VM versions. VM/ESA Version 1 Release 1.0 became available in mid-1991 with two varieties: the 370 feature and ESA feature. VM/ESA-370 feature is a replacement for VM/SP and a migration path to the "true" VM/ESA of the ESA feature. VM/ESA 370 feature is essentially the last version of VM/SP. Comments about VM/SP usually apply to VM/ESA 370 feature as well. VM/ESA Version 1 Release 2 was released in December 1992, and consists of only the ESA feature. All VM sites are expected to move, sooner or later, to VM/ESA.

A feature summary chart in Fig. 0.1 shows recent major versions of VM and their features. Since VM/XA and VM/ESA are so similar, most information related to VM/ESA applies equally to VM/XA. Exceptions are pointed out where needed.

Trademark Names

IBM, RACF, SQL/DS, VM/XA SP,VM/ESA, PS/2, System/370, ESA/370, ESA/390, System/390, OS/2, and Micro Channel are trademarks of the

Hardware supported	VM/SP VM/ESA-370	VM/SP with HPO	VM/XA SP VM/ESA-ESA
CPU models	9370, 43xx 303x, S/370	308x, 3090, 4381, 303x, S/370	308x, 3090 4381 (some models) ES/9000
Number CPUs	1 or 2	1 or 2	Up to 64
Real Storage	Up to 16MB Up to 32MB (ESA)	Up to 64MB CP control blocks only in low 16MB	Up to 512MB
Expanded Storage	Not applicable	For paging	For paging and minidisk cache
Virtual Storage	Up to 16MB	same as VM/SP	Up to 999MB (XA) Up to 2047MB (ESA) plus ESA dataspaces
Uses	370 mode CMS and guests.	same as VM/SP	370, XA, ESA CMS and guests.
Maximum channels	Up to 16	Up to 32	Up to 128
I/O devices	All current IBM device families, except 3390	Adds support for cached 3380	All current IBM devices

Fig. 0.1 VM versions.

International Business Machines Corporation. XMENU, V/SEG, and KPROBE are trademarks of VM Systems Group. XAMON and XAMAP are trademarks of Velocity Software, Inc. PROREXX, VMMONITOR, VMSECURE, and VM DIRECT are trademarks of Systems Center Inc. ACF2 is a trademark of Computer Associates, Inc. FOCUS is a trademark of Information Builders, Inc. DEC is a trademark of Digital Equipment Corporation. Apple and Macintosh are trademarks of Apple Corporation. UNIX is a trademark of Unix System Laboratories. KEDIT is a trademark of Mansfield Software Group. uni-XEDIT is a trademark of The Workstation Group. Personal REXX is a trademark of Quercus, Inc. Contact is a trademark of The Adesse Corporation. Novell is a trademark of Novell Corporation.

Notes on Words

In this book, the word "data" is unrepentantly used as a collective, singular noun (the phrase "data is" is used, instead of "data are"). Gender-free pronouns are used throughout.

Chapter

1

VM Concepts

VM has a tradition of flexibility and adaptability unparalleled by IBM's other operating systems. VM is the only operating system that runs on all models of the System/370 and System/390 processor lines, from the smallest to the largest configurations. VM provides an unequaled range of compatible, scaleable performance. VM applications have access to a wider range of computing power, without porting or recompiling, than applications written for any other system.

Consequently, VM is used in a wide range of mainframe and distributed environments. IBM customers license more than 20,000 copies of VM, far more than MVS. IBM itself uses VM more than any other 370/390 operating system, with (at year-end 1990) over 2,400 internal IBM mainframes and 25,000 MIPS (Millions of Instructions Per Second).[1] By comparison, MVS runs on only 550 systems, totaling 8,000 MIPS.

VM also has a wide range of application domains. With CMS, VM is used for interactive problem solving, program development, electronic mail and text editing, and numerically intensive computing, as well as commercial data processing and database applications. VM is also host to guest operating systems running the entire array of applications available on System/370 and 390 hardware. VM is used to support "guest" environments running other operating systems for production, test, and development.

---

[1]This book occasionally refers to "MIPS," as a rough measure of computing power, though they should more properly be described as "Meaningless Indicator of Performance." This is discussed further in Chapter 3, "System/370 and System/390 CPU Architecture."

VM's flexibility is due to its basis as a virtual machine operating system. This encouraged its authors to implement functions in separate components with formal interfaces between them, rather than in a single complex operating system. This caused VM to be designed as a modular system when this was still a revolutionary concept. In fact, "VM" is really a family of operating systems—VM's components—which cooperate with one another, instead of a single operating system responsible for everything.

This has helped keep each VM component relatively simple, compared to other operating systems. The Control Program (CP) component, which manages virtual machines and real hardware resources, doesn't have to worry about the file system or user interface. The Conversational Monitor System (CMS), which provides the user command language, program interface, and file system, doesn't concern itself with hardware control or distribution of resources to multiple users.

Separation of function has helped VM grow to handle tasks of increasing complexity without making complexity visible and intrusive everywhere. It has made it far easier for implementers to make enhancements to VM, since the compartmentalized nature of VM reduces the possibility of unforeseen side effects. This book will illustrate how this principle has helped VM respond and grow in a changing computing world.

Fundamental VM Concepts

VM systems are managed by a Control Program, called *CP*, which controls the real system. CP provides a *virtual machine* for each user of a VM system. A virtual machine is a simulated image of a complete System/370 or System/390 mainframe. Each user has an individual virtual machine and can start it, crash it, or run programs on it without interfering with other users.

Virtual machines are created when users *logon* to CP. CP services each virtual machine in turn by providing brief time-slices of CPU service (instruction processing time on the system's "central processing units") to each one, before switching to the next one.

The list of users able to logon to a VM system is described in the VM *directory*, a special file maintained by system administrators. The directory contains the *userid* and password for each user, and the virtual machine configuration each user is given.

Like real machines, virtual machines are specified with different amounts of storage and disk space. Each userid is also assigned *privilege classes* that specify which commands can be issued. System operator and administrator userids have system control privilege classes not given to general users. Numerous other processing options are also specified in each user's directory entry.

VM Components

VM is divided into *components* that implement different functions. This allows each component to be less complex than operating systems that provide all services from a common body of code. Isolation of the programs used to create these components, and well-defined interfaces between them, makes it easier to change one component without creating bugs in other components. In fact, it is common practice at many VM sites to upgrade to a new release of VM one component at a time. This reduces risk and makes it easier to debug problems.

The VM components are:

- CP—Control Program
- CMS—Conversation Monitor System
- GCS—Group Control System
- TSAF—Transparent System Access Facility
- AVS—APPC/VM VTAM Services
- DVF—Dump Viewing Facility

By far, the most important components are CP and CMS, and the majority of this book discusses them. The other components provide support roles that are either invisible to general users, or provide services to CMS applications.

The following paragraphs briefly introduce the components and discuss their characteristics. Subsequent chapters discuss them in detail.

CP—Control Program

CP is the only VM component that runs on the "bare" hardware. The other components operate within virtual machines running under CP, and use services CP provides.

The VM Control Program can be roughly divided into two functional areas:

- Real machine operation—Administers real computer system hardware, controlling system start-up and shutdown, and other support tasks. This is the role most like that performed by standard operating systems, and includes the traditional scheduling and dispatching of work, and execution of service requests from users.
- Virtual machine operation—Provides the illusion of a virtual machine for each logged-on user. In addition to facilities provided by real 370 and 390 computers, virtual machines have access to an array of programming services including I/O, debugging, and inter-user and inter-system program-to-program communication.

While CP is not formally divided into these two areas, most of its modules can be said to fall into one or the other of them, or into a number of "glue" functions that provide support infrastructure for both of them. We will investigate the concepts and facilities of these parts of CP in later chapters.

CMS—Conversational Monitor System

Most VM users interact with the *Conversational Monitor System* (CMS). CMS provides the following functions:

- Command language
- CMS file system commands and system calls for file access and directory services
- XEDIT—The system product editor
- Program management services for loading and executing programs
- Memory management services for allocating and returning virtual storage, and for loading and removing named segments of code and data shared among users.
- Interrupt services for handling error conditions and external events
- The REXX procedures language for writing *EXECS* (command procedures called "shell files," "CLISTS," or "batch files" in other systems). Older CMS EXEC and EXEC 2 languages are also supported. REXX is a complete programming environment; many CMS applications are written entirely in REXX.
- Screen and window services
- Application programmer interfaces, including services for writing cooperative applications. Recent additions to this interface are the APPC/VM program-to-program protocol, and CMS Pipelines. These are discussed in later chapters of this book.

In addition to its own program interfaces, CMS provides many program interfaces defined by MVS and DOS/VSE. "OS simulation" and "DOS simulation" in CMS provides enough compatibility to simplify developing and testing MVS and DOS/VSE applications under CMS, or moving applications between them and CMS.

CMS was a single-tasking operating system, though IBM recently shipped a version that provides processes and threads in the style of OS/2 and Mach. CMS also provides interrupt service routines that make it possible to write multithreaded applications.

GCS—Group Control System

GCS is a multitasking supervisor mostly used to implement the SNA product suite under VM. GCS provides emulation for MVS macros for I/O, storage, task, and program management. This allowed IBM to port to VM SNA related products like VTAM and NETVIEW, without rewriting the parts of these products that use these MVS facilities.

A few sites use GCS to create multitasking applications since CMS does not yet directly support multitasking. GCS is discussed in more detail in the section "Group Control System (GCS)" on page 332.

TSAF—Transparent System Access Facility

TSAF lets multiple VM systems in a TSAF collection share remote access to common resources, such as CMS files and SQL/DS databases. VM systems in a TSAF collection are connected to one another via communications lines, and use a protocol named *Advanced Program-to-Program Communication/VM* (APPC/VM). TSAF is discussed in further detail in Chapter 14, "VM Communications."

AVS—APPC/VM VTAM Services

AVS extends the scope of TSAF by allowing APPC/VM communication between VM and systems to flow over an SNA network. VM systems can share resources both with other VM systems and non-VM systems using the SNA LU6.2 protocol. AVS is discussed in Chapter 14, "VM Communications," and in the section "Advanced Program-to-Program Communication/VM (APPC/VM)" on page 372.

DVF—Dump Viewing Facility

DVF is a debugging tool used to process storage dumps from the other components. It provides the **DUMPSCAN** command, a dump reading and formatting program that displays storage dumps and formats the contents of control blocks. DUMPSCAN is programmable, and can be extended by programmer-written "macros" to automate diagnostic functions. DVF is almost exclusively used by system programmers, and is not further discussed in this book.

VM Contributions to Operating System Principles

VM introduced a number of key operating system principles, and has influenced the design of many system environments. The following sections describe some of the concepts developed, popularized, or proven effective on VM.

Virtual machines

VM pioneered the concept of the virtual machine by providing multiple computer images on a single physical computer. Virtual machines operate independently of one another, and may run different operating systems and even different computer architectures.

Each user of a VM system has the image of a System/370 or System/390 computer for private use, running its own operating system. The basis of the interface between VM's Control Program and users running on it is the System/370 or System/390 *Principles of Operation*, a formal and complete document specifying the behavior of IBM mainframes. This provides the important capability of being able to run different operating systems on the same computer for test, migration, or consolidation purposes, and have them operate as if they were individual real computer systems.

CP implements the 370 or 390 architecture for each user, with few restrictions, mostly involving dependency on specific CPU models' behavior and timing. In compensation, VM provides users with an "extended machine" that includes numerous useful facilities not present in real 370 or 390 computers.

CP virtualizes hardware, both directly emulating hardware facilities and providing abstract versions of their functions. For example, VM provides a compatible emulation of the System/390 and 390 hardware IPL (bootstrap load) function, and an abstraction of the concept that IPLs a previously saved system's memory image by its name, in a single step without a bootstrap process. This reduces CPU processing, and lets multiple users share a read-only reentrant copy of the same software. Most VM users run CMS from a shared *named saved system*.

CP provides abstractions for numerous facilities, sometimes with the purpose of eliminating messy details, and sometimes to provide an augmented virtual machine with features not present on any real machine. For example, CP provides I/O calls that relieve virtual machines of responsibility for real-machine details of disk device geometry, I/O error handling and interrupt processing. This is typical of I/O access methods provided by an operating system, but CP provides the same service to operating systems.

Abstractions that augment the virtual machine environment include VM's *IUCV* (Inter-User Communication Vehicle), which lets separate virtual machines communicate with one another via a message passing protocol, and its logical extension *APPC/VM* (Advanced Program-to-Program Communication), which lets virtual machines communicate with processes residing on the same or different systems, whether running VM (or IBM compatible hardware) or not.

Few systems provide virtualization as thoroughly as VM's Control Program, but the concept of abstracting hardware functions into virtualized capabilities has influenced computer science in many areas. Literature from other parts of the computing world sometimes refer to, for example, a "Smalltalk virtual machine" or a "virtual disk."

Micro-kernel supervisors

The innermost portion of an operating system is often referred to as its "nucleus" (especially for IBM systems) or its "kernel." The VM Control Program introduced and popularized the concept of a "micro kernel" operating system, used to provide a fundamental set of core primitives to processes running on top of it. Typically, the micro-kernel provides facilities for device control, real storage management, process management, and message passing between independent processes. This is very much the spirit of CP.

This is in contrast to operating systems in which most facilities are imbedded in the kernel. In such systems, like MVS and UNIX, facilities like the file system, database managers, security managers, per-process virtual storage management, and sometimes even editors, file utilities, and compilers are implemented in the kernel or require "hooks" to kernel facilities not available to "normal" programs. In VM, most of these functions are performed by virtual machines, with CP support for most low-level aspects of physical resources. In general operating system terms, many VM functions are implemented in *user space* instead of *kernel space*.

The micro-kernel approach has several advantages: the total operating system environment is layered, and each layer can be much simpler and easier to understand and construct than a composite system that performs all functions in one scope of control. Since parts of the system are implemented in separate compartments or layers, they can be replaced by component parts with the same function. A failure in a process outside the kernel is far less likely to crash the entire system than a failure in the kernel.

This is not to say that the goal is to keep the kernel as sparse as possible. The function set in the kernel must be rich enough to efficiently construct higher level services in user space, without including every conceivable function and producing another monolithic operating system.

A kernel-provided application interface that routes service requests from client to server, such as VM's IUCV, lets functions be implemented either by the kernel or by user processes. Functions may float between kernel space (CP) and user space (virtual machine) without altering application interfaces, depending on implementation choices concerned with performance trade-offs or refinements in functionality.

For example, CP once made all security decisions, but security and access control can now be routed to security manager virtual machines for additional flexibility and control. Remote terminal access was once built into CP, but is now provided by VTAM, VM/Pass-Through, and TCP/IP service machines. Printer support was once handled only by CP, which took print files from the system spool and sent them to channel-attached printers.

Remote printing is now provided by RSCS (Remote Spooling Communication Subsystem), and by AFP (Advanced Function Printing), which also provides sophisticated font, character set, and forms processing.

These subsystems let complicated tasks be performed without building the necessary support into CP, and let the subsystem builder employ the program interfaces available to virtual machines. Improving program services for virtual machines is a better investment than building program interfaces within CP, since a richer program interface for virtual machines is available to more developers.

On the other hand, VM/ESA's ISFC (Inter-System Facility for Communications) lets workstations communicate with VM applications at extremely high data transfer rates. I/O operations previously performed by a service virtual machine can be done directly via CP, thus reducing instruction path lengths, and allowing data to be transmitted at channel speeds. In this case, the opportunity for higher performance is the reason for moving the function into kernel space, where it becomes part of the augmented virtual machine model. Alternatively, inter-CPU message processing can be viewed as an innate system function that belongs in the kernel function set.

Kernel-based operating systems are now available in other system contexts. The Mach operating system provides an application interface largely compatible with UNIX, but with most facilities removed from the kernel. Other new operating systems, like Microsoft's Windows/NT, rediscover this CP design principle.

Interaction between microcode and software

As discussed in Chapter 3 "System/370 and System/390 CPU Architecture," most computer systems use a combination of hardware circuits and microcode, special programs imbedded in the computer, to implement the view of the computing system visible to its applications. Microcode can also provide high-performance implementations of heavily used software code sequences, a technique proven with VM.

Some aspects of virtual machine emulation could not be efficiently implemented purely in software. This led IBM to replace high-frequency CP code paths with microcoded routines, resulting in dramatic performance improvements. Microcode can speed up virtualization for the same reasons that a built-in "multiply" instruction is faster than multiplying by performing repeated addition in software. Microprogram instructions reside in fast control storage memory, can initiate multiple concurrent operations, and can directly address real CPU buses and data latches provided by the circuitry.

Microcode additions to System/370 were used repeatedly to improve VM performance. This concept was eventually used to increase performance of DOS/VSE, VS1, and MVS as well. Similar enhancements were provided for the APL interpreter via APL assist microcode on the 370/145 and 370/148, though this was not repeated on later CPUs. IBM processors and operating systems increasingly integrate the use of microcode and system software, a concept proven in VM. Almost all modern computers, including RISC workstations and personal computers, use microcoded routines to some extent.

Virtual storage

Virtual storage is a key operating system principle that profoundly affects all modern operating systems. Virtual storage lets programs address a range of contiguous storage addresses, independent of real storage assignments or the amount of storage actually installed on the computer. Virtual storage was not introduced by VM, but VM proved how effectively it could be used and pioneered its exploitation.

Before virtual storage, operating systems like OS/360 and pre-Berkeley versions of UNIX shared real storage by "swapping" entire application program images in and out of storage, or simply reserving a contiguous block of real storage for an application's duration, whether it was used or not. These operating systems had to move applications in and out of storage on an "all or nothing" basis; more conservative and batch-oriented systems simply left applications in storage until they completed. Storage fragmentation often made it impossible to find enough storage to handle application needs without preempting other users, or even rebooting the computer. These problems significantly complicated the use of early computer systems.

Virtual storage solves both problems by making it possible to retain in real storage only currently needed storage locations of running applications, and by separating the logical view of storage from the physical storage locations they are assigned to. Real storage fragmentation is irrelevant because adjacent virtual storage addresses can be assigned to non-contiguous real storage locations. Main storage is used more efficiently because unused storage locations can be stored on external media until needed again.

These benefits were only hypothetical in VM's early years. The first implementations of VM were built when virtual storage performance properties were not well understood. Early virtual storage operating systems, such as the Atlas Ferranti and the Manchester MU5, were known to have serious performance problems, for reasons not yet clear. Seminal work by Peter Denning and Laszlo Belady codified the working set concept and determined the properties of different storage replacement algorithms. Most commercially available systems (and even laboratory systems) lacked virtual storage, and at best swapped entire applications in and out of storage.

VM demonstrated that highly efficient virtual storage systems could be built, at a time when the question of virtual storage was, "Can it be made to work with real workloads?" Even when virtual storage operating systems became popular, VM showed that extremely high ratios of virtual to real storage size could be supported without performance problems, if sufficiently robust I/O and storage subsystems were provided.

VM also showed that replacing file I/O with virtual storage access could improve performance. Virtual storage had been viewed solely as a way to leverage main storage to fit more applications. VM established that it was almost always cheaper for applications to refer to data in virtual storage, and let the underlying operating system fetch it, if needed, via paging. This principle was subsequently accepted in other system environments as well.

Device independent file I/O

CMS provided a disk-model independent file system at a time when most programs or control language scripts, at least in the IBM marketplace, had to be intimately aware of disk device geometry. CMS showed, in the 1960s, that a file system could transparently and efficiently map a uniformly structured file space onto different disk media.

Compared to contemporary 1960s and 1970s "physical I/O" and "logical I/O" supervisors, and to subsequent MVS access methods, CMS introduced I/O interfaces that were both easy to program and flexible. The only comparable file system experience then was the highly successful UNIX file system, which added generality, and the elegant innovation of the tree-structured file directory, but is comparatively inefficient and non-robust.

Multiple application program interfaces

CMS provides its own application program interface, but also accepts program calls used in IBM's OS and DOS family operating systems. This was done for very pragmatic reasons (to allow compiled language code to run under VM without having to change the language implementations), but proved that a single operating system could accommodate multiple "foreign" program interfaces. This is again an important issue, as Microsoft, IBM, Apple, and UNIX vendors compete with one another, and claim to provide not only their native APIs, but those of their competitors as well.

The REXX programming language

Most interactive systems provide a form of *EXEC, shell, script* or *clist* (command list) language to create higher level commands by combining system commands. Such languages have been available for many years with differing degrees of power and ease of use, for systems as diverse as CMS, TSO, Wylbur, UNIX, and PC-DOS. The assumption underlying these languages was that most work was performed by the commands invoked by the EXEC, with a thin layer of control added by the EXEC itself, so little effort was expended to making them good for general programming. Consequently, most EXEC and shell languages were cumbersome or cryptic when used to write nontrivial programs.

The REXX language, developed by IBM's Michael F. Cowlishaw and introduced in VM/CMS, revolutionized EXEC languages by combining structured programming and data manipulation capabilities of modern programming languages with shell-oriented features from CMS's EXEC 2. Quoting Cowlishaw:[2]

> It became clear to me that a new language was needed, one based on the more classical syntax and semantics used by languages in the tradition of ALGOL, PASCAL, and PL/I, yet including the command and string programming facilities that EXEC 2 had proven to be so effective and powerful.

Cowlishaw designed REXX to be both powerful and easy to use by selecting language features for the convenience of the programmer instead of the language implementer. REXX shields programmers from computer-imposed idiosyncrasies like binary arithmetic and word size, while providing a powerful set of built-in functions. REXX uses an elegant, structured syntax without cumbersome conventions. REXX also includes content-addressable *stem* variables, a natural and easily understood type system that doesn't require that variables be declared with a specific data type, and powerful primitives for arranging and parsing character text.

For the first years of its existence, REXX only existed on VM/CMS, where it became the language of choice for many applications, in addition to its role as a command shell. The enthusiasm generated by REXX users on VM, and its obvious strengths, soon won converts in other computing environments as well.

Since then, REXX has been implemented on a wider range of computing systems than any other control language. IBM designated REXX the System Application Architecture (SAA) Procedures Language, not MVS JCL or TSO CLIST, and has produced REXX implementations for MVS, AS/400, OS/2, and AIX. IBM is also researching object-oriented REXX and implementations for its CICS transaction processing system under MVS and DOS/VSE. On non-IBM platforms, REXX is now available for MS-DOS, many versions of UNIX, VAX VMS, Tandem, and Amiga.

The spread of REXX is not due to marketing pressure from IBM or any other vendor: it grew due to its obvious technical excellence. REXX is a new way of programming inspired by VM facilities, pioneered on VM, and now providing added productivity throughout the computing world.

High performance interactive computing

VM grew to popularity in a world dominated by batch systems, when the standard interaction with a computer system was submitting (even the verb is subservient) a punched card job deck to a computer operator, and re-

---

[2] *The REXX Handbook*, Editors Gabriel Goldberg and Phil Smith III, McGraw-Hill 1992, pg. 4.

ceiving a printed listing much later. It's hard to picture this now, when computer terminals and personal computers are ubiquitous, but the notion of interactive systems was once radical and controversial. VM proved, years before any other interactive operating system had credibility in the commercial marketplace, that timesharing systems could improve productivity and provide excellent interactive capabilities at low cost.

VM also pioneered the idea that subsecond interactive response times were both highly valuable and achievable. Other timesharing systems, such as TSO, were noted for high resource requirements and slow response times. VM/CMS proved that this was not necessary, and set a standard for low cost-per-user timesharing that other operating systems still struggle to match.

Personal computing

The virtual machine concept gives each user of a VM system a "personal computer." Before microcomputer technology made desktop computer systems possible, VM users had their own personal systems, transparently sharing the same physical hardware, yet customized for individual preferences and tasks.

Users in separate virtual machines can customize and apply their personal systems as they choose, and operate however they like without interfering with others, much as with "real" desktop personal computers. This provides a predictable, secure, simple style of computing now used everywhere.

Additionally, VM's ability to run on large shared computers (as well as departmental and even desktop systems) provides the capability to exploit economy of scale, and eases resource and data sharing, while still providing individualized computing.

VM deeply influenced personal computing. It is surely not accidental that both VM/CMS and MS-DOS have COMP (compare), COPY, RENAME, ERASE, PRINT, TYPE, SORT, and FORMAT commands with almost the same meanings, as well as the concepts of the "A-disk," "B-disk," "C-disk," and so on.

Client-server computing

Since completely isolated virtual machines prevented cooperative processing, and precluded sharing programs and data, message-passing mechanisms were invented early in VM's history to allow communication between processes. This led to the pervasive use of "service virtual machines" or "servers" to implement both applications and system functions on behalf of clients (users). It is very natural and common to implement VM facilities this way. A variety of program tools help make this easy.

This made VM the originator of cooperative and client-server processing, a style of computing that has only recently become popular outside VM. A

Local Area Network (LAN) provides the same function VM introduced fifteen years ago by inter-user communication protocols: a high-bandwidth, reliable mechanism for communication between machines. The advent of LAN hardware allowed other parts of the computing world to rediscover client-server computing for personal computers and UNIX systems.

VM facilities for cooperative applications have become increasingly powerful and general. Subsequent chapters will discuss them in detail from a number of perspectives.

VM Application Environments

VM is used for diverse application environments. The next few sections describe the most common ways VM is used.

CMS program development

VM has been described as "written by programmers, for programmers," and consequently is a comfortable environment for creating and testing new programs. VM's editor, command language, and REXX procedures language provide a powerful and convenient, yet easily learned and used, platform for developing and maintaining programs. I've seen many cases in which a newly hired programmer is given a VM userid and a terminal, and is productive within days without formal training or even manuals. No other system I know of combines this much ease of use, expressive power and functional richness. CMS is used to develop CMS programs, of course, but it is also frequently used to develop software to be run on systems, such as DOS/VSE and MVS, which are less congenial for programmers.

CMS InfoCenter

VM/CMS ease of use and expressive power has long made it popular for end-user computing, which IBM dubbed the "InfoCenter" in the early 1980s. Even before this term was invented, there was a vigorous industry segment providing VM timesharing to commercial clients. Decreased costs of hardware in the 1980s, and increased acceptance of VM and the InfoCenter concept, brought timesharing "in-house" into company-owned data centers formerly used only for batch. The current trend is to "outsource" both batch and interactive computing, often into shared facilities, proving that every trend eventually comes full-circle.

VM's command language has proven natural and easy to use, especially when compared to other command-language driven operating systems. This makes VM an application enabler for knowledge workers, since it empowers them to perform their own computing without assistance (or interference) from official DP development staffs. Armed with standardized applications, productivity tools and fourth-generation languages (such as FOCUS, SAS, APL, QMF, and many others), users can provide their own applications solutions to a remarkable extent.

PROFS and OfficeVision/VM, and office automation

One application that has contributed heavily to the spread of VM is IBM's PROFS (Professional Office System), which has been replaced by Office Vision/VM (usually abbreviated as OV or OVVM, though many people persist in calling OfficeVision "PROFS").

PROFS provides a variety of electronic office functions: electronic mail for single and distributed computer systems, document processing for individual authors and groups, calendaring, and scheduling. Advanced functions include the ability to proofread a document for use of words in context (that is, not using the word *there* when *their* was needed), and checking for words higher than a specified school grade level. Synonym facilities make it possible to select alternatives when the original words are "too hard."

Many companies installed VM purely to run PROFS. It has been estimated that there are approximately two million PROFS and OfficeVision /VM users in the world. PROFS lets companies leverage their computer networks to provide inexpensive electronic office and mail functions. PROFS and OV are particularly small consumers of resources, so it is an extremely cost-effective e-mail environment.

VM is also the host for "groupware" applications that allow many users to interact and work cooperatively. Two such applications are the Contact conferencing and bulletin board system from The Adesse Corporation, IBM's Grouptalk, and the bulletin board facility built into OfficeVision. These products let VM users have electronic dialogues, distribute and update documents, send and receive mail, and search files based on keywords.

Numerically intensive computing (NIC)

Ease of programming, expressive power, and low overhead, combined with powerful System/370 and System/390 hardware, make VM a valuable method of performing numerically intensive computing, usually for scientific applications. VM's scalability lets smaller applications be developed on smaller and less expensive 370 or 390 models, and executed on high-end systems without program change.

VM is used for "number crunching" at the U.S. National Science Foundation Supercomputing center at Cornell University, at Stanford Linear Accelerator Center (SLAC), NASA sites, the European physics consortium CERN, and other research and engineering institutions in the academic and industrial worlds.

In early years, a 370/168 running VM at Cornell University was the first IBM mainframe to be connected to an FPS Computing (formerly Floating Point Systems Inc.) array processing auxiliary processor. More recently, VM is used in supercomputer environments to solve applications with massive CPU time requirements. These systems are usually equipped with the Vector Facility (VF) feature of IBM 3090 and ES/9000 systems, which allows multiple floating point calculations to be executed at the same time. For example, an ES/9000 model 900 equipped with six CPUs and VF units runs the 1000-by-1000 Linpack benchmark at 1.457 gigaflops (billion floating point operations per second) compared with the eight-CPU Cray Y-MP/832, which runs at 2.144 gigaflops.[3] Clearly, IBM also makes supercomputer systems.

Guest VM environment

VM lets a System/370 or 390 family computer flexibly run multiple operating systems at the same time. This is used to test new system versions, to convert from one version to another, and to operate separate workloads on the same physical computer system. This is discussed in Chapter 17, "Guest Machines."

Service virtual machines

As mentioned earlier, VM applications are frequently implemented via *service virtual machines*, which respond to requests from clients (users). SVMs are used to implement popular application systems, such as PROFS, OfficeVision/VM, and SQL/DS. SVMs are also used to implement system facilities: security (RACF, VMSECURE, and ACF2), and network communications (VTAM, TCP/IP, RSCS, VM/Pass-Through). For years, the trend in VM has been to implement new functions partially or completely in service virtual machines.

IBM has developed rich protocols to make it easy to write SVMs for client-server applications. The most recent protocols support applications in which the client and server are on separate computers, and different types of computer separated by a network.

SVM's are equivalent to UNIX *daemons* and MVS *started tasks*. An advantage UNIX and VM share, compared to MVS, is that SVM's are programmed no differently than normal userids logged on at a terminal. This makes it possible for applications programmers to easily write SVMs using the same REXX EXECs and other tools they use for interactive sessions.

[3] "Large Computers," page 35, IEEE Spectrum, January 1992.

Chapter

2

Using VM

This section introduces VM/CMS fundamentals for readers not already VM users. You can skim this section if you are familiar with VM.

CMS is a single-user operating system that runs in a virtual machine. Multiuser access to VM is provided by CP, which gives a private copy of CMS to each user. Most of CMS resides in a single, shared copy in real storage (called a *named saved system*) to make better use of computer memory, but each user's copy of CMS executes independently from other users. A CMS user can alter his or her CMS session, crash it or restart it without having any effect on other users of the system, much as a PC user can reboot a PC without affecting other PC users.

Logging onto VM

CP displays a logo screen on each terminal connected to it. The logo contains a greeting panel, which is usually customized by VM system programmers to identify the VM system. It also contains input areas for inserting a VM userid and password, or for issuing one of the few VM commands allowed before logging on. The IBM-provided logo is shown in Fig. 2.1.

A user logs on by typing his or her userid and password in the area provided for them, and pressing the Enter key. The password field is a nondisplay field, so the password is not printed. Users can also press the Enter key without filling in the blanks: CP clears the screen and displays a list of permissible commands. The user can then type LOGON followed by the userid. CP prompts the user for the password, and then proceeds as if both were specified from the logo screen.

```
VM/ESA ONLINE

                      VV          VV MM          MM
                      VV          VV MMM        MMM
                      VV          VV MM M      M MM
                      VV          VV MM  M    M  MM
                       VV        VV  MM   M M    MM
                        VV      VV   MM    M     MM
              EEEEEEEEEEEEE   SSSSSSSSSSS      MAAAAA
              EE          VV SS      MM  SS      AA    AA
              EE           VVSS      MM         AAM     AA
              EE            VSS      MM        AAMM      AA
              EEEEEEEEEEE     SSSSSSSSSSS   AAAAAAAAAAAAA
              EE                        SS  AA           AA
              EE                        SS  AA           AA
              EE               SS       SS  AA           AA
              EEEEEEEEEEEEE   SSSSSSSSSSS   AA           AA


Fill in your USERID and PASSWORD and press ENTER
(Your password will not appear when you type it)
USERID   ===>
PASSWORD ===>
                                                   RUNNING   VMESA
```

Fig. 2.1 IBM-provided VM logo.

VM displays a number of messages during logon. There is usually a logon message with system news (for example, announcing new software available on the system). This is equivalent to the TSO broadcast or UNIX motd (message of the day). There may be additional messages indicating that the user has reader files (mail files) awaiting processing. Most userids automatically IPL a copy of CMS, so the next messages are typed by CMS as it starts processing.

A VM session lasts until the user logs off via the `LOGOFF` command. An operator command, `FORCE`, lets the system operator terminate a logon session if necessary. Users are not automatically forced off the system after a period of inactivity, as is common with MVS/TSO, unless an installation has explicit procedures to do so.

A user can disconnect a session from a terminal by issuing the `DISCONN` command. This can be done for security reasons when leaving a terminal, to prevent somebody else using the unattended userid. A user may also disconnect when going to another location, if he or she has work in progress and doesn't want to logoff. CP automatically disconnects a user when certain terminal I/O errors occur, or if the user powers off the terminal without logging off.

The LOGON command reestablishes a terminal session with a disconnected virtual machine; the terminal need not be the same terminal that the user disconnected from. CP displays the message **RECONNECTED** instead of **LOGGED ON**, to indicate that the userid has been reconnected to a terminal, instead of being newly logged on. CP may issue a read to the terminal, giving the user a chance to terminate or continue the disconnected session. The usual response is to issue the command **BEGIN** to continue processing.

VM/ESA 1.1 provides a **LOGON HERE** variation of the LOGON command for users that forgot to disconnect before going to another office. LOGON HERE verifies the logon password, and then disconnects the session from its original terminal, and logs it on again "here" at the new terminal. This is illustrated in Fig. 2.2. In this example, I try to logon to my userid, but I get an error message because it's logged on at a different terminal. I then use LOGON HERE, and CP disconnects my userid from its terminal and lets me logon at my new location.

A disconnected session can be idle until the user reconnects, or can be running a program. If the program crashes or issues a read to the console (which is not currently connected to a user at a terminal), CP automatically forces the userid off the system after a fifteen minute grace period, to give a user or programmer a chance to reconnect to the userid and correct the problem.

AUTOLOG and XAUTOLOG

VM lets virtual machines be logged on without a terminal via the **AUTOLOG** and **XAUTOLOG** commands. These commands are issued by userids with class A or class B privileges. Class G users can XAUTOLOG another user if the target

```
LOGON JEFF
HCPLOG054E Already logged on GRAF  0009

Enter one of the following commands:

  LOGON userid            (Example:  LOGON VMUSER1)
  DIAL userid             (Example:  DIAL VMUSER2)
  MSG userid message      (Example:  MSG VMUSER2 GOOD MORNING)
  LOGOFF
  UNDIAL
LOGON JEFF HERE
ENTER PASSWORD  (IT WILL NOT APPEAR WHEN TYPED):

DISCONNECTED FROM GRAF  0009
There is no logmsg data
FILES:  NO RDR,  NO PRT,  NO PUN
RECONNECTED AT 17:38:22 EST FRIDAY 01/27/92
```

Fig. 2.2 LOGON HERE.

user's directory entry lists the class G userid name in an XAUTOLOG or AUTOLOG statement. AUTOLOG and XAUTOLOG perform essentially the same task, however XAUTOLOG adds syntax that allows additional flexibility bringing up the AUTOLOGed userid, and has a class G form.

At IPL time, CP automatically XAUTOLOGs a userid named AUTOLOG1, which most sites use to automate system operation. This mostly consists of XAUTOLOGing the service virtual machines that provide network, database, and application services. CP also XAUTOLOGs userids that collect accounting, performance monitor, and system error data.

Standard Virtual Machine Configuration

Virtual machines are defined with a predetermined amount of virtual storage and a set of input/output devices. Both of these can be altered during the LOGON session by CP commands. The standard assignments for a CMS user are described below.

Disk space

Disk space for VM users is usually allocated in *minidisks*. A minidisk is a contiguous band of disk space assigned to an individual VM userid; actual disk volumes are carved up into many minidisks.

CP is unaware of minidisk contents. The virtual machine operating system, usually CMS, defines a file system structure on the minidisk. The CMS **ACCESS** command reads a minidisk's file directory, thus making its files visible. CMS automatically accesses a set of standard minidisks when a user logs on; other disks can be accessed or released as needed. The CMS file system is described in Chapter 10, "Using CMS," and in detail in Chapter 12, "The CMS File System."

Linking to other user's disks

The **LINK** command logically connects other users' minidisks to a virtual machine. LINK commands are controlled by passwords or security managers. Once you have LINKed to a disk you can issue the **ACCESS** command to make its files visible. The format of the LINK command is:

```
LINK userid vaddr1 [AS] vaddr2 mode [PASS=] password
```

where **AS** and **PASS=** are optional keywords, and:

- **Userid** is the userid being linked to.
- **Vaddr1** is the device number of the disk being linked to in the other user's directory entry.

- `Vaddr2` is the device number at which the disk is to be accessed in your virtual machine.
- `Mode` specifies whether the disk is to be made read/only or read/write.
- `Password` specifies, if the disk is password protected, the LINK password needed to access the disk. Different passwords are used for read, write, and "mult access" links to a disk.

  The link modes are:

- `R`—The user is given read access to the disk, unless another user already has the disk in write state.
- `RR`—The user is given read access, even if the disk is write-linked.
- `W`—The user is given write access unless another user has the disk linked for either read or write. In this case the disk is not made available.
- `WR`—The user is given write access unless a user has the disk linked. In this case, the disk is read-linked.
- `M`—The user is given write access unless the disk is write-linked by another user, in which case the disk is not made available.
- `MR`—The user is given write access, even if the disk is read-linked by another user. If the disk is write-linked, the disk is made read-only.
- `MW`—Disk is given write access, regardless of whether another user currently is write-linked to it. This mode should **never** be used for CMS-format disks because it can destroy the CMS file directory in the minidisk.

  The following link modes are new with VM/ESA 1.1:

- `SR`—The disk is given a "stable read" link to the disk. This works like R, except that another user cannot subsequently create a write-link.
- `SW`—The disk is given a "stable write" link to the disk. This works like W, except that another user cannot subsequently create a write-link.
- `SM`—The disk is given a "stable multiple" link to the disk. This works like M, except that another user cannot subsequently create a write-link.
- `ER`—The disk is given an "exclusive read" link to the disk; no other user is permitted to be linked to it.
- `EW`—The disk is given an "exclusive write" link to the disk; no other user is permitted to be linked to it.

In addition to, or in place of passwords, a security manager may be used to grant or deny a link to a disk based on rules specifying which userids are allowed to link to a disk. Password protection is built into VM; security managers with access rule protection are available from a number of vendors, as will be discussed later.

Console

Terminal input and output is done to the virtual machine "console." VM provides both line mode and fullscreen command and application environments. When in line-mode, CP controls the appearance of the terminal display, as described later in this chapter. Users can work with CMS's fullscreen environment, which uses window areas to display different messages.

Virtual unit record devices

Line printers, card readers and punches, also called *unit record* devices, let computers print reports and both produce and read punched card decks. Real punches and readers are obsolete, but virtual card input and output is used to transmit files and mail from user to user or system to system. Virtual printers are also used to create reports, which may be sent to another user or directed to a real printer.

Every user has a reader, printer, and punch queue of files awaiting processing. The reader queue contains files from other userids' virtual printers or punches. The printer and punch queues contain files sent to a real system printer or punch, though the latter use is vestigial. Reader, printer, and punch files reside in spool disk areas controlled by CP. CP automatically allocates spool space when a user writes the first record of a virtual punch or printer file.

The CP **SPOOL** command specifies the userid to which output of a virtual punch or printer should be routed. For example, the command **CP SPOOL PUNCH TO DANIEL** directs punch output to userid DANIEL. **CP SPOOL PUNCH OFF** and **CP SPOOL PUNCH TO SYSTEM** reset the destination of a punch file to point to the system queue, which is directed to a real punch device. The SPOOL command can also be used to specify a spool file class (used by installation convention to identify different types of file), the number of copies of a file to produce, and a variety of other options.

When an output punch file is closed, it is routed to the input reader queue of the userid it was SPOOLed to. CP and CMS commands let the target userid read, purge (erase), hold (exempt from read operations) reader files, or transfer them to other users. Output sent to a virtual printer is treated like data sent to a virtual punch. Like punch output, print output can be sent either to a virtual reader, or sent to the system print queue for printing on a real printer.

A reader queue with several mail files is shown in Fig. 2.3. Each file can be purged, browsed, loaded to disk, or processed directly by an application.

The console is also a unit record device, and data displayed on it can be spooled much like a virtual printer or punch. The command **CP SPOOL**

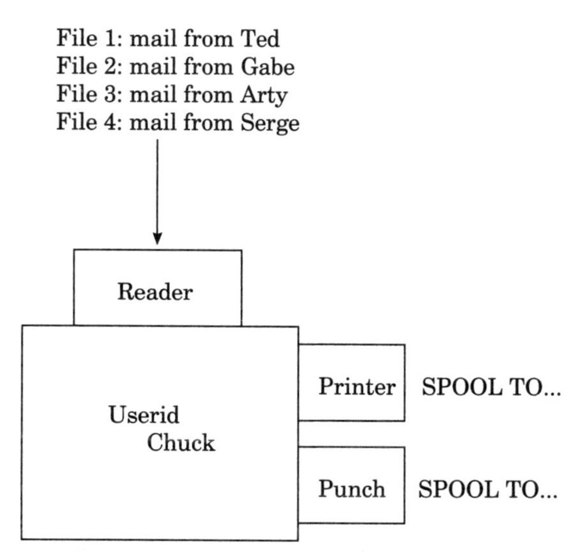

Fig. 2.3 Spool reader queue.

`CONSOLE START`, for example, starts collecting system messages and user input in a spool file. When a user logs off, or issues the command **`SPOOL CONSOLE STOP CLOSE`**, CP closes the console file and sends it to its destination. Console SPOOL files are used to log all messages and inputs in a session.

VM Screen Handling

Most users access VM from IBM 3270 terminals, or from PCs or workstations emulating 3270s. 3270 terminals are display devices, usually containing at least 24 vertical lines and 80 character columns of data. Host applications can read and write data to and from any of the screen positions. Some 3270 terminals can display color and graphics (pictures, bar charts, graphs), others can only display character text. 3270 terminals are controlled by 3174 or 3274 cluster controllers, which buffer screen data and respond to host commands.

VM applications divide the 3270 display screen into formatted fields, each of which is assigned a number of attributes: color, reverse-video or blinking appearance, intensity (normal, high, or nondisplay for passwords), and whether or not the field can be typed. Input fields are said to be "unprotected," since they are not protected from being overtyped by the user. VM has a standard screen format, described below. In addition, applications can control the screen and fully specify its appearance.

The 3270 keyboard

3270 terminals, in addition to the normal typewriter keyboard characters, have special keys for editing or controlling the layout of characters on the screen, and for requesting special attention from the system. Some keys are used identically in all IBM mainframe environments; others have special assignments in VM. Several keys used to edit the contents of the 3270 screen, without host intervention, are:

- `INSERT` pushes existing characters to the right of newly typed characters, rather than overtyping them.
- `DELETE` deletes the character under the cursor.
- `RESET` resets error conditions—like trying to type into a protected field—and turns off `INSERT` mode.
- `ERASE EOF` erases characters from the current cursor position to the end of the formatted field.

3270 control units buffer keyboard input until an attention generating key is pressed, usually the Enter key. This contrasts with minicomputers, workstations, and personal computers, which interact with the user on a character-by-character basis.

A 3270 user can type hundreds of keystrokes before requiring attention from the host processor. Intelligence distributed to the controller relieves hosts and networks of considerable overhead. Otherwise, host systems would have to process interrupts for each keystroke received from hundreds or thousands of terminals. This would make it almost impossible for centralized computers to support large terminal networks. Buffered input also lets networks send keyboard input in large bursts of data, instead of having to inefficiently transmit individual characters to the host.

The negative consequence of this architecture is that mainframe applications cannot respond to individual keystrokes. Many PC and workstation applications use their ability to process each keystroke to format documents as they are typed, while mainframes can only format text after the Enter key has been pressed. This is an important difference between mainframes and other computer types, and determines the types of work for which they are best suited. Personal computers and workstations are more responsive to keyboard input in a way that is very useful for word processing, while mainframes are more effective for applications involving many networked terminals.

Several keys signal the host for predefined special actions. The Program Function (PF) and Program Access (PA) keys are especially significant for CMS terminal usage. There are up to 24 PF keys, labeled from PF1 to PF24, each of which can be assigned a command string, as described later in this chapter. The PA1 and PA2 keys have special meanings in VM, described later in this chapter.

Fullscreen and line-mode operation

Many VM applications are *fullscreen* applications, and control the appearance of the 3270 screen. Applications can be written to use the fullscreen interfaces provided by CMS, which includes windowing services, or work in *line-mode*. Line-mode applications read and write individual lines of text from and to the terminal. The user's terminal is also referred to as the CMS *console*.

When a line-mode application is running, or when CMS's fullscreen windowing services are not used, CP controls the appearance of the data displayed on the screen, using a standard format. CP formats the 3270 display into three areas, as shown in Fig. 2.4.

- The *output area* occupies all but the last two lines of the screen. Responses from system commands are displayed in this area.
- The *input area* occupies the last two lines of the screen. VM positions the keyboard cursor at the beginning of this area when it is ready to receive a command.
- The *status area* displays the current status of the logon session and the VM system identifier name, in the right-most characters of the bottom

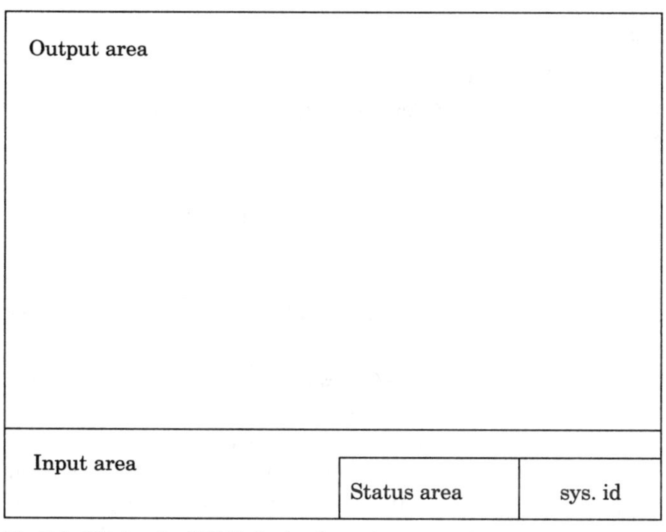

Fig. 2.4 CP standard 3270 display format.

line of the screen. The different status meanings are described later in this chapter. The system identifier is assigned by the VM system programmer that defines the system.

On 3270 terminals with appropriate optional features, users can specify different colors and screen attributes (blinking, or reversed video) for each of the screen areas.

When data is entered from the input area, CP redisplays the line in the output area, followed by system responses. Output lines are displayed on successive lines of the terminal.

Users can usually enter new commands or data whenever convenient; they usually do not have to wait for previous processing to finish. When a command is entered, the terminal is temporarily "input inhibited," and the keyboard is locked (will not accept further input). Most terminals display a small clock symbol to indicate that the user should wait. VM unlocks the keyboard as soon as it receives the input line and redisplays it, so the next command can be typed while previous commands are executing. This is markedly different from TSO, which locks the keyboard until the previously entered command completes.

Input lines are "stacked" in memory in first-in, first-out order until they are processed by the CMS command interpreter or an application. This is the basis of the "CMS stack," a software facility CMS applications use to place lines in stacks of input, which subsequent programs read as if they were reading from the console. This lets one program feed inputs to another by automating keyboard interactions.

Status area contents

The bottom right portion of the VM screen is the status area, describing the state of the terminal conversation between VM and the user. The status values and their meanings are:

- `RUNNING`—The CMS session is running, and has not issued a read to the terminal. It does not mean that a CMS program is running, it just means that CMS is running and that the session has not entered one of the other states.

  Most commands are executed when the CMS session is in RUNNING state. When the user presses the Enter key, VM reads the contents of the input area, redisplays it on the next available line of the output area, and clears the input area for the next command.

  If the Enter key is pressed when the input area is empty, CMS issues a read to the terminal, which places the screen in VM READ state. This is CMS's way of saying, "You got my attention...what do you want?" The user can enter a command at that time, just as when the terminal is in RUNNING state, or just press Enter again to return to RUNNING state.

- `VM READ`—CMS or an application wants input from the user. This may be the next CMS command (if the command `SET AUTOREAD ON` has been issued), or input data for a user program.
- `CP READ`—CP itself is prompting the user for input, for example when requesting a password. VM also issues a CP READ if the PA1 key is pressed; this is a convenient way for bypassing the virtual machine and its applications to talk directly to CP. The `CP TERMINAL BRKKEY` command lets users specify a different "break key" or turn off the break key altogether. Input typed when a CP READ is displayed is sent to CP, not to the virtual machine. The `BEGIN` command tells CP to let the virtual machine begin executing again.

  Infrequently, a CP READ results when a virtual machine operating system fails (usually called an `ABEND`, for "abnormal end"). When this happens, VM displays an error message describing the problem and displays a CP ENTERED message. The usual recovery action is to issue the command `IPL CMS` to "initial program load" a fresh copy of CMS and continue running.

  CP READ can be prevented by issuing the command `SET CONCEAL ON` or placing `OPTION CONCEAL` in the user directory. CONCEAL protects a session from being placed in CP READ. When CONCEAL is set, a CP READ is usually translated into an "attention interrupt" to the virtual machine. In case of a virtual machine ABEND, CP automatically reIPLs the virtual machine, and passes it the reason for the reIPL.
- `MORE`—The output area of the screen is full, and more data is waiting to be displayed on the screen. VM holds the contents of the screen for 50 seconds, then sounds an audible alarm on the terminal (it usually sounds like a "beep"), waits an additional 10 seconds, and then clears the screen. This gives the user a chance to read the screen output before continuing.

  This method contrasts with systems like MS-DOS and UNIX, in which terminal output can "fly off the top of the screen," unless controlled by a filter like *PG* or *MORE*. TSO is like VM in this regard, and treats the 3270 as a page-mode device by default, but with different conventions for indicating and handling full screens.

  To continue processing without waiting for the timed display (the usual situation) the user tells CP to continue either by pressing either of the 3270 CLEAR or PA2 keys. The CLEAR key clears the entire screen; CP then displays the next output at the top of the screen. The PA2 key is preferred because it is slightly faster. VM does not need to repaint the display, and does not erase text typed in the input area.

  To lock the contents of the screen, the user can press the Enter key, which places the screen in HOLDING state. Starting with VM/ESA release 2, users can specify the MORE delay period instead of using the IBM default times.

- **HOLDING**—The output area of the screen is full, and one of the messages on the screen is a "priority" message, such as a message from another user. To make sure that priority messages are seen, VM holds the screen contents until the user manually clears the screen via the CLEAR or PA2 keys. A user can toggle the screen between MORE and HOLDING by pressing the Enter key.
- **NOT ACCEPTED**—The last command was not accepted by VM. This usually means that the previous command is still being processed, and the user should wait for it to be completed. Some commands "disable interrupts," and don't allow commands to be stacked while they are running.

VM screen handling sounds more complicated than it is, and very quickly becomes natural. The part that most confuses novices is an unexpected CP READ, because familiar CMS commands aren't recognized. The trick to remember is to issue a BEGIN command to resume virtual machine execution. The best method is to use the **CONCEAL** option described above.

CMS also provides a fullscreen environment with pop-up windows, entered by the command **SET FULLSCREEN ON**. Messages can be directed to different *virtual screens* used for different purposes, and then displayed on windows on the terminal. For example, messages from other users can be directed to a "pop-up" window. Windows can be hidden, displayed, or changed in size and location on the physical display. Fullscreen CMS is further discussed in the chapters on CMS. Many users spend their entire VM sessions within fullscreen applications like OfficeVision/VM, in programming or editing environments like XEDIT, ISPF, and the APL2 session manager.

Program function keys

VM lets users reduce typing by assigning predefined input text to PF keys. An *immediate* PF key is equivalent to typing the PF key's text in the input area and pressing the Enter key. A *delayed* PF key places the PF key data in the input area and positions the cursor after the rightmost character. The user can modify the line's contents by overtyping it or using the 3270 editing keys, and then press Enter. Users can also define PF keys that insert substitution text into a predefined template before sending the line to VM.

For example, the following commands associate the string **FILELIST** with PF2. Pressing PF2 is equivalent to typing this command and pressing the Enter key. The **NODISP** form eliminates the usual input redisplay:

```
cp set pf2 immed filelist
cp set pf2 nodisp filelist
```

The following command assigns the HELP command to PF1 as a delayed PF key. When PF1 is pressed, the command **HELP** appears in the 3270 command input area. The user can then add the name of the command or message whose help file should be displayed:

```
cp set pf1 del help
```

This can also be done by setting up a PF key with substitution text. The following commands associate PF1 and PF3 with fixed text and insert place holders for variable data:

```
cp set pf1 substitu help &1
cp set pf3 substitu fortvs2 &1 (opt(3) &2 &3 &4
```

To use these keys, the user types in the variable data on the input line and then presses the PF key. The first word in the input area is substituted where `&1` appears, the second word is placed where `&2` appears, and so on. The first of these commands lets the user type a command name in the input area and obtain help information for it by pressing PF1. The second command lets a user type the name of a FORTRAN program and compile it by pressing PF3. Additional words on the input line are passed to the FORTRAN compiler as compiler options. Substituted words can be used with immediate, nondisplay, and delayed PF keys.

A PF key can also be set up as a "retrieve" key to let users reissue previously entered input lines without retyping them. CP remembers a small number of recently entered input lines; repeatedly pressing the retrieve key displays previously entered lines in the input area, where they can be altered and reissued. The standard way to reissue an incorrectly typed command, for example, is to retrieve the command line, correct it, and press Enter. The following command makes PF10 a retrieve key:

```
cp set pf10 retrieve
```

Application programs also use PF keys as short-cuts for command sequences. Most applications, with the notable exception of Office Vision/VM, use PF1 as the "help" key, and use PF3 as the "end"or "exit" key. OfficeVision/VM, by default, uses PF9 and PF12 for these functions.

Line Editing

Before VM processes an input line from a terminal, it scans it for "line editing" characters that alter how the line is interpreted. Line editing can be used to correct typing errors, or to enter several commands in a single line. If you are familiar with UNIX, this is similar to the use of the line-kill, erase, and escape characters. If you are familiar with TSO, this is similar to the line and character delete characters specified by the TSO **PROFILE** command. Line editing is turned on by default, but can be turned off by issuing the command **SET LINEDIT OFF**.

Character and line delete

The *line delete character*, by default the "cents" sign, deletes the entire line from its beginning. The *character delete* character, by default the "at-sign" ("@"), deletes the last character typed, and is one way to correct a typing mistake. Multiple character delete characters can be typed, to remove characters up to the beginning of the line. For example, the input line

```
copyfool@@@ile * data a = = b
```

is interpreted as

```
copyfile * data a = = b
```

3270 terminals, which let you correct input without host intervention, have largely eliminated the need for character and line delete characters. To make corrections on a 3270, you simply backspace the cursor and then overtype the input line, or use the INSERT and DELETE keys to alter displayed text. To erase an entire input line, you move the cursor to the beginning of the input field, usually by hitting a hardware TAB or NEXT FIELD key, and then press the ERASE EOF ("erase to end of field"). Character and line delete remain useful on teletypewriter-like terminals.

Line end character

The most important line editing character is the *line end* character, by default the "pound sign" ("#"). CP segments input lines into multiple logical lines, as if the Enter key had been pressed after each of the segments between line end characters. For example, the input line

```
query users#indicate#query time
```

is interpreted as if the three commands had been entered separately.

```
query users
indicate
query time
```

```
* Start a number cruncher
load bigmodel (start
Execution begins...

11:15:13 * MSG FROM JULIE  : Do you have the results yet?

#cp msg julie it's running right now!

11:15:46 * MSG FROM JULIE  : Okay, thanks
Ready;

tell julie it's done now!
Ready;
```

Fig. 2.5 Using #CP to issue commands while a program is running..

This is often convenient for starting up multiple commands. For example, you might issue the following sequence of commands to erase old program output, compile a Fortran program, and then start running it:

```
erase * output a#fortvs2 myprog#load myprog#start
```

Command sequences can be assigned to a PF key, so they can be issued with a single keystroke.

The most important use of the line end character is to send a command directly to CP. To communicate directly with CP without CMS processing it at all, type #CP before the command. When CP reads a command from the terminal that begins with #CP (assuming the line end character has not been changed), it processes the command without sending it to the virtual machine.

This is useful, for example, if you want to issue a CP command while CMS is running a command that takes a long time. For example, you can issue **`#CP INDICATE USER`** to see how much CPU time you've used in a command while it continues to run. If #CP were omitted, CP would pass the command to CMS, which executes it when previous commands have completed.

In Fig. 2.5, a user sends a message to a friend while a program is running: the command executes even though CMS is already running a program.[1] While the program is running, you must use the CP command **`MSG`** to send a message to another user's screen. After the command completes, either MSG or the CMS **`TELL`** command can be used. TELL is nicer in a number of ways, since it uses a nickname file to obtain the VM userid and system id to send a message to, while MSG requires the actual VM userid and can only

---

[1] Illustrations from VM screen snapshots in this book use the asterisk ("*") to indicate comments. VM treats lines beginning with asterisks as comments.

send a message to users on the same system. Unfortunately, TELL is a CMS command, and can't be used until the previous command finishes.

Escape character

The final line editing character is the "escape" character, by default assigned to the "quote" character ("). The character following the escape character is used as is, without being interpreted as a line editing character. The mnemonic association for remembering that the quote character is used for escape is that one is "quoting" the following character. Use of the escape character is illustrated in Fig. 2.6.

Changing line editing characters

Different line editing characters can be specified via the CP TERMINAL command. Different characters can be substituted for the defaults, or the function can be turned off, as illustrated in Fig. 2.7.

System message handling

As shown in Figs. 2.5 and 2.6, messages from other users can appear on your terminal screen. VM lets you suppress these and other messages if you want to work undisturbed, and lets you control the format of other messages. Each of the following message categories can be individually controlled:

- `MSG`—Messages sent by the CP MSG command. When a MSG is received, the 3270 sounds an audible alarm and displays the message. If you are in XEDIT or another fullscreen application, MSG output is not displayed until you press Enter (unless you are using CMS Windows, which provides a pop-up window for MSG display).
- `WNG`—Messages sent by the CP warning (WNG) command. Warnings are "stronger" than normal messages, and can be sent only by system operators. WNG messages can break in on a screen display even when a fullscreen application is being displayed.
- `IMSG`—Informational messages resulting from a command. For example, when you detach a minidisk or other virtual device via the CP DETACH

```
18:42:23 * MSG FROM HEALY   : How can I check my program's CPU use
18:42:34 * MSG FROM HEALY   : while it's running?

* send a message containing the line end character to another user
tell healy To do that, type "#cp indicate user
Ready;
```

Fig. 2.6 Using the ESCAPE line editing character.

```
* change the linedel character
cp terminal linedel !
Ready;

* turn off logical line end
cp terminal linend off
Ready;
```

Fig. 2.7 Line editing characters.

command, CP responds with a **Detached** message. More commonly, CP also issues an informational message when a spool file arrives from another user.

- **EMSG**—Error messages from CP and other components.

Each of these message types can turned ON or OFF via the CP SET command; the current settings are displayed by the **QUERY SET** command. For example, **SET MSG OFF** disables MSG commands. A user trying to send a message to you receives an error message stating that you have MSG OFF. The **CP TERMINAL BREAKIN** command lets you specify whether messages from CP, including MSG output, break-in on fullscreen panels immediately, or only when the user presses the break key, which is usually the 3270 PA1 key.

EMSG provides an option that allows a message to be displayed but controls its appearance. VM error messages are of the form **xxxmmmnnnns text** where **text** is readable message text, **xxx** identifies the VM component name, **mmm** is the module name in the component that generated the message, **nnnn** is a 3- or 4-digit message number, and **s** is a severity code (**I** for informational, **W** for warning, **E** for error, **S** for severe error, **T** for terminal errors, and **R** when a response is required). EMSG is actually somewhat a misnomer, since not all messages indicate errors.

For example, the ACCESS command can generate the following message:

```
access 300 u
DMSACC724I 300 replaces U (300)
DMSACC723I U (300) R/O
Ready;
```

DMS is a CMS message. HCP is a VM/ESA CP message, and DMK is a 370-mode CP message. **ACC** designates that module DMSACC produced the message, **724** is the message number, and **I** denotes an informational message.

EMSG can be set to **ON**, **OFF**, or **TEXT**. **ON** and **OFF** enable or suppress the message. TEXT turns off the message prefix and only types the message text. CMS and GCS use DIAGNOSE 5C, as explained in Chapter 16, "CP DIAGNOSE Functions," to control whether to display all, part, or none of an error message.

In general, it is best to leave EMSG set to ON. The message prefix makes it possible to use the HELP command to explain messages. You can enter HELP followed by the error message prefix for an explanation of the error message. The module portion of the prefix, ACC in the preceding example, is omitted because multiple VM modules may generate the same message. An explanation of the above message can be obtained by issuing the command:

```
help dms724i
```

Chapter

3

System/370 and System/390 CPU Architecture

System/370 and System/390 architecture uniquely shape VM, in a way different from conventional operating systems, because VM has the special task of emulating CPU architectures for its users. This chapter describes portions of System/370 and 390 architecture especially relevant to understanding VM. It also explains computer design principles that affect both hardware and software development. You may wish to skim this chapter if you are familiar with System/370 CPU architecture. Understanding real System/370 family machine concepts is key to understanding how VM implements virtual machines.

System/370 and System/390 Evolution

IBM mainframes represent a continuous, compatible evolution of design based on System/360, and extended through System/370, System/370 Extended Architecture, and now System/390. This degree of continuity of function and compatibility is unique in the computer industry, and a key reason for IBM's many-years dominance. The very notion of a computer architecture is one of the innovations provided by IBM with its 360 line.

System/360

In the early 1960s, IBM sold incompatible lines of computers for commercial and scientific applications. The 7090 family of computers was used for scientific computing, while the 1401 and 7080 families were used for commercial data processing. Programs written for one computer could not easily be ported to another. Sites outgrowing a 1401 could not easily upgrade to a 7080, since they were also incompatible, even though they were both used for commercial applications.[1]

IBM decided to provide a general-purpose family of computers that would use the same architecture for both commercial and scientific applications, and on both small and large models. Customers would be able to upgrade to larger systems without rewriting their applications, and the single system would be easier for IBM to support than multiple incompatible ones.

In 1964, IBM announced System/360, a series of compatible computers with a wide range of price and performance. With System/360, IBM introduced the notion of a well-defined computer architecture, which specifies the "principles of operation" of a conforming system: the intrinsic data types and semantics of all instructions (even incorrectly specified ones), the organization of storage, and interface to input/output devices. The architecture even specified areas in which different 360 models could have different behavior due to timing differences, as well as allowable subsets, extensions, or deviations in function.

Except for a few well-documented exceptions, each 360 model ran the same instruction set. The exceptions were the 360/44, which added special instructions for laboratory environments, the low-end model 360/20, which only had a subset of the 360 instruction set, and the 360/91 supercomputer, which omitted most of the packed decimal instructions used for business applications (the 360/91 was intended for scientific applications). Technically, a 360 could be ordered with only subsets of the instruction set, but most models were ordered with the "universal" instruction set. In any case, the few deviations were IBM's problem, and were not generally visible to application programmers. For example, IBM provided software for the 360/91 to emulate the missing decimal instructions.

In almost all cases, a correctly written program written for one 360 model would run on any other 360. A company could upgrade over the performance range of 360 models from a tiny 360/30 with 64K of memory up to a 360/91 supercomputer with 6MB of storage (at the time, a massive amount of main storage). Vendors could write software that could be marketed without change for the entire 360 customer base. Additionally, all 360 models could use the same I/O devices, so a system's CPU could be upgraded while retaining its complement of disk and tape drives, printers, and consoles. This also aided IBM's goal of making it possible for a site to upgrade from one model to another.

System/360's compatibility was a remarkable advance at the time, and

---

[1] It's impossible to write these sentences in 1992 without a sense of deja vu, as IBM again offers incompatible computer lines: mainframes, AS/400, RS/6000, and PS/2.

gave IBM a tremendous advantage over its competitors. IBM knew that they "bet the company" when they introduced System/360, since they faced the risk that their customers would refuse to undertake the arduous conversion from their existing equipment to System/360, and if forced to convert at all, might easily convert to non-IBM equipment.

The gamble payed off, and made IBM into the industry giant we are familiar with today. It also made IBM resolve that future upgrades would be upwards compatible, to avoid a similar risk later. This philosophy was far-sighted and valuable for IBM and its customers, but also had a negative consequence: innovation could be shackled by the need to preserve compatibility. Other companies without an installed base would more easily respond to technology opportunities.

System/370

In 1970, IBM announced the System/370 line of computers, an upward compatible replacement for System/360. System/370's increased computing and I/O speed, and most importantly, storage addressability revolutionized the use of IBM computers and added interactive computing to the System/360's batch heritage. System/370 models had several times as much real storage as a comparable System/360 model. Even a moderate sized model like the 370/158 would typically have 2MB of storage, compared to the 0.5MB or 1MB of storage of a 360/65.

Most significantly, System/370 used *dynamic address translation* (DAT) for *virtual storage*. Though the first two models of the System/370 series, the 370/155 and 370/165, did not provide DAT, later models made virtual storage an indispensable part of mainframe computing. Applications could refer to storage operands using virtual storage addresses instead of real storage addresses; hardware would convert the virtual address into the corresponding real address, or generate a page fault if the virtual storage location was not currently assigned to real storage.

Virtual storage leveraged real storage, increasing the effective size of available storage, by making it possible to keep resident in "real" storage only the data and code areas actually referred to during program execution. Details of virtual storage are discussed in "System/370 and 390 Dynamic Address Translation (DAT)" on page 58. The impact of virtual storage on computing is discussed in "System/370 and Virtual Storage Computing" on page 84.

Extended Architecture/370 (XA)

By the late 1970s IBM was increasingly aware that limitations of System/370 architecture, inherited from System/360, restricted the size and effectiveness of IBM systems and the applications running on them.

System/370 programs use 24 bits (3 bytes) of address to refer to main storage, and therefore can only address a total of 16MB of storage for programs and data (24 address bits provide 2**24 unique addresses—16 megabytes or 16,777,216). This meant that IBM systems could not be used to solve problems requiring large arrays, or manage networks with thousands of terminals (and using an in-storage descriptor for each of them). Other computer manufacturers were able to address larger storage sizes, in some cases on minicomputers.

Also, System/370 I/O operations required too much attention from the CPU, causing overhead and reduced performance for I/O intensive applications. Finally, System/370 only allowed CPU complexes with up to two CPUs, making it impossible to provide large systems with many CPU "engines" for parallelism and fault tolerance, and increased capacity.

IBM announced a new architecture for its mainframe computers: *Extended Architecture*, usually referred to as *XA*. XA provides 31-bit addressing, which lets applications address up to 2 gigabytes (2GB) of storage. XA expanded addressability while preserving compatibility with existing applications.

32-bit addressing was not used, since it would have caused problems for applications that use signed arithmetic instructions when manipulating addresses. A 32-bit address with the high-order bit on would be treated as a negative number instead of a very large positive number—making many programs fail. For example, the **BXLE** (Branch on indeX Low or Equal) and **BXH** (Branch on indeX High) instructions use signed arithmetic. Programs with these instructions would fail when used with very large address values if 32-bit addressing was used. IBM provides instructions that perform 32-bit unsigned arithmetic, but there was no way to guarantee that existing programs would use them for address calculation, instead of the more commonly used signed arithmetic instructions. Consequently, the extra bit of addressing capability was sacrificed for compatibility.

A larger problem was posed by many existing programs, including IBM compilers and operating systems, that assumed that only the low-order 24 bits of an address were significant. For example, many programs used the fact that System/370 addresses occupied only 3 bytes, to squeeze flag values or small integers in the high-order byte of a word. Programs written this way would fail in 31-bit addressing, since the high-order byte would be interpreted by hardware as an address, and since changes to that byte would now destroy the 31-bit pointer value stored in the word.

To make it possible for applications to be migrated smoothly to 31-bit addressing, IBM provided 24-bit addressing even in XA environments, and lets applications control whether they run in 24 or 31-bit addressing modes. This will be discussed under CMS programming. Fortunately, programs written in high level languages don't need to be specially coded for 31-bit addressing. This is primarily a concern for assembly language programmers.

XA also offloads I/O path handling to the hardware, both freeing the CPU to run applications and increasing I/O responsiveness. XA is also oriented around the idea of a "processor complex" in which several CPU engines share memory and I/O devices. Each CPU in a 370-XA complex has a unique processor identification, a number from 0 to 63. This improved on the System/370 design, which was oriented around uniprocessor (single CPU) systems, and only allowed dual processor systems as an exception.

Enterprise System Architecture/370 (ESA) and ESA/390

The 2 gigabyte address range provided by XA was not enough for large applications. The idea of using larger address words to refer to virtual storage was rejected because System/370 family systems provide 32-bit words and arithmetic, and larger address sizes would have been difficult to implement compatibly. XA also didn't provide a suitable method for structuring large programs that shared in-storage data between cooperating applications.

Instead, Enterprise System Architecture/370 (ESA/370) extends addressing capability by allowing an individual application to address many 2GB *data spaces*, in addition to its *primary address space*, for a total addressable storage of 2TB (2 terabytes). This is sometimes called "horizontal address growth," compared to the type of increased addressability that would have been provided by larger address words. ESA/390, available on ES/9000 processors, adds to ESA/370 capabilities by providing *VM dataspaces* designed for CMS, and the ESCON channel architecture.

Personal/370

IBM System/370 and its successors are almost always considered mainframe architectures, used only in centralized data center environments. Even though 9370s, smaller 4300 computers, and rack-mounted ES/9000 models run without special cooling and power facilities, and can be placed in office environments, IBM's main computer line is viewed as existing only in the specialized "glass house," raised-floor computing center.

In fact, IBM has implemented the System/370 architecture and VM on personal computers several times. The first desktop 370 systems were the XT/370 and AT/370. These machines used adapter cards mounted in a standard PC/XT or PC/AT. The adapter cards contained highly modified Motorola 68000 and Intel 8087 chips, and implemented enough of the System/370 architecture to let a single virtual machine execute. They ran a hybrid version of VM called VM/PC. VM/PC let users run VM/CMS applications on their personal computers. Unfortunately, the performance of these systems were restricted by the 640K limit of the MS-DOS memory model, and by slow instruction rates of approximately 0.1 MIPS.

IBM researchers in the IBM Fellows Department at the Kingston, New York laboratories subsequently produced the 7437 Technical Workstation. The 7437 added a tower-style box that connected to a PS/2 via a cable. The result was a completely compatible System/370 computer system with 16MB of main storage that ran VM/SP as a PC-DOS or OS/2 application. The 7437 ran at approximately 1 MIPS, about the same processing power as a 4341 or a 9370 model 60, on a processor that was compatible enough to pass the standard IBM architectural integrity checks used to validate 3090s. It ran standard VM/SP, letting a desk-side system be used as a self-contained, single-user VM site, complete with languages, database systems, and network attachments via local area networks and communications lines.

IBM recently enhanced the 7437 to produce the *Personal/370 (P/370)*. The Personal/370 reduces hardware requirements to a single add-in card for a Micro-Channel PS/2 running OS/2, and increases computing power by a factor of 3. The resulting system runs at 3.5 MIPS, approximately the same speed as a low-end 4381 mainframe, at a remarkably low cost. P/370 systems provide multiple 3270 windowed sessions with full 3270 graphics capability for direct and LAN attached displays. P/370 systems can connect to one another and to "real" 370 systems as peers via LAN, RSCS, VTAM, and VM/Pass-through connections. Minidisks can be shared between P/370 and host 370 systems. The Personal/370 is a truly exciting breakthrough, and shows that VM can be used in a personal computer or workstation system in distributed environments.[2]

Multiprocessor systems

CPU complexes with multiple CPU "engines" and multiple concurrent instruction streams are an important trend in computer systems. Hardware limitations provide incentives for multiprocessor systems. High end processors push commercially proven circuit technology, packaging, and design to their limits. It is difficult and expensive to dramatically increase the speed of a CPU once the limitations of a particular hardware technology have been reached.

As a result, IBM and other vendors increasingly build systems with multiple CPUs combined in a single *processor complex*. Considerable effort has been spent developing parallel computer systems, and algorithms that work well on them. Parallelism comes in a number of varieties. One type of system, descended from the Illiac IV, uses many processing elements to perform the same operation on different data items. Current machines with this architecture include *The Connection Machine*, Intel's *Hypercube*, and IBM's RP-3 parallel computer.

These systems provide a high level of raw computing power for a single application. This is useful for applications whose processing is inherently parallel and can be divided into many simultaneously executing elements. Massively parallel systems may have hundreds or thousands of identical processing elements working on the same problem.

---

[2] For further information on the Personal/370, contact: P/370 Marketing, IBM Corporation, P.O. Box 950, Department A72A Building 705. Poughkeepsie, New York 12602, Telephone (914) 435-8485, or (800) 633-7437 if calling from within the United States.

Although IBM has experimented with massively parallel computer systems, their commercial efforts emphasize a different type of parallel execution. IBM mainframes use a relatively low level of parallelism (at this writing, up to eight CPUs) to increase the processing capacity of a single computer system controlled by one operating system. An extension to IBM's FORTRAN compiler extends this capability by letting each CPU in a pair of processor complexes running VM execute the same FORTRAN program in parallel.

Multiprocessor systems provide "horizontal growth," since capacity increments are provided by additional CPUs working side-by-side on the same or different applications. VM and MVS let individual applications run on multiple CPU engines at the same time for increased throughput, but efforts have been focused on increasing system throughput and fault tolerance rather than the speed of a single application. IBM multiprocessor systems can survive the loss of failed CPUs and continue operating with reduced performance. Consequently, most IBM development efforts have been directed towards allowing parallel execution of their operating systems, reducing bottlenecks caused by resource contention and allowing parallel execution of key components.

IBM's first experiences with general-purpose multiprocessor operating systems were in the 1960s. At the time, their operating system designs prevented effective use of multiple CPU engines. The addition of a second CPU engine provided far less than a doubling of computer power, and no systems had more than two CPUs.

Since then, multiprocessor effectiveness has been increased by improving resource serialization and reducing cross-system interference. Current systems provide increasingly greater levels of lock granularity to allow parallel acquisition of resources by different CPUs, and replicate private copies of resources to each CPU to permit access free of any lock contention.

IBM provided a multiprocessor in the 1960s with the 360/65MP, composed of two 360/65 CPUs sharing common main storage. More MP configurations were provided with System/370: the 370/158 and 370/168, and later, the 3031, 3032 and 3033, could be ordered in uniprocessor (UP) configurations, with one CPU, or with two CPUs in attached processor (AP) or multiprocessor (MP) configurations. An MP system was composed of two UP systems, and could be split into a pair of UP systems by throwing switches. An interconnection unit coordinated inter-CPU signalling and cache management, AP systems were built by adding a second instruction processor, without additional channels or main storage, to a UP system.

System/370-XA included multiprocessors as a fundamental part of their design. The 3081 and 3084 provided 2-way (dyadic) and 4-way (quadratic) multiprocessors, and better integrated the operation of the separate CPUs.

Among current processors, IBM's largest system is the ES/9000 Model 982, a 8-way multiprocessor with over 400 MIPS. Other vendors also offer multiprocessor systems: Amdahl also markets an 8-way high-end processor.

System/370 architecture only supports 1 or 2 processors, so VM/SP and HPO systems are limited to uniprocessors and dyadics. VM/XA and VM/ESA have architectural support for systems with up to 64 processors (and allow virtual machines with up to 64 CPUs), far more than IBM and IBM-compatible manufacturers are expected to implement in the near future on real computers.

System/370 and System/390 CPU Architecture

System/370 and System/390 systems consist of one or more central processing unit (CPU) instruction processors, I/O processors called *channels*, and main storage shared by both CPUs and channels, as shown in Fig. 3.1.

Instructions and data types

A System/370 or 390 CPU contains circuits for fetching, interpreting, and executing instructions residing in main storage. The CPU fetches the contents of storage containing the next instruction, interprets the instruction type to determine which operation it requests, evaluates the effective addresses of its storage operands, and executes the requested instruction, as illustrated in Fig. 3.2.

An instruction may be 2, 4, or 6 bytes in length, depending on its complexity, and contains an operation code, or "op-code" in its first byte. For

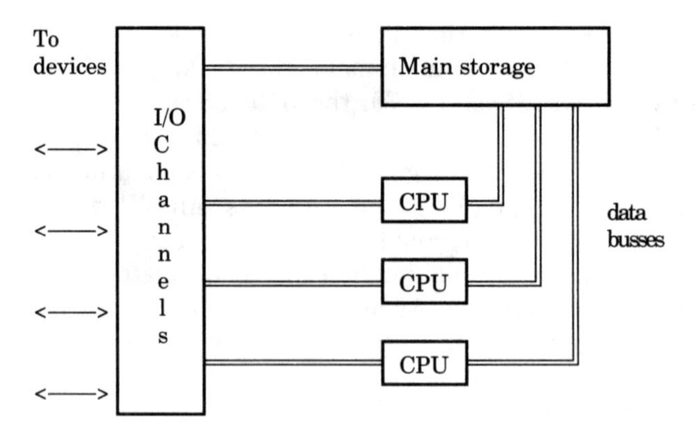

Fig. 3.1 System/370 and 390 block diagram.

```
do forever
  fetch next instruction
  decode instruction type
  fetch operands to internal data busses
  execute instruction
   if a BRANCH instruction, set next instruction address from
          branch operand value
   else next instruction address is at next storage location
end
```

Fig. 3.2 Instruction processing cycle.

example, the instruction with the value `1827` has op-code `18`, which stands for `LOAD REGISTER`, and copies the contents of register 7 to register 2.

The smallest addressable storage location is the 8-bit byte, which is arranged into 2-byte *halfwords*, 4-byte *words* (also called *fullwords*), and 8-byte *doublewords*, each aligned on a storage address evenly divisible by its length in bytes. System/370 numbers bits from the left, starting with bit zero. A 32-bit fullword has bits numbered from 0 to 31; bit 0 is the most significant bit, and contains the sign for 2's complement arithmetic, and bit 31 is the least significant bit.

Binary numbers are either 2 or 4 bytes in length, and floating point numbers are either 4, 8, or 16 bytes in length, with the longer data types providing a larger range of values (for integer data), or greater precision (for floating point).

Binary arithmetic is performed with 2's complement arithmetic, and both signed and unsigned arithmetic instructions are available. Floating point numbers contain a sign bit and a seven bit exponent in the leftmost byte, and a mantissa that is either 3, 7, or 15 bytes in length, depending on whether the number is single, double, or extended precision. Decimal data values are of varying length, with the length of the operation specified in the instruction. Each byte contains a pair of binary coded decimal digits with the values from 0 to 9. The last byte of a decimal number contains a decimal digit and an encoded positive/negative sign.

370/390 instructions provide a variety of arithmetic operations (add, subtract, multiply, divide, and so on) for binary, floating point, and decimal data types. Sixteen 32-bit *general purpose* registers are used for integer data and the addresses of storage operands. Four 64-bit floating point registers are provided for floating point instructions. The results of most arithmetic and logical operations are stored in the registers. Sixteen *control registers* describe CPU processing options such as which external interrupt types are enabled, the location of the current virtual storage segment translation table and so on. Finally, on ESA processors, a set of sixteen *access registers* contain storage addresses for dataspaces.

Most arithmetic and logical instructions specify a "target" register, and a source operand that may be either another register or a storage value. An "add" instruction adds a storage value to a target register; an "add register" adds the contents of two registers, overlaying the contents of the first operand with the sum. The latter instruction is called a "register-register" (RR) instruction. The former instruction may be a "register-storage" (RS) or "register-index storage" (RX) depending on whether the instruction format provides array indexing by combining a "base address" with an "index value."

Data manipulation operations are provided for bit and character data. Bit values can be set, cleared, and inverted using OR, AND, and exclusive-OR, as well as shifted either left or right. Individual bits, or combinations of bit values can be tested in a single instruction. Characters are stored in bytes of storage, using IBM's EBCDIC character set.

A number of powerful instructions are available to copy or compare blocks of storage, translate characters to different values based on a translation look-up table, and format decimal data into edited, displayable format. For example, individual instructions can translate character strings from EBCDIC to ASCII, search a block of storage for specified byte values, logically OR two blocks of storage, or format a packed decimal number into display format with properly positioned currency symbols (e.g., the dollar sign). These instructions are part of the reason IBM mainframes are considered *Complex Instruction Set Computers* (CISC), compared to *Reduced Instruction Set Computers* (RISC), such as Sun Microsystems' SPARC, Hewlett Packard's Precision Architecture, and IBM's own RS/6000.

Unfortunately, not every 370/390 operation type and addressing mode is available for every instruction, and the complier writer of assembly language programmer must be familiar with a list of idiosyncratic rules. For example, there are instructions to add binary and floating point data from a register or storage to a register, but not to add a register's contents to memory. There are add, substract, multiply and divide instructions for fullword integers, floating point, and decimal numbers, but no divide halfway instruction. There are seperate instructions for each permitted combination of addressing mode and data type, instead of a single ADD or MULTIPLY instruction for all operands. Not all instructions set the condition codes disussed below. ADD and SUBSTRACT instructions do, but MULTIPLY and DIVIDE do not.

The lack of an *orthogonal* instruction set has been one of the chief criticisms of System/360 and its descendants. Other architectures, such as the PDP-11, VAX (a decidedly CISC-style CPU), and Motorola 68000, provide more *regular* (few "special cases") instruction sets, which makes it easier to write compilers and assembly language programs. Fortunately, end users and higher-level language programmers need not be concerned with these issues, and assembly language programmers soon become skilled at coping with and exploiting the idiosyncrasies of the instruction set.

Another controversy, alluded to above, is the conflict between CISC and RISC CPU architectures. RISC machines execute only simple instructions, but executes them in single or a few CPU clock cycles, compared to complex instructions that may require many clock cycles to execute. RISC machines conserve chip space, making more on-chip storage available for fast registers. As a result, RISC machines are often reported as having very high instruction rates (MIPS rates) that may not correspond to actual application performance. For example, some RISC machines lack integer multiplication instructions, and use repeated *multiply-step* instructions to perform a multiplication.

This makes comparison of MIPS rates across architectures a poor basis for performance comparisons. In fact, widely varying MIPS rates can be produced on the same CISC CPU by selecting which instructions are executed. For example, a single CPU on an IBM 3090S model is nominally rated in performance reports as approximately 17 or 18 MIPS, but I've benchmarked it at 69 MIPS by selecting only RISC-like instructions.[3] Reasonably, IBM has long abandoned MIPS ratings as a meaningful comparison of computing power, though the industry and trade press persists in using them.

Condition codes

Many (but not all) instructions set a *condition code*, a 2-bit PSW result field (with values 0, 1, 2, or 3) that can be tested by a *conditional branch instruction*. For example:

`CR`	`5,6`	Compare registers 5 and 6, using signed arithmetic, and set condition code.
`BL`	`LESS`	Branch to label LESS if contents of register 5 are less than register 6.
`S`	`6,X`	Subtract storage location X from register 6
`BP`	`POS`	Branch to label POS if result of subtraction is positive (Branch on Positive).

The condition code is also set by instructions used for I/O operations and system control. For these instructions, the condition code indicates the success or failure of the requested operation. For example, condition code 0 on an SIO (`START I/O`) instruction indicates the I/O operation was successfully initiated, while condition code 3 indicates that the device was not operational.

---

[3] I always say, "Give me a benchmark result, and I'll contrive a benchmark that proves it (or its opposite)."

Storage addresses

Instructions refer to storage via addresses contained in a general purpose register, added to a fixed *displacement* value embedded in the instruction, and sometimes an *index* value contained in a second register. The *effective address* of a storage operand is computed by adding the contents of the base and register registers to the binary number contained in the displacement value of the instruction.

If the register specified for the base or index register is zero, its contents are ignored and the value 0 is used instead. Since the displacement field of an instruction is 12 bits long, it can contain values between 0 and 2^{12}–1 (4095). Consequently, the first 4K bytes of storage (page 0) can be addressed without a base register. IBM operating systems make use of this by putting globally accessed data in low-address storage. Page 0 also contains reserved locations the hardware uses to store information about the current or recent state of the CPU, as discussed below.

System control instructions

Special instructions are used for system control. They initiate or halt I/O operations executing on the channels, store and set clock and timer values, control storage management, and a host of other special functions. These instructions can only be executed when the CPU is in *supervisor* or *privileged* state. Most applications run in *problem* state and cannot issue these instructions.

The *Program Status Word* (PSW) describes the current state of a processor: the address of the next instruction to be executed, whether or not *privileged instructions* can be executed, the current condition code setting, whether *dynamic address translation* is in effect, which *interrupt classes* will be recognized by the CPU, and other attributes. These are explained below.

As mentioned earlier, every CPU contains control registers that contain processor state information, and control timers, virtual storage translation, hardware event tracing, and enable or disable interrupts for different types of event. Access registers modify the effective addresses used for instructions, as described in the section on storage concepts.

DIAGNOSE instruction

The DIAGNOSE instruction is very frequently used in the VM environment as the method for making service requests to CP. Originally, DIAGNOSE was used on System/360 computers to perform model-dependent operations, usually in machine-check (CPU failure) handling routines. DIAGNOSE could be used to invoke diagnostic microcode or to turn on red lights on the computer's front panel.

The DIAGNOSE instruction has been extended on 3081 and later computers as MSSFCALL (Monitoring and Service Support Facility Call). A DIAGNOSE 80 instruction is issued by CP when varying off or varying on (disabling or enabling) a CPU engine in a multiprocessor complex, usually for hardware maintenance purposes. DIAGNOSE 80 is also issued when writing a new I/O configuration via the I/O Configuration Program (IOCP).

Such esoteric functions are rarely coded and are documented as having CPU model dependent behavior. The DIAGNOSE instruction is used so infrequently that IBM assembly language has no built-in mnemonic for it. DIAGNOSE therefore could be safely appropriated for a new purpose in a virtual machine. In VM, DIAGNOSE is now almost exclusively thought of as the way a virtual machine communicates with CP.

Timer facilities

Timing facilities are provided by several high resolution clocks: the time-of-day clock ("TOD clock"), a clock-comparator, which generates an alarm clock-like interrupt, and a CPU timer which runs when the CPU is processing instructions, and causes an interrupt when a period of time has elapsed.

Each clock is 64 bits in length, with a precision equivalent to updating bit position 51 every microsecond. The TOD clock is set by the SET CLOCK instruction and inspected by the STORE CLOCK instruction, and is continuously incremented by hardware.

The clock-comparator, set and inspected by the SET CLOCK COMPARATOR and STORE CLOCK COMPARATOR instructions, generates an external interrupt when the TOD clock value exceeds the comparator value. The interrupt is generated as long as the TOD clock value exceeds the comparator, instead of only at the moment it passes it. Otherwise, clock-comparator events would be missed if the CPU happened to be disabled for interrupts at the moment of the alarm. After the clock comparator value is reached, a program should set the comparator to a new value higher than the current time of day. The clock comparator can also be disabled by turning off the clock comparator interrupt bit stored in one of the CPU's control registers. Clock comparator interrupts are deferred as long as the interrupt is "masked off" by a zero value in this bit.

The CPU timer is also an alarm clock, but it is decremented from a starting value, and contains an interval value rather than a time of day. It is set and inspected via the SET CPU TIMER and STORE CPU TIMER and is often used for measuring time-slices of CPU service provided to a user.

System/360 and System/370 also provided a lower resolution clock called the interval timer. The interval timer operated by decrementing the value in storage location 50 (hexadecimal), and generating an external interrupt when the value reached zero. The interval timer is 32 bits in length, and is updated at a rate equivalent to subtracting 1 from bit position 23 300 times per second, though the actual clock resolution may be lower on individual CPU models. The interval timer is not available in XA and ESA machines, though it is available in System/370 mode virtual machines running in VM/XA or VM/ESA.

The System/370 and System/390 clocks are better than the System/360 interval timer, obviously because they provide higher resolution, but also because they represent a better method of managing CPU clocks. A clock value retained in main storage cannot be used as an reliable representation of the current date and time, since it can be overlaid by software, and is certainly overlaid if a new system is loaded into memory. Clock updates to main memory causes contention for the data busses that connect CPU circuits with main storage. Restricting clock access to special instructions isolates clock values from software interference, and coincidentally makes it easier to implement virtual machine clocks. This will be discussed when virtual machine timers are described.

Interrupt processing

System/370 and System/390 hardware generate *interrupts* to alter the flow of control and switch processor states when real-world events happens. The CPU is switched from the currently executing program to an *interrupt handler*.

Technically, a *program exception* results from an incorrectly specified or failing instruction, and an interrupt is produced by an external signal, such as an I/O device signalling a completed operation. In practice, both categories are commonly referred to as interrupts.

When an interrupt occurs, the hardware performs a "PSW swap" to switch control from the interrupted program to the interrupt handler for the category of event. Each interrupt class described below has a pair of PSW locations reserved for it in page 0 of real storage.

Interrupts are normally acknowledged at the beginning of processing a new instruction. The CPU saves the current PSW in the *old PSW* low-storage location associated with the interrupt class, and loads a new PSW from the *new PSW*. The new PSW normally is a supervisor state PSW pointing to an interrupt handler in the operating system. The following events occur when an interrupt is signaled:

- Overlapped hardware events are allowed to complete. Many CPU models allow overlapped execution of instructions and data movement. Interrupt processing serializes and completes in-progress work.
- The current PSW is stored in a fixed storage location. Different locations are used for each event class, and are called the "old I/O PSW," "old SVC PSW," and so on.

- A new PSW ("new I/O PSW," "new SVC PSW") is loaded from its fixed storage location, sometimes called an "interrupt vector."
- Execution continues at the instruction address in the new PSW.
- The interrupt handler saves the general registers and old PSW contents and processes the event.

The flow of control for instruction processing, including interrupt processing, is illustrated in Fig. 3.3.
The interrupt types are:

- *External*, which includes timer, inter-CPU signaling, and console external interrupt events.
- *Input/Output* indicates that an I/O event has occurred. This might be the completion of a previously started I/O command, an *unsolicited* interrupt indicating that a device is requesting attention, or, on newer processors, a change in the I/O configuration.
- *Supervisor call (SVC)*, is voluntarily caused when a program executes the SVC instruction. SVC calls are used for CP program linkage and for invoking operating system functions in most 370/390 operating systems. SVC instructions are two byte instructions. The first byte is the SVC operation code, and the second byte is an *SVC number* from 0 to 255.

  SVC is used in all IBM operating systems: it allows programs to ask the system to perform a service function. In essence, it is a combined sub routine call and context switch into the operating system.

```
do forever
  if an interrupt occurred do
      Synchronize hardware events
      Store current PSW into fixed [old PSW] location
      Load new PSW from [new PSW] location
    end
  fetch next instruction
  decode instruction type
  fetch operands to internal data busses
  execute instruction
    if a BRANCH instruction, set next instruction address from
                 branch operand value
    else next instruction address is at next storage location
end
```

Fig. 3.3 Instruction processing with interrupts.

SVC instructions are used instead of simple subroutine calls because operating system code may execute in supervisor state instead of problem state. The SVC instruction causes both a branch into the operating system and a switch into supervisor state. Additionally, the addresses of operating system procedures are usually not known to application programs.

IBM operating systems use the SVC number, and parameters contained in general registers (usually registers 0 and 1) to describe the service being requested.

- *Program check* indicates that an invalid computation state has occurred. Program checks may result from errors, such as dividing by zero or attempting to store into protected storage. Program checks also implement virtual storage: an attempt to refer to virtual storage not currently resident in real storage results in either a *translation exception* or a *segment exception*, both usually referred to as a *page fault*. This is not an error condition, and is handled by fetching the referenced storage location into real storage and reissuing the instruction. The system response for an error program check usually is to terminate or ABEND ("abnormal end") the failing program. The response for a page fault is to bring the desired virtual storage into main storage.

  The most important program check from the perspective of VM is the *privileged operation exception*, often called a *privop* exception, which results when a program attempts to execute a privileged instruction. System/370 VM systems use privileged operations to virtualize the 370 architecture, as will be discussed later.

  System/360 and its descendants execute in one of two states: *supervisor state* (also called *privileged state*) and *problem state*. A program running in supervisor state can execute all the instructions defined to the processor. A program running in problem state can only execute instructions suitable for "solving problems," that is, running application programs.

  Instructions requiring supervisor state include the instructions for performing I/O, for handling storage protection and dynamic address translation, and for switching state between supervisor and problem state. These are called *privileged* instructions. An attempt to execute a privileged instruction while in problem state results in a program check and suppression of the instruction.

  The original intention of supervisor state was to ensure that an application program could not accidentally or maliciously gain control of the computer and overwrite data belonging to the operating system or other applications.

- *Machine check* is signaled by CPU circuits when they detect an uncorrectable hardware failure. For example, a machine check results if there is a permanent failure reading or writing real storage, or a parity error in an internal circuit.

The recovery action for a machine check depends on the type of failure and the operating system in use. On older IBM computers, software would attempt to retry the failing operation. On current systems this has already been done by microcode and hardware, making additional attempts futile. Instead, the operating system attempts to configure the failing component "offline" (remove it from use), and either restart or abort the failing process.

If an entire CPU fails in a multiprocessor system, CP places the virtual machine that was executing on it in halted state, and takes the failed CPU offline (unless it was the sole remaining processor in the system), and schedules its work for other CPUs. VM continues to operate, however with reduced performance. Similar recovery actions are taken after failures in other hardware components, such as blocks of main storage or I/O channels.

Interrupts can be *maskable* or *non-maskable*. Maskable interrupts are controlled by bits in the PSW: if the bit is on, the interrupt is said to be enabled, and the event is acknowledged and processed as just described. If the interrupt is off, the interrupt is deferred in hardware until the interrupt class is enabled.

Machine check, external, and I/O interrupt classes can be disabled and enabled by loading a PSW with the appropriate bit settings, or by using the instructions `SSM` (Set System Mask), `STOSM` (Store Then Or System Mask), and `STNSM` (Store Then And System Mask). SSM sets interrupt classes from memory locations, STOSM and STNSM save the current interrupt classes in main storage, and then set a new value by either OR-ing it with new classes (to enable additional classes) or AND-ing them (to disable classes).

Microprogrammed Control

System/360 and its descendants were made possible by IBM's introduction of microprogramming to control computer logic, possibly IBM's most significant hardware contribution ever. Micro-coded features have been extremely important to VM's development.

Before System/360, commercially available computer systems largely used custom hard-wired logic to implement computer instruction sets. Circuit gates were directly activated by decoding instruction opcode values. New circuits had to be fabricated if there was a mistake in how an instruction worked, or if a new addressing mode or instruction was to be added. Complicated semantics in instructions required complicated circuitry, which was difficult to scale down to inexpensive systems, especially before very large-scale integrated (VLSI) circuits.

IBM wanted System/360 to have a wide range of price and performance to let companies select the 360 model large enough for current needs, and compatibly upgrade as business increased. System/360 models used a variety of implementation techniques, including different circuit technologies for CPU logic and main storage, depending on the price and performance needed for a particular model. Discrete logic would have made it very difficult to inexpensively implement the 360 architecture across the entire processor line.

In addition, IBM wanted to ease conversion from 7090 and 1401 family systems by emulating their instruction sets. A 360 could execute both System/360 programs and programs from one of the older environments. This was clearly too complex to be implemented purely in various hardware technologies.

IBM solved these problems by using hardware as a microprogrammable controller. The microprogram interprets the 360 instruction set (as its preferred environment), and 1401 or 7090 instructions as needed. The actual CPU could be relatively simple, and not implement the programmer's view of the 360. The actual 360 is provided by the microprogram residing in the CPU's control storage read-only memory. In its most simple form, a microprogram could look like the pseudo-code in Fig. 3.4.

Low-end models use "vertical microcode," which specifies many serial steps to implement the stages of instruction fetch, decode, and execution. For example, the microcode program for an "add from memory to a register" instruction could include microinstructions to do the following:

- Evaluate storage operand address and place in memory address register.
- Fetch storage operand address to CPU's memory data register.
- Wait for storage to deliver the operands to the CPU.
- Move memory data register to adder circuit input.
- Send register contents to other input of adder circuit.
- Enable the adder circuit latch.
- Move the output of the adder to the register operand.

On low-end models, the memory bus width may be shorter (one or two bytes) than the width in bytes of the operand, so each of the "fetch" and "move" steps actually requires separate steps to move each operand byte.

```
do forever
   fetch next instruction
   decode instruction type
   fetch memory operands
   call microcode subroutine to implement that instruction
   compute next instruction address
end
```

Fig. 3.4 Pseudo-code for simple microprogrammed instruction processor.

This results in low CPU performance, but it allows the architecture to be implemented with a minimum of expensive discrete logic. Similar techniques were used by Intel when implementing the 8088 and 80386SX processors, which have narrower internal data paths than the storage and address data they operate on, and by Digital Equipment Corporation (DEC) in building microprocessor versions of PDP-11 and VAX architecture computers.

Faster models use "horizontal microcode" to specify multiple actions executed in parallel. For example, microcode for an add instruction could simultaneously fetch both operands for input to the adder circuit, while updating the program counter to point to the next instruction and fetching its contents, and so on. Higher-end models implement increasingly larger portions of the architecture in hardware, and use discrete logic to decode and execute the most frequently used instructions. Top-of-the-line 360s dispensed with microcode entirely.

Microprogrammed control remains extremely popular in contemporary computer designs from IBM and other vendors. As before, designers choose discrete logic or microprogram control (or programmed logic arrays) based on criteria for speed, cost, part availability, space available on an integrated circuit, and heat dissipation. All current IBM CPUs use microcode for many functions, including esoteric capabilities like built-in local and remote diagnostic facilities. For instance, an IBM 3090 or ES/9000 "calls home" to an IBM support site if a hardware fault occurs. This is not the type of facility one would implement purely in hardware.

In addition to IBM CPU families, Intel and DEC processors, math coprocessors, and CPUs from Motorola and other vendors (including RISC computers) all rely heavily on microcode. Amdahl also uses microcode in its CPUs, but sometimes prefers to call it *macrocode*. Microcode is also referred to as *firmware*, a name that indicates that it is more mutable than hardware but less than software. IBM has recently started calling microcode *Licensed Internal Code*, to emphasize its proprietary nature.

Manual Operation

System/370 and 390 computers, in addition to the normal process of executing instructions, can be placed in "manual mode" by system operators to execute control and diagnostic functions:

- `SYSTEM RESET` performs the architecturally defined system reset operation to place a machine in its initial status (no system running, no I/O operations or errors pending).
- `SYSTEM CLEAR` performs a system reset and additionally clears storage to zeros.

- IPL causes an *Initial Program Load* to read an operating system from a device, and start execution. This process is often called "bootstrap loading" or "booting" on non-IBM computers. IPL firsts performs a system reset and then loads the first part of an operating system into storage and starts it.
- SYSTEM RESTART implements the hardware restart function, which stores the current PSW at main storage location 8 and then loads the PSW at location 0. System restart is usually used when an operating system "hangs" and doesn't respond to commands. A restart makes VM take a storage dump and reIPL.
- DISPLAY displays storage and register contents.
- STORE alters contents of storage and registers with operator-specified values.
- STORE STATUS stores the contents of hardware registers into main storage. This is used to save the contents of registers that are either not directly addressable by software, or would be altered by an IPL, before IPLing a "standalone dump" program to save the state of a computer for debugging.
- STOP places the virtual machine in stopped state.

These functions are performed at the computer system's hardware console, which is driven by a *service processor*. Each of the above functions is also provided by CP for virtual machines, via CP commands with exactly the same names as those above (STORE, IPL, and so on).

Real CPUs also provide commands to reconfigure storage, CPU engines, and I/O channels. Hardware facilities can be enabled or disabled. In some cases, a CPU complex can be physically partitioned into two equal halves: an ES/9000 model 900 with 6 CPU engines can be split into two 3-engine halves, each with half the main storage and I/O channels. Each system can then IPL a different operating system and operate as a separate system image.

Systems with the *Processor Resource/System Management* feature (later 3090 systems, and all ES/9000) can *logically partition* a CPU complex into multiple computer system images, in effect, using a VM environment built into the CPU's hardware and microcode.

IPL function

Initial Program Load (IPL) starts an operating system. IPL performs a system reset to clear pending interrupts and error conditions, and, if requested by the system operator, clears storage and registers to zero values. An IPL is also called a *system load*; when storage is cleared it is called a *load clear*.

IPL then starts a *channel program*, an I/O command interpreted by the system's I/O channels, that reads 24 bytes of data from the IPL device into location zero in main storage. The channel program then branches to location 8, causing the contents of locations 8 to 15, and usually 16 to 23 as well, to be interpreted as channel commands to read additional data from the IPL device into main storage. The IPL device can be any 370 device that responds to a *read* operation, but is typically a disk drive. IBM operating systems usually refer to the IPL disk as the *system residence volume*, since it contains the executable operating system code.

The first eight bytes of storage, locations 0 to 7, are then loaded as a new PSW. At this time, the hardware IPL function is complete, and the code branched into acts as a bootstrap program to read the rest of the IPLed operating system into memory and initiate operations.

System/370 and System/390 Storage Concepts

Modern computing systems have a hierarchy of storage levels, with small, fast memories at the top of the hierarchy, and large and slow memories at the bottom. Storage sizes at each level depend on economic factors based on underlying hardware technology. Fast memories are available in smaller sizes than large ones because it is more expensive to fabricate faster memories than slower, and because it is difficult to package large amounts close enough to the CPU to avoid propagation delays.

Computing systems increasingly provide large address spaces to applications. Programs can directly refer to large amounts of storage, without regard for the amount of storage actually installed on the computer. Discrepancies between the amount of storage physically present and the amount used by applications are handled by a combination of hardware and software. IBM uses System/370 and 390 hardware *dynamic address translation* (DAT), described below, as the basis of a hierarchy of storage media addressed as virtual storage.

IBM storage hierarchies use, in order of decreasing speed: high-speed cache storage main storage, expanded storage, disk devices, and offline media like tape and optical disk.

Cache memories

Caches are high speed buffers used to speed access times to data. Caches are both faster and smaller than main storage. Even with the large difference between the cache and main storage sizes, average access time to storage is closer to cache time than that of main storage. This is necessary for high-end computer systems, whose cycle times are far shorter than main storage access times.

CPU cache storage is allocated in units called *cache lines*. When a byte of main storage is referenced, hardware promotes it and the remainder of the cache line it belongs to into the high-speed cache. The first reference to a cache line is therefore at normal memory speeds, and subsequent references at cache speeds. The size of a cache line is CPU dependent. On a 3090, for example, a cache line is 128 bytes long. When the cache is full, the cache line that has been least recently used (unused for the longest time) is selected for replacement. This selection algorithm is called *LRU*, and is discussed again later.

A storage hierarchy's effectiveness is often expressed as a *hit ratio*, the fraction of storage requests satisfied without having to access slower media. Hit ratios depend on the relative sizes of the adjacent levels in the storage hierarchy, and on storage reference patterns of the programs being run.

Each CPU in a multiprocessor system has its own private cache. Cache "snooping" techniques provide cache coherency by invalidating cache contents altered by a channel or a different CPU. HPO and VM/ESA align key control blocks on cache line boundaries to reduce the number of cache lines required to retain information in cache. They also avoid inter-CPU cache interference by using private data areas for each CPU whenever possible.

Main storage

Main storage is called *first-level* or *real* storage, to distinguish it from *second-level* or *virtual* storage. In VM systems, it is also called *host* storage since it belongs to and is controlled by the CP "host" instead "guests." Main storage is also called *central* storage to distinguish it from the *expanded* storage available on ES/9000 and 3090 CPUs. Second-level storage is also called *guest real* storage, since it looks like real storage from the virtual machine's perspective. If the guest system also is a virtual storage operating system, like MVS or VM itself, it creates *third-level* virtual storages for its users.

Storage is divided into units called *pages*, 4096 (4K) bytes in length, and beginning at a storage address evenly divisible by 4096. Main storage pages are called *page frames*. Page frames may be allocated to CP program and data areas or to virtual machines.

In multiprocessor systems, a *prefix register* translates real storage references to page 0 to a different page in real storage. Each CPU's prefix register contains a different value, so each CPU can refer to a different page of data as page 0. The translated real storage address is referred to as the *absolute* address. This lets each CPU use its own page 0 as a read/write area for PSW swaps, register save areas, and other scratch pad purposes.

Storage locations are protected from unauthorized access by a protect key mechanism: Associated with each 4K page frame, and on smaller and older processors, with each 2K block of storage, is a 4-bit *storage protect key*. On each storage reference, the CPU compares the storage protect key with the protect key stored in the executing program's PSW. If the PSW key is different from the assigned storage key, the CPU signals a *protection exception* program check, except for programs with PSW key 0, which is allowed to read and write all storage locations.

The 4-bit protect keys only allow 15 unique protected applications (there are 16 different bit combinations, less one because key zero programs can access all of storage) and therefore cannot be used for general storage protection between applications. The primary method in VM and MVS to protect storage is to provide each application a unique *address space*; all of an application's storage references refer to its own address space and not to the virtual storage of other users. Storage protect keys are used to prevent applications from overwriting storage they can address but should not alter.

A storage protect key can be assigned to a block of storage via the Set Storage Key (`SSK`) and Set Storage Key Extended (`SSKE`) instructions. The PSW protect key can be altered by loading a new PSW via the `LPSW` (Load PSW) instruction, or by issuing the `SPKA` (Set PSW Key From Address) instruction. These, and other instructions that manipulate protect keys, are supervisor state instructions. This ensures that applications cannot alter storage assigned to the operating system or other users.

CP runs largely in key 0. Much of CMS runs in virtual key 0, and CMS applications run in protect key 14, to protect CMS control blocks from being over-written by incorrectly written applications. CMS applications run in supervisor state and can easily switch to key zero and then alter storage; however they can only alter storage in their own virtual machine, so no security exposure exists. Under no circumstances can a CMS virtual machine overwrite real storage, since its storage addresses are virtual, not real storage addresses.

Expanded storage

Expanded storage is semiconductor storage used as a logical extension of main storage for paging and I/O buffering. Expanded storage is accessed almost as quickly as main storage, but is available in larger amounts. Expanded storage is not addressable at the byte level, as is main storage. Instead, each 4K block of expanded storage is identified by its block number, and is transferred to or from main storage by the `PGIN` (page in) or `PGOUT` (page out) instructions.

Since 4K byte expanded storage blocks are identified by 32-bit integers, IBM mainframes can address 2^{32} blocks of 4096 bytes of expanded storage. This is equivalent to 2^{48} bytes, or 16,583 gigabytes of data. Current IBM processors have up to 8GB of expanded storage, so there is considerable room for expansion within this addressing scheme.

IBM is expected to provide shared expanded storage between mainframes. This will allow cooperating operating systems to share gigabytes of control and application data at memory speeds, instead of communicating through communications devices or shared disk drives.

System/370 and 390 Dynamic Address Translation (DAT)

Operating systems on System/370 and 390 use *dynamic address translation* (DAT) to implement virtual storage. DAT converts each virtual address into a real memory location if the virtual storage location is currently assigned a location in real memory. If the virtual storage location is not resident in real storage, DAT generates a *translation exception* program check, usually called a *page fault*.

The failing instruction is suppressed, and hardware causes a context switch to the operating system. The system retrieves the page from external paging media and redispatches the application. If the page was previously unreferenced, a fresh page containing binary zeros is given to the page faulting application. IBM operating systems usually place applications in *page wait*, blocking execution until the user page has been fetched into storage. IBM mainframe operating systems provide program interfaces to let multitasking applications continue execution after a page fault.

DAT is enabled by a flag in the PSW. When in use, each address generated by a program is a virtual address and is translated by hardware into a real memory address. When DAT is off, program addresses are real storage addresses and must correspond to a storage location installed in the computer's real memory. CP runs with DAT disabled.

370-mode systems use only 24 bits of an address value to refer to storage, and can therefore address up to 16MB of real or virtual storage. XA and ESA systems run in 31-bit mode, allowing addressability of 2GB of data and can provide both 24-bit and 31-bit addressability to its applications. The XA architecture has instructions for switching between 24-bit and 31-bit addressing. As mentioned earlier, 32-bit addressing is not used, in order to prevent the sign-bit being relevant to address arithmetic.

Segment and page addressing

DAT hardware performs a double table lookup to convert virtual storage addresses into real addresses. Virtual addresses are are divided into a *segment* number, the page within the segment, and a page displacement into the page. Segments are 64KB in VM/SP and VM/HPO, and 1MB in VM/XA and VM/ESA. Pages are 4K bytes in length.

Control register 1, also called the *segment table origin* (STO) register, points to the current *segment table* in main storage. DAT takes the high order bits of each virtual storage address, and uses it as an array index into the segment table. Each segment table entry contains a pointer to the page table describing the pages in the segment.

The next bits of the virtual address are used as an index into the *page table*. The page table entry includes a main storage address, which is the real storage page address of the *page frame* that page has been assigned to. DAT hardware then adds the remaining bits of the address to the real address, and uses that for the real storage address. This mapping is shown in Fig. 3.5 for an address mapping to segment 2, page 0.

Segmented addressing reduces the size of tables needed to translate virtual addresses to real. IBM architects anticipated that large sections of a user's address space would be unused. Page tables occupy more storage than segment tables, but can be omitted for unused segments.

Virtual machines need segment tables large enough to address the highest-numbered segment they can address, but can omit page tables for unused page ranges. This saves considerable table storage for CMS users. CMS IPLable saved systems, and applications saved in "discontiguous shared segments" reside in segment ranges discontiguous from the virtual machine's storage size. This lets many CMS users share a single copy of a program in main storage, and also lets them share the segment tables for the common storage areas. CP allocates segment tables for all the addressable segments, but doesn't need segment tables for the unused parts of the address space.

Page faults

Entries in both the segment and page tables contain valid/invalid bits, which indicate whether there is a main storage page for the specified virtual address. If both the segment and page entries for a virtual address are marked "valid," then the page is said to be *resident*, and the storage reference is allowed to proceed.

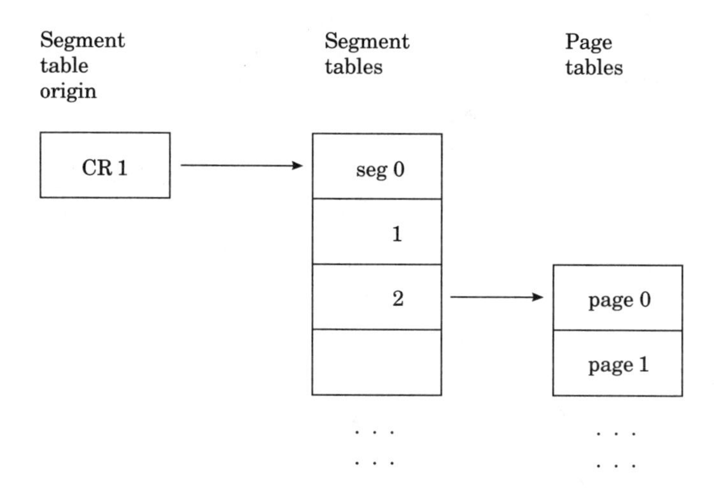

Fig. 3.5 Dynamic address translation.

On each successful main storage access, hardware automatically marks a page's page table entry as "referenced." For write accesses, a "changed" bit is set as well. CP uses these bits to decide which pages should be kept in memory, and which pages have been altered and must be be written to expanded storage or disk before they can be reused.

If either the segment or page are marked invalid, hardware generates the page fault mentioned earlier. CP allocates a real page frame with the required virtual storage contents, either by reading a page from disk or expanded storage into memory, or for previously unreferenced virtual storage pages, by clearing a page frame to all zeros. CP then marks the page and segment tables of the user to now include this page as resident, and redispatches the user at the instruction that previously faulted.

A single instruction may page fault multiple times if it or its storage operands reside in multiple pages. Storage-to-storage instructions like MVC (MoVe Characters) can fault as many as 6 times. The instruction itself can span a page boundary and reside partially in two nonresident pages, as can each of its two operands. The instruction is suppressed until each of the storage operands is resident in memory. System/370 and 390 hardware conceptually "pretests" each instruction's operands for being resident before permanently changing any operand. A specific hardware implementation may either pretest storage operands or discard temporary results if a storage location is found to not be resident.

The "long" instructions, MVCL (MoVe Characters Long) and CLCL (Compare Logical Characters Long) are exceptions to the "suppress and retry" rule. These instructions copy or compare up to 16MB of virtual storage in a single execution, so it is impractical to pretest and suppress execution. Instead, these instructions are designed to be restartable in case of an interrupt like a page fault. Both instructions use pairs of registers containing address and length values for their source and destination storage operands. As the instruction proceeds, the addresses are incremented and remaining lengths decremented to adjust for the storage already processed. If an interrupt occurs, the instruction can be restarted and continued.

Clearly, both "long" and standard instruction methods for handling page faults represent significant complexity for an implementation to deal with, and require commitments in microcode and circuitry. Proponents of RISC architectures argue that this is a defect of CISC computers, and that the added CPU complexity is not justified by the flexibility of allowing instructions and operands to span multiple pages.

Translation lookaside buffers

Dynamic address translation is not without expense, even for storage references that do not page fault. Considerable real storage is allocated for these tables. To reduce the real storage requirements of idle logged on users,

VM/SP, HPO, and VM/ESA migrate inactive segment tables to disk. This was not made available in VM/XA, but was reinstituted in VM/ESA. Without this feature, a maximum size virtual machine of 2047MB would require 8MB of real storage for segment tables as long as it was logged on.

Machine cycles are used to translate addresses from virtual to real. The double table lookup is expensive, since it requires fetching and examining multiple words from main storage for each program reference to storage. To reduce this cost, 370 and 390 systems use a *translation lookaside buffer* (TLB) containing the most recently translated page addresses. Each CPU in a multiprocessor contains its own TLB.

A TLB is a small, fast "content addressable memory," indexed by virtual storage address. If a TLB entry matches the segment and page of a storage reference, the address previously translated for it can be used. If there is no matching table entry, hardware performs the translation and saves the result in the TLB. TLBs are of limited size, and the hardware discards the least recently used translation value when adding to a full TLB. The TLB has to be emptied when VM switches to a different virtual address space (e.g. another VM user), since their virtual addresses correspond to different real addresses.

The most significant cost of virtual storage, however, is the expense of using a bounded real storage to simulate an arbitrarily larger amount of virtual storage.

Virtual storage replacement strategies

The sum of all users' virtual storage is usually larger than real storage. A replacement strategy selects data to be kept in faster media, or literally, which data is to be moved to slower media. Different algorithms try to predict which virtual storage locations are the best candidates to retain in real storage.

The optimal algorithm (called `MIN` to indicate "minimum cost") keeps in the top of the hierarchy data that will be needed in the near future, by replacing the data that will not be needed for the longest time. Unfortunately, this is not generally implementable, since storage references are not known in advance.

Instead, replacement algorithms try to predict future storage references of a program by keeping track of its recent history. There are a number of algorithms based on this idea, the best known of which is the *Least Recently Used* (LRU) algorithm. This algorithm selects for replacement the allocated slot which has not been used for the longest time. A storage location that has not been used recently is not likely to be needed in the near future. LRU is a good approximation of MIN.

LRU requires that a "last access time" variable be updated for each access to storage. This is infeasible for replacement algorithms implemented in software, without considerably higher hardware costs. LRU is used for cache and TLB management, but not for software implemented virtual storage, at least, not on System/370 and 390.

Instead, storage management algorithms for System/370 and System/390 approximate LRU by periodically inspecting *referenced* and *changed* flags set by hardware during storage references. This software approximation of LRU is called "CLOCK." The methods used by VM are discussed in the section "Free list replenishment" on page 169.

Development of good replacement strategies was a vital step in making virtual storage concepts usable in realistic environments.

Chapter

4

System/370 and System/390 I/O Architecture

System/370 and System/390 input/output (I/O) architectures influence VM's design just as CPU processing does, because VM emulates real system I/O processing for virtual machines. In some ways, this is even more challenging than virtual CPU processing, because VM must simulate details external to the CPU. VM has evolved with IBM's changing I/O architectures, reflecting the increasingly more sophisticated methods used for input and output. This chapter discusses aspects of I/O processing that have influenced and motivated VM's development. As with the previous chapter, you may prefer to skim this material if you are familiar with System/370.

I/O Architecture Design Considerations

Good I/O architectures are essential for general purpose computing systems. System/360's success was attributed largely to its I/O architecture, and to availability of large and fast (for the times) disk drives. This made it possible for System/360 users to use disk-resident multiprogramming operating systems, and use disk-based applications. This was a significant advance over the tape and card-oriented processing of the early 1960s. IBM has continued to improve I/O capabilities with each generation of mainframe.

A key requirement of an I/O architecture is that processing should not be limited by the slow speeds of input/output devices. This has several meanings: First, input/output subsystems should be able to deliver data to the computer quickly enough to keep the CPU busy. Balanced computer systems have sufficient I/O resources to keep computation from "drying up" while waiting for I/O to complete.

A further requirement is that I/O processing be efficient with CPU resources. Operating systems should be economical with the CPU processing to perform I/O; CP is noted for short I/O support instruction pathlengths. In mainframe architecture, this also means that execution of I/O operations is distributed to specialized I/O processors, to let CPUs continue with other tasks after starting an I/O operation. In System/360 and its descendants, this is done using specialized channels. Channels on ES/9000 systems are actually powerful special-purpose computers. Channel programs, initiated by the CPU, can be long sequences of I/O commands executed by the channel without host attention. CP simulates channel properties for its virtual machines.

Ironically, the advent of personal computers and workstations has reintroduced computer systems whose CPUs directly perform I/O operations and wait for them to complete. Direct comparisons of "MIPS" ratings between these systems and mainframes are extremely misleading, since they don't include the many MIPS dedicated to I/O processing. Channels allow mainframes to offload work that must be performed by the actual CPU in PCs and workstations. In fact, each of dozens of channels on 3090 and ES/9000 processors are RISC processors estimated to execute at 20 MIPS.

Mainframe I/O architectures increasingly distribute intelligence to outboard devices, and decouple CPU operations from I/O processing. This increases the possibility for throughput by encouraging concurrent operation of CPUs and many I/O devices.

System/370

System/370 addresses I/O devices by a three- or four-digit hexadecimal number, with the first one or two digits specifying the channel number, and the last two digits specifying the device on the channel, as shown in Fig. 4.1. This is the origin of the notation "cuu" that is frequently used to describe a device.

System/370 CPUs start an I/O operation by issuing a Start I/O (`SIO`) or Start I/O Fast Release (`SIOF`) instruction. This tells the channel to inspect a fixed low-storage location called the *channel address word* (CAW), at location X'48'. The CAW contains the address of the first *channel command word* (CCW) of a channel program. The channel accepts the program if it is not busy and no error states (malfunctions of device or channel) are detected. If the channel is busy, CPU software either tries to start the I/O operation over an alternate channel path (if one has been installed), or queues the I/O operation until the current operation completes.

The CPU and the channel continue processing independently after the I/O instruction completes. SIO and SIOF both result in condition codes, and

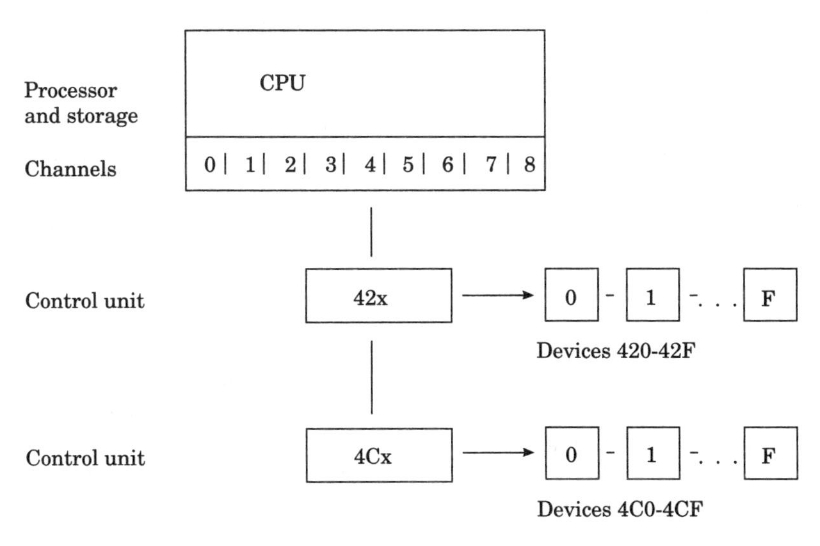

Fig. 4.1 System/370 I/O structure.

a conditional branch can test whether the I/O started successfully. When the channel program completes, the channel places status information in the channel status word in main storage, and generates an interrupt to the CPU that started the I/O.

An SIO instruction does not complete until the I/O command has been transmitted to the peripheral device. This allows the SIO to return a condition code indicating whether the physical device accepted the I/O operation. This is a long delay relative to the speed of the computer and may cost thousands of instruction times on fast CPUs. Upgrading a CPU does not necessarily reduce the time of an SIO instruction, since most of its execution time is outboard to the CPU, and consists of transmitting a signal to and from a distant device.

SIO was available with System/360, and still works with System/370 systems. SIOF was introduced with System/370, and terminates quickly with a preliminary condition code that reflects whether or not the channel could accept the command. This lets the CPU continue processing while the channel subsystem transmits the I/O command to the device.

When SIOF completes with CC=0, it indicates that the I/O was accepted, but does not guarantee that the I/O operation will be successful. If the device was busy, the channel generates a *deferred condition code* interrupt. This tells the CPU that the previously started I/O operation wasn't accepted. The CPU must reissue the I/O when the channel or device generate an interrupt to indicate that it is available.

CP emulates both SIO and SIOF for virtual machines using virtual devices, which need not map onto a real device, and channel commands located in virtual storage. When a virtual machine issues an SIO, it remains in instruction simulation, and cannot issue further instructions until CP can issue a real SIOF to the device. CP delays virtual machine execution until the real SIOF (if one is needed) so it can place the I/O operation's condition code in the virtual machine PSW. Virtual machines can continue CPU processing before the I/O operation is issued if they use SIOF and enable block multiplexing. Control register 0 mode has a bit setting that defines whether block multiplexor channels are in multiplex mode. CP emulates this feature of System/370 by allowing or refusing I/O operations on an in-use virtual channel based on the contents of virtual control register 0.

When a channel program completes, the channel notifies the CPU by an interrupt, after storing status information in the *channel status word (CSW)*, at location X'40'. The CSW contains the address following the last command executed by the channel, and a number of status indicator bits. The status indicators are vital for determining if the I/O event completed normally, and includes the fields "channel end" (CE), which indicates that the channel reached the end of the channel program, "device end," "busy," "unit check," and several others. CP converts the CSW's channel command address into the corresponding virtual storage address in the virtual machine, and places it and the other CSW data in the virtual machine's CSW.

Channel queueing

Channel queueing, available in ES/9000, 3090, and 308x processors, provides additional decoupling of a CPU's speed from its devices. These processors can accept a SIOF instruction even if the path is busy.

If the path is busy because the channel is busy, hardware restarts the I/O when the channel becomes free. If the control unit is busy, a 10 millisecond timer is started. If the path becomes available before the timer expires, the channel restarts the I/O without telling the CPU about the temporary delay. This saves CPU cycles because the operating system does not have to reexecute its I/O scheduling routines. It also improves I/O performance because the I/O device is restarted as soon as it becomes available. Without hardware queueing, an I/O operation is not retried until the CPU enables for interrupts, receives an interrupt for the completed I/O, and reissues the delayed I/O.

Extended Architecture and Enterprise System Architecture

IBM designers realized that System/370 I/O required too much CPU intervention, and too closely coupled I/O operations to individual CPUs and channel paths. System/370 requires that a CPU specify the path to the I/O device. SIO and SIOF instructions explicitly name the channel and control unit the I/O is directed to. If the channel path is busy, the CPU must requeue the I/O on an alternate path, or restart it when the path becomes free.

When a device responds to a System/370 host, it must send data to the same CPU and channel path the I/O started on. I/O event completion is delayed until the original CPU is enabled for interrupts, and the same channel path is idle, even if another channel path to an interrupt-enabled CPU is available.

XA and ESA architecture disassociate I/O operations from specific CPUs or channels, and offload work, most notably path selection, to an external I/O data subsystem, illustrated in Fig. 4.2. This reduces the CPU time needed to drive I/O, shortens the response time before the system responds to an interrupt, and improves use of channel paths.

XA I/O operations specify a device's *subchannel number*, which names a device but doesn't specify the control unit or channel path to it. This is a key difference between 370 and XA I/O, because 370 I/O instructions specify path information.

System programmers specify path information when they run the *Input Output Control Program (IOCP)*. IOCP input specifies every device in-

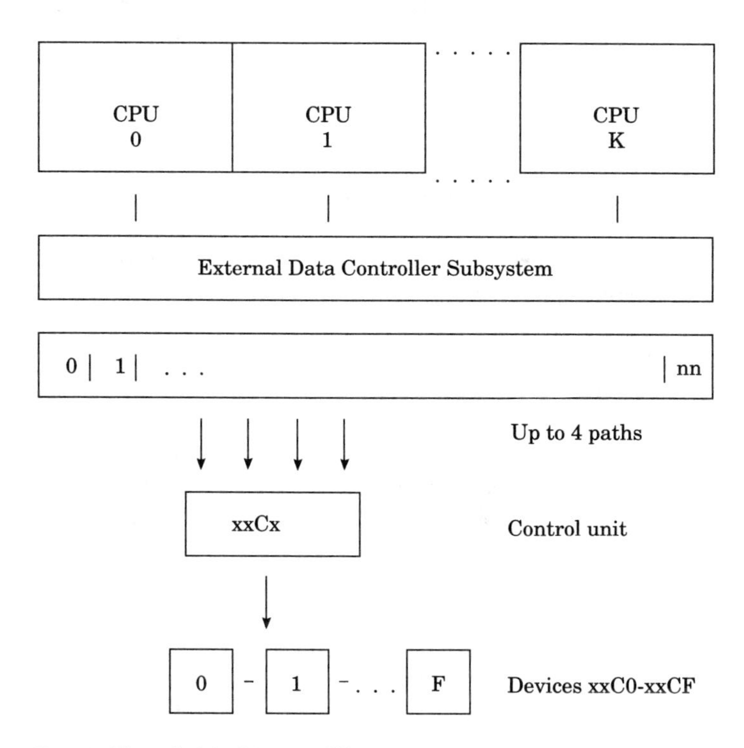

Fig. 4.2 Extended Architecture I/O structure.

stalled on a system (in groups, to reduce typing). A device's description includes its device number, a programmer-selected number used to identify the device in operator commands, the device's model (e.g., a 3390 disk drive), and the control units it is attached to. Similarly, a control unit's definition includes the list of channels it is connected to. IOCP assigns each device a subchannel number, and records its device number, device characteristics, and the channel paths between it and the CPU complex.

Human-entered commands refer to the device number, the device's external name, and I/O operations refer to the subchannel number. CP's RDEV control block describes every device, and can be indexed by either device or subchannel number. For convenience, device numbers are usually arranged with the same notation as System/370 device addresses, even though their numeric values no longer indicate the real channel and device path used in I/O operations.

IOCP information is stored in an *I/O Control Data Set* (IOCDS). An IOCDS is loaded into the CPU's *hardware storage area* by system operator commands after changing the hardware configuration available to the host. The HSA is a block of real storage reserved for the CPU itself, and unaccessible to software routines. Operator commands for manipulating IOCP information are processed by microcoded support routines built into the CPU. During system operation, the HSA contains information describing the status of every device.

CPUs issue I/O to a device via the Start Subchannel (`SSCH`) instruction. SSCH is used with an Output Request Block (`ORB`), which specifies device and control information. The I/O subsystem determines which physical channels to the device are available, and starts the operation along an idle path.

This is more efficient than the System/370 method of issuing an I/O operation along one path, and then retrying on alternate paths until a free path is found. In XA, an I/O operation is not delayed unless all physical paths to a device are busy. A device can signal to any CPU in the processor complex, across any channel path that connect them. *Dynamic path reconnect* improves device responsiveness and makes XA's I/O performance much better than System/370's.

VM/XA and VM/ESA emulate XA I/O operations for virtual machines running in XA or ESA mode, using a process analogous to 370-mode I/O emulation described previously. In addition, VM/XA and VM/ESA support 370-mode virtual machines, and translate virtual 370-mode I/O operations to and from the XA mode operations used on the real hardware.

Channels

A *channel* is a special-purpose computer that controls I/O operations and transfers data between outboard (external) devices and main storage. The channel orders the sequence of actions needed to perform a complete I/O

Selector	High-speed devices, one active I/O at a time
Byte multiplexor	Low-speed devices, multiple active I/Os Data interleaved on individual byte basis
Block multiplexor	High-speed devices, multiple active I/Os Data interleaved on block basis

Fig. 4.3 System/370 family channel types.

operation while the CPU proceeds with other work, and transfers data between the peripherals and main storage.

There are three channel types, used for different types of devices: the *byte multiplexor*, the *selector*, and the *block multiplexor* channels. (Channel characteristics are summarized in Fig. 4.3.) There is no mechanical difference between them; channel types are specified via firmware or the IOCP, and take effect with the next *Power On Reset* (POR).

Byte multiplexors are used for relatively slow devices like line printers and slow-speed telecommunications, and can perform multiple simultaneous I/O operations. The "byte mux" is so named because it can interleave (multiplex) data transfer between devices and memory for different devices on a byte-by-byte basis.

Selector channels are used for fast devices, such as tape drives. When a selector channel is transferring data between main storage and a device, it is monopolized ("selected") by the device, and cannot service any other device or I/O operation until the operation completes. An attempt to issue a new I/O operation to the channel results in a "busy" condition code, and the request is ignored. If you have a long bank of tape drives on the same channel, only one of them is actually under the control of the channel at any one time.

Selector channels, and to a lesser extent, byte multiplexor channels, have been replaced by the block multiplexor channel. Although actually available for late, high-end 360 models, the block multiplexor is generally considered one of System/370's improvements over System/360. "Block mux" channels drive high-speed devices like selectors, but can interleave data transmission between storage and different devices on a block-by-block basis, that is, between individual READ or WRITE commands. Block multiplexor channels are used for disk and tape I/O and for faster versions of device types formerly driven by byte channels, such as NCP (SNA/VTAM style) terminal I/O and 3800 printers.

An I/O request to a block channel with active channel programs does not necessarily result in a "busy" condition. The request can be accepted, and either execute or result in a later rejection, called a "deferred condition code." The meaning of "busy" is changed from "already doing work" to "already doing work, and unable to accept more."

The attention of a multiplexing channel is required during a READ or WRITE operation, since it is the interface between the device and the computer's main storage, but can be released (disconnected) during parts of a channel program that don't require access to main storage. During these commands, usually device positioning commands, the channel can be used to service other devices. A block multiplexor can therefore be transferring data from one disk while other disks on the same channel are positioning themselves, either by moving the access arm or by rotating a desired record until it is under the read/write head.

A channel is wired via a bus arrangement to *control units*, each of which controls a group of devices. Control units may be "daisy chained" (as it is called) by routing channel cables through multiple controllers. The last control unit on a channel cable includes a "terminator" to mark the end of the circuit. Each control unit responds to a separate range of I/O addresses, and responds only to commands passed from the channel that fall within its range.

Enterprise System Connection (ESCON)

When IBM introduced System/390 in September of 1990, they also introduced their first truly new channel architecture since System/360. ESCON channels provide higher data transfer rates, let devices be much further from the host computer than System/360 and 370, and make it easier to configure and change data centers while they are in use.

Previous IBM channels transmitted data over heavy copper "bus and tag" cables. Control and data signals travel in parallel between host and device controllers over separate signal wires. Randomness in signal speed in these wires causes signal impulses to arrive at different times ("timing skew"). To keep skew within acceptable tolerances, devices on parallel channels can be no further than 400 feet from the host computer.

In many data centers, the 400-foot cable restriction becomes almost intolerable, and it becomes almost impossible to physically install all needed peripherals close enough to the CPUs to which they must be connected. Additionally, devices can only be added or removed from parallel channels when the host system is quiesced, since the channel circuit has to be broken, risking an electrical spike.

ESCON architecture replaces parallel channels with *serial* channels based on fiber-optic technology. Electromagnetic pulses (which must be shielded) over heavy copper cables are replaced by LED (light emitting diode) signals transmitted over fiberglass strands. Signals are transmitted in bit-serial manner instead of byte-parallel. Complete bytes are assembled and disassembled at the ends of the strand, either by new parallel channels, ESCON *converters* (which convert parallel traffic to and from serial), or ESCON-capable devices.

ESCON allows higher data transfer speeds than parallel channels: 10MB per second and higher compared to 4.5MB. ESCON also lets devices be as many as 23 kilometers away from the CPU, and lets channel to channel (CTC) adapters connect CPUs up to 60 kilometers from one another. This provides flexibility in data center configuration, and lets companies share peripherals between CPUs in multiple sites.

ESCON channels are far lighter than parallel cables—an important benefit for technicians who move them, and for building planners. Parallel channel cables are so heavy that their weight must be considered when designing the weight-bearing capacity of a data center floor.

Since data is transmitted via light instead of electricity, devices can be added to or removed from a host configuration without risk of electrical disruption. IBM uses this to allow coordinated device change management in multi-CPU, continuously operating data centers.

Channel interface to the CPU

A channel shares main storage with the CPU and other channels, and communicates with the CPU using condition codes and data in storage. I/O instructions tell a channel to start executing a *channel program* built by system software. When the program ends, the channel interrupts the CPU and provides status information. Channel programs are composed of eight-byte long *channel command words* (CCWs). Individual channel commands are single low-level I/O operations, such as "seek to this cylinder," "sense I/O error conditions," "read," "write," and "search."

For example, an I/O operation to read a single record from a disk file uses a channel program with several channel commands. A "command chaining" flag in each channel command indicates whether another command follows it in storage. This is extremely valuable for system performance, since it allows a series of primitive I/O operations to be performed without individual host notification. A complicated I/O command can be scheduled and started as a group, and the host only has to service a single interrupt when it completes.

Even logically separate I/O operations to the same device can be chained together by appending a Transfer In Channel (`TIC`) command to the end of channel programs. A TIC acts like a "branch" instruction on the host CPU, and can be used for looping or for joining separate programs into a single I/O. This helps further reduce CPU overhead needed to schedule I/O and process I/O interrupts.

A number of commands release the channel so it can be used for another device. Disk "seek cylinder" commands release the channel, as do tape positioning commands. The devices request attention from the channel after completing the positioning command.

Control Units

Control units handle the low level device-oriented details of device control. Even channels look at I/O operations in a way that is relatively device-type independent. A *read* channel command looks the same to a channel whether for a tape drive or a disk, even though different mechanical and electronic events occur.

Control units on a channel share a common bus. Each responds only to commands directed to the address range assigned to the control unit, and ignores other message traffic.

Control units are designed for a single or small number of closely related devices, and are aware of the timing and device geometry characteristics of the devices they control. Most control units are powerful microprogrammed computers, capable of executing millions of instructions per second, and use programs loaded from floppy diskettes (during Initial Microprogram Load or IML) to implement control logic.

Most controllers manage a group of devices of the same type. Controllers usually are much more "intelligent" than devices, and handle their control aspects while relegating only truly low-level mechanical and electronic operations to devices. This design choice shares expensive logic instead of replicating intelligence in each device unit. Exceptions to this rule are 3745 communications controllers and 3900 high speed laser printers, both very complex and containing integrated controllers.

More typical are disk control units, which, for example, perform the low-level work of locating a desired record on a disk track. The control unit compares the identification of the data currently under the magnetic read-write head to the search argument given by the channel. This is a timing-critical operation and requires dedicated attention from parts of the control unit.

This makes a disk control unit, such as the 3990 disk storage director, a complicated high-powered computer in its own right. A 3990 can arbitrate I/O requests to devices under its control from as many as eight CPUs, transform data from bit-serial to bit-parallel form and transmit data to the channel interface at 4.5MB per second, or transmit at 17MB per second on ESCON serial channels. Disk controllers can diagnose and retry many types of I/O errors without host intervention.

A control unit can allow a channel to process other I/O requests while an I/O operation is running, just as a channel allows the CPU to perform other activities during an I/O. This has always been true for certain long-running I/O operations such as tape rewind, even on selector channels. These commands can be programmed as the last command in a channel program. This lets the channel become idle and report a "channel end" (CE) to the CPU, which can then start a channel program to another device. The first device is operated by the control unit, which reports a "device end" (DE) back to the channel and CPU when the rewind finishes.

With the advent of the block multiplexor channel, IBM introduced control units able to perform more processing independent of the channel. The most significant of these is the ability of a disk control unit to operate without the channel for most of the duration of an I/O operation. Disk devices *disconnect* from a control unit during disks' rotational and seek delays. This is discussed below in the section on Direct Access Storage Devices.

Most control units can be attached to multiple channels, making devices and data accessible from multiple host systems. It also provides fault tolerance because each host can access devices under the control unit as long as one of their channel interfaces is functional. Finally, this improves performance, since all channel interfaces on a control unit can concurrently service I/O operations.

Figure 4.4 illustrates two CPUs connected to the same devices via a pair of cross-connected disk controllers. System "A" has channels 1 and 2 cabled to the A and B interfaces of one controller, and channels 3 and 4 cabled to the A and B interfaces of the other controller or storage director. The opposite channel interfaces are reserved for the channels originating from System "B."

In this diagram, both CPUs can concurrently execute multiple disk I/O operations, with up to 4 devices transmitting data at the same time. Other disks may be busy moving access arms or waiting for data to rotate under the read-write head. Each CPU can continue to access the disk drives, with reduced performance, after a failure of either the storage director or of all but one channel and channel interface combination. This arrangement is used in almost all IBM data centers. It provides both high performance and insulation from outages caused by a single point of failure.

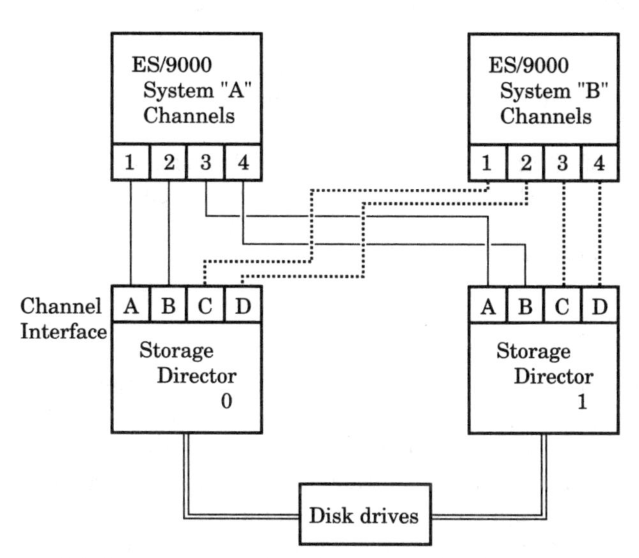

Fig. 4.4 Cross connected channels, control units, devices.

I/O Devices

At the end of the subchannel path, from the CPU's point of view, and at the bottom of the scale of distributed intelligence, are I/O devices. I/O devices are responsible for physical data media, and include electromechanical transport mechanisms to store and transmit data.

Most devices have a minimum amount of logic, suitable for converting the analog information in, for example, magnetic flux on disk media, into binary digital data. A device may also convert data between bits serially received from the device to complete bytes transmitted to the control unit.

In addition, a device is also responsible for performing error detection and correction through the use of parity bits or ECC (error correction codes). The controller may use this information to request a retry of an I/O operation if a parity error was detected. Most error retries can be performed without CPU intervention. Some errors are temporary and do not recur when the I/O operation is retried. IBM operating systems record both temporary and permanent I/O errors; most installations regularly run error reports to identify devices that require service.

Direct Access Storage Devices (DASD)

Disk drives, often called *Direct Access Storage Devices* (DASD) in the IBM mainframe world, contain platters of magnetic media, with data recorded on both sides of each platter. In some models, one side of one platter is used to record timing information.

Data is sensed by read/write heads that move in and out of the stack of platters and read or write data by sensing or changing magnetic flux on the disk surface. Platters are arranged in concentric tracks, each a given radius from the center of the disk drive. The data in all tracks at the same radius is called a cylinder, and contains the amount of data that can be read without moving the access arm.

IBM uses a number of different architectures for addressing and managing disk storage, discussed below. As with other changes in their computing architecture, they reflect the trend towards distributing intelligence and decoupling operations from host control.

Count key data architecture

Most System/370 DASD use the *Count Key Data* (CKD) architecture, IBM's traditional disk architecture since System/360. Each record on a CKD disk consists of count, key, and data fields separated by gaps, and is identified by a *seek address* composed of cylinder and track numbers, and record number within a track. A gap also appears between each record. Records stored on disk are often referred to as a *block*, to distinguish them from application records (such as lines in a program file), which may occupy only part of a block. The number of *logical records* that fit in a block is sometimes referred to as the *blocking factor*.

The count field contains the seek address and the length of the key and data portions. Consequently, each disk record is self-identifying: many I/O commands use the count field to specify which disk record is to be read or written. Programs can format a track to contain different numbers of records of different sizes, based on application needs. CMS uses a small number of standard "good" block sizes to simplify programming and to shield users from details of disk geometry.

The key field, which may be omitted, contains a search key used by the application: channel commands can search for a record with a matching key (e.g., a person's name or customer code). A number of host access methods use this hardware feature to offload searching operations to the disk controller.

Additionally, each track contains a home address record following the index point of the disk. The home address contains its cylinder and track address and flags that indicate whether the track is usable or defective; it is used to ensure the access arm is properly calibrated and is seeking to the right locations. Additionally, the first record on a track, called *record 0* (R0), contains the address of an *alternate track* if the track is defective. A simplified illustration of a CKD track appears in Fig. 4.5.

Clearly, System/360 and System/370 DASD were designed to cope with unreliable disk drives. This was a key factor in System/360's lifetime because disks were far less reliable than current devices. This is largely due to the less accurate mechanical control possible at the time. This was also caused by the use of mountable disk volumes that were mounted and dismounted by operators, much as tape drives still are today. Later IBM disk drives used sealed units with built-in access arms, which allowed better calibration of access arm and media.

CKD I/O operations start with a seek to a given cylinder and track. If this is an I/O operation initiated by an application, the operating system (CP, MVS, or

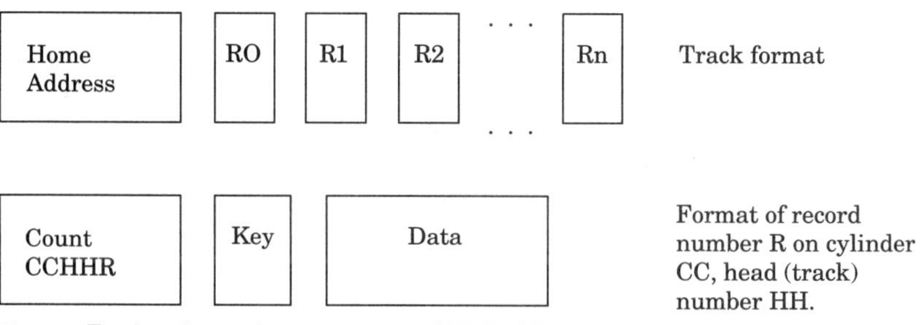

Fig. 4.5 Track and record organization in CKD DASD.

VSE) appends a SET FILE MASK command to prevent applications from moving the read/write arm beyond the extent of the disk area belonging to the user.

Successive commands search for a specified record, and read or write data from or to disk. An optional SET SECTOR command, described below, tells the channel to disconnect while the data is rotating towards the access arm. A sector can be considered as specifying the angular position of data on the circumference of a track. The following example shows a typical CKD channel program:

```
CCW  SEEK,SEEKADDR,CC          seek to cylinder/head
CCW  SETFILEMASK,MASK,CC       restrict subsequent seeks
CCW  SETSECTOR,CC              specify reconnect sector
CCW  SEARCH,SRCHARG,CC         search for desired record
CCW  TIC,*-8                   search again if not found
CCW  READ,BUFFER,0,BUFLEN      read the record
```

The search argument may be a key in the usual sense of a random access (e.g., VSAM) file or a count record address. The SEARCH command compares the current record's count field to that of the record under the read/write head. If they match, the next channel command is skipped. Otherwise, the TIC command branches the channel program to issue the search again. CC indicates command chaining, and tells the channel that the channel program continues with the next main storage location. Additional commands could be appended to the channel program to read or write additional blocks.

Fixed block architecture

IBM uses the *Fixed Block Architecture* (FBA) on its rack mounted 3310, 3370, 9332, 9335, and 9336 devices, devices usually attached to smaller System/370 and ES/9000 computers. FBA disks store data in 512 byte blocks, in a manner similar to how data is stored on personal computer and UNIX systems. Blocks are identified by linear block numbers, starting at zero, without cylinder or track geometry. FBA disks have cylinders and tracks, of course, but these details are hidden within the controller.

FBA simplifies I/O programming, and reduces the number of interactions between the storage controller and the host channel. Instead of SEEK and SEARCH commands, FBA channel programs use DEFINE EXTENT and LOCATE, to tell the controller the range of disk locations that may be referenced in the channel program, and the locations needed for a subsequent read or write operation. DEFINE EXTENT takes the place of CKD SEEK and SET FILE MASK, and additionally specifies whether or not WRITE or diagnostic commands will be permitted in the channel program. LOCATE takes the place of the SETSECTOR, SEARCH, TIC sequence, and tells the controller whether a

READ or WRITE command will be used after the desired record is reached. A typical FBA channel program is shown below:

```
CCW  DEFINEEXTENT,CC,extent        specify extent of I/O operation
CCW  LOCATE,location,CC            specify location of 1st disk record
                                     in I/O operation
CCW  READ,BUFFER,0,BUFLEN          read the record
```

DOS/VSE and VM support FBA disks. MVS never was altered to support this device architecture, partially because it would have been such a difficult change to introduce in the hundreds of device-sensitive places in MVS code, and partially because FBA disks were only installed on the small systems MVS didn't run on.

Extended count key data

FBA's benefits were extended to large system DASD with the 3390 and some 3380 models via a hybrid of FBA and CKD channel commands called Extended CKD (ECKD). ECKD also uses DEFINE EXTENT and LOCATE commands, but uses the CKD format of disk data. This provides media and program compatibility with CKD. In fact, CKD channel programs can be used on 3390s, although with a cost in performance.

ECKD lets the controller decouple device timing from channel and host access, a distinct improvement over CKD, which requires synchronous transfer of data from the media to main storage when the data passes under the read/write head. Since the LOCATE command specifies whether the following operation is a read or write, the controller and channel can perform anticipatory data transfer before the device is positioned over the desired disk location. On a write operation, the controller can receive data from the channel and store it in a buffer until the disk is ready to a receive it. On a read operation, the controller can receive data from the disk as soon as it is ready, and present it to the channel when it eventually issues the read command. This helps avoid the effects of RPS misses, discussed below.

ECKD was originally used for the 3380 *speed matching buffer* feature, used when 3380 disk drives were attached to systems with channel speeds slower than the 3380's data transfer rate. ECKD makes it possible to use ESCON channels for disk drives in locations distant from the CPU, without concern for signal propagation delays.

Disk performance

The time to perform a disk I/O falls mostly into the following categories:

1. Seek time moving the arm to the cylinder. The time depends on the distance between the prior and new seek locations, and is zero if they are the same.

2. Rotational latency time, the time needed to rotate the needed data under the disk read/write head and acquire the attention of the channel.
3. Data transfer (read or write). This is the only part of the I/O operation improved by faster channels.

A disk's access arm must be moved to the cylinder that contains the needed data. If the arm is not already positioned over the right cylinder there is a delay called *seek time*. There may also be a delay changing between tracks of the same cylinder. Most drives cannot switch between the last record of one track and the first record of another track within one revolution.

When several files or minidisks on the same volume are in use at the same time, the access arm must seek back and forth between them. This is called *head contention*, and it is extremely damaging to the performance of any system. Head contention is reduced by spreading frequently used files over many different disk volumes, or clustering them near one another on the volume, rather than on opposite ends.

Rotational latency is the time it takes for the desired data to rotate to the read/write head, and is uniformly distributed between 0 (the data was right under the read/write head) and a full revolution (the data just missed the head, and has to rotate completely to get to it again). IBM 3390 disks rotate at 4200 RPM (revolutions per minute), and have a maximum delay of 14.2 milliseconds. Other IBM disk drives rotate at 3600 RPM, and have a maximum rotational delay of 16.7 milliseconds. The average delay is one-half the maximum.

Rotational position sensing (RPS) lets a channel service other disks while waiting for rotational delay. CKD programs use the SET SECTOR command to specify the *sector* number preceding the data record. The sector number identifies an angular position relative to a fixed index marker position. When SET SECTOR is encountered, the channel disconnects from the channel program until the specified sector is reached. When the sector rotates under the head, the control unit tells the channel to reconnect and finish the channel program.

There is a brief period of time, called the *RPS window*, during which the channel can successfully reconnect to the device. If the channel does not connect during the RPS window, because it is busy servicing another device, the disk spins past the desired record, and the data is not available until a full additional revolution. Failure to reconnect is called an RPS miss, and causes a delay of a full revolution. The delay may be repeated, with equal likelihood, each subsequent time the RPS window comes up.

VM/ESA "dynamic pathing" greatly reduces RPS delays. An I/O device can reconnect to any channel attached to it, and an RPS miss occurs only if all channels attached to a bank of DASD are busy during the RPS window. In

System/370 operating systems like VM/SP, the reconnect can only occur over the channel that initiated the I/O operation, making misses far more likely.

ECKD disk drives also reduce or eliminate the effect of RPS misses. On write operations data is buffered in the control unit at the time of the write, and is copied to disk as soon as the data is rotated under the access arm. On read operations, data is copied from disk to controller storage, and thence to the channel when it becomes available without waiting for another disk revolution.

Cached DASD controllers

As with virtual storage, disk accesses frequently show locality of reference. This makes it possible to use buffers of smaller and faster memory to speed disk access times. IBM and other vendors provide control units with semiconductor cache storage. Cached controllers, such as the IBM 3880-13, 3880-23, and 3990-3, have between 16MB and 512MB of cache.

All of these controllers improve DASD performance by satisfying reads of previously read data from cache storage without going to actual DASD media. *Read hits* for data already in cache avoid seek and rotational delays, the largest components of the time to perform a disk I/O operation. For example, I/O operations normally requiring 20 to 25 milliseconds may be reduced to 4 milliseconds.

This can be very effective for data that is mostly read. Disk reads are satisfied from cache storage at channel speed if the associated track contents are in cache. On a cache miss, the controller uses the LRU algorithm to displace the longest unused track, and stages into storage the requested record and any records following it on the same track.

IBM's 3990-3 disk controller caches writes as well. The 3990-3's *DASD Fast Write* (DFW) feature accepts data from the channel into semiconductor buffers, and signals the CPU that the write operation is complete; writing to the actual disk is done asynchronously. This lets disk writes proceed at channel speed just like cached reads. VM benchmarks with DFW have reported 75% improvements in I/O response times for some applications.

The 3990's buffer uses nonvolatile semiconductor storage to ensure data integrity. The buffer stores output data until the data is successfully written to disk, and can handle DASD errors or power supply failures. VM/ESA provides the CP operator commands `COMMIT`, `DESTAGE` and `DISCARD` to control data residing in storage cache but not yet written to data. They allow the operator to force data to be written to disk, or to discard data in cache when the target disk volume is failing.

The storage in the 3990 also lets it perform *dual copy* for selected disk volumes. Dual copy lets installations define pairs of disk volumes: when a host system writes to the primary disk volume, the controller asynchronously writes the same data to the alternate copy without host intervention. If the primary volume fails, the system automatically switches to the duplicate volume. The 3990 maintains a bit-map to record which disk tracks have changed when one of the volumes in a pair is unavailable, and can resynchronize disk contents by copying data from the current volume to its alternate.

Chapter

5

VM/CMS Origin and Development

Today's VM system has evolved to adapt to new methods in hardware technology, networking, and most importantly, ways of using computers.VM had the good fortune to have been conceived with a design that made this evolution possible while remaining consistent with previous VM versions. This has helped retain the value and investment in VM applications, even while they are enlarged and enhanced.

Early Timesharing with CTSS

VM has its roots in the landmark *CTSS* system produced at MIT in the mid-1960s. CTSS, the Compatible Time-Sharing System, was one of the world's first interactive systems. Previously, systems ran in batch mode, or programmers had to wait their turns for dedicated time periods to use the computer. The CTSS project, under the direction of Professor Fernando Corbató revolutionized the use of computers by allowing a single computer to time-slice between many users, and provide quick response to them in an interactive manner. While "many" and "quick" had far different meanings then than they do now, the stage was set for future interactive computing environments.

CTSS ran on pre-System/360 IBM processors (IBM 709, 7090, and 7094) and has influenced all interactive systems since then. Many CTSS designers went on to create MULTICS, which in turn inspired UNIX. CTSS also influenced IBM's TSS/360 (Time-Sharing System/360) and CP/67 (Control Program/67). The Association for Computing Machinery (ACM), the pre-eminent computing science organization, presented Professor Corbató the 1990 Turing Award in recognition of his contribution to computing systems.

System/360 operating systems

In the mid-1960s, IBM introduced System/360, which provided architecturally identical computer systems with a range of price and performance. Incompatibilities between System/360 systems were essentially limited to those due to capacity: a program written for a large system might not fit in the memory of a smaller one. This turned out to be a very important incompatibility in practice, and determined the course of IBM operating system development for the next 25 years.

IBM wanted System/360 sites to run a single operating system called OS/360. OS/360 provided batch execution facilities, including program support for data management on disk and tape, memory management, and an arcane *Job Control Language* (JCL) for specifying batched execution of jobs.

It became clear that the extremely complex (critics said far too complex) OS/360 would be shipped too late for many customers' needs, and would require much more main storage than was available on many 360 models. No organization in the world had ever attempted a software project as complicated as OS/360, and nobody understood the complexity and problems of such a project.[1]

This dilemma led to the introduction of multiple operating systems with different programming conventions, and targeted for different-sized 360s. The tragedy of the 360, with respect to compatibility, was that the hardware was compatible, but the operating systems running on it were not. This led to one of VM's earliest roles: using the same hardware to run incompatible operating system environments.

Most System/360 sites ran DOS/360, which ran batch jobs and small transaction processing systems on low-end 360 models like the 360/30. Though unglamorous, DOS/360 running on small 360s was the workhorse of the 360 processor line. DOS provided batch data processing for payroll, general ledger, accounts processing, and other prosaic applications, and was key to the automation of corporate data processing.

Larger sites ran one of two varieties of OS/360: OS/MFT (Multiprogramming with a Fixed number of Tasks), and OS/MVT (Multiprogramming with a Variable number of Tasks).[2] These systems provided file and job management facilities not available with DOS, but required considerably more

---

[1] The story of the struggle to produce OS/360 was described in the book *The Mythical Man-Month* by Fred Brooks, OS/360's main designer. Aptly, the cover of the books shows a dinosaur trapped in the La Brea tar pits. This excellent book should be read by anybody involved in large software projects, though today we no longer refer to "man-months."

[2] A third variety, OS/PCP (Primary Control Program), let small System/360 systems run OS/360, but only let one task execute at a time. In practice, most small 360s ran DOS, and PCP was eventually withdrawn.

hardware resources. OS/MFT could run on moderate-sized systems, and the more sophisticated OS/MVT required even more hardware to run. MVT provided more facilities, including far more flexible memory management, multitasking application capabilities, and a timesharing option (TSO) to let programmers create and test programs at a terminal before they ran in production. OS/360 versions were largely, but not completely compatible with one another. Applications could be moved from one variety of OS/360 to another with little or no change. OS/360 applications were incompatible with DOS/360.

CP/40

The next step leading to the development of VM was the experimental system CP/40, which ran on a customized System/360 model 40 at IBM's Cambridge Scientific Center in Massachusetts. CP/40 introduced the concept of the *virtual machine*, as an extension of the still-experimental notion of virtual storage. It proved that, if provided hardware support for address translation, a System/360 computer could create multiple virtual computers, which could run different operating systems and be used for different purposes.

One of the operating systems was the *Cambridge Monitor System*, called CMS, which provided facilities for user interaction and programs much in the flavor of CTSS. CP/40 had Control Program (CP) for controlling the real system, and CMS for user interaction, thus introducing concepts, commands, and conventions still in use in VM/ESA.

CP/67

CP/40 ran only on an experimental 360/40 modified to provide dynamic address translation for virtual storage. CP/40 was ported to the System/360 model 67, IBM's first production virtual storage computer, and renamed CP/67.

The 360/67 was a virtual storage implementation of the 360/65. The 360/65 most epitomized System/360 design principles and was the basis of the later 370/168, 3033, and 3090 systems. It was also the model IBM used to test features that would become standard in later hardware generations. IBM's first multiprocessor was introduced as a dual-processor 360/65. The 360/67 translated applications' virtual address references to real storage addresses, if the associated block of data was resident in real storage. If the virtual address did not map to a real storage address, the 360/67 interrupted processing, so the operating system could bring the block of storage from disk into storage. Though the mechanics were different from System/370 dynamic address translation, many of the concepts were the same.

The 360/67 was intended for timesharing, and a new and ambitious operating system, TSS/360, was being written for it. Unfortunately, TSS/360, while introducing novel and useful concepts, was programmed using the same "horde of programmers" method that almost buried OS/360.

CP/67 began to be used for timesharing and program development, and for guest systems running multiple copies of OS/360 and DOS/360. New functions were quickly added to CP/67 and shared by a number of research sites within IBM. When the TSS/360 project collapsed under its own weight, CP/67 increasingly was applied outside IBM. Soon a significant client base used CP/67 virtual machines and interactive computing.

Nonetheless, the growth of CP/67, and of timesharing on IBM equipment in general, was curtailed by the limited distribution of its hardware platform. The 360/67, while a production model in the System/360 series, was only one model in a processor line with a wide range of price and performance. Sites with smaller or larger computing needs and budgets were excluded from using CP/67. More seriously, virtual storage was only available on the 360/67, which was therefore considered a "special purpose" system.

Timesharing itself was considered a "special purpose" application in a world that was almost exclusively batch-oriented, even for program development. The time for generally available interactive computing had not yet arrived.

System/370 and Virtual Storage Computing

When System/370 was announced, it notably lacked virtual storage, and there was concern that IBM had abandoned this concept. In 1972, IBM ended these doubts by announcing virtual storage models of System/370 computers, and new operating systems to use this capability: OS/VS1 to replace OS/360's MFT, OS/VS2 to replace MVT, DOS/VS to replace DOS/360, and VM/370 to replace CP/67. IBM announced that future enhancements would come only in the new operating systems, making it necessary for all of their customers to convert from their "functionally stabilized" operating systems (to use IBM's words) to their replacements.

DOS/VS and OS/VS initially allowed all executing jobs to share a single 16MB address range on computers with far less real storage. Previously, programs were shoe-horned to fit into the storage actually installed on a computer. This was a sharp constraint on application and system development in a world in which a small 360 might only have 64KB of main storage, and a large one might have a single megabyte.

IBM later released OS/VS2 Release 2, which provided a 16MB address range for each application. IBM named this system *Multiple Virtual Storage* (MVS) to emphasize the fact that each application had a potential *address space* of 16MB, instead of sharing the single 16MB address space with other applications and the operating system itself (a capability which was already available in VM/370 and even CP/67).

IBM devoted the bulk of its development resources to increasing MVS functionality and its ability to recover from software and hardware errors, while maintaining compatibility with JCL and program interfaces from OS/360. MVS became IBM's "strategic" operating system. IBM expected and encouraged VM, OS, and DOS users to convert to MVS, especially for batch production and CICS telecommunication environments.

Unfortunately, the sheer size and complexity of MVS made it execute very slowly on the machines available then, and difficult to program and change (even by IBM). Adherence to OS/360 JCL and conventions made MVS difficult to use. Nonetheless, MVS made possible the large applications and networks that came to typify enterprise-wide computing.

Increased storage addressability had far-reaching consequences. First, the mainframe computing world had to undergo conversion to new and slightly incompatible operating systems, a process entailing risk and significant effort. Secondly, the increased real and virtual storage sizes available on System/370 enabled interactive computing, by making it possible to keep in storage parts of the program and data storage of many users at the same time. These factors made VM increasingly important.

VM/370

VM/370 was essentially an enhanced version of CP/67 ported to System/370. Based on the only virtual storage operating system from 360, it had a head start compared to DOS and OS/360. The most significant difference between CP/67 and VM/370 was the replacement of code that used the 360/67 method of implementing virtual storage with code to support System/370's Dynamic Address Translation (DAT). CMS was relatively unchanged, but was renamed from Cambridge Monitor System to *Conversational Monitor System*, the name it still retains.

System/370 exposed VM concepts to a larger audience, and defined the main purposes for which VM continues to be used.

Operating system conversion

As the 1970s progressed, IBM's DOS and OS installed base converted to DOS/VS and OS/VS to exploit virtual storage capabilities and, in an increasing number of cases, simply to support new I/O devices not known to the older operating systems.

Many customers found VM essential for converting to these new operating systems. At the time, there was no alternative, short of dedicated test CPUs, to run a new operating system in parallel with the existing production environment. VM reduced the risk of converting to a new operating system by permitting more comprehensive testing. Customers could ensure that the new operating system environment was reliable and compatible with existing applications before using it for their production work.

Since VM lets system programmers do their testing during normal daytime hours, instead of three in the morning, it was not surprising that system programmers were among VM's biggest fans. In many companies, system programmers discovered that VM could be used for a lot more than just converting operating systems, and began to promote its use for CMS-based timesharing by application programmers and end-users.

CMS-intensive workloads

An increasing number of sites began to use CMS for interactive program development and end-user computing. CMS was noted for flexibility and efficiency. VM was (and remains) capable of providing fast response times to large numbers of users, and runs well on both small and large systems.

VM soon gained the reputation of being user-friendly and easy to learn, and became a standard method of delivering interactive computing services. A remote computing services industry soon sprang up to offer timesharing service for decision support, database access, graphics, and applications written by end-users, rather than by programming departments.

A number of installations decided to use VM and CMS as their primary computing platform, using it for production purposes as well as ad-hoc interactive computing. This category became increasingly important.

Program development for DOS and OS

Many sites decided to use DOS/VS and OS/VS1 for their batch and transaction processing workloads. These systems have much lower resource requirements than MVS, allowing their users to purchase much less expensive computers than if they used MVS, though without features available in MVS.

The most noticeable lack in DOS/VS and OS/VS1 is the absence of a good timesharing environment for interactive programming and testing. Many sites use CMS instead of the program development facilities of DOS/VS and OS/VS1. Developers code, compile, and test their programs under CMS, before sending them to a guest system for final test and production.

Numerous MVS sites also came to use CMS, even though MVS/TSO provided an interactive environment, for the pragmatic reason that VM/CMS provides better response times and can service between two and five times as many logged-on users as TSO on the same computer equipment. Some sites use one CPU for production work, and a second CPU for timesharing and system testing under VM.

IBM added code to CMS to support DOS and OS facilities, making CMS more suitable for developing and running programs intended for execution under DOS or OS family systems. As mentioned earlier, some sites used this capability to run the applications purely under CMS, and dispensed with DOS or OS systems altogether.

The combination of VM/CMS with either DOS/VS or OS/VS1 turned out to be extremely popular, since each provides facilities the other lacks, and the aggregate system turns out to be both cost effective and flexible. It has been estimated that over half VM sites maintain some type of guest system, and that most OS/VS1, DOS/VS, and (subsequently) DOS/VSE sites ran VM.

Parallel production and test

Many sites use VM to provide separate test and production environments for their applications. This provides safety for critical applications by allowing new programs to be tested in a realistic environment, especially for application interfaces not supported by CMS.

A single CPU could run several test and production guests, as well as programmers running CMS. IBM added 370 microcode and handshaking software to the VM control program, DOS/VS, and OS/VS1 to let guests run more efficiently in a virtual machine. In some cases, guest systems actually ran faster in a virtual machine than on the "real" computer. This was not the case with MVS, which for many years ran extremely slowly under VM. For DOS/VS and VS1 sites, VM was an extremely attractive alternative to both MVS and to purchasing additional CPUs for test environments.

The doubtful decade

All this did not sit well in some influential parts of IBM. The favored operating system in these circles was MVS. According to MVS advocates, MVS was already the best platform for batch and transaction processing, and interactive computing could be handled by MVS's Time-Sharing Option (TSO). This caused IBM to devote the bulk of its development efforts to MVS. VM lagged behind MVS in a number of important areas, such as being able to support the latest hardware devices when they were shipped. The same chill was felt by DOS/VS users, who had access to CICS and batch facilities at much lower costs than with MVS.

However, while MVS does provide important and unique capabilities, virtual machine environments, efficient, easy-to-use interactive computing, and good performance on small processors are not among them. Part of the problem was MVS' almost total orientation towards batch production jobs, and later, teleprocessing systems like CICS (which appear like jobs from the perspective of MVS). MVS designers continued to underestimate the value of end-user computing, especially interactive computing.

MVS's Time-Sharing Option was particularly noted for being unfriendly to users. TSO requires massive (especially in the context of CPUs available in the 1970s and early 1980s) amounts of computer resources, and produces uncomfortably long response times. As ironically noted by the popular VM advocate, Kent Taylor (now retired from IBM), "TSO may be slow, but it sure is hard to use."

Even TSO's name clearly indicates that interactive computing was viewed as an optional extra in MVS, a mere adjunct to the serious business of the system. It really wasn't important, from this perspective, to provide sub-second response times to interactive users, or to give them an easily used command language. It required the insistence of VM-oriented experts like IBM's Walter Doherty to convince the industry that productivity for interactive computer users was of paramount importance, and that the best way to provide it was to deliver interactive response times in the area of one-tenth of a second. The explosion of end-user computing that began in the mid-1970s made this VM-based view increasingly dominant.

While IBM's official stance was to encourage conversion to MVS, an increasingly large number of sites inside and outside IBM were convinced that VM was too valuable and effective to let die. Their vocal and vigorous insistence on VM forced IBM to devote resources to VM, and helped keep VM alive despite active efforts within IBM to kill the product entirely. Despite the mixed signals sent by IBM, VM/370 continued to grow in use and importance.

VM/System Product (VM/SP)

IBM eventually realized that they needed VM, both to operate guest virtual machines and to provide high-performance, high-functionality, easily used timesharing. Consequently, IBM decreed VM "strategic," and announced VM/SP (VM/System Product).

Unlike VM/370, which was provided free of charge, VM/SP was subject to a license fee. This was part of IBM's change from being purely a hardware vendor (and giving software away), to treating both software and hardware as products. This was very valuable for VM and other IBM software products: IBM, like most companies, pays more attention to revenue-generating products than for projects that consume resources (like staff and hardware) without directly and visibly contributing to the bottom line. The revenue streams produced by software allowed IBM to devote more resources to software development and support, and fostered a stream of enhancements.

VM/SP was based on VM/370 Release 6, and combined VM/370 features with those in the previously optional IBM "System Extensions Program Product" (SEPP) enhancement. VM/SP provided a dramatic increase in VM functionality. It improved MVS guest support, and added support for IBM's SNA networking protocol, a new CMS file system with better performance and elimination of file size restrictions, a new EXEC language (EXEC 2), and the extremely popular XEDIT editor. This announcement, and the introduction of the extremely successful IBM 4300 series of computers, increased VM/CMS growth.

The improved file system, EXEC language and editor made CMS even more attractive as a productivity tool. In the old file system, individual files were restricted to 65,535 records, making it unusable for larger applications. EXEC 2 removed restrictions in the original EXEC language, making it increasingly popular to create applications purely in EXEC, without recourse to traditional compiled languages and their compile, link, and run cycle. EXEC 2 could be used as a macro language to make application systems programmable, a capability immediately exploited by XEDIT and DMS/CMS (an IBM fullscreen application display tool).

XEDIT expanded the capabilities of end-users and programmers. A very powerful screen editor, XEDIT is also highly programmable and customizable for individual preferences, making it one of the most "CMS-like" of CMS applications. The ability to program XEDIT from EXEC 2 started a trend of EXEC-programmable application systems. XEDIT became popular enough to be implemented on other computer systems. Other implementations include KEDIT for MS-DOS and OS/2 from Mansfield Software Group, and uni-XEDIT for UNIX from The Workstation Group.

VM/SP made VM easier to fit into SNA networks. SNA support, even with its cumbersome initial implementation for VM (it then required a guest DOS/VS or VS1 system) let VM participate in the networks employed by large corporations. This was essential for VM's acceptance in the commercial marketplace, where most sites had large investments in SNA networking and did not want to maintain an incompatible VM network as well.

The new 4300 processors (originally, the 4331 and 4341 models) boosted VM growth by making it possible to place small VM systems in locations previously out of reach of IBM mainframe technology. Departmental systems could be set up in office locations without special cooling or electrical power, yet were compatible with VM running in "raised floor" data center locations.

4300 systems helped IBM compete against minicomputer offerings from other vendors. These machines also did not require raised floor or special cooling or power. Unlike these vendors, IBM could offer a scaleable product that could run applications without change on systems ranging from a 0.1 MIPS 4331-1, suitable for a department, up to the then current top of the IBM line, the IBM 3081 at 14 MIPS. VM was very important to IBM in this arena, especially since MVS could not run on smaller 4300s.

The reduced costs possible with 4300s encouraged many companies to bring interactive systems "in house," instead of buying computer resources from remote computing system vendors. The availability of in-house timesharing systems decreased the cost of interactive computing and helped CMS grow even more.

VM/SP was enhanced over the next several years to include new functions, the most notable of which was the introduction of the REXX procedures language. Developed by Michael Cowlishaw of IBM, REXX was first made public in VM/SP Release 3. REXX has since been adopted as IBM's SAA Procedures Language for VM/CMS, MVS/TSO, OS/400 and OS/2. REXX is also available on a variety of other systems, including MS-DOS, UNIX, Amiga, VAX VMS and Tandem.

Many other features were added to VM/SP, including end-user facilities like the NOTE, PEEK, FILELIST, RECEIVE and SENDFILE commands, the Shared File System, and CMS Windowing services. National Language Support was added to let users get system messages in their own languages instead of English. These are all discussed in subsequent chapters.

IBM also added system-oriented enhancements such as the Alternate Nucleus Support for increased system reliability, the PER command for machine-level debugging, native SNA support, and TSAF (Transparent System Access Facility) for multi-host access to database and file data. The last release of VM/SP, Release 6, added the *Shared File System* (SFS), which provides enhanced file sharing for CMS files, and the ability to organize files in tree-structured directories.

VM High Performance Option (HPO)

While VM/SP features helped VM move away from its "lean and mean," but sometimes sparse, heritage, it wasn't keeping pace with enhancements in IBM's hardware line. VM/SP was designed for a much smaller mainframe than was becoming available. Algorithms suitable for midsize processors were inadequate for systems with many times more CPU and storage capacity, and supporting hundreds of logged on users.

VM/SP was incapable of addressing more than 16MB of main storage, even though IBM was introducing machines with several times as much memory. VM/SP also could not exploit new hardware features such as cached disk drives and expanded storage, which provided faster access to data for applications and paging. VM/SP paging algorithms required applications to page fault their working sets (virtual storage being referred to by the application) one page-I/O and disk rotation at a time, adding delay and overhead to large applications.

IBM introduced the *High Performance Option* (HPO) to better exploit new hardware features and relieve these constraints to system growth. HPO was an extra cost feature to VM/SP. Small VM sites that had no need for HPO functions could continue to use the inexpensive VM/SP, while large VM installations needed HPO's features, and could use the increased performance on large CPUs to justify HPO's license fees. The changes were solely in the CP component. Other parts of VM remained the same.

HPO added support for main storage sizes up to 64MB, supported cached DASD for faster disk reads, and used the expanded storage on 3090s as a high-speed paging device. HPO also introduced *swapping* of user pages[3] to allow multiple pages to be transferred in a single I/O operation and disk rotation, thus reducing paging delay and overhead. HPO also improved the scheduler and dispatcher for more efficient operation with large numbers of logged-on users, and introduced more efficient locking mechanisms to let multiprocessor VM systems run with less overhead.

HPO made it possible for VM to efficiently run large application systems and manage complex environments, sometimes exceeding a thousand logged-on users. Quite a few installations continue to run HPO.

VM/XA

Even the changes introduced to VM by HPO were insufficient to handle the next set of hardware advances. This led to a revolution in VM's design and implementation, which produced VM/XA and today's VM/ESA systems. VM customers can now fully exploit the 31-bit addressing and I/O capabilities of XA and ESA architectures.

IBM used an internal version of VM/XA to implement and test MVS/XA, but was slow to produce a full-function version of VM/XA that could replace VM/SP or HPO. Interim VM/XA systems were made available to customers (VM/XA Migration Aid, and VM/XA System Facility), but they were largely used for running guest operating system environments requiring XA-mode guests, that is, MVS/XA.

It wasn't until late 1989 that a "real" VM/XA was made available to customers: VM/XA System Product (VM/XA SP). The CP component of VM/XA SP was a complete rewrite of the CP in VM/SP and HPO, reflecting the difference in underlying hardware architecture, and the need to support both 370-mode and XA-mode guests. This also gave IBM the chance to give CP code a long-needed cleanup. Twenty-year-old operating systems tend to grow barnacles of patches and outgrown implementation ideas too deeply ingrained to be removed. VM/XA was rewritten from the ground up, providing the chance to start afresh.

VM/XA SP CP is a true 31-bit operating system (unlike MVS/XA and MVS /ESA, which still have numerous 24-bit dependencies), and fully exploits hardware features of 3081 and 3090 processors. VM/XA SP also exploited a new hardware facility: *interpretive execution*, which revolutionized the mechanism by which a hypervisor manages virtual machines. Interpretive execution also made it possible to add hardware-managed virtual machines, in its *logical partitioning* features of 3090 and ES/9000 processors.

While VM/XA's CP was a complete rewrite, CMS was an evolutionary

---

[3] MVS had swapping from its inception. Unfortunately, MVS originally used swapping to transmit control blocks between disk and storage; user pages were individually read and written until later MVS versions.

change from previous versions. VM/XA SP CMS is *bimodal*: CMS executes in both 370-mode and 370/XA-mode execution, and uses both 24-bit and 31-bit addressing. New interfaces were added to use 31-bit addresses, and to support XA architecture, while preserving older program interfaces. Internal algorithms were changed to better handle large virtual storage sizes, since virtual machines could now grow from 16MB of storage to 999MB.

Bimodal CMS was called CMS 5.5 (and later CMS 5.6), since it was based on VM/SP CMS 5, and did not include features built into VM/SP CMS 6. This was a result of IBM's haste to deliver a 31-bit, XA-mode version of CMS, and build in the "extra" functions of VM/SP6 later. Also, some CMS 6 features, such as the Shared File System, would require additional development effort to let them efficiently operate in the much larger system environments of VM/XA.

VM/ESA

IBM subsequently extended XA's concepts with *Enterprise System Architecture/370* (ESA/370 and ESA/390), which lets an application address multiple 2-gigabyte address spaces. IBM introduced VM/ESA in 1991, which not only supports these new hardware facilities, but finally joined all the functions of VM/SP and HPO with support for XA and ESA architectures.

IBM announced two varieties of VM/ESA Release 1.0: ESA feature, described above, and a 370 feature. The 370 feature of VM/ESA is a migration vehicle for VM/SP sites converting to VM/ESA, containing the same CMS and other key components as the ESA feature, but a 370-mode CP based on VM/SP. It is essentially "VM/SP Release 7."

Both features of VM/ESA use the same CMS code, making CMS applications for VM/ESA compatible in either ESA or 370-mode systems. VM/ESA Version 1, Release 1.0 provides CMS 7, a compatible upgrade of both CMS 5.6 and CMS 6, providing the functions of both. CMS 7's main points are that it provides the bimodal addressing capabilities of CMS 5.6, with the SFS and APPC/VM communications protocol available with CMS 6.

In December 1991, IBM started shipping an updated version of VM/ESA, Release 1.1. The transitional 370 feature was eliminated, and new facilities were added for additional hardware exploitation and flexibility. Among the new facilities is support for *VM dataspaces*, which let CMS applications flexibly share large amounts of in-storage data, and view disk-resident data as a logical extension of virtual storage. VM/ESA 1.1 includes CMS 8, which incorporates CMS Pipelines, formerly an extra-cost software product. Additionally, SFS is extended to include *System Managed Storage*, which lets installation use policy rules to control the performance, backup, migration, and retention properties of data. VM/ESA 1.1 also adds support for ESCON and ES/9000 technology, and the ability to use dual-copy (disk mirroring, performed in hardware) and cached writes on the latest IBM disk drives. Unlike the "doubtful decade," VM now includes software support for IBM's latest hardware features.

IBM increased VM/ESA functions with VM/ESA Release 2, shipped in December 1992. VM/ESA Release 2's most important new facility is dynamic CP reconfiguration, which allows alteration of system options and I/O configuration data while the system is running. Previously, local customization information was stored in the CP nucleus and could only be changed by changing configuration modules, creating a new CP nucleus, and re-IPLing VM. Additionally, VM/ESA includes support for virtual disks and adds the Server Tasking Environment to CMS to provide programming interface to create multitasking and multiprocessor applications.

The VM User Community

To a large extent, VM became what it is today because of its enthusiastic and vocal user community. Even in the days of CP/40 and CP/67, VM was largely championed and extended by its users, who preferred it to IBM's officially sanctioned and sponsored solutions.

The VM user community had great influence on VM's evolution and was essential for VM's actual survival. Members of the IBM user groups SHARE and GUIDE made it very clear that they intended to use VM/CMS instead of MVS or TSO, and demanded that IBM commit resources to VM support and development. This was necessary to counter the efforts of factions in IBM that attempted to have VM terminated. This would have been a disaster for IBM, as well as for VM's users, since IBM had no other credible end-user interactive computing environment.

Many VM facilities first appeared as local enhancements written at customer sites, and then distributed electronically or on "tools tapes." Since VM came with complete source code, experts at IBM and customer sites were able to learn exactly how VM worked, and could invent enhancements and fix bugs by adding to distributed code. Even though system modification requires skill and creates an element of risk, it also can provide remarkable opportunities to make computer systems more fit for solving problems—the purpose for which we buy them.

VM experience with local enhancements was highly beneficial for the entire VM customer base and IBM. Everyone gained from the enriched facilities in VM provided by VM's users. The only comparable experience has been in the UNIX world, in which many UNIX facilities were added at user sites, most notably at the University of California at Berkeley. MVS also benefited from local enhancements, but to a lesser extent since little of MVS was available with source code. The JES2 and JES3 job entry subsystems, essential parts of MVS, are notable exceptions, since they are based on HASP and ASP subsystems created and enhanced at user sites.

Local enhancements were quickly distributed in the VM user community, and became ubiquitous at sites both inside and outside IBM. Some were so popular that IBM technicians asked if you were using them. I recall a debugging session with an IBM programmer who asked if I had installed the powerful PER debugging command from the University of Maine, so we could use it instead of the standard VM/SP TRACE command. (I had. We did.)

VM facilities written at user sites and then adopted (with author's permission) or independently redeveloped by IBM include the PF key command retrieve facility, disk read-ahead caching (written at the Stanford Linear Accelerator Center, SLAC), the previously mentioned PER command, block paging (Mitre Corporation), shadow table processing (Texas Instruments), chained drum I/O and drum to disk page migration (Cornell University, Pratt and Whitney), the CMS system profile "SYSPROF EXEC," CP alternate nucleus facility (numerous varieties, though Princeton University's implementation was the most popular), RSCS support for dialup lines and ASCII devices, and many, many bug fixes.

If one includes features originated outside the official VM development organization, this list must be extended to include massive contributions developed elsewhere in IBM, including the REXX language and the LEXX Live Structured Editor (both by Michael F. Cowlishaw), XEDIT (Xavier de Lamberterie), CMS Pipelines (John Hartmann), the RSCS (Tim Hartmann (no relation), and Ed Hendricks), and PVM (Noah Mendelsohn, Bill Anzick, and Don Ariola) communications packages, DIRMAINT, and many others. These products would also not have been possible without general availability of VM source beyond the programmers with official "need to know."[4]

VM is no longer shipped with all of its source code, due to IBM's controversial "Object Code Only" (OCO) policy, initiated in 1983, in which IBM stated that IBM would increasingly distribute software products without source code. Many VM users feel this has had a very harmful effect on VM.

Fortunately, IBM has softened its approach to OCO, and has even shipped source for modules formerly distributed OCO. A more moderate approach, in which only modules containing "trade secret" information are OCO, seems to have been adopted. Even before this welcome turnaround, which can be credited to the vigorous efforts of the user community, most of VM's key CP and to a lesser extent, CMS components remained available with source code. The ability for customers to use source code to debug, understand, and occasionally fix or extend VM has always been present.

System programmers with expertise in VM's internal workings benefit IBM and the entire VM installed base, since these individuals continue to fix

---

[4] Biographical notes on VM developers are largely due to "VM and the VM Community: Past, Present, and Future," Melinda Varian, Proceedings of SHARE 73, August, 1989, pp. 779–844.

bugs and devise enhancements. This does not imply that IBM is incapable of fixing its own bugs or conceiving its own enhancements. Rather, there is a pool of expertise that IBM and its customers all implicitly draw upon for problem corrections and new solutions.

No other operating system has this advantage for vendor-user cooperation and synergy. Even UNIX, which technically is available with source code, is effectively OCO for most of its users. Only academic institutions can obtain the UNIX source code without a massive license fee, precluding access by commercial institutions that are not computer system or software vendors. The source code made available rarely includes the proprietary enhancements UNIX vendors use to provide product differentiation from other vendors' UNIX dialects. Current UNIX system vendors discourage the sale of source licenses to user sites. It is very difficult for a UNIX site to get the source code that produces the binary software they are actually running.

VM user groups and meetings

The VM user community also gets together at a number of meetings sponsored by user groups. The largest user groups are SHARE and GUIDE; both of which have VM projects and sessions, but are not exclusively oriented towards VM. It was at SHARE that the teddy bear was adopted as VM's official mascot, symbolizing the warm and cuddly nature of VM/CMS. Parenthetically, the MVS mascot started off as the turkey (they chose this themselves) due to the terrible performance problems MVS suffered at the time; this was deemed undignified and was later changed to the bald eagle. DOS/VSE people adopted the cat as their symbol, due to IBM's attempts to kill that product as well.

A number of regional VM user groups meet on a regular basis. Some of the long-standing VM groups in the United States are the Metropolitan VM Users Group (MVMUA), serving the New York metropolitan area, Los Angeles VM Users Group (LAVMUG), Chicago Area VM Enthusiasts (CAVMEN), Mid-West VM Users Group, New England Users of VM (NEUVM), and Hillgang (Washington D.C. area). Some of these groups charge membership fees, others are free.

VM users from all over the world meet at the annual VM Workshop, held every summer at a college campus in the United States. VM system programmers and users meet in an informal atmosphere and exchange technical information, experiences, tutorials. A feature is the Workshop "Tools Tape," based on contributions from the attendees. The contents of the tools tape include system programmer tools and modifications to VM, user productivity tools like spelling checkers and file scanning programs, and complete applications such as problem tracking systems and compilers.

VMSHARE

The "electronic home" of the VM user community is the VMSHARE electronic conferencing system. VMSHARE is available to companies that are members of SHARE and affiliated user organizations including GUIDE, SHARE Europe, and Australasian SHARE/GUIDE. VMSHARE is used by VM programmers from around the world to communicate news about VM, warn others about problems or describe how to circumvent or correct them, ask for help, offer code to share, and to brainstorm and ask for advice.

First implemented by programmers at Tymshare, and offered on Tymshare's own VM system, VMSHARE access was free to members of VM sites belonging to SHARE. VMSHARE eventually moved to McGill University with expanded services and a nominal annual membership fee, where it is accessed by VM experts and neophytes from North America, Europe, and Australia.

VMSHARE is a vital avenue of information and opinion about VM. It is used to collect votes on SHARE resolutions, and is a very active forum on the hot issues of the day. It is widely read by IBM developers and management, some of whom have their own userids on VMSHARE and log on to answer technical questions or solicit opinions. This has been a welcome way to survey opinions from VM users working in a variety of contexts, helping avoid conflicts and incompatibilities early in the proposal and design phase of a VM enhancement. The contents of the VMSHARE conference are also copied to "shadow" conferences in IBM and in BITNET and the Internet.

The software used to create VMSHARE is now a commercially available conferencing and bulletin board system under the name *Contact*. Contact is marketed by the Adesse Corporation, which continues to furnish a free copy to McGill University for VMSHARE's use.

Chapter

6

VM System Definition and Access

This is not a book on how to do VM system programming, but a discussion of some aspects of creating and maintaining a VM system will be useful for understanding objects in a VM system and how to use them.

VM's model of computation consists of the underlying kernel, CP, and the virtual machines running over it. From CP's perspective, every virtual machine is a user, even if it is a virtual machine that implements "system-like" facilities, such as network access or security control. Defining a VM system therefore consists of defining CP's configuration, the configuration of the users registered to it, and the software executing in the user's virtual machines.

CP System Definition

A VM system is built by collecting executable software for CP and the other VM components, and by specifying the objects known to them. CP resides in a nucleus which is written on disk by the system generation process. It is loaded into main storage and started by hardware commands issued from the computer's console when starting a VM system.

This last process is called *Initial Program Load* (IPL), IBM's name for loading an operating system into an inactive computer system. In other environments, this is called *bootstrap loading* or *booting*, thus referring to the method in which operating systems "pull themselves up by their bootstraps" to initialize themselves. The computer is normally IPLed from a disk device, although it can be IPLed from tape or other input devices for special purposes.

The nucleus consists of hundreds of modules, several of which must be customized for each installation:

1. HCPSYS specifies the names of the disk volumes to contain CP's nucleus, checkpoint and warm start areas, and the names of *CP owned* disk volumes that can be used for spooling, paging, temporary disk (T-disk), and directory areas.

   Other HCPSYS statements specify the system's identification, security options, and the names of VM userids automatically logged on as the system operator and recipients of accounting, performance monitor, and diagnostic information. HCPSYS also specifies the maximum amount of main storage installed on the system and how much storage to be reserved for the "V=R" (virtual=real) area. This is discussed in the chapter on guest operating systems.
2. HCPRIO specifies the "real I/O" configuration: the device types, features, and addresses of the input/output devices installed on the real computer system. HCPRIO contains the "real device blocks" (RDEVs) for each device; an RDEV describes the state of every real device on the system. CP obtains the subchannel associated with each RDEV at IPL time by retrieving information stored in the IOCP.
3. HCPBOX defines a VM logo for 3270-family display terminals. Changing HCPBOX is an optional but customary method for system programmers to demonstrate creativity. Useful contents of the logo screen often include system identification and the phone numbers of the data center's help desk hotline.

After creating these files and assembling them to produce object code, the system programmer uses the `VMFBUILD` command to create a nucleus, which is written to disk and IPLed whenever VM is brought up. In 370-mode versions of VM (VM/SP, HPO, and the 370 feature of VM/ESA), CP modules have names beginning with `DMK` instead of `HCP`; the corresponding modules for the functions mentioned above are DMKSYS, DMKRIO, and DMKBOX.

VM/ESA Release 2 eliminates the need for these local customization modules. CP now reads configuration, system option, and customized logo information from standard CMS files. This long-awaited enhancement to VM eliminates the system generation process and makes it possible to institute system changes (such as add new real devices, or change the current logo) without having to create a new system nucleus and reIPL the system. This increases system programmer productivity and makes it easier to provide continuous system operation.

VM starter system

One might think there is a Catch-22 problem defining HCPSYS and HCPRIO, since they apparently require an operational VM system be present in order to build a VM system. To solve this, IBM distributes a *starter system* with each new version of VM. The starter system is a stripped-down copy of VM designed to be able to run on any hardware configuration. It provides just enough of a VM system to perform system programming tasks needed to build a complete system.

The starter system tape is IPLed from tape to run the *DASD Dump Restore* (DDR) utility to restore the starter system to disk. When the starter system is itself IPLed, it asks the system programmer to type in device addresses for a small number of critical devices. The starter system can then be used to "bootstrap" a complete VM system defined for the site.

Maintenance userids

Sites already running VM usually ignore the starter system, and just use their existing system to create new versions and test them in a virtual machine. VM system programming is usually done from a VM userid traditionally referred to as `MAINT`, since it is used for maintenance purposes. MAINT contains separate minidisks for source code, object code, updates, and control files for the different VM components. Different versions of VM are not combined in a single maintenance userid.

In practice, the actual VM userid need not be MAINT. Using a different userid is helpful when converting to a new version of VM. Since each version is maintained from its own userid, this lets both old and new versions have unique names.

Installing a new version of VM involves creating a new maintenance userid, loading the IBM-distributed product tapes onto its minidisks, customizing it, delivering an IPLable nucleus to a volume, and then testing it before placing it in production.

CP Disk Areas

In addition to the CP nucleus, a VM system requires several essential disk data areas:

1. Page areas, used for contents of CP and user virtual storage that overflow from main storage. Paging is critical in all virtual storage operating systems; how VM handles paging is discussed in Chapter 8, "VM Storage Management."
2. Spool areas, used for reader, print, and punch files. Spool files are used to transmit files between users or systems. For example, the CMS command `SENDFILE`, writes a CMS disk file to spool, where it resides on the "reader queue" of a recipient user. The spool is often used as a temporary holding location for electronic mail, data awaiting processing, or files awaiting transmission to other sites
3. Warmstart and checkpoint areas, used by CP to log the disk locations of

spool files. Essentially, these areas include the index describing the contents of the spool areas. CP reads these areas at IPL time to rebuild the structure of the files saved in spool.

4. User directory, which describes all users registered to a VM system. The directory is discussed later in this chapter.
5. T-disk, a pool of temporary disk space that can be requested by users when needed. Users are assigned permanent disk space via the directory, but can ask for temporary disk space for work areas. A T-disk is released when a user explicitly detaches it or logs off the system. For example, the following command defines a 10-cylinder temporary disk with device number 1AA:

```
cp define t3380 1aa cyl 10
```

The user can format the disk, as described in Chapter 12, "The CMS File System," and use it for temporary file work areas.

A system-wide option can be set to automatically clear T-disk areas whenever the system is IPLed or users detach a T-disk, to prevent users getting unauthorized access to residual data remaining on disk. This option, which was added as part of the implementation of the Department of Defense (DoD) C2 standard level of security, overwrites the entire freed disk area before it is reused. VM's default action is to overwrite enough of a detached T-disk to make its file directory unusable. However, it is possible for a user to acquire T-disk space without reformatting it, and then use specially written programs to read data placed there by the disk location's previous owner. Clearing the disk locations makes this impossible.

Before a nucleus can be used, the system programmer uses the `CPFMTXA` command (`CPFORMAT` in VM/SP and HPO) to format these areas (except for T-disk space, which is formatted by users when they acquire temporary disk space). CPFMTXA prompts the user for the disk cylinder ranges to be formatted, and then writes uniform 4096-byte blocks across the specified extent.

CPFMTXA also writes an *allocation map* to cylinder zero of the disk volume. The allocation map marks each cylinder as being used for *SPOL* (spooling), *PAGE* (paging), *DRCT* (directory), *PERM* (permanent data, including minidisks and the CP nucleus), or *TDSK* (temporary disk).

The VM User Directory

The *user directory* is the central definition point for all userids and resources. Every VM user is assigned a *userid* in the directory. The *directory entry* for a userid specifies its name, password, and a number of resources and attributes assigned to the userid when it logs on to VM. Most importantly, a directory entry specifies a userid's initial *virtual machine configuration*: the amount of virtual or real storage and the initial complement of I/O devices assigned to the user. The directory entry also specifies accounting, security and privilege class information, and communications parameters for the userid. Many more userids may be defined in the directory than are logged onto VM at any one moment.

Source and object directories

The directory is maintained in a CMS file by convention called *USER DIRECT*, although it can have any valid CMS file name. This is referred to as the *source directory*, since it can be edited and maintained with CMS commands. The directory is normally maintained by VM system programmers or administrators. Most sites run a directory manager product that lets them distribute directory control to user departments, and let users adjust parts of their own directory entries.

In its simplest form, the USER DIRECT file is a single CMS file consisting of fixed length, 80-character records—in other words, a punched-card format file. In fact, in its earliest days, the USER DIRECT file was frequently maintained in punched card decks and read through the system card reader.

Directory statements follow a simple format: the first blank-delimited word in a statement specifies the type of statement, usually the name of the object being defined. Subsequent words fill in information needed for that statement type. Columns 73 to 80 of each record are ignored, allowing them to be used for sequencing. Lines beginning with an asterisk ("*") are comments and ignored.

CP does not read the source directory. Instead, the `DIRECTXA` command (`DIRECT` in VM/SP and HPO), which runs under CMS, is used to read USER DIRECT and create or update the *object directory*, a disk-resident control block structure representing the source directory. DIRECTXA parses the source directory, checks for syntax errors or inconsistencies (such as defining the same user twice), and then writes the object directory to disk (assuming DIRECTXA has write-access to the disk that will contain the new or updated directory).

The directory area should be large enough to store two copies of the object directory. If the area is large enough, the DIRECTXA command will write a directory to the unused portion of the directory area, and then, if the directory was successfully written, switch a disk pointer to the "active" half of the directory area. This helps protect against disk errors creating a partially-updated directory.

If the userid running DIRECTXA has a suitable *privilege class*, which will be discussed shortly, it will also notify CP that the directory has been replaced and that the disk locations it resides in are now different. CP will then consult the new disk locations when a user attempts to logon or refer to a directory-managed resource.

The DIRECT statement

The first statement in a USER DIRECT file is the `DIRECT` statement, which specifies the object directory's volume identification and device type. The format of this statement is shown in Fig. 6.1. In this example, the directory is placed on a 3380 disk volume with the volume serial label (*volser*) VMSRES. The '123' indicates that DIRECTXA will write the directory to device 123. This device is a virtual device defined in the userid running DIRECTXA, and need not have any relation to the actual device number of VMSRES.

Userid definition

A user is defined by the `USER` statement. Following directory statements are interpreted as applying to this user, until the next USER statement is encountered or the end of the directory source. Sample user directory entries are illustrated in Fig. 6.2. The USER statement specifies the userid's name, password, default and maximum virtual storage, privilege classes, and optionally allows specification of different characters for line editing.

The VM userid and password can each be up to eight characters long. The userid must not be one of a number of reserved words. This includes keywords like SYSTEM, NOH, OFF that are used as part of the syntax in VM commands. If `SYSTEM` were a legal VM userid, the command `CP SPOOL PRINTER SYSTEM` could be interpreted as either "direct print files to the system printer," or "direct print files to userid SYSTEM."

Privilege classes

Privilege classes determine the "power" or "authority" of a VM userid by specifying which commands it can issue.

Access to CP commands is controlled by associating each command with one or more privilege classes. A user must have one of the privilege classes in order to execute the command. For example, the `SHUTDOWN` command,

```
Format of the DIRECT statement:

  DIRECT <device number> <device type> <volser>

Example:

  DIRECT 123 3380 VMSRES
```

Fig. 6.1 DIRECT statement in user directory.

```
USER CMSUSER1 password 4M 32M G
* CMS user that sometimes runs large-storage applications
IPL CMS
CONSOLE 009 3215
SPOOL 00C 2540 R
SPOOL 00D 2540 P
SPOOL 00E 3211 CLASS A
* Read-only access to CMS public system disks
*                       CMS S-disk
LINK MAINT 190 190 RR
*                       Help file disk
LINK MAINT 19D 19D RR
*                       System extension Y-disk
LINK MAINT 19E 19E RR
MDISK 191 3380 050 010 VMUSR1 MR RPASS WPASS MPASS
MDISK 192 3380 130 100 VMUSR2 MR
* Read-access to a friend's 191 "A-disk"
LINK FRIEND 191 193 RR
```

Fig. 6.2 Sample directory entry for a CMS user.

which shuts down the entire VM system, requires privilege class A, which is normally assigned only to system operators and administrators.

Up to 32 privilege classes, specified by the letters A to Z and the numbers 1 to 6, can be defined in a VM system, although the default assignments from IBM only use classes A to G. A user can be assigned one, several, or all of the privilege classes, although standard users are normally only assigned class G for "general user."

Privilege class protection is a very robust protection method. Class G users are very reliably prevented from circumventing VM's access control mechanisms. Only on a very infrequent basis is there a report of a program bug in CP that allows a user to gain privileges not explicitly granted by privilege class. This is part of the reason for VM's reputation as a highly secure operating system.

The default IBM privilege classes are as follows:

- A—System Operator. Can FORCE userids off the system and can SHUTDOWN the entire VM system, LOCK or RESERVE real storage for users, and do the actions included in class B. Obviously, access to this class should be carefully protected.
- B—System Resource Operator. Can ATTACH and DETACH real devices, such as tape drives, to different users, or issue the VARY command to make hardware resources unavailable to VM. Often used by programs that act as tape management systems.
- C—System Programmer. Allows commands to affect system performance tuning switches, and allows display and alteration of real storage. Normally

assigned to system programmers. Access to this class should be protected even more than access to class A. A knowledgeable class C user can store into his or her VMDBK to assign the remaining privilege classes. Class C also includes the privileges assigned to Class E.

- D—Spooling Operator. Lets the operator manipulate all files in the system reader, print, and punch queues. The operator can purge files, "hold" them to prevent their being processed, transfer them to new owners, and direct them to system printers and punches. The operator can also start and stop system printers.
- E—System Analyst. Allows performance switch setting, and lets the analyst follow the resource consumption of other users and display real storage. Also lets system programmer define and purge saved segments.
- F—Hardware Service Engineer. Allows the engineer to run hardware diagnostic programs that bypass CP's normal error handling and I/O command filtering.
- G—General user. Able to execute commands that affect the operation of his or her own virtual machine.

Commands can be assigned different privilege classes than the ones set up by IBM. This facility, called *User Class Restructure* (UCR) allows finer granularity of which commands can be executed by a userid.

For example, it might be useful to allow additional userids to issue the FORCE command, for example Help Desk staff, but restrict the SHUTDOWN command. This can be done by creating a *class override* file, in which the FORCE command is assigned to an additional class, say, class K for "kill," as well as the original class A. After the OVERRIDE command is issued, userids with either class A or class K can issue the FORCE command. Alternatively, SHUTDOWN could be assigned a different privilege class that is assigned to only the system operator userids.

Users can issue the CP command COMMAND to display which CP commands and DIAGNOSE instructions they can execute. The output of the COMMAND command can be processed by a program to determine if a particular command is allowed. This is illustrated by the REXX program shown in Fig. 6.3. This program uses CMS Pipelines to retrieve the output of the COMMAND command, and search it for a specified command.

Directory option and flag settings

The directory is also used to specify a wide variety of processing options for each virtual machine. Much of this will be discussed elsewhere, but the

```
/* May I issue this command or DIAG? */
address command
parse upper arg what .
'PIPE CP COMMAND | ',          /* Get the list of okay commands */
  'split | ',                  /* split one per line            */
  'find 'what' | ',            /* find the specifed command     */
  'count lines | ',            /* count successful hits         */
  'var maybe'                  /* save in a REXX variable       */
if maybe<>0                    /* 0 indicates no match          */
then say 'Yes, you may'
else say 'No, you may not'
```

Fig. 6.3 MAYI EXEC to test command authorization.

most important directory option statements include the following:

- `MACHINE` specifies whether a virtual machine logs on in 370, XA, ESA, or XC architecture mode of operation. For example, the following statement causes the virtual machine to logon in ESA mode:

  ```
  MACHINE ESA
  ```

  The architecture name may be followed by the number of virtual CPUs. 370-mode virtual machines cannot use more than two virtual CPUs. The `CPU` statement, discussed below, specify attributes of each virtual processor. The CP command `SET MACHINE ESA|XA|XC|370` can be used to change architectures at run-time.

- `OPTION` specifies miscellaneous details of virtual machine operation: how the virtual machine handles timer events, whether it should be allowed access to a *Vector Facility* unit, whether it can create accounting data, whether the system running in it should handle missing interrupts for incompleted I/O operations, and a variety of other specifications.

- `CPU` specifies, for multiprocessor virtual machines, the CPU address of each virtual processor, whether it is the "base" (primary) CPU for the virtual machine, and whether it should be given a dedicated real CPU engine, for example:

  ```
  USER VMTEST MACHINE
  ESA 2
  CPU 0 BASE
  CPU 1
  ```

  Virtual CPUs can be added or removed by the `DEFINE CPU n` and `DETACH CPU n` commands. Virtual CPUs can be dispatched concurrently if the real CPU has multiple CPU engines, or execute in interleaved manner on the same CPU engine. This is useful for guest systems testing multiprocessor software in a virtual machine, or for production guest systems requiring more than one CPU's computing power.

SHARE specifies the user's share of the processing resources of the system, expressed relative to other users, or as an absolute percentage of the system. For example, the following statements specify an absolute share for an MVS guest system, and a high relative share for a network service machine:

```
USER MVSGUEST password 64M 96M G
SHARE ABSOLUTE 10%
...
...
USER VTAM password 10M 16M BG
SHARE RELATIVE 1000
```

- IUCV specifies which virtual machines, resources, or CP system services a user can connect to. This is discussed in "Inter-User Communication Vehicle (IUCV)" on page 358.

Minidisk specification

Private user disk space in VM is divided into contiguous disk areas called *minidisks*, specified by the MDISK statement. CP makes no assumptions or restrictions on the use of a minidisk. It is up to the operating system running in a virtual machine to impose a file system or data structure on the contents of the minidisk, for example, as done by CMS. CP performs physical I/O operations to the device on behalf of the VM user.

Minidisks are therefore a natural way of providing disk space to virtual machines, each of which runs a private copy of an operating system and may perform its own storage and file management. Minidisks provide transparency for operating systems that are used to complete disk volumes. A minidisk merely looks like a smaller than usual disk volume.

In a multiuser timesharing environment like TSO or UNIX, interactive users work with a common supervisor and file store. In VM, each CMS userid has a own private allocation of disk space, the minidisk space assigned to it, that it can manage without interference from other users. The advantages and disadvantages of this approach, and the Shared File System, which provides an explicit multiuser file system, are discussed in a later chapter.

An MDISK always belongs to a specific VM userid, the one whose USER statement it follows. The first operand of the MDISK statement is a *device number*, a hexadecimal number by which the device is referred to in VM commands and I/O operations.

The MDISK statement also specifies the volume label and device type of the real disk volume the minidisk resides on, the starting cylinder or disk block assigned to the minidisk, and its length. The start location and length of a minidisk, or equivalently, its start and end locations, are often referred to as its *extent*. CP ensures that I/O requests are not permitted to read or write to disk locations outside the minidisk extent. CP does not, however, ensure that the directory administrator properly allocates disk space to minidisks. It is all too easy for an administrator to define minidisks that overlap one another or an extent known to CP but not the directory (extents defined in HCPSYS or assigned for paging, spooling, directory, or T-disk).

In this case, the very likely result is destroyed data and applications. Fortunately, software tools and methods evolved years ago to prevent this. IBM provides a `DISKMAP` command to check for overlaps, and system programmers define "cover" minidisks to account for disk space assigned to CP functions. This makes minidisk allocation safe but excessively manual, so most sites use directory management software to automate the process and guarantee safely allocated disks.

The MDISK statement also assigns each minidisk a *minidisk mode* which specifies whether the userid is given read-only or read-write access to the disk when logging onto the system. The MDISK statement uses the same definitions as the link modes described in "Linking to Other Users' Disks" on page 20.

An optional modifier, `V`, can be added to `MW` minidisks. CP emulates the hardware reserve-release feature for `MWV` disks. Reserve-release is used by some operating systems to ensure serialized write access to critical disk areas shared between multiple CPUs. Virtual reserve-release lets VM simulate multi-CPU complexes with shared disk drives.

Following the disk mode are up to three passwords which may be used when other users issue the CP LINK command to temporarily add the minidisk to their virtual machine configurations. In order, they are the *read-password*, *write-password*, and *mult-password*. The LINK command includes a mode specification like those above (except without the "V" option for reserve-release), and the LINKing userid must specify the password appropriate for the LINK being attempted. Unfortunately, VM doesn't make it possible to grant `MR` access, which is safe, without also granting `MW`, which is dangerous. One password must do for each variety of R, W, or M links. This is solved by using security manager products like RACF or VMSECURE for more flexible resource control.

LINKs can be established in the directory via the `LINK` statement. The LINK statement is similar to the CP LINK command. It names the MDISK to be linked to by its owning userid and device address, and specifies the device number the linking userid knows it by. As with the MDISK statement and the LINK command, the directory LINK statement uses link-modes to specify whether the userid gets read-write, read-only, or no access at all, based on whether other users are linked to the disk when the user logs on.

```
USER MVSTEST passwood 32M 64M BG
* Test MVS/ESA guest system
MACHINE ESA 2
CPU 0 BASE
CPU 1 IPL 240
* Device statements follow: device type followed by virtual
* address, then further operands
CONSOLE 00A 3270
* Define local 3270s for tape library operators
SPECIAL  B00  3270
SPECIAL  B01  3270
SPECIAL  B02  3270
* Dedicate the DASD volumes used by the guest
* The first number is the virtual device number.
* the second is the real device number.  Note that virtual
* addresses need not be matched to real hardware addresses
DEDICATE  240  600
DEDICATE  241  601
DEDICATE  242  735
DEDICATE  243  D44
DEDICATE  244  898
DEDICATE  245  89A
DEDICATE  246  C5F
DEDICATE  247  122
DEDICATE  248  111
```

Fig. 6.4 Directory entry for an MVS/ESA test system.

Other devices

The directory defines additional virtual devices that are assigned to the userid or created for it when the user is logged on.

The `CONSOLE` statement defines the console device for the virtual machine: its device number and whether it emulates line-mode devices like the IBM 3215 teletypewriter, or acts as a 3270 full screen device. CMS userid consoles are defined as linemode devices, since CMS fullscreen I/O uses a separate software protocol. 3270 mode is defined for guest operating system consoles.

The directory can also be used to specify additional terminal devices via the `SPECIAL` statement. SPECIAL defines additional 3270 or teletype style devices that can be administered by virtual machine software. Usually, the CONSOLE device is used to control the virtual machine itself, and frequently is a guest operating system's operator's console. Terminal devices defined in SPECIAL statements are usually assigned to users and applications running in the guest.

The SPECIAL statement also can be used to define a virtual *channel-to-channel adapter* (CTCA), or its successor, the 3088. A CTCA is a fast point-to-point communications line, used for inter-system communication between operating systems running on different real or virtual CPUs. Both VM and MVS use CTCAs to coordinate activities and transmit file and terminal data at high speed in a multi-system complex of CPUs. Systems on each side of a CTCA use READ and WRITE commands to receive and send buffers to their communication partner. Virtual CTCAs are emulated totally by CP software: no hardware facility is required.

The `SPOOL` statement defines virtual line printer, card reader, and card punch devices. Different model virtual printers can be defined to correspond with special features of the IBM 1403, 3211, and 3800 printers. For example, a program can write 3800 datastreams to a virtual 3800, along with font and overlay information.

VM/ESA Release 2 introduces the `VDISK` statement, used like MDISK except it defines a *virtual disk* instead of a disk extent. Virtual disks reside in pageable storage and are used for high-speed transient files. VDISKs are discussed further in Chapter 9.

Finally, devices can be defined in the directory by the `DEDICATE` statement, which simply assigns a specified real device, of whatever type, to a virtual machine whenever the userid logs on. Dedicated devices are used exclusively by the userid they are currently assigned to, although the `DETACH` and `ATTACH` commands can be used to remove a device from a virtual machine and assign it to another. A device can be dedicated to more than one user in the directory. The first user to log on acquires the device. Subsequent users receive error messages indicating that dedicated devices are unavailable.

Virtual machine I/O to dedicated devices can be done with less CPU overhead in CP than simulated or shared devices. This is especially valuable for guest operating systems, since it can let VM eliminate overhead of interpreting guest I/O instructions. An MVS/ESA guest system directory entry suing DEDICATE statements is shown in Fig. 6.4.

Directory profiles

Many statements in a user's directory entry are identical to corresponding statements in other users' entries. For example, a CMS userid needs LINKs to the CMS public minidisks, definitions for virtual console, reader, printer, and punch devices, and specifies that the user IPL CMS. Instead of duplicating these statements for thousands of userids in the directory, common statements may be placed in a `PROFILE`, which can then be referred to when defining a standard user. A PROFILE is shown in Fig. 6.5.

PROFILEs are especially useful when part of the common environment is changed, for example, to LINK to an additional disk or IPL a different system. If the information is stored in one place, the change can be made by changing a single PROFILE entry.

A popular, but not "IBM standard" method with similar effect is to use an

```
DIRECT 123 3380 VMSRES
PROFILE CMSUSER
* Common system to IPL, and spool devices for CMS users
 IPL CMS
 CONSOLE 009 3215
 SPOOL 00C 2540 R
 SPOOL 00D 2540 P
 SPOOL 00E 3211 CLASS A
 LINK MAINT 190 190 RR
 LINK MAINT 19D 19D RR
 LINK MAINT 19E 19E RR
USER CMSUSER1 passwd1
 PROFILE CMSUSER
 MDISK 191 3380 001 010 MR VMPK01
USER CMSUSER2 passwd2
 PROFILE CMSUSER
 MDISK 191 3380 011 010 MR VMPK01
USER CMSUSER3 passwd3
 PROFILE CMSUSER
 MDISK 191 3380 021 010 MR VMPK01
```

Fig. 6.5 Definition and use of directory profiles.

"IPLER" program. An IPLER is a special IPLable program that "front-ends" the normal CMS IPLable system and performs set-up tasks such as defining common devices and linking to CMS system disks before IPLing the "true" CMS.[1]

An advantage of IPLERs is that they can be programmed to make choices for different circumstances, for example, pick different or additional public disks or different CMS systems based on the userid's current virtual machine storage size, or whether the userid is currently running in 370 or XA mode. A number of IPLers are available in the public domain, and can be obtained from VMSHARE, the "Waterloo mods" tape, or the "Workshop tape" distributed at the annual VM Workshop.

Directory Managers

As mentioned earlier, directory maintenance can be both time-consuming and error-prone. VM's built-in facilities may be completely adequate for small and moderate sized sites, since new minidisks may only be created infrequently, and processed by the system programmer that installed the VM system. Most directory activity is performed on the relatively infrequent occasions that a new user is registered in the system, or a user has exhausted the disk space in his or her minidisks, and needs more space.

---

[1] The concept of the IPLER was invented and first implemented by larry brenner, formerly of cornell universityand now at IBM.

In large VM systems, these situations occur frequently enough to be burdensome if basic directory maintenance methods are used because:

- Directory maintenance is error-prone and requires too much skill, especially for allocating space for new minidisks. This is acceptable for small sites in which the single administrator is also the system programmer, but is assigned to less technical staff in larger sites.
- It is too manual and time-consuming.
- Only one userid can alter the USER DIRECT file at a time, so directory changes have to be single-threaded through a single administrator.
- Whoever updates USER DIRECT has total control of the directory and all passwords in it, so directory maintenance can't be distributed to different user groups. This makes it impossible, for example, to let managers in user departments distribute space allocations to users or look up their subordinate's passwords in case they forget them.

These shortcomings because obvious years ago, and a number of directory manager products, and several public-domain tools, became available to solve these problems. The two most popular products are VMDIRECT from System Center, Inc., and Directory Maintenance Program Product (DIRMAINT) from IBM.

Both of these products address the issues cited above. Multiple directory administrators can be defined, and can concurrently work on creating or altering userids. Disk space can be automatically allocated from pools of available space, without risk of accidentally overlapping a newly allocated disk over a previously created one. Both products provide commands to rename userids, transfer minidisks from one user to another, and to enlarge, contract, delete, move, or add minidisks. Both products also let users change their own passwords and can be used to make periodic password changes mandatory.

VMDIRECT offers additional facilities for distributing user control: users can be set up as directory managers for collections of userids. Directory managers can be authorized to allocate disk space from a private pool of disk space, or to look up or change passwords for their userids without having the ability to edit a directory entry. This ensures they cannot change the privilege classes of their userids or make other unauthorized changes, providing secure distributed directory maintenance.

System Startup

VM is IPLed when the system operator uses the LOAD function to reset the CPU and load a new nucleus from a disk volume called the *system residence volume*. CP's IPL routines "bootstrap" load the nucleus into storage and initialize the system for execution. CP determines the physical environment it is running with, and then initiates CP functions.

VM/ESA and VM/XA determine the number of CPUs (instruction processing engines) installed on a multiprocessor complex by testing the architecturally defined CPU addresses from 0 to 63, stopping when reaching the first nonexistent CPU identifier. CP determines the amount of storage installed on the system by issuing the Test Block (**TB**) instruction, which indicates whether storage addresses are available and properly functioning.

Most IBM operating systems formerly referenced successively higher addresses until a program check error indicated that they had gone past the end of addressable storage. TB improves on this by validating the integrity of the addressed 4K byte block of storage, in some cases by writing and rereading data test patterns. TB indicates by an error code whether storage is failing. Real storage can contain ranges of addresses that are unavailable because they are failing or because they have been assigned to the Hardware Storage Area (HSA) for I/O device information.

CP also determines the presence and availability of all I/O devices attached to the system. In 370-mode versions of VM, CP issues a **TIO** (Test I/O) instruction for every device specified in DMKRIO. TIO returns condition codes indicating whether the device is ready, busy, or unavailable. XA and ESA VM systems issue **TSCH** (Test Subchannel) instructions with subchannels numbered sequentially from 0, and increment the subchannel number until the hardware returns a condition code indicating "no more devices." CP uses IOCP information to relate the subchannel number (internal I/O device name) to the device number (external device name) and stores the information in the corresponding RDEV control block.

The most important devices at IPL time are the operator's console and the disk CP-owned disk volumes containing paging, spooling, and directory areas. The console device is selected from a list of console devices specified in HCPRIO. VM tries each listed console until it finds one that is operational. The system operator userid is named in HCPSYS; by convention, the userid is OPERATOR. CP reads the volume serial label on each disk device, and, if the volume is CP-owned, makes it available to the system for paging, spooling, and other system purposes.

CP automatically logs the operator onto the system. CP asks the operator to specify how to initialize the spooling subsystem, and whether the current stored date and time need to be changed. The operator can specify the following:

- **WARM** is used when the system was previously stopped by the **SHUTDOWN** command, and retrieves data from *warm start* and *checkpoint* disk areas to quickly reconstruct the status of the spooling system. Additionally, it reloads the previous logon message (LOGMSG), and enables the printers and terminals that were active when the system was last running.

- FORCE is used when VM was abnormally terminated and did not have the chance to save warm-start information. VM/SP and HPO FORCE starts could take extremely long times, as CP traversed disk spool control blocks to reconstruct the spooling system.

  VM/SP and HPO also had a CKPT (checkpoint) start that acted like FORCE, except cancelled the IPL if parts of the spool were unavailable, for example, if spool volumes were not powered up. In these circumstances, VM/ESA displays the missing spool volume's names and the number of spool files that would be missing, and then asks the operator if VM should continue processing anyway.
- COLD discards current spool contents.

A system IPL console screen is shown in Fig. 6.6.

After locating the system directory and initializing spooling, CP autologs AUTOLOG1 and userids that collect system performance, accounting, and error information. System initialization is now complete from CP's perspective. AUTOLOG1's PROFILE EXEC is coded by installation system programmers, and typically AUTOLOGs security, network and database service machines.

Operator Console

In systems like MVS or DOS/VSE, the operator uses commands and messages totally different from those seen by a normal user, and can only use one of a small number of previously selected consoles. For example, the MVS operator issues system commands with a syntax different from any other part of MVS, and cannot issue commands provided by MVS's interactive component, TSO. In contrast, there is nothing "magic" about the VM operator function. The operator is a standard VM userid whose capabilities are controlled by the privilege classes and limits set in its directory entry. Unlike the UNIX *root* user, the VM operator has no special security privi-

```
17:44:19 START ((WARM|FORCE|COLD) (DRAIN) (DISABLE) (NODIRECT))|(SHUTDOWN)
17:44:32 WARM
17:44:32 NOW 17:44:32 EST FRIDAY 01/27/92
17:44:32 CHANGE TOD CLOCK (YES|NO)
17:44:37 NO
17:44:37 The directory on volume VMSRES at address 0365 has been brought online.
17:44:38 HCPWRS2513I
17:44:38 HCPWRS2513I Spool files available    3123
17:44:39 HCPWRS2512I Spooling initialization is complete.
17:44:50 HCPAAU2700I System gateway VMNET1 identified.
```

Fig. 6.6 System IPL messages at operator's console.

```
USER OPERATOR password 2M 16M ABDEG
* System operator
IPL CMS
CONSOLE 009 3215
SPOOL 00C 2540 R
SPOOL 00D 2540 P
SPOOL 00E 3211 CLASS A
LINK MAINT 190 190 RR
LINK MAINT 19D 19D RR
LINK MAINT 19E 19E RR
MDISK 191 3380 001 005 VMUSR1 MR
```

Fig. 6.7 Sample directory entry for system operator.

leges or access to files. Other userids, if authorized by their directory privileges, can issue the same commands as the primary system operator. If the operator logs off, the next class A userid to logon becomes the system operator. The directory entry for a system operator is shown in Fig. 6.7.

The only special things about VM's system operator are that it is automatically logged on at a predefined system console and it receives all unsolicited system messages (for example, I/O error messages and messages CP generates when users log on or off). By convention, the operator also receives all messages sent from other users to the userid named **OPERATOR**, even if the userid is not OPERATOR. This allows writing programs that send messages to the operator that work in any VM system.

The OPERATOR userid can be moved to any terminal after the system is brought up. Frequently, the operator userid is disconnected from the console, as described in Chapter 2, and runs a part of VM called the *Programmable Operator* (PROP). PROP uses the *MSG system service, described later, to intercept messages that would otherwise be displayed on the operator's console. PROP filters messages through a set of rules, and takes programmed responses to system events. PROP can be used to automate computer operations (except for physical tasks like mounting a tape volume in a tape drive).

Single Console Image Facility (SCIF)

VM lets console output of a disconnected machine (called the *primary user*) be directed to the console of a different user (called the *secondary user*). The CP **SEND** command lets a secondary userid issue commands to the primary userid. SEND has two formats, to let the secondary user send a command either to the primary virtual machine, or to CP on the primary machine's behalf:

`CP SEND <userid> command` equivalent to normal console input

`CP SEND CP <userid> command` equivalent to #CP input

Messages appearing on the secondary user's console are prefixed with the primary virtual machine userid. CP also notifies the secondary user when the primary machine issues a read to the terminal. An arbitrary number of disconnected primary virtual machines can be directed to the same secondary virtual machine, letting a single user or operator control the execution of multiple virtual machines. The normal fifteen minute time-out period is not used when a disconnected user has a secondary console. SCIF usage is illustrated in Fig. 6.8.

SCIF is enabled by placing the secondary virtual machine's userid on the CONSOLE statement in the primary user's directory entry. The example shown below designates OPERATOR as the secondary userid for CMSUSER3:

```
USER CMSUSER3 password 2M 4M G
IPL CMS
CONSOLE 009 3215 OPERATOR
```

The primary user can determine the secondary user by issuing the **QUERY SECUSER** command. The **SET SECUSER** command, introduced with VM/ESA Release 2, lets privileged userids change the secondary console userid.

A secondary userid can itself be disconnected, provided that it is connected to either the *MSG or *MSGALL system services, described in "CP System Services" on page 366. These services let a program in a virtual machine intercept messages that would otherwise appear on the console. This is commonly used to implement *automated operations* in VM systems. A virtual machine, running programs like the Programmable Operator described below, can catch SCIF messages and issue SEND commands to respond to them without human intervention.

```
send servant1 exec job1
Ready;
SERVANT1 : Running JOB1 EXEC

send servant2 exec job2
Ready;
SERVANT2 : Running JOB2 EXEC

SERVANT1 : Finished with JOB1
SERVANT1 : Ready;
SERVANT2 : Finished with JOB2
SERVANT2 : Ready;

send cp servant1 logoff

SERVANT1 : CONNECT= 00:40:32 VIRTCPU= 000:22.17 TOTCPU= 000:24.52
SERVANT1 : LOGOFF AT 13:43:51 EST WEDNESDAY 01/08/92
```

Fig. 6.8 Single Console Image Facility.

The Programmable Operator (PROP)

The Programmable Operator (PROP) is the built-in VM program for automating system and application operations. A PROP machine uses *MSG to intercept messages directed to it, including messages routed to it via SCIF. PROP uses routing tables to filter messages based on their textual content and origin and pass them to action routines. Routing tables select action routines based on the class of message (message generated by CP or a virtual machine, command from a user or operator, and so on), and the message's text (for example, select all messages containing LOGOFF).

Action routines can be written in either assembly language or REXX; REXX is clearly the language of choice because of its expressive power, safety, and the ease with which it interacts with VM commands. Action routines are passed the description of the message that caused them to be invoked: the type of message, the origin virtual machine and VM system, and the message text.

Users can interact with PROP machines by issuing the standard CP MSG command. Routing tables specify which users are authorized to issue privileged commands (for example, stopping PROP). Users may additionally issue the FEEDBACK command to place comments on PROP's log files. Installations can add action routines to let users request a variety of services in a controlled manner, such as asking a PROP machine to AUTOLOG or FORCE virtual machines belonging to them.

PROP is usually programmed to send exception messages, or messages requiring human intervention, to a *logical operator*. PROP can route messages to logical or programmable operator userids on different systems. A single point of control can be created for distributed VM systems connected by a network.

Many large IBM sites use NetView, IBM's standard network monitoring tool, to provide automated operations for MVS and SNA networks; PROP provides the *Programmable Operator/Netview Message Exchange* (PMX) to route messages to NetView. This lets installations use the same automation package for all of its mainframe environments.

VM Security and Access Control

VM has always been an extremely secure operating system. It is highly resistant to traditional attacks on computer systems, most of which try to compromise security by fooling the operating system into giving "superuser" or "authorized program" privileges to the attacker.

VM's high degree of security is largely due to the user isolation provided by the virtual machine computing model. The interface between CP and programs running in virtual machine is well defined and rigid. Programs executing in general user virtual machines can neither display nor store into memory occupied by CP or other virtual machines, and cannot cause them to branch into storage locations whose contents were defined by a penetrator.

This is an important advantage over systems like UNIX, in which a very significant portion of kernel operation resides in user program space and is coercible. This is part of the reason UNIX has such a sorry history of frequent penetration by "crackers." MVS also suffers from this problem, but to a lesser extent, because many MVS data areas reside in a *Common Storage Area* (CSA). Programs can be written to snoop CSA storage locations belonging to other users. It is much harder to penetrate your neighbor's (virtual) computer when it is essentially a different computer system than the one you are using, as it is under VM.

VM makes it very easy to reliably protect files from unauthorized access. Unlike systems like TSO or UNIX, a VM user cannot even see the names of files owned by other users without permission from their owners. VM's default actions provide security; many other systems allow unrestricted access to files unless each file is explicitly requested.

As with many systems, access to userids and data is subject to password protection. A password is needed to LOGON to any VM userid (no "anonymous" userids are provided), or to LINK to any disk that doesn't have the password `ALL`, which permits all users to LINK to it. Separate passwords are used for read and write links. A minidisk without a password cannot be linked by any user. Only the owner of the disk can access its contents.

Passwords are often compromised because people pick easily guessed passwords (common words, the name of a spouse, the current month and year, and so on), and rarely change them. This was exploited by the famous 1988 Internet worm, which penetrated thousands of UNIX systems. Part of its attack was to use the words in a spelling dictionary as the list of passwords, and keep trying the words until it was able to logon.

Fortunately, VM protects itself from this type of attack. After an installation-specified number of invalid LOGON passwords, CP sends warning messages to the system operator and journal files, and disables the userid and terminal. Similar action is taken for excessive invalid LINK passwords.

When processing USER DIRECT, the DIRECTXA command compares each logon password to an installation-specified list of restricted passwords contained in a CMS file named RPWLIST DATA. Userids specifying one of these passwords are placed in "NOLOG" state, in which they are defined in the directory (so they can receive spool files and can be LINKed to), but cannot log on. This helps prevent selection of easily guessed passwords. The reserved password NOLOG also places users in NOLOG state.

Passwords entered on the command line are visible and a potential security breach. If the password is omitted, CP prompts the user for the password, and reads the password from a nondisplay (non-echoing) field. An HCPSYS option lets a site prohibit passwords entered on the LINK or LOGON command line. This does not apply to the initial logon screen from the

VM logo, because the password field in the logo screen is a nondisplay field.

LINK passwords can be securely avoided by having a directory administrator place static minidisk links in the system directory, as shown in Fig. 6.2. This allows previously authorized disk links without passwords, under the control of installation administrators, but is time-consuming and inflexible. Static links are only useful if the disks needed by an application are known in advance and change infrequently.

Minidisk passwords are insufficiently flexible, since they can be divulged, and since they provide equal access to every file on a minidisk. The logon password to a userid is normally known only to the userid's owner, but minidisk passwords must be given to every user authorized to LINK to the minidisk and access the data contained on it. LINK passwords appear in EXECs that issue LINK commands, and are therefore compromised if the disks containing the EXECs are not equally protected.

This makes it very hard to contain "leakage," since many people may have access to a password. When the password has to be changed, perhaps because it was found to have been divulged, every user linking to the disk has to be given the password all over again.

These shortcomings have been addressed by security manager products and security features added to VM. VM/XA SP2.1 and VM/ESA systems have been certified as meeting the Department of Defence C2 level of security, which specifies a degree of control over resources and the ability to create reliable audit trails of accesses (and attempts to access) for each resource. VM is certified to provide a *Trusted Computer Base* when used in specific configurations including security manager products.

Trusted service machines

Many sites create trusted service machines to provide users protected access to system resources and data. Service machines of this type never run programs created by its clients, which would open it to attack; instead, they receive messages containing requests from users, and determine whether or not they should be processed. PROP is an example of an application that can securely validate requests from users before executing them.

VM lets service machine applications execute as *surrogates* of other userids. For example, a virtual machine used to run batch jobs from many users can assume the access rights of the jobs submitters. While running a job submitted by UserA it would run with UserA's ACIGROUP and rights, and thus only be able to access minidisks and SFS directories accessible by UserA.

This method is used to prevent attacks in which a user program subverts a server program that has more rights than the user, and assumes its capabilities. This method was also used by the 1988 Internet worm, which exploited a bug in a UNIX utility to gain control over its operation. Instead, VM servers that run user code (and therefore could possibly be subverted by them) can run with only the rights of the submitter.

Access control interface authorization

Requests to LOGON, LINK to a disk, execute CP SPOOL or TAG commands, and even issue CP DIAGNOSE calls can be intercepted and sent to a service machine called an *external security manager* (ESM). CP uses the *Access Control Interface* to pass validation requests to the ESM. An ESM can use authorization rules to determine if access should be granted or denied. This technique can be used to replace or supplement the built-in password mechanisms. The ACI interface is discussed in "CP System Services" on page 366.

By far the most commonly checked requests are attempts to LOGON to a userid or to LINK to a minidisk. ACI validates the following actions:

- LOGON at a terminal.
- LINK to a minidisk.
- SPOOL, CLOSE, TRANSFER, or TAG a spool file to a destination.
- AUTOLOG and XAUTOLOG a disconnected userid.
- Store into real CP storage. The command for this is protected by privilege class C; the ACI provides further validation checking, and adds the ability to log uses of the command
- Generate TRSOURCE system trace data, which can contain the contents of protected CP storage locations.
- DIAGNOSE D4, which lets a class B assign an *alternate userid* to a surrogate machine working on behalf of a client.
- DIAGNOSE E4, which lets a user with directory OPTION DEVINFO or OPTION DEVMAINT inspect real disk information.

LOGON, LINK, and the spool file commands are available to all users. As mentioned above, the remaining commands are restricted by privilege class or directory options, but the ACI interface provides extra checking and logs their usage. This permits finer control over access capabilities. For example, an operator might have class B, in order to issue the CP ATTACH command, but should not be able to issue DIAGNOSE D4. The User Class Restructure (UCR) mentioned earlier can also be used to assign different privilege classes to DIAGNOSE codes.

The ACI interface can be used to audit all CP commands and DIAGNOSE instructions, and these additional program services:

- VMCF, IUCV, or APPC/VM connect and sever
- Create, purge, or open a spool file
- Create, purge, or open a system data file in spool

This lets CP and an ESM protect "logical resources," such as the right to IUCV connect to a userid or send a spool file to it, as well as the physical resources previously discussed.

Most security products provide a variety of flexible authorization rules to control resources. Most rules are based on identifying the requestor as being among the set of users permitted to access a resource. CP provides the `ACIGROUP` statement in the directory to let users be grouped into collections for security purposes. Security managers can use group-wide rules to grant or deny access to a resource to all members of an ACIGROUP.

Additional flexibility is provided specifying expiration dates on rules, or only permitting access to a resource when a user is signed on at a known terminal location. This is an effective method of excluding penetration by "crackers" dialing in from external networks.

Security manager products

A number of security products are available for VM systems, all providing rules-based security. They compete with one another in providing the most flexibility in specification of rules, and providing additional features like allowing automatic expiration of rules, and requiring users to change passwords on a periodic basis.

IBM provides the *Resource Access Control Facility* (RACF) product, which is compatible with the MVS version of RACF. RACF running on multiple VM and MVS systems can share the same rules database and use the same commands and screen panels. DIRMAINT can be used to force users to change expired passwords, and DIRMAINT and RACF can be made to coordinate their activities with one another.

Computer Associates (CA) provides *ACF2/VM*, which is compatible with ACF2/MVS and can share a rules database with it. Unlike other security products for VM, ACF2/VM does not use the ACI interface. Instead, ACF2/VM is installed by patching itself into the CP nucleus to front-end many internal decision points. This lets ACF2/VM control actions the ACI interface doesn't intercept, but it also adds the risk that IBM changes will break undocumented (and therefore changeable) program interfaces ACF2/VM relies on. Consequently, the system programmer must cautiously apply IBM fixes in consultation with CA's support staff, and may have to delay installation of fixes that affect ACF2/VM until new ACF2/VM code is available. The system programmer also must use a non-standard method to create a new VM nucleus, and has a more difficult time diagnosing system problems, because the running system no longer matches the source code or IBM's diagnostic references.

The most popular security product for VM is *VMSECURE* from System Center Inc., which includes the previously mentioned VMDIRECT product. VMSECURE includes rules-based authorization like the other products, and allows flexible distribution of security management to individual users and workgroups. Unlike the other products, which are MVS-ish in style, VMSECURE is very well integrated into VM. On the other hand, RACF and ACF2 let institutions with both MVS and VM share the same methods, commands, and security rules database between all their operating environments.

Special Considerations for Directory Availability

The directory is one of the most crucial parts of a VM system. If it is damaged, a VM system can be unusable, so it is worth taking extra precautions to ensure its availability. Backup copies of both source and object directories should be kept in order to recover from a hardware failure that makes the primary copies unreadable.

Since the source directory is a simple CMS file, it can be backed up by copying it to another physical disk volume on a periodic basis. Making a copy on the same minidisk or physical volume is not adequate protection since the volume could be made unavailable due to a disk head crash.

The object directory requires additional planning, since it is a CP object and not as easily manipulated by CMS commands as a CMS file. VM will not initialize properly if no object directory is available, so it is essential that a recent directory be maintained on a CP-owned volume at all times. When a VM system is IPLed, CP looks for an object directory on the disk volume used as the IPL device. If CP cannot find one, it examines CP owned volumes in ascending device address order until it finds one.

To make a backup object directory, copy the source directory to a second file, and change the DIRECT statement to specify the volume label and device type of the backup device. Then use the DIRECTXA command to write the object directory to disk. DIRECTXA should be executed from a class G userid (general user, without system operator privileges) to ensure that CP does not make that directory the active (in-use) directory.

VM's Alternate Nucleus facility can be used to place VM nuclei on an emergency volume, and a copy of the directory placed there. Under normal circumstances, this directory would be ignored if it has a higher device address than the normal IPL volumes, but would be used during an emergency by IPLing that address. The volume need not be used as an alternate nucleus, since CP will use the directory on it if it cannot find one at a lower address, but IPLing from this volume ensures that the emergency directory is selected. This is useful if the normal object directory is partially damaged, since it guarantees that a valid directory is used while the normal one is rebuilt.

Chapter

7

Control Program Organization

Like conventional operating systems, CP contains routines for initiating I/O operations, handling interrupts, scheduling work, managing memory, performing error recovery, and a host of other tasks.

Functionally, CP can be viewed as consisting of programs that directly support virtual machines, and programs that manage the real machine. CP routines handle

- explicit service requests from virtual machines, such as DIAGNOSE, console function commands, and I/O requests
- implicit service requests from virtual machines, such as when a virtual machine page faults by referring to a storage location not resident in real storage
- resource scheduling and management
- statistics gathering for performance information, accounting, hardware error data collection

CP Nucleus

CP programs reside in the *resident nucleus* or the *pageable nucleus*. Both parts of the CP nucleus are loaded from disk when VM is IPLed, but modules in the resident nucleus remain in storage at all times, while pageable modules are read into main storage as needed. CP modules are resident or pageable depending on their functions and the way they are called. Modules for storage management or the I/O supervisor clearly cannot be paged out, nor can many other modules that provide low level functions for the rest of CP.

CP's pageable modules are paged in and out of main storage much like users' virtual storage. CP runs without dynamic address translation, letting CP execute slightly faster than other virtual storage systems because its storage references are not subject to translation. Virtual machines also run faster, because their previously translated virtual storage addresses remain in the translation lookaside buffer (TLB) while CP is running. TLB contents can be reused if CP redispatches the same virtual machine last executing on a CPU. This makes it unnecessary for CP to purge the TLB and let virtual storage references refill the TLB. CP attempts to *fast dispatch* users to take advantage of this.

Although CP doesn't use dynamic address translation, CP has a virtual address space just like virtual machines. CP modules reside at virtual storage addresses assigned when the CP nucleus was created by the system programmer, even though the modules reside in arbitrary and changing real storage locations at run time. The CP virtual address space is also used for spool and user directory buffers and other data areas.

For example, in Fig. 7.1, the CP LOCATE command displays the address of the CP variable HCPIUGID (the IUCV message identifier), which resides in the resident module HCPIUG, and the CP virtual storage location of the entry point HCPLNKIN in the pageable module that implements the LINK command, HCPLNK. HCPLNK may reside in different real storage locations at different times, and may not be in real storage at all, but is always uniquely located by its virtual storage address.

Pageable modules are up to 4096 (4K) bytes in size, and reside entirely within a single page. This guarantees that an entire module is loaded when the module is read into storage. The CP program loader, executed when a CP nucleus is built, packs multiple pageable modules into the same virtual page. When a module's contents span a page boundary, it is assigned the next virtual page address and starts at the beginning of the page.

Pageable modules are *reentrant* (never alter their code and data contents). CP copies its pageable modules to paging media at IPL time, without removing them from storage. CP never writes a nucleus page back to disk

```
* Display real storage location of resident symbol
#cp locate hcpiugid
HCPIUGID = 03DBF414 RESIDENT
* Display CP virtual storage location of LINK command module, HCPLNK,
* primary subroutine entry point HCPLNKIN.
#cp locate hcplnkin
HCPLNKIN = 03FC9028 PAGEABLE
```

Fig. 7.1 CP LOCATE of pageable and resident modules.

when it is replaced for another purpose, because there is always an identical copy on paging media. Since CP runs with DAT off, CP actually refers to its programs with real storage addresses, and manually brings each pageable module into real storage, as described in the following section.

CP Module Call Mechanism

CP routines use the `CALL` (370-mode VM) or `HCPCALL` macro to call other CP modules. Two types of subroutine linkage are used, depending on the attributes of the calling and called modules.

CP uses a fast code path to call resident modules that are assigned a *static savearea*, by loading the module's real storage address into a register and branching to it. This is called a *BALR call*, since the call was implemented in 370-mode VM systems by a *BALR* (branch and link) instruction. This expression is still used in VM/ESA for tradition's sake, even though the *BASR* (branch and store) instruction is used now.

Static saveareas are storage locations permanently assigned to individual modules, and reside in the prefix page allocated to each CPU. Modules invoked by BALR calls use their static saveareas to store their caller's registers and for work areas. Static savearea modules are lowest-level routines (for example, the routine one calls to obtain a dynamic savearea), and must never release control of the processor by returning to the dispatcher, starting another CP task, enabling interrupts, or waiting for a page-in or other event. Doing so would make it possible for a different thread of execution to call the routine, and overlay its savearea. Any routine that might lose control of the processor, which includes any module in the pageable nucleus, must be called with a dynamic savearea.

When a CP module calls a pageable module or a resident module that uses a dynamic savearea, HCPCALL calls it indirectly with the aid of a resident service routine. This is referred to as an *SVC call*, since the 370-mode VM implementations used an SVC instruction to branch to the service routine. HCPCALL now branches directly to the service routine HCPSVC (which is faster than using an SVC instruction), passing it the virtual address of the called module in CP's virtual address space. The service routine acquires a savearea from a pool of free storage, and connects it to the list of saveareas owned by the current thread of execution.

Each savearea contains the register values of the calling module, including the address of the previous savearea, parameter values, the base address of the calling module, and the location at which it issued the HCPCALL. This makes it easy, in case of a system failure and a storage dump, to follow the savearea chain backwards from the point of failure and locate all the inter-module calls and parameter registers used in a thread of execution.

When calling a pageable module, HCPCALL generates an **LRA** (Load Real Address) instruction using the virtual address of the called routine as its storage operand. If the module is resident, LRA completes with condition code 0, and returns the real address of the module. This instruction explicitly translates virtual addresses to real addresses, even when DAT mode is not enabled. Pageable modules are distinguished from resident modules by having a virtual storage address higher than the address of the last resident module. The **HCPCPE** (in VM/XA and ESA) and **DMKCPE** (VM/SP and HPO) modules mark the end of the resident nucleus.

Otherwise, the paging supervisor is called to read the module from auxiliary storage into main storage. In CP jargon, this is called *TRANS-ing* a module, short for *page transfer*. When the page transfer is complete, the execution thread is resumed, and the called routine receives control at its real storage address. Since DAT is not turned on, the called routine is entered with its base address set to the real storage address at which it was loaded, rather than the virtual storage address at which it was referred to by the HCPCALL external reference.

In VM/XA and VM/ESA, HCPCALL invokes the inner macro **HCPMDLAT** ("module attributes"), which contains the residency requirements of each module, as well as indicating whether or not it executes only on the CP master processor. HCPCALL uses this information to determine the type of code to generate for the call.

VM/ESA 1.1 introduces *fast dynamic linkage*, which reduces the number of instructions needed to call frequently used dynamic linkage routines. Fast dynamic linkage uses an in-line calling sequence instead of branching to HCPSVC, and omits a number of tests. It can only be used when calling a module resident in storage, and cannot be used to call a module that requires execution on the master CPU processor in a multiprocessor complex. These requirements are not checked at run time.

Control Blocks

CP uses a variety of control blocks to describe internal objects. Many control blocks represent service requests, such as IOBLOKs and TRQBLOKs (I/O and timer services), which are frequently allocated and deallocated as the service requests are generated and completed. Other control blocks represent logical or physical resources with longer lifetimes, such as the allocation map of available pages in a SPOOL area, or the description of a real device attached to the system.

One of the most important control blocks is the Virtual Machine Definition Block, or **VMDBK**. The VMDBK is the VM/XA or ESA representation of a logged on virtual machine. Virtual machines with multiple virtual processors have multiple VMDBKs: a *base* for the primary virtual CPU in a virtual multiprocessor, and *adjunct* VMDBKs for the other virtual CPUs. CP creates a VMDBK when a user logs onto VM, with initial contents based on the information contained in the directory entry and on the LOGON command. The **VMBLOK** is the corresponding VM/SP and HPO control block.

The VMDBK describes the state of the virtual machine throughout its session, and changes to reflect the activities of the virtual machine. For example, flags in the VMDBK indicate whether the userid is running, idle, or waiting for a resource or request to complete. CP commands like DEFINE, LINK and DETACH alter a virtual machine's configuration after it is logged on, in some cases subject to limits specified in the directory. Still other control blocks describe virtual machine properties, and exist for the duration of the virtual machine.

CP Free Storage Management

CP uses a pool of *free storage* for dynamically acquired control blocks. Free storage routines are invoked thousands of times per second in a complex VM system to allocate and deallocate control block storage. Considerable research has been devoted to make storage management as efficient as possible. Different versions of CP use algorithms of increasing sophistication to provide short path lengths for storage requests, and to handle storage fragmentation and multiprocessor overhead.

VM/ESA routines obtain and return control block storage from free storage managers by issuing **HCPGETST** (get storage) and **HCPRELST** (release storage) macros. These macros generate calling sequences to call HCPFRE entry points. VM/SP and HPO routines call **DMKFRE** and **DMKFRET**. A typical call to allocate a block of storage specifies the amount of storage needed, and returns with the address of the acquired block of storage. Calls that deallocate storage specify the address and length of the area being returned. CP requires that entire blocks of storage be returned. Partial deallocations of a block are not permitted.

Incorrect allocation and deallocation of storage is one of the most insidious problems in operating systems or complex applications. Programs that acquire storage but never release it eventually cause systems to run out of storage, a problem sometimes referred to as a *core cancer*. Programs might also attempt to continue to refer to storage after it has been released and possibly reallocated (the *dangling pointer* problem), or release an unallocated block or a different sized block of storage than was acquired.

A *free storage trap*, optional in VM/SP and HPO, but built into VM/XA and VM/ESA, detects some of these errors. Storage management routines append a trailer area to the allocated block of storage to hold self-identifying information. The trailer contains a unique "eyecatcher" constant value that identifies it as part of an allocated block of storage, the module name and address of the requesting routine, and the original size of the storage request. When a CP routine releases a storage block, the storage manager computes the address of the trailer by adding the length of the returned block to its address, and uses it to validate the storage deallocation request.

If the trailer area no longer contains the eyecatcher value, either a different sized area is being returned than was acquired, the trailer area was overwritten because of an invalid address pointer, or the area was already released and the eyecatcher altered. If the eyecatcher is present, then the length stored in the trailer is compared to the length of the deallocation attempt. If they differ, then the deallocation call specified an incorrect length that happened to point to another control block's trailer area. Each of these situations is a fatal error: CP takes a storage dump for subsequent debugging and reboots the system.

This type of problem is usually easy to debug because the dump contains the storage block's requestor location and the size of the area originally allocated, as well as the size of the deallocation request. If the sizes do not match, the two routines can be compared to determine why they disagree. If storage was exhausted due to a core cancer, the offending program can be easily identified since the module name of the acquiring program is in each of the unreleased storage blocks, as well as the address of the statement that acquired the unreleased block. If a program stored data beyond the bounds of its block of storage, it will likely destroy the trailer, and be caught as soon as it returns the storage. In each case, it is valuable for CP to detect the error and collect the diagnostic information as soon as possible. These self-checks help make CP reliable because this category of error can be caught early in unit test, and never survive to show up in software shipped to IBM customers.

Of course, the best bug is the one that doesn't happen. To prevent errors caused by typographical mistakes, VM/XA and VM/ESA usually allocate and deallocate control blocks by name. Storage management routines always use the proper length for a specified control block, thus eliminating the entire category of error of allocating or deallocating the wrong length.

VM/SP and VM/HPO free storage management

VM/SP and HPO require a previously declared free storage pool for its control blocks. The VM systems programmer defines the FREE area size in the configuration module `DMKSYS`.

Experience with CP storage requests showed that many requests are for small blocks of storage. Free storage management divides storage into subpools containing linked lists of like-sized blocks of storage. Allocation can be done very quickly for popular storage size by taking the first element of the appropriate subpool linked list; deallocation is also done very quickly by adding a new linked list element. Both of these are unit time operations: they complete in the same time regardless of the amount of storage in use. Low asymptotic execution time for allocation and deallocation is essential for large system performance. Adjacent blocks are periodically merged to form larger blocks to avoid fragmentation. Blocks of storage too large for one of the subpools are allocated by searching a storage chain for a large-enough contiguous area of storage. Additionally, on CPUs equipped with ECPS, most free storage calls are processed by microcoded assists.

If CP needs free storage and none is available in the FREE area, it logically *extends* the FREE area by taking a page from the pool of real storage used for pageable data, the *Dynamic Paging Area* (DPA). Extending has very negative effects on VM/SP and HPO performance. CP prevents virtual machines from running during extends, since they may issue requests that require additional storage, and only allows CP tasks to run if they release real storage, such as page-out operations. Extending is usually prevented by providing a sufficiently large FREE specification.

HPO also reserves a pool of *prime storage* for each CPU. Prime storage is cache-aligned main storage allocated to an individual CPU, and is used for high-frequency storage allocations that are related only to an individual CPU. This reduces storage management CPU path lengths, since inter-CPU synchronization can be omitted, and improves cache utilization by reducing cross-processor cache invalidation and reducing cache working sets.

VM/XA and VM/ESA free storage management

The growth of real storage from 16MB to hundreds of megabytes could have been a source of intolerable overhead if storage management running time grew proportionally to storage size. VM/ESA and VM/XA storage routines were therefore designed for asymptotic efficiency, to be able to handle extremely large real and virtual storage sizes.

Storage management routines were also redesigned to eliminate the negative consequences of extending, to reduce storage fragmentation, and to more efficiently handle storage requests in multiprocessor systems. VM/XA and VM/ESA storage management is based on the experience gained with VM/SP and HPO (for example, it still uses subpools), but removes the restrictions in the earlier implementations.

The preallocated FREE storage area is eliminated. Instead, pages for CP control blocks are acquired and returned to pageable real storage as needed. In essence, VM/XA and ESA extend all the time, but the extend process has been made nondisruptive, partially by ensuring that a pool of storage is always kept available for storage requests. This keeps CP from entering emergency situations in which it cannot dispatch user work because it has exhausted control block storage.

VM/XA and VM/ESA developers noted that many control blocks tend to be associated with an individual virtual machine, and that different types of control blocks had different lifetimes ranging from milliseconds to days, or could be clearly associated with a single CPU in a multiprocessor complex.

This is exploited several ways to improve speed of allocation and deallocation, and reduce fragmentation of storage.

Control blocks associated with an individual virtual machine are stored with the VMDBK describing the virtual machine. The VMDBK is allocated a page frame of real storage, even though the VMDBK control block is much smaller than 4096 bytes. Control blocks related to a userid are allocated, when possible, from the unused part of its VMDBK. This reduces the CPU path length to acquire or release storage for a user-related control block. Multiprocessor locking can be omitted because only one CPU has control over a VMDBK at any moment, and therefore access to the VMDBK is implicitly serialized. Since most control blocks associated with a virtual machine are stored in the VMDBK, these control blocks cannot contribute to fragmentation of generally allocatable free storage.

This principle is used more generally by *processor local* pools of real storage retained for each CPU. Each CPU can freely dip into its free storage pool without executing locking code to ensure serialized access. This reduces multiprocessor overhead and simplifies CP coding logic. Local storage is replenished when the available storage reaches a low-water mark, and is added in page increments. Most storage requests can be satisfied without spinning on a lock for global storage, and inter-CPU cache invalidation is eliminated.

CP Trace Table

CP records recent events in a *trace table*. The trace table is used by systems programmers and IBM's support center to diagnose system crashes and other problems. Trace table entries are created for procedure calls and returns, I/O events, storage allocation and deallocation, and many other events. If a system crash occurs, a dump is taken of real storage contents, including the trace table. The trace table is also sampled for performance statistics during normal execution by performance monitoring products, such as IBM's *Real Time Monitor*.

In VM/SP and HPO, the trace table is a single contiguous block of main storage residing below the 16MB line. Routines trace execution by storing 16-byte trace entries in the table, and then advancing the pointer to the next available trace entry. When the end of the table is reached, the pointer is reset to the beginning of the table. When running on a multiprocessor system, compare-and-swap logic is used to serialize access to the trace table pointer. The pointer always contains the address of the next available trace element location. In a storage dump created by a crash, the crash occurred after the trace table entry just before the trace table pointer. The customer or IBM system programmer debugs the crash by working backwards from the point of the crash.

VM/ESA and VM/XA allocate a trace table area for each CPU in a system. Each processor updates its own trace table without compare-and-swap overhead or interference from other processors, thus reducing the CPU cost of retaining trace information. Instead of using a single block of storage, each trace table is actually a bidirectional linked list of page frames. Each processor keeps a pointer to the current trace table entry in the current trace page, and advances it as needed. In case of a crash, dump reading utility programs use time-stamps in the different CPU's trace tables to merge trace entries in time-sequence order.

Virtual Machine Operation

The creation of virtual machines is CP's unique capability. Its other capabilities (managing real storage, performing I/O, scheduling, and dispatching work) are in the same domain as other operating systems.

A VM/ESA or VM/XA virtual machine may be a System/370, Extended Architecture/370, Enterprise System Architecture/370, or Enterprise System Architecture/390 system, or run in *Extended Configuration* (XC) mode, a specialized ESA/390 mode that exists solely in virtual machines. It may have up to 64 CPU processors, and a complement of I/O devices and main storage. Multiple virtual CPUs for a single virtual machine may be dispatched simultaneously on different real CPUs, just as real CPU multiprocessors provide concurrent execution. VM/SP and HPO virtual machines are restricted to uniprocessors (with the exception of SPMODE guests, described in Chapter 17) running System/370 architecture.

CP simulates all details of interrupts and interrupt classes, storage protection, I/O instructions, and address translation described in the *Principles of Operation* manual for a virtual machine's architecture. This is done through a mixture of hardware, microcode, and software. Parts of this job are increasingly performed in microcode and hardware, as illustrated in the following sections.

System/370 Virtualization

The combination of supervisor state execution and virtual storage makes it possible to *virtualize* the System/370 architecture. Virtual storage lets separate applications use the same virtual addresses to refer to different real storage addresses, thus providing an independent address space for each user, just as would be the case if they were all on separate real CPUs.

CP intercepts privileged operation exceptions resulting from supervisor instructions issued from problem state programs, allowing controlled simulation of the instructions that require emulation or suppression when performed in a virtual machine. This ensures they are simulated in accordance with architectural rules for 370 computers without interfering with one another.

Consequently, virtual machines run in problem state, even when running operating system code that normally runs in supervisor state. CP can therefore detect instructions that control main storage protection, interrupt handling, virtual storage addressing, input/output devices, and state switching between privileged and problem states.

For this reason, the real system always runs with I/O and external interrupts enabled when a virtual machine is executing, even if the virtual machine is disabled for interrupts. This ensures that CP always regains control of the CPU on I/O or timer interrupts. Similarly, virtual machines always run with dynamic address translation (DAT) enabled using page and segment tables provided by CP, to ensure that they only access their own virtual storages.

Only CP is aware of the real I/O configuration, and maps virtual device addresses to real I/O addresses before executing I/O commands. In many cases CP totally simulates I/O operations without requiring I/O to a real device. Similarly, CP manages and allocates real storage, and only it can execute instructions that affect the real computer's address translation and storage protection.

When a virtual machine changes state, for example switches between supervisor and problem states, CP sets flags in the virtual machine's `VMBLOK` to indicate the virtual processing state, without changing the real hardware state. Execution states are shown in Fig. 7.2.

If a privileged operation occurs when the virtual machine is in simulated problem state, CP *reflects* a privileged operation exception to the virtual machine operating system, just as a real machine would. If the virtual machine is in virtual supervisor state, CP simulates the instruction in conformance with rules in IBM's hardware *Principles Of Operations* manuals.

VM/SP and HPO CP runs virtual machines by loading CPU registers with the virtual machine contents, and then issuing the Load PSW (`LPSW`) instruc-

Execution state	Virtual PSW	Real PSW
CP	not applicable	supervisor state, interrupts disabled, dynamic address, translation (DAT) off
Virtual machine supervisor	supervisor state	problem state, interrupts enabled, DAT on
Virtual machine application	problem state	same as above

Fig. 7.2 Virtual and real supervisor states in System/370 VM.

tion to start executing instructions in the virtual machine. Execution continues in the virtual machine until interrupted by one of a number of events: a real timer expires to end the user's time-slice or signal the start of a CP task, an I/O operation completes and interrupts the CPU, or the programs running in the virtual machine cause one of several types of interrupt.

This is actually somewhat complicated. Virtual PSW and control registers must be converted to corresponding values suitable for loading on the real machine. The final step loads the virtual machine's registers and virtual PSW. The last instruction is a LPSW instruction that branches into the virtual machine's code. Execution does not resume after the LPSW instruction when the virtual machine is interrupted. Instead, CP execution resumes at the first-level interrupt handler for the hardware interrupt class that interrupted the virtual machine.

SVC instructions in the virtual machine

The supervisor call (SVC) instruction illustrates simulation originally performed by CP software, later made faster by specialized microcode, and ultimately integrated into CPU architecture with VM/XA.

An SVC instruction from a virtual machine should cause a context switch to the virtual machine's supervisor, not to CP. CP's simulates this by reflecting interrupts back to the virtual machine. The virtual machine's PSW is stored in the SVC old PSW in its virtual page 0, and its next PSW is loaded from the SVC new PSW location.

This was handled by CP software in 370-mode versions of VM. The SVC interrupt would cause a context switch to CP's SVC interrupt handler, which determined whether it was entered from CP or a virtual machine. If a virtual machine was running, CP would perform the virtual PSW swap just described, and return to the dispatcher to continue processing.

Virtual SVC simulation was a cause of overhead in early VM systems running on old processors, especially when running guest operating systems that frequently executed SVC instructions. An inexpensive, built-in instruction on real machines required two context switches to simulate for a virtual machine. Microcoded assists, described in "VMA and ECPS Microcode Assists in System/370" on page 134, were introduced to solve this problem.

Privileged operation simulation

Like SVCs, privileged instructions may be simulated by microcode, or may cause CP to gain control to simulate the privileged instruction.

If the virtual machine is in virtual problem state, the privileged exception is reflected to it. This is handled just like reflecting an SVC interrupt, except that the program check old and new PSWs are used instead of the SVC PSWs.

The following events occur when a privileged instruction is executed in a virtual machine:

1. The virtual machine executes a privileged instruction.
2. Microcode determines if it can handle the simulation without help from CP. If it can, CP remains unaware of the privileged operation. Otherwise, hardware returns control to CP by generating a privileged operation exception and loading CP's program check new PSW.
3. CP's program check handler examines the state of the machine at the time of the interrupt. If CP was running, the system terminates itself. CP should always execute in privileged state and should **never** generate a privop exception (or other program check).
4. CP simulates the privileged instruction.
5. If the virtual machine is still runnable, it is dispatched again.

Step 4 is a complex activity which depends on the instruction executed and the state of the virtual machine. Some situations are relatively simple to simulate, and can be handled by a short sequence of code. An `SSM` instruction to disable the virtual machine for interrupts takes very few instructions to simulate. All CP has to do is change flags in the virtual machine's `VMDBK` or `VMBLOK` to indicate its new interrupt status.

Other cases require additional processing. Simulating an SSM instruction that enables the virtual machine for interrupts may require executing code to reflect pending interrupts. By far, the most complicated instructions to simulate are the I/O instructions, as described in "Virtual Machine I/O" on page 189.

One privileged instruction is simulated in a way that lets operating systems determine whether they are running under CP or on native hardware. The `STIDP` (Store Processor ID) instruction returns the CPU model type (such as "3090"), the CPU serial number, and a one-byte CPU version code. CP returns a unique version code of all one bits (hexadecimal FF). IBM operating systems use this to determine if they should use DIAGNOSE interfaces to communicate with CP, or, if running natively, use *active wait* (discussed later in this chapter) when waiting for work.

VMA and ECPS microcode assists in System/370

Microcode assists boost performance in one of two ways: by intercepting and handling events that would normally require software intervention, and by providing high-level instructions that replace entire software subroutines.

The first category also avoids costly context switching between virtual machines and CP, thus eliminating the overhead spent switching states and flushing main storage cache. When handled by a software interrupt, the interrupt handler must preserve the state of the system at the time of the interrupt by saving registers, gaining addressability to the proper processing routing, and then reversing the process to return to the interrupted program. Microprograms can directly process the intercepted event via a subroutine call or in-line code.

Microcode is also faster than conventional software instructions because it can directly manipulate the internal buses, registers, and logic circuits in a particular CPU model, and can initiate multiple operations for parallel execution. Microcode avoids the fetch-interpret-execute cycle of normal host instructions.

Virtual Machine Assist (VMA) is a microcoded extension to System/370 architecture for VM/SP and HPO, which uses the first of the two methods just described. VMA speeds privileged operations and SVCs from virtual machines by executing in microcode logic that CP would normally perform in software. When a VMA-assisted event occurs, microcode handles virtual machine state switching and instruction simulation without CP intervention. CP is unaware of the event, and incurs no software overhead at all

VMA is standard on all current IBM mainframes running 370-mode VM. On some older CPUs, such as the 3033, VMA was an "RPQ" (request for price quotation) feature, and could be quite expensive. VMA is available on most but not all non-IBM System/370 compatibles. VMA is also not available for second level machines, except when the first level VM is VM/ESA or VM/XA running on a CPU with SIE Assist microcode. VMA may be partially or totally turned off for users running with TRACE debugging commands in effect, since CP has to trap events in software to perform the debugging operations.

VMA dramatically speeds virtual SVC simulation. VMA microcode completely performs the PSW swap previously performed by software, unless virtual page 0 had been paged out or the new PSW was invalid or loaded a virtual machine wait state. VMA exits to CP's SVC handler in these cases.

VMA also handles many privileged operations, and exits to CP software for instructions it cannot process. It also exits to software when a privileged operation changes the dispatchability of a virtual machine, or if a virtual page was required and not resident. For example, VMA normally handles LPSW instructions, but exits to CP software when a virtual machine loads a PSW that places it into a "wait state." VMA lets CP software process the LPSW so CP knows that the virtual machine is no longer runnable. I/O instructions are generally too complex to be handled by VMA.

Extended Control Program Assist (ECPS) is a VM/SP and HPO microcoded assist available on 9370, 43xx, 370/138, 370/145, 370/148, 370/158, and 3031 processors, with model dependent variations in function. IBM has never implemented it on their "high-end" processors, possibly because they erroneously assumed that their largest accounts would only run MVS, or because they thought that the high end CPUs would be so fast that microcoded assists would not be needed.

The most important feature of ECPS is the Control Program Assist (`CPA`) facility, which moves high-frequency CP code paths to microcode. CPA replaces CP software for

- allocating and releasing blocks of real storage
- locking and unlocking pages of real storage
- translating and untranslating real and virtual CCW storage addresses
- CP module-to-module CALL and RETURN for pageable modules
- finding virtual machine device control blocks
- dispatching a virtual machine
- virtual storage management

For these functions, CPA replaces an entire CP subroutine's execution with a single instruction. The microcode instruction is a long-running one, compared to a simple `Load` or `Store`, but it is much faster than the software subroutine it replaces.

ECPS replaces VMA with an extended VMA (`EVMA`) that adds support for additional privileged operations. ECPS also adds a function called Virtual Interval Timer Assist, or `VITA`. System/360 and System/370 (pre-XA) CPUs have an interval timer maintained by decrementing a binary counter at location 80 (hexadecimal) in real storage. When the value reaches zero, an external interrupt signals the end of the interval. The timer can be updated or inspected at any time by altering or reading the contents of location 80.

VITA updates the location 80 timer of the dispatched virtual machine 300 times per second, far more frequently than CP would do it via software, and with less CPU cost. System/370, XA, and ESA systems provide more accurate timers (the time-of-day, CPU timer, and clock comparator) that are only accessed by privileged operations, and do not require continuous updates to virtual storage. XA and ESA systems do not have the interval timer.

Interpretive execution in VM/XA and VM/ESA

The System/370 method of running virtual machines was elegant and worked well for years, but a more sophisticated method was implemented for XA and ESA environments. New versions of VM had to handle virtual machines running in a number of architectures, and therefore had to smoothly move between executing in XA or ESA mode in CP to executing in 370, XA, or ESA mode when running a virtual machine. This is not a facility built into the XA or ESA instruction set. There is no way for a real CPU in XA-mode to suddenly start running in 370 mode.

The microcode assists that had evolved over the years were ad hoc, not extensible, and not available on every system. The redesign needed for VM/XA and VM/ESA provided an opportunity to start afresh, and provide an architected method for switching control between a host operating system and guests of varying types.

This method is called *interpretive execution*, and is implemented with assistance from XA and ESA hardware. Instead of the sequence of setup code needed in System/370, the VM/XA and VM/ESA dispatchers dispatch a user by passing the user's VMDBK to microcode via the **SIE** (Start Interpretive Execution) instruction. SIE is executed from a module called **HCPRUN**, since it runs the current user.

VMDBK contents are used by microcode to determine the type of interpretive environment to provide the virtual machine. The facility supports 370, XA/370, ESA/370 and ESA/390 mode virtual machines. In concept, the interpreted machine need not even be an IBM mainframe architecture.

The virtual machine executes until interrupted by the same type of events as in System/370. An event that drops the CPU out of interpretive execution is called an *SIE intercept*. When a virtual machine drops out of SIE, CP regains control at the next sequential instruction following the SIE. In essence, SIE acts as a subroutine call to the virtual machine, instead of the GOTO-like method used in System/370.

With System/370, a CP interrupt handler must save the processor's state, and figure out what was happening at the time of the interrupt. For example, it has to determine whether CP or a virtual machine was running at the time of the interrupt. Eventually the flow of control makes its way back to the dispatcher.

Interrupt processing with SIE is simpler and more efficient than the System/370 method. After a SIE intercept, CP still has addressability to the user's VMDBK, and can directly update its information and call whatever routines are needed to process the intercept. "Fast path" situations, in which simulation processing is trivial and the user can be resumed, can be done with a shorter code path than in System/370.

The increased integration of the SIE facility makes possible increased emulation in hardware. SIE takes the place of VM/SP's VMA, EVMA, and VITA, and handles virtual SVCs and many privileged operations without software intervention. In addition, SIE handles shadow page table mapping of first to third level storage when a virtual storage operating system runs under VM/ESA, a function performed in software in VM/SP and HPO.

DIAGNOSE Instructions in the Virtual Machine

Since SVC instructions are simulated for applications requesting services within a virtual machine, a different mechanism was needed to allow virtual machine applications to request services from CP. The **DIAGNOSE** instruction was chosen for this purpose.

A DIAGNOSE instruction executed from virtual supervisor state is a service request to CP, and extends the virtual machine environment to include capabilities not in any real machine. If executed from virtual problem state, a DIAGNOSE instruction results in a privop exception reflected back to the virtual machine. DIAGNOSE functions are discussed in Chapter 16.

Console Function Mode

Virtual machines may be in console function mode, like real machines. CP commands simulate many hardware console switches, buttons, and commands provided on real CPUs and described in "Manual Operation" on page 53, notably:

- `SYSTEM RESET`
- `SYSTEM CLEAR`—CP actually discards real storage and disk locations assigned to virtual storage locations, instead of clearing them to zero. On the next virtual reference to a location, CP provides a page containing zero values.
- `IPL`—In addition to simulating true hardware IPL, VM also lets virtual machines IPL *named saved systems*; preinitialized systems that are usually reentrant and shared by multiple users. This is how most users run CMS.
- `SYSTEM RESTART`
- `DISPLAY`
- `STORE`
- `STORE STATUS`
- `BEGIN` begins virtual machine execution after it has been stopped. Execution can be resumed at a different location than the point at which it was interrupted by specifying a branch address.
- `STOP` places the virtual machine in stopped state.

Each of these commands operates within the context of the virtual machine: DISPLAY and STORE refer to the storage locations that appear first level to the virtual machine operating system, yet are actually second level virtual addresses from the perspective of CP. Userids with system programmer privilege classes can display and store CP's "host," storage locations.

Additional commands have no analogue on real machines, such as `DEFINE` and `DETACH`, which change the virtual machine configuration. Other CP commands display information about the system: the current time, whether an individual user is logged on, the CPU utilization of the system, the amount of computer resources consumed since logging on, and many others. Additional commands control real and virtual I/O devices, spool files, the colors used for terminal output, and many other options.

Virtual machines can be placed in console function in several ways. The user can press the 3270 PA1 key, or the virtual machine can load a *disabled wait* PSW (a PSW that places the virtual machine in wait state, but is enabled for no events). CP interprets this as the virtual machine "hanging up." Additionally, virtual machines are briefly in console function mode while executing CP commands via DIAGNOSE function 8.

Virtual IPL

The IPL function provides an interesting example of a real machine function VM interprets both literally—imitating the hardware facility—and liberally, via an abstraction of the IPL process.

A virtual machine can IPL from a virtual device, typically a disk device, although tape volumes and even the virtual card reader may be IPLed. CP precisely simulates the hardware IPL function.

VM designers could have written code in CP to directly simulate the I/O and PSW manipulation implicitly caused by an IPL, but this would have involved duplicating code for simulating I/O operations initiated from a virtual machine.

Instead, they cleverly have CP copy one of its modules, the virtual machine IPL simulator (DMKVMI in VM/SP and HPO, and HCPVMI in VM/XA and VM/ESA) into virtual machine storage and execute it like any other virtual machine instructions. This code executes I/O instructions compatible with the virtual machine architecture, which CP modules interpret like other virtual machine I/O operations.

IPL of a saved system is handled quite differently. After performing a system reset, CP sets up the virtual machine page and segment tables to map its virtual storage address references onto the virtual storage contents of the saved system image, thereby making it immediately addressable by the virtual machine. CP also sets the virtual machine to start executing at the next instruction after the point where the saved system image was saved.

Saved system IPL is more efficient, since the operating system need not be loaded piecemeal into storage. Most saved system contents are reentrant, and are shared by all the users IPLing it, so only one copy of the saved system resides in real storage.

Tracing and debugging commands

CP provides console function commands for machine level debugging, used to display and alter virtual machine storage or registers, and to trace execution. These commands are used for assembly-language program or operating system debugging. IBM provides high-level symbolic debuggers for their FOR-

TRAN, COBOL2, C, PL/I, Pascal, and APL2 language implementations.

While a full description is beyond the scope of this chapter, the following are the primary capabilities of the VM machine-level debugging commands:

- **DISPLAY** displays the contents of storage or registers. It can display storage in a variety of styles, including translation of hexadecimal values into EBCDIC characters, and translation of machine code instructions into assembler language opcodes. For example:

`cp display g`	display general purpose registers
`cp display g0-5`	display general registers 0 to 5
`cp display 848.10`	display 16 (hexadecimal 10) bytes starting at hexadecimal location 848
`cp display i20000-200ff`	display the contents of locations 20000 to 200ff in instruction format
`cp display psw`	display the current PSW

- **STORE** alters storage or registers, usually when the tester or debugger realizes that a stored value is incorrect and wishes to correct it manually and continue. It is also used to set up new values for different test cases:

`cp store g0 64`	store hexadecimal 64 into register 0
`cp store 2c 0`	store the value 0 into location 2c

- **TRACE** follows the path of execution of a virtual machine. It can track execution on an instruction-by-instruction basis, or let execution continue until specific locations are reached or particular storage locations or registers are altered. The latter capability is almost essential for solving "storage overlay" errors, in which some unknown program overlays the contents of storage that doesn't belong to it. For example, the following command detects a storage overlay in which a program set the contents of location 10 (hexadecimal) to zero:

```
cp trace store into 10.4 data 0
```

  TRACE can select other types of event: all successful branch instructions, for example, or specified SVC or DIAGNOSE instructions. All of these trace options can be refined by restricting them to address ranges in the tested virtual machine.

  TRACE can also be used to trigger other debugging commands. For example, the following command causes VM to halt the virtual machine when an SVC 40 (MVS or OS simulation EXTRACT macro) is executed, and display the contents of general registers 0 and 1:

```
cp trace svc 28 cmd display g0-1
```

I use the following TRACE command to debug programs in which I have placed a "breakpoint" instruction:

```
cp trace g0 data 81828384 range 20000-5fffff
```

This TRACE command stops execution if register 0 is set to an unlikely value from within a range of program addresses. By deliberately inserting a LOAD instruction to do this at the beginning of code sections I may need to debug, I can leave breakpoints in production code with negligible overhead (the cost of a single LOAD instruction), and enable the breakpoint as needed by issuing the TRACE command. This is especially valuable if I do not know in advance where in storage the program will be loaded, but need to trap its execution (in this case, I omit the *range* specification).[1]

This is only a small part of the TRACE command's capabilities. TRACE is a powerful tool for machine-level debugging, far more flexible than the limited facilities available at "real machine" consoles. For further reference, see the *VM/ESA CP Command Reference*.

- `VMDUMP`—When all else fails, the standard way to collect diagnostic information is to take a storage dump for later processing. The VMDUMP command partially or completely dumps storage at programmer request. VMDUMPs are nondestructive: the status of the virtual machine is not altered. Virtual machine execution continues as soon as the dump is written to spool.

  Dumps are directed to VM userids where they can be loaded to disk and processed by dump analysis programs like IBM's Dump Viewing Facility (DVF) or VM Systems Group's KPROBE. These tools provide sophisticated dump analysis facilities such as control block formatting and pointer chain traversal. Both can be extended by writing "macros," programs in REXX or EXEC 2 to automatically execute DVF or KPROBE commands.

Dispatching

Virtual machines are selected for execution by the CP *dispatcher*. The dispatcher chooses virtual machines from lists of virtual machines selected by the *scheduler*, and performs fine-grain control over user processing.

The dispatcher performs the low level work of starting virtual machines and CP tasks. CP tasks run until they complete or voluntarily surrender control, in both cases by returning to the dispatcher. Virtual machines execute until they either are preempted by a real world event, request a service

---

[1] I learned this trick by reading the source code to utility software written by Dick Johnson, now at IBM, when he was at the Stanford Linear Accelerator Center (SLAC).

that places them in a wait state, become idle, or exhaust a short burst of CPU time called a *minor time-slice*.

The dispatcher acts on the instructions of the scheduler, and passes information back to it, for example, when a virtual machine becomes idle. The dispatcher runs many times per second, as virtual machines are started and interrupted by real-world events.

Scheduling and dispatching are oriented around queues of users that are either active or waiting for service. Virtual machines are scheduled by placing their VMDBKs on a dispatcher list. Different virtual CPUs for multiprocessor virtual machines can be dispatched at the same time by dispatching the VMDBKs that represent each virtual CPU.

Dispatch list processing

VM/SP scans the dispatch list for a user to run. This includes virtual machines that are in short duration page or I/O wait. If they were in long duration wait, they would have been dropped from queue.

As the number of concurrent users increased on larger processors, the dispatcher spent more time scanning this list, and skipping over virtual machines that could not be run. Consequently, the HPO dispatch list was changed to include a "true run list," which only contains virtual machines that are in fact runnable. When a virtual machine goes into a page or I/O wait, it is taken out of the true run list. The dispatcher no longer has to scan past virtual machines that cannot be run. This shortens the time the dispatcher spends searching for work.

VM/ESA algorithms for dispatching users were made more efficient, largely because separate dispatch lists are maintained for each processor. With these changes, it became cheaper to leave "temporarily not ready" users in the dispatch list than to move them to and from the run list.

CP Internal Tasks

CP runs its own tasks to handle external events and requests for service. The dispatcher always runs CP tasks before running virtual machines. In CP jargon, CP tasks are *stacked* for later execution, and are *unstacked* by the dispatcher and branched to.

Tasks are frequently used to create and process asynchronous threads of execution. Many CP routines are written to segment work into parallel tasks instead of performing long-executing tasks serially. This lets CP make better use of multiprocessor systems, since work can be distributed to more than one processor.

More importantly, this lets CP respond quickly to external events like I/O interrupts. CP runs disabled for interrupts except when running a virtual machine, or when passing through the dispatcher. Operating systems try to run disabled for interrupts for the briefest durations possible, in order to reduce the time between an I/O interrupt and when it is processed. Processing interrupts quickly makes it possible to initiate a queued I/O request sooner, and drive devices closer to their maximum throughput.

CP enables interrupt processing in the dispatcher before starting a CP task or virtual machine. By breaking work into smaller units, CP makes additional passes through the dispatcher, and gets additional chances to see if any I/O interrupts have occurred. This also eliminates the overhead of starting a virtual machine and immediately taking an I/O interrupt that would switch back to CP.

CP has a VMDBK with the pseudo-userid name SYSTEM, used for overhead functions that cannot be attributed to a specific virtual machine. The SYSTEM VMDBK is always dispatched before virtual machines.

Creating and running CP tasks

A CP routine creates a CP task by performing the following steps:

- Acquires storage for the control block describing the task. This is called the **CPEXBLOK** in VM/SP and HPO and **CPEBK** in VM/XA and VM/ESA.
- The CPEBK is filled in with the registers to be loaded by the dispatcher when it unstacks the task. This sets up the program and data addressability for the task. Usually, one or more registers will point to a data element to be processed.
- The interrupt return address (IRA) for the task is stored in the CPEBK. This is the branch address that the task will be started at when it is run. If the interrupt return address is in a pageable module, the program creating the CPEBK calls a service routine to bring it into real storage from paging media, if not already resident, and to lock it (prevent it being paged out) for the duration of the task.
- The address of the VMDBK for which the task is being executed is stored in the CPEBK; it is either the address of a virtual machine VMDBK or the pseudo-userid SYSTEM.
- The CPEBK is stacked for execution on a VMDBK (the system VMDBK for global system tasks), and the VMDBK is made dispatchable. The dispatcher checks for a waiting CPEBK before running the virtual machine owned by a VMDBK. The task may be placed on either the global VM dispatch list, or on the local dispatch list of a particular CPU. A specific CPU is needed if the CPEBK requires execution on VM's master CPU, or if a hardware feature, such as the Vector Facility, installed on a particular CPU is required.

When the dispatcher unstacks the CP task, it loads the registers contained in the CPEBK, and then branches to the interrupt return address. The task begins execution using the data passed to it in its parameter registers.

Timer and I/O tasks

CP also creates tasks to process timer and I/O events. When a timer is set, a **TRQBK** (timer request block, called a **TRQBLOK** in 370-mode VM systems) is set up indicating which CP code to run when the timer expires. It is set up like a normal task, except that a time of day is stored in the TRQBK, and a service routine is called to enqueue the timer on a list of pending timer events in time sequence order.

VM/XA and VM/ESA uses a sophisticated hashing algorithm to allow quick insertion and removal of time requests. 370-mode versions of VM use a linked-list insertion method which is less efficient on large systems. Timer service routines set a hardware clock to interrupt execution at the time of the first queued timer event. When the timer event occurs, the TRQBK is sent to the dispatcher for execution, and the hardware timer is set up for the next later time event.

A similar **IORBK** (I/O Request Block) is used for I/O events. Contents of the IORBK include the real device number, the address of the channel command program to start on it, and the IRA and register contents to use when the I/O event completes. A synchronous I/O call format is also provided in VM/XA and VM/ESA for tasks that cannot proceed until the I/O they requested is complete.

Multiprocessor Effectiveness

Many operating systems contain *serially reusable resources*, which can be inspected or updated by only one program at a time. A control block representing a free-storage list is such a resource, since two programs must not be allowed to claim the same storage locations. If multiple users are allowed to work with a serially reusable resource at the same time, and their execution is interleaved due to time-slicing or other delays, the resources could be updated in inconsistent and disastrous ways.

Operating systems prevent this by updating shared resources under the protection of sections of code called *critical regions*, which are guaranteed exclusive use of specified resources. Almost all operating systems have some mechanism for controlling access this way, although they may refer to it as *locking*, or *ENQ-ing* a resource.

For example, storage management routines must ensure that the same piece of real storage isn't allocated to different CPUs requesting storage at the same time; routines that update a linked list or a counter value must make sure that they have exclusive access to the variables being updated.

Consequently, CPUs allocating and deallocating serially reusable resources must coordinate their activities to prevent deadlocks and misallocation of resources, and sometimes a CPU must wait until a critical resource is released. As a result, part of the instruction processing power from added CPUs is consumed by overhead or contention for resources.

The potential for "multiprocessor overhead" increases as more CPUs are added to a complex. IBM has recognized this as an important constraint on growth, and has expended considerable efforts to reduce multiprocessor overhead. Current versions of VM provide almost linear growth in CPU capacity for most workloads: doubling the number of CPUs in a system almost doubles the effective capacity. The evolution of methods used in VM are discussed in the following sections.

Resource serialization

Critical regions were originally implemented, on computer systems containing only a single CPU, by disabling hardware interrupts, as shown in Fig. 7.3. This guaranteed that the critical region would execute from beginning to end without losing control of the CPU. Specifically, timer and I/O events would be disabled, thus preventing preemptive dispatching for time-slices or I/O events.

Multiprocessor systems made disabling interrupts insufficient. A process could disable interrupts on one processor to ensure exclusive control of one CPU, but other CPUs sharing memory with it could still overlay its storage locations.

Hardware designers solved this problem by introducing hardware interlock instructions to guarantee exclusive control to storage locations, even when multiple CPUs are involved. System/370 and System/390 use the Compare and Swap (`CS`), Compare Double and Swap (`CDS`), and infrequently, the older Test and Set (`TS`) instructions to ensure serial access to storage. These instructions only allow a single CPU to update a storage location at a time. If several CPUs try to update the same storage location at a time, only one CPU "wins" and changes the storage location. The other CPUs get a nonzero instruction condition code and have to try again.

To update a serially controlled storage location, a program loads the prior value of a word or double-word storage location, computes the next value

```
DISABLE all interrupts
.
. Exclusive control of the system: Update critical variables
.
ENABLE interrupt classes disabled just disabled
```

Fig. 7.3 Uniprocessor serialization.

(possibly a counter or "ownership" value, or the new head of a linked list), and then issues CS or CDS to get the updated storage value and replace it with new computed value.

If the storage location was not already being updated, the update is performed and the instruction completes with a zero condition code. If another CPU was updating that storage location at the time, the new value is placed in a register and the instruction completes with a non-zero condition code. The program can then derive the next value to store in that location and try again. This process is illustrated in Fig. 7.4.

Compare-and-Swap logic can create logical locks whose access can be synchronized across multiple CPUs. In its simplest form, a lock can be "available," and contending processors can attempt to acquire it by storing a unique process identifier into an agreed-upon lockword. The processor that manages to save its identification in a lock has acquired it.

Depending on the nature of the lock and the resource being protected, a process that fails to acquire a lock may defer its own execution till the resource is available ("try later"), or it may enter a *spin loop* in which it repeatedly tries to acquire the lock until it becomes available. This is sometimes done because the CPU time to defer the process and select another one is longer than the expected delay period. It is also done when the lock is needed for a fundamental control block needed for dispatching, and the waiting CPU literally cannot do anything other than wait for the lock to be available.

Resource locking

IBM's first multiprocessor operating system was a version of OS/360 MVT modified for the System/360 65MP dual processor. However, OS/360 design never anticipated multiprocessor operation, and there was no way to structure its spaghetti-like use of disabled interrupts into a series of locks that would allow proper access to resources without deadlock.

For the sake of expediency, to let the 65MP system be used at all, a single system interlock was used to control entry to the operating system. The CPU owning the lock could freely access OS/360 control blocks, but the other CPU either had to be either running user application code or waiting in a spin loop until the lock freed up.

Since all but the most CPU intensive applications (typical of numerical analysis) frequently call the operating system for services, at least one of the two 65MP processors spent most of its time "spinning its wheels" fruitlessly. This made OS/360 multiprocessing largely ineffective for most real application environments. IBM learned from this lesson, and planned both MVS and VM to use a locking scheme for controlling resources.

Multiprocessing was not initially available in VM, but was introduced with VM/370 Release 4 in the late 1970s. The initial implementation provided in-

LOAD current value in storage CALCULATE new value COMPARE-AND-SWAP If unsuccessful, start again at the first step

Fig. 7.4 Multiprocessor serialization.

adequate reliability, but it established the scheme of multiprocessor resource control later used in VM/SP and HPO.

VM/SP and HPO use a series of locks to guarantee exclusive access to storage and logical resources. Locks may be acquired and released thousands of times per second, causing noticeable overhead, as each CPU updates or assigns locked resources.

Examples of resource controlled by locks include dispatch lists of users waiting for service, I/O device control blocks, and storage management control blocks. Lock granularity was often too coarse. Some locks controlled too many resources, so ownership of the lock by one CPU prevented access to any of the resources from other CPUs. Many functions required ownership of a "global system lock," causing lock contention delays. Too often, one processor controls a lock and the other processor must wait until the lock is freed.

Master and auxiliary processor serialization

VM/XA and VM/ESA were designed for multiprocessor environments, and use the experience gained with HPO to improve performance and reliability. They require fewer lock accesses, and increase granularity by decreasing the scope of resources protected by individual locks

VM/XA and VM/ESA designate one CPU as the *master processor*, and the other processors as *alternate processors*. CP functions are coded to either run only on the master processor or on any available processor. Master-only routines are implicitly serialized without extra lock management.

To make this possible, many resources have been replicated for each processor. For example, each CPU has private lists for users it is dispatching and for real storage that it can access. A CPU may have to occasionally "go back to the well" and serialize on a global resource, for example, to obtain additional real storage if the private pool has been exhausted, but the rate is far lower than in older VM versions, which relied heavily on global lists that were serialized on every access.

Depending on workload, it is possible for the five alternate processors on an ES/9000-900 to saturate the master processor with requests for service that require executing on the master. Examples of master-only services are console function mode operation (the interpretation of CP commands issued from virtual machines), processing of the *Virtual Machine Communication Facility* (VMCF) inter-virtual machine communication protocol, and some parts of virtual I/O simulation. Master-processor contention is a potential bottleneck for large and VM/ESA systems, but tends not to cause trouble for most workloads. To a large extent this contention is manageable, for example, by recoding VMCF applications to use IUCV or APPC/VM.

Private dispatch lists

In VM/SP, each processor looks at a common dispatch queue in order to find work to dispatch. When work becomes ready to run but the active processor is already occupied, it uses the Signal Processor (`SIGP`) instruction to wake the other processor. This can happen when the other processor is idle, or when it is active but processing work of lesser priority.

Signaling causes CPU overhead, as processors transmit and receive "shoulder-taps." The use of a common dispatch queue also reduces the effectiveness of the cache storage installed in most CPUs.

Each CPU in a multiprocessor system has its own cache. For consistency purposes, a main storage location can only be buffered in one cache at a time. By sharing a common dispatch queue, the VM/SP dispatcher running on one CPU continually invalidates the other CPU's cache contents, slowing storage references. This effect is difficult to measure because it is timing dependent and does not result in software executing additional instructions. Instead, individual instructions take more time, which cannot be detected by system software.

In HPO, VM/XA and VM/ESA, each CPU has a private dispatch list, which it can access without cache contention. If the private dispatch list, called the *Processor Local Dispatch Vector* (PLDV), becomes empty, the CPU looks at other CPUs' dispatch list for work to run. This occurs less frequently than when all CPUs use the same list, so fewer cache lines are invalidated.

Active wait

When there is no work to be done in a multiprocessor, VM versions after VM/SP repeatedly scan the dispatch list until work arrives, instead of entering a wait state. This "active wait" seems wasteful at first, since each processor runs at 100 percent utilization at all times, but is actually quite useful. Other processors no longer need to set up and issue signals to wake up a sleeping CPU. When work arrives, it can be processed sooner because the CPU is already running the dispatcher, instead of having to work its way there from the external interrupt handler.

Clearly, there is no disadvantage to running the CPU in a loop when there is no other work for it do. Fortunately, active wait is not used when VM runs under VM.

Active wait is run with CP in PSW protect key 3. True CPU utilization can be displayed on the System Activity Display (SAD) frame, on CPUs that have them, by excluding CPU activity in this protect key. The hardware monitor (usually a horizontal bar chart of CPU utilization for each CPU in a system) will display the CPU utilization not spent in active wait.

System Resource Allocation

Schedulers in every operating system control how much computer resource a user receives. In multiprogramming environments, different users compete for system resources, and schedulers allocate resources to them based on their importance and resource requirements. Schedulers are an important part of how operating systems implement the policies of the computer system's owners.

The VM scheduler does this by selecting virtual machines to be in the "multiprogramming set" of users to be run by the dispatcher. The scheduler monitors resource requirements of each user, overall system load, and the externally specified importance of each virtual machine. The primary factor for deciding whether a ready-to-run user can enter the multiprogramming set is determining whether its working set can fit in available main storage.

The VM scheduler's goals are to provide a "fair share" of CPU and storage resources to each user over relatively long periods of time, except where biased by installation policy, and to ensure good utilization of these resources. It makes "coarse grain" decisions about which users are allowed to run. Additionally, the scheduler is strongly oriented towards providing quick response to interactive users with short running transactions.

Preferential treatment is appropriate for service virtual machines (SVMs) that provide service to other users, since delays they experience are experienced by their clients as well. This is especially important for servers that provide interactive access to the system, such as VTAM service machines. This is also appropriate when key virtual machines, such as guest operating systems, have resource requirements larger than their fair share of the system.

The scheduler evaluates the workload both on an event basis, for example, when a virtual machine completes a transaction, and on a periodic basis, to monitor system performance and make recommendations to the dispatcher.

Scheduler timing operates over longer time periods than the dispatcher, periodically evaluating the progress of each running user. In 370-mode VM, the scheduler uses time periods called *queue slices*, made up of a number of dispatcher CPU time slices. VM/XA and VM/ESA schedulers run at the end of *elapsed time slices* (ETS), instead of after a quota of consumed CPU time. This reflects their orientation towards system rather than CPU scheduling, and causes the scheduler to evaluate the status of users even if bottlenecks make them unable to absorb CPU resources.

Scheduler queues and virtual machines

Some operating systems have naive resource schedulers, and are unable to handle heterogeneous workloads (mixes of both "light" and "heavy" resource-consuming applications) and concurrently provide both good response time for interactive users and good throughput for batch-like applications. For example, the simple "round-robin" method of scheduling resources to each user in turn, used in most UNIX implementations, insufficiently distinguishes between interactive user and batch processes, making it too easy for background applications to elongate terminal response time.

This type of scheduling existed in very early versions of VM, where its weaknesses were quickly revealed. Systems running interactive users together with compute-intensive batch jobs or guest operating systems need a scheduler that differentiates between the kinds of service needed for interactive and non-interactive users. The "Wheeler Scheduler," an optional scheduler for VM/370 written by IBM's Lynn Wheeler, provided this kind of sensitivity to user category, and was the basis for later schedulers in VM/SP, HPO, and VM/ESA.

VM categorizes users by sorting them into a multilevel queue system. The scheduler places virtual machines with a recent history of interactive behavior on a list called Q1. The dispatcher gives these machines quick service by giving them frequent but short time slices. Virtual machines executing medium and long transactions are on queues called Q2 and Q3. These users receive fewer but longer time slices. This lets VM provide short response times to interactive users who need frequent short bursts of service, and gives longer but less frequent chunks of CPU time to batch users.

A virtual machine is said to be *in-queue* if it is on one of these lists, collectively known as the *dispatch list*. Membership in these queues is based on a virtual machine's current processing state, recent resource consumption, and overall system load.

Before being placed in-queue, a virtual machine is placed in an *eligible list* of machines waiting to receive service. The lists E1, E2, and E3 contain virtual machines waiting to enter Q1, Q2, and Q3. The scheduler holds virtual machines in eligible lists if their addition to the multiprogramming set would cause excessive storage contention. Under normal circumstances, virtual machines are moved to the dispatch list without delay. As is described later, VM uses this method to prevent a virtual storage performance problem called *thrashing*.

Each scheduler list is ordered by *deadline priority*, which is derived from virtual machine priority or share settings, recent resource consumption, and scheduler biases. A deadline is a time of day by which a user should have received a given amount of service. Lower deadlines correspond to earlier times and therefore faster service.

Time-slice and transaction duration

The dispatcher lets each virtual machine execute a quota of CPU time called a *true* or *minor* time slice before it dispatches another user. The duration of a time slice is called a *quantum*, and is scaled by CPU speed.

After a number of true time slices, a VM/SP or HPO user is said to have used up a queue slice. A queue slice marks the end of a transaction, and is the amount of CPU time a virtual machine is allowed to absorb before it is reevaluated by the scheduler. Transactions also end when a user becomes idle. The time for an interactive queue slice is scaled by CPU speed to be sufficient for "typical" trivial transactions. Noninteractive slice durations are a multiple of the interactive slice length.

In VM/ESA, a transaction is given a fixed time in-queue to compete for resources or become idle. A virtual machine is queue-dropped after it has been in-queue for an elapsed time slice (ETS) even if it received no service. This prevents fruitlessly high multiprogramming levels. ETS time is increased and decreased to try to categorize 85% of all transactions as interactive. Longer ETS times factor in effects of storage and I/O waits.

Scheduler state transitions

If a virtual machine becomes idle before its queue slice ends, it has performed a *voluntary queue-drop*. This is typical of truly interactive transactions. When an idle virtual machine becomes ready to run again, it goes back into Q1.

If a Q1 transaction does not complete in its queue slice, it receives an *involuntary queue-drop*, and it is moved to the eligible list E2. If its working set does not exceed the number of available page frames, it is placed in Q2, where it receives fewer but longer bursts of service.

If a transaction does not complete in a Q2 slice, it is considered noninteractive and is again queue-dropped and placed on E2. A virtual machine arrives in E3, and subsequently Q3, if it has run several Q2 queue slices without becoming idle. Q3 is used for large transactions; Q3 users receive longer and fewer slices than Q2 and have poorer deadline times than Q1 and Q2 users.

There are several reasons to decrease frequency and increase duration of queue slices as a transaction lengthens. Q1 transactions need frequent short bursts of service for good interactive response. Short queue stays detect transactions that exhaust their queue-slices without completing, and therefore require nontrivial CPU resources. This avoids wasting high-priority service on batch-like transactions.

Lengthening the duration of a nontrivial transaction also reduces start-up overhead. A long-running transaction is more likely to have a large working set, and may have to reestablish it each time it is placed in queue. Those pages may have been paged out since the last time the virtual machine ran. When the virtual machine runs again, it page faults its working set back into memory with significant delay. By providing the virtual machine with long slices, VM gets more productive computation done for the initial overhead.

Queue-drop processing

As just described, CP uses queue-drops to revise estimates of the type of transactions being run and the type of resources they have been receiving. The scheduler adjusts the projected working set of a dropped virtual machine to get a more recent view of its memory requirements. It therefore has a better estimate of whether a user will fit in memory when placed back in queue.

The scheduler also uses queue-drops to review a user's rate of progress relative to the rest of the system. This is used to determine if a virtual machine is getting more or less than its fair share of the system and needs to be slowed down or speeded up to equitably distribute resources.

Virtual machines also queue-drop when they become *idle*, or *dormant*. Idle virtual machines have loaded a wait state PSW (Program Status Word) indicating they are waiting for an external event to occur, but have no DASD or tape device I/O waiting. This is called a *long wait* to distinguish it from short waits for I/O operations. A long wait normally means that the virtual machine has completed a transaction and is waiting for work, although it could also be waiting for a file to arrive on the virtual reader, or for a VMCF, IUCV, or APPC/VM message.

The end of a transaction lets the scheduler recategorize the workload characteristics of the virtual machine. The next transaction is initially classified as interactive, since the user might have completed a "heavy" transaction and will now be performing a series of trivial interactions.

The scheduler also uses the fact that a virtual machine is idle to better manage main storage. Storage management routines more willingly claim real storage pages belonging to idle users, who are not expected to reuse them in the short-term future, and use them to service the current storage demands of active users.

In VM/SP, a virtual machine may erroneously be treated as idle during terminal I/O, such as when a command is echoed from the input area to the output area of a 3270 terminal. The inappropriate queue activity causes CP overhead, although usually not at levels significant with the small number of users on VM/SP systems.

HPO, VM/XA, and VM/ESA use a *queue-drop delay* timer of 300 milliseconds to determine if a virtual machine is inactive. The userid is queue-dropped if the virtual machine remains idle when the timer expires. This prevents erroneously queue-dropping users that are briefly inactive within a transaction. Additionally, VM/ESA and VM/XA are aware of users in wait state for inter-virtual machine communications, and treat them differently from truly idle virtual machines.

Biased resource distribution

The "fair share" orientation of the scheduler can be biased in favor of important virtual machines by providing VM external indication of their higher priorities.

VM/SP and HPO user priorities are specified in the user directory, or by the **SET PRIORITY <userid> nn** command, where **nn** is a value between 0 and 99. User priority is used to calculate the virtual machine's deadline time; the lower the priority, the smaller the derived deadline, and the better the service.

The SET FAVOR <userid> nn command can also be used in VM/SP and VM/HPO to guarantee a user a specified percentage of the CPU. The value **nn** is a percentage between 1 and 99. This command is used to ensure that a critical user gets sufficient CPU, regardless of system load from other users.

The **SET SHARE <userid>** command adjusts service to users in VM/ESA, combining the functions of SET PRIORITY and SET FAVOR. **SET SHARE <userid> ABS n%** is similar to VM/SP's SET FAVOR with percentage, except that it specifies a percentage of the entire VM system instead of a single CPU. On an ES/9000 model 900 with six CPU processors, an absolute share of 16% provides the equivalent of a dedicated CPU on demand.

SET SHARE <userid> REL nnn assigns relative portions of system resources to users. Resources neither assigned to absolute share users nor used by CP are distributed in proportional amounts. A user with a relative share of 200 absorbs CPU service twice as fast as a user with a share of 100, provided both are competing for resources in a CPU constrained system.

VM/ESA gives a *hot-shot* burst of high priority service to a user that has a terminal interaction while running a medium or long transaction. CP briefly treats the virtual machine as interactive instead of batch-like to provide good response for the keyboard interaction. CP then slows the virtual machine down by an equivalent amount to prevent it getting an unfair long-term advantage.

For example, a user might issue **#CP INDICATE USER** or **#CP QUERY TIME** to see how a program is progressing, or an **HX** command to halt its execution. Response to these commands could be slow if they execute at the priority of the long running command.

VM/ESA implements "#CP" commands by dispatching the user that issued it. Response to these commands could be delayed if treated with the same priority as the transaction in progress. Hot shot bias lets the user get quick response to CP and other short commands independent of the resource consumption of the virtual machine. After the hot-shot period, VM/ESA briefly lowers the virtual machine's priority to make sure that it absorbs no more than its assigned share of system resources.

VM/ESA also gives a *lock-shot* boost to users that are holding an internal VM lock. This helps a virtual machine release system resources for other users.

System Data Collection

Most operating systems generate data for system management: performance data for tuning and capacity planning, accounting data for chargeback to users and cost recovery, and error logging of hardware errors. CP sends the following types of data to collector virtual machines:

- performance monitoring data
- system accounting data
- hardware error logs
- software error symptoms
- dynamic device configuration changes in ESCON hardware

VM/SP and HPO only collect the first three of the above types of data, and use a different method to collect each one. Accounting data is sent to the reader of a virtual machine specified during system generation in the form of 80-character card images. This is a historical artifact left over from when VM accounting data was sent to a real card punch. VM was then enhanced to write accounting data to a virtual reader instead of real punched cards. Accounting cards can be processed with the same commands as any other reader file. Performance monitor data is also sent to a virtual machine's reader, but using a format that required the use of special DIAGNOSE programming. Error records are written directly by CP to a specially formatted disk area identified to CP during system generation.

These methods had a number of deficiencies. Different mechanisms meant that CP had to have unique code for each type of data recording, and that installations had to write different procedures for processing each type of data. Additionally, the use of spool files required too much I/O processing. CP had to write the data to spool disks, and then the virtual machine had to read it from spool, often merely to write it to CMS disk files. This was especially costly for performance data, which can be extremely voluminous.

VM/XA and ESA send information to collector machines via the IUCV protocol. A collector service machine for each of these data types connects to a CP System Service IUCV function in order to establish a conversation with the data source in CP. CP system services are described in "CP System Services" on page 366. Each time CP has data to send to a virtual machine for processing, it issues an IUCV `SEND` to the service machine, which issues a `RECEIVE` to copy data from CP storage into a virtual storage buffer. The application can then log it to a CMS disk file or process it directly from storage.

Monitor data collection

VM/ESA and VM/XA handle monitor data slightly differently than the other types of data. The high rate at which monitor data is created makes it impractical to issue IUCV SEND and RECEIVEs for every monitor record. Instead,

CP writes monitor data to the *monitor saved segment*, and uses IUCV to tell the monitor collection machine when data is available in the segment.

Unlike normal saved segments, which contain virtual machine data saved by the SAVESEG or SAVESYS command, the monitor segment is continually written to by CP and read from by authorized virtual machines. CP and a virtual machine share a common portion of addressable storage in a controlled manner, with only read access permitted from the virtual machine. CP uses normal mechanisms for writing to a virtual storage page. Monitor segment pages may be paged in and out of real storage just like other saved segment and user pages.

IBM provides a CMS program called MONWRITE, which attaches the monitor saved segment as part of its address space, and connects to the *MONITOR IUCV system service. When CP writes a page of data to the segment, it sends an IUCV message over *MONITOR that indicates the type of data placed in the segment, and its address within it. MONWRITE writes the data to disk or tape and issues a response to CP to let it know the page can be reused. Products from other vendors, such as XAMON from Velocity Software, and VMMONITOR from Systems Center, Inc., also connect to *MONITOR to gather performance data, and additionally analyze it. Under VM/XA, only one virtual machine at a time could connect to *MONITOR; VM/ESA lets multiple virtual machines connect to *MONITOR.

Monitor data gives installations an extremely detailed view of the performance characteristics of its VM systems. Data reduction tools from IBM and other vendors provide reports, charts and analysis for performance tuners and capacity planners.

Monitor data in VM/ESA is divided into categories called *domains*:

- General system domain: overall system performance
- Monitor domain: configuration data
- User domain: information about users including resource consumption and scheduling status
- Scheduler domain: scheduler queue transition and work flow data
- Seek domain: DASD seek information
- I/O domain: real device utilization and timing information
- Processor domain: work dispatched and utilization of each CPU
- Storage domain: utilization of real, expanded, and auxiliary storage

Monitor data is either *event* or *sample* data. The scheduler and seek domains contain event data, and the system domain contains sample data. The remaining domains contain both event and sample data. Event data is collected whenever a system event occurs, such as an I/O operation or a transaction.

Sample data consists of periodically collected counters and timers, and is further subdivided into *single sample* and *high-frequency sample* data. The different sample times are used to record counters and flags that change with differing frequencies. For example, single sample information records CPU utilization in an interval, and high speed frequency includes virtual machine execution state sampling.

Chapter

8

VM Storage Management

CP manages real storage resources, and provides virtual storage address spaces for itself and virtual machines, using auxiliary media to hold data that does not fit in real storage. This chapter discusses VM virtual and real storage management.

Virtual Storage Management in VM

VM/ESA presents each logged on user the image of a virtual computer containing up to 2047MB of unique address space. This is limited to 999MB in VM/XA, and to 16MB in VM/SP and HPO. Additionally, CP itself has an address space of 2048MB (2GB). In VM/ESA, both CP and virtual machines may have multiple auxiliary dataspaces of up to 2GB in size; this is described in "VM Dataspaces" on page 173. In practice, most virtual machines have only their primary address space, usually referred to as its virtual machine size, and most are a few megabytes in size.

A user's view of storage is not related to the amount of storage installed in the computer or storage requirements of other users. Virtual storage contents that do not fit in main storage are kept on slower media and read (*paged in*) or written (*paged out*) to and from main storage as needed. Unallocated pages that have never been referenced by a virtual machine exist in neither real nor backing storage.

Purposes of virtual storage

Virtual storage exploits the tendency of most programs to exhibit *locality of reference* for storage references made in a short interval. That is, references to instructions and data tend to be clustered to a relatively small set of storage locations, called the *working set*. A program's working set is usually far smaller than its total code and data size, and varies as the program moves from one execution phase to another.

Virtual storage systems keep the working sets of applications in real storage, rather than their total program and data storage areas. Other storage locations are kept on slower media and brought into real storage when programs refer to them. An application only needs enough real storage to contain its working set.

An attempt to refer to a program or data location not currently in real storage results in a *page fault* interrupt, which switches control to the operating system. The operating system reads the required virtual storage location from auxiliary storage into real storage, possibly writing out an unused storage location to make room for it, and then lets the interrupted program resume execution.

This makes it possible to concurrently run programs whose aggregate storage requirements far exceed the amount of real storage installed on a computer system. Additionally, virtual storage systems eliminate the need to have physically contiguous blocks of storage for users, since contiguous virtual addresses are translated into real storage locations which need not be contiguous.

The working set principle is used many places in VM, for example, in the CMS file system, and in other systems as well. The dramatically cheaper and larger main storage that has become available since VM's origin has increasingly validated this concept. Originally, it was essential that the paging subsystem be highly efficient, as VM's is. Systems with unsophisticated paging mechanisms, such as UNIX, can now exploit this principle since storage prices are low and main storage sizes high. Increasingly, operating systems provide methods to refer to file data in virtual storage without explicit I/O operations. Almost all modern operating systems use virtual storage to let many users or many programs execute with little regard to the amount of storage installed on the computer.

CP delays execution of a page-faulting virtual machine until the page it referred to can be brought into real storage, unless *page fault handshaking*, described later, has been established between CP and the virtual machine. If a page fault is for a previously unreferenced page, CP clears a new

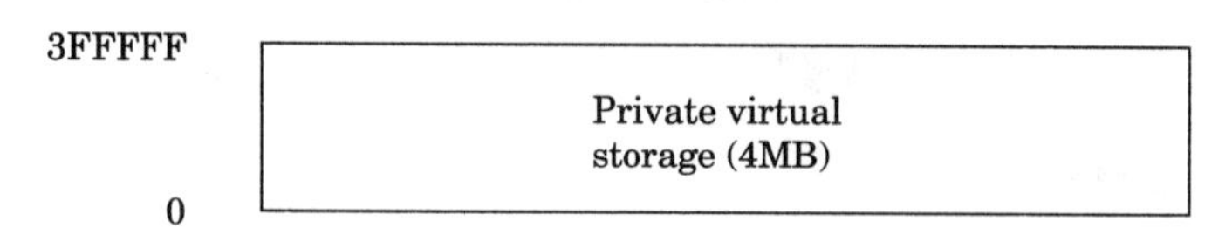

Fig. 8.1 Virtual machine storage without shared segments.

page to zeroes and gives it to the virtual machine. Otherwise, CP reads the contents of the page into real storage from disk or expanded storage, a large capacity semiconductor memory typically used as a paging device on mainframe systems. Although details vary, the same process is performed in all virtual storage operating systems.

Shared segments and named saved systems

Storage visible to a virtual machine may be private, consisting of data locations numbered from 0 up to the virtual machine's size (`VMSIZE`) minus 1. That is, a virtual machine with 4MB of virtual storage can address storage numbered 0 to 3FFFFF (hexadecimal), as shown in Fig. 8.1 (although, as we'll see shortly, relatively few virtual machines address only their private address space). Storage references outside this range are invalid, and cause a program check. Private storage contents are entirely controlled by the virtual machine operating system.

VM also provides logical extensions to a virtual machine's private storage called *Named Saved Systems* (NSS) and *DisContiguous Saved Segments* (DCSS), used by almost all virtual machines running CMS. The most common purpose for saved segments and systems is to share reentrant code between many users. This dramatically improves response time and system performance, since each user shares the same copy in real memory. In this context, saved segments are also called *shared segments* or *shared systems*. CMS itself, GCS, and many CMS products, reside in shared systems or shared segments.

Segments begin on an address boundary determined by the CPU architecture: a 64KB boundary on 370-mode VM systems, and a megabyte boundary in VM/XA and ESA. The starting address of a saved segment need not adjoin the end of a virtual machine's private storage (in fact, the segment's start and end addresses may even reside *within* the virtual machine's private address range), hence they may be discontiguous.

For example, in Fig. 8.2, the virtual machine's last private address is at the end of its VMSIZE, 3FFFFF, but the PRODUCTA segment begins at 700000. The storage locations between the end of the virtual machine and the beginning of PRODUCT1 remain unaddressable, as are the locations between the end of PRODUCT1 and the beginning of the CMS nucleus. Refer ences to "gap" locations result in program checks.

Many products (APL2, GDDM, VSAM, VS FORTRAN, OfficeVision/VM, ISPF, C/370, Syncsort, SAS, SQL/DS, FOCUS, XMENU, and numerous others) can be installed in saved segments. Typically, a small "stub" module for each product is read from disk into private storage. The stub module attaches the segment to the virtual machine and branches to it. Saved segments are attached to a virtual machine via DIAGNOSE 64 (described in Chapter 16), and invoked in CMS by the `SEGMENT` command. Saved systems are invoked when

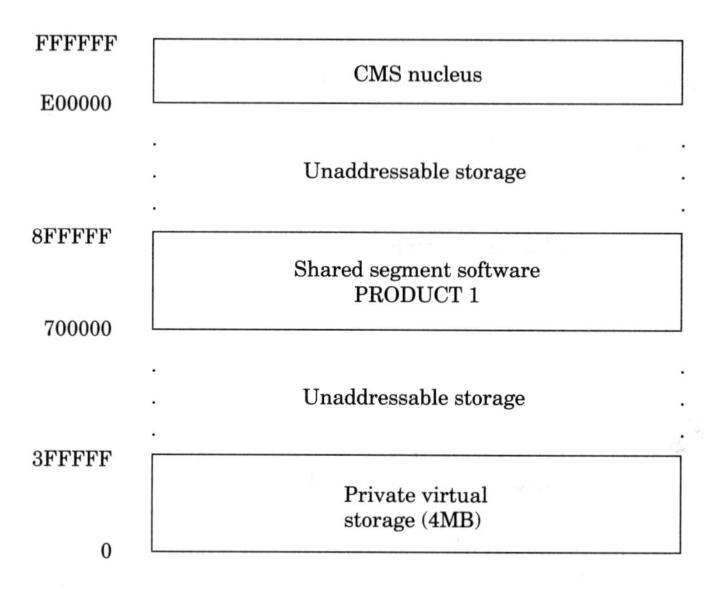

Fig. 8.2 CMS virtual machine storage with shared segments.

a virtual machine IPLs the named saved system (for example, `IPL CMS`). In both cases, CP associates part of a virtual machine's segment tables with a segment table describing the saved system or segments. Virtual machine storage references therefore point to the shared storage.

Shared segments improve response times by reducing real storage requirements, and by making it more likely that programs are in real storage when referenced. Shared pages are retained in storage just like virtual machine pages, subject to paging based on their pattern of reference. However, shared segment and shared system pages may be referenced by many users, so used pages (common code paths, instead of occasionally executed routines) are more likely to remain resident in storage than private virtual machine pages. System-wide storage requirements are decreased because a single real-storage copy of a product serves all of its users. This lets VM systems leverage real storage, compared to workstation systems in which each user of an editor or language compiler uses a different copy in real storage.

Shared segments can improve response time even when there is little or no code sharing. CP is highly optimized to perform paging operations quickly, and can page a segment's contents into storage faster than CMS can read a MODULE file from disk. Since shared segment contents are brought into storage via page fault, only referenced locations are read into storage. In contrast, the entire contents of a MODULE file are read from disk to storage, whether subsequently used or not.

In VM/SP and HPO, saved segments and systems are defined in a CP system generation module named **DMKSNT** (system name table). Macros in DMKSNT specify the virtual storage locations the segments will occupy, and the disk locations they are saved in. The name table is changed by updating DMKSNT, creating a new CP nucleus, and reIPLing VM. The **SAVESYS** command saves the contents of virtual storage into the assigned disk locations. Subsequent references to the NSS use the saved storage values.

VM/XA and VM/ESA system programmers can create saved segments and systems at any time. The **DEFSYS** command defines a saved system, and **DEF SEG** defines a new saved segment. These commands create a special spool file called a *System Data File* (SDF), which resides in spool disk space. The **SAVESEG** and **SAVESYS** commands store the current contents of virtual storage into a previously defined NSS.

When first defined, an NSS file is a class S, or *skeleton*, file. This indicates that its addresses and attributes have been established, but no contents have been assigned to it. When SAVESEG or SAVESYS is executed, the spool file becomes class A, indicating that it is *active*. If there already was a class A SDF with the same name, it is marked class P to indicate that it is *pending purge*. CP purges the old version of the spool file when the last user connected to it logs off or releases it.

Both types of NSS may be defined with one or more ranges of virtual addresses. Different page ranges can be defined as shared by all users attached to the segment, usually for read-only access, or exclusively owned by each virtual machine loading the segment. In the latter case, unique copies of the saved pages are assigned to each user loading the segment.

VM/XA and VM/ESA allow multiple named segments to be combined into a *segment space*. The segment space must begin on a segment boundary, like a regular saved segment, but *segment space members* may begin or end on any page boundary. This makes it easier to combine related products together in a single physical segment. For example, a VM site might combine the APL2 and GDDM segments into a single segment space, as shown in Fig. 8.3, since APL2 uses GDDM for its session manager. An application loading a member of a segment space implicitly loads the entire space.

CMS provides a similar facility by letting a single *physical segment* provided by CP contain multiple *logical segments*. Logical segments may begin and end on individual 4K boundaries, and may contain shared code, REXX EXECs, file directories, or any other programmer defined object. Segment directories, built from *LSEG* (logical segment) and *PSEG* (physical segment) files prepared by system programmers, let CMS map a structure onto the CP- defined segment.

Logical segments and segment spaces provide overlapping functions by allowing granular allocation of segments within a hardware defined segment. CMS logical segments were introduced with VM/SP Release 6, which does not have the segment spaces available in VM/XA and VM/ESA. Similarly, the version of CMS available with VM/XA did not support logical segments. VM/ESA

```
q nss name aplgddm map
FILE FILENAME   FILETYPE  MINSIZE  BEGPAG  ENDPAG  TYPE  CL  #USERS  PARMREGS  VMGROUP
0072 APLGDDM    DCSS-S    N/A      00A00   00DFF   —     A   00000   N/A       N/A
0070 AP2R30S1   DCSS-M    N/A      00A00   00B3F   SR    A   00010   N/A       N/A
0119 ADMASS00   DCSS-M    N/A      00B40   00DFF   SR    A   00002   N/A       N/A
Ready;
```

Fig. 8.3 Segment space containing both APL2 and GDDM.

provides both facilities, and lets system programmers choose the method they prefer. An advantage of CMS logical segments is that they reduce the amount of programming needed to use data or programs residing in shared segments.

It can be challenging to plan the location of segments, since segments that may be used at the same time must be assigned non-overlapping addresses. For example, FOCUS, OfficeVision/VM and ISPF (which is called from OfficeVision) are all installed in shared segments. If users invoke FOCUS applications within OfficeVision/VM, then the system programmer must ensure that their shared segments do not overlap. Other users inevitably use a different set of products, and make it necessary to install other products at non-overlapping locations.[1] After a while, it is hard to find any private space left over for the user. This is especially a problem in the 370-mode environment, in which users are restricted to a total address range of 16MB.

The V/SEG family of products from VM Systems Group, Inc., helps solve this problem by letting the system programmer define "families" of segments containing a product. For example, when an application calls for the FOCUS segment from within OfficeVision, they select the FOCUS segment that overlaps neither OfficeVision nor ISPF. Ultimately, the most effective way to provide non-overlapping saved segments is to convert users from 370-mode to XA-mode virtual machines, and locate their shared segments above the 16MB line. 370-mode users can only refer to virtual storage addresses below 16MB, making it hard to find nonconflicting addresses for products. XA-mode provides ample virtual storage addresses to assign each product its own range of storage locations.

CMS provides the **SEGMENT** command (and a related SEGMENT macro for assembly language programs) for loading and purging saved segments. The SEGMENT command lets CMS load saved segments when the virtual machine size exceeds the starting address of the saved segment, as shown for a user with a large VMSIZE in Fig. 8.4.

The **SEGMENT LOAD** command uses DIAGNOSE 64 to determine which storage locations are used by the saved segment, and ensures that these lo-

[1] This is not a contrived example!

cations are not in use by the CMS session. If CMS has allocated data areas from the address range occupied by the segment, the command issues an error message. Otherwise it issues DIAGNOSE 64 again to load the segment into storage. **SEGMENT RESERVE** tells CMS to not use the storage locations associated with a shared segment. It is good practice to issue a SEGMENT RESERVE for a segment you know you will use later. This ensures that no program allocates a control block or other shared segment in its location.

Further discussion of how shared segments are used is left for the CMS chapters. The following sections describe storage management methods used to efficiently provide private and shared virtual storage.

Segment protection

Virtual machines could store into shared pages on older CPUs without the *segment protect* facility. When switching between users, CP had to check for changes to shared pages by testing the *change bit* associated with each shared page resident in real storage. When CP found altered, shared pages,

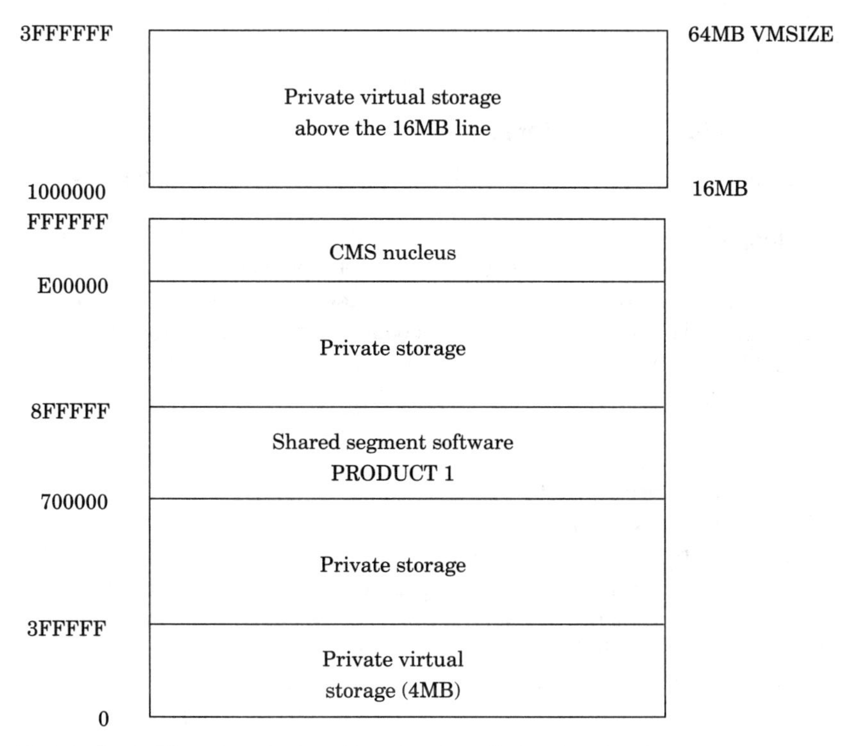

Fig. 8.4 Large XA-mode virtual machine storage, with shared segments.

it made them *nonshared* by assigning the user a private copy of the shared segment or system they reside in. CP also read fresh copies of the changed pages from disk or expanded storage so other users could continue to access the original contents.

The normal storage protection feature controlled by storage keys could not be used, since a virtual machine program can switch to any protect key. Scanning for changed shared pages accounted for up to 20% of the CP overhead on System/370 and 303x processors.

An additional cost occurs when VM/SP runs on a multiprocessor system. If pages are shared on both CPUs, a user could alter a page before the CP dispatcher on the other CPU had a chance to detect the change. To prevent this, VM/SP keeps two copies of each shared segment, increasing storage requirements.

HPO, VM/XA, and VM/ESA avoid this waste by using the segment protect facility installed on all current processors. Segment protection lets these versions of CP define pages as "read-only" regardless of users' storage protection keys. This causes a program check when a program stores into the shared segment. CP no longer keeps a copy of each segment for each processor, and doesn't scan shared segment "change" bits when dispatching users. Segment protect is another example of an architectural enhancement added to provide hardware assistance to software routines.

CP Distribution of Real Storage

Real storage is controlled by CP and is divided into the following areas:

- The Prefix Page, called the Prefix Storage Area or PSA in VM/SP and HPO, contains hardware defined areas such as interrupt vectors, pointers to CP's globally used control blocks and routines, and most commonly used constant values. The prefix page resides in page 0 of memory (storage locations 0 to 4095) which can be addressed by any CP routine without the use of an address register (base register).

  A hardware facility called *prefixing* lets each CPU in a multiprocessor address a different page frame as page 0. Every CPU has a *prefix register* whose contents are added to addresses that fall within 0 to 4095 to map the storage references to unique pages in storage. The term *absolute storage* is used to refer to a real storage location to which prefixing is not applied.

  Each CPU in a multiprocessing system uses its own prefix page for data private to that processor. A global "common area" is used for data shared by all CPUs. In VM/SP and HPO multiprocessor systems, common data is stored in an *absolute PSA*, which is organized the same as the per-CPU PSA. This let uniprocessor code be quickly refit to multiprocessor operation by using the same identifiers and storage locations, by only requiring that the routines address the proper PSA. In VM/XA and VM/ESA, a unique *system common area* was defined to contain data that is global for the entire system.

- A VIRTUAL=REAL area can be established when a CP nucleus is created. It allows a single virtual machine to run without address translation or paging. V=R guests can run under VM with essentially the same performance as when running native.

  VM/ESA, when running on ES/9000 and 3090 E, S, or J processors, can use the "Multiple Preferred Guests" feature, to run up to five additional virtual machines as VIRTUAL=FIXED guests. V=F machines run with the same performance benefits as V=R.
- The CP resident nucleus contains CP modules that remain resident in real storage at all times.
- The free storage area, in VM/SP and VM/HPO, is a reserved storage area for CP control blocks. In VM/XA and ESA, control blocks are allocated from free storage, as is described below.
- The trace table, in VM/SP and VM/HPO only, is a circular buffer of recent events used for diagnostic purposes. VM/XA and VM/ESA allocate trace tables differently, as discussed in "CP Trace Table" on page 130.
- The Dynamic Paging Area (DPA) contains user virtual storage, shared virtual storage, and CP's pageable nucleus. CP also uses this area for spool and directory file pages, for VM/ESA control blocks, and for VM/SP and HPO control blocks that overflow (*extend*) the predefined FREE area.

VM real storage distribution is shown in Fig. 8.5.

Real Storage Management

User storage, the CP pageable nucleus, and spool buffers are allocated from pages in the dynamic paging area. The status of each page is recorded in the `FRAMETBL` (page frame table) in VM/ESA and VM/XA, and the `CORTABLE` in VM/SP and HPO (so called due to its origin when computer's memories were made of ferrite, donut-shaped cores).

A frame table entry (`FRMTE`) describes the status of each page. Frames can be associated with one another by linked-lists chained through FRMTE words. A page can be marked as

- free (not in use for any purpose)
- owned by a user
- shared (e.g., in a shared segment)
- locked for an I/O buffer

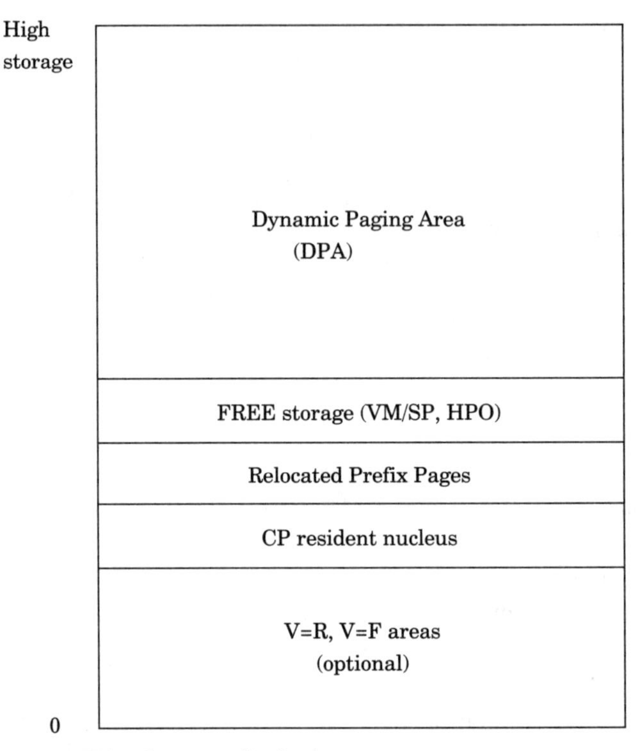

Fig. 8.5 VM real memory distribution.

- locked by the class A LOCK command
- used by CP
- offline—VM handles failing page frames by marking them offline and not using them for any purpose.

Virtual machine storage categories

Real storage is also called first-level storage, since it is never subject to dynamic address translation. Storage CP provides to a logged on user is called *guest-real* or *second-level* storage. If the guest runs a virtual storage operating system, like MVS or VM itself, the virtual storage it creates for its applications is called *third-level* storage or *guest-virtual* storage.

Virtual machine storage is usually pageable, and is sometimes called *virtual=virtual* (V=V), since the virtual address space of the guest resides in virtual storage. CMS almost always runs in V=V virtual machines. Some guest operating systems, notably DOS/VSE and VS1, run well in a virtual=virtual machine.

A single virtual machine's guest-real storage can be permanently assigned to host-real storage. That is, its storage can be locked into fixed storage addresses. This eliminates paging for the virtual machine and makes possible a number of VM options for higher performance and availability. Such users are said to have *virtual=real* (V=R) storage, since their virtual storage locations are assigned to the equivalent real storage locations. This is almost always reserved for guest virtual machines, not CMS.

When VM/ESA runs on an ES/9000 or a 3090 CPU equipped with the *Multiple Preferred Guest* (MPG) facility, a guest can also be one of up to five virtual=fixed (V=F) machines. These are like V=R virtual machines, except that MPG microcode adds a constant offset to each virtual address to produce the real storage address. MPG is not available when VM is running in a partition created by the *Processor Resource/System Manager* (PR/SM) facility. Production workloads should be avoided for VM/ESA guests when VM itself runs in a partition.

Page fault handling

When a user has a page fault, CP takes an unused page frame, and schedules a page-in from paging disk if the page was previously used and a copy is on disk. When the page-in completes, CP updates page and segment tables to include the newly resident page, and then reexecutes the instruction that failed.

This process is called *demand paging*, and is how pages are acquired in VM/SP. A VM/SP user page faults his or her working set into memory one page at a time. The other versions of VM demand page too, but also read and write pages in blocks, a technique called *swapping* or *block paging*. The basis of this difference, which is discussed later, is that page faults and page I/O delays can be reduced by reading blocks of pages in a single I/O.

There are cases in which it is useful to let a virtual machine continue operation while a page fault is being resolved. VM has long supported *VM/VS handshaking* to let DOS/VSE and VS1 guest operating systems keep running after a page fault. Since VS1 and DOS/VSE are multiprogramming systems, a guest task may page fault but still have other tasks ready to run. CP, DOS/VSE, and VS1 have been programmed to support *page fault reflection* in which the guest system is told when a first level page fault occurs. The same interface can be used for other guest operating systems as well.

Handshaking is controlled by the `SET PAGEX` command. PAGEX is turned OFF when a virtual machine is IPLed, since the guest system may not yet be ready to handle faults, it can be turned on afterwards. When handshaking is on, CP passes an interrupt to the guest when it page faults. The guest then can continue processing if it has any other work to run. When CP resolves the page fault, it passes another interrupt to the guest, which now knows that the prior task is runnable again. More than one avoided page wait can be in effect at one time.

An additional form of handshaking is provided by VM/ESA for virtual machines running in XC-mode, a VM/ESA extension of ESA architecture for virtual machines discussed later in this chapter. The **PFAULT** macro lets programmers ask CP to pass the virtual machine an external interrupt when a page fault occurs or is resolved, similar to the original VM/VS handshaking.

Assigning real storage to virtual machines

Service virtual machines and guest operating systems may need a protected allotment of real storage to achieve adequate performance. The class A **LOCK** and **SET RESERVE** commands guarantee real storage for these users. These commands should be used cautiously, since they remove pages from the pool of storage CP algorithms manage. Their primary use is to ensure that critical userids have low page rates by giving them preferential access to real storage.

LOCK command keeps specified virtual pages in real storage, whether referenced or not, until the virtual machine logs off, performs a virtual SYSTEM RESET operation, or the UNLOCK command is issued. LOCK should be used only when there is prior knowledge of which pages in a virtual machine are critical for performance. Since frequently referenced pages would tend to remain resident anyway, LOCK provides a space-time trade-off: possibly inactive pages are guaranteed to remain resident to ensure minimal page reference times when they are needed.

SET RESERVE is more flexible; it specifies a number of page frames to set aside ("reserved") for a given virtual machine. The actual set of pages reserved in storage may change, depending on the access patterns of the virtual machine, but the resident set size is not allowed to drop below the reserve set. The reserved page count can be adjusted upwards or downwards for a critical virtual machine until its page rate remains acceptably low. SET RESERVE is a better choice than LOCK in most circumstances.

Both commands are illustrated in Fig. 8.6, along with the **QUERY FRAMES** command, which shows the distribution of real storage page frames into V=R, resident nucleus, paging, trace table, and RIO370 areas. Pageable storage is again divided into available, pageable nucleus, reserved, locked, CP save area, and free storage control block pages.

Guest operating systems are often executed in virtual=real (V=R) machines, in which virtual storage locations are mapped one-for-one onto real storage locations with identical addresses, or virtual=fixed (V=F) virtual machines, in which virtual storage locations are mapped into fixed storage locations. Unlike the normal virtual=virtual (V=V) userid, the virtual storage contents of these virtual machines are never paged out of main storage. V=R and V=F machines are discussed in the chapter on guest operating systems.

```
cp set reserve vmvtam 750
Ready;
cp lock pvm 0 0
Command complete
Ready;
cp query frames
SYSGEN  REAL    USABLE  OFFLINE
065536  064928  064930  000000
V=R     RESNUC  PAGING  TRACE   RIO370
014976  000976  048858  000120  000000
AVAIL   PAGNUC  LOCKRS  LOCKCP  SAVE    FREE    LOCKRIO
044326  001492  000218  000001  000030  002791  000000
Ready;
cp query reserve
VMVTAM  RSV=000750 ACT=000750
REQUESTED FRAME TOTAL=000750; ACTUAL FRAME TOTAL=000750
Ready;
```

Fig. 8.6 SET RESERVE, LOCK, QUERY FRAMES commands.

Free list replenishment

VM maintains a list of unused pages, called the *free list* in VM/SP and HPO, and the *available list* in VM/XA and VM/ESA. These pages can immediately be used to satisfy storage requests.

Most pages are made available by CP storage management, described in the next two sections. CP selects new page frames to replenish the free list when its size drops below a threshold value. Keeping a pool of free pages prevents a user having to wait for a page-out to write the frame's prior contents to disk before his or her page can be read in.

Page frames also become free when virtual machines relinquish virtual storage. Page frames containing released virtual pages are immediately added to the free list, and backing slots on paging media are marked available. CMS storage management issues a *release page* DIAGNOSE, DIAGNOSE 10 (or DIAGNOSE 214 in VM/ESA), to free up real storage pages when applications release storage and when commands start. Pages are also released when virtual machines log off, redefine storage size, perform a *system clear* function, or IPL saved systems.

VM/SP and HPO free list replenishment

When the free list size drops below its threshold size, VM/SP and HPO scan the CORTABLE for a page that has its *reference* bit turned off. As CP passes over referenced pages, it turns their reference bits off so the next pass over the CORTABLE will allocate them if they remain unreferenced. In VM/SP the threshold size is a number of pages just higher than the number of users in the dispatch list. In HPO, the size of the threshold can be set by operator command for additional control. The low threshold should be raised if CP's defaults are too low and the free list occasionally becomes empty, as reported by system monitoring programs like IBM's *VM Monitor Analysis Program.*

When CP reaches the end of the table, it "wraps around" to its beginning. When CP finds an unreferenced page, it remembers its position in the table, and starts the search there the next time a scan is made. If CP started from the beginning of the CORTABLE for each search, it would select recently used pages from the beginning of the table, instead of "old" pages positioned later in the table.

If CP selects a page frame belonging to an active user, the page is considered *stolen*. Stealing can mean that too many users are running to fit in main storage, and that they are continually stealing from one another to maintain their working sets. Some stealing occurs under normal system loads.

VM/XA and VM/ESA Available List Replenishment (ALR)

VM/ESA maintains both low- and high-threshold available page counts for each CPU in a system. Each CPU in a multiprocessor complex has a private available list, reducing inter-CPU contention for storage management. Free list replenishment starts when the available list size drops to the low threshold, and continues until the high threshold is reached. Both thresholds are dynamically adjusted to keep enough storage for the available list without wasting storage. The low threshold is increased when storage demands increase, to make sure that free pages are available if a burst of storage requests occur.

Available list replenishment algorithms are based on virtual machine storage needs instead of frame table contents, in recognition of the fact that some users are more important than others and should have their pages protected. In particular, idle (dormant) users should not have their pages protected from selection.

VM/ESA periodically orders each user's resident pages from least to most recently referenced. A *reorder task* runs after a user has absorbed a measure of virtual CPU time. This *reset interval* is adjusted up or down depending on storage demand. The reset period is shortened if storage demands are high. The reorder task partitions resident pages into a working set list of referenced pages, and a list of unreferenced pages. Long term unreferenced pages move to the end of this list. A special reorder task processes CP virtual address spaces and saved segments every 30 seconds.

The *steal task* obtains free storage when the available list reaches its low threshold. It combines users' page lists with knowledge about user activity to select good candidates for reassignment: pages that are expected to remain unused. The steal task first selects an in-queue user or saved system and moves its unused pages to the free list. If this provides enough free storage, the process stops without further action. This balances storage consumption of running transactions against incoming work. A different user or shared system is selected each time the steal task is called.

If additional pages are needed, the steal task performs a first *demand scan* pass to search for pages using the following order: long-term dormant users (idle 20 seconds or more), dormant users, the system pseudo-userid itself, saved segment pages, eligible users, and users in the dispatch list. The steal task takes any resident page from long-term dormant users, and unreferenced pages from the other users. It does not take a page if it would cause a virtual machine's resident pages to drop below its working set size, as measured by the scheduler, or its reserved page count.

If this scan does not free enough pages, CP repeats the search, this time taking pages from users' working sets. This pass is rare on systems that are not storage overcommitted. If page frames are still needed, CP makes a third pass by taking pages from saved segments and systems, dormant users, eligible users, and users in the dispatch list.

Like other versions of VM, VM/ESA provides DIAGNOSE 10 to let virtual machines release a group of pages. However, IBM designers noted that applications frequently re-referenced storage in virtual addresses they had just released, causing significant overhead releasing storage and using it again. VM/ESA 1.1 introduced DIAGNOSE 214, which improves this by letting virtual machines request a *pending page release*, in which groups of pages are released, but not immediately returned to the available list. Instead, pages are retained by the virtual machine until available list replenishment requires additional page frames. This reduces overhead because virtual machines can cancel a pending request if they are about to reuse the storage addresses. CMS storage management in VM/ESA use DIAGNOSE 214 this way to provide CP better "hints" about its future storage references.

VM/ESA provides the **REFPAGE** macro to let applications describe a page reference pattern. CP uses this information to bring pages into storage before they are used, and to write to secondary storage pages that will not be needed for a long period of time. REFPAGE is only available for VM/ESA virtual machines running in XC-mode.

This is especially valuable for very large numerically intensive programs that work with immense arrays. Programmers can use their knowledge of how an application works to predict which array elements will be needed next. Many programs sweep through an array repeatedly, and just-referenced locations will not be reused until the next pass through the array.

REFPAGE lets application programmers tell CP which pages will be needed by providing a list of page addresses, or by describing a block of storage references with a specified pattern. A block of storage references may proceed in ascending or descending address order (many matrix operations work with decreasing subscript values), and may touch a *span* of pages, while not referring to a set of *skipped* pages. The REFPAGE INFORML format provides a list of pages to be referenced, and REFPAGE INFORMB describes a block of storage references.

Storage influence on the scheduler

The first virtual storage operating systems introduced a performance problem called *thrashing*. Systems thrash when real storage is too small for the virtual storage requirements of users, and when paging systems are too slow to keep up with the page traffic needed between main storage and auxiliary media.

Thrashing systems spend much of their time running the storage manager, as users continually steal working set pages from one another instead of performing productive work. While the ultimate answer is to provide sufficient real storage and faster paging subsystems, a scheduler can prevent thrashing by controlling the multiprogramming set of active users to reduce the degree to which real storage is overcommitted.

VM schedulers avoid thrashing by not running users whose working sets will not fit in available storage. CP holds virtual machines in eligible lists when main storage is overcommitted. They are assigned to lists named E1, E2, and E3 depending on whether they are waiting to enter Q1, Q2, or Q3. Eligible list users receive no service, and usually have no resident main storage. Virtual machines actually enter one of the eligible lists on every queue transition, but move immediately into the dispatch list under normal system load conditions.

An eligible virtual machine is placed in-queue if main storage becomes free, or is delayed long enough for its deadline priority to be better than that of an active machine. In the latter case, this may mean moving a virtual machine from in-queue to eligible status to make room for it.

Eligible lists reduce storage load so in-queue users can actually keep their working sets in main storage and run efficiently. Users receiving service will complete their transactions sooner, and eligible users will eventually get their turn. Eligible lists are an emergency response to an overloaded storage system, and are empty unless storage is overcommitted.

The **SET FAVOR <userid>** command tells VM/SP and VM/HPO to exempt a user from being placed in the eligible list. Under VM/XA and VM/ESA, the **SET QUICKDSP <userid> ON** command has a similar effect. QUICKDSP users are assigned to a scheduler list called Q0, which has no corresponding eligible list, and therefore never go into eligible state. These commands are valuable for large working set virtual machines, especially guest operating systems and service machines. They only have an effect if eligible lists are being created.

VM/XA and VM/ESA let an installation control creation of eligible lists by class of user. The **SET LDUBUF** and **SET STORBUF** commands respectively specify the degrees by which paging devices and main storage can be overcommitted. They allow different tolerances for Q1, Q2, and Q3 users. An installation can protect interactive response in different degrees by specifying that Q3 users are quickly placed in eligible lists during heavy loads, followed by Q2 and Q1 users in increasingly heavy loads. The default settings for these commands are too conservative for most installations, and create eligible lists in situations where they are not required. Most installations should not use the default values.

VM/XA and VM/ESA provide preferential service for interactive users, even when storage is overcommitted and eligible lists are present. *Transaction class blocking* favors Q1 and Q2 transactions by not allowing Q3 transactions to start if a shorter one is waiting on an eligible list. A user on E2 blocks an E3 user from entering queue; E1 users block both E2 and E3. When elapsed time slices of transactions end, their storage becomes free and eligible transactions can start. If no transactions from a longer class are active, VM/ESA places the shorter transaction in-queue whether it fits or not. CP takes even stronger action if a user has remained on the E1 list for approximately one-half second, by preempting a Q2 or Q3 user (moving it to E2 or E3) to make its storage available for the interactive user.

VM dataspaces

VM/ESA provides *VM dataspaces* when running on ESA/390CPUs. Dataspaces let CP and CMS applications efficiently address and share massive amounts of storage. Dataspaces also help applications partition their storage for different purposes.

Dataspaces are auxiliary *address spaces* of byte-addressable storage up to 2GB (2 gigabytes) in length. The term *address space* is usually associated with MVS, in which it is often used to identify a uniquely executing *job*. It emphasizes the fact that applications running under MVS have unique Multiple Virtual Storages (hence MVS's name) each potentially able to address up to 2 gigabytes of storage.

Every logged on virtual machine also has its own address space, which is referred to as its base address space. VM/ESA uses ESA/390 hardware to let CMS applications define multiple dataspaces. Dataspaces are only used for data, not for data and executable programs like a primary address space.

Dataspaces are addressed via *access registers*, numbered from 0 to 15, instead of the normal general purpose registers. Access registers contain main storage addresses; when the virtual machine is in *access register mode*, instruction references to storage use locations pointed to by the access register, in addition to storage addressed by general purpose registers. A single program can refer to both address space and data space data to access multiple 2GB size address ranges.

Reasons for dataspaces

A virtual machine can directly address up to 2,047MB of virtual storage. In some applications, even this is not enough storage—rarely because the entire 2,047MB address range is full of data, but because it becomes difficult to reserve contiguous storage for large data structures.

This limit, while obviously large, prevents the straightforward solution of large problems, and would prevent full exploitation of new ES/9000 and compatible processors with more than 2GB of central and expanded storage. (It has been said that it is annoying to exhaust a virtual resource, since you can't just purchase more of it.)

Dataspaces also make it easier for an application to flexibly share its virtual storage with other virtual machines, while retaining control of which parts of storage the other virtual machines can view or change. Without dataspaces, most VM applications share data via message-passing protocols such as IUCV. This is far less efficient than simply referring to the contents of virtual storage. Thousands of CPU instructions are used when communicating virtual machines send IUCV messages to request information, receive the request, reply with the answers, and then receive the reply message. This limits performance of key applications like SQL/DS and SFS. When using VM dataspaces, virtual machines can share data with as few as 4 CPU instructions.

CMS use of dataspaces

VM started supporting dataspaces with VM/XA, for ESA-mode virtual machines running on ESA/370 hardware. ESA/370 dataspaces are used by MVS/ESA to implement *hiperspaces*, which are used analogously to VM's minidisk cache. VM does not use ESA/370 dataspaces for itself or for CMS applications.

For ESA/390, the dataspace concept was enhanced to allow reference from virtual machines running without dynamic address translation. ESA/370 dataspaces require a DAT-mode guest, which handles its own virtual-to-real translation. This is inconsistent with CMS, which defers real storage management to CP. To handle this, IBM introduced ESA/XC, where XC stands for *eXtended Configuration.*

VM/ESA CMS virtual machines can run in XC-mode, an upward compatible extension of XA-mode and ESA-mode operation that lets non-DAT virtual machines operate in access-register mode. XC-mode virtual machines can use VM/ESA's application programmer interface to define dataspaces and specify how they can be shared with other users.

The `ADRSPACE CREATE` function, available through the CMS Callable

Service Library (CSL) creates a VM dataspace. Dataspaces have names, which include the userid of the creating virtual machine, and can be accessed by name from other virtual machines. The creating virtual machine also specifies an access list defining the users that can share the data, and whether they can share in read-only or read-write mode.

SQL/DS and the Shared File System (SFS) both exploit VM dataspaces. Both rely heavily on data transmitted between client and server virtual machines, and use dataspaces to speed inter-user data sharing.

CP use of dataspaces

CP also uses dataspaces for its own purposes. CP has a primary address in which CP code resides and executes. CP also creates dataspaces for system, virtual free storage, and "null" address spaces. These address spaces are used for CP bookkeeping and residence of control blocks. CP also creates PTRM address spaces. Up to 16 of these pseudo address spaces may be created to contain information about page tables which can be paged out of real storage to expanded storage or disk.[2]

Auxiliary Storage Management in VM

Virtual storage pages that have not been recently used are selected for *replacement*, to make room for working set pages, and are written to auxiliary media. Since devices used for paging have different speeds and capacities, IBM operating systems manage a hierarchy of storage devices, and try to satisfy as many storage requests as possible from the fastest devices.

The auxiliary storage manager is responsible for handling page transfers between main storage and backing storage. It is designed to quickly read pages from auxiliary storage to satisfy page faults, and quickly write pages to free their main storage page frames for allocation.

Paging devices

The fastest paging device is expanded storage, a large-capacity semiconductor storage device available on IBM 3090s, ES/9000s and compatible processors. On a 3090, a 4K page frame can be transferred between expanded and central storage in 75 microseconds, comparable to the time for normal storage-to-storage copy of 4,096 bytes.

The next fastest paging devices are *solid-state DASD* (SSD) like the STC 4305, Amdahl's EDAS, and the Intel 3805. SSD disks combine memory chips with microcode to emulate disk devices. SSDs exhibit properties needed for

---

[2] This information courtesy of a VMSHARE append by Jim Hennessy, of IBM's Endicott Programming Laboratory.

demand paging: short latency times and high data transfer rates. Typical service times for these devices are 4 milliseconds and lower, compared to "real" DASD times near 20 milliseconds. Sites with SSDs use them as the preferred device type in the paging hierarchy. Most installations page onto less-expensive moving head media like 3380s and 3390s. VM/ESA and VM/XA paging algorithms optimize the use of these devices.

Each version of VM uses a different method of selecting the location to write a page. No choice is made on page-ins, since the needed page resides on a specific device and must be retrieved from it. Page areas are normally placed on the fastest DASD devices in the system.

Demand paging, swapping, and block paging

VM/SP reads and writes pages individually on a demand basis, although it attempts to try to *chain* page I/Os to the same device. This results in separate I/O scheduling and interrupt handling for each page. Each page I/O usually requires a separate disk rotation.

Recent disk devices are large and fast moving-head disks. Fixed-head media (incorrectly called drums) like the IBM 2305 used in the 1970s and early 1980s, were excellent demand paging devices. They had high rotational speed and no seek delays, but were expensive and had limited capacity. Modern disk devices like the 3380 and 3390 incur seek and rotational delays for each I/O, but have high data transfer rates and track capacities. Paging algorithms in MVS and VM exploit these devices' properties by reading and writing pages in blocks, instead of singly.

Block paging shares the cost of head motion and rotational delay among a group of pages. As discussed in the chapter on the I/O subsystem, the largest components of a disk I/O's time are the head motion and rotational delay. By reading or writing a group of pages in a single I/O, only one seek and rotational delay is incurred for the entire group.

Block paging reduces the overhead of initiating a page transfer by grouping pages into *big pages*. Block paging saves overhead by sharing the overhead costs of I/O scheduling and interrupt processing for the entire block, and also frees a group of pages at once on swap-out. This lets recent VM designs eliminate the page-by-page selection of free pages used in VM/SP.

VM block paging exploits virtual storage locality of reference by forming groups of pages from within the same megabyte of virtual storage address. Pages that are used at the same time at one moment will tend to be used together a few moments later. Page references also are usually clustered by virtual storage address, since program sections and data areas tend to have *hot spots*.

HPO and VM/ESA both use this temporal (time) and virtual address locality of reference to select groups of pages to be written in a single I/O operation. These pages are from the recent working set of the user that owns it, but have not been used recently. When the user subsequently page faults on a page in the swap or block set, VM reads the entire block in a single I/O. There is a high probability that other pages from the same swap set will be referenced, but at no additional cost, since they have already been read into storage.

As mentioned earlier, systems programmers use the CPFMTXA or CP-FORMAT utilities to allocate areas on CP-owned volumes for paging and spooling and format their disk locations into page-sized blocks. CP writes pages to page area by preference, and write overflow pages to spool areas if page areas are full, after warning the system operator. Page and spool I/O is almost identical, except that paging in a spool area is always done on a single-page basis.

VM/SP and HPO paging

While VM/SP only performs demand paging, HPO uses both demand paging and swapping. HPO swapping reads and writes pages in groups called *swap sets* instead of one at a time.

HPO uses separate disk areas for paging and swapping, each of which must be specified in DMKSYS. The systems programmer specifies the location of each swap area and a swap set size to be used for the entire system. HPO also swaps pages to and from expanded storage. This does not reduce I/O initiation costs, but it lets HPO reuse the programs used when swapping to DASD, but with a faster device.

VM/SP distinguishes between preferred and nonpreferred paging devices. Preferred slots are selected from fixed-head media until they are all used or the page's owner has exceeded his or her SET SRM MAXDRUM quota. VM/SP selects devices in the order of 2305 (no longer manufactured) and equivalent fixed-head devices such as the STC 4305, followed by the optional fixed-head (0 time seek) areas present on some 3380 and 3350 models.

If no fixed head slots are available, VM/SP selects slots from the fastest available moving-head devices, VM/SP selects pages in round-robin fashion from each device type until it is full, before moving to the next slower disk device.

HPO adds additional provisions for controlling paging and spooling. Macros in DMKSYS specify areas on CP-owned volumes for

- swapping (SW), for writing and reading blocks of pages
- preferred paging (PP) for fastest demand paging
- general paging (PG), for overflow from PP space
- page migration (PM), for receiving unreferenced pages from PP space
- spooling (PS), for overflow paging and spooling

Multiple swap or preferred paging levels can be defined if devices with different performance characteristics are being used. For example, preferred paging can be allocated to both expanded storage and solid state DASD, if they are available, with normal disk drives used for general paging. Expanded storage can be used for both paging and swapping. The amounts allocated to each should be tuned to cause the fewest I/O operations to overflow to disk media. The `QUERY PSTOR` command can be used to display expanded storage utilization.

HPO allocates a page to the fastest available level in the hierarchy. For example, a demand page-out is written to the area described by the first TYPE=PP macro that has available slots. A user can be prevented from taking too large a share of preferred paging media by using the `SET SRM MAXPP` command, which specifies the maximum preferred page slots a user can have. This quota can be used to ensure that sufficient slots on fast media are available for interactive users.

HPO migrates unreferenced pages from preferred areas to *page migration* areas. This prevents higher speed paging devices being wasted on pages that are written out and not referenced again. CP periodically selects an unused page slot from the top of the hierarchy and copies it to a slower device.

Migration is influenced by a time-limit that specifies the minimum age since last reference for a page before it can be migrated. A high-usage disk-full threshold tells CP when page migration is needed to free up preferred page space. Migration can be encouraged by issuing the privileged command `MIGRATE` to cause unused pages to move from fast to slower paging media. MIGRATE can be applied to a specific user, or specified without an operand, in which case all users are examined for pages suitable for migration.

After a hierarchy level is chosen, HPO uses a technique called *N-select* to select the DASD volume to use. In N-select, a device dependent number of pages are selected for each volume before moving to the next one. *N* is usually the number of pages that fits on a single disk track, for example, 10 on 3380 DASD. N-select reduces the number of times that CP has to choose a device for a page. CP selects the lesser of the value *N* that applies to the device type and the number of page slots available in the current cylinder. This method also makes it more likely that several pages can be chained together and written in a single I/O operation.

VM/ESA and VM/XA paging

VM/ESA improves on HPO swapping with a flexible combination of swapping and demand paging. VM/ESA does not use special page areas for swapping. Instead, VM/ESA writes up to 20 pages in a single I/O operation when contiguous page slots are available at the current cylinder on the selected page device. Block paging is encouraged by over-allocating page areas to make it more likely that runs of contiguous page slots are available. VM/ESA does not block page to expanded storage, since there are no I/O blocking or rotational delay savings.

When an application page faults on a page contained in a block, VM/ESA reads the entire block into storage in a single I/O operation. The channel program is ordered so the faulted page is read first, even if this causes the total I/O operation to take an extra rotation. The READ command for the faulting page is set up to generate a *program controlled interruption* (PCI), which tells CP that the needed page is now in memory. CP restarts the user while the channel program continues reading the remainder of the block group into storage.

For example, Fig. 8.7 shows a block of seven pages belonging to a user on a single disk track. If an application page faults on page 4, CP starts a channel program that starts reading the block of pages with page 4. The channel generates a PCI as soon as page 4 is transferred to memory, and continues reading the rest of the block. Pages 5, 6, and 7 are read in the same revolution as page 4, and pages 1, 2 and 3 are read in the next revolution. The read operation would span multiple tracks if the block of pages resided on more than one track.

As a result, VM/ESA restarts a page-faulting application sooner than HPO. IBM studies showed that transactions could often perform useful processing when only the faulted page from a swap set was added to a user's already resident set.

Page area selection is simpler in VM/ESA and VM/XA than in VM/SP or HPO. VM/ESA always pages to expanded storage if available, and migrates old pages from expanded storage to disk to retain a minimum quota of available expanded storage space.

VM/ESA does not provide a disk device hierarchy for paging. It monitors the response times and request queue lengths of each page device, and selects for page-out the one with the best service times. This automatically selects the fastest device with free paging space, and balances load between multiple devices. As a result, VM/ESA paging is easier to administer than

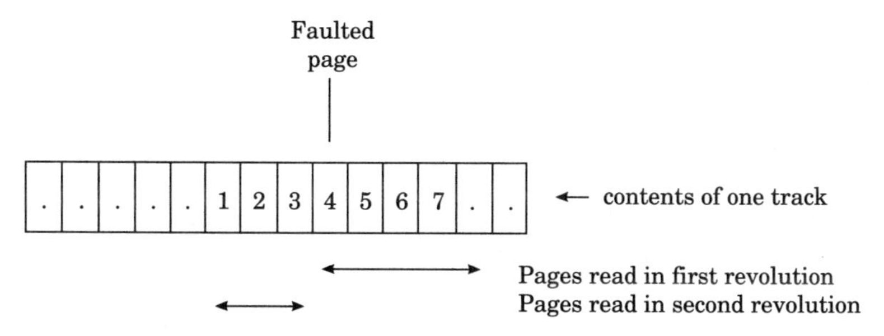

Fig. 8.7 PCI channel program for page read.

paging in VM/SP and HPO.

VM/ESA dynamically uses all page space for both single page and blocked page I/O. Block paging uses a dynamically calculated block size on each block write, based on the user's page references and the number of contiguous page slots on the DASD cylinder currently selected for output. Page areas should be overallocated by at least four to one to provide runs of empty page slots on DASD.

This arrangement improves the handling of *free-loader* pages brought into storage by a block read but subsequently unreferenced. In VM/ESA, these retain their DASD slots when removed from main storage. In HPO, free-loader pages must be written to demand paging media since they are no longer part of a swap set in swap areas.

VM/ESA always uses expanded storage, if available, as the preferred paging device. A migration task runs periodically to move unreferred expanded storage pages disk media; this is the normal method that pages are written to disk in a VM/ESA system that has sufficient main and expanded storage.

CP's stores pages directly from main storage to disk when the migration task does not free up expanded storage quickly enough to keep up with storage requirements. A high store rate, relative to the migration rate, indicates that there is insufficient expanded storage to buffer pages before they are old enough to be migrated.

VM/ESA and VM/XA do not migrate pages between different disk types. Pages are migrated from expanded storage to disk, but not from fast disks to slower. The XASSD software product from Velocity Software, Inc., adds page migration to VM/ESA and VM/XA for sites with an investment in electronic disk drives.

IBM expects expanded storage to be the primary paging device for large VM systems. Pages should only go to moving head media when migrated out of expanded storage. VM monitoring software reports the rate at which pages are migrated to DASD from expanded storage, or directly written from memory because no expanded storage was available.

Page slot allocation

CP's allocation strategy tries to reduce head motion to page devices. CP divides disk cylinders into page slots, and keeps a bit map indicating which slots are available and which are in use.

VM/SP uses a "zig-zag" allocation algorithm: pages are allocated from the physical center of the paging area defined on the volume, first on one side of the center, and then on the other. This works well with small page areas and low I/O rates, since it keeps the disk head near the center of the volume. The zig-zag algorithm performs poorly with large paging areas and high page rates, since the head winds up shuttling over previously allocated pages to and from the opposite sides of the page area.

To remedy this, HPO and VM/XA use the *moving cursor* algorithm. This technique, also called (in non-IBM literature) the *elevator* algorithm for disk scheduling, starts at one end of the paging area, and moves the head forward to the next cylinder with a free page slot. When the end of the page area is reached, the cursor (or elevator) changes direction (*reflects*), or starts over again at the beginning of the area.

This algorithm allocates a *moving wave* of new pages. Since recently written pages are more likely to be referred to than pages written a long time ago, this helps cluster seeks. Performance can suffer in HPO if page areas are too large, since the head has to cross a larger number of cylinders to retrieve page-ins from cylinders distant from the cursor. To prevent this, HPO page areas should be kept small enough that the *reflect time* remains under 5 minutes.

VM/ESA and VM/XA modify the elevator algorithm to restart its sweep when 75% of the slots behind the cursor are available. This helps cluster seeks to the same cylinders of the volume, and means that, unlike HPO, a page area can be over- allocated for peak capacity without causing longer seeks. The large number of unoccupied slots in the used area behind the cursor provides runs of slots for block paging.

Prepaging

Interactive response is best when a user's working set is already resident when his or her transaction starts. A newly active user may page fault repeatedly until the working set is resident in main storage. This process is serial and can elongate response time.

HPO attempts to reduce this delay by preloading into memory a "starting set" of pages from the user's working set before the user is run. The risk, of course, is that pages will be prepaged and never get referenced by the user. VM/ESA does not prepage. IBM feels that block paging and expanded storage make prepaging unnecessary. This reduces complexity, and eliminates the overhead possible when pages are prepaged into memory but are unused.

Chapter

9

CP Input/Output Administration

This chapter describes input/output (I/O) processing in CP. Virtual machine I/O is described in the chapters on the CMS file system, communications, and guest operating systems.

VM, like IBM's other mainframe systems, illustrates the evolution of I/O methods from its System/360 origins. Additionally, it provides stylized I/O operation used to decouple applications from details of actual devices.

VM provides a highly efficient I/O subsystem with an extremely short instruction path length. This is made possible by separation of logical I/O (provided by virtual machines), from physical I/O, provided by CP. VM has been observed to compete with MVS systems for access to shared disks so effectively that MVS could not gain access to the disks, even when running on a CPU several times faster than VM's.

CP I/O Processing

CP performs I/O for itself and for virtual machines. Most CP-generated I/O is disk I/O for spooling, paging, and directory access, although CP also performs I/O to terminals, printers, and tape drives (for dumping spool contents to tape).

CP routines create I/O request blocks and then call the I/O scheduling routine, as described below.

I/O scheduling

CP describes I/O requests in a control block called an `IORBK` (I/O Request Block) in VM/ESA, and an `IOBLOK` in 370-mode I/O. A routine wishing to perform I/O acquires storage for the I/O request block, fills in its contents, and then calls the I/O scheduling routine.

The information in an IORBK or IOBLOK includes the following:

- the device number (ESA or XA systems) or device address (370 mode VM) of the device to be driven
- the address of a channel program in real storage to be executed on that device
- the VMDBK or VMBLOK of the user for whom the I/O operation is being performed (the pseudo-userid `SYSTEM` if not associated with a specific user)
- the Interrupt Return Address (IRA) of the CP routine to regain control when the I/O operation completes
- for disk devices, the first cylinder or block location addressed by the channel program (used to schedule disk seeks; VM normally sorts queued disk seeks to minimize seek lengths)

370 I/O in VM/SP and VM/HPO

CP routines start I/O by creating IOBLOKs and calling the routine `DMKIOS` (`IOS` stands for "I/O Supervisor"). DMKIOS returns immediately to the caller, which can continue processing during the I/O operation, or as is more common, call the dispatcher to wait until the operation is complete.

Devices in 370-mode CP are represented by the `RDEVBLOK` (Real Device Block), `RCUBLOK` (Real Control Unit Block), and `RCHBLOK` (Real Channel Block). These control blocks describe the type of each device, and their current status, and contain the anchors for linked lists of pending IOBLOKs.

DMKIOS starts I/O to a device if it is not currently busy executing a previous I/O operation (indicated by a flag in the RDEVBLOK) and its control unit and channel paths are free. If the device is busy, the IOBLOK is placed on a linked list of requests to that device. Similar queues and flags are maintained at the control unit and channel level. DMKIOS dequeues and starts the first IOBLOK on each list when the associated real resource becomes free and notifies the CPU via an interrupt.

If the device has multiple channel or control unit paths, CP attempts to start the I/O on each of the alternate paths. If none of the paths are available, CP creates "mini-IOBLOKs" that are linked to the original IOBLOK, and enqueues them on the alternate paths. When a path becomes free, CP dequeues the IOBLOK, possibly chaining from a mini- to the primary IOBLOK, and then issues the I/O operation.

When the I/O event completes, CP unstacks the current IOBLOK and restarts the waiting CP process at its interrupt return address.

XA I/O in VM/XA and VM/ESA

CP routines call HCPIOS with an IORBK describing the I/O operation, and an RDEV control block describing the device. To simplify coding and slightly improve performance, a new entry point was added to HCPIOS that doesn't return to the caller until the I/O operation completes. Measurements of 370-mode VM showed that most CP routines branched to the CP dispatcher immediately after calling DMKIOS to wait until their I/O events completed. In other words, asynchronous execution was rarely used in a single thread of CP execution.

The synchronous interface is coded like a traditional subroutine call in a higher level language. Execution continues in the calling CP module immediately after the HCPIOS call when the I/O event has completed (or failed). CP code is shorter since calling routines need not code their own exits to the dispatcher, and more reliable, since the possibility of doing it incorrectly is removed. Routines that start I/O operations and continue executing while the I/O operation proceeds are written as in VM/SP and HPO.

XA-mode I/O queuing is much simpler than System/370's, thanks to the enhancements provided by XA and ESA architecture. Since path management is handled by XA hardware, I/O operations are only queued when the individual device is busy. No alternate path retry or mini-IOBLOK queuing is needed because hardware automatically starts the I/O operation on the first available path.

Real Device Control

CP provides privilege class B operator commands to make real devices available to the system, remove them from use or assign them to an individual user.

VARY command

The VARY command makes a device or range of devices usable (*online*) or unusable (*offline*) for system access. An offline device cannot be assigned to or used for any function; devices are typically taken offline when they are serviced. For example, if the hardware engineers at a site were to perform preventive maintenance on a disk drive with device number 753, the system operator would issue the commands illustrated in Fig. 9.1 to logically remove them from the system.

Errors and interrupts from offline devices are ignored; XA and ESA systems disable the subchannel assigned to the offline device, thus ensuring that a failing or serviced device cannot cause a host interrupt.

The VM/XA and VM/ESA VARY command can also make a channel path to a device online or offline. Again, this would be used if the channel, or the control unit path between the channel and devices, were to be serviced. I/O

```
* Take a disk volume offline for service
vary off 753
0753 varied offline
1 device(s) specified; 1 device(s) successfully varied offline
Ready;

* After the engineers say the device is usable:
vary on 753
0753 varied online
1 device(s) specified; 1 device(s) successfully varied online
Ready;
```

Fig. 9.1 VARY command.

to the devices would proceed along the remaining channel paths. The VARY PATH command is illustrated in Fig. 9.2.

Attachable devices

Devices can be assigned to an individual user via the `ATTACH` command, shown in Fig. 9.3. The ATTACH command specifies the real device number of the device, which must be in "free" (available) state, the userid to receive the device, and an optional virtual device number. The virtual device number defaults to the real device number if omitted. An attached device is detached from its current owner via the `DETACH` command.

This is how VM applications use tape drives, for example, although most sites use a tape management system, such as IBM's Attachable Media Manager, or VMTAPE from System Center, Inc. Tape management packages ATTACH the tape device to a user after verifying that the correct tape was mounted. By convention, CMS uses tape devices at virtual device numbers 181 to 187, and 281 to 287.

Tape devices can also be assigned to a user by the `GIVE` command, available in VM/ESA and VM/SP Release 6. GIVE differs from ATTACH in several ways: The device is previously attached to the virtual machine issuing GIVE, instead of being free, and is specified by its virtual instead of its real device number. Also, the tape drive can be returned to the tape manager when the user detaches it or logs off, with the tape volume rewound to its load point. For example, the following command transfers ownership of the tape drive at virtual device number 181 to another user, and retrieves it when the user DETACHes:

```
cp give 181 to keith 181 return
```

The tape manager can verify the contents of the tape volume returned to it. This can also be used for applications that create a tape volume in one virtual machine and process it in another: the same tape device and volume can be passed between virtual machines without manual intervention to mount and ready tape drives.

Disk volumes can be attached to a user, like tape drives, or to the entire VM system. The latter makes the minidisks defined on the volume available to users. Instead of a userid and a virtual address, the ATTACH command specifies the keyword SYSTEM, and the volume serial label of the disk drive, for example:

```
cp attach 360 to system vmpk01
```

Volumes attached to the system can only be detached from the system if no minidisks are currently in use.

In VM/ESA, disk volumes specified in the *CP-owned volume list* or *user volume list* are implicitly attached to the system at IPL time. Both lists are defined in the configuration module HCPSYS. CP-owned volumes are dis-

```
query paths 753
DASD 0753 online
Path status for device 0753: online - 1E 2C 5A 68, offline - NONE
Ready;
* Disable channel 1E so the controller interface to it can be serviced
vary off path 1e from 753
Vary path 1E offline command initiated
Vary path 1E offline command complete
Ready;
query paths 753
DASD 0753 online
Path status for device 0753: online - 2C 5A 68, offline - 1E
Ready;
* After the engineers say the channel interface is usable:
vary on path 1e to 753
Vary path 1E online command initiated
Vary path 1E online command complete
Ready;
cp query PATHS 753
DASD 0753 online
Path status for device 0753: online - 1E 2C 5A 68, offline - NONE
Ready;
* Display all devices reachable by channel path 1E
cp query chpid 1e
Path 1E online to devices 0740 0741 0742 0743 0744 0745 0746 0747
Path 1E online to devices 0748 0749 074A 074B 074C 074D 074E 074F
Path 1E online to devices 0750 0751 0752 0753 0754 0755 0756 0757
Path 1E online to devices 0758 0759 075A 075B 075C 075D 075E 075F
Ready;
```

Fig. 9.2 VARY command.

```
* Detach a tape drive from a user and give to another
cp query 100
TAPE 0100 ATTACHED TO DENNIS   0181 R/W
Ready;
cp detach 100 from dennis
TAPE 0100 DETACHED DENNIS  0181
Ready;
cp query 100
TAPE 0100 FREE
Ready;
cp attach 100 to loretta 181
TAPE 0100 ATTACHED TO LORETTA 0181
Ready;
tell Loretta Your tape is up now!
Ready;
```

Fig. 9.3 ATTACH and DETACH commands.

tinguished from user volumes in that they can contain directory, paging, spooling, and T-disk extents. CP-owned volumes can also be removed from the system, but only if neither minidisks nor CP areas are in use. In practice, this is only possible for volumes defined to contain directory or T-disk cylinders, since page or spool pages will inevitably be allocated to any volume defined with page or spool areas. User groups have asked IBM to provide operator commands that "drain" a spool or page volume by prohibiting allocation of new pages to a specified volume. Eventually, as users logoff and spool files are processed, the volume would be emptied and freed for allocation.

370-mode systems specify a CP-owned list in the module DMKSYS. User volumes need not be explicitly attached to the system in order for their minidisks to be used. Although it seems an unnecessary complication to have to attach volumes containing minidisks to the system, the VM/ESA method is useful in practice, since it makes it much easier to prevent users from LINKing to minidisks on a volume being taken out of service for maintenance.

Real unit record device commands

`START` and `DRAIN` shown in Fig. 9.4 are privilege class D commands used to start and stop CP-controlled real printers, readers, and punches (although the latter two are obsolete). START should not be confused with the CMS START command, which runs a program loaded into CMS storage. This collision of command names is not a problem for most users because only system operators get privilege class D. The START command specifies the output device, the spool classes to be printed or punched on it, and which form has been loaded into the printer. It can also specify an *image library* that contains font definitions.

The DRAIN command reverses the START command. Output is allowed to end after the currently printed file completes. A `FLUSH` command can be used to cancel the file currently being printed.

Virtual Machine I/O

Every virtual machine contains a virtual I/O device configuration. CP maps virtual devices onto real or simulated devices. Virtual machines perform an I/O operation to a virtual device either by executing a native System/370 or 390 I/O instruction, such as Start I/O (SIO) or Start Subchannel (SSCH), or by issuing a DIAGNOSE I/O call.

For native I/O instructions, CP faithfully emulates the 370, 370/XA, or 390 architecture running in the guest machine. VM/ESA and VM/XA map 370-mode guest I/O instructions into XA-style I/O instructions, and map the resulting condition codes back into the equivalent 370 condition codes. DIAGNOSE code simulation is less complex.

To simulate an I/O instruction to a disk, CP must do the following:

1. *Locate virtual device control blocks* corresponding to the device specified in the I/O instruction. If there is no corresponding virtual device, CP reflects back an error indication. For native I/O instructions, it uses the same error indication that would appear on a real CPU if I/O instructions were directed to a nonexistent device.
2. *Copy the user's channel program to CP data areas*. This guarantees that a cleverly written user application cannot tamper with a channel program.
3. *Check the channel programs for validity*. CP validates channel programs to make sure they don't overwrite shared storage or seek past the extent of a minidisk.
4. *Page in user buffers* since I/O channels require real addresses, the user's buffers must be moved to real storage, and locked for the duration of the I/O operation.

```
* Allow spool class P files, to print on printer 00E with payroll
* special forms
cp start 00e class p form payroll
PRT 000E STARTED SYSTEM CLASS P
Ready;

* After printing the checks, drain the printer
cp drain 00e
Ready;
```

Fig. 9.4 START and DRAIN commands.

5. *Translate channel command buffer addresses*. Virtual storage addresses in the channel program are replaced by the corresponding real addresses. Since the real channel program is in CP space, the user is prevented from subverting CP by placing different real storage addresses in the channel command. Otherwise, a user could "break" CP by overwriting it with machine code read from disk, or snoop by writing CP data areas to disk files.
6. *Queue and start the I/O operation*. An IORBK or IOBLOK is prepared, and either HCPIOS or DMKIOS is called to schedule the actual I/O operation.
7. *Reflect a condition code to the virtual machine* corresponding to the condition code received when the I/O was sent to the real device.
8. *Reflect an I/O interrupt* to the virtual machine when the I/O completes and the user is enabled for interrupts, and redispatch the virtual machine. Ending status is placed in architecturally specified virtual machine storage locations.

During the I/O instruction, a virtual machine is said to be in *simulation wait*, since CP is simulating a privileged operation for it. For native 370 and 390 I/O instructions, a virtual machine is allowed to continue execution after the I/O instruction has been issued, and is said to be in *I/O wait* if it subsequently loads a wait state PSW with the I/O interrupt class enabled.

When the real channel or device signals completion of the I/O event, CP reflects the I/O event back to the virtual machine. For native I/O instructions, CP presents the architecturally defined I/O interrupt and channel status information. For DIAGNOSE I/O, CP places result information in the program PSW and general purpose registers.

V=R and V=F guest I/O

As described earlier in this chapter, CP normally translates buffer addresses supplied in guest I/O operations from second level storage addresses into real storage addresses. When the guest runs a virtual storage operating system, it has already done this to convert the third level storage addresses into second level.

CCW translation can be eliminated for V=R and V=F guest I/O operations, allowing reduced CPU overhead, by issuing the command `SET CCWTRANS OFF` after guest IPL. I/O operations to minidisks and devices simulated by CP (spool, console, and virtual CTCAs) always undergo CCW translation.

When VM/ESA or VM/XA run on a CPU with the `SIE assist` feature, microcode provides an *I/O assist* that eliminates CP intervention for V=R and V=F guest I/O operations. I/O instructions to dedicated or attached real devices are handled completely in microcode, without the normal privileged operation intercept and simulation performed for virtual machines. This is a tremendous performance enhancement, and lets guest operating systems run at almost native performance under VM. I/O assist is clever enough to translate System/370 I/O instructions into native XA-mode I/O instructions for 370 mode guests.

The command `SET IOASSIST ON` is used to enable I/O assist. When IOASSIST is in effect, INDICATE USER for V=R and V=F guests commands show a "+" sign after the I/O count, indicating that CP only counted the I/O operations it processed in software:

```
cp ind user mvsguest
USERID=MVSGUEST MACH=ESA STOR=0064M VIRT=R XSTORE=NONE
IPLSYS=DEV 01A0 DEVNUM=00066
PAGES: RES=000000 WS=000000 LOCK=000000 RESVD=000000
NPREF=000000 PREF=000000 READS=000000 WRITES=000000
XSTORE=000000 READS=000000 WRITES=000000 MIGRATES=000000
CPU 00: CTIME=00:38 VTIME=011:46 TTIME=011:55 IO=000871+
        RDR=000000 PRT=000000 PCH=000000
```

DIAGNOSE I/O

VM avoids considerable overhead by providing a streamlined I/O interface for CMS based on the DIAGNOSE instruction discussed in Chapter 16. The synthetic DIAGNOSE interfaces use simplified I/O protocols more easily simulated than the general, and powerful complete 370/390 I/O architecture.

DIAGNOSE I/O operations are synchronous, that is, a virtual machine cannot continue execution until the I/O operation is complete. This eliminates multiple trips through the dispatcher to

1. restart the virtual machine after starting the I/O operation.
2. place the virtual machine in idle-state if it decides to wait until the I/O is complete. This is almost invariably the case because DIAGNOSE I/O is mostly used by single-tasking CMS applications.
3. reflect the I/O interrupt when the I/O operation completes.

Like IPL-able saved systems, DIAGNOSE I/O is an abstraction of a real-machine facility devised for the virtual machine environment. Both produce an augmented machine environment by eliminating some of the messy details of the real CPU environment. In this case, it provides a much shorter CPU instruction path length as well.

DIAGNOSE 18 is the standard method CMS uses for disk I/O in VM/SP and HPO, and is also supported under VM/ESA for virtual machines running in 370 mode. DIAGNOSE 18 provides a synchronous I/O instruction that performs complete path management and error handling. CMS calculates the cylinder, track, and record number of a CMS block, and generated either SEEK, SET SECTOR, and SEARCH or DEFINE EXTENT and LOCATE channel commands to move the access arm to the right position to read or write the disk.

DIAGNOSE 18 uses a standard, simplified channel program format, permitting a shortened path through CP's channel command translation.

DIAGNOSE 20 provides synchronous I/O to tape, DASD, attached printers, and other unit record devices. Like DIAGNOSE 18, DIAGNOSE 20 is the interface provided under VM/SP and HPO, and supported under VM/ESA for compatibility reasons.

VM/XA and VM/ESA CMS use DIAGNOSE A4 for disk I/O. Like DIAGNOSE 18, DIAGNOSE A4 provides CMS a synchronous I/O instruction with complete path and error handling. DIAGNOSE A4 is specifically designed for CMS disk I/O, and provides access to CMS disk information by CMS block number. This lets CMS view a minidisk as an array of uniformly sized disk blocks, and relegates details of disk device geometry to CP. Instead of copying, validating, and translating a channel program, CP uses the block numbers supplied by CMS to calculate seek addresses for preformatted channel programs. This reduces the complexity of I/O processing in both CMS and CP. CMS is relieved of device dependency issues, and CP is relieved of the burden of channel command translation and verification. The result is shortened code paths and higher efficiency in both VM components.

DIAGNOSE A8 is the ESA replacement for DIAGNOSE 20, and can be used for all devices, except for consoles, 3270 devices, and channel-to-channel adapters.

Minidisk I/O

Minidisk I/O is like other simulated I/O, except that CP validates disk seek addresses. Minidisk cylinder addresses range from 0 to *N*-1, where *N* is the minidisk size. CP ensures that all seek addresses are in the proper cylinder range, and then adds the minidisk's starting cylinder address to create the real channel program seek address.

CMS minidisk I/O is usually performed using either DIAGNOSE 18 or DIAGNOSE A4, although some high-performance sort/merge and file copy products continue to use their own channel programs. Guest operating systems use native I/O instructions. Except for (sometimes) smaller disk sizes, guest systems are usually unaware that their disks are minidisks instead of complete volumes.

Minidisk Cache (MDC)

When VM/ESA or VM/XA runs on a processor with expanded storage, it can use the *Minidisk Cache* (MDC) facility to dramatically speed disk reads for CMS applications. MDC, introduced with VM/XA, has a remarkable effect on I/O performance.

Most CMS file accesses are reads instead of writes. CMS often reads MODULE, EXEC, XEDIT, TEXT, TXTLIB, and LOADLIB files. Certain files are "popular" and frequently read by CMS users. Consequently, CMS files exhibit locality of reference just as virtual storage access does. The same disk contents may be read by multiple users concurrently or within a short period of time. This makes global buffering of disk reads in memory extremely effective for eliminating disk accesses. VM uses expanded storage both for paging and for caching minidisk contents.

MDC can eliminate most I/O to S- and Y-disks and other public minidisks, and is used by SFS and SQL/DS. I have seen MDC speed access to SQL/DS databases from 150 to over 1,000 reads per second, and CMS I/O intensive applications to rates exceeding 3,500 reads per second. CMS applications benefit from MDC without effort from application or system programmers, except that minidisks must be formatted with 4K blocks. MDC only caches 4KB blocked minidisks because expanded storage is allocated in 4KB pages.

By default, MDC is enabled for all 4K formatted CMS disks, unless the DASD volume the disk resides on is shared by multiple VM systems. Minidisks written by multiple systems must be excluded from caching to prevent data integrity errors. Otherwise, one system could satisfy disk reads from cache contents after another system has updated the disk's contents. Applications would read the in-cache parts of files, instead of changed blocks on disk. A volume can be specified as a shared device in HCPRIO, or via the `SET SHARED ON <disk real address>` command. A minidisk can also be exempted from MDC processing by following its minidisk entry in the CP directory with a `MINIOPT NOMDC` statement.

MDC also should be turned off for minidisks with a high ratio of writes to reads, such as accounting, performance data, spooled console collection disks, and SFS and SQL/DS logs. These disks inherently cannot benefit from minidisk caching, and their few reads only dislodge more useful blocks.

Reads to CMS and SFS files or SQL/DS databases are satisfied from cache if the associated block is in expanded storage. Otherwise a read to DASD is started. When the read completes, data is placed in cache to buffer future reads. If several users read the same disk block while it is in transit from disk, CP remembers that they are all waiting for the same data, and satisfies all their reads when the disk block arrives in storage.

An arbiter decides how much expanded storage to use for paging and how much to use for cache. The arbiter shifts expanded storage to MDC if system I/O wait is higher than page wait, and assigns expanded storage pages to minidisk blocks on an LRU basis.

Each user is assigned a fair share of how many blocks he or she can insert into cache per minute. This prevents a user from monopolizing the cache by accessing a large set of data once. If the cache isn't full, pages beyond the fair share are added to cache anyway, but become replaced if other users cause cache insertions. This lets a user's cache allotment grow quickly when expanded storage is available, yet not slow other users when expanded storage is full. The directory option NOMDCFS can be used for SFS servers and SQL/DS databases, to specify users that deserve more than their fair share of expanded storage.

MDC is almost completely self-tuning, and requires very little attention to operate efficiently. Information on MDC performance and utilization is provided by VM/XA's INDICATE LOAD command and the Real Time Monitor (SMART).

The arbiter gives precedence to paging over minidisk cache when allocating expanded storage. If insufficient expanded storage is available, paging will push MDC out of the cache, and most CMS reads will go to disk. If a sudden surge in paging occurs, the arbiter may not respond quickly enough to allocate expanded storage to paging, causing disk paging instead.

The CP RETAIN XSTORE command controls expanded storage allocation by setting upper and lower bounds on the amount of expanded storage used for MDC. Even a small amount of expanded storage can have a very helpful effect for frequently used files. The following commands set a lower bound of 10MB of expanded storage and an upper bound of 96MB, and then show how much of expanded storage is used for MDC paging, or attached to a user (in this case, no userid owns dedicated expanded storage):

```
#cp retain xstore mdcache 10m 96m
XSTORE MDC retained min=10M, max=96M


#cp query xstore
XSTORE= 256M online= 256M
XSTORE= 256M userid= SYSTEM usage= 82% retained= 256M pending= 0M
XSTORE MDC min=10M, max=96M, usage=37%
XSTORE= 0M userid=  (none)  max. attach= 0M
```

Dedicated and attached devices

Dedicated and attached devices are treated identically by CP, except that dedicated devices are assigned to the owning userid via the DEDICATE directory statement, and attached devices are assigned by the privilege class B ATTACH command. Dedicated devices are essentially given to a virtual machine by an implicitly issued ATTACH command.

In most cases, virtual machine I/O to attached devices is similar to I/O for other devices. CP performs the channel command translation, I/O scheduling and error handling it performs for other devices, with the exception of microcode-assisted I/O for V=R and V=F guest operating systems, as described in “V=R and V=F Guest I/O” on page 190. CP uses a shorter instruction path length for attached disks than minidisks, since it doesn't have to translate disk seek addresses or check for invalid seek addresses beyond a minidisk extent.

Dedicated devices also allow VM to support devices that VM does not yet utilize. For example, VM/XA SP2.1 does not provide support for 3390 disks using its DASD Fast Write feature (VM/ESA does, however), yet can make these disks available to MVS guests. A VM system programmer can define a real device as an "unsupported device," and then attach it to a virtual machine. CP will then pass guest-issued channel commands to the real device without interference.

Spool devices

Some devices are emulated by CP without corresponding commitment of a real device. Most popular among these are spooled devices and consoles.

As mentioned in the section "Virtual Unit Record Devices" on page 22, most users have virtual reader, printer, and punch devices. The punch and reader are normally used to send and receive files to and from other CMS users, as well as mail files, or files transmitted from other computers. Print files can also be transmitted to the reader of another user, or can be directed to a real system printer.

Spooled printer and punch files created on these devices are written to CP spool disk areas. The CP `SPOOL` command specifies the destination for an output file, as well as numerous other file attributes. A `TAG` command specifies tag information, simple character text associated with the file, interpreted by the application that receives the file.

The SPOOL command also optionally specifies a spool file class for files created on a virtual device. The class is a single letter or numeric digit, with no meaning to VM itself, but used by applications to categorize files. *Font*, *form*, and *file control block* information can be specified to request special forms handling (like preprinted forms, or character sets). The SPOOL command also may specify a `copy count` indicating the number of copies of the file to print, or to be read by a virtual machine.

When a file is closed by the CP CLOSE command or the user logging off, the file appears on the input queue of the virtual machine to which it was directed by the CP SPOOL command. If the file was not directed to another userid, it goes to VM's system print or punch queues, and awaits output on a system printer or card punch. The latter is obsolete; not too many real card reader/punch devices remain in existence.

The virtual machine interface to virtual spool devices is extremely simple. CP accepts the channel commands used with actual readers, printers and punches. These are normally simple read and write command sequences, one command per line or card-image. Input files can also be processed by DIAGNOSE 14, which provides a direct interface to spool file contents. DIAGNOSE F8 lets applications determine the origin of a spool file by retrieving identification information associated with spool files by trusted virtual machines. These diagnose instructions are described in Chapter 16.

CP opens a new spool file when a virtual machine creates it by writing its first record. In 370-mode VM systems, a VM Spool File Block (`SFBLOK`) identifies the file and contains its origin and destination, the date and time of creation, spool class, and other information. Individual page-sized sections of the file are identified by Spool Page Buffer Link Blocks (`SPLINK`), maintained as a bidirectional linked list originating in the SFBLOK.

Spool files are processed by traversing the SPLINK chain originating at the SFBLOK. If the copy count was greater than one, it is decremented and the file is prepared for rereading. When the copy count reaches zero, the SPLINK chain is followed to return the file's disk blocks to available spool space. For a large file, this can take an extremely long time, since CP has to traverse the file's disk-resident linked list.

VM/ESA uses similar control blocks. A Spool File Control Block (`SPFBK`) identifies a spool file, and Spool File Map Page Blocks (`SPMBK`) and Spool File Data Page Blocks (`SPDBK`) respectively contain bit maps describing the disk locations of the file, and the actual file contents. A file is processed by chaining through each of the SPMBKs of a file. The allocation bit maps let VM/XA and ESA purge spool files and return their disk locations to available space much faster than 370 mode VM.

Console I/O

Virtual consoles operate in either 3215 or 3270 mode; the 3215 is a line-mode teletypewriter device supporting simple single-line read and write commands. The console can be in 3215 mode even when the real device is a 3270 display terminal. This makes line-mode terminal input and output easy to program, because CP handles 3270 attributes and screen formatting.

A console can also be placed in 3270 mode, which lets virtual machines use 3270-format channel programs. This provides direct compatibility for guest operating systems that use their own 3270 console support. Console mode is specified by the directory CONSOLE statement and the `TERM CONMODE 3215` or `TERM CONMODE 3270` commands.

CMS always uses CONMODE 3215. When in non-fullscreen command mode, CMS uses the simple 3215 command set for line-mode I/O, and lets CP control the 3270 screen appearance. CMS uses DIAGNOSE 58 to perform fullscreen I/O. DIAGNOSE 58 is normally used for a user's logon terminal, but can also be used for a 3270 terminal DIALed or ATTACHed to a virtual machine.

DIAGNOSE 58 lets CMS applications partially or fully control the display's appearance. When DIAGNOSE 58 operates in line-mode, the screen is divided into CP's standard output, input, and status areas. In line-mode, DIAGNOSE 58 applications can write up to a full screen of data in a single I/O call, with data starting at a specific line of the display. DIAGNOSE 58 also operates in fullscreen mode, and lets applications completely exploit 3270 features and control the format of screen input and output.

Channel-to-Channel Adapter (CTCA) and 3088

The channel-to-channel adapter (CTCA) and its replacement device, the 3088 multisystem adapter (most people refer to them interchangeably as *CTCA*) let different computer systems communicate with one another at channel speeds. A CTCA provides point-to-point communications between programs running on two CPUs, and can be thought of as a bidirectional data pipe. A WRITE command from one CPU generates an I/O interrupt on the other CPU, which can issue a READ command to obtain the information sent from the other system. CTCAs transmit data at full channel speed, so they are very suitable for high-volume data transmission.

CTCAs are used for inter-CPU communication between operating systems or key system services. VM uses CTCA for RSCS, TSAF, VM Pass-Through, and VTAM links to adjacent computer systems. They also connect "loosely coupled" MVS systems working in cooperation. MVS uses 3088s to implement GRS and JES3 subsystems. CTCA and 3088 devices can be assigned to virtual machines by the ATTACH command, or by the directory DEDICATE statement.

Additionally, CP completely simulates CTCA and 3088 in software, so "virtual CTCA" and "virtual 3088" devices can be used for inter-virtual machine communication. Each virtual machine issues the CP DEFINE command to create a virtual CTCA or 3088, and then one of a pair of virtual machines issues CP COUPLE to logically connect it to its partner.

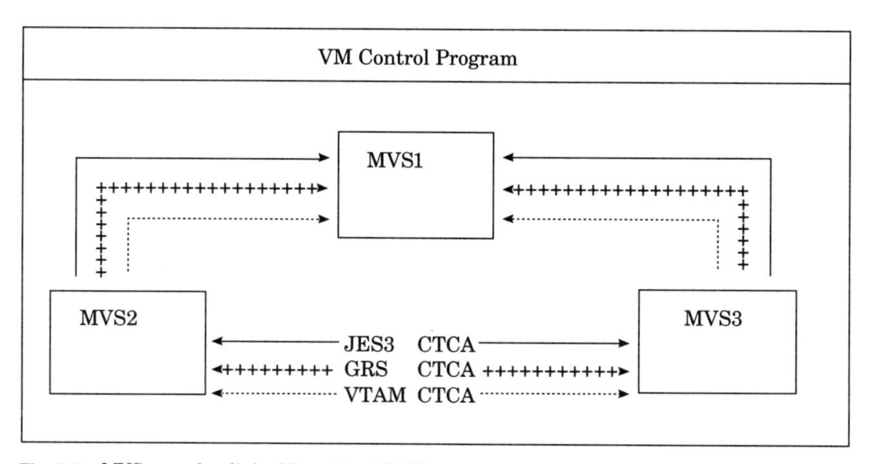

Fig. 9.5 MVS complex linked by virtual 3088s.

For example, virtual 3088 connections can be used in VM to test an MVS multisystem complex: 3088 connections would be defined between each MVS guest system for JES3, GRS, and SYSPLEX connections, as shown in Fig. 9.5.

Virtual CTCAs and 3088s also provide network connectivity for guest systems: an arbitrary number of guests can be connected via virtual 3088s to a VTAM service machine with a physical attachment to a front-end communications controller. This provides each guest full network access, as if each had direct connections to the front-ends. This can be used to let guest system users logon to the guest, to transmit files or access them via the Shared File System, or to run SNA LU6.2 applications.

Chapter 10

Using CMS

The preceding chapters have concentrated on fundamental aspects of how VM works. This and the following chapters focus on how VM is applied, starting with its most important capability, the CMS interactive environment.

CMS is one of the most flexible and natural interactive computing environments available. CMS provides both ease of use for novices, and functional power for expert users. The CMS editor, command language, and REXX procedures language make it easy for end-users and programmers to be productive with neither formal training nor the assistance of "gurus."

The heart of CMS is its emphasis on personal computing. Each user has a private machine with its own set of devices, files, and storage. The machine can be configured for personal preferences, and can be kept as isolated as a standalone desktop personal computer, or linked to other services via LAN-like connections.

Command Orientation

Some computing environments use menus or a graphical user interface (GUI). In these systems, users tell the computer what to do by using aids sometimes described as WIMPs (Windows, Icons, Mice, and Pointers).

Instead, CMS users tell CMS what to do by issuing commands. There are exceptions: ISPF, available under both CMS and TSO, is a menu-based system that uses PF keys and menu choices for system interaction, and largely makes command entry unnecessary. Users select from options on menus, and "fill in the blanks" for file identifiers and program options.

```
PROFILE EXEC    A1
GAUSS   FORTRAN A1
SYSTEM  NETID   S2
```

Fig. 10.1 Typical CMS file identifiers.

Additionally, the CMS FILELIST and RDRLIST commands provide a point-and-shoot style of file handling, described below. Many users spend their entire VM sessions inside fullscreen applications or productivity aids like FILELIST. Nonetheless, the primary way to interact with CMS is to enter commands.

CMS File System

Typical interactive computer users spend most of their time manipulating or referring to files. Although Chapter 12, "The CMS File System," provides a detailed look at the CMS file system, it is discussed here to provide background for CMS command processing, general usage, and programming.

VM users own *minidisks* and *directories*, each containing a collection of files. CMS provides a wide variety of commands for creating, erasing, copying, editing, transmitting, and otherwise manipulating files, as will be discussed later.

A minidisk is a private allocation of disk space assigned to a user, much like the hard disk on a personal computer, although its contents can be shared with other users. A minidisk is assigned a numeric *device number*. File directories are provided by a CMS facility called the *Shared File System* (SFS). A directory is like a personal computer file system residing on a local area network file server. The user can access and create files on it, but it is not physically attached to the user as a device; a file server manages access to the actual disk resources. Files residing in directories are more flexibly shared than files in minidisks.

File naming conventions

Files are identified by an eight-character *filename* and a *filetype*. A *filemode* letter specifies which minidisk or SFS directory a file is on. If you are familiar with MS-DOS, it is similar to referring to a disk drive by its drive letter (such as `C:`). Files are not visible to a CMS session until the `ACCESS` command, discussed below, reads a minidisk or SFS directory's file descriptors into virtual storage.

Filename and filetype, and the filemode number, are permanent attributes of a file (unless erased or renamed), while the filemode letter only becomes associated with a file when the minidisk or directory it resides in is

ACCESSed. The full name of a file when it is named in a command or program is the filename, filetype, and filemode, separated by blanks. Typical CMS file identifiers are illustrated in Fig. 10.1.

ACCESSing disks and directories

Users can have many minidisks and directories, but only ACCESS the subset of them they want to work with at one time. ACCESS assigns a filemode to a minidisk or directory and makes its contents visible to the CMS session. The `RELEASE` command reverses the effect of ACCESS. CMS users ACCESS and RELEASE different disks and directories while working with different sets of files.

For example, when the command `ACCESS 193 B` is issued, all the files on the 193 disk are now visible to CMS and can be referred to, as shown in Fig. 10.2.

By convention, certain minidisks and directories are automatically accessed when CMS IPLs. By convention, filemode “A” is a user’s personal disk space and work area, filemode “S” contains CMS and is shared by all users, and a “Y-disk” contains compilers and other commonly used programs and files. Individual sites may have other standard disks. When a user logs on, CMS automatically accesses the disk at virtual device number 190 as the S-disk, 191 as the A-disk, and 19E (these are hexadecimal numbers) as the Y-disk. A user can also be set up without a 191 disk, and instead use an SFS directory as the standard disk area.

The default device addresses and the associated filemodes are illustrated in Fig. 10.3. Many VM installations have local procedures that add more disks when a user logs on.

Some minidisks or directories belong to the user, others belong to other users or the system administrator and can only be read from or written to with their permission. The `LINK` command, described in “Linking to Other User’s

```
* access the files on the 193 disk at filemode C
access 193 b
Ready;
* list the 'EXEC' files on the disk
listfile * exec b
COMPILE   EXEC B1
RUNDEMO   EXEC B1
Ready;

* Access the files in the '.TOOLS' directory at filemode C
access .tools c
Ready;
```

Fig. 10.2 Accessing a minidisk and a directory.

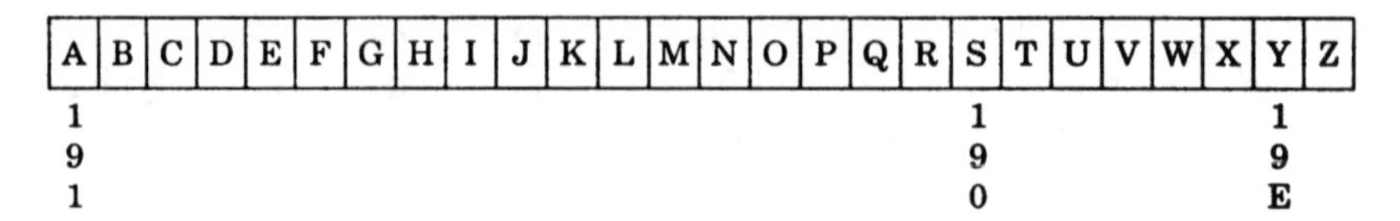

Fig. 10.3 Filemodes accessed during CMS IPL.

Disks" on page 20 is used to gain read or read/write access to another user's minidisk. Only the ACCESS command is used for SFS directories.

Filemode search order

A filemode can be thought of as a slot in a table of 26 entries. The filemode letter determines the position of the disk or directory in the CMS search order. CMS searches each accessed filemode in alphabetical order for command resolution, and for file access by many commands.

For example, if the command "compile" is issued, CMS will search each accessed disk or directory in alphabetical order for COMPILE EXEC, and if not found, for COMPILE MODULE. This makes it easy to "front-end" public commands and files with customized versions by placing private versions of a file on a disk accessed earlier in the search order.

Special filetypes

Filenames and filetypes may be selected by the user, but some filetypes have special meanings to CMS or CMS applications. For example, CMS recognizes files with filetype `MODULE` as executable programs, and files with filetype `EXEC` as command scripts.

Many CMS commands assume that files they work with have certain filetypes. For example, the IBM C/370 compiler assumes that input source files have filetype C, and produces output files with filetype TEXT and LISTING, as shown in Fig. 10.4. Library filetypes (MACLIB, TXTLIB, LOADLIB, and CSLLIB) store related programs as *members* of library files containing hundreds or thousands of programs, instead of retaining them as individual files. The `GLOBAL` command tells CMS which libraries to search for compiler source input (MACLIB, or *macro library*), or for binary program input (the other library types).

Additionally, CMS commands associate default file characteristics with certain filetypes. For example, the system editor XEDIT assumes that documentation files filetype MEMO or SCRIPT are edited in mixed-case, and that COBOL programs contain uppercase fixed length 80 character records, and so on. Another example is the PRINT command, which assumes that files with filetype `LISTING` contain carriage control (print format) information in the first column of each line. A list of command filetypes and their standard uses is shown in Fig. 10.5.

Command Processing

CMS executes one command at a time, either entered from the terminal or issued internally from another command. VM commands are identified by the first word in the command line. Command names are case insensitive, and may be entered in either upper or lowercase. CMS always translates the command name to uppercase before looking for its program file. CMS searches each accessed disk in alphabetical filemode order for an executable file with the same name as the command. Commands may be EXEC files, which are command files usually written in the REXX language, or object code procedures in program files called MODULEs.

When a command completes, CMS types a *ready message*, and waits for the next command. The ready message also displays non-zero return codes of commands that indicate an error condition. The ready message has long and short formats. The short format simply types `Ready;` while the long for-

```
* list the C program
listfile hello
HELLO    C          A1
Ready;

* run the C/370 compiler with options to create LISTING file
cc hello (list source
Ready;

* list the C program and compiler output
listfile hello
HELLO    C          A1
HELLO    LISTING    A1
HELLO    TEXT       A1
Ready;

* create an executable version of HELLO
cmod hello
Ready;

* list the C program, compiler output, and executable program
listfile hello
HELLO    C          A1
HELLO    LISTING    A1
HELLO    MODULE     A1
HELLO    TEXT       A1
Ready;

* Run the program
hello
Hello, world!
Ready;
```

Fig. 10.4 C/370 use of filetypes.

Filetype	Usage
	(Executable program files)
EXEC	CMS command procedures in REXX, EXEC2, or EXEC languages
XEDIT	XEDIT command procedures in REXX or EXEC2
REXX	REXX language filters for CMS Pipelines
MODULE	Executable program images from compiled languages
	(Compiler input and output)
LISTING	Report files from compilers and utility programs
TEXT	Object code produced by compilers
MACLIB	Macro libraries searched by assemblers and compilers
APLWSV2	APL2 workspace
ASSEMBLE	Assembler language program source
BASIC	BASIC language programs
C	C language programs
H	Header file input to C compilers
COBOL	COBOL programs for the VS COBOL and COBOL II compilers
FORTRAN	FORTRAN programs
PASCAL	Pascal programs
PLI	PL/I programs
PLIOPT	Alternate file type for PL/I programs
	(Program library files)
TXTLIB	Object code libraries searched by LOAD command, in addition to TEXT files
LOADLIB	Relocatable code libraries produced by LKED command
CSLLIB	Callable Subroutine Libraries
	(Note and documentation files)
NOTEBOOK	Log of mail sent to and received from other users
MEMO	Memo files
SCRIPT	Input to the Document Composition Facility processor

Fig. 10.5 Common CMS filetypes.

mat types the amount of virtual CPU time (CPU time spent by CMS) and total CPU time (virtual CPU plus CP CPU time) consumed by the command, and the current time of day. The commands `SET RDYMSG SMSG` and `SET RDYMSG LMSG` specify the format, as shown in Fig. 10.6.

Types of command

If both an EXEC file and a MODULE have the same name, CMS selects the EXEC file. This makes it easy to front-end MODULES with EXECs that perform set-up operations. For example, a MORTGAGE EXEC might issue `FILEDEF` (file definition) commands before invoking a MORTGAGE MODULE created from a FORTRAN program. If a user types `mortgage` CMS will look for a MORTGAGE EXEC before looking for a MORTGAGE MODULE.

The user can also type `exec mortgage` at the command line, to explicitly tell CMS to only look for MORTGAGE EXEC.

The command `SET IMPEX OFF` ("set implied EXEC off") tells CMS to not run EXECs unless the "exec" command is specified. This is useful when you want to bypass EXEC processing for a given run of a program. The different combinations of EXEC and MODULE processing are illustrated in Fig. 10.7.

Many CMS commands are built into the CMS nucleus, and reside in neither an EXEC nor a MODULE file. The nucleus routine DMSFNC contains a command lookup table that the command interpreter, DMSINT, scans before looking for a MODULE file. When one of these commands is found CMS simply branches to the appropriate routine in the CMS nucleus. These commands are said to be *nucleus resident*. IBM selects nucleus routines based on function and frequency of use. For example, the `LOADMOD` command is both a CMS command and the internal function used to load MODULEs into storage for execution. Clearly it cannot reside in a MODULE file itself.

The CMS nucleus also contains commonly used commands like ACCESS, FILEDEF, RELEASE, LISTFILE, and most SET and QUERY subcommands. Each of these commands once was a small *transient area* module, but IBM recoded them to be reentrant and moved them to the CMS nucleus. This improved performance by eliminating I/O operations needed to load these programs from disk.

CMS also lets programmers create *nucleus extensions* that are treated like nucleus entry points. The `NUCXLOAD` command loads a MODULE or a member of a LOADLIB into storage; it remains there until explicitly purged or cancelled by an error. A nucleus extension can be repeatedly invoked without having to reread it from disk. CMS searches the list of currently loaded nucleus extensions before scanning the list of nucleus resident functions or searching for a MODULE. This lets nucleus extensions "front-end" internal nucleus commands and MODULE files on disk, and call them after performing other processing (such as logging its use or adding the command line arguments).

If a command is neither a CMS nucleus resident command nor an EXEC or MODULE file, CMS passes the command to CP for execution. This way,

```
set rdymsg smsg
Ready;

erase banana memo
DMSERS002E File BANANA MEMO not found
Ready(00028);

set rdymsg lmsg
Ready; T=0.01/0.01 15:47:31
```

Fig. 10.6 CMS Ready Message.

```
* list the files named 'mortgage' on my A-disk
listfile mortgage
MORTGAGE EXEC      A1
MORTGAGE MODULE A1
Ready;

* Run the program front-ended by the EXEC
* The MORTGAGE EXEC types 'hello' and 'goodbye' messages;
* Other messages are from MORTGAGE MODULE
mortgage
Hello — about to run mortgage program
Your mortgage has 25 years more to go.
Goodbye — mortgage program finished
Ready;

* turn off implied exec
set impex off
Ready;

* Run the mortgage program alone
mortgage
Your mortgage has 25 years more to go.
Ready;
```

Fig. 10.7 Implied EXEC command search.

users don't have to remember which commands are CP and which are CMS. If the command name is mistyped, CMS will type the message `Unknown CP/CMS command` to emphasize that neither it nor CP recognized the command name.

As with EXECs, the user can preface a command name with the word `CP`, to tell CMS to send the command directly to CP without looking for a like-named EXEC or MODULE. This is very slightly more efficient, since the double file search is omitted. The performance difference is normally too insignificant to make it worthwhile for commands entered from the terminal, although it is advisable for commands executed within a loop inside an EXEC.

CMS can be asked to not pass commands to CP unless the prefix `CP` is used, by executing the command `SET IMPCP OFF` ("set implied CP off"). Implied and explicit CP command execution is illustrated in Fig. 10.8. Since there is no MSG command in CMS, the CP MSG command is not recognized when IMPCP is turned off.

EXEC commands can be used to front-end CP commands, just as they can front-end MODULES, as illustrated in Fig. 10.9. In this example, a LOGOFF EXEC has been coded to ask the user if he or she is really ready to LOGOFF.

The contents of LOGOFF EXEC are in Fig. 10.10. Normally, it is not a good idea to make EXEC or MODULE files with the same names as built-in commands, especially if you share your programs with other users. This example is innocuous, however, and illustrates command search order.

Even though CMS routes commands to CP, it is sometimes convenient to know which commands are part of CMS, and which are part of CP. This can usually be deduced by the command's function. Most CP commands are concerned with the virtual machine aspects of a session, such as virtual machine storage size and devices attached to the virtual machine. Since CMS provides all file and program management functions for the session, all commands that manipulate files or run programs are CMS commands. Consequently, `DEFINE` and `DETACH`, which add or remove devices in a virtual machine, and `LOGOFF`, which ends a virtual machine session, are CP commands. `RENAME`, `ERASE`, and `COPYFILE`, which do to files exactly what their names suggest, are CMS commands.

Abbreviations

VM uses a "minimum truncation" scheme to recognize command names. For example, the command `COPYFILE` can be abbreviated as COPY. Manuals and HELP screens usually list commands with the minimum truncation shown in uppercase letters, and the optional characters shown in mixed case. COPYFILE would be documented as `COPYfile`.

For example, the `PRint` command, which, reasonably enough, prints a file, can be abbreviated to two characters, and is invoked by any of the following command lines:

```
print
prin
pri
pr
```

Experienced VM users tend to type the shorter forms of each command to save typing, allowing a high degree of conciseness. Less experienced users are more likely to use the longer command forms, since their

```
* Send a message to a friend
msg pete lunchtime yet?
Ready;

* Turn off 'implied CP' command search
set impcp off
Ready;

msg pete lunchtime yet?
Unknown CP/CMS command
```

Fig. 10.8 Implied CP command search.

```
* Issue logoff, and let the front-end EXEC catch it
logoff
Are you SURE you want to logoff now? Enter "yes" or "no"!
no
Okay, no logoff yet.
Ready;

* bypass the EXEC by specifying CP
cp logoff
CONNECT= 00:40:32 VIRTCPU= 000:01.17 TOTCPU= 000:01.23
LOGOFF AT 12:13:21 EST WEDNESDAY 01/08/92
```

Fig. 10.9 EXEC front-end to a CP command.

mnemonic names make them easier to remember. Commands in EXEC files should be fully spelled out for readability. As with implied EXEC and CP command processing, there is a slight overhead for processing synonyms. When a command synonym is typed, CMS searches accessed disks for an EXEC and then for a MODULE with the synonym name. CMS then expands the command to its full name and searches again. The overhead is too insignificant to consider for commands entered at the terminal.

CMS does not provide short forms for commands that can potentially destroy data, such as `ERASE` (erase disk files) or `FORMAT` (initialize a disk by formatting its contents). Commands that can cause data loss should not be too easily invoked; two letter sequences like `rm` should be avoided.

Common commands

Figures 10.11 and 10.12 show some of the most commonly used CP and CMS commands, with upper and lowercase used to show their minimum truncations. Both LOGON and LISTFILE have the same minimum truncation, but there is no possibility of conflict. LOGON can only be executed before the user has logged on, and LISTFILE can only be executed when a user is logged on and running CMS. Figure 10.13 shows commands frequently used by programmers.

Both CP and CMS have QUERY and SET commands. This is not a problem, since CMS passes to CP any operands it does not recognize. If you type `query time`, a CP command, CMS recognizes that it is not a CMS query option, and ask CP to handle it.

Immediate commands

When you type in a command while another command is running, CMS searches for it in a table of *immediate commands*. If the command is not found in the table, it is stacked for execution after the current command completes. Otherwise, the currently running command is interrupted and the immediate command is executed. Immediate commands are usually used to control the execution of the command, or to terminate it. Immediate commands are two-character sequences, for easy typing. The most important immediate commands are `HX` (which stands for "halt execution"), `HT` ("halt typing") and `RT` ("resume typing").

HX cancels the currently running command and returns the user to the command line. HT and RT are used when a program generates a lot of terminal output, and you don't want to see all of it. HT tells CMS to discard terminal output lines. The program continues to run and send messages to the console, but CMS ignores them. RT tells CMS to start displaying the messages again. It is common to start a command, decide you don't want to see its output, and issue HT. For long running commands, such as copying several hundred files from one disk to another, RT and HT can be issued periodically to check on the command's progress. Other immediate commands are listed in Fig. 10.14.

CMS provides the `IMMCMD` command and assembler macro to let applications create immediate commands, by defining an immediate command name and a program that corresponds to it. Like CMS's built-in immediate commands, user-created immediate commands are branched to even when another program is executing. This facility can be used to write commands that can be interrupted while they are running, in order to change their execution or report on progress.

CMS Customization

Before running the first user command, CMS executes an EXEC named the `SYSPROF EXEC`. This is a "system profile," which issues commands common to all users. SYSPROF EXEC is set up by IBM and installation system programmers to execute commands common to all users, for example, accessing disks that contains public libraries.

After the system profile completes, CMS runs a personal `PROFILE EXEC` that the user may have provided. This lets the user customize his or her session with option settings, screen colors, synonyms, program function key

```
/* LOGOFF EXEC: LOGOFF after confirmation */
address command              /* Do *not* use implied CP or EXEC routing */
say 'Are you SURE you want to logoff now? Enter "yes" or "no"!'
parse upper pull yesno .     /* read in upper case, take first word */
if yesno = 'YES'             /* Insist on exact match for safety */
then 'CP LOGOFF'
else say 'Okay, no logoff yet.'  /* reassurance message */
```

Fig. 10.10 LOGOFF EXEC.

Command	Usage
	(Control virtual machine session and devices)
`Logon`	log onto VM
`LOGoff`	log off VM
`DISConn`	disconnect a session from the terminal
`Ipl`	'Initial Program Load' a fresh copy of CMS into the virtual machine
`LINK`	link to another user's disk
`DETach`	detach a virtual device
`DEFine`	define virtual devices or storage size
	(share information with other users)
`SPool`	direct print or punch output to a destination or select types of reader files to process
`TAG`	associate attributes with print or punch files
`Msg`	send a message to another user's screen.
	(Obtain system information and control option settings)
`Query`	query CP session attributes: which options are in effect, the current time of day, and so on
`SET`	specify CP session options
`INDicate`	show system load or user resource consumption

Fig. 10.11 Common CP commands.

assignments, and other preferences. An example of a PROFILE EXEC is shown in Fig. 10.15. After the PROFILE EXEC completes, CMS is ready to process commands entered from the terminal.

Both the system profile and the user profile usually complete quickly. An entire CMS session may be performed from within the PROFILE EXEC if the PROFILE places a user in an application program and then logs off when it finishes.

CMS lets users make their own synonyms and abbreviations for commands. For example, a user wishing to type *delete* or *rm* instead of *erase* can create a synonym file and use the CMS `SYNONYM` command to tell CMS to use ERASE whenever *delete* is typed. Synonym files contain the original command name, the synonym or abbreviation, and the minimum accepted length. Fig. 10.16 illustrates how I could set up the TSO and UNIX commands for erasing a file as synonyms for the CMS ERASE command, in the unlikely event that I wanted to do so. The `SET SYNONYM OFF` command disables synonym processing.

CMS sessions can also be customized by using the `DEFAULTS` command. The DEFAULTS command displays and sets options for a number of common CMS commands. Options are set in a global variable file (LASTING GLOBALV) that is saved between CMS sessions. Figure 10.17 shows the DEFAULTS command being used to list the current options, and then change the number of lines displayed by the PEEK command.

Many CMS commands, controlled by the DEFAULTS command, such as

PEEK, NOTE, and FILELIST run application profile EXECs or XEDIT macros. Users can specify their own profiles via the DEFAULTS command, and use them to set different program function key assignments, set screen colors, and otherwise customize their behavior. To a large extent this is possible because these programs are actually EXEC commands that use XEDIT, discussed below, as a screen display manager.

The System Product Editor, XEDIT

XEDIT, the standard text editor provided with VM, is widely regarded as a powerful and easily used text editor, certainly in the context of mainframe ed-

Command	Usage
	(get help on commands and methods)
Help	Obtain help on VM commands, messages, tasks.
	(control minidisks and file directories)
ACcess	access a minidisk or directory to make its files visible
RELease	release a minidisk or directory
FORMAT	format a disk for storing CMS files
	(manipulate files)
Xedit	edit a file with the VM system editor
BROWSE	browse a file (provided with the CMS Utilities Feature)
ERASE	erase a file or directory
Rename	rename a file
COPYfile	copy a file to a different location or name
COMpare	compare two files
PRint	Print a file
Listfile	list files based on their filenames and types
FILEList	fullscreen, scrollable version of LISTFILE. Files can be selected for processing by cursor actions
FLIST	alternate full-screen file list program in CMS Utilities
TAPE	position tape volumes, copy files between tape and disk
	(share information with other users)
NOTE	Send a note to a user or list of users. Uses your personal nickname file for userids
TELL	Send a message to another user or list of users' screen. Also uses the nickname file
PEEK	Browse a file, such as a mail file, in the reader queue
RECEIVE	Load (receive) a file from reader to disk
SENDFile	Send a file to a user or group of users
RDRlist	View the list of files in the reader queue
	(Control option settings)
Query	query CMS session options
SET	specify CMS options
SYNonym	specify command synonyms and abbreviations

Fig. 10.12 Common CMS commands.

Command	Usage
	(Use language processors)
APL2	run the APL2 interpreter
CC	run the C/370 compiler
COBOL2	run the COBOL2 compiler
COBOL	run the VS COBOL compiler
HASM	run Assembler H for assembly language programs
FORTVS2	run the VS FORTRAN compiler
PLIOPT	run the VS Pascal compiler
	(Create and run programs)
GLobal	specify program libraries
LOad	load object code from compilers into memory
START	start execution of a loaded program
Genmod	save a program image into a MODULE fine

Fig. 10.13 Common CMS commands for programmers.

itors. XEDIT is too rich a subject to fully describe in a short section, although I will try to convey some of its flavor. For further information, I recommend you consult the *XEDIT User's Guide*, James C. McMaster, McGraw Hill, 1993.

Text editors often create strong personal preferences and loyalties in their users, and sometimes feelings of intense dislike. Editors are important because users spend much of their time editing or viewing data in files. A good editor makes these tasks easy and pleasant. XEDIT is a very good editor, since it makes a wide variety of editing tasks easy to do with few keystrokes, and with a syntax that is easily understood and learned by novices. The ability to extend XEDIT with macros written in REXX further extends its power. XEDIT is also used as a fullscreen display manager, as previously mentioned, and is used to create common CMS commands like FILELIST, RDRLIST, NOTE, PEEK, MACLIST, and CSLLIST.

I have used XEDIT, EDGAR, the old CMS EDIT command, ISPF, TSO EDIT, TECO, UNIX's ed and vi, SunOS text edit, and a variety of word processors on personal computers, but find XEDIT to be the most natural, generally suitable, and powerful text editor for general-purpose editing. This book is written using both XEDIT, and KEDIT, an XEDIT-compatible editor for MS-DOS and OS/2 produced by the Mansfield Software Group.

XEDIT can be used both with line-mode and fullscreen 3270 terminal sessions, although it is designed for 3270 terminals. This book assumes you are accessing it from a 3270 terminal. XEDIT allows direct input and replacement of text by overtyping data displayed on the screen. XEDIT is also a line-oriented editor, since many XEDIT subcommands refer to a *current* or *focus* line or operate on a range of lines.

XEDIT efficiently edits files as large as virtual storage even if they are many megabytes in size. XEDIT can edit an arbitrary number of files in a single session. When multiple files are edited, they are said to be in a *ring*. Repeatedly entering the XEDIT subcommand without specifying a file switches between each of the files in the ring. Additional files can be edited at any time from within XEDIT by issuing the XEDIT subcommand followed by a file identifer. If the file specified is already in the ring, it is displayed, otherwise it is read from disk and added to the ring.

XEDIT screen appearance

XEDIT can display one file at a time, multiple files in different parts of the screen, or multiple views of the same file. The screen can be split horizontally, vertically, or into rectangular sections to display the files in the ring, or provide multiple views of the same file.

The XEDIT screen is divided into the following areas:

- Header line—displays file information for currently displayed file.
- Status line—displays XEDIT status information.
- Command line—used to enter XEDIT commands. This can be placed on different parts of the screen based on user preference.
- File area—displays the file being edited. The current line is highlighted. A *scale line* can be displayed over the file area to display column numbers, and a *tab line* can display tab settings.
- Prefix area—is used for *prefix area commands* that insert, delete, copy, move, or manipulate lines and their contents. The prefix area can be placed to the left or right of the file area, be numbered or unnumbered, or be turned off altogether.

Additionally, users can *reserve* lines on a screen and place their own messages in them. This is usually done in XEDIT macros.

An XEDIT screen is shown in Fig. 10.18. In this example, which uses the standard XEDIT screen format, the prefix area is on the left, and the com-

HB	Halt Batch; stop a CMSBATCH job
HI	Halt Interpretation; stops REXX EXECs
HX	Halt eXecution; stops the running program
HT	Halt Typing; stops terminal output
RT	Resume Typing: resumes terminal output
TS	Trace Start; trace REXX EXECs
TE	Trace End; stop tracing REXX EXECs
HO	Halt Tracing; used for CMS program tracing
SO	Suspend Tracing; used for CMS program tracing
RO	Resume Tracing

Fig. 10.14 Immediate commands.

```
/* My Profile EXEC */
address command                         /* strict command search order */
'SET RDYMSG SMSG'                       /* Ready; - not Ready plus times */
/* Set immediate (executed immediately) and delayed (command is */
/* placed in the input area and executed by hitting ENTER) PF keys */
'CP SET PF1 IMMED APL2'                 /* PF1 key puts me in APL2     */
'CP SET PF2 DEL FORTVS2'                /* PF2 puts a FORTRAN command line */
                                        /* in the input area and leaves it */
                                        /* there so I can fill in the fileid */
'CP SET PF3 IMMED #CP IND USER'         /* PF3 shows my current CPU usage */
'CP SET PF10 RETRIEVE'                  /* PF10 retrieves prior input lines */
/* specify screen contents colors (also can be specified in */
/* directory entry */
'CP SCREEN CPOUT YELLOW'                /* output from CP */
'CP SCREEN VMOUT WHITE'                 /* output from CMS */
'CP SCREEN INREDISP TURQ'               /* input line redisplay */
'CP SCREEN INAREA YELLOW'               /* input area */
'CP SCREEN STATAREA RED'                /* status area */
'CP LINK GAMES 191 193 RR'              /* Link to public games disk */
' ACCESS 193 B'                         /* Make its files visible */
'ACCESS .TOOLS C'                       /* Access personal tools directory */
say 'Welcome to your CMS session!'
```

Fig. 10.15 Example of a PROFILE EXEC.

mand line is identified by an arrow. The top of the file is identified by a "Top of File" marker, and the top line identifies the file, shows its current record length, truncation column, and other information.

An additional file can be edited by moving the cursor to the command line to the right of the arrow, and entering the subcommand XEDIT. For example, if the command `xedit demo memo` were entered, XEDIT would display the screen shown in Fig. 10.19. In this case, there is no file with that name, so XEDIT displays an empty file. The status area at the bottom of the screen now indicates that 2 files are in the XEDIT ring.

Using XEDIT

The *current line* is the current cursor into the file, and the default *target* of commands like DELETE and CHANGE. XEDIT highlights the current line to make it stand out from other lines in a file. The current line pointer can be moved by pressing PF7 to scroll the file backward, PF8 to scroll forward, and a variety of commands that change the current line pointer, including `Locate` (which finds a string), `UP n` and `DOWN n`, which move up or down *n* lines, and `FOrward n` and `BAckward n`, which scroll the screen display *n* screen images. PF10 scrolls horizontally by moving the screen image to the left and then to the right.

File contents can be changed by overtyping the contents shown in the file area or entering commands. The file area can be overtyped with text, and the 3270 editing keys can be used to insert, erase, or move characters in a line totally without host intervention. New lines can be added by issuing the command XEDIT subcommand `ADD` or `INSERT`, or by moving the cursor to the prefix area and typing `A` or `I` at the point you wish to insert the new line. Multiple lines can be added by specifying a number after the command line or prefix command. Lines can be duplicated by using the prefix area command `"` (the quote mark is traditional markup for duplicating text).

Lines can also be altered from the command line. The most commonly used command for this is `Change`, which can be abbreviated to `C`. The typical form of the Change command is: *change /oldstring/newstring/ <lines> <instances>*. The *<lines>* and *<instances>* modifiers are optional and default to 1. For example:

`change /Tuesday/Wednesday/`	affects one occurrence on one line
`c/now/later/ 5 *`	affects all occurrences on next 5 lines
`c/bad/good/ * 1`	affects first occurrence on each following line

The `SET CASE` command specifies whether text in a file is translated to uppercase (`SET CASE Upper`) or left in mixed case (`SET CASE Mixed`), and whether Change and Locate commands are case-sensitive. `SET CASE M R` indicates mixed case text, and specifies that Change and Locate “respect” the case of the text strings. `SET CASE M I` tells XEDIT to ignore the case. Default case settings are based on the file type. SCRIPT files, for example, are mixed case and case-sensitive.

XEDIT makes it easy to add, delete, move, or copy lines of text. The simplest way is to move the cursor to the prefix area and enter `D` for Delete, `C` for Copy, and `M` for Move (copy lines and delete from original location). Multiple lines can be indicated by specifying a number (for example, the prefix command `D5` deletes 5 lines), or a range of lines bracketed by pairs of `DD`, `MM`, or `CC` prefix commands. Move and Copy require specification of a target location to move the lines to. This can be indicated by the prefix command `F` (position the new lines following the indicated line), or `P` (position the new lines preceding the indicated line). For example, in Fig. 10.20, lines

```
* display the synonym file 'jeff synonym'
type jeff synonym
ERASE DELETE 3
ERASE RM     2
Ready;

* enable the synonyms
synonym jeff
Ready;
```

Fig. 10.16 Synonym processing.

```
defaults list peek
The following is a list of your default options for the PEEK command:
        PROFILE PEEKPROF FROM 1 FOR 200
To change these default options enter DEFAULTS SET PEEK Opt1 <Opt2..>
Ready;

defaults list note
The following is a list of your default options for the NOTE command:
        PROFILE NOTEPROF SHORT NOLOG NOACK NOTEBOOK ALL
To change these default options enter DEFAULTS SET NOTE Opt1 <Opt2..>
Ready;

* Change PEEK default to show first 1,000 records of a spool file
defaults set peek for 1000
Ready;
* Change NOTE default to log mail and to request acknowledgement
defaults set note log ack
Ready;
```

Fig. 10.17 DEFAULTS command.

68 to 71 will be deleted, a new line will be added after line 76, and line 72 will be moved after line 74.

Prefix line groups need not all be defined, moved, copied, or deleted on the same screen. For example, a DD range of lines can be started on one screen and its other side left undefined until the user scrolls up or down to the right position to place the other DD pair. The same effect holds for MM and CC pairs. XEDIT displays a `block pending` message to remind the user that a block of lines remains unclosed.

XEDIT targets

Many XEDIT commands are based on the XEDIT *target*, which identifies the scope of lines a command affects. The simplest target is a relative line number, such as `-5` or `5`, that moves the current line pointer backward or forward 5 lines. A target can also be a line number in the file, such as `:60`, which represents the 60th line in the file. Targets can be entered on the command line to change the current position in the file, or can be used as a prefix to a command:

`:405`	move to line 405 in the file
`5 change /old/new/`	move down 5 lines, then change `old` to `new`
`top`	move before the first line in the file
`bottom`	move after the last line in the file

More interesting targets are based on string searches. XEDIT represents strings within delimited pairs of identical characters, as shown in the preceding *change* command. The first nonblank character entered where a string is required is used as the character that brackets the string target.

For the *locate*, the standard bracketing character is the forward slash (/), and the *locate* can be omitted when it is used. The following commands all have the same effect, and move the current line pointer to the next line containing the word XEDIT.

`locate /XEDIT/`	fully spelled out, standard form
`locate ,XEDIT,`	alternate delimiters
`l /XEDIT/`	use abbreviation
`/XEDIT/`	skip command name altogether

Reverse searches are performed by prefacing the target with a "-" sign. String targets can combine strings in a combination using AND, or OR and NOT logic:

`-/guppy/`	search backwards for a line with guppy
`locate /fish/&/bicycles/`	line with both fish and bicycles
`/fish/|/bicycles/`	line with either fish or bicycles

A line's name can also be a target. Line names are assigned by the SET POINT command. A line name is a character string beginning with a period; once defined, a line target can be referenced through its name.

`set point .here`	current line is names .here.
`.here`	XEDIT positions the current line at here
`set point .there`	current line is named .there
`.there change /later/now/`	move to .there and issue "change"

A line name can also be assigned by typing the line name in the prefix area adjacent to the line. Overtyping the prefix area at line 75 in Fig. 10.20 with ".on" associates that name with the line containing the command "EXEC XCLOCK."

```
PIPELINE MEMO    X2  V 80  Trunc=80 Size=114 Line=0 Col=1 Alt=0
===== * * * Top of File * * *
      |...+....1....+....2....+....3....+....4....+....5....+....6
===== Pipeline tools and tips
=====
===== This file contains CMS Pipelines notes that will be
===== updated on a periodic basis.  I encourage contributions
===== and will be documenting and coordinating programs
===== to be placed on the public disks.  There are
===== already some nice tools on the public disks that are of
===== general interest, so I will be sending more notes soon!

====>
                                              X E D I T  1 File
```

Fig. 10.18 Default XEDIT screen.

```
DEMO    MEMO    A1  V 80  Trunc=80 Size=0 Line=0 Col=1 Alt=0
DMSXIN571I Creating new file:


===== * * * Top of File * * *
      |...+....1....+....2....+....3....+....4....+....5....+....6
===== * * * End of File * * *


====>
                                               X E D I T  2 Files
```

Fig. 10.19 Initial XEDIT screen for empty file.

Named lines are used like line number targets, with the additional benefit that XEDIT adjusts their positions in the file to compensate for added and deleted lines. Mnemonic names can be assigned to lines, making it easy to locate specific positions in a file. The command `QUERY POINT *` displays all of the defined names and their line number positions in the file.

Targets can be used in combination to flexibly control the range of lines controlled by a command.

`:0 /Carrier/`	search for the first instance of `Carrier` in the file (move to the top of the file then search)
`c/Tuscany/Provence/ /Spain/*`	change each instance of Tuscany to Provence until a line containing Spain is found
`.here put .there other file a`	move the current line to the line named .here, and copy lines up to .there into the file OTHER FILE A

This provides a powerful shorthand for the experienced XEDIT user, and helps programmers automate editing functions in XEDIT macros.

PROFILE XEDIT

The screen appearance and the meanings of the program function keys can be customized to suit the preferences of the user. Screen colors, the format of the prefix area (left or right side of the screen, or turned off; with or without file sequence numbers), the location of the command line and where messages are displayed, synonyms and program function key settings, all can be set by PROFILE XEDIT every time a user edits a file.

A PROFILE XEDIT is executed every time an XEDIT session is started, analogous to the PROFILE EXEC started when users IPL CMS. A typical PROFILE XEDIT is shown in Fig. 10.21.

FILELIST

Groups of files can be manipulated by the `FILELIST` command, which presents a fullscreen display of files on accessed disks, as illustrated in Fig. 10.22. FILELIST sorts files in descending date order, so the most recently created or changed files are shown at the top of the display.

FILELIST selects a subset of files for processing based on the command line arguments. Unless told otherwise, FILELIST selects all files present on the A-disk or directory. For example:

`filelist`	selects all files on A-disk
`filelist * exec a`	all EXEC files on A-disk
`filelist * exec a`	all EXEC files on all accessed disks
`filelist abc*`	all files on A-disk beginning with ABC

The screen in Fig. 10.23 was produced by entering the command `file list sfs*`.

FILELIST allows "point and shoot" manipulation of files. For example, to edit the file SFSUSER MEMO, the user only has to place the cursor on the line containing it and press PF key 11. FILELIST lets the user type in commands under the column labeled *Cmd*. Typing `erase` before one of the file identifiers and pressing the Enter key erases the specified file. The nonblank portion of the screen can be overtyped, and several commands can be typed in on different lines before pressing Enter and executing them.

FILELIST provides a syntax for substituting parts of the file identifier into a generated command line. The string / expands into the selected file's filename, type, and mode. Modifiers n, t, and m expand into the selected file's filename, filetype, and filemode, respectively, and can be combined. For example, if the line `copyfile / /nt b` is typed over the line containing SFSUSER MEMO, FILELIST expands the line to `COPYFILE SFSUSER MEMO A SFSUSER MEMO B`.

```
FULLSCR  EXEC  A1  V 130  Trunc=130 Size=76 Line=68 Col=1 Alt=0
====>
0dd68  'SET  CMSPF  8 Forward   NOECHO #WM WINDOW FORWARD = 1'
00069  'SET  CMSPF  11 Right    NOECHO #WM WINDOW RIGHT = 20'
00070  'SET  CMSPF  23 Session  NOECHO SESSION VMC'
0dd71  'SET  CMSPF  12 IUCV     NOECHO EXEC IUCVMSG'
0m072 colors = 'BLUE RED WHITE PINK YELLOW TURQ GREEN'
00073  /* Randomly select a color (for fun) and use it for the */
00f74  /* clock we'll put in the top of the screen */
00075  'EXEC XCLOCK' Word(colors,random(1,7)) '(NOTOP'
i0076  'VSCREEN WRITE CMS 1 20 25 (RES PROT HIGH DATA' userid()
00077  * * * End of File * * *
```

Fig. 10.20 Prefix commands to delete, copy, and move lines.

```
/* My PROFILE XEDIT */
parse arg fn ft fm . '(' options  /* Get command line info */
'LOAD' fn ft fm
if rc <> 0 then exit rc
if pos(' 'ft,' PASCAL C PLI')<>0 then /* one of these types? */
  do /* override default XEDIT characteristics */
    'SET CASE MIXED IGNORE' /* Case-insensitive locate */
    'SET MARGINS 1 72'
  end
'SET COLOR FILEAREA TURQ'      /* Pretty Turquoise file area      */
'SET COLOR CMDLINE RED'        /* Easily spotted command line */
'SET COLOR CURLINE YELLOW' /*  and current focus line           */
'SET NUM ON'                   /* I like numbered prefix area     */
'SET PF5 MACRO SPELL'          /* Invoke spellcheck via PF5       */
```

Fig. 10.21 A PROFILE XEDIT.

The list of files can be sorted by pressing the PF keys listed in the legend at the bottom of the screen. FILELIST is an XEDIT application, making the full expressive power of XEDIT available for selecting files. XEDIT commands can be entered on the command line (the line with the cursor arrow), including the `ALL` command to display all lines containing an XEDIT string specification. For example, the subcommand `ALL /NOTEBOOK/|/MEMO/|/SCRIPT/` displays all lines listing NOTEBOOK, MEMO, or SCRIPT files.

The MACLIST command shown in Fig. 10.24 provides a similar "point and shoot" interface for MACLIBs. A MACLIB is a library of program text included by language processors at compile time. Maclib members, usually called *macros* or *copy files* typically contain record structure definitions or common code sequences that the compiler or assembler expands in line. As with FILELIST, PF keys can be used to sort the list or edit individual members.

Sending and Receiving SPOOL Files

The CMS `NOTE` and `SENDFILE` commands sends mail and disk files to other users by punching them to other users' virtual readers, as shown in Fig. 10.25. Files can be read to disk using the `RECEIVE` command. `PEEK` and `RDRLIST` allow users to inspect their reader queues, and browse, purge, or load reader files to disk.

The PEEK command lets users view files on their reader queues and then discard them or load them to disk. The `RDRLIST` command provides a FILELIST-like display for reader files, as shown in Fig. 10.26. Files can be PEEKed or received to disk by moving the cursor and pressing a PF key.

NOTE, SENDFILE, PEEK, RDRLIST and RECEIVE are EXECs, and use the `NETDATA` command to create and read spool files. NETDATA uses a data format that lets arbitrary record formats be transmitted via 80-byte card images. NETDATA format is recognized by MVS/TSO, so it can be used to transmit files between VM and MVS.

CMS provides `PUNCH` and `READCARD` commands to punch and read simple card image files. The `DISK` command, like NETDATA, uses a spool file format that can represent arbitrary file formats in card images. The `DISK DUMP` command places a file on the virtual punch in this format, and `DISK LOAD` reads it to disk with its original file identifier and format. The `CARD` command, written at Cornell University by Larry Brenner (now at IBM), is a very high performance replacement for PUNCH, READCARD, and DISK. Unlike SENDFILE, these commands require the user to issue SPOOL and TAG commands to direct spool output to a destination. All of these commands predate SENDFILE and RECEIVE, and have largely been superceded by them. The CARD command is still the fastest of this family of commands.

SENDFILE, RECEIVE, PEEK and NOTE use the CMS *nickname* facility, provided by the `NAMEFIND` command, to convert user-specified nicknames into VM userids, and for files sent to remote destinations, remote site destinations as well. RECEIVE accepts files created with PUNCH and DISK DUMP, so users need not determine which command created a file before loading it to disk.

Fullscreen CMS and Session Services

With VM/SP Release 5, IBM introduced a windowed, fullscreen environment for CMS. In addition to the traditional VM screen layout described in "VM

```
 JEFF    FILELIST A0  V 108  Trunc=108 Size=1322 Line=1 Col=1 Alt=0
Cmd Filename Filetype       Fm   Format    Lrecl Records  Blocks  Date      Time
    CPULOG   920127         A1        V       60      26       1 1/29/92 17:13:14
    PETEG    NOTEBOOK       A1        V      126    7579      83 1/29/92 16:58:40
    JULIE    NOTEBOOK       A0        V       80    6228      69 1/29/92 16:48:25
    PASSTHRU DATA           A1        V       80     676       6 1/27/92 17:46:15
    CLAUDE   NOTEBOOK       A0        V       84    1426      20 1/27/92 17:42:16
    JEFF     MEMO           A0        V       73    3484      45 1/27/92 17:32:51
    SKAFF    NOTEBOOK       A1        V      110    1352      15 1/27/92 17:25:05
    STEVENS  NOTEBOOK       A1        V       87    7315      74 1/27/92 17:22:02
    LASTING  GLOBALV        A1        V       60      26       1 1/27/92 17:18:39
    VMMAINT  DIR            A0        V       71     931       9 1/27/92 17:17:28
    MDH      NOTEBOOK       A0        V       80     316       4 1/27/92 15:07:43
    COSTS    MEMO           A1        V       71      45       1 1/27/92 14:55:49
    SPORER   NOTEBOOK       A1        V       78     320       5 1/27/92 12:57:32
    VOELKER  NOTEBOOK       A1        V       86    1191      11 1/27/92 12:39:06
    JAY      NOTEBOOK       A1        V       80    1060      11 1/27/92 10:15:02
    KEITH    NOTEBOOK       A0        V       80     647       7 1/27/92  7:29:07
1= Help    2= Refresh 3= Quit   4=Sort(type) 5=Sort(date) 6=Sort(size)
7= Backward 8= Forward 9= FL /n 10=       11= XEDIT    12= Cursor
====>
```

Fig. 10.22 FILELIST screen.

```
 JEFF  FILELIST A0  V 108  Trunc=108 Size=12 Line=1 Col=1 Alt=0
Cmd Filename  Filetype   Fm  Format  Lrecl  Records Blocks  Date Time
    SFSCMDS   CONSOLE   A1   F        132        77      3  12/17/91 16:15:44
    SFSUSER   SCRIPT    A1   V         73       286      3  12/12/91 17:02:22
    SFS       MEMO      A1   V         73       148      1  12/06/91 13:18:33
    SFSLIM    EXEC      A1   V         71         5      1  12/06/91 12:47:09
    SFSUSER   MEMO      A1   V         73       210      3  11/12/91 18:46:24
    SFSUSE    CONSOLE   A1   V        104       426      5  11/03/91 22:10:42
    SFSFOIL   MEMO      A1   V         65       451      4  11/01/91 13:57:18
    SFSGRANT  CONSOLE   A1   V         72       364      3  10/30/91 17:35:41
    SFSADMIN  CONSOLE   A1   V         74       189      2  10/30/91 16:45:55
    SFS       CONSOLE   A1   V         81       381      5  10/30/91 16:32:55
    SFSGONE   EXEC      A1   V         68        19      1  10/25/91 12:17:35
    SFSTEMP   EXEC      A1   V         72        41      1  10/22/91 18:15:46
1= Help   2= Refresh 3= Quit  4=Sort(type) 5=Sort(date) 6=Sort(size)
7= Backward 8= Forward 9= FL /n 10=      11= XEDIT   12= Cursor
====>
                                                        X E D I T 1 File
```

Fig. 10.23 FILELIST display from "filelist sfs* * a".

Screen Handling" on page 23, users can issue the command `SET FULLSCREEN ON` to enter a fullscreen, windowed environment. Fullscreen CMS is also referred to as CMS Windows when emphasizing its windowed nature.

Fullscreen CMS is based on *session services* that provide an application interface to windowed screen output. Session services can be used without going into fullscreen CMS, so users can retain the traditional VM screen format, while making use of a flexible and convenient display interface.

Fullscreen CMS uses *virtual screens* and *windows*. Program input and output can be directed to virtual screens, which may be displayed in a window on the physical screen. A virtual screen has size, color and highlighting attributes, its contents can be scrolled forward and backward (to see early parts of a session) and may optionally be logged to disk files.

CMS provides the following default virtual screens:

- CMS—general session input and output
- NETWORK—file and mail transmission output messages received from RSCS
- MESSAGE—messages sent from other users via the MSG command
- WARNING—messages sent from operators via the WNG command
- STATUS—fullscreen CMS status information
- XEDIT—XEDIT terminal session input and output

Users can define additional screens via the `VSCREEN DEFINE` command, and use the `VSCREEN WRITE` command to place text on it in any row/column position. Additional commands read from the screen, define colors and highlighting, reposition windows on the screen, hide or display windows, and perform a variety of other functions.

Fullscreen CMS can be a valuable productivity aid. It lets users create and browse logs of their session's activities, scroll back and forth in a session window, direct terminal I/O to a virtual screen, and work with overlapped windows. It provides pop-up windows so asynchronous messages, such as the arrival of mail, don't interrupt the screen the user is working with.

For example, in Fig. 10.27, I received a mail file while in the NOTE command composing mail to send to another user. Without session services, when I next pressed Enter after the file arrived, VM would clear the screen and display the "RDR FILE FROM" message. I would have to clear the screen again to restore the original screen contents. With session services, I get a concise pop-up window that doesn't overlay the rest of the screen.

Figure 10.28 shows what happens after I send the file created in Fig. 10.27; I had issued the command `NOTE PETEG` while in XEDIT. When I returned from NOTE to my XEDIT session, the messages created by NOTE appeared in the CMS window that popped up in my XEDIT screen. The file I am editing happens to be Pete's EXEC that he uses to customize fullscreen CMS to his preferences. Windows also can pop up while in the fullscreen CMS command environment, as shown in Fig. 10.29.

Windows can be scrolled, moved, maximized (enlarged), or minimized (shrunk) by executing WINDOW and VSCREEN commands, or by issuing single-character *border commands*. Border commands are executed by placing the cursor on a border's corner and entering a one character mnemonic com-

```
JEFF    MACLIST A0 V 130 Trunc=130 Size=35 Line=25 Col=1 Alt=8
Cmd Member name  Index   Records Library name Library type Mode
    IPARMLX      18496      98   HCPGPI       MACLIB       R2
    IUCV          2972    2053   HCPGPI       MACLIB       R2
    MAPMDISK      1645    1326   HCPGPI       MACLIB       R2
    PFAULT        1271     373   HCPGPI       MACLIB       R2
    REFPAGE        522     748   HCPGPI       MACLIB       R2
    SFBLOK       18336     159   HCPGPI       MACLIB       R2
    SPLINK       18252      83   HCPGPI       MACLIB       R2
    VMCMHDR      18136     115   HCPGPI       MACLIB       R2
    VMCPARM      18046      89   HCPGPI       MACLIB       R2
    VMUDQ            2     519   HCPGPI       MACLIB       R2
    VRDCBLOK     17928     117   HCPGPI       MACLIB       R2

1= Help    2= Refresh 3= Quit  4=Sort(name) 5=Sort(index) 6=Sort(size)
7= Backward 8= Forward 9= FL /n 10=        11= XEDIT   12= Cursor
====>
                                                   X E D I T 1 File
```

Fig. 10.24 MACLIST screen.

```
The sending user session looks like:

sendfile profile exec a phsiii
File PROFILE EXEC A1 sent to phsiii at VMSG on 02/28/92 16:13:48
Ready;

The receiving user session looks like:

RDR FILE 0009 SENT FROM GABE   RDR RECS 0031 CPY 001 A NOHOLD NOKEEP
q r all
ORIGINID FILE CLASS RECORDS  CPY  HOLD  DATE  TIME      NAME     TYPE  DIST
GABE     0009 A PUN 00000031 001  NONE  02/28 16:13:48  PROFILE  EXEC  VMSG
Ready;
receive
File PROFILE EXEC A1 created from PROFILE EXEC A1 received from GABE
Ready;
```

Fig. 10.25 SENDFILE and RECEIVE commands.

mand. For example, to scroll a window backward to see earlier contents, type the border command B and press Enter. To move a window to a new location, place M in one of the window's corners, move the cursor to the desired new location, and press Enter.

Additionally, the session services provided with fullscreen CMS are a flexible and easy-to-use application program interface for screen display. Programs written in REXX and other languages can use session services to create attractive displays with multiple colors and windows. A number of vendor products and publicly available tools use session services for terminal display. For example, the small EXEC shown in Fig. 10.30 displays the time of day in any XEDIT application.

Fullscreen CMS was not initially well-received by CMS users, and remains controversial. It was introduced when relations between IBM's VM development organization and the VM user community were strained, and its design suffered from having had little review by its potential users. The implementation suffered from serious defects, not all of which have been corrected. It's worth reviewing this to show how well-meaning developers can create problems.

One problem was that fullscreen CMS did not detect when programs used DIAGNOSE 58, the in-place fullscreen I/O interface, to alter a screen's appearance. Fullscreen CMS only rewrites the parts of the display that have changed, a valuable optimization for users connected to VM via remote terminals and slow lines. Unfortunately, after a DIAGNOSE 58 program ran, CMS would think that the screen contents were largely unchanged, even when the screen's appearance was totally different. For example, after returning from FLIST (a program similar to FILELIST) invoked from fullscreen CMS, a user would see a bizarre mixture of FLIST output and the CMS fullscreen panel. The user had to press the CLEAR key to cause CMS to rewrite the display.

XEDIT uses CMS session services, so XEDIT and XEDIT-based applications (such as NOTE, PEEK, RDRLIST, NAMES and HELP) are compatible with one another. This meant that session services were in use whether a user used fullscreen CMS or not. For example, the scenario just described occurred when FLIST was called from XEDIT. Eventually, most programs were converted to cooperate with CMS session services. CMS was trained to better detect when console I/O was performed without the use of session services, and to repaint the screen when needed for a consistent screen image.

Another problem was the introduction of commands with un-CMSlike syntax. New commands for fullscreen processing had names like SHOW (a window), POP, DROP, HIDE, SHOW, GET, PUT, CLEAR, and WRITE, precluding the use of these useful verbs for other CMS commands—including commands already written at customer sites. At the request of VM user groups, IBM retracted these commands and made them operands of the VSCREEN and WINDOW commands.

Finally, fullscreen CMS suffers by comparison with windowed programming environments available on personal computers and workstations, because the 3270 display is less suitable for this type of interface. Although 3270 displays use colors and graphics and can be equipped with mice, the 3270 interface is less convenient, and screen appearance less attractive, for windowed applications than high resolution displays. Nonetheless, CMS session services provide a valuable service by giving CMS a powerful, easily used and universally available display manager, and by letting mainframe applications use windowed displays.

The Live Parsing Editor, LEXX

A highly positive experience is provided by the Live Parsing Editor (LEXX). Written by Mike Cowlishaw, the inventor of REXX, LEXX provides an intelligent text editor that is sensitive to file contents. LEXX was designed for

```
JEFF    RDRLIST A0  V 108  Trunc=108 Size=4 Line=1 Col=1 Alt=0
Cmd Filename Filetype   Class   User      at Node   Hold    Records  Date  Time
  VMFINS     CONSOLE    CON T   VMESA11   VMC       NONE         42  02/27 11:16:12
  $$$TLL$$   IPL        PUN A   VMESA11   VMC       NONE     125861  02/27 11:18:40
  DAILY      REPORT     PRT A   ACCOUNT   VMC       NONE      46183  02/27 11:22:01
  BACAS      NOTE       PUN A   JCB       VMC       NONE         16  02/29 22:00:51

1= Help    2= Refresh 3= Quit    4=Sort(type) 5=Sort(date) 6=Sort(user)
7= Backward 8= Forward 9= Receive 10=        11= XEDIT   12= Cursor
====>
                                                          X E D I T 1 File
```

Fig. 10.26 RDRLIST screen.

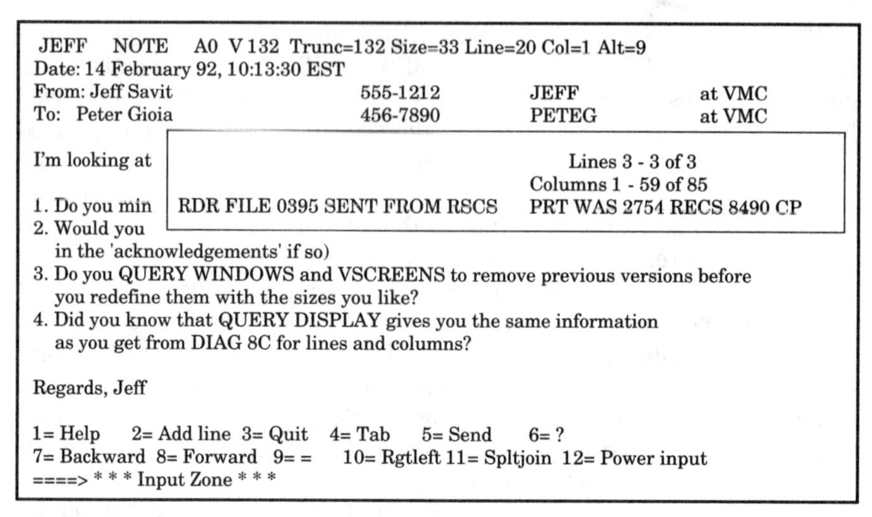

Fig. 10.27 Window pop-up while in NOTE.

the authors of the New Oxford English Dictionary, became a software product for VM/CMS, and is now also available under OS/2 and AIX.

LEXX is aware that files have structure, and uses this knowledge to display files on the screen in a way that suggests their structure. LEXX also allows files to be manipulated in units meaningful to the type of document. The "live parsing" aspect of LEXX is that LEXX recognizes changes in the structure as soon as you press Enter: there is no reformatting step. This is about as close as "What you see is what you get" as can be expected on a mainframe 3270 terminal. LEXX fully uses the capability of 3270 terminals to display different colors, font and type faces (such as italic and bold characters) to emphasize the meanings of different parts of a file.

IBM provides parsers for REXX and GML files, and documents how users can write additional parsers. This provides a powerful, extensible editing environment. For example, LEXX knows that Generalized Markup Language (GML) documents (such as this book) contain both text and markup tags to describe how text should be formatted. GML tags indicate the beginning of paragraphs and chapters, and indicate whether text should be printed in bold or italic type. LEXX uses its understanding of GML to show a document's structure while its being edited. For example, a chapter section is indented slightly to show that it is subordinate to the contents of the chapter it is part of. If you start a new paragraph by entering the tag :P, LEXX immediately opens up a new paragraph and indents it to show which subchapter it belongs to.

For example, on a 3270 screen with color and graphics, GML tags are displayed in turquoise, highlighted phrases are bright yellow, italic phrases and document citations are displayed in italic, and chapter headings are bold yellow. I can't illustrate colors here, but LEXX displays a GML document something like the illustration Fig. 10.31.

LEXX provides a GML command to control editing. Subcommands move the current focus position to the next or previous section or chapter of the document, display the table of contents of the document, and display the document in *galley mode*. In galley mode, the tag words are removed, as shown in Fig. 10.32.

LEXX also recognizes the structure of REXX program files. REXX programs contain comments, program text, and literal fields inside quoted strings. LEXX displays each of these types of text in a different color and font. If you forget to close a comment, LEXX displays the remainder of the file in the color associated for comments. The mistake, and its location, are indicated by screen appearance as soon as you hit enter. It is almost impossible to produce an "unclosed comment" or "unclosed string" error when using LEXX. A LEXX screen of a REXX program is shown in Fig. 10.33.

LEXX provides a variety of other editor features including an advanced autosave feature. LEXX writes the contents of a file to a specially named disk file if a user-specified time period has elapsed without an explicit save to disk. LEXX performs an autosave even if the user doesn't touch the keyboard. If the system crashes, edited files can be recovered from the autosave files. Since

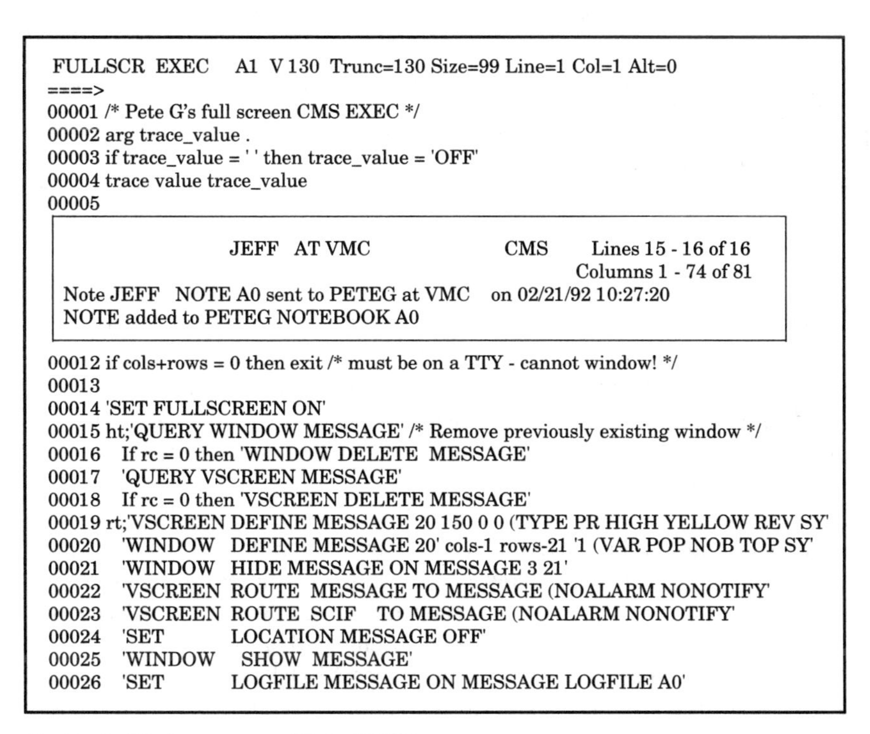

```
 FULLSCR EXEC    A1  V 130  Trunc=130 Size=99 Line=1 Col=1 Alt=0
====>
00001 /* Pete G's full screen CMS EXEC */
00002 arg trace_value .
00003 if trace_value = ' ' then trace_value = 'OFF'
00004 trace value trace_value
00005
 +----------------------------------------------------------------+
 |              JEFF   AT VMC             CMS      Lines 15 - 16 of 16 |
 |                                                 Columns 1 - 74 of 81 |
 | Note JEFF   NOTE A0 sent to PETEG at VMC    on 02/21/92 10:27:20  |
 | NOTE added to PETEG NOTEBOOK A0                                 |
 +----------------------------------------------------------------+
00012 if cols+rows = 0 then exit /* must be on a TTY - cannot window! */
00013
00014 'SET FULLSCREEN ON'
00015 ht;'QUERY WINDOW MESSAGE' /* Remove previously existing window */
00016   If rc = 0 then 'WINDOW DELETE  MESSAGE'
00017   'QUERY VSCREEN MESSAGE'
00018   If rc = 0 then 'VSCREEN DELETE MESSAGE'
00019 rt;'VSCREEN DEFINE MESSAGE 20 150 0 0 (TYPE PR HIGH YELLOW REV SY'
00020   'WINDOW   DEFINE MESSAGE 20' cols-1 rows-21 '1 (VAR POP NOB TOP SY'
00021   'WINDOW   HIDE MESSAGE ON MESSAGE 3 21'
00022   'VSCREEN  ROUTE  MESSAGE TO MESSAGE (NOALARM NONOTIFY'
00023   'VSCREEN  ROUTE  SCIF   TO MESSAGE (NOALARM NONOTIFY'
00024   'SET         LOCATION MESSAGE OFF'
00025   'WINDOW      SHOW  MESSAGE'
00026   'SET         LOGFILE MESSAGE ON MESSAGE LOGFILE A0'
```

Fig. 10.28 Window pop-up while in XEDIT.

```
                                        Fullscreen CMS  Columns 1 -   13:07

erase old file
Ready;
+--------------------------------------------------------------------+
|                          Messages                                  |
|                                                                    |
| 13:07:24 MSG FROM JOANN   : Are you there?                         |
+--------------------------------------------------------------------+
PROFILE EXEC A1
Ready;

PF1=Help      2=Pop_Msg  3=Quit      4=Clear_Top     5=Filelist     6=Retrieve
PF7=Backward  8=Forward  9=Rdrlist  10=Left         11=Right       12=Cmdline
====>
```

Fig. 10.29 Message pop-up while in CMS fullscreen mode.

```
/* Provide a digital clock while in XEDIT                        */
/* Run this once per CMS session before going into XEDIT        */
address command
parse upper arg color '(' opts
if opts  = '' then opts  = 'TOP'            /* default location */
if color = '' then color = 'BLUE'           /* default color    */
'WINDOW  DELETE STATUS'
'VSCREEN DELETE STATUS'
'WINDOW  DEFINE  STATUS 1 9  1 71 (FIXED NOBORDER POP' opts 'SYSTEM'
'VSCREEN DEFINE  STATUS 1 9  0 0 (TYPE PROTECT' color 'SYSTEM'
'WINDOW SHOW STATUS ON STATUS 1 2'
'SET LOCATION STATUS OFF'
```

Fig. 10.30 XCLOCK EXEC.

files are frequently and automatically saved, little data is likely to be lost.

This contrasts with editors like XEDIT and ISPF, which autosave only after a specified number of changes, and only after the user presses Enter or a PF key. With those editors, a user with autosave turned on can still lose a significant number of changes if he or she doesn't make that one last change that reaches the autosave limit.

LEXX allows selection of text on units that span line boundaries: PF10 selects a logical unit of the file text, like an entire paragraph. PF4 and PF5 copy or move the selected text to a new location in the document. LEXX also provides an *Undo* facility to remove changes more flexibly than the XEDIT RECOVER command, which lets users recover changed or deleted lines.

LEXX is not a replacement for XEDIT, since XEDIT provides a number of features that are not in LEXX, such as update processing. XEDIT is also faster and better suited for many editing applications. Nonetheless, LEXX is a powerful editor that can be used to increase productivity for many applications.

Fourth-Generation Languages

CMS hosts a wide variety of non-IBM fourth-generation languages such as FOCUS, RAMIS, NOMAD, SAS, and SPSS. These languages provide improved programmer and end-user productivity by using nonprocedural statements (that relieve the programmer of dealing with details of flow-of-control) to formulate and solve problems.

Database systems

CMS also hosts a variety of database systems that allow end-user and programmer access to organized data. Perhaps the most important of these database systems is IBM's SQL/DS (Structured Query Language/Data System). SQL/DS is a relational database that stores data in tables. SQL/DS commands let programmers select records based on their values, merge tables based on common key values, update and insert records, and a wide variety of other operations. End users can work with interactive SQL on a command basis by using the ISQL command, or by using the high-level Query Management Facility (QMF), which lets users select records without having to enter commands.

SQL/DS can be used for both ad hoc end-user queries and for production data processing applications. Many sites use SQL/DS to store critical data in databases containing millions of records. SQL/DS can be accessed from fourth generation languages like FOCUS and SAS, and can be used in production applications written in COBOL, PL/I, APL2, C, and FORTRAN, and from REXX using either IBM's RXSQL or VM Systems Group's DB/REXX products.

```
Document:VMCHAP1 SCRIPT A1   At: "each user"..          16:09

  :H2.Fundamental VM concepts

      :P.VM systems are managed by a Control Program called
      :HP2.CP:EHP2., which controls the real system.  CP provides
      a :HP2.virtual machine:EHP2. for each user of the VM system.
      A virtual machine is a simulated image of a complete
      System/370 or System/390 mainframe; each user has his or
      her own virtual machine and can start it, crash it, or run
      programs on it without interfering with other users.
```

Fig. 10.31 LEXX display of a GML document.

```
Document: VMCHAP1 SCRIPT A1    At: "each user"..            Browse 16:11
   Fundamental VM concepts


   VM systems are managed by a Control Program called CP,
   which controls the real system.  CP provides a virtual
   machine for each user of a VM system.  A virtual machine is
   a simulated image of a complete System/370 or System/390
   mainframe; each user has his or her own virtual machine
   and can start it, crash it, or run programs on it without
   interfering with other users.


PF1 Help   PF2 Opencl  PF3 Quit  PF4 Copy    PF5 Move    PF6 ?

PF7 Up     PF8 Down    PF9 =     PF10 Select PF11 Splitj PF12 Focus
```

Fig. 10.32 GML document in galley format.

```
   /* Initialize the service machine environment */


   address 'COMMAND'
   owner = 'JEAN'
   target = 'MINE'
   'CP MSG' monitorID userid() 'is up and running'
   Call LOGMSG 'Restarted'
   'CP SPOOL PUNCH RSCS'
   'CP TAG DEV PUN' target

   parse upper source...filename filetype filemode execfname.
   Do forever
     'WAKEUP (RDR'
     if rc < > 4 then
       do
          ' CP MSG' owner filename filetype 'stopping'
          ' CP MSG' owner 'Unexpected Wakeup event'
          exit rc
       end
     call READER
   End
   Exit

PF1 Help  PF2 Opencl  PF3 Quit  PF4 Copy    PF5 Move    PF6 ?
PF7 Up    PF8 Down    PF9 =     PF10 Select PF11 Splitj PF12 Focus
```

Fig. 10.33 LEXX session with a REXX program.

SQL/DS databases can be accessed from remote VM systems in a TSAF collection or VTAM network. SQL/DS can also be accessed from workstations connected to VM by a TCP/IP network.

Chapter

11

CMS Programming Environment

CMS provides a very rich programming environment. CMS provides powerful applications enablers in the form of REXX and CMS Pipelines, and also provides a wide variety of program interfaces, including simulated program interfaces from OS/MVS and DOS/VSE. This lets CMS be used as a development system for other environments, as well as a host for its own applications.

A key facet of the CMS programming environment is that programmers have full access to the CMS facilities in their virtual machine. Multiuser systems usually restrict useful program interfaces to "authorized programs" or "super-users." CMS, due to its personal computing orientation, lets users fully exploit its capabilities without demanding special privileges. One of the direct results of this style of program access is that VM lets all programmers perform tasks that are "special" on other systems, such as defining new commands, tracing application and system execution on an instruction basis, and even setting up interrupt handlers.

The REXX Procedures Language

REXX is both a programming language and the standard EXEC language used for building CMS commands from basic commands. REXX is frequently the language of choice for building applications, due to the ease with which it can be used to quickly produce working programs.

REXX's presence is so ubiquitous in CMS that many nonprogrammers use it, even if just to automate a common sequence of commands. The presence of a single flexible, efficient, and easily used procedures language is one of the reasons that CMS is such a highly productive environment for both end users and programmers. No other operating system, not even UNIX, has a single EXEC/procedures language that is as powerful, universally available, and easily learned and understood.

A key REXX concept is that expressions not known to the language are passed to an *external environment*. REXX interprets statements (*parse, say, do, if, select, call*, assignment statements, and so on), and sends other clauses, usually commands, to the enclosing environment. For example, the SORT and LISTFILE commands in the literal strings in Fig. 11.3 and Fig. 11.4 are not REXX statements, and are sent to CMS for execution.

The environment is controlled by the REXX *address* instruction. The default in EXECs is address CMS, which sends commands to the CMS command environment using the same command resolution as if the commands were entered from the CMS command line (implied EXEC and implied CP are used if in effect for the CMS session). This is illustrated in Fig. 11.1.

Most EXECs use *address command*, which sends commands to CMS without implied CP or EXEC command search. This makes EXECs run faster, since CMS doesn't search for nonexistent EXECs every time a command is entered. It also makes programs more robust, since it ensures that an EXEC with the same name as a VM command is not accidentally executed instead of the normal CMS command. *Address command* makes programmers do a little more typing to add the *CP* and *EXEC* prefixes for commands that need them, as shown in Fig. 11.2, but is well worth it for the improved performance and reliability.

REXX is not limited to *address CMS* and *address command*. The CMS and command subcommand environments are always available, and subcommand environments are also provided for XEDIT, CMS Pipelines, DMS/CMS, ISPF, GDDM, SQL/DS, XMENU, and other programs. VM/ESA added a unique subcommand environment, *address CPICOMM*, to perform program-to-program communications, as described in "Advanced Program-to-Program Communication/VM (APPC/VM)" on page 372. The default environment is normally established by the program that invokes the REXX procedure. XEDIT macros default to address XEDIT, for example.

```
address CMS /* the default */
/* CMS searches for a LINK EXEC, then a LINK MODULE, before */
/* passing the command to CP */
 'LINK PUBLIC 191 193 RR'
/* CMS searches for an ACCESS EXEC before finding the nucleus */
/* resident ACCESS command */
 'ACCESS 193 B'
/* CMS looks for a SENDFILE EXEC, finds it, and runs it */
 'SENDFILE CURRENT DATA B TO WORKERS'
```

Fig. 11.1 Address CMS.

```
address COMMAND     /* send to command enviroment */
 /* there is no CMS LINK command so the next line is unrecognized */
  'LINK PUBLIC 191 193 RR'
 /* REXX passes the command directly to CP for execution */
  'CP LINK PUBLIC 191 193 RR'
 /* REXX passes the command directly to CMS */
  'ACCESS 193 B'
 /* there is no CMS SENDFILE MODULE or built-in command so the */
 /* following command is not recognized */
  'SENDFILE CURRENT DATA B TO WORKERS'
 /* REXX sends the command to CMS as an EXEC */
  'EXEC SENDFILE CURRENT DATA B TO WORKERS'
```

Fig. 11.2 Address COMMAND.

Any application program can declare a subcommand environment using the CMS SUBCOM interface, and use it to communicate directly with REXX programs. REXX provides an application interface that lets external programs both get and set the contents of REXX variables. In its simplest form, this is used to set the return code variable *rc* to indicate the success or failure of the previous command, but is also used to let REXX and subcommand environments completely interact with one another. This lets REXX act as a universal macro language, a capability increasingly exploited in other operating systems as well. REXX macros enhance applications by making them user-programmable, and by extending the variety of commands they provide.

REXX's inventor, Michael Cowlishaw, was much more concerned that REXX should be convenient for its users than for the extremely few programmers that would create a REXX implementation. He therefore designed REXX to provide a natural form of expression and hide details of hardware from the programmer. For example, REXX lets variables take on different data types and sizes at different times, and permits run-time specification of numeric precision. These and other language features make compilation very difficult. The REXX implementation in CMS, written by Cowlishaw himself, and most other implementations, interpret REXX programs instead of compiling them into native machine code.

Interpreted programs can require more CPU resources than programs that are compiled into machine code. IBM provides a REXX compiler program product that creates System/370 object code from REXX source programs. The REXX compiler implements the full REXX language and allows much faster execution. The compiler also provides programmer tools not available with the built-in interpreter, such as a cross-reference listing to show where variables are used, and a listing that shows statement nesting in *do*, *if*, and *select* statements.

System Center, Inc., also provides a REXX compiler for CMS, called, *PROREXX*. PROREXX is an example of a *translator* instead of a true compiler. Instead of producing machine code, it converts a REXX program into an easily interpreted internal format, which can be more quickly executed than text-format REXX statements. The obvious advantage for System Center, Inc., is that PROREXX can be ported to a non-System/370 platform more easily than a true compiler.

REXX is just one of the many contributions VM has made to the computing world. Although developed on CMS, REXX is now also available on MVS/TSO, AS/400, OS/2, and MS-DOS, many versions of UNIX, VAX VMS, Tandem, and Amiga. REXX is far too broad and rich a topic to adequately cover in a short section of this book. The examples of REXX code sprinkled throughout this volume convey, I hope, the flavor of the REXX language and how it is used. I recommend the following books for further information:

- *The REXX Handbook*, edited by Gabriel Goldberg and Phil Smith III, McGraw-Hill (1992).
- By REXX's inventor: *The REXX Language, a Practical Approach*, M. F. Cowlishaw, Prentice-Hall (1985, 1990).
- *Modern Programming Using REXX*, by Bob O'Hara and Dave Gomberg, Prentice-Hall (1985 and 1988).
- *Programming in REXX*, by Charles Daney, McGraw-Hill (1992).

The CMS Stack

A traditional part of the CMS environment is the *program stack*, a buffer of text lines in virtual storage used in place of keyboard input. Lines read from the terminal are actually read from the stack until it is exhausted. The stack is like the *standard input* concept in UNIX and MS-DOS, except that the stack is used in preference to the terminal instead of replacing it. Also, lines are explicitly placed in the stack, instead of being placed there by redirecting standard output.

The stack lets applications simulate keyboard input or pass data from program-to-program. For example, the CMS `SORT` command asks the user to supply a range of columns to sort. The stack can be used to feed preprogrammed inputs to SORT, as shown in Fig. 11.3.

Lines are added to the stack by the `CMSSTACK` function and by the REXX statements *queue* and *push*. These functions, respectively, add lines to the stack in FIFO (First In, First Out) and LIFO (Last In, First Out) order. The CMS command `SENTRIES` (stack entries), and the REXX function *queued()* return the number of lines remaining in the stack. Many commands optionally place output on the stack instead of typing it. For example, the

```
/* SORT command asks for a column range, so we place it in the stack */
queue '1 8'                /* sort columns 1-8 of a file */
'SORT UNSORTED INPUT A SORTED OUTPUT A'
```

Fig. 11.3 Use the stack to provide prompted inputs.

```
'LISTFILE * * A(STACK'  /* put LISTFILE output in the stack */
do queued()             /* one iteration per file */
  parse pull fn ft fm .
  .....
end
```

Fig. 11.4 LISTFILE (STACK.

```
/* Process every accessed disk */
'QUERY DISK (STACK'
do queued()
  parse pull . . mode .
  'MAKEBUF'                        /* make a buffer */
  bufno = rc                       /* save its number */
  'LISTFILE * *' mode '(STACK'     /* stack a line for each file on disk */
  do i = 1 to queued()             /* process all lines in current buffer */
    parse pull fn ft fm .          /* get each file identifier */
    'EXEC TALLY' fn ft fm          /* Run a command on each file */
  end
  'DROPBUF' bufno           /* remove the buffer, restore prior state */
end
```

Fig. 11.5 Using MAKEBUF and DROPBUF to create a stack level.

`LISTFILE`, `QUERY`, and `EXECIO` commands provide STACK, FIFO, and LIFO options to place data in the stack, as shown in Fig. 11.4.

CMS lets programs declare multiple program stack buffers. The `MAKEBUF` command creates a stack level buffer and returns a buffer number in the return code variable. The `DROPBUF` command releases a stack level. This lets programs place data in the stack and process it without disturbing previous stack contents. Otherwise, a program that places data in the stack and processes the number of lines returned by *queued()* would consume data already in the stack and possibly intended for other programs.

For example, in Fig. 11.5, the `QUERY DISK (STACK` places one line in the stack for each accessed minidisk or SFS directory. The outer loop processes each line, and creates a stack level for the lines placed in the stack by `LISTFILE`.

```
q = queued()              /* remember number of lines in stack */
'LISTFILE * * A(LIFO'     /* stack new lines LIFO order */
do i = 1 to queued()-q    /* process only newly added lines */
  parse pull fn ft fm .
  .....
end
```

Fig. 11.6 Using LIFO stacking to preserve stack contents.

Another method is to stack lines in `LIFO` order and remember the number of lines to process, as shown in Fig. 11.6.

CMS Pipelines

CMS Pipelines is a powerful extension to CMS developed by John Hartmann of IBM Denmark. CMS Pipelines was inspired by, and is a rich superset of UNIX's *pipe* and stream editor *sed*. Like REXX, Pipelines started as an internal-use tool in IBM, and then was released as an informal program offering in Europe. Users clamored for access to Pipelines, and IBM first released it as a licensed product for all of its sales areas, and then, responding to user acclaim, added it to CMS in VM/ESA Version 1 Release 1.1. Since CMS Pipelines was so recently added to the standard VM product line, it is not yet as well known as REXX. For that reason, and because few texts discuss Pipelines, I'll cover CMS Pipelines in a little more detail than some of the other tools available in the CMS environment.

Unlike UNIX pipes, CMS Pipelines are line-oriented, instead of character-oriented, due to the fundamental differences between the UNIX and VM file models. CMS Pipelines extends the pipeline concept by allowing multi-dimensional pipelines and dynamically changeable pipeline topologies, instead of the purely left-to-right pipes provided in UNIX and MS-DOS. Unlike those system's pipes, CMS Pipelines also syntax checks an entire pipeline specification before executing any of it, instead of partially executing a pipe only to halt with undetermined results if a syntax error is found.

CMS Pipelines is widely considered to be the most important enhancement to CMS since the introduction of REXX. It encourages the use of *pipethink*: a nonprocedural, functional style of programming that bypasses traditional imperative programming methods.[1] This relieves programmers and end users from the step-by-step details of specifying flow of control, loops, and assigning data to variables. Pipelines can be used in conjunction with traditional programming methods to enhance programming effectiveness.

---

[1]Programmers on the way to mastering pipethink are said to be plumbers. Naturally, there are both apprentice and master plumbers!

Pipelines consist of simple programs called stages that pass data from one to another. The output of one stage automatically becomes the input of the following stage. A typical pipeline might look like this:

```
pipe stage1 | stage2 | ... | stageN
```

The PIPE command invokes CMS Pipelines, and the vertical bars are *stage separators*. Pipelines can be invoked from the CMS or XEDIT command lines, or imbedded in REXX programs.

A stage receives input lines from the stage to its left and processes them. Output lines, if any, are sent to the stage to the right. Data flows through a pipeline just like water flows through a real pipe. As with real pipes, each filter or junction may change the flow. I compare pipes to a bucket brigade, in which people in a line pass buckets of water to their neighbors on the right. This emphasizes the idea that each stage receives a single line of input, processes it, passes it to its neighbor, and then turns to the left to await another input. This contrasts with pipe implementations in other systems that run each stage to completion before starting the next stage, and write intermediate data to files. CMS Pipelines multitasks each stage in the pipe specification, and passes data between stages very efficiently.

Stages are device independent, and don't care whether the origin of the data is a disk or tape file or the captured output display from a command, or whether the output is destined to be written to a disk file, displayed on the console, or discarded. This encourages program reuse, since stages and entire pipeline specifications can be reused without change for a variety of inputs and outputs.

Pipe device drivers

Pipelines are connected to the outside world by *device drivers*, special stages that read or write data to external sources. Device drivers may refer to actual devices, like tape or disk files, or they may be conceptual devices that supply or consume data, such as the CMS stack, REXX variables, and literal strings (input only, of course). A list of device drivers is shown in Fig. 11.7.

For a trivial example, the following line is a simplified version of the CMS TYPE command:

```
pipe disk my data a | console
```

This pipeline uses the *disk* device driver to read from the CMS file "MY DATA A" and passes its contents, line by line, to the device driver *console*, which types them on the console. The < symbol is a synonym for the *disk* device driver, and indicates input from a disk file. This should look familiar to UNIX and MS-DOS users, where it represents redirection of standard in-

Driver	Type of data
	(Physical devices)
disk	Read or write a CMS file. "<" and ">" are synonyms
>>	Append to a CMS file
diskupdate	Update records in a CMS file
tape	Read or write a tape file
console	Read or write to the terminal
punch	Write to virtual punch
printer	Write to virtual printer
reader	Read from virtual reader
	(Abstract devices)
stack	Read or write the CMS stack
var, stem	Read or write a REXX variable or stem
CMS	Issue a CMS command
CP	Issue a CP command
XEDIT	Read or write lines from XEDITed file
XMSG	Send data to XEDIT message line
starmsg	Intercept messages from *MSG system service
hole	discard output data ("send to black hole")

Fig. 11.7 Partial list of CMS Pipelines device drivers.

put. The *disk* device driver can also be abbreviated to > for disk output, and >> appends to a file.

Some device drivers' behavior depends on where they appear in a pipeline specification. For example, the *disk* device driver reads from a file if it is the beginning of a pipe, but writes (with replacement) CMS files if it appears elsewhere. Similarly, *console*, *tape*, and *stack* drivers read when the beginning of a pipe, and write otherwise. If not the last stage in a pipeline, these stages pass data to the following stage as well. The following example reads a CMS file, copies it to a second disk file, a tape, and the virtual punch:

```
pipe < large file | > copied file a | tape | punch
```

Pipe filters

CMS Pipelines would not be very interesting if all they did was copy data from one place to another. Instead, CMS Pipelines stages can select and edit the data passing through the pipe. For example, the following pipe selects only records containing the string "hue," and changes every instance of the string "red" to "blue":

```
pipe < red colors | locate /hue/ | change /red/blue/ | > new colors a
```

CMS provides a wide list of *filter* stages like *locate* and *change*. A very partial list appears in Fig. 11.8.

Using Pipelines

CMS Pipelines makes a lot of tasks very simple. Suppose I want to select from a VM accounting data file only the records that correspond to users logon sessions. These records contain the string "01" in columns 79 and 80. I can collect them by issuing the following:

```
pipe < 01151992 account | locate 79-80 /01/ | > 01151992 USERS A
```

The alternative, without Pipelines, would be to write a small program to read each record and write out the records containing the 01 type field. CMS Pipelines lets me describe the output that I want in a functional, declarative way, rather than forcing me to write an imperative program (no matter how simple) that has to deal with handling the end of the file and reading each line.

If I wanted to count the new lines, I could add the following stages to the above Pipeline:

```
.. > 01151992 USERS A | count lines | console
```

Filter	Function
	(Selection filters)
locate	Select lines containing a string
nlocate	Select lines not containing a string
find	Select lines beginning with a string
nfind	Select lines not beginning with a string
take	Select the first (or last) n records in a stream
drop	Throw away the first (or last) n records in a stream
lookup	lookup records in one input stream based on key values in a different input stream
	(Data arrangement filters)
strip	Remove leading and/or trailing characters (usually blanks)
pad	Pad input records to a given length with a pad character
split	split records into multiple records
join	join multiple records into single ones
sort	sort records by column ranges
change	Change record with XEDIT-like specification
xlate	Translate character codes in a string
specs	Rearrange data according to pairs of input-output specifications

Fig. 11.8 Partial list of CMS Pipelines filters.

Each record is passed to the count filter which, instead of passing records immediately to the right, counts input records until an end-of-file is signaled, and then writes the count of records. *Count* is an example of a *buffering* stage, since it logically cannot produce any output till it has consumed all input records. Another buffering stage is *sort*, which sorts its inputs based on column specification. It also cannot produce its first output record until it has read the last input.

Pipelines can do a lot of work from the CMS command line, but are even better when combined with REXX. For a simple example, I frequently filter accounting data in the way described in the previous example. To save myself typing, I use the EXEC shown in Fig. 11.9. Since I'm using an EXEC that is repeated often, I want to pretty up the output. Instead of just typing the number of filtered lines, I use the *specs* to rearrange the data lines according to specifications of input output pairs. *Specs* uses pairs of input and output specifications, which may be column or word ranges or literal data. In this case, I insert the literal text "I kept " starting in output column one, followed by the entire input record (column 1 to *), followed by additional literal text.

Because this is a REXX program, literal data passed to Pipelines is enclosed in apostrophes while REXX variables substitute the changing parts of the command. This is an example of a *portrait style* pipeline specification. Long horizontal pipelines are too hard to read, and eventually don't fit conveniently in the screen display. Splitting them up vertically into separate lines (implicitly concatenated by REXX) makes them easier to read. Some Pipeline plumbers prefer to put the stage separators on the left of the stage in an even line, while others keep them on the right. CMS Pipelines comes with an XEDIT macro named **FMTP** that converts a horizontal pipeline into portrait format.

CMS Pipelines doesn't simply throw away records that are not selected by a *locate*, *find*, or other selection filter. Data can be written to a *sec-*

```
/* Select only logon/logoff records from an accounting file */
address command
parse upper arg fn ft fm fn2 ft2 fm2 .
if fn2 = '' then fn2 = '01' /* default new fileid, if needed */
if ft2 = '' then ft2 = ft
if fm2 = '' then fm2 = fm
'PIPE <' fn ft fm ,
  '| locate 79-80 /01/',
  '| >' fn2 ft2 fm2 'F 80',
  '| count lines',
  '| specs /I kept / 1 1-* next / records./ next',
  '| console'
```

Fig. 11.9 REXX EXEC with Pipe to filter accounting data.

```
'PIPE (endchar ?) < ' fn ft fm , /* "?" ends a pipeline segment */
  '| a: locate 79-80 /01/',
  '| >' fn2 ft2 fm2 'F 80',
  '| count lines',
  '| specs /I kept / 1 1-* next / records./ next',
  '| console',
'?', /* end of first pipeline, beginning of second */
  'a: | > other' ft2 fm2 'F 80', /* save other stuff */
```

Fig. 11.10 Secondary output from Pipe.

ondary output stream, if one is defined. To do this, one defines a label at the selection stage, and then refers to it later in a second pipeline segment. An *endchar* marks the end of a linear pipeline segment. The primary output flows to the stage to the right of the selection stage, as usual, and *secondary output* flows to the stage segment with a label reference to the selection stage.

For example, the pipeline in Fig. 11.10 takes data not selected by *locate* at label *a:* and sends it to the secondary output defined in the second segment. The second segment takes its input and writes it to a file, but could pass the data through other stages, and even send it back to a stage in the first segment. Many other selection filters, such as *find*, *nfind*, and *chop* have secondary, or even tertiary outputs (the first reference to a label is a secondary stream reference, the second is a tertiary stream, and so on) for the data not sent along the primary stream. Several commands support multiple input streams, to allow merging of several streams of information.

Pipelines users very quickly start using Pipes to solve a variety of data massaging applications. For example, a user at my installation wanted to process account report files he was given, but they were formatted for printing, instead of data processing. I wrote the EXEC shown in Fig. 11.11 to strip unneeded data records, eliminate duplicates (parts of the file were repeated), and then sort them in descending dollar value (what he wanted to do anyway).

The EXEC shown in Fig. 11.12 uses CMS Pipelines to perform the same task as the EXEC in Fig. 11.5 with much less work. The first line issues the QUERY DISK command, the second line throws away the QUERY DISK header line, and the third line uses the spec filter to create lines of the form "listfile * * X," where *X* is one of the accessed disks. The next lines pass the LISTFILE commands to CMS for execution, and take their output and create EXEC TALLY commands. The CMS and CP device drivers take the input streams passed to them and send them to their respective command environments. Console output resulting from the commands are passed to the following stage.

```
/* Sort accounting reports. Eliminate unneeded, duplicate records  */
/* Writes new file with filename CHARGES to same disk as input     */
address command
parse upper arg fn ft fm .
'PIPE (name JON)',
  '<' fn ft fm ,                                   /* Read this file */
  '| locate 50-55 /VM/',          /* Lines with such a string cols 50-55 */
  '| spec 41.8 1 115-128 10',         /* select userid and total charge */
  '| sort 10-* d',                     /* sort in descending cost order */
  '| unique 1-* first',         /* report dupes: take 1st instance only */
  '| > CHARGES' ft fm                  /* ft names which report it was */
```

Fig. 11.11 Example of data massaging Pipelines.

```
/* Use a Pipe, instead */
'PIPE cms query disk',        /* issue command and grab output */
  '| drop 1',                 /* drop the standard header line */
  '| spec /listfile * * / 1 12-13 next', /* create LISTFILE * * fm */
  '| cms',                    /* execute generated LISTFILEs */
  '| change //exec tally /'   /* create EXEC TALLY lines */
  '| cms',                    /* execute the TALLY commands */
  '| console'                 /* let it all appear on the console */
```

Fig. 11.12 Pipeline program to process all accessed files.

```
/* ALLMODES REXX subroutine */
'PIPE cms query disk',            /* issue command and grab output */
  '| drop 1',                     /* drop the standard header line */
  '| spec 12-13 1',               /* filemode in either column 12 or 13 */
  '| strip',                      /* remove leading or trailing blanks */
  '*:'                            /* send it to output stream */
```

Fig. 11.13 Pipeline filter to provide accessed disks.

CMS Pipelines lets users make up their own filter and subroutine stages, usually written in REXX. For example, a user frequently needing the filemodes of all accessed disks and directories, could write a small filter consisting of the lines in Fig. 11.13.

The "*:" characters represent a *connector*, indicating that the stream of data emerging from that end of the pipe should be connected to the pipe section this subroutine connects to. This subroutine would be used with a pipeline specification in the form:

```
pipe allmodes | change //listfile * * / | cms .....
```

I use the QSYSTEM filter in Fig. 11.14 to list all the virtual machines currently using a physical disk volume, if I need to vary it offline for hardware maintenance.

QSYSTEM takes as input the device address that is being serviced, and issues the QUERY SYSTEM command to list the users with links to minidisks on it. The *callpipe* command dynamically invokes Pipes to add another (in this case, the first) pipeline stream to the set of active pipes. *Callpipe* is a pipeline tool that dynamically changes a pipeline's topology by creating new streams of data. For example, if a pipeline is passed a stream of file identifiers, callpipe can be used to place each file's contents in the pipe.

The following commands break *qsystem* output into one line per user, and sends them to the next stage of the calling pipeline sequence. I can take the output of this pipeline to send a message to each user by using this:

```
pipe qsystem 321 | specs /WNG / 1 1-8 next / please logoff!/ next | cp
```

The *specs* places the literal string *WNG* in the first positions of the output record, places columns 1 to 8 of the input in the next available positions, and then appends *please logoff*. The final stage issues the assembled WNG (warning) command to each user. Other programmer-defined pipe filters can be used to extend the set of available tools for pipe-building.

These are system-related examples, but Pipelines can be used for true problem-solving applications. The program in Fig. 11.15 uses *lookup* to match two files based on common key portions, a typical data processing application. *Lookup* uses primary and secondary input streams: records in one stream are placed in storage, sorted, and then compared to successive records of the other stream. *Lookup* output is sent to three output streams.

```
/* list users using a disk volume */
/* Usage: pipe qsystem <device> | ...other stages... */
parse upper arg cuu .
if cuu = '' then exit 999
'callpipe (name QSYSTEM)',
  'literal QUERY SYSTEM' cuu     /* QUERY SYSTEM <device> */
  '| cp 150000 ',                /* Give to CP with big buffer */
  '| drop 2 ',                   /* discard header lines */
  '| split at , ',               /* separate lines per user */
  '| strip ',                    /* no leading trailing blanks */
  '| chop 8 ',                   /* select and align userids */
  '| pad 8 ',
  '| sort unique ',              /* remove dupes for users with */
  '| *:'                         /* multiple links, then to output */
```

Fig. 11.14 Pipe subroutine to list users on a disk volume.

```
/* Use Pipelines to match 2 files on common key, and merge
   needed fields into an output file */
address COMMAND
/* Command line contains file ids of the key file and data file,
   and the matched record output file */
parse arg kfn kft kfm dfn dft dfm mfn mft mfm

'PIPE (end \)',
   '<' kfn kft kfm ,               /* Read the key file                  */
  '| spec 1.14 1 28.6 next',       /* desired key file fields only       */
  '| l: lookup 1.8 1.8',           /* Match records from both files      */
  '| join 1 / /',                  /* Join the pair of records           */
  '| spec 1.14 1 / / next 15.7 next 31.21 next / / next 51.3 next',
  '| >' mfn mft mfm 'F' ,          /* Matched records..primary output    */
  '\ <' dfn dft dfm ,              /* secondary input is the data file   */
  '| spec 1.8 1 21.21 next 65.3 next', /* desired data fields only       */
  '| l:'                           /* Meet at lookup stage to merge      */
exit rc
```

Fig. 11.15 Non-linear pipeline used with LOOKUP.

The primary output stream contains pairs of records where the key ranges from the key and data files matched. In this case the pairs of records are joined into a single record and placed in a file. The secondary and tertiary output of *lookup* contains the records in each input stream that were not matched by corresponding records in the other input.

CMS Pipelines also lets programmers create their own filter stages, usually written in REXX, that can be used just like the ones it supplies. For example, the program in Fig. 11.16 uses the REXX interface to CMS Pipelines to read successive lines, evaluate the column specification passed in the command line, and finally output a total.

CMS Pipelines does not make you trade efficiency for expressive capability. It is incredibly efficient, especially for file I/O. It takes a great deal of effort to write a program that performs as well as Pipelines for tasks that read and write files while selecting and altering records. Since the traditional way to process files with several transformations is to write intermediate copies to disk, CMS Pipelines, which processes each record in storage, is almost always far faster. CMS Pipelines is not a toy: it can be used for sizeable data processing applications.

These examples just scratch the surface of what CMS Pipelines can do. It is a powerful enabling technology that is just beginning to be exploited. For a more in-depth introduction, I recommend you read the IBM document *CMS Pipelines Tutorial*, GG66-3158, J. Hartmann, L. Kraines, and J. Lynn, J. Gobeille editor, February 1990.

CMS Global Variables

The GLOBALV command defines *global variables* that can be created, set, and referred to by multiple EXECs, and can retain values across sessions. This is a useful tool for creating applications sharing a pool of data values between multiple commands, and for remembering program options and user preferences between sessions. For example, the DEFAULTS command saves preferences in GLOBALV variables.

Global variables can have the following durations:

- A single CMS IPL. These variables are retained in virtual storage.
- A single CMS session from LOGON to LOGOFF, even if CMS is reIPLed. Data values are saved in a file called SESSION GLOBALV. Users define the beginning of a new session (essentially) by erasing SESSION GLOBALV.
- Permanent variables that persist between CMS sessions. Data values are saved in a file called LASTING GLOBALV.

Global variables can be partitioned into separate groups of variables to avoid name collisions. A group is specified by using the SELECT clause when retrieving or storing individual variables, with the same effect as qualified names in languages like PL/I. Different applications use their own groups to ensure that their variable names are distinct from variables used by other programs.

The GLOBALV command can be issued directly from the terminal in order to list or set variables, but is usually issued from within an EXEC. The most

```
/* ADD REXX: add a column or word range. Pete Gioia     */
/* Input:  Strings with numberic column                 */
/* Output: Total of numeric column                      */
/* Parameters: column range of input (optional)         */
signal on error /* normally till end of file (RC=12)    */
arg colspec .
if colspec = '' then colspec = '1-*'
Tot = 0
do forever
  'readto in' /* reads next line from input stream into 'in' */
  'callpipe var in | spec' colspec '1 | var num' /* select field */
  Tot = Tot + Num
end

ERROR:
if RC = 12 then 'OUTPUT' Tot /* RC=12 indicates EOF - no problem */
exit RC*(RC<>12) /* 0 if RC=0 or RC=12; neither are error states */
```

Fig. 11.16 ADD pipeline filter.

convenient way to access variables is to use **GLOBALV GET <variable>** and **GLOBALV PUT <variable>**. The GET function obtains the value of the specified variable from storage or a GLOBALV file, and copies it into the REXX variable with the same name. The PUT function does the opposite function, by storing the contents of a REXX variable. The PUT subcommand stores a value for the duration of a CMS IPL; PUTS places the value in SESSION GLOBALV, and PUTP (permanent) saves the value in LASTING GLOBALV.

A global variable is used in COMMAND$ EXEC in Fig. 11.17 to retain the cost of the current VM logon session using an installation's chargeback policy. The GLOBALV command selects the variable $SAVE from the group named COMMAND$ (it is good practice to base the name of a private variable group on the command's name), and either issues GET to retrieve the value, or PUT to save it.

The first time COMMAND$ is invoked, no previous value has been saved: the EXEC issues commands to cause it to be invoked at the end of every command, and saves the initial session cost. On every subsequent invocation of this EXEC, the $SAVE variable has a previous value, and the EXEC displays the current session cost and the cost of the most recent command. The $SAVE variable is not a permanent or session variable, so it is reset if the user logs off or reIPLs CMS.

A permanent global variable is used in Fig. 11.18. APL2 applications use a unique APL ID to identify themselves when communicating with APL2 programs running in other virtual machines. APL2 uses this for its own version

```
/* COMMAND$: Get cumulative cost and cost of last command */
address COMMAND
$ = vmcost() /* Current logon session cost from local
                vmcost() routine */
'GLOBALV SELECT COMMAND$ GET $SAVE' /* get saved prior cost */
msg = 'Estimated session charge is $'space(format($,8,2))'.'
if $save <> '' then do  /* If we have a saved prior cost */
  if $save <= $          /* and it's valid, compute difference */
  then msg = msg 'Last command cost' $ - $save
 end
else do          /* No saved cost if first time since IPL */
  'NUCXLOAD COMMAND$ (ENDCMD'          /* Load end-of-command routine */
  'EXECLOAD COMMAND$ EXEC'             /* And this EXEC, to save I/O */
   $save = $                           /* remember current cost */
  'GLOBALV SELECT COMMAND$ PUT $SAVE'
  exit                          /* we'll talk when the endcmd runs */
 end
say msg
$save = $
'GLOBALV SELECT COMMAND$ PUT $SAVE'
```

Fig. 11.17 GLOBALV used to calculate cost of previous command.

```
/* APL2 EXEC: Front end APL2 MODULE to adjust command line, if needed */
address command
parse arg arglist
if pos('ID',argline) = 0 then do     /* No ID specified */
  'GLOBALV SELECT APL2ID GET APLID' /* Do we remember it? */
  if aplid <> '' then arglist = 'ID('strip(aplid)')' arglist
  else do  /* No saved ID - see if one was assigned */
    'PIPE < APL-IDS USERLIST | find' userid() ', /* find userid */
         '| spec word 2 1 | var aplid' /* pick 2nd word as ID */
    if rc=0 & symbol(aplid)<>'LIT' then do
        arglist = 'ID('strip(aplid)')' arglist
        'GLOBALV SELECT APL2ID PUTP APLID' /* remember it! */
      end /* of: found id in userlist */
   end /* of: no id saved in LASTING GLOBALV */
 end /* of: no ID() specified in command line */
'APL2' arglist   /* Call APL2 module with supplied id() */
exit rc
```

Fig. 11.18 GLOBALV used to remember APL2 userid.

of global shared variables, in which APL2 programs can share selected program variables for read or write access with other virtual machines. To use this, each APL2 user must specify a unique APL ID number. The APL2 EXEC reads the APL userid from LASTING GLOBALV. If it wasn't found, it searches a file containing VM userids and their assigned APL IDs. If the APL ID is found, GLOBALV PUTP saves it permanently to eliminate future searches.

NAMEFIND

CMS provides another useful data-manipulation tool in the **NAMEFIND** command, which looks up values associated with a nickname. Nickname data is stored in **NAMES** files, which contain entries located by nickname. The file **userid NAMES**, where *userid* is the VM userid, contains nickname information used by the NOTE, SENDFILE, RECEIVE, and TELL commands. Other NAMES files can be built for application purposes.

NAMES file entries consist of entries identified by a user-specified *nickname*, and a set of arbitrary identifier names called *tags*, and the values assigned to them. Each tag and value pair is of the form :tagname.tagvalue. For example, a NAMES file might contain the following lines:

```
:nick.jeff     :name.Jeff Savit      :userid.JBS
                    :phone.555-1212
:nick.jcb      :name.John Bacas      :userid.JCB
```

The command “namefind :nick jeff” displays all the information associated with my nickname, and “namefind :nick jcb :userid” displays John's userid

```
namefind :nick peteg :userid
PETERG
Ready;
namefind :nick dennis
:nick DENNIS
:userid DJM
:node VMSYSA
:notebook DENNIS
:name Dennis M.
Ready;
```

Fig. 11.19 NAMEFIND.

tag. Searches need not only be done by nickname: they can be performed using any unique identifier for a nickname entry. For example, "namefind :userid jcb :nick" would display the nickname associated with the userid JCB.

NAMEFIND output can be sent to the terminal or to the stack, where it can be processed by an enclosing EXEC. IBM uses NAMES files with the NOTE, SENDFILE, RECEIVE, and TELL commands to look up the userid, notebook and node names associated with a nickname. Output from NAMEFIND is shown in Fig. 11.19.

Languages

The VM/CMS environment hosts a wide variety of programming languages, including Ada, APL2, BASIC, COBOL, RPG, Fortran, PL/I, C, Pascal, Modula-2, SNOBOL, PROLOG, LISP, SIMSCRIPT, and, of course REXX.

By and large, CMS implements the programming model defined in each language. For example, PL/I programs acquire storage via the ALLOCATE statement, and perform file I/O with the GET, PUT, READ, and WRITE statements. The high-level language programmer codes for the language model, not for CMS. There are occasional exceptions, due to CMS restrictions. For example, PL/I multitasking is not available in the single-task CMS environment.

Program Linkage Conventions

CMS invokes modules with the following standard register contents:

- R0 contains the address of an *Extended Parameter List*, or `EPLIST` containing the command line used to invoke the program. The EPLIST is optional, and is described further below.
- R1 contains the address of a tokenized parameter list, or `PLIST` containing the command line chopped into adjacent, uppercase, 8-character tokens. Words longer than 8 characters are truncated, and shorter words are padded on the right with blanks. The end of the list is indicated by an

8-byte *fence* containing all one-bits (8 bytes of hexadecimal 'FF'). For 24-bit mode addressing applications, R1 also contains, in its upper byte, a flag describing whether the program was called with an EPLIST, as well as other linkage attributes.

- R12 and R15 contain the entry point address of the routine. R15 is used as the entry point address by convention in all IBM systems, but is also used as a work register. As a convenience to the programmer, CMS places the entry point address in R12 as well, where the program can use it as the module's base register. On exit, R15 contains the program's return code: a return code of zero indicates successful execution.
- R13 contains the address of a save area provided by CMS. The application stores its callers registers in the save area by using the STM (store multiple) instruction, and reloads them by issuing the LM (load multiple) instruction. The save area is mapped by the USERSAVE macro, and also contains a copy of the call type byte.
- R14 contains the return address the program branches to when it finishes execution.

The tokenized parameter list was present in CMS since its earliest days, and makes it easy for applications to scan their command lines. Instead of parsing the beginning and ending of each word, the application simply marches through a list of 8 byte tokens until it reaches the fence. The CMS command-line interpreter calls a scanner routine that converts the user's command line into the tokenized PLIST, and appends the fence. For example, the CMS command, "erase my data a(type" becomes

```
PLIST    DC    CL8'ERASE   '   8-byte tokens for each word
         DC    CL8'MY      '
         DC    CL8'DATA    '
         DC    CL8'A       '       DC     CL8'(        '
         DC    CL8'TYPE    '
         DC    8X'FF`          End of PLIST fence
```

The CMS command interpreter locates the command based on the first word in the PLIST, as described in the section on SVC 202 processing. The command can process each of the words in the parameter list with a minimum of logic.

While this is convenient, it is also unusable for words longer than 8 characters or for lowercase strings. With VM/SP, IBM added the extended parameter list, which is in the following format:

```
EPLIST   DC    A(cmdname)  Address of command name
         DC    A(begarg)   Address of beginning of arguments
         DC    A(endarg)   Address of end of arguments
         DC    F'0'        User communication word
```

```
* Trap the first instruction of the 'test' command
cp trace inst range 20000.4
Ready;
test this is a command line
 -> 00020000 STM  90ECD00C >> 000095F4   CC 0

* We're stopped at the beginning of the program. Show registers 0, 1
 display g0-1
GPR 0 = 00000E08 0B000848
* Display tokenized Plist from R1 address
 d t848.30
R00000840 C5E7C5C3 40404040 E3C5E2E3 40404040 F6 *EXEC  TEST
R00000850 E3C8C9E2 40404040 C9E24040 40404040    *THIS  IS
R00000860 C1404040 40404040 C3D6D4D4 C1D5C440    *A     COMMAND
R00000870 D3C9D5C5 40404040 FFFFFFFF FFFFFFFF    *LINE  ........
* Display extended Plist from R0 address
 display e08.10
R00000E08 00000740 00000747 0000075D 00000000 F6
* Display verb and arguments from EPLIST addresses
 display t740-750
R00000740 A385A2A3 404040A3 8889A240 89A24081 F6 *test     this is a
R00000750 40839694 94819584 40938995 85404040    * command line
```

Fig. 11.20 Tokenized and extended CMS Plists.

For example, in the ERASE command used in the previous example, A(cmdname) would contain the address of the ERASE verb, A(begarg) would point to the letter "M" in MY, and A(endarg) would point to the end of the command string. The relationship between the tokenized and extended parameter list is shown in Fig. 11.20.

This convention lets commands process long command line operands, although this can require more programming effort for parsing. To a certain extent, this applies solely to assembly language programmers. PL/I programmers access the command line parameters as a varying length character string, C programs use the standard *argc* and *argv* variables, and REXX programmers have the convenience and flexibility of the *parse arg* instruction. IBM introduced the **PARSECMD** command and macro to make this easier. PARSECMD parses a command line string according to a user-specified description file. This is discussed in the section on national language support (NLS).

The presence or absence of an extended parameter list, as well as other options, is signaled by the **CALLTYP** flag. In 24-bit addressing applications, this flag appears in the high-order byte of R1 (where it does not interfere with address references to the PLIST). For 31-bit applications, the flag is placed in the USECTYP field in the USERSAVE pointed to by register 13. The call type values are as follows:

- X'00'—PROGRAM: No extended parameter list was supplied.
- X'01'—EPLIST: An extended parameter list was supplied.
- X'02'—SUBCOM: The program is invoked by the SUBCOM program interface. SUBCOM lets applications declare named entry points that can be invoked as commands via SVC. For example, XEDIT defines SUBCOM entry points, active during an XEDIT session, that can be invoked as a command by REXX macros.
- X'03'—NONUCXE: An extended parameter list was supplied, but command processing should bypass searching for a nucleus extension. This is often used by nucleus extensions that front-end a command, in order to call the "true" command whose invocations they intercept.
- X'04'—NONUCXT: Like NONUCXE, except that no extended parameter list was supplied.
- X'05'—FUNCTION: Calls a REXX function or subroutine.
- X'0B'—CMS: Simulates command invocation from the terminal, and passes both the tokenized and extended parameter lists. CMS performs full command search, using implied CP and EXEC search if they are in effect.

Program loading and MODULE creation

Language processors produce TEXT files containing object code, the names of separately compiled programs and data areas, and address constants. The **LOAD** command loads object code from TEXT files into memory, resolving external references to procedures (for example, FORTRAN subroutines and C functions), and relocating address constants relative to the origin address the programs are loaded at. The **INCLUDE** appends additional TEXT files to the programs already loaded into memory. The result is a program image loaded into virtual storage, ready to be started up immediately, or saved on disk for future execution.

External references are resolved by looking for TEXT files on any accessed disk with the same name as the external symbol, or by searching for a TEXT file stored within a TXTLIB ("text library"). For example, if a Fortran program MAIN calls a subroutine named RANDU, the LOAD command will search for a file named RANDU TEXT, and failing that, search through a list of *globalled* TXTLIBs for a member named RANDU. The **GLOBAL TXTLIB** command specifies which libraries to search. Each IBM language product comes with its own libraries, with the exception that C/370 and the PL/I Optimizing compiler share a common library.

LOAD uses CMS *loader* tables to resolve program addresses. As programs are loaded into storage, their entry point names and addresses are added to the tables, and the names of subroutines they refer to are entered in the table and marked as "undefined." Automatically loaded subroutines themselves may cause other files to be loaded into memory. The process continues until all external references have been satisfied, or all available TEXT and TXTLIB files have been searched.

If there are missing subroutines, the LOAD command types an error message listing the external symbols it could not satisfy. Loader tables are also used while a program is running. Applications can dynamically load programs via the **LOAD**, **LINK**, or **XCTL** macros. If the called program is already loaded into storage, CMS uses the address it resides at, otherwise it searches for an appropriately named TEXT file or TXTLIB member.

Once a program has been loaded into memory, it can be immediately executed by issuing the command **START**, or alternatively, the START option can be specified on the LOAD command. For example, a Fortran program can be compiled and loaded into storage by the following two commands:

```
fortvs2 zork
load zork(start
```

The **GENMOD** command saves a loaded program to disk as a MODULE file, which is a ready-to-run saved program image. MODULEs make it unnecessary to perform the LOAD and search process each time a program is run. MODULEs also let programs be invoked as commands. CMS invokes the internal function **LOADMOD** to read the saved program image from disk into the storage locations it was loaded into when it was created. The following commands create the ZORK command from the ZORK source:

```
fortvs2 zork
load zork
genmod zork
```

Programs are usually loaded at the default load address, hexadecimal 20000, the beginning of the user area (exceptions are described below). Programs can also be loaded into explicitly specified locations, for example, to create a planned overlay structure.

The LOAD option **ORIGIN TRANS** loads a program in the CMS *transient area*, an 8KB area starting at hexadecimal location E000. Transient area modules are used for small utility programs that may be invoked from within a command residing in the user area. Transient area commands are not reread from disk if invoked twice in succession. Instead, the copy already residing in storage is reused. EXEC command performance can be improved by re-executing the same transient command before using a different one, avoiding "transient area thrashing" that repeatedly reads module files from disk.

Transient area programs must be *serially reusable*. Specifically, they must reinitialize all their data areas every time they are used. Otherwise, residual storage values from their previous execution would be used when the command is reissued.

By default, address constants in a loaded program are non-relocatable, and the resulting program image can only execute in the storage locations it was loaded into when built. This is an inconvenience when creating applications that issue CMS commands. Such programs may attempt to invoke other programs loaded at the same storage addresses—CMS does not permit this.

The RLDSAVE option on the LOAD command avoids this problem by saving *relocation dictionary* information with the loaded program image and resulting MODULE file. The relocation dictionary contains the location of every address constant in the MODULE. Each address constant can then be adjusted for different origin addresses when CMS loads the program for execution. A relocatable MODULE can therefore be loaded to any unused storage location in a virtual machine, instead of its original address. The minor cost of relocatable MODULEs is that they occupy more disk space than non-relocatable ones, and take a little more CPU time to load into storage. The ability to freely invoke commands from one another is well worth the slight overhead.

The CMS loader compatibly handles programs written to exploit XA-mode storage addressing and older programs written for 24-bit addressing. Programs in TEXT files have **RMODE** and **AMODE** attributes that specify the *residency* and *addressing* modes they require for applications. Programs with RMODE 24 have 24 byte addressing for program data, and can only reside below the 16MB address line. Programs with RMODE ANY or RMODE 31 can reside either above or below the 16MB line. Programs with AMODE 24 use 24-bit addressing, and can only be passed parameters that reside below the 16MB line. AMODE ANY applications can refer to data in any storage address. CMS automatically copies parameter lists to locations below the 16MB line when invoking an AMODE 24 command.

The CMS loader attempts to load programs into the most general locations compatible with their RMODE settings. For 370-mode virtual machines, all programs must execute below the 16MB line, and are loaded by default at the beginning of the user area. In XA and ESA mode virtual machines, CMS attempts to load the program above the 16MB line if permitted by its RMODE, and uses the largest available contiguous block of storage as the initial load address.

If the load process starts by loading 31-bit RMODE programs above the line and then encounters a below-the-line TEXT file, it discards the partially constructed load image above the 16MB line, and restarts the process below the line. The command **SET LOADAREA 20000** tells CMS to load programs at 20000 when in XA mode, even when their RMODEs permit execution above the line. This option, the default for 370-mode machines, ensures compatibility for modules built in XA-mode environments but executed in 370-mode. **SET LOADAREA RESPECT**, the default in XA and ESA-mode, uses the "best" above-the-line location available.

AMODE and RMODE attributes are propagated into the loader tables for in-storage invocation of the program, and are saved with the MODULE file when GENMOD is issued. AMODE and RMODE options on the LOAD and GENMOD command lines let the user override the information saved with TEXT decks.

Application Program Interfaces

CMS provides several application program interfaces (APIs) for compiled and assembly language programs:

- Native CMS
- OS/MVS
- DOS/VSE
- Callable Subroutine Library, also used with REXX programs

The native interface is invoked by assembler macros, and is implicitly invoked by commands and OS and DOS simulation. Among the many CMS program macros are the following:

- CMSSTOR—Obtain or release a block of virtual storage. CMS also supports an older DMSFREE macro, which provides the same functions, but only supports storage below the 16M address line.
- SUBPOOL—Declare or remove of named subpool of storage. CMSSTOR calls can acquire storage from a named subpool. All the storage belonging to a subpool can be released in a single macro call.
- FSREAD, FSWRITE, FSOPEN, FSCLOSE, FSPOINT—Perform file I/O. These macros are discussed further in Chapter 12.
- CMSCALL—Invoke another CMS command.
- LINEWRT, LINERD, CONSOLE—Write and read from the CMS console. WRTERM and RDTERM macros are supported for compatibility, and work with applications operating below the 16M line.
- APPLMSG—Generate a message line with substituted text values, and optionally display it on the console. Message text can be included in the

program's body, or can be loaded from a *message repository*. Message repositories are part of national language support (NLS). Applications can display messages in different languages by selecting different repository files.

- LINEDIT—Generate a message line with substituted text. This macro predates APPLMSG, and neither uses a message repository nor operates above the 16M line.
- CMSSTACK—Place a line in the CMS stack
- PARSECMD—Parse command line arguments according to a template.
- ANCHOR—Locate an "anchor" control block in virtual storage. This lets applications find a control area whose location may be unknown until run-time. IBM provides a registering service that assigns anchor word names to applications.
- NUCEXT—Load or purge a nucleus extension program preloaded into virtual storage.
- HNDEXT, HNDIO, HNDINT, HNDSVC—Set up or clear interrupt handlers for external, I/O, and SVC interrupts.
- ABNEXIT—Set up or clear an exit to be called when a program abnormally terminates (crashes).

CMS SVC Interface

As in IBM's other operating systems, CMS system functions are invoked by SVC (supervisor call) instructions. SVC instructions usually indicate which function is requested via the SVC number, a value from 0 to 255 in the second byte of the instruction. MVS and DOS/VSE use a wide value of SVC numbers, mostly clustered in the numeric values under 100. To avoid collision with these SVCs, CMS uses only SVCs 201 to 204 for its own purposes. Other SVC numbers are implicitly passed to OS or DOS simulation. Applications can issue the `HNDSVC` macro to specify routines to receive control when specific SVC instructions are issued.

SVC 201 is used by the `CMSRET` macro, and causes CMS to return from a program invoked by any of the other CMS SVCs to the previous SVC level. The CMSRET macro lets the programmer specify which general purpose and floating point registers should be returned to the caller with new values. The fullword after the SVC 201 instruction contains a 16-bit bit-map for the general registers followed by a 4-bit field for the floating point registers. If a bit is on, the corresponding register value is given to the returning program, instead of restoring the caller's original register contents.

SVC 203 is generated by some CMS macros, such as DMSFREE and DMSEXS, and uses an encoded halfword value immediately after the SVC instruction to specify which function is used. The expansion of these macros is usually of the form:

```
LA    R0,some_value     Set parameter register
LA    R1,other_value    Set parameter register
SVC   203               Call CMS
DC    H'xxxxx'           Value interpeted by CMS
...
```

CMS uses the halfword following the SVC instruction as a branch table index into a lookup table in the CMS module DMSFNC. This table contains the addresses of numerous CMS routines at unchanging offsets. CMS adds the absolute value of the halfword to the address of the table, selects the address constant at that location, and branches to it. This provides an extremely quick method for deriving the nucleus address of modules implementing SVC functions, but is less "open" and extensible than the SVC 202 and SVC 204 methods discussed below.

CMS adds 2 to the SVC old PSW address to return to the instruction after the halfword code. The sign of the halfword value specifies the action CMS should take if there is an error. If the value is negative, CMS returns to the application with an error indication in register 15. Otherwise, CMS ABENDs (abnormally ends) the program.

SVC 202 and 204 are closely related. Both invoke commands and system functions by name, instead of by a numeric value. Most CMS functions are invoked through SVC 202 or 204, instead of using a different SVC number for each function (as is standard in MVS and DOS), or using a different SVC 203 halfword value. This provides a much larger name space for creating new functions (there are only 256 possible SVC numbers) or having to worry about collisions with previously assigned code values.

CMS locates a routine called by SVC 202 or 204 by searching the list of nucleus extension routines loaded into storage, and then searches a table of internal commands and their addresses listed in DMSFNC. If the requested command is in neither table, CMS searches the accessed disks or SFS directories to locate the command. In other words, the same mechanism is used to invoke system functions and user commands, which adds generality and lets user applications transparently look like part of the system.

SVC 202 was present in CMS in its earliest days when CMS stood for the *Cambridge Monitor System* (the number 202 was selected, it is claimed, because 202 in hexadecimal is CA, which stood for Cambridge). SVC 204 is the 31-bit, bimodal-CMS version of SVC 202, introduced because SVC 202 relies on 24-bit addresses.

SVC 202 uses the following calling sequence to invoke a CMS command:

```
LA    R0,EPLIST          R0 := @extended parameter list
LA    R1,PLIST           R1 := @parameter list
```

```
ICM   R1,B'1000',CALLTYP   'Call type' in upper byte
SVC   202                  Call CMS
DC    A(error_exit)        Error exit address (optional)
```

This calling sequence is restricted to 24-bit applications for two reasons: the high order byte of R1 contains a flag value, and therefore is explicitly a 24-bit-only interface. Second, CMS determines whether the address of an error exit routine follows the SVC instruction by comparing the byte following the SVC to zero. Since no instructions have a zero-value opcode, this test works only with 24-bit addresses. As with SVC 203, CMS ABENDs the application if an error occurred and the programmer did not provide an error exit. The programmer can also provide the constant address of 1 for the error exit. In this case, CMS branches to the next sequential instruction, and the programmer checks for an error by testing the return code in register 15.

SVC 204 callers pass flag information through R15, thus letting R1 be used for full 31-bit addresses. SVC 204 is normally invoked through IBM macros, instead of being "hand-coded" as SVC 202 frequently was. For example, the CMSCALL macro is used to replace the in-line code sequence shown above. When the called program completes, register 15 contains its return code. The CMSCALL macro lets the programmer specify an error routine address or ask CMS to ABEND the application.

When an AMODE 31 application is invoked, CMSCALL places 31-bit addresses in its registers, and lets its parameter reside anywhere in storage. When an AMODE 24 application is invoked, CMS relocates its arguments below the 16M address line, if necessary, and places the traditional call type flag in R1 for compatibility.

OS simulation

CMS simulates application interfaces in MVS by mapping MVS/XA system calls into native CMS functions. This is referred to as *OS simulation*, a name that has not changed since the operating system CMS emulated was OS/360. CMS also provides DOS simulation by emulating the system calls used under DOS/VSE.

OS and DOS simulation is far from complete (CMS would then have to be extremely complex), but is sufficient to let most higher level language applications, and assembler language programs that do not refer to MVS or DOS control blocks, run on either CMS and MVS or CMS and DOS/VSE without change. In particular, most high-level language compilers running under CMS use OS or DOS simulation to execute. CMS's willingness to simulate program interfaces from MVS and DOS/VSE lets IBM use the same compilers, libraries and compiled code under CMS, MVS, and DOS/VSE. I will focus on MVS simulation because most higher-level language implementations for CMS use the MVS API.

Higher level language programs use their standard statements for invoking system functions like file I/O, timer support, and storage management. These statements compile into the control blocks and call formats recognized by MVS. When compiled code or language support libraries issue a system call, CMS automatically maps the OS/MVS-style requests into the underlying macro, as shown in Fig. 11.21.

CMS automatically converts OS/MVS-style requests into the corresponding CMS macro. In some cases there is no equivalent CMS macro, and assembly programmers under CMS use the MVS-compatible macro even if they have no need for compatibility with MVS. A table of some of the MVS macros simulated by CMS appears in Fig. 11.22.

Not all macros and macro options are simulated, and some are only partially simulated. For example, the MVS **EXTRACT** macro has options to return addresses of MVS control blocks that are not simulated under CMS. The **ENQ** and **DEQ** macros, which serialize access to logical resources, are meaningless in a single-user environment like CMS and are ignored. Under MVS, the **ATTACH** macro creates an asynchronously executing subtask. Under CMS, ATTACH invokes a new program, but the program that invoked it does not continue execution until it completes.

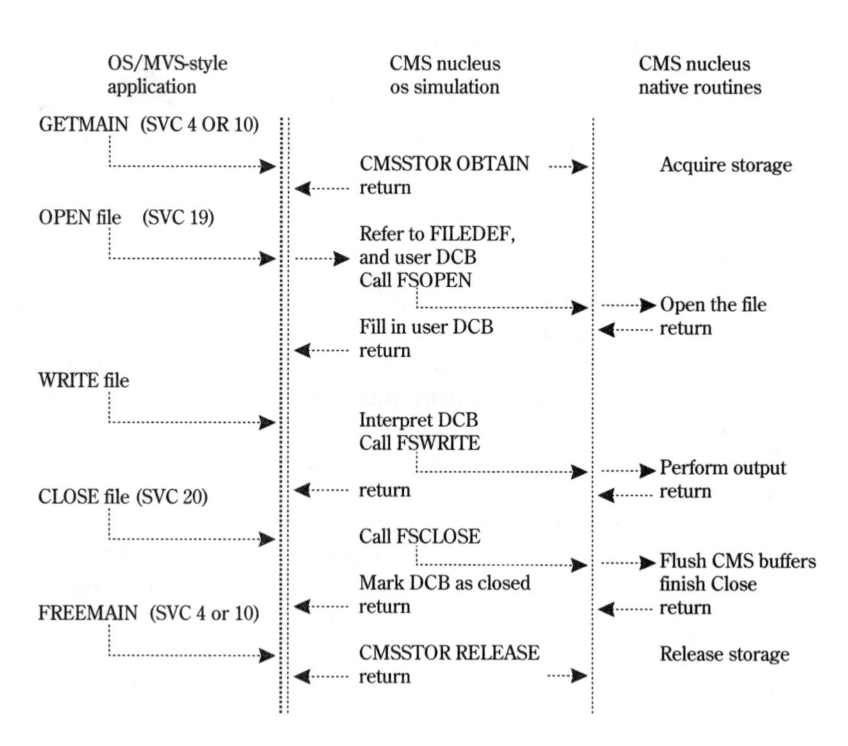

Fig. 11.21 OS/MVS simulation flow.

MVS macro	CMS equivalent	Notes
	(Storage management)	
GETMAIN	CMSSTOR	Acquire virtual storage
FREEMAIN	CMSSTOR	Release virtual storage
	(Interrupt and event handling)	
STAE, ESTAE	ABNEXIT	Set up error exits
TIME	n/a	Obtain date and time of day
STIMER,TTIMER	n/a	Set or cancel a timer 'alarm'
WAIT, POST	n/a	Wait for or signal an event
STAX	HNDINT	Specify terminal attention exit
	(Program management)	
LOAD	n/a	Dynamic module load
LINK	n/a	Link to a separate load module
ATTACH	n/a	Create subtask
	(Input/Output)	
TPUT,TGET	LINERD,LINEWRT	Terminal input/output
WTO	LINEWRT	'Write To Operator'
OPEN	FSOPEN	Open a file for processing
GET, READ	FSREAD	Read a logical record or block
PUT, WRITE	FSWRITE	Write a logical record or block
CHECK	n/a	Test for a completed I/O
CLOSE	FSCLOSE	Close a file
FIND	n/a	Open a member of a library
STOW	n/a	Save a member of a library
NOTE	FSPOINT	Direct access I/O
POINT	FSPOINT	Direct access I/O
RDJFCB	n/a	"Read Job File Control Block"
DEVTYPE	n/a	Obtain device characteristics

Fig. 11.22 Partial list of OS/MVS simulation and native macros.

Callable Subroutine Library

The CMS Callable Subroutine Library provides a wide variety of programming services to higher level languages. CSL routines can be called from REXX, PL/I, COBOL, Fortran, C and Pascal, using the Call statement in each language, and from assembly language programs. Calls are actually made to the interface subroutine *DMSCSL*, which invokes the CSL routine whose name is passed as a character string in the first parameter to DMSCSL. The second parameter is always the integer return code provided by the CSL call. Remaining parameters depend on which CSL routine was invoked. CSL call syntax is illustrated in Fig. 11.23.

CSL functions are named with an easily remembered convention. All begin with the characters `DMS` (the standard IBM prefix for CMS components), followed by a suffix that names the operation (`GET`, `DE` for "delete," `CR` for "delete," `CL` for "close"), and the object being processed (`DIR` for "directory," `LO` for "lock," `ALI` for "alias"). Names are abbreviated to allow the command verb to fit in eight characters. One could make the case that

```
FORTRAN:
  Call DMSCSL(rtnname,retcode,parm1,...,parmN)

COBOL:
  Call "DMSCSL" USING rtnname,retcode,parm1,...,parmN.

PL/I:
  Call DMSCSL(rtnname,retcode,parm1,...,parmN);

Pascal:
  DMSCSL(rtnname,retcode,parm1,...,parmN);

C: /* must use & to pass parameters that receive values */
  dmscsl(rtnname,&retcode,parm1,...,parmN)

REXX: /* Pass REXX variable names */
  csl('rtnname retcode parm1 ... parmN')   /* or, */
  call csl 'rtnname retcode parm1 ... parmN'
```

Fig. 11.23 CSL call syntax in different languages.

longer identifiers should have been made possible to make them more easily readable, albeit harder to type.

CSL provides too many functions to enumerate here. Many functions provide direct access to facilities normally provided by system commands, such as the ability to copy, erase, and rename files, grant and revoke file authorizations, create or erase SFS directories, and many others. The file system calls are described "SFS Callable Subroutine Library Functions" on page 308.

A valuable CSL call lets programs interact with the CMS command and REXX environments. The **DMSCCE** procedure lets programs issue REXX EXECs, which can then execute any desired combination of commands. Programs can also use CSL calls to get and set the values of REXX variables in EXECs that invoke them. The REXX program in Fig. 11.24 sets two REXX variables. The C program in Fig. 11.25 prompts the user for the names of REXX variables, obtains them via a call to the CSL routine DMSCGR, and displays them.

Extract/Replace

One of the most important CSL functions is **DMSERP**, the *Extract/Replace* function, which provides access to most of the environmental switches that control the behavior of a CMS session.

Before IBM provided the extract/replace function, programs that interact with the CMS system environment resorted to a variety of methods for obtaining system information. Programmers often had to use assembler language subroutines to obtain this information, which frequently meant that systems programmers were needed. Programmers used undocumented (and therefore changeable) program interfaces and storage locations. This made conversion to a new release of CMS a potentially risky experience for assembly language programs. Programs in FORTRAN, COBOL, PL/I and other higher level languages that use interfaces defined in their language definitions and the *IBM Programmers Guide* manuals rarely were affected by changes to CMS releases.

```
/* REXX variable made available to C */
address command
happy = 'I am so happy'
sad   = 'I am so sad'
'EXECOS CSLDEMOC'
```

Fig. 11.24 REXX program used to demonstrate CSL calls.

```
/* CSLDEMOC - Example of how to invoke a Callable Services Library
   function from a C programme */
#include <stdio.h>
#include <ctype.h>
#define RXSTRLN 256
/* pragma linkage is necessary to tell the compiler to build an
   OS-format plist for the called subroutine */
#pragma linkage(dmscsl, OS)
main()
{
  extern void dmscsl();
  unsigned char rxvar_name[RXSTRLN], rxvar_val[RXSTRLN];
  long int rxname_len, rxval_out = 255l, rxval_full, cslcode;
  int i;

  printf("Please enter the name of a REXX variable.\n");
  scanf("%s", rxvar_name);
  rxname_len = strlen(rxvar_name);
  for (i = 0; i <= rxname_len; i++)
    rxvar_name[i] = toupper(rxvar_name[i]);
  dmscsl("DMSCGR  ", &cslcode, rxvar_name, &rxname_len,
       rxvar_val, &rxval_out, &rxval_full);
  if (cslcode == 0) {
    printf("%s's value is \"%s\".\n", rxvar_name, rxvar_val);
    printf("The full length is %ld.\n", rxval_full);
  }
  else printf("CSL return code %ld\n", cslcode);
}
```

Fig. 11.25 C program using CSL calls to get REXX variables.

REXX programmers have always had access to many system variables by issuing CMS and CP commands and displaying the message text, or by inspecting storage. Unfortunately, neither method is a sanctioned programming interface. For example, programs can be broken if IBM or an installation alter the format of a message, or if a user uses the **SET LANGUAGE** command to generate messages in a language other than American English.

VM user groups asked IBM to provide a stable program interface to CMS environmental variables, a request sometimes stated in the form "Document and officially support the interfaces built into CMS." In some cases IBM did exactly that, but in other cases they wanted to provide an application program interface that allowed them to change CMS without breaking a documented interface customers relied on.

The Extract/Replace function in CSL provides exactly this capability. It provides a generalizable method to let applications query (extract) and set (replace) a wide variety of system variables, ranging from the current version of CMS, to the number of lines in the console stack, to whether of not implied EXEC (IMPEX) is turned on or off. Some of these items were available to REXX or assembler programs; others were only available to programs dependent on the current CMS implementation. DMSERP provides a general program interface that can be expected to remain compatible over different releases of VM.

DMSERP is called with the following arguments, in this example using PL/I syntax:

```
Call DMSCSL('DMSERP  ',       /* Invoke extract/replace   */
            retcode,          /* return code from CSL     */
            funct,            /* 'EXTRACT' or 'REPLACE'   */
            numArgs,          /* number of arguments      */
            infoname,         /* extract/replace variable */
            buffer,           /* receives EXTRACT data,   */
                              /* or supplies REPLACE data */
            datatyp,          /* datatype flag            */
            buflen);          /* buffer length            */
```

IBM documentation refers to the extract/replace variable as the *information name*, or *infoname*, to emphasize that variables are identified by preassigned names. Not all of the variables can be altered by extract/replace—a disk cannot be changed from read-only to read-write status by replacing the value associated with the infoname "CMS_READ_ONLY_DISK." The current replaceable items are variables that can also be changed by existing CMS commands, which may not be accessible to compiled programs. A REXX program using Extract/Replace is shown in Fig. 11.26.

This particular infoname wouldn't be requested by a REXX program because the *storage()* function returns the same result, however the same technique can be used for data not retrievable by REXX functions or CMS commands. What is really important is that a PL/I program, which has no built-in access to this type of information, now can retrieve it through CSL

```
/* Play with Extract/Replace routines */
rc = 0; narg = 0
inam = left('VIRTUAL_MEMORY_SIZE',20)
xbuf = left(' ',4)
xLEN = 4; dtyp = 4
inam = left('VIRTUAL_MEMORY_SIZE',20)
call csl 'DMSERP RC EXTRACT NARG INAM XBUF DTYP XLEN'
vmsize = c2d(left(xbuf,4)) /* binary number into string */
say 'Virtual memory size is' vmsize 'bytes =' vmsize/1024 || 'K'
```

Fig. 11.26 REXX Extract/Replace example.

```
/* Demonstrate Extract/Replace in PL/I */
testerp: proc options(main);
 dcl dmscsl  entry options(asm inter),
    rtnname  char(8) initial('DMSERP'),
    rc       fixed bin(31),
    funct    char(8) initial('RESET'),
    numargs  fixed bin(31) initial(0),
    infoname char(20),
    buffer   fixed bin(31),
    cbuffer  character(8),
    buflen   fixed bin(31) initial(4),
    datatype fixed bin(31) initial(4),
    xlen     fixed bin(31);
 call dmscsl(rtnname,rc,funct); /* Issue RESET */
 funct   = 'EXTRACT'; infoname = 'VIRTUAL_MEMORY_SIZE';
 call dmscsl(rtnname,rc,funct,numargs,infoname,buffer,
          datatype,buflen);
 put edit('Virtual memory size is',buffer,' bytes')(a,f(12),a);
 put edit(' = ',buffer/1024,'K')(a,f(4),a);
 infoname = 'INITIAL_FILE_POOL_ID';
 buflen  = length(cbuffer);
 call dmscsl(rtnname,rc,funct,numargs,infoname,cbuffer,
          datatype,buflen);
 put edit('Initial file pool',cbuffer)(col(1),a,a);
 infoname = 'CURRENT_FILE_POOL_ID';
 call dmscsl(rtnname,rc,funct,numargs,infoname,cbuffer,
          datatype,buflen);
 put edit('Current file pool',cbuffer)(col(1),a,a);
end testerp;
```

Fig. 11.27 PL/I Extract/Replace example.

with only a few lines of code. The PL/I example in Fig. 11.27 retrieves the same information, plus the initial and current SFS filepool assigned to the user.

Optional parameters can specify search parameters for selecting results from CMS variables with multiple occurrences. For example, the information name "DISK_BLKSIZE" requires specification of a disk.

The following is a very small subset of the information names accessible by extract/replace. The total list can be obtained by issuing the command "help routine dmserin":

- CMS_XA_MODE—Indicates if the virtual machine is in XA mode.
- VIRTUAL_MEMORY_SIZE—Virtual machine storage size.
- NO_TYPE_HT—The "Halt Typing" flag is in effect to suppress typing CMS console output (this flag can be changed by issuing REPLACE).
- NUM_FILES—The number of files in a disk or directory.
- DEV_TYPE—The encoded device type for a specified virtual device.
- DEV_INT_ADDR—The storage address of the interrupt routine address for the specified device.
- FILE_NUM_REC—The number of records in the first CMS file matching the supplied search criteria.
- FILE_DIRECTORY_ID—The fully qualified SFS directory containing a file matching the search criteria.

Coordinated resource recovery

CMS provides *coordinated resource recovery* (CRR), which uses *two-phase commit* to commit or rollback changes made in a series of transaction steps called a *Logical Unit of Work* (LUW). SFS uses CRR to either fully commit or backout changes to a file. In fact, CRR is implemented in an SFS filepool server, normally named VMSERVR. Options in the filepool server configuration file tell it to act as a CRR server instead of a normal SFS file system.

CRR is also used to synchronize changes made by a single application executing in multiple VM systems, an essential part of reliable distributed applications. Two-phase commit ensures that all partners in a distributed application are ready to commit their changes before any of them commit them. This prevents having a distributed database or file change that occurs only in some of the systems running the application.

CMS commands normally execute with a default LUW. CMS also provides CSL calls that let programmers define and terminate multiple LUWs in the same command. All file changes made in a single LUW can be committed or rolled back at the same time.

For example, a CSL application could decide after doing part of a file update that the file changes have to be aborted if the data was found to be invalid. The application could rollback all of the changes to the file. All write operations done to that point, even across multiple files, would be nullified. CSL provides the following calls to manage LUWs:

- DMSGETWU—Get a unique logical unit of work.
- DMSRETWU—Return a unit of work and commit its changes.

- DMSQRYWU—Query the current unit of work's name.
- DMSPURWU—Purge a unit of work and its changes.
- DMSCOMMIT—Commit changes associated with a work unit.
- DMSROLLB—Roll back changes associated with a work unit.

Fullscreen Dialogue Managers

In addition to the fullscreen programming interfaces provided by CMS Session Services, CMS application programmers have access to a variety of commercially available fullscreen panel and dialogue managers. Among the most popular are `XMENU` from VM Systems Group, Inc., IBM's Display Management System/CMS (`DMS/CMS`) and Interactive System Productivity Facility (`ISPF`), also from IBM.

XMENU and DMS/CMS let programmers define new screens with a "what you see is what you get" panel interface, ideal for menus and "fill in the blanks" applications. Programmers create panels using either XMENU's XMEDIT command or DMS/CMS's PANEL command, by typing fields in the positions they will occupy on the screen when the application is being used. These utilities let the programmer define color and highlighting attributes for each field.

Applications using these products can be written in REXX, PL/I, FORTRAN, COBOL, or other languages. Programs select a screen by name, and display its contents by calling the display package. The display manager fills in program variables with data from the screen: the name of the key pressed by the user (Enter, a PF key, or one of the other 3270 keys), and input values filled in by the user. XMENU has a number of features not supplied by DMS/CMS, such as the ability to return to the calling program after a timeout interval or after receiving an SMSG interrupt from another virtual machine. The former capability can be used to create real-time displays for programs that periodically update screen information.

ISPF has a completely different orientation, due to its TSO origin. ISPF is both the standard editor used under TSO, as XEDIT is used under CMS, and also a menu-oriented system that hides the details of TSO from TSO users. Instead of using native TSO commands to run compilers or copy, erase, and rename files, TSO users traverse ISPF menus for invoking compilers, manipulating files, and so on. ISPF dialogues use *panel*, *message*, *table input*, and *skeleton* libraries containing a mixture of annotated screen contents and procedural code. ISPF lets programs access and update tables of information, display messages, and interact with the built-in ISPF BROWSE and EDIT functions to provide an integrated environment with similar "look and feel" for each application. ISPF functions let programmers DISPLAY a panel, or SELECT a set of hierarchical menus. Functions for controlling variables let programmers define, get, and put the contents of variables in a global pool of variables available to all panels in an application.

Writing fullscreen applications in ISPF requires far more effort than using either DMS/CMS or XMENU. However, ISPF is available in both MVS and CMS, making it an attractive tool for applications written for both operating systems. ISPF is largely used, as an interactive environment, by new CMS users accustomed to TSO. ISPF is used as a dialogue management system by IBM and other vendors that write applications that may run either in MVS or in CMS. For example, the interactive debuggers for IBM's FORTRAN, PL/I, COBOL, and C use ISPF to display the running program, the contents of variables, and to read commands.

IBM's Graphical Data Display MANAGER (`GDDM`) is an additional display manager for specialized purposes. GDDM can be used to write text displays, but its primary purpose is to produce graphics displays: pie, bar, and line charts, as well as arbitrary graphics images. IBM provides a rich set of program calls to display text, ellipses and areas with filled colors, patterns or shading, draw lines and arrows of various thicknesses and patterns, and many other types of object. GDDM's Interactive Chart Utility (`ICU`) makes it easy for nonprogrammers to create standard business graphics from tabular data entered interactively or read from files. Graphics can be displayed on suitably equipped 3270 terminals (not all support non-text data) or on a printer driven by RSCS or Advanced Function Printing.

GDDM applications can be written using standard IBM languages. A subroutine call interface is available for FORTRAN, COBOL, PL/I, C, and other languages that use the standard IBM linkage conventions. APL2 uses GDDM to provide a fullscreen session manager, similar to the fullscreen CMS environment, as well as an auxiliary processor programmable interface to displaying GDDM data. Most APL2 programmers spend their entire logon sessions inside the APL2 session manager, running and editing APL2 programs, and even executing commands to the host CMS environment.

IBM markets a GDDM/REXX interface product, GDDM-REXX, that lets REXX interact with GDDM as a subcommand environment. GDDM-REXX subcommands let REXX programs define windows, draw lines, select colors, create filled areas, write annotated text, and so on. Graphics applications can be created with very short REXX programs.

Message Handling

Programs traditionally write messages to their users using message text in the program body. This is initially convenient, but makes it necessary to change and recompile every program containing a message whenever its text is changed. If a common message is changed (for example, "File not found"), then the change must be repeated in every program that generates the message.

Worse, this technique means that different program versions must be maintained if messages are provided for multiple languages. IBM wants its systems to be equally accessible in many languages (recall that the "I" in "IBM" stands for "International"), and introduced National Language Support (NLS) with VM/SP Release 5.

NLS message repositories

NLS messages are separated from program text and placed in *message repositories*. Programs refer to messages by message number via either the **XMITMSG** command or the **APPLMSG** macro, and NLS selects the matching message in the currently selected repository.

IBM supplies message repositories for American and United Kingdom English, German, Japanese (using the Katakana character set), Dutch, Spanish, French (with both Canadian and French national dialects), and other languages. The default language is American English, and installations can install the additional languages. The **SET LANGUAGE** command adds or deletes a language from the currently selected set of language repositories.

Repository files have the filetype **REPOS**. User-created repository files have filenames of the form **XXXUME**, where *xxx* is a three letter code you pick to identify the application, and UME stands for *User MEssage*. The **GENMSG** command converts the repository file into a TEXT file that can be loaded into storage by the SET LANGUAGE command. IBM uses TEXT files because normal program management methods can be used to load them into storage, and because TEXT files can be included in program images used to build a CP or CMS nucleus.

Repository files contain a control line and lines describing each message the application displays, as illustrated in Fig. 11.28 for a sample utility called "TRACESVC," courtesy of Keith Landovitz of Merrill Lynch.

The first line is the control line, which defines the substitution symbol to be used in the following text description lines, and the number of digits to

```
& 3
* printed responses (messages 1-4, format 1)
00010101 0                    SVCTRACE OFF
00020101 1                    SVCTRACE ON
* typed responses (messages 1-4, format 2)
00010201I SVCTRACE OFF
00020201I SVCTRACE ON
* error messages
00100101S Error found in PVC table: check DLCS
00200101E SVC tracing is already on
00300101E SVC tracing is not on
00400101E SVC tracing is already active
00500101S Error &1 reading file &2 &3 &4 from disk or directory
```

Fig. 11.28 NLS message repository file.

display for message numbers. In this example, the character "&" is used to indicate a variable field, and the application generates 3-character message numbers.

The subsequent lines describe each message. Columns 1 through 4 contain the message number, and columns 5 and 6 specify a message format for a message that can have different appearances. Columns 7 and 8 contain the line number of the message, and are needed for messages that produce several lines of output. Column 9 contains a severity code, using the flags described in Chapter 2. The appearance of a message is controlled by the SET EMSG command described in that chapter: the full message format, complete with message number and severity code, is displayed only when EMSG is ON.

This repository file can be converted to a TEXT file by issuing the command **GENMSG TSCUME REPOS TSC**, where TSC is the application identifier chosen for the program. The command **SET LANGUAGE (ADD TSC USER** adds the repository to the set of currently selected languages. An application can use the XMITMSG command to select and display messages by number, for example **XMITMSG 001 (APPLID TSC**. To type message 5 (the last line of the file), TRACESVC provides character strings to substitute in the positions occupied by &1 &2 &3 and &4. REXX code generating this message might look like this:

```
PIPE <' fn ft fm '| stem data.'
if rc<>0 then do
   'XMITMSG 005' rc fn ft fm
   exit rc
  end
```

Language repositories separate programs from messages, making it easy to port applications to different national languages, or simply add new message contents. Instead of changing procedural code for each language, programmers and translators need only provide new REPOS files.

Command line and response syntax

Command line options parsed by a command suffer the same potential limitations as messages, since they are typically coded using a single language and use hard-coded constants for keyword values. The CMS PARSECMD service, available to assembly language programs and programs written in REXX or EXEC2, parses command input according to a syntax specified in **DLCS** (Definition Language for Command Syntax) files. Keywords can be changed or added by providing a new DLCS file, without requiring program changes. The same facilities can be used to parse user responses to prompts issued by a program, such as the "Are you sure?" message displayed by the FORMAT command.

The :DLCS statement specifies the name of the application and the language the DLCS file is written in. The following statements define the syntax needed to invoke the command: the :CMD keyword identifies the command (multiple commands may be identified in the same DLCS file), :KW identifies command keywords, and so on. The **GENCMD** command converts the DLCS file into a TEXT file that can be loaded into memory via the **SET LANGUAGE** command. The DLCS file for the "TRACESVC" utility program is shown in Fig. 11.29.

DLCS checks the syntax of common operand types. Many CMS commands use operands that are file identifiers, virtual device addresses, SFS directory names, and so on. Instead of manually checking that an operand is a correctly specified SFS directory name, for example, a programmer can use the DLCS *function definition* (fcndef) **DIRID** to state that an operand should be a valid directory.

The PARSECMD command checks commands and responses entered by users and places values from the command line in program variables. An EXEC using the DLCS file in Fig. 11.29 could use the command **PARSECMD TRACESVC(APPLID TSC** to parse the contents of the command line according to the DLCS specification.

PARSECMD assigns values to the REXX stem variables *token.* and *code.*, and returns a nonzero return code if the command line doesn't match the specified syntax. Variables *token.0* and *code.0* contain the number of token and validation code values set by PARSECMD. The *token.i* variables contain the contents of the *i'th* command line token, and the *code.i* variables contain the associated validation code. Validation codes indicate what type

```
:DLCS TSC USER AMENG :;
:CMD 00 TRACESVC TRACESVC 8 :;
  :KW.1 ON     2 :;
    :OPT KWL(<PRINT 5> <TYPE 4> <BOTH 4>) :;
  :KW.1 OFF    3 :;
  :KW.1 SUSPEND 3 :;
  :KW.1 RESUME  3 :;
  :KW.1 SET    3 :;
    :OPR KWL(<GRCALL 6> <GRRET 5> <FRCALL 6> <FRRET 5>
          <GRMOD 5> <PLIST 5> <CALL 4> <RETURN 3>)
        REPEAT :;
    :OPT KWL(<PRINT 5> <TYPE 4> <BOTH 4>) :;
  :KW.1 CLEAR  5 :;
    :OPR KWL(<GRCALL 6> <GRRET 5> <FRCALL 6> <FRRET 5>
          <GRMOD 5> <PLIST 5> <CALL 4> <RETURN 3>)
        OPTIONAL REPEAT :;
    :OPT KWL(<PRINT 5> <TYPE 4> <BOTH 4>) :;
```

Fig. 11.29 DLCS file.

of operand was found by PARSECMD. Some of the codes are COMMAND (command name) FN (filename), FT (filetype), DIRID (SFS directory id), INTEGER (integer), HEX (a hexadecimal number), and ALPHANUM (an alphanumeric string).

A good technique for *yes/no* options is to allow the user to specify a number as well as the words *yes* and *no*. This technique, used by IBM commands like FORMAT and RECEIVE, makes it possible to use the same input whether the user is working in English or another language (0 always has the same meaning). This is convenient for users, and makes it easier to write EXECs that stack responses to commands and work in multiple languages.

Parallel Programming with VM

VM systems, and IBM mainframes in general, operate in parallel at the system and application level.

IBM's VS FORTRAN compiler allows parallel execution of a single FORTRAN program on multiple ES/9000 or 3090 CPU engines. In the VM implementation, a single virtual machine is defined with multiple virtual CPUs, and the FORTRAN program executes in parallel on each virtual processor. Compiler directives in the FORTRAN source code tell the compiler which loops can be executed in parallel. An extension to FORTRAN allows a program to spawn a copy of itself to an adjacent networked ES/9000 or 3090 system, and thereby run a single parallel FORTRAN on multiple systems.

Server tasking environment

Multiprocessing application capability is also provided by IBM's Server Tasking Environment/VM (`STE/VM`) program. STE/VM is a free program, incorporated into VM/ESA Release 2, that provides multitasking for applications written in IBM's C/370 or assembly language. Like parallel FORTRAN, it lets multiple CPUs work on a single application. Unlike FORTRAN, threads of execution run on each machine doing different work, as opposed to executing the same loop in parallel.

STE/VM is not a general purpose CMS multitasking facility. Instead, it is a special-purpose tool for creating high-performance service virtual machines. STE/VM programs make use of CP's ability to create virtual multiprocessor systems to provide true parallel operation. The base CPU of the virtual multiprocessor, CPU0, runs CMS as usual, and all requests for CMS services are executed on this processor. A task interface, explicitly programmed by the application, creates new threads of execution. For example, a call to *ThreadCreate* creates a new execution thread and returns its identifier to the calling program. At this point, both the initial and new threads continue execution in parallel. STE/VM provides procedures for interprocess signaling and control.

Vector facility

Vector computing is a special version of parallel processing. Vector processors use arrays of registers to perform a floating point arithmetic operation on arrays (vectors) of operands at the same time. This can dramatically speed up the execution of numerically intensive computing by computing many expressions at the same time.

Vector processing is provided by optional *Vector Facility* (VF) units available for ES/9000 and 3090 processors. One VF can be attached to each ES/9000 or 3090 CPU in a multiprocessor complex. Typical vector instructions add a scalar value to a vector, add or multiply vectors, or perform a simultaneous multiply and add. Vector Facility execution is pipelined. The vector facility simultaneously fetches its many operands, processes them, and stores the results.

Vector facilities provide very high floating point performance when used with suitable applications. Good applications are floating point intensive programs with loop operations that can be performed in parallel. A loop can not be vectorized if values used as inputs in one loop iteration are produced by previous iterations. Many applications, especially linear algebra applications that perform matrix and array arithmetic, are especially well suited for the vector facility. In some cases, entire loops are replaced with vector instructions.

The IBM VS FORTRAN compiler and APL2 interpreter exploit the vector facility for increased performance, by identifying vectorizable expressions and generating vector instructions to compute them, instead of scalar instructions performed repetitively. FORTRAN programs must be compiled with the VECTOR option to make the compiler generate vector instructions. A number of compiler directives can be supplied to help the compiler detect vectorizable loops, although the compiler can vectorize programs without them.

APL2 automatically uses the vector facility, when one is present, without programmer intervention. Since APL2 is an interpreted language, it need not pregenerate serial or vector code. Instead, the APL2 interpreter decides at run-time to use either scalar or vector code sequences, depending on the operators and the size of the operands being evaluated. There is a constant-time cost for initiating a vector instruction, so the APL2 interpreter uses vector instructions only for vector or matrix operations long enough to repay the initial overhead. APL2 is also aided by the vector orientation of the APL2 language. APL2 operates on vectors and matrices more naturally than any other language, making it easy for APL2 to recognize vectorizable expressions. For example, if X and Y are 1,000 element floating point vectors, APL2 automatically vectorizes the expression X+Y.

Chapter

12

The CMS File System

The file system is a vital component of any operating system. A viable operating system must ensure that data can be reliably stored and retrieved. To be competitive it must do so with adequate performance for the type of applications for which it is targeted.

Additionally, the style of file facilities in a computing system determines how that system can be used. Batch-oriented operating systems like MVS require that file information be predeclared before files can be created, and impose a high cost for creating or referring to files that are not currently in use.

This chapter discusses the CMS file system in depth, describing its user and application interfaces and comparing it with other file systems.

File System Overview

The CMS file system was designed to be suitable for a variety of applications, with emphasis on flexibility and ease of use. It provides device independence, generality, dynamic allocation of disk space, and high performance.

Interactive users usually refer to many small files (program source and executable files, memos, documentation, help files, and so on) instead of a few large files, as is common in batch applications. CMS file system design was based on this observation, and therefore emphasizes efficient and convenient access to multiple files. Consequently, CMS does not require prior declaration of file attributes such as record length, file size, or whether a file will be accessed sequentially or randomly.

CMS file access is noted for its efficiency. File operations have an extremely short CPU instruction path-length, and data is automatically transferred in large blocks to reduce elapsed times. This reduces CPU overhead by reducing the number of I/O calls needed to read or write a file. It also reduces elapsed time since larger amounts of data are transferred in a single disk rotation. This contrasts with MVS and DOS/VSE, where file blocking requires explicit programmer action for each file, and with UNIX and MS-DOS, where file performance is limited (although slowly improving).

CMS uses sophisticated methods for searching file directories to make locating and "opening" files inexpensive. The low cost of locating a file, usually called STATE-ing (as in "stating whether or not a file is present"), is especially crucial, because CMS frequently searches for files containing executable programs, EXECfiles, program source files, and relocatable object code.

The low cost for locating files lets CMS efficiently store programs in individual files, instead of in program libraries, as in MVS and DOS/VSE. This simplifies CMS program development and usage and eliminates the cumbersome library maintenance needed in those systems. CMS's search order makes it easy to "front-end" commands with private versions for testing and private customization.

These properties influence how CMS is used, and the way CMS applications are structured. In his IBM Technical Report *Why CMS?*, Pat Ryall (now at Apple Computer) described the CMS file system as a key part of what is meant by "CMS- like": easy-to-use and efficient.

Minidisk and SFS file systems

CMS provides two different but compatible methods for storing files: minidisks and the Shared File System (SFS). In the original CMS file system, files reside on minidisks and are read and written by I/O instructions issued by CMS. Minidisks are contiguous extents of disk space, defined in the CP directory and owned by a single VM userid. Temporary minidisks can also be assigned from a pool of temporary disk space via the CP DEFINE command. Temporary disks, usually called *T-disks*, are used as work areas and are returned to the system when a user logs off or DETACHes them.

The minidisk file system design was based on the virtual machine paradigm. Individual users have private file storage contained on their minidisks, which they may choose to share with other users for read or write access. Minidisk file storage is similar to the hard disk of a personal computer: a private fixed-size disk space entirely controlled by a single user. Minidisks provide extremely high performance for most applications, but impose restrictions on how easily data can be organized and shared.

CMS also stores files in the *Shared File System* (SFS). SFS provides tree-structured file directories, similar to those in UNIX and MS-DOS, and provides file-level granularity of access control and update synchronization. SFS files reside in SFS filepools, service virtual machines that use their own minidisk space to define logical file structures for multiple concurrent users. CMS automatically creates program-to-program connections between users and filepool servers to perform file access. SFS files can be accessed remotely from VM systems connected by an SNA network. SFS does not normally provide the raw efficiency of minidisk I/O, but its added functionality makes it attractive for a wide variety of applications.

File System History

The CMS file system has been remarkably stable in organization and function since it was introduced with CP/67. It has undergone two major revisions since then: the introduction of the *Extended Disk Format* (EDF) for minidisks, and the introduction of SFS.

Conventional Disk Format (CDF)

The original CMS file system, introduced in CP/67, was used with little change through VM/370. This file system stores data in 800 byte long blocks, and automatically maps user-specified record lengths into the 800 bytes transferred to and from disk. The 800 byte size fit well on the small track capacities of the 2311 and 2314 disk drives of the 1960s, and did not require large buffers in main storage (an important consideration when main storage sizes were small).

This file system was designed for small files and small disk drives. It therefore had limitations that became restrictive when larger applications and disk media were used with CMS. Most painful was the restriction that a file could have no more than 65,535 records. The control block describing a file, the *File Status Table* (FST), described below, and the control block used to access a file, the *File System Control Block* (FSCB), had only 16-bit record counters, hence the small maximum file size. The small block size also made it necessary to issue many disk reads or writes to process a file, and wasted disk space in inter-block gaps between 800 byte blocks.

Extended Disk Format (EDF)

A new file system, the *Extended Disk Format* (EDF), was introduced in the late 1970s to remove limitations in the original file system (retrospectively named *Conventional Disk Format*). EDF FSTs and FSCBs use 32-bit file record counters and let files have up to 2,147,482,647 records. EDF also allows disk block sizes of 512, 1,024, 2,048, and 4,096 bytes for increased time and space efficiency.

EDF became a standard part of VM when VM/SP was introduced, while CDF was retained for compatibility purposes. Finally, with VM/ESA, IBM retracted CMS support for CDF and removed its software modules from the CMS nucleus. All further discussion of CMS files in this chapter is based on EDF.

Shared File System (SFS)

The next major change to the CMS file system did not appear until the *Shared File System* (SFS) was introduced in VM/SP Release 6. As is discussed in detail, SFS relieved the difficulties in structuring and sharing changing data that are inherent in the minidisk file system.

CMS File Identifiers

As described in "File Naming Conventions" on page XXX, files are named by their filename, filetype, and filemode, collectively referred to as the file identifier. Filename and filetype are up to eight characters long, and are specified when the file is created or renamed. Filenames and filetypes consist of letters, numeric digits, and the special characters #, @, +, –, and _. Letters are normally uppercase: a few programs (notably OfficeVision) create files with lowercase letters to make it difficult for users to accidentally erase or alter them (the CMS command processors normally fold identifiers to uppercase before using them.)

The filemode is a two-character field, consisting of a *mode letter* between A and Z (lowercase is not used), followed by a *filemode number*. The filemode letter identifies which minidisk or directory a file resides on, while the filemode number specifies optional processing options for the file. The filemode number is a single digit value ranging from 0 to 6, with the following meanings:

- Filemode 0—is used to hide a file from users that have read-only access to a disk. This should be used as a convenience to hide the clutter of personal files when users read one another's disks. This is **not** a secure method for hiding files, since a number of methods can subvert filemode 0 "protection" and gain access to filemode 0 files. In fact, VM/ESA provides the ACCESSM0 command to let installations control whether users view filemode 0 files on read-only disks. Files on minidisks are protected by protecting access to the minidisk. SFS files are individually protected by **GRANT** and **REVOKE** commands.
- FILEMODE 1—default processing.
- FILEMODE 2—treated identically to filemode 1, but is often used to indicate subsets of files on a disk. For example, the public S-and Y-disks have both filemode 1 and filemode 2 files, but CMS automatically accesses only the filemode 2 files.
- FILEMODE 3—erase after read. This is used for "scratch" files that are erased after use.
- FILEMODE 4—indicates files in OS simulated data set format. This tells CMS to simulate OS format control information for varying length files, not normally maintained for CMS files.

- FILEMODE 5—is used like filemode 1, but is also used to indicate file subsets.
- FILEMODE 6—indicates, for files on minidisks, that the file should be updated in place, instead of to new disk blocks as updates are made. For SFS files, filemode 6 is treated the same as filemode 1, since different methods are used to indicate "in-place" update.

ACCESS options

As mentioned in Chapter 10, the ACCESS command makes files on a minidisk or directory visible to a CMS session. ACCESS can also be used to make a minidisk a *read-only extension* of a different filemode, or to view only a subset of the files it contains. Examples of the ACCESS command are shown in Fig. 12.1.

How ACCESS and filemode search work

The ACCESS command reads the Master File Directory (`MFD`) from disk into virtual storage. The MFD contains descriptive information for every file on the minidisk, in a control block called the File Status Table (`FST`). When in storage, the file directory for a minidisk is pointed to by a control block called the Active Disk Table (`ADT`). ADT entries are chained from a fixed position in CMS low storage, and are chained in a linked list in filemode alphabetical order.

The volume label of a minidisk contains the "disk origin pointer" to the disk block containing the minidisk's file directory. ACCESS reads the volume

```
* access a disk as a read-only extension of itself, to prevent
* accidental erasure or changes
access 195 d/d
DMSACP723I B (195) R/O
Ready;

* subset access: only view files with filetype DATA on 200 disk
access 200 i/i * data
DMSACP723I I (200) R/O
Ready;

* access the SFS directory containing the SCRIPT files of this book
access .vmbook.script g
Ready;

* access Arty's REXX program library stored in SFS
access arty.rxsocket h
Ready;
```

Fig. 12.1 ACCESS command.

label, and then reads the disk block it points to locate the first FST in the file directory. The file directory is itself a special file, with a filename containing a binary value of 1 right adjusted in an 8-byte field of zeros, and a filetype of `DIRECTOR`. The low numeric value of the filename causes its FST to be sorted into the first position of the disk-resident copy of the file directory.

For read/write accessed disks, CMS also reads into storage the minidisk's *allocation map*, which contains a bit for each block of disk space, indicating whether or not it is currently allocated to a file. The allocation map is also a special file, located in the second FST in the disk copy of the file directory. The filename is the binary value 2, and the filetype is `ALLOCMAP`.

CMS scans in-storage FSTs whenever searching for a file on an accessed disk or directory, and refers to or changes the FST contents when files are manipulated: "opened" for read or write access by an application, erased or renamed. CMS rewrites changed portions of the file directory and allocation map to disk when file changes are committed via the `FSCLOSE` macro, the `FINIS` CMS service, or by higher-level language statements that invoke them.

Changed directory data is written to different disk blocks than the ones they already reside on. This provides file system integrity in case of software or hardware errors. If the new directory blocks are successfully written to disk, CMS points the disk origin pointer to an alternate location. This way, the contents of the CMS file directory are either successfully changed or not changed at all. Alternate disk origin pointer locations are used, and are flip-flopped each time the directory is saved.

For SFS directories, the ACCESS command has the same effect of making the file name-space on the specified directory visible. The SFS server and the CMS client both cache file information in virtual storage.

CMS `STATE` routines search the in-storage file tables using an efficient hashing algorithm. This makes searches for files extremely inexpensive, since disk I/O is replaced by searches within virtual storage. The search algorithm is designed to minimize the number of pages touched while searching for files, and remains efficient even when thousands of files are on a minidisk. File searches in accessed disks require no disk I/O, and cause few page faults.

By contrast, most other systems read file directory information from disk-resident catalogs, "volume table of contents" or directories. Usually, it takes multiple disk I/O operations to locate and open a file, making the initial access of a file costly. MVS is especially expensive in this area, but the same effect can be observed on an MS-DOS personal computer by issuing the DIR command on several subdirectories and watching the hard disk's activity light.

As an additional optimization, CMS records whether any files in a set of "preferred filetypes" are present on a minidisk. A 16-bit table is maintained in the ADT, with a bit assigned to important filetypes like EXEC, MODULE, TEXT, XEDIT. A bit is turned on if at least one file of the associated filetype is present on the disk. When searching for a file with one of the preferred filetypes, STATE simply checks the associated preferred filetype bit. If the bit is off, the disk or directory can be skipped, and STATE can continue with the next ADT. This is an important optimization for CMS command resolution, since CMS frequently searches for MODULE, EXEC, TEXT, and XEDIT files.

Shared copies of file directories

Minidisks containing commonly used files are frequently read-accessed by many users at the same time. Since it would be wasteful to keep hundreds or thousands of in-storage copies of the same minidisk directories, CMS provides methods for sharing file directories in saved segments. This reduces the working sets of each user by the size of the directories, and reduces the overall storage requirements of an entire VM system.

Storage references to shared directory contents occur frequently enough to keep directory pages resident in main storage most of the time. Almost all references to the directory are satisfied from real storage instead of causing page faults, both reducing system overhead and improving system response time. The shared directory also lets CMS IPL more quickly since control blocks need not be read from disk.

Shared file directories were first made available for the S-and Y-disks every CMS user accesses. Their directories are saved at the end of the CMS nucleus, after the executable code. During CMS initialization, CMS reads the label of the S- and Y-disks to obtain the time and date the disks were last changed. If either disk was changed since CMS was saved, CMS types a warning message and then reads the directory as if it were unshared. VM system administrators resave the CMS nucleus after changing either the S-disk or Y-disk.

Similar performance can be provided for other minidisks that are read-shared by many users. The SAVEFD INIT and SAVEFD SAVE commands create a file directory in a discontinuous shared segment. When this is done, the ACCESS command uses the shared copy instead of reading the file directory into private storage. If the disk is changed, a system administrator issues the SAVEFD SAVE command to bring the shared copy up to date.

Preparing File Areas for Users

System administrators assign disk space to users. Minidisk space is assigned via the directory, as described in "Minidisk Specification" on page 106. SFS file space is provided to users by *enrolling* them in an SFS filepool, and specifying a quota of disk space for the user.

The `FORMAT` command prepares a minidisk for CMS file system use. FORMAT writes uniformly sized blocks across the entire minidisk, and creates an empty file directory.

```
format 193 b
DMSFOR603R FORMAT will erase all files on disk B(193).
Do you wish to continue? Enter 1 (YES) or 0 (NO).
1
DMSFOR605R Enter disk label:
my-193
DMSFOR733I Formatting disk B
DMSFOR732I 5 cylinders formatted on B(193)
Ready;
```

Fig. 12.2 FORMAT command.

The FORMAT command is easy to use, but is normally done by a system administrator or by a directory manager product when a new disk is being prepared for a user. FORMAT should **not** be used on an existing disk, since it erases the disk's prior contents. Fortunately, FORMAT issues a prompt to ask the user if he or she is sure. An example of using FORMAT is shown in Fig. 12.2.

Disk block size considerations

Minidisk blocks may be 512, 1,024, 2,048, or 4,096 bytes in length. Uniform block sizes for all data on a minidisk shields users and applications from the complexities of CKD and ECKD cylinder and track addressing, while still making good use of physical device properties. Obviously, CMS blocks map very naturally into FBA disk architecture.

CMS automatically blocks application I/O into the minidisk block size, without user or programmer intervention. From the point of view of users and programs, a CMS minidisk contains *N* uniformly sized blocks of disk space numbered from 0 to *N-1*, regardless of the actual device arrangement of tracks and cylinders. In this regard, CMS is more like UNIX or MS-DOS than MVS or DOS/VSE.

FORMAT picks the most space efficient block size for the disk model being used, although a block size choice can specified. CKD and ECKD disk drives impose a space penalty called the *inter-block gap* (IBG). Differing track capacities and IBG sizes determine the most space-efficient block size for each disk type.

There is always a trade-off for performance when selecting a block size, whether in CMS or in other operating systems. Small blocks are memory and disk space efficient, but more I/O operations are needed to read or write a file. It usually costs a full disk rotation each time an I/O operation is performed. Large blocks reduce the number of I/O operations and rotations, but may require so much storage that paging is increased, which in turn causes delays.

Block sizes in CMS are good compromise values, and avoid the problems of extremely small or large blocks. 4,096 byte (4K) blocks are usually the most efficient CMS block sizes for recent IBM disk drives like the 3380 and 3390. 4K blocks yield the fastest I/O since they transfer more data in a single I/O request, although this effect is minimized by the multiblock read-ahead and write-behind policies discussed later. 4K byte blocks are necessary for using the minidisk cache (MDC) facility, a very important performance option in VM/ESA.

File Properties

CMS file I/O is record-oriented. Individual READ and WRITE operations transmit an entire record to or from the application. CMS automatically maps the record length into the underlying disk block size the data is stored in. No "end of line" or "end of record" characters are stored in the file.

Files have either *fixed-length* or *variable-length* records. In fixed-length record files, all records must have the same length, called the *logical record length* (LRECL). In variable-length record files, the length of each record is specified when it is written, and provided to the application when it is read from disk. Unlike MVS, the maximum LRECL for a file need not be predeclared when using CMS's own file system primitives. However, programs using OS simulation routines, which include programs using the native I/O statements in COBOL, PL/I, and Fortran, must follow the MVS rules and specify in advance the size of the largest record to be placed in a file.

CMS files contain up to 2,147,482,647 records. Each record may be between 1 and 2,147,482,647 bytes in length, except for varying length record files, which can only have records of up to 65,535 bytes.

CMS automatically converts file I/O operations into the disk's block size by converting the record lengths of the file into the appropriate number of blocks needed on the minidisk. Records may be smaller or larger than the disk's block size: CMS fills a block with multiple application records until it is full. Records span multiple disk blocks if they are large or the record length does not evenly divide into the block size. CMS does this all automatically without any effort from users or programmers.

Random and sequential access

All CMS files can be randomly accessed (also called direct access) by record number. `FSREAD` and `FSWRITE` macros for assembler programs, and the Callable Service Library (`CSL`) routines for REXX, assembler, and high-level languages, let programmers specify record numbers when reading or writing a file. Input/output statements in PL/I, FORTRAN, COBOL, and other languages also allow sequential and random access to CMS files. APL2 provides an especially innovative method: in addition to providing standard file operations, APL2 lets a CMS file be associated with an array variable. This lets the APL2 programmer process the file by indexing into the array, assigning values to it, and otherwise manipulating it with the same syntax as a program variable.

Files are not specially defined to allow direct access. Random access is available regardless of whether a file contains binary or character data, or has fixed or variable length records. However, random access is faster with fixed length records.

File update

Files can be updated by reading and rewriting records in sequential or random access order. One restriction is that a record in a varying-length record file cannot be replaced with a longer record. When this happens, CMS truncates the remainder of the file.

CMS uses a new disk block when a record in a file is rewritten to a minidisk. This helps provide file integrity in case of a system or application crash, since the contents of the file remain unaltered until the file is closed. Long-running applications (especially continuously operating service machines) that repeatedly update a file can exhaust the free disk blocks on a minidisk. This can be prevented by periodically closing the file to discard obsolete blocks.

If the file has the update-in-place attribute (filemode 6), the file is actually rewritten in place using existing disk blocks. This saves disk space, but can result in a partially updated file in case of a system failure. SFS provides the equivalent of in-place update, but by default writes shadow disk blocks for file changes until a file's changes are *committed*. File commits occur when the file is closed, or if a CSL system call is used to commit file updates while leaving the file open.

File space allocation

CMS allocates disk blocks as needed from free blocks in a minidisk or SFS file pool as applications write records to files. CMS does not require that a file's maximum size be predeclared when it is created, as is necessary in MVS and DOS/VSE. In this regard also, CMS is much more like UNIX and MS-DOS than IBM's other mainframe operating systems.

CMS maintains an *allocation map*, which records the in-use status of every disk block in the minidisk. A bit is present for each block of disk space in a minidisk, and is set to '1' if the associated disk block is in use. When a file is erased or truncated, its blocks are deallocated by turning on the corresponding bits in a deallocation bit map. The file directory is written to disk when the last open output file is closed or the disk is released. At that time, the deallocation bit map is merged into the allocation map to add the newly freed blocks.

The allocation map resides on disk, and is read into storage by the ACCESS command. ACCESS only reads the allocation map into storage if a disk is accessed in read/write mode, since the contents of read/only disks are never allocated or deallocated. Disk space allocation is therefore very fast, since the data structure describing available space is both compact and retained in storage.

When a file's first block is written, CMS allocates a block of disk space for it and puts the block number in its FST. If the first block fills, CMS allocates additional disk blocks for the file's data, and for a *pointer block* used to locate data blocks. CMS then puts the block number of the pointer block in the FST and continues writing the file. A CMS file therefore never actually resides solely in two disk blocks: it either occupies one disk block, or three or more.

A pointer block has enough room for multiple data blocks. When a pointer block is full, CMS expands the file by creating an additional level of pointer blocks to point to lower level pointer blocks. A very large file has a multilevel tree structure on disk, which can be efficiently traversed for both random and sequential access. An example of a pointer structure is shown in Fig. 12.3. In it, the file directory contains multiple FSTs, the first of which has pointer blocks that in turn point to data blocks.

Dynamic space allocation provides a productivity advantage over systems that require preallocation, because these systems force users and pro-

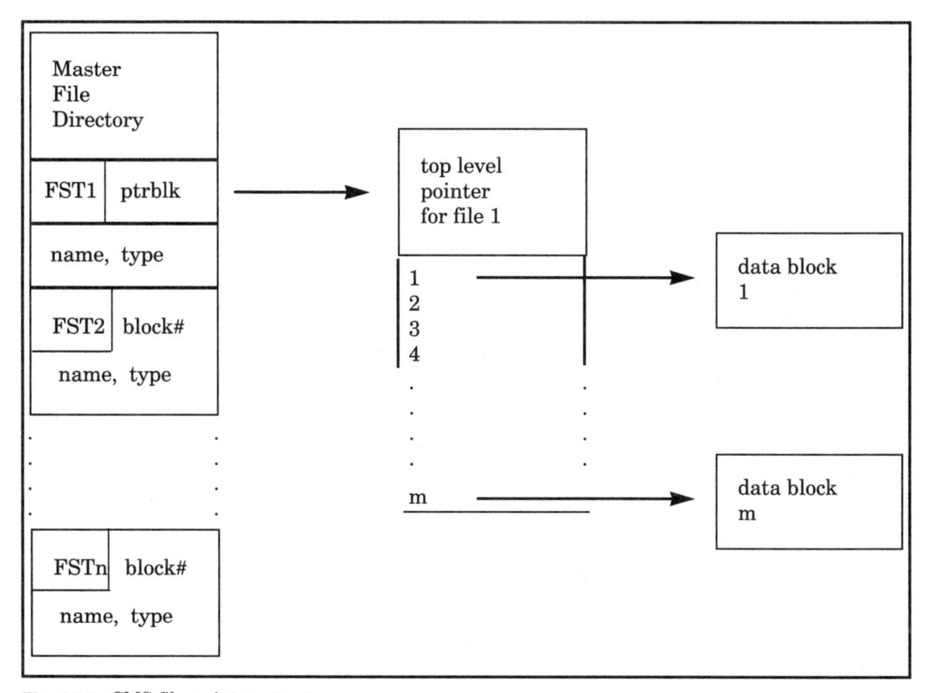

Fig. 12.3 CMS file pointer structure.

grammers to estimate and specify every file's size. Since the penalty for underestimating a file's size is a crashed application, many MVS and DOS/VSE space estimates are larger than needed, resulting in wasted disk space. CMS avoids both problems by allocating disk storage automatically and only as needed. A user cannot monopolize disk space by endlessly writing to files, since file sizes are restricted by minidisk or SFS quota sizes.

CMS provides a high level of granularity for disk space allocated to a file. The minimum space allocation for a CMS file is a single disk block, at most 4K bytes. This is only one-tenth of a track on a IBM 3380 disk drive. Minidisks are allocated in units of cylinders on CKD and ECKD disk drives, and in 512 byte block units on FBA devices.

MVS and DOS/VSE allocate at least a track of disk space for each file. They use SET FILE MASK channel programs, which operate at the cylinder or track level, to prevent a user's program from reading or writing outside the bounds of its own files (and thus browsing or destroying other users' data). Since a minidisk belongs to a single user, CMS files residing on it can be freely mixed on the same disk track.

The maximum disk space wasted in a CMS file is the unused portion of a 4K block. On average, one-half of the last block allocated to a file is wasted space. The percentage of the last block used is a random variable ranging from "almost empty" to "totally full," with one-half full being average. On a minidisk formatted with 4K byte blocks, an average of 2K bytes is wasted per file. Minidisks with many small files may be more space efficient when formatted with a smaller block size.

Sparse files

CMS allows *sparse* files: files that have "missing" record numbers. For example, a file might have records numbered 1, 6, 22 and 10000, without having the intervening records numbered 2, 3, 4, and so on. This file would only occupy as much disk space as needed for four records! Sparse files are useful for random access files keyed by numeric values.

Sparse files are created by writing the specific record numbers desired in the file, using any access method listed in this chapter. When an application tries to read a record not present in the file, CMS returns a buffer containing zero values. Records can be added to a sparse file by specifying the record number when writing it.

Sparse files can be created by random access I/O statements in assembly language, PL/I, FORTRAN, and COBOL, and by REXX programs using EXECIO or CMS Pipelines. An EXEC that creates a sparse file using EXECIO is shown in Fig. 12.4. The console output from its execution is shown in Fig. 12.5. Note that the file only occupies 5 disk blocks, even though it has records numbered between 1 and 2,600.

```
/*SPARSE EXEC: create sparse file from REXX */
address command
Fileid = 'DEMO FILE G'

/* a set of record numbers to use as file keys */
keyvalues = '23 16 47 2600 123 1 17 19 11 125 159 1006'

/* Create a sparse file */
do i = 1 to words(keyvalues)
   recno = word(keyvalues,i)
   output_value = '<<< This is record' recno '>>>'
   'EXECIO 1 DISKW' fileid recno 'F 80 ( VAR OUTPUT_VALUE'
end
'FINIS' fileid                        /* close the file */
'LISTFILE' fileid '(DATE'

/* Read each of the record created above, in random order */
do i = 1 to words(keyvalues) /* at least as many reads as records */
   /* Randomly select on of the words in the list */
   recno = word(keyvalues,random(1,words(keyvalues)))
   'EXECIO 1 DISKR' fileid recno '( VAR OBTAINED_VALUE'
   say 'Record' recno 'contians' obtained_value
end
```

Fig. 12.4 SPARSE EXEC to create a sparse CMS file.

```
randio
FILENAME  FILETYPE  FM FORMAT   LRECL  RECS  BLOCKS  DATE     TIME
DEMO      FILE      G1 F        80     2600  5       12/16/91 19:01:52
Record 123 contains <<< This is record 123 >>>
Record 17 contains <<< This is record 17 >>>
Record 16 contains <<< This is record 16 >>>
Record 1 contains <<< This is record 1 >>>
Record 16 contains <<< This is record 16 >>>
Record 16 contains <<< This is record 16 >>>
Record 125 contains <<< This is record 125 >>>
Record 159 contains <<< This is record 159 >>>
Record 2600 contains <<< This is record 2600 >>>
Record 123 contains <<< This is record 123 >>>
Record 17 contains <<< This is record 17 >>>
Record 123 contains <<< This is record 123 >>>
Ready;
```

Fig. 12.5 Output of SPARSE EXEC.

As an optimization, CMS does not store on disk any block with all sparse records (zero byte values). This is indicated internally by a pointer block containing the value 0. Block number 0 cannot be part of any CMS file because it is reserved for other purposes, so the associated block is known to be sparse. Sparse files can be made non-sparse by accident, so they should not be altered by editing or appending records via COPYFILE's APPEND option.

Contiguous and fragmented minidisk space

Free disk space may be fragmented on a minidisk that has been used for a long period of time, since free space "holes" are created when files are erased or replaced. CMS files can be scattered over an arbitrary number of noncontiguous disk locations, so there is no functional difference between disks that have fragmented space and those that do not. There is, however, a potential difference in performance. Scattered file locations can lower performance since the disk access arm may have to be moved several times to read a file's contents.

CMS minimizes fragmentation by allocating disk blocks in a "moving wave" across the minidisk. New disk blocks for output are selected in increasing block number order until the highest numbered free block on the disk is used, and then wraps around to low-numbered free blocks. This makes it very likely that blocks written at the same time are allocated from contiguous or nearby disk locations.

A minidisk can be defragmented by copying its contents to a freshly formatted minidisk. This is usually only worthwhile for minidisks whose performance is critical, such as public system minidisks. Modern disk drives' fast seek times, disk caching, and the allocation method just described make this an increasingly less important optimization.

Read-ahead and write-behind

CMS optimizes file reads and writes when file blocks are allocated to the same cylinder. IBM research into file system behavior showed that most files are read from beginning to end, instead of partially or randomly. CMS exploits this by joining multiple I/O operations to reduce head and rotational latency, and the number of DIAGNOSE I/O calls to CP.

When an application reads a block of data from disk, CMS "reads ahead" to additional blocks as well, if they happen to be on the same cylinder. When the application reads the next block, it is already in storage and can be provided without additional delay. On output, CMS performs "write behind" by saving multiple output blocks and writing them in a single I/O operation.

Anticipatory reads and deferred writes save CPU time by reducing the number of DIAGNOSE calls made to CP. Since each DIAGNOSE has a fixed overhead cost, CPU time is saved by doing as much as possible in a single request. Elapsed time is reduced because multiple blocks are transferred with a single rotation and disk head motion, instead of a separate rotation and (potentially) an additional seek for each block. If the subsequent blocks are on the same DASD cylinder as the first one, then reading or writing them is almost "free" since they can be transmitted without additional disk head motion, and often in the same DASD rotation as the first block. CMS "read ahead" and "write behind" can dramatically speed up I/O processing, and make selection of an optimal block size less significant.

The degree of buffering is controlled by a CMS installation option. The buffer size is specified in the local customization module DMSNGP created before CMS is built. The default value is 12KB of storage, which allows a read-ahead of three 4KB blocks, and can go up to 99KB. Higher values provide better performance in environments that have low paging rates. Care must also be taken to not consume too much virtual storage when running virtual machines that "just barely" fit into storage.

File System Interfaces

As mentioned in Chapter 11, CMS provides both native and simulated MVS and DOS/VSE program interfaces. The native file interface provides assembly language macros for opening, closing, reading, and writing files. This is often called the "FS macro" interface, since the IBM macro calls all begin with the letters FS:

- FSREAD—read a record from a file.
- FSWRITE—write a record from a named file.
- FSSTATE—determines if a file exists, and if it does, return information about it to the caller.
- FSOPEN—determine a file for access. This is an optional call, since the first FSREAD or FSWRITE to a file implicitly opens a file.
- FSCLOSE—close a file, by writing any pending buffers to disk, and releasing internal buffers and control blocks representing it.
- FSERASE—erase a file.
- FSPOINT—reposition the file's read or write record pointer to a different position in the file. This is used in direct access applications. FSPOINT is optional, since record numbers can also be specified in FSREAD and FSWRITE. Separate read and write pointers are maintained for a file, allowing different parts of a file to be worked on at the same time.

The FS macros use the actual CMS filename, filetype and filemode of the file being processed. This makes it easy to write applications that internally determine which files they want to access. File identifiers can be read into program variables from the CMS command line, the terminal or a CMS file, and then used by the macro call. No convention of allocating an actual file to logical filename ("ddname" in MVS) is used.

FS macros allow sequential and direct access to CMS files. The record number for the next read or write in a FSREAD or FSWRITE macro defaults to the next sequential record, but can be specified if random access is used.

The FSPOINT macro also can be used to change the file pointers. A file can be accessed both for input and output at the same time, allowing direct-update applications.

FS macros are flexible and very easy to use, provided you can program in assembly language. Higher level languages use either OS file simulation, discussed below, or the Callable Subroutine Library.

OS simulation

CMS simulates MVS *access methods*, each of which is used for different purposes:

- QSAM—Queued Sequential Access Method, for buffered sequential input and output.
- BSAM—Basic Sequential Access Method, for unbuffered sequential access.
- BDAM—Basic Direct Access Method, provides random access based on a record's position within a file.
- BPAM—Basic Partitioned Access Method, for access to library file ("partitioned data set") members.
- VSAM—Virtual Storage Access Method. VSAM provides sequential access (called "entry sequenced") and direct access based on record number (called "relative record"), much like BSAM and BDAM, but it additionally provides keyed access based on application-specified alphanumeric keys. This is called "key sequenced" data, and lets applications retrieve records based on customer id, transaction name, or other identifiers. VSAM support under CMS requires the VSE/VSAM program product.

QSAM, BSAM, BDAM, and BPAM simulated files can reside on CMS minidisks and SFS directories, and, for read-only access, on volumes formatted by MVS or DOS/VSE. This allows their use for CMS-only applications, and for read-sharing of data with MVS systems. VSAM files reside on DOS-format minidisks or volumes, and can be used for CMS-only applications or for sharing data with DOS/VSE systems.

The `FILEDEF` command establishes a logical connection between a specific file and the `DDNAME` specified in the application's OS style DCB. FILEDEF is equivalent to the MVS JCL `DD` statement or TSO `ALLOCATE` command, For example, a PL/I program that applies updates to a master file might used FILEDEF statements like those in shown in Fig. 12.6.

Other application interfaces

CMS provides CMS Pipelines and the EXECIO command for EXECs. Both provide flexible methods for reading and writing CMS files to and from REXX variables. CMS Pipelines provides high level methods for filtering and

```
/* Set up file definitions and run update program DAILY */
'FILEDEF INPUT   DISK MASTER FILE A'
'FILEDEF CHANGES DISK NEWEST UPDATES B'
'FILEDEF OUTPUT  DISK NEW    MASTER A'
'FILEDEF SYSPRINT TERMINAL'
'DAILY' /* update program in PL/I, COBOL, or other compiled language */
```

Fig. 12.6 EXEC with FILEDEF command for OS simulation application.

arranging data, and is being increasingly used in place of the older EXECIO. SFS files and directories can be manipulated via CSL calls, discussed in "SFS Callable Subroutine Library Functions" on page 259.

Device Independence

CMS file I/O is disk model independent, so CMS applications can be moved to new generations of disk drive without changing programs or procedures. CMS programs *can* access "low level" device characteristics of a disk drive if they insist, but need not be concerned with the number of tracks in a disk cylinder or number of bytes in a track. There is rarely advantage to doing so.

CMS applications are even shielded from the architecture of the physical device, whether it be the *Fixed Block Architecture* (FBA) used on 3370 devices, *Count Key Data* (CKD) format used by 3380 disk devices, or the *Extended Count Key Data* (ECKD) format used by 3390 disks.

This contrasts with systems like MVS, which require programmers to specify disk model dependent information for each file created. Optimal MVS block sizes, for example, depend on the file's logical record length and the device type being used. Consequently, converting MVS or DOS/VSE applications to a new device requires new block sizes be laboriously calculated and specified for each file.

Minidisk I/O

CMS uses DIAGNOSE instructions, discussed in Chapter 16, to request disk I/O operations, instead of native System/370 and XA I/O instructions. These are intercepted by CP, which then performs the physical disk I/O.

In VM/SP and HPO, CMS reads and writes to minidisks by creating channel programs and issuing DIAGNOSE 18. DIAGNOSE 18 accepts a subset of the channel command repertoire in order to reduce CP effort interpreting and translating channel programs. This increases performance, since this interface between CMS and CP can be interpreted much more efficiently than the general I/O capability of the 370 and 390 architecture.

VM/ESA CMS uses DIAGNOSE A4 instead of DIAGNOSE 18. Instead of converting the block number and type of operation into a channel program and passing it to CP, CMS passes the block number, minidisk address, block size of the disk, buffer location and type of operation to DIAGNOSE A4. CP uses this information to generate the type of channel program appropriate for the device. This provides better performance than DIAGNOSE 18 because channel program translation and interpretation is no longer needed. It also simplifies CMS design, since it no longer has to be concerned with device geometry (capacity of a track, number of tracks per cylinder, and so on).

Most DIAGNOSE operations are synchronous, and the CMS userid is placed in a wait state until the I/O operation is complete. It usually makes little sense for CP to return control to the CMS userid after initiating an I/O operation. CMS would normally enter a voluntary wait state until the I/O completed. Holding the CMS userid in wait state eliminates overhead dispatching the userid, having it signal a wait condition, and redispatching it when the I/O operation completed.

Reserved Disk Areas and *BLOCKIO

The CMS `RESERVE` command tells CMS to reserve all unused disk blocks on a minidisk and assign them to a single unique file id. If a LISTFILE command is executed against this disk, it looks as if one file entirely fills it.

RESERVE is used by SQL/DS and SFS. These applications use the *BLOCKIO DASD Block I/O system service, described in "CP System Services" on page 366, to perform asynchronous disk I/O based on disk block numbers. Database and file servers perform their own disk storage management, internally allocating disk blocks for tables or files, and request I/O operations by sending messages to *BLOCKIO.

RESERVE is usually issued as soon as a minidisk is formatted, and ensures that contiguous blocks are made available to the database application (so it can suballocate from within a single extent). RESERVE marks the disk blocks as "in use" to ensure that another program doesn't allocate them.

Every block of data within a reserved file can be addressed by its block number within the minidisk. This is calculated by adding its relative position within the file to the offset in the minidisk at which the file starts. Even a minidisk with no files uses several disk blocks to contain the file directory and allocation map. *BLOCKIO applications use the CMS `DISKID` service to obtain the number of file system overhead blocks, and the origin of the reserved file.

Problems with Minidisk Sharing

A weakness of the minidisk file system is the relative difficulty of sharing changing data. If several users are linked "read-only" to a minidisk while another user is writing new files to it, the read-only users cannot use the new files until they reACCESS the disk.

A minidisk can be safely LINKed in write mode by at most one user. If a disk is LINKed and ACCESSed in write-mode by more than one user, the result is almost invariably a corrupted minidisk file directory. Each user ACCESSing the disk reads its file directory and allocation map into storage, and then updates them without cooperating with the others.

Depending on the order in which the minidisk is changed, a disk block can wind up being allocated to multiple files, for example, or both allocated to a file and present in the available block list. Usually, if this has happened (and most VM security systems prohibit this), the minidisk's contents have been corrupted. The only recourse is to salvage undestroyed files and restore the remaining contents of the minidisk from a backup copy.

Non-CMS File System Access

CMS supports read-only access to MVS or DOS/VSE datasets on minidisks or full disk volumes formatted with MVS or VSE Volume Table of Contents (VTOC). This support is limited to certain dataset organizations. This allows one-direction sharing of data between CMS and MVS or VSE applications. A program product from The Adesse Corporation gives CMS read-write capabilities for these file organizations.

Additionally, CMS VSAM (Virtual Storage Access Method) provides both read and write access to VSAM objects on OS or DOS-format disks. CMS VSAM is a version of DOS/VSE VSAM ported to run under CMS, so it is not surprising that both versions of VSAM can access the same files. This can be used for CMS applications that need keyed direct access to files, and can be used to share data between VSE and CMS programs. The data sharing is less useful for sharing data with MVS systems, since current MVS systems use a different catalogue structure than the one supported by VM and VSE. VSAM sharing capabilities will be limited until all three versions of VSAM support the same format of VSAM catalogue.

	FS macros	OS simulation (except VSAM)	VSAM	CSL	EXECIO CMS Pipelines
Languages	Assembler	Assembler and compiled languages	same as OS sim.	same as OS, plus REXX	REXX, EXEC 2
Disks	Minidisks, SFS	Same as FS macros, plus OS format disks	OS or DOS format disks	SFS	Minidisks, SFS, and OS format disks

Fig. 12.7 File interface applicability.

Chapter

13

Shared File System

Despite its performance, ease of use, and flexibility, the CMS file system has several deficiencies. CMS files can be no larger than the minidisks on which they reside, making it necessary to find large amounts of contiguous disk space for large files. Because files cannot span minidisks and minidisks cannot span disk volumes, the largest contiguous free space on a single disk volume determines the largest file that can be created.

When a user needs more disk space, a system administrator must copy the minidisk's contents to a larger minidisk. Directory manager tools make the mechanical aspects of this task easy, but it normally must be done when the disk's owner has detached the disk or is not logged on, thus making it inconvenient for a user to increase disk space. The unit of allocation of disk space depends upon the device type. The system user or administrator must convert the amount of space needed into the cylinder capacity of the disk model being used.

Manipulating large numbers of files is cumbersome because, unlike PC-DOS or UNIX systems, CMS files on minidisks cannot be organized into subdirectories. Only a single user can write to a CMS minidisk at a time, and read-only users of a disk are not notified of disk changes, making it difficult to share changing data.

CMS files were accessed easily only from a single VM system, thus making it cumbersome to share data among VM systems. IBM introduced the Inter-System Facility (ISF) for HPO, and later, Cross-System Extensions (CSE) for VM/XA and VM/ESA, to let multiple VM systems share access to CMS minidisks. Each system accessing shared data had to reside in the same computing center, however, to have physical connections to the shared disk drives.

These limitations were solved by the *Shared File System (SFS)*, which separates the logical view of data from the physical method used to store it. SFS was introduced in VM/SP Release 6, but didn't get much exposure because few sites converted to this version of VM. With VM/ESA, SFS became available at large VM sites, and so was exploited by more users.

Compared to minidisk files, SFS files are organized and shared more easily by users of the same or different VM systems because SFS files are relieved of hardware-characteristic based size restraints.

SFS functions

Data in SFS can be organized, shared, and updated more naturally than in traditional CMS minidisks. SFS lets users structure data into tree-style directories, much like in MS-DOS and UNIX, and multiple users can read and write files in the same SFS directory without interfering with one another.

SFS disk space is allocated in 4KB units, regardless of disk type, so neither user nor administrator must remember device characteristics. The quota allocated to a user can be increased or decreased at any time, without requiring the user to logoff or stop using files.

SFS also lets one user update a file while many users are reading it. Under application control, files either can be accessible during updates or can be locked to prevent access during updates. If they are accessible, users can see the most recent, fully committed version of a file, or individual changes as they are made. Separate file authorizations can be specified for each file, thus providing flexible control file access.

SFS is IBM's first remote file system. Therefore, SFS files can be shared over a network among multiple VM hosts. Applications read and write files that reside in remote locations exactly as they read and write files on local disk drives. For example, a VM system in San Francisco can run an application that reads files in an SFS filepool in Chicago, and write them to a filepool in New York.

SFS is also the basis for IBM's emerging VM implementation of System Managed Storage (SMS). First introduced in MVS, it is intended to provide a single consistent view of data, independent of the media upon which it resides. Rules can be defined to specify a file's performance requirements, the frequency with which it should be backed up, and how long backup and archival copies should be retained. SMS also supports automatic migration and recall of inactive data. Files can be migrated to a compressed disk file format—migration level one—if they have not been referred to in a specified number of days, and then will be migrated to off-line storage—migration level two—after a second interval of continued disuse. Programs can recall a migrated file explicitly through DFSMS commands, or implicitly by opening a file for read access. Not all SMS functions are available in VM yet, but IBM is expected to roll out new functions. Some of them, such as device selection, really are needed only in MVS.

Differences between minidisk and SFS file access are summarized in Fig. 13.1.

File sharing controls

SFS lets users specify who can access data on a file-by-file basis, rather than on a minidisk level, with the `GRANT` and `REVOKE` commands. File update also

	Minidisk	SFS
Read sharing	any number of users	any number of users
Write sharing	one user per minidisk, Readers don't see changed or added files without reACCESSing disk	one user per file. Changed, new files are visible to readers as soon as committed
Access control	Rules specified for entire minidisk	File-by-file permission
File Organization	Flat namespace on each minidisk	Tree-structured directories and aliases
Maximum file size	As large as minidisk, which can be no larger than a single disk volume	As large as the SFS pool, which can be arbitrarily large
Space allocation	In cylinders or blocks. Cylinder capacity varies by model	4K block quotas, regardless of disk type
Data location	Minidisk must reside on disks attached to VM system that user is on	Data can be accessed from any VM system in a TSAF collection or SNA network
Performance	Very high	Increased overhead (with exceptions)
Application Interfaces	OS/MVS simulation for Higher Level Language and assembler language, FSREAD/FSWRITE macros for assembler language	Minidisk interfaces, plus the Callable Subroutine Library (CSL) for both HLL and assembler language

Fig. 13.1 SFS and Minidisk file system comparisons.

occurs at the file level, allowing individual files to be written or updated by only one user at a time although they may be read by many users. Default and explicit lock mechanisms let users control when a file can be updated.

SFS provides consistent access to changing data. When a file is changed, SFS's default action lets users see the most recent committed version of a file, thus providing data integrity by preventing access to partially updated files. Changed data is written to *shadow disk blocks*. If the transaction is "rolled back" under program control or if the application crashes, the shadow disk blocks are discarded and the original file remains intact.

When a file is closed or committed, its new disk locations become permanent and are used by the next user to open the file. The original disk locations are retained as long as one of the users reading the old version of a file has the file open.

SFS also provides a "commit without close" option, in which changes to a file can be committed to disk without closing the file and losing current file positions and buffer contents. CSL calls let applications specify that readers of the file should be able to see changes to the file as soon as they are made, without waiting for a commit or close operation. SFS lets changes to a file be rolled back or committed under program control.

The `FILEATTR` command, shown in Fig. 13.2, overrides the default behavior and the `NORECOVER` attribute indicates that a file cannot be rolled back once it is changed. The `INPLACE` option indicates that changed disk blocks are rewritten in their original disk locations, though users reading the file may have to reopen the file to read newly added records. These options are appropriate when disk space and processing costs must be conserved, or when file changes must be immediately visible to all users of a file.

Files can be locked to ensure that they are not updated or referred to during an application's execution. Locks can be *exclusive*, so only the lock

```
 listfile * data c(d
FILENAME FILETYPE FM   FORMAT  LRECL    RECS    BLOCKS DATE    TIME
TEST     DATA     C1   F          80      10    1      1/21/92 17:17:57
Ready;
 query fileattr test data c
Directory = VMSYSU:JBS.USERS.CLAUDE
Filename Filetype Fm   Type    Recovery       Overwrite
TEST     DATA     C1   BASE    RECOVER        NOTINPLACE
Ready;
 fileattr test data c norecover inplace
Ready;
 query fileattr test data c
Directory = VMSYSU:JBS.USERS.CLAUDE
Filename Filetype Fm   Type    Recovery       Overwrite
TEST     DATA     C1   BASE    NORECOVER      INPLACE
Ready;
```

Fig. 13.2 FILEATTR command.

holder can read or write the file, or shared so they can be read but not altered. CMS implicitly locks files that are opened for output. XEDIT locks SFS files for the duration of an edit session, unless the **NOLOCK** option is specified on the command line. Programs also can explicitly set and release locks via CSL calls and the **CREATE LOCK** command.

SFS filepool servers

SFS data resides in *filepool* server userids, which control minidisks containing SFS data and respond to user requests to read and write data. Filepool servers run a multitasking CMS application similar to SQL/DS, letting filepool servers concurrently handle multiple requests from users and issue overlapped I/O operations to minidisks.

Filepool servers do not use normal DIAGNOSE I/O. Instead, they use the asynchronous ***BLOCKIO** CP system service. ***BLOCKIO**, which is also used by SQL/DS, is an IUCV service implemented in CP that allows asynchronous, overlapped disk I/O operations while the server continues to execute. CP returns a completion message to SFS when a previously initiated I/O operation completes.

The filepool server maps the directory tree file structures of its users onto the minidisks that are assigned to it. Users do not LINK to the minidisks containing the data, because their CMS sessions don't read and write to the disk drives containing the files.

Instead, users are enrolled into an SFS filepool and given a quota of disk space, which can be adjusted by administrators. When files are read or written, CMS automatically creates an Advanced Program to Program Communication (APPC/VM) message and sends it to the filepool server. APPC/VM is described in the Chapter 15 section, "Advanced Program to Program Communication/VM (APPC/VM)." If the filepool server is on a different VM system, CP sends the message over a VTAM network or TSAF link to the system running the filepool server.

SFS access and naming conventions

Files in SFS directories use the same filename, filetype, and filemode conventions as minidisks. As with minidisks, files are made visible to the CMS session via the **ACCESS** command. Once a directory is accessed, its files are used almost exactly like files residing on an accessed minidisk. For example:

```
access <directory id> b   -- rather than,
access <disk address> b
```

SFS does not use the *current directory*, *working directory*, or PATH concepts of UNIX and MS-DOS. In these systems, part of the directory tree becomes the current name space of the files against which commands operate. A search path is defined for locating disk resident commands and files outside the current directory.

CMS, instead, allows multiple currently-accessed directories, and uses its traditional alphabetical filemode search across each accessed minidisk or directory to implicitly define access paths.

To view different parts of the directory tree at the same time, **ACCESS** the desired subdirectories at different filemodes. This is a little like the ability in MS-DOS to refer to multiple disk drives at once, and have a different subdirectory be the "current" directory on each drive.

SFS lets users create *aliases* to files via the **CREATE ALIAS** command, which is similar to the alias provided by the UNIX ln command. An alias lets a single file be known by different names in the same or different directories. A single directory can contain aliased files from multiple directories, making it easy to work with files located in various parts of the SFS directory structure simultaneously.

SFS directory names

Directories are named by:

1. SFS filepool id, which usually can be omitted. The filepool id ends in a colon (":"). If it is not specified, it defaults to the current filepool, which is set by the command **SET FILEPOOL <filepoolid>**. The standard filepool for user data is **VMSYSU**, but installations can create additional filepools for their applications.
2. Userid, the VM userid of the owner of the directory. If omitted, it defaults to your userid.
3. Directory id. The directory is separated from the owning userid by a period ("."). Sub-directory names also are separated by periods. IBM uses periods where MS-DOS uses backslash ("\") and UNIX uses forward slash ("/"). If "." is specified by itself, it indicates the root directory of the user. When I first saw this, I felt it was an unnecessary difference in notation from the other two systems. I've since come to feel that this is a good idea for two reasons: it ensures that CMS directory identifiers are distinct from UNIX and MS-DOS ones, and, because MVS uses periods to indicate levels of qualification for "datasets," it will provide compatibility with MVS syntax in case CMS and MVS ever share a distributed file system.

The following are valid directory specifications, and can appear as the first operand of ACCESS:

vmsysu:jeff.	Userid JEFF's top directory
vmsysu:jeff.users.harley	Fully qualified subdirectory name

`jeff.users.jon`	Filepool id allowed to default
`.`	Your top directory
`.fruit.bananas`	Bananas subdirectory within fruit

Directory names are used in **ACCESS** commands in the same way as minidisk device numbers, as illustrated in Fig. 13.3.

You can save typing by specifying a "+" or "–" to move up or down in the tree, relative to a previously accessed directory. The **+fm** notation tells CMS to start at the directory accessed at the specified file mode, and then move to the specified subdirectory below it; **–fm** tells CMS to move to the parent of the directory accessed at that filemode, and then move to the subdirectory below it. This notation is illustrated in Fig. 13.4. If you are used to MS-DOS, this is similar to using relative and parent directory pathids (e.g., MS-DOS `..\nextdir`).

Some CMS commands create "scratch" or "work" files on disk. To prevent accidentally writing these files into other users' directories, CMS accesses other users' directories in read-only mode. This can be overridden by the **FORCERW** option of ACCESS if WRITE authority to the directory is available, as described in the Chapter 13 section, "Granting access to files and directories." **FORCERW** is illustrated in Fig. 13.5.

Managing SFS objects

CMS includes commands for creating, erasing, and renaming SFS directories, and for controlling access to them and their files.

Creating directories

Every user registered in an SFS filepool automatically has a "top" directory, specified as "." (In UNIX, this is the "home" directory.) To make additional

```
* access your top (root) directory as "A"
access . a
* access Daniel's top directory (if allowed)
access daniel. b
* access Jeff's games directory (if allowed)
access vmsysu:jeff.games c
* access Jeff's games directory, assuming current filepool
access jeff.games c
* access my program directories:
access .progs.source d
access .progs.source.header e
access .progs.source.c f
access .progs.executable g
```

Fig. 13.3 ACCESS commands for SFS directories.

```
access .users b
* Access .users.rush
 access +b.rush e
* Access .users.doris by
"backing up" from .users.rush
 access -e.doris f
```

Fig. 13.4 Relative directory names.

```
access myboss.reports b (forcerw
Ready;

copyfile status report a = = b
Ready;

release b
Ready
```

Fig. 13.5 FORCERW option for R/W access of another user's directory.

directories, use the **CREATE DIRECTORY** command. This is the CMS equivalent of MS-DOS and UNIX **mkdir** and, fortunately, can be abbreviated as CRE DIR. For example:

```
create directory .flora
Ready;

cre dir .flora.fruits
Ready;

cre dir .flora.vegetables
Ready;

cre dir .flora.vegetables.greens
Ready;

cre dir .flora.vegetables.legumes
Ready;
```

The directory structure created by the above commands is shown in Fig. 13.6.

Erasing directories

IBM did not add a new command to CMS to erase directories. Instead, the **ERASE** command was enhanced to allow it to erase directories as well as files, as shown below:

```
erase .documents.oldproject
```

By default, **ERASE** will not erase a directory if any files are still in it; the option **FILES** makes it less fastidious:

```
erase .documents.oldproject (files
```

Displaying directories and files

CMS provides commands for displaying and traversing directory trees. **LISTDIR** displays fully qualified directory names within a subtree. Its default action is to display all the directories belonging to the user issuing the command. If an operand is specified, **LISTDIR** displays the directory tree under the specified directory. **LISTDIR** output is shown in Fig. 13.7.

The column labeled **Fm** contains a hyphen if the disk is not accessed; otherwise it contains the filemode under which the directory is accessed.

CMS includes the fullscreen command **DIRLIST** to traverse a directory structure. **DIRLIST**, shown in Fig. 13.8 presents the same information as **LISTDIR** but, like **FILELIST**, allows "point and shoot" selection of a directory. For example, moving the cursor to the line for the **.USERS.HARLEY** subdirectory brings up a FILELIST display for the files in that directory.

The existing **QUERY SEARCH** command was enhanced and **QUERY ACCESSED** was added to show the search order and names of accessed directories, as shown in Fig. 13.9.

Renaming directories

IBM also extended the **RENAME** command to support directories. Directories can be renamed freely, but cannot be assigned to a different filepool or VM user. For example:

```
rename .documents.current .documents.old
```

SFS also includes the **RELOCATE** command, which lets users move files and directories to different locations in their directory tree structures. For example:

```
* Move all TOMATO files from .vegetable to .fruits
relocate * tomato .flora.vegetables to .fruits
```

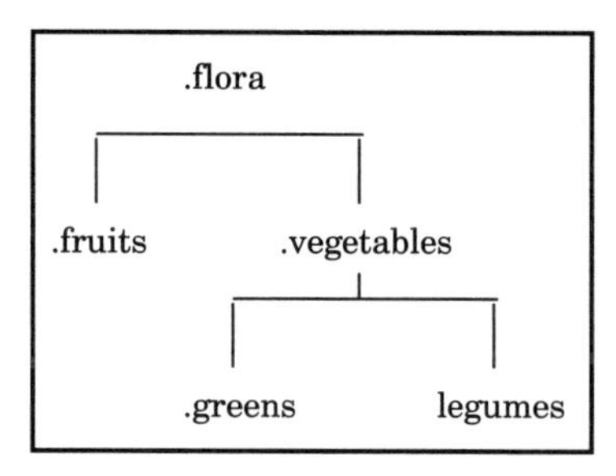

Fig. 13.6 Sample tree structure.

```
listdir
Fm Directory Name
- VMSYSU:JEFF.
- VMSYSU:JEFF.MVMUA
- VMSYSU:JEFF.PERF
- VMSYSU:JEFF.PERF.CONS
- VMSYSU:JEFF.PERF.CPULOG
- VMSYSU:JEFF.PERF.XAMAP
- VMSYSU:JEFF.TOOLS
- VMSYSU:JEFF.USERS
- VMSYSU:JEFF.USERS.BRODIE
- VMSYSU:JEFF.USERS.DORIS
- VMSYSU:JEFF.USERS.HARLEY
- VMSYSU:JEFF.USERS.HERSKOVITZ
- VMSYSU:JEFF.USERS.PETEG
Ready;
listdir .users
Fm Directory Name
- VMSYSU:JEFF.USERS
- VMSYSU:JEFF.USERS.BRODIE
- VMSYSU:JEFF.USERS.DORIS
- VMSYSU:JEFF.USERS.HARLEY
- VMSYSU:JEFF.USERS.HERSKOVITZ
- VMSYSU:JEFF.USERS.PETEG
Ready;
```

Fig. 13.7 Output of LISTDIR command.

```
Ready;

* Move all SCRIPT files in .documents.current to .documents.old
Relocate * script .documents.current to .documents.old
Ready:

* Move the .sample.files directory into the .production.version *
directory. relocate .sample.files to .production.version
Ready;
* now there is a .production.version.sample.files directory
```

Granting access to files and directories

SFS allows highly granular access control to SFS files and directories. File permissions specify the right for a user to read or write a file, and directory permissions specify the rights of users to view or alter the contents of a directory by seeing the names of the files, or by creating, erasing or renaming them.

Access can be allowed or denied on an individual basis by using the `GRANT` and `REVOKE` commands. These commands can be applied to VM userids, names in a `NAMES` file (thus allowing nicknames for VM userids and for lists of VM userids), and `PUBLIC`. In the last case, all users who can connect to the filepool can access the file.

File authorization can be for READ or WRITE access. Directory authorizations are:

- READ lets users see a list of directory files.
- WRITE lets users add directory files.
- NEWREAD lets users read future files.
- NEWWRITE lets users write to future files.

The format of the GRANT command is:

```
GRANT AUTH <fn> <ft> <dirid> TO userid | nickname | public(<options>
```

Here, <fn> and <ft> can be specified with "*" and "%" wildcard characters to indicate groups of files. The <dirid> is specified as above, and <options> include the authorization types just specified.

A user can be allowed to READ or WRITE individual files without being allowed even to see the names of other files or to add files to the directory. For example:

```
grant auth zork exec .games to friends (read
grant auth .data.client1 to client1 (read
grant auth .logdir to workers (newwrite
grant auth * exec .public.execs to public (newread
```

CMS provides both line-mode and fullscreen commands for displaying the authorization rights to files and directories. For example, the display in Fig. 13.10 shows that the top directory of COMETS:HALLEY. can be read-accessed by all users but written to only by GALILEO and KEPLER.

SFS performance

When using SFS rather than minidisks, there is the possibility of decreased performance because SFS I/O operations require communications between

```
TXJEFF  DIRLIST  A0  V 319  Trunc=319 Size=10 Line=1 Col=1 Alt=0
Cmd  Fm Directory Name
      -  VMSYSU:JEFF.USERS
      B  VMSYSU:JEFF.USERS.BRODIE
      -  VMSYSU:JEFF.USERS.DORIS
      -  VMSYSU:JEFF.USERS.HARLEY
      -  VMSYSU:JEFF.USERS.HERSKOVITZ
      -  VMSYSU:JEFF.USERS.PETEG

1= Help        2= Refresh      3= Quit    4= Sort(fm)    5= Sort(dir)    6=Auth
7= Backward    8= Forward      9=         10=            11= Filelist    12=Cursor
```

Fig. 13.8 DIRLIST command.

```
ac .users.brodie b
Ready;
q search
JBS191    191   A     R/W
-         DIR   B     R/W   VMSYSU:JEFF.USERS.BRODIE
MNT319    319   P     R/O
ESA190    190   S     R/O
MNT300    300   U     R/O
MNT31A    31A   X     R/O
MNT19E    19E   Y/S   R/O
Ready;
q accessed
Mode      Stat  Files  Vdev  Label/Directory
A         R/W   1342   191   JBS191
B         R/W      6   DIR   VMSYSU:JEFF.USERS. BRODIE
P         R/O      9   319   MNT319
S         R/O    280   190   ESA190
U/U       R/O    276   300   MNT300
X         R/O   1342   31A   MNT31A
Y/S       R/O    872   19E   MNT19E
Ready;
```

Fig. 13.9 QUERY SEARCH and QUERY ACCESSED.

the user and SFS server. However, performance may increase when using SFS, because it can help users avoid expensive methods for sharing data in minidisks.

SFS file operations usually are not as efficient as file operations to a minidisk. Rather than directly executing a DIAGNOSE instruction to perform disk I/O, CMS must prepare an APPC/VM message to the filepool server and transmit it. The message is interpreted by the server, which performs the actual I/O.

Nonetheless, several factors mitigate the potential loss in performance. SFS uses the *BLOCKIO system service to allow it to perform multiple concurrent I/O operations and also buffers file input and output to and from the client machine, so these operations remain efficient. Some operations are executed as special cases for efficiency. For example, a COPYFILE command issued to make a copy of a file within a filepool is executed entirely within the filepool, rather than as a series of transactions between the server and the client userid.

SFS can perform concurrent overlapped I/O operations because filepools typically use disk space that is spread over several disk volumes. Files read by many users simultaneously may be processed faster if they are moved from a single minidisk to SFS, because several disk volumes might simultaneously be performing I/O operations, rather than processing one at a time on the single volume containing the minidisk.

VM directory entries for SFS servers running on processors with expanded storage for minidisk caching should include the statement OPTION NOMDCFS. This tells CP to allow the server to have more than its "fair share" of minidisk cache blocks, and is appropriate because the SFS server handles I/O operations for multiple users.

ES/9000 VM *dataspaces*, discussed later, can remove almost all inter-virtual machine overhead of communicating between client and filepool servers, making SFS I/O potentially as efficient as minidisk I/O.

SFS performance must be compared to its alternatives. Without SFS, many applications must create a file on a work disk, and then transmit it via the spool to a virtual machine that owns the desired target disk. The combination of SENDFILE and RECEIVE—and their numerous equivalents—is far more expensive than using SFS to place the data on the desired target directory. When files are "shared" that way, the same data is read and written from disk several times, making SFS an extremely efficient alternative.

SFS lets installations grant larger quotas of disk space to users than they need without wasting space. With minidisks, a too-high space allocation wastes disk space. An excessive allocation in SFS, however, has no effect because unused disk space remains available for other users. Larger disk quotas let users avoid creating temporary disks ("T-disks") when they need temporary work areas. T-disks must be formatted every time they are used—a very significant I/O cost—because the entire contents of the temporary disk must be written, even if only a fraction of the minidisk space will be used. SFS users can create their temporary files and erase them when they no longer are needed without this overhead.

SFS also provides more effective allocation of disk space when disk space must be conserved. SFS allocations are not subject to space fragmentation or cylinder boundaries like miniqdisks. Space allocation can be controlled with a high level of granularity, down to the 4KB block level, while minidisks must be allocated in cylinder units.

```
 ASTRO  AUTHLIST A0  V 165  Trunc=165 Size=4 Line=1 Col=1 Alt=0
Directory = COMETS:HALLEY.
Grantee      R    W    NR  NW
<PUBLIC>     X    -    X   -
GALILEO      X    X    X   X
KEPLER       X    X    X   X

1= Help       2= Refresh   3= Return   4= S(Grantee)   5= Sort(W)     6= Sort(R)
7= Backward   8= Forward   9=          10=             11= Sort(NW)   12= Sort(NR)
====>
                                                                  X E D I T  1 File
```

Fig. 13.10 AUTHLIST display

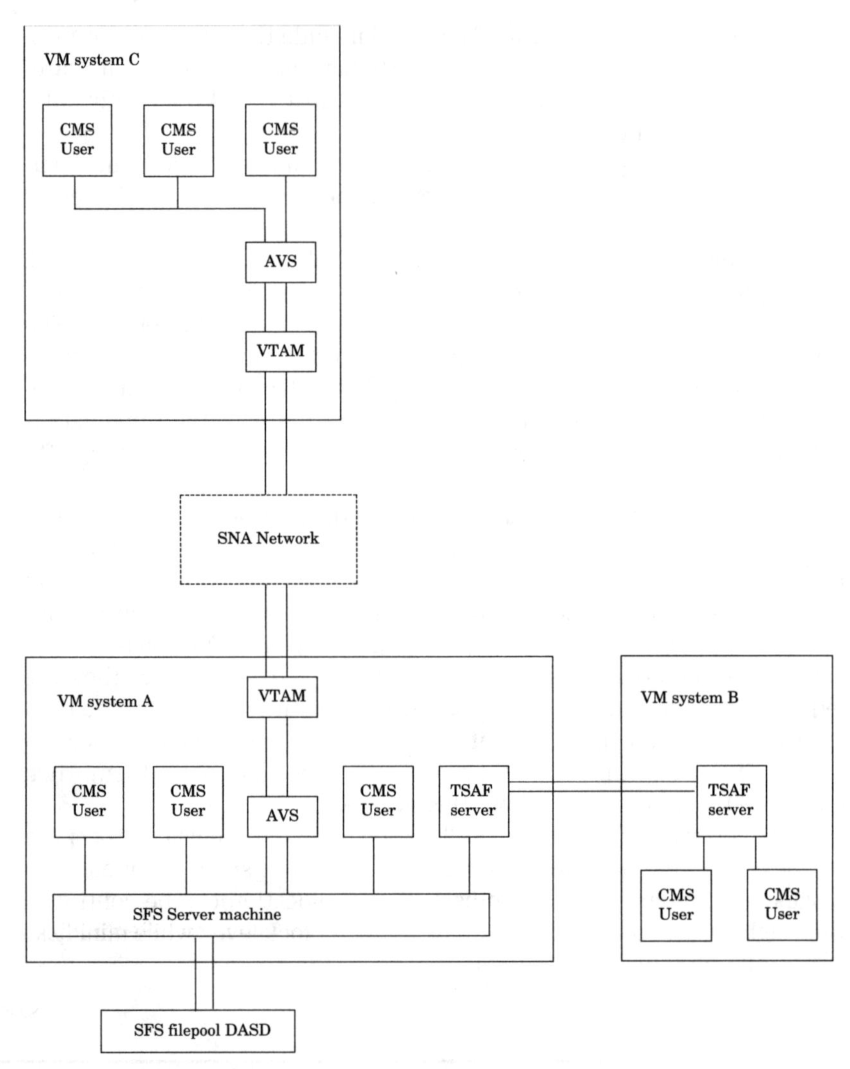

Fig. 13.11 Local and remote access to SFS files.

Remote access to SFS files

SFS files can be accessed across an SNA network or TSAF collection, giving VM a transparently accessed networked file system on the same communications lines used for interactive traffic. VM systems in a TSAF collection communicate with one another across CTCA links or bisynchronous lines.

VM systems also can use *APPC/VM VTAM services (AVS)* to convert APPC /VM messages to and from SNA LU6.2. This lets VM systems communicate with one another across an intervening SNA network. In Fig. 13.11, VM systems A and B are in the same TSAF collection, and system C is connected to them by an SNA network.

Directory control directories and VM dataspaces

The SFS directories described above are called *file control* directories because they allow file level authorization and access control. SFS directories also can be designated as *directory control* directories—usually called *dircontrol*—and allows higher performance at the expense of decreased control over individual files.

Dircontrol directories are more like minidisks than filecontrol directories because they can be accessed in read/write mode by only one user at a time. They should be used for infrequently updated files or for files that are updated by only a single VM userid at a time.

These directories improve performance by requiring few authorization checks. A user can access all the files in a dircontrol directory with only a single check for proper authorization, whereas filecontrol directories require a check for each file.

Files in dircontrol directories can be placed in VM dataspaces when running on ES/9000 processors equipped with expanded storage. Users can access files in dataspaces via direct memory reference rather than APPC/VM communication between SFS server and client applications. The instruction path length for a retrieving a disk block in a dataspace can be as small as four in-

```
* Create a new directory control directory
create directory .production.library (dircontrol
Ready;

* Change an existing directory from filecontrol to dircontrol
dirattr comet.datafiles (dircontrol
Ready;

* Let the userid 'produser' update the production library
grant auth .production.library to produser (dirwrite
Ready;

* Let everyone read the production library
grant auth .production.library to public  (dirread
Ready;

* place the production library in a dataspace for fast access
dataspace assign .production.library
Ready;
```

Fig. 13.12 Directory control directories.

structions, if the data is resident in memory, compared to the thousands of instructions that would be needed for normal APPC/VM message flow and disk I/O. This, therefore, is an ideal way to provide high performance for mostly-read files shared by multiple users.

If data is already in real storage, it is accessed without cost or delay. If data is resident in expanded storage because it was migrated out of central storage, the entire 4KB block is copied to real storage at memory-to-memory speeds and then made available. Highly shared data will tend to remain resident in real or expanded storage without programmer intervention and can be accessed at semiconductor memory speed, providing remarkable performance improvements to many applications.

SFS exploits another capability of VM dataspaces: *minidisk mapping services*. The contents of a minidisk can be mapped one-for-one to the contents of a dataspace. A minidisk consisting of *N* 4KB byte blocks numbered from *0* to *N-1* can be directly referred to as virtual storage in a dataspace N pages in length.

Rather than explicitly issuing I/O operations to read from disk, SFS applications simply refer to disk contents as if they were already present in real storage. This is referred to as *data in virtual* or *data in storage*, because applications just refer to data without regard to its physical location. This also has been called *single level storage*, because data always is referred to by storage reference, even if it really resides on disk.

SFS issues program calls to CP to associate a dataspace with a minidisk and to terminate the association. Mapped data can be updated as well as read, so data that is paged out is written asynchronously to disk. Application programs also can request that data be saved on disk to ensure that a good copy resides on permanent media. SQL/DS is another VM application that uses dataspaces and minidisk mapping for enhanced performance.

Dircontrol directories are created by specifying the option `DIRCONTROL` when using the `CREATE DIRECTORY` command, or by using the `DIRATTR` command to modify the attributes of an existing directory. `GRANT` commands provide read or write access to the entire directory's contents, rather than to individual files contained in it. The rights `DIRREAD` and `DIRWRITE` grant users read and write access to the entire contents of the directory.

Commands manipulating dircontrol directories and dataspaces are shown in Fig. 13.12.

SFS Callable Subroutine Library functions

In addition to the application program interfaces available with minidisk files, CMS provides Callable Subroutine Library (CSL) functions for more expressive power. These functions provide a rich set of file-related services, letting calls be made from assembler, and from such higher-level languages as REXX, C, FORTRAN, COBOL, Pascal, and PL/I.

```
/* The following REXX program section uses CSL routine DMSEXIFI to check
   whether or not a given SFS file exists. It then uses CSL calls to open
   the file and read its first record. Note that the directory need not
   be ACCESSed! */
  parse upper arg fileid
  f_len = length(fileid)
  commit = 'COMMIT'; c_len = length(commit)
  /* help rexx csl wrong: says RC variable is set */
  Call csl('DMSEXIFI rtnc rsnc fileid f_len
             commit c_len')
  if rtnc<>0 then do
     Say 'File does not exist as specified' ,
          || ', Return code is ' rtnc  ,
          || ', Reason code is ' rsnc
     exit rtnc
   end
  accesstype = 'READ CACHE OLDDATEREF'
  a_len       = length(accesstype)

  Call csl('DMSOPEN  rtnc rsnc fileid f_len' ,
             'accesstype a_len token')
  if rtnc<>0 then do
     Say 'Unable to open' fileid,
          || ', Return code is  'rtnc  ,
          || ', Reason code is  'rsnc
     exit rtnc
   end
  say 'Assigned token (file handle)' token
```

Fig. 13.13 CSL routine to open a CMS file, Part 1.

One benefit of CSL is that its calls have identical effects regardless of the language from which they are called. Built-in I/O statements in different languages sometimes have idiosyncrasies or jargon that make it difficult to share program methods and code. For example, a FORTRAN direct access file is called a REGIONAL(1) file in PL/I.

CSL calls can open, close, read, and write files in SFS filepools. CSL calls let files read or write by record number, and read or write multiple blocks simultaneously. When a file is opened for update access, CSL calls can be used to determine whether changes to the file should be made visible to users already reading it ("update-in-place"), or written to shadow blocks until the file is committed. File level CSL calls include:

- DMSEXFI and DMSEXIST determine if a file exists, and return status information either in supplied variables or a buffer.
- DMSOPEN opens an SFS file.
- DMSREAD reads a file.

```
      /* no. records to read. must be 1 if RECFM V */
data_length = 4096                /* length to read (bytes) */
buffer  = copies(' ',4096)
buflen  = length(buffer)
position = 0               /* indicate next sequential record */
Call csl('DMSREAD  rtnc rsnc token records data_length' ,
         'buffer buflen bytes_read position')
if rtnc<>0 then do
   Say 'Error reading file' ,
         ||', Return code is ' rtnc  ,
         ||', Reason code is ' rsnc
   exit rtnc
  end
say bytes_read 'bytes_read'
say substr(buffer,1,min(79,bytes_read))

Call csl('DMSCLOSE rtnc rsnc token commit c_len')
if rtnc<>0 then do
   Say 'Error closing file' ,
         ||', Return code is ' rtnc  ,
         ||', Reason code is ' rsnc
   exit rtnc
  end
```

Fig. 13.14 CSL routine to read from a CMS file, Part 2.

- DMSWRITE writes a file.
- DMSCLOSE closes a file.
- DMSCOMM commits changes to a file without closing it.

One of the convenient aspects of CSL file access is that files being operated on need not reside on accessed directories. Unlike other CMS file interfaces, file objects can be handled without being ACCESSed!

REXX code in Fig. 13.13 uses CSL calls to determine whether a file exists and then opens it. It is not necessary to ensure that the file exists before opening it; it is done here for illustration. DMSOPEN returns a "token" value used to refer to the file while it is open. The code in Fig. 13.14 uses this token to read the first record of the file, and then closes it. Note that the file could have been read randomly and for more than one record at a time.

CSL calls also let applications perform many of the file and directory manipulation functions provided by CMS commands, making it easy for an application to incorporate much of the power of the file system. Some of the functions provided are:

- DMSERASE erases a file.
- DMSRENAM renames a file.

- DMSFILEC copies a file. This is very efficient because the SFS filepool server copies internally without APPC/VM traffic with the requesting userid.
- DMSGRANT grants file access to another user.
- DMSREVOK revokes file access.
- DMSCRALI creates an alias name for a file.
- DMSCRLOC creates a lock to control access by other users.
- DMSDELOC deletes a lock.
- DMSCRDIR creates a directory.
- DMSDEDIR deletes a directory.
- DMSOPDIR opens a directory for reading.
- DMSGETDI gets (reads) directory information.
- DMSCLDIR closes a directory.
- DMSRELOC relocates a directory to a different position in the file tree.
- DMSQLIMA determines the space quotas for all users in a filepool.
- DMSQLIMD deblocks data from the buffer returned by DMSQLIMA.
- DMSQLIMU determines a user's space quota.

For example, the REXX program in Fig. 13.5, by Daniel Friedman of Merrill Lynch, displays quotas for all users in an SFS filepool.

SFS provides the `CREATE NAMEDEF` command to associate an identifier with a file or directory name. CSL programs can refer to the namedef rather than to hard-coded filenames, making it easy for programs to operate on different files and directories. Namedefs persist until they are replaced by a new name definition (with the `REPLACE` option), or until they are removed with the `DELETE NAMEDEF` command.

Defining SFS filepools

VM/ESA has three standard filepool servers: VMSERVS for system data, VMSERVU for user data, and VMSERVR for coordinated resource recovery (CRR). An installation can add as many other filepools as it likes, using installation-specified names.

Figure 13.16 contains an example of a VMSERVU directory entry. Several of the directory statements contain special settings needed for an SFS filepool server:

1. The `user` statement gives the server 32MB of virtual storage. A high storage value is recommended to provide SFS storage for buffers.

```
/* Obtain quotas for all users in a specified filepool */
arg subpool .
if subpool = '' then subpool = 'VMSYSU'
poolen = length(subpool)
/* first call just to get number of enrolled users */
Call CSL 'DMSQLIMA reta reasa subpool poolen buffl 32'
Call CSL 'DMSQLIMD retd reasd buffl 32 1 numr nume uid sgrp maxblk' ,
  'comblk thresh'
number = nume
size = nume*24 + 8        /* now we know what buffer size to use */
Say 'Number of users enrolled =' nume
Say ' '
Say 'Userid   Stor. Grp   Max blks   Commit blks   Threshold'
Call CSL 'DMSQLIMA reta reasa subpool poolen buff size'
Do n=1 to number
  Call CSL 'DMSQLIMD retd reasd buff size n numr nume uid sgrp' ,
    'maxblk comblk thresh'
  sgrp = right(sgrp,6)
  maxblk = right(maxblk,12)
  comblk = right(comblk,10)
  thresh = right(thresh,10)
  Say uid sgrp maxblk comblk thresh '%'
end
```

Fig. 13.15 CSL calls to obtain SFS limits.

2. The `OPTION` statement defines special options recommended or necessary for SFS servers:

   - `MAXCONN` specifies the maximum number of users who can connect to the filepool at any one time.
   - `QUICKDSP` ensures that the filepool server always can get service from the scheduler.
   - `APPLMON` lets the server generate CP MONITOR data for gathering performance data about SFS operations.
   - `ACCT` lets the server generate accounting data, so the installation can bill back CPU time spent servicing SFS clients.
   - `NOMDCFS` stands for "no MiniDisk Cache Fair Share," and indicates that the SFS server should be allowed to get more than its proportional share of the system's expanded storage. This is a good policy because the SFS server performs I/O for multiple users.

3. `IUCV` allows all VM users to make an IUCV connection to the SFS server. Users who are not registered to SFS will be rejected by SFS itself.
4. `IUCV *IDENT` indicates that the SFS server is able to declare a global resource (RESANY GLOBAL), which allows the resource—the filepoolid and its data—to be visible across an SNA network.
5. `SHARE` gives the server a high VM priority. This, along with QUICKDSP,

ensures that SFS is not delayed waiting for resources.

6. FONT1>MACHINE XA lets the server use storage that is defined beyond the 16MB line. The server also could be defined as `MACHINE ESA` or, to enable VM dataspaces, `MACHINE XC`.

Each SFS minidisk is used for a special purpose:

- CONTROL disk describes every 4KB data block in the *storage groups* defined to the filepool. The size of the control disk determines the maximum amount of data that can be placed in the filepool. If it is too small, the FILESERV REGENERATE command can be used to enlarge it, but only when the filepool is not in use.
- CATALOG disk describes all the objects contained in the filepool, and is altered when objects in the filepool are created or altered. The catalog also is called *storage group 1*.
- LOG disks store copies of changes to the catalog disk since its last backup, which can recover catalog information in case of a disk failure. SFS maintains two identical logs, thus allowing data recovery even if the catalog and one of the log files are damaged.

  When a backup is made of the catalog data, the log files are emptied. SFS automatically schedules a backup to a destination—predefined by the systems programmer—when the log disks become full. Minidisk

```
USER VMSERVU password 32M 64M G 1
 OPTION MAXCONN 2000 QUICKDSP APPLMON ACCT NOMDCFS
 IUCV ALLOW
 IUCV *IDENT RESANY GLOBAL
 SHARE REL 500
 MACHINE XA
 IPL CMS
 CONSOLE 009 3215 T
 SPOOL 00C 2540 R
 SPOOL 00D 2540 P
 SPOOL 00E 3211 CLASS A
 LINK MAINT 190 190 RR
 LINK MAINT 19E 19E RR
 MDISK 191 3380 4 2 VMDSK9 MR
 MDISK 301 3380 237 36 VMDSK1 MR
 MDISK 302 3380 1499 16 VMDSK5 MR
  MINIOPT NOMDC
 MDISK 303 3380 16 16 VMDSK9 MR
  MINIOPT NOMDC
 MDISK 304 3380 32 13 VMDSK2 MR
 MDISK 305 3380 1025 745 VMDSK3 MR
```

Fig. 13.16 USER DIRECT entry for an SFS filepool server.

```
ADMIN MAINT JEFF DANIEL PETE JULIE KEITH
BACKUP
ACCOUNT
SAVESEGID CMSFILES
FILEPOOLID VMSYSU
USERS 1000
```

Fig. 13.17 VMSERV DMSPARMS example.

caching should be turned off for log disks, because they are mostly written to, rather than read.

- *User data storage groups* store actual user data and are numbered starting from group two. A storage group can consist of an arbitrary number of minidisks and clients. Users are assigned to a specific filepool when they are enrolled into SFS.

  Additional groups can be defined to simplify data backup and restore functions. To provide consistent file views, a storage group is disabled while it is being backed up. Using multiple storage pools reduces the time service is interrupted for any individual SFS client.

When using the default IBM definitions, userid VMSERVS implements the filepool VMSYS, and VMSERVU implements VMSYSU. These filepool names are always local to a VM system, and cannot be accessed by remote VM systems in a network. There is no requirement to provide filepools with these names, and other names can be used to make global file sharing possible. The CRR server—normally VMSERVR—is recommended, because it stores the status information needed to implement two-phase commit and transaction rollback.

The name of the virtual machine running the filepool is not significant. Instead, the server determines the name of the resource it defines—and declares it to VM and the network in which VM participates—from the POOLDEF and DMSPARMS files contained on its A-disk.

When started by the `FILESERV START` command, a filepool server reads the file with its userid for the filename and for the filetype DMSPARMS, which resides on any accessed minidisk. The DMSPARMS file, as illustrated in Fig. 13.17, specifies key information about the filepool:

- `ADMIN` lists the userids of the default administrators that control the pool. Additional administrators are defined by the `GRANT ADMIN` command.
- `BACKUP`, indicates whether control data backups should be created. This normally is turned off only for CRR servers.
- `ACCOUNT`, tells the server to generate accounting information.

- SAVESEGID specifies the name of a saved segment containing the SFS server code. This statement is optional. If omitted, SFS will load the code from disk files. Using the saved segment improves performance because each logged on SFS filepool server will share the same code in real storage.
- FILEPOOLID is the name of the filepool that the server implements.
- USERS specifies the maximum numbers expected to connect to SFS simultaneously.

A system programmer creates a DMSPARMS file when defining an SFS filepool. The command FILESERV GENERATE uses the contents of the DMSPARMS file and input from the system programmer defining the filepool, to create a POOLDEF file with the name of the filepoolid—in this case VMSYSU POOLDEF—shown in Fig. 13.18.

The POOLDEF file specifies the assignment of minidisks to SFS functions. The FILESERV GENERATE command formats the minidisks and writes their initial empty contents.

Summary

SFS is an important advance for CMS file access. With it, users can choose between minidisks for high-performance access to private data, or can use SFS for more flexible access and easier sharing between users and systems.

```
MAXUSERS=1000
MAXDISKS=500
DDNAME=CONTROL          VDEV=301
DDNAME=LOG1             VDEV=302
DDNAME=LOG2             VDEV=303
DDNAME=BACKUP  DISK     FN=BACKUP     FT=DATA    FM=D
DDNAME=MDK00001         VDEV=304         GROUP=1
DDNAME=MDK00002         VDEV=305         GROUP=2
```

Fig. 13.18 VMSYSU POOLDEF example.

Chapter

14

VM Communications

VM provides a remarkable number of options for communications and connectivity. VM can be accessed for interactive use from a wide variety of terminals and terminal emulators. VM also supports a large set of formal and defacto protocols for inter-CPU communications.

VM is as comfortable with non-IBM communication protocol suites like TCP/IP, as it is with standard IBM terminals and IBM's *System Network Architecture*. VM's ability to provide compatible interoperability with a variety of networking methods makes it the best-suited of IBM's mainframe operating systems for interfacing with the "open systems" and personal computer worlds.

3270 Terminal Access

The standard VM terminal is an IBM 3270, described earlier in "VM Screen Handling" on page 23, or a personal computer emulating one. IBM 3270 terminals are arranged in *clusters* attached to 3274 or 3174 control units (usually referred to as 3270 controllers). VM supports 3270 clusters attached to a channel, or remotely through 3705, 3725, or 3745 communications controllers. Many personal computers are equipped with software and hardware to emulate 3270 terminals. The 3270 family of devices also includes simple line-printers; these printers (usually models 3286 or 3287) are cabled to a 3270 controller just like a display device.

The traditional VM 3270 is connected to a channel attached controller, and is usually called a "local 3270." This is the simplest and highest-performance terminal connection available for mainframes. Terminal I/O is performed by CP without the use of a "terminal access method," as under MVS. This shortens the instruction path-lengths for transmitting a datastream from an application to the display and for processing attention interrupts from the keyboard. Channel attachment provides enough data bandwidth to make the time to "paint" a full screen of data too short to be observed. A CMS user on a local 3270 can move through XEDIT, FILELIST, and other display screens without perceptible delay in response. It is even possible to write programs that perform screen animation (motion), a feat not normally associated with mainframe systems.

Local terminals have been restricted to users within close physical proximity to the host computer, due to the former limits of 400 feet for channel attached devices, the distance between the CPU and the 3270 controller, and up to 2,000 feet of coaxial cable between the controller and the 3270 terminal. System/390's ESCON architecture makes it possible to place 3174 controllers kilometers from the data center, and still provide the same performance as local terminals. Almost-local response times have been provided for many years via channel-extender devices provided by Paradyne and Dataswitch.

VM also supports remote 3270 clusters attached to the host via a front-end controller. Remote 3270 terminals on the same cluster share a single line through which all data passes. The major disadvantage of remote 3270s is the far lower data bandwidth available for remote connections. As many as 32 users might be sharing a single 9,600 bits per second line. These users will suffer poor response time no matter how fast the host system.

VM supports remote 3270 clusters using bisynchronous (`BSC`) protocol at rates of up to 19.2KB (an upper bound imposed by hardware, not software). VM/SP and HPO support remote clusters defined by `CLUSTER` and `TERMINAL` macros in the system-generation module `DMKRIO`. VM/Pass-Through (PVM) is used to drive remote clusters under VM/ESA.

SNA, discussed below, allows higher remote 3270 data transfer rates. It also supports a new 3270 communications controller protocol, *Distributed Function Terminal* (DFT) mode. DFT mode, compared to the original 3270 architecture (now called *Control Unit Terminal*), provides additional usability functions, such as higher data transfer rates, Token Ring LAN attachment, and the ability to define multiple logical host sessions on the same terminal and cable.

Dial-Up Terminals

ASCII terminals, often operated as line-at-a-time "teletype" devices, are popular for remote dialup access. CP supports teletype compatible ASCII devices as half-duplex, linemode terminals connected to the host through a 3705 family front-end processor. VTAM also supports teletype devices. Technically, there is a separate telephone number for each frontend processor line and modem set. Typically, users dial into a hunt group of telephone numbers connected to the same type of modem; the hunt group connects the user to an idle modem.

Most dialup terminals are now actually personal computers. Popular personal computer packages allow a PC to emulate commonly used terminals such as the DEC VT100 or IBM 3101.

These terminals, and PCs that emulate them can be connected via 37×5 front-end processors, and by 7171, 3708 or 3174 protocol converters. The 9370 and 9221 models of ES/9000 include integrated ASCII subsystems, to provide terminal emulation without the need for additional hardware. Increasingly, software or hardware protocol converters map "glass teletype" terminals and PCs into simulated 3270s, often providing full-duplex and type-ahead features not directly provided by VM. Value-added networks like Tymnet and Telenet also provide conversion facilities to create simulated 3270s.

Some PC products provide built-in protocol conversion to provide 3270 terminal emulation and file transfer, typically by interacting with a companion product residing on the mainframe. Two such product families are *Simware* from Simware Inc, and *Relay* from Microcom, Inc. Both products let a personal computer dial into VM from a remote location and get full 3270 terminal emulation, plus the ability to perform file transfers between the host and PC. Both systems provide scripting capabilities to automate dialogues between personal computer and host, and can be used to shield users from the mainframe user interface.

Virtual Terminals

CP lets virtual machines define and control "virtual terminals": terminals that are software artifacts instead of hardware devices. This capability is used for a number of innovative applications, but the original purpose is to let communications software connect networked terminals to a VM system without having to pre-define them. This allows terminal I/O and network control to be extracted from the VM nucleus and implemented in virtual machines.

CP creates virtual terminal data streams with the same code it uses for real ones. At the point where terminal device drivers would normally call CP's low level I/O routines, they instead call the interface modules that route screen traffic to the virtual machine creating the virtual terminal. Consequently, virtual terminals are highly compatible with real ones. VM provides two methods for creating virtual terminals, both discussed below.

Logical Device Support Facility (LDSF)

The Logical Device Support Facility (LDSF) is one of VM's innovative features. LDSF lets applications create "logical devices," simulated 3270 terminals created under application program control. Logical devices are usually called *LDEVs*; virtual machines that create them are called *LDEV hosts*.

CP treats logical devices like locally attached 3270-family display devices. Instead of writing to and reading from physical 3270s, CP "writes" 3270 datastreams to the virtual machine creating the logical device, and "reads" input from the virtual machine. LDSF is programmed using a combination of DIAGNOSE 7C, to pass LDSF requests to CP, and external interrupts from CP when data or status information is arriving on a logical device. Details on the program interface to LDSF is described in Chapter 16.

When an application creates an LDEV, CP places a VM logo screen on it and notifies the LDEV host. The LDEV host can then send a LOGON command to initiate a VM logon session, followed by the screen interactions needed to run an application. LDSF was created for VM/Pass-Through (PVM), and is also used by TCP/IP's Telnet application. PVM and TCP/IP service machines receive keyboard input from remote systems, use LDEVs to simulate keystrokes as if the remote user were logged onto a real 3270, and send simulated display output back to the remote user.

Logical devices are also used by session manager programs, which let a user at a single terminal create and logon to multiple sessions, and hotkey between them. One of the most popular of these is the SESSION program, a program generously made available to the public by its author, Arthur Ecock of the City University of New York. Mr. Ecock also distributes a REXX function package, RXLDEV, which makes LDEV functions directly usable from REXX programs. Both programs are available on the Waterloo VM library and VM Workshop Tools tapes.[1]

LDSF can also create logical printers. This can let VM route print traffic to an application program which can write it to disk, filter it, send it to a networked device, or otherwise manipulate it.

Console Communications Service (*CCS)

Console Communications Service (*CCS) is a generalization of LDSF which allows creation of line-mode as well as 3270 terminals. *CCS uses the IUCV message passing protocol instead of DIAGNOSE to create and manipulate simulated terminals. A separate communications path is maintained between CP and the *CCS host virtual machine for each simulated terminal. This lets the *CCS host more easily pace traffic over its virtual terminals. CP and the

---

[1] The Waterloo VM library can be obtained by contacting the University of Waterloo , Department of Computing Services (ATTN: Jack Hughes, mail stop MC2053), in Waterloo, Ontario, CANADA N2L 3G1. The VM Workshop Tools tapes can be obtained by attending the Workshop, or asking for a copy from one of the attendees.

*CCS host issue IUCV SEND and RECEIVE commands to transmit screen contents and keyboard input to one another. The *CCS program interface is described in "CP System services" on page 372.

*CCS was introduced for VM's SNA support. A VTAM Service Machine (VSM) connects to the *CCS system service to identify itself as a *CCS host and create sessions. *CCS is also used by TCP/IP to create line-mode Telnet sessions.

VM/Pass-Through (PVM)

VM/Pass-Through, usually referred to as PVM, is a simple, inexpensive, yet powerful method of networking VM systems for terminal and printer access. PVM's primary purpose is to let VM users logon to remote 3270 hosts, although it also lets programs simulate logons and run preprogrammed scripts, or pass program-to-program messages across a network.

PVM started in 1977 as an internal tool called V6 (because its original site already had service virtual machines named V0 to V5) written by Noah Mendelsohn, and became a program product in 1980 with new development and support from Bill Anzick and Don Ariola. PVM came to be used at hundreds of VM sites shortly after being made publicly available. PVM's immediate popularity was due to the ease with which it could be installed and used, the obvious value of being able to logon to a remote host, and its low overhead.

PVM virtual machines communicate with one another in peer-to-peer fashion over BSC lines or channel-to-channel adapters. Users on either system can connect to the partner system. PVM also routes traffic to indirectly connected hosts. In Fig. 14.1, for example, the systems can connect to one another, using the link between systems B and E as an intermediate path for connections between the two cities. Clusters of nearby systems can route traffic through communications hubs, as in this example, allowing multiple systems to share (or cost justify) high-speed long distance lines. VM users in a PVM network can connect to any system to which there is an indirect path, although response time deteriorates as the number of intermediate nodes increases.

PVM also lets VM users logon to a remote system that runs neither VM nor PVM by emulating a 3274 control unit. In this mode, PVM responds to orders from a remote host system just as a 3274 controller would. Since the remote host thinks that it is communicating with a control unit instead of a system, there is no provision for intermediate nodes, and logons can only be made from the VM system to the remote host, and not the other way around.

A user on a VM system logs onto a remote system by entering the CMS command PASSTHRU, if already logged onto the local VM system, or by en-

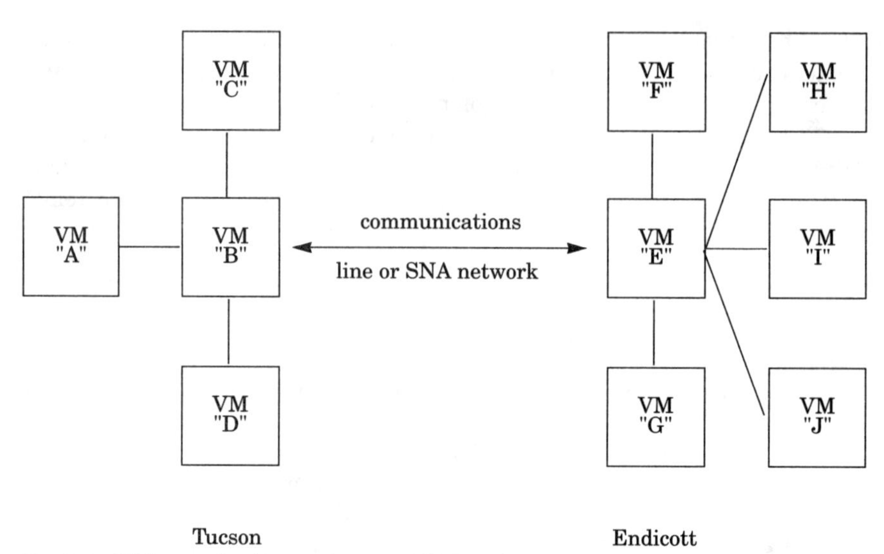

Fig. 14.1 PVM network with two clusters of CPUs.

tering the command `DIAL PVM` from the VM logo. The PASSTHRU command creates a conversation with the PVM virtual machine, and exchanges keyboard and screen data via the VMCF protocol. When the DIAL command is used, the PVM service machine directly drives the user's terminal.

In both cases, PVM displays a panel with system names, as shown in Fig. 14.2. The user selects a system by placing the cursor over the name of the system he or she wants to logon to, and presses the Enter key. Each node is prefaced by a one letter code indicating what type of node it is: L for the local VM system, N for a PVM host node, and S for a simulated 3270 node. The next thing the user sees is the logo or greeting screen of the remote system. The PVM service machine at the remote system uses LDSF to create a 3270 with the same physical characteristics as the one the user is logged onto (number of screen rows and columns, and presence of color and highlighting features).

PVM provides a number of additional useful facilities for users logged on at their local VM sites. A user can specify *temporary disconnect* and *notepad* program function keys to let the user briefly return from the remote session to the local system, and to append the remote session's screen image to a local disk file. PVM also provides the PVMIUCV facility, which lets IUCV applications communicate with applications residing on a separate VM system.

MPVM is a PVM feature that provides multiple session support for CMS users. MPVM provides a selection screen much like the standard PVM screen, but with user-specified nicknames. Multiple sessions can be established with local or remote systems, and users can switch between them and the local system via a "hotkey." An escape key can be specified to let a user execute a command on the local system without temporarily disconnecting from a remote session.

MPVM provides a programmable session manager which lets programmers automate dialogues with local or remote systems. MPVM "macros," written in REXX, let applications merge data from several systems into a single display, capture screen information and process it, and automate keyboard input.

PVM also provides special facilities for multiple system control. PVM is the communications medium linking multiple VM systems together in a *Cross System Extension* (CSE) complex, and transmits control information between VM systems sharing common spool areas and user populations. PVM also provides remote operator capabilities for unattended 4300 computers. The ROCF (Remote Operator Console Facility) lets PVM simulate a remote CPU's hardware console for distributed 4300 processors. Operators at a central site can IPL and control remote systems.

PVM communication methods

PVM originally performed its own I/O operations over dedicated BSC point-to-point communication lines. These communication lines could not be shared with other applications, such as RSCS, making it necessary for installations to provide multiple individual links between adjacent systems in a PVM network. This added cost made it difficult to perform network management and reconfiguration in case of a failed host or communications circuit. This problem was partially mitigated by line-driver modifications from the University of Maine

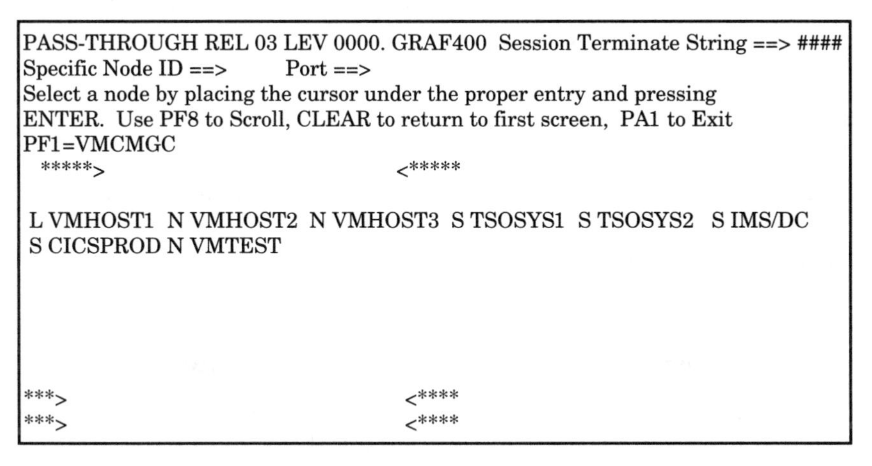

```
PASS-THROUGH REL 03 LEV 0000. GRAF400  Session Terminate String ==> ####
Specific Node ID ==>        Port ==>
Select a node by placing the cursor under the proper entry and pressing
ENTER.  Use PF8 to Scroll, CLEAR to return to first screen,  PA1 to Exit
PF1=VMCMGC
  *****>                                      <*****

 L VMHOST1  N VMHOST2  N VMHOST3  S TSOSYS1  S TSOSYS2   S IMS/DC
 S CICSPROD N VMTEST





***>                                          <****
***>                                          <****
```

Fig. 14.2 PVM selection screen.

that let PVM and RSCS share the same physical line. With PVM providing interactive traffic and RSCS transmitting files, the combination often fulfilled most of the communication needs between two locations.

PVM is now a VTAM application and can use SNA for its physical transport, in addition to its original BSC and CTCA links. PVM uses the APPC line driver to connect to VTAM and pass APPC/VM messages to a PVM server on a remote host. A PVM Gateway (PVMG) server machine runs under GCS and simulates an SNA *Logical Unit Type 2*. This lets PVM connect to SNA applications, and lets users connect to PVM like other SNA services. Previously, SNA users that wanted to logon to a link provided by PVM had to connect to a VM system and then logon or issue the DIAL PVM command.

SNA links let companies replace multiple communications lines between sites with a smaller number of higher speed lines, as well as making available a number of other SNA benefits discussed later in this chapter. PVM provides line drivers for each type of communication resource it supports:

- BSCA—Point-to-point BSC link over a leased line, used for connection between PVM nodes.
- CTCA—Channel-to-channel adapter connection between PVM nodes.
- 3088—The successor device to the CTCA. It provides added capabilities for long distances over ESCON channels and connections to 3172 and 8232 LAN channel stations to workstations.
- APPC—Connects PVM nodes via an SNA network. The PVM server uses APPC/VM macros, which the AVS component of VM maps into SNA LU6.2.
- IUCV—Connects PVM to a PVMG gateway server on the same VM host. This is similar to the APPC line driver, except that PVMG is a VTAM application specifically designed for interaction with PVM.
- 327X—PVM emulates a 3274 or 3174 controller for a non-PVM host.
- R3270—PVM drives remote BSC 3274 and 3174 controllers. Support for remote 3270 clusters was removed from CP when VM/XA and VM/ESA were introduced; the PVM R3270 line driver provides the same function outside CP.
- ROCF—The line driver for ROCF operator consoles

Remote Spooling Communications Subsystem (RSCS)

The Remote Spooling Communications Subsystem (RSCS) transfers files between systems. In a number of ways, RSCS is the quintessential VM facility: it is simple, easy to understand and use, and provides valuable functions with little fuss or overhead.

RSCS provides elegant and easily used file and mail transmission for networked computers. RSCS makes it easy for users to send files and electronic mail to remote computers, encouraging exchange of programs and mail. RSCS is also the primary method used in VM systems for printing on network-connected printers.

RSCS's name is due to its extension of VM spooling to remote systems named by an 8-character *node id*. RSCS lets users send files, notes, and messages to users on different systems as easily as to users on the same VM system. The CMS NOTE, SENDFILE and TELL commands use nickname files to let users specify destinations for one or more users without regard for their network locations, or let you specify the node name explicitly:

```
sendfile mvmua roster to jwagner at pucc  explicit node id
sendfile mvmua agenda to members          nickname for a list of
                                          users at different nodes
tell jwagner please add to your files     cross-system terminal
                                          message
```

SENDFILE and related commands send files to the RSCS machine's virtual reader along with with TAG information specifying their destination system nodes and userids. RSCS transmits files through the network to their destination node's RSCS. The remote RSCS writes the file on to the VM spool and transfers the file to the destination user's reader queue. It is easy to send files to other locations using low-level VM commands. For example, the following commands have essentially the same effect as the first SENDFILE in the previous example:

```
cp spool punch to rscs               direct files to RSCS userid
cp tag device punch pucc jwagner     specify destination node, user
punch mvmua roster                   place file on RSCS's reader
```

Origins of RSCS, and RSCS networks

RSCS is the basis for international networks linking thousands of computer systems and many thousands of users. It started as an IBM internal tool named CPREMOTE, used to let a pair of CP/67 systems transmit files to one another over a BSC communications line. CPREMOTE's author, Ed Hendricks, along with Tim Hartmann, produced RSCS by adding support for a variety of communications protocols, including support for batch-oriented *RJE* (Remote Job Entry) stations used to transmit punched cards to mainframes, and receive printouts in return. RSCS provided file transmission to remote CPUs and remote workstations (which bear no resemblance to what we call workstations today!) in the same package.

Hendricks and Hartmann subsequently added the ability for RSCS nodes to transmit files through intermediate nodes, using a store-and-forward protocol. RSCS files are received on the spool at intermediate nodes, and then transmitted to the next system en route to the final destination. This lets files make progress towards their destination even if connecting links or systems are down, and ensures that a system or communication failure anywhere along the transmission path does not cause lost data. In Fig. 14.3, spool files sent from NEWSON at System A to VARIAN at System D are received at system B and sent onto system C, and then finally sent to System D.

Hendricks and Hartmann provided a simple routing mechanism: each RSCS node only needs to know the next location to send files for each destination. They also added the ability to transmit interactive messages and commands, and a line-driver that was compatible with the NJE/NJI protocol used by the MVS JES2 and JES3 subsystems.

An informal network called *VNET* soon sprung up within IBM as system programmers "borrowed" communications lines to connect their systems to the nearest adjacent RSCS node. By 1979 there were almost 300 hosts connected to VNET; this number passed 1,000 in 1983 and is now over 3,000. Most of these hosts are VM systems, although compatible MVS systems also participate. VNET is IBM's nerve system, and lets IBM employees exchange mail, programs and information at locations all over the world.

RSCS became the basis, outside IBM, of the U.S. academic network BITNET (Because It's Time Network), Canadian NETNORTH, and the European Academic Research Network (EARN). These networks are all connected to one another, of course, and to the Internet. RSCS lets researchers, programmers, and other computer users communicate with one another throughout the world. RSCS networks tend to have more complex topologies and more nodes than PVM networks, because more people have need to exchange mail and files with computer users at other sites than have reason or authorization to logon to computer systems belonging to other institutions.

Since source code is supplied for RSCS, programmers at many sites have been able to add important features to RSCS, including distributed operator authority and the ability to automatically handle incoming dialed connections, many of which have been adopted by IBM.[2] IBM provides a number of well-defined exit points in RSCS to make it easier for customers

[2] I used the former of these facilities using a version developed at the City University of New York, and wrote a version of the latter (the eventual IBM version was much better than the one I did, but I needed mine several years before it appeared in the product).

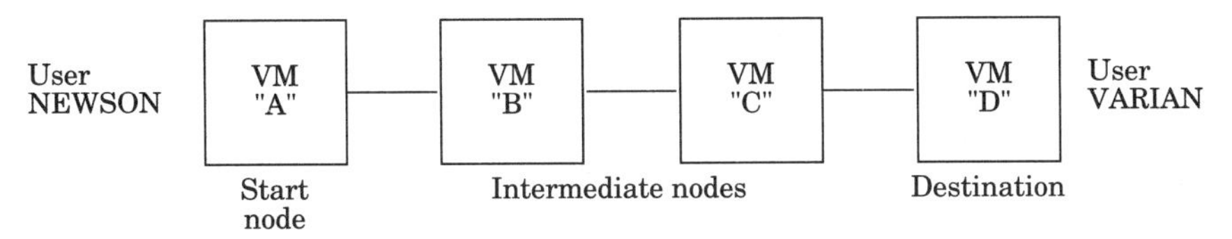

Fig. 14.3 Message flow through a simple RSCS network.

to make local customization to RSCS without having to learn the internals of RSCS operation. Installations can code user exits to control accounting, set file size limits (so people don't try to transmit large databases during peak network load periods), and so on.

RSCS links and protocols

RSCS maintains conversations along *links* to remote computers and intelligent terminals running either another copy of RSCS or a program compatible with one of the industry-standard protocols RSCS supports. A link can be in CONNECT state, meaning that a conversation has been established between the two partners, in ACTIVE state, indicating that a START command was issued but the remote system has not responded, or INACTIVE state. RSCS maintains a queue of spool files awaiting transmission along a link. Queues can be ordered in first-in, first-out (FIFO) order, in priority order, or in order of ascending file size.

RSCS supports a wide variety of standard line protocols for host-to-host, and host-to-dumb terminal communication:

NJE (Network Job Entry) protocol is common to all IBM mainframes, and provides a framework for transmission of files, executable jobs (files run as control streams on an MVS system), inter-user messages, and operator commands. NJE is the basis of VNET and the other networks discussed earlier. An NJE header accompanies each file to describe the file's contents, and its origin and destination nodes and userids.

NJE is a peer-to-peer protocol. Both systems in a conversation can initiate the transmission of files or commands to the other in a symmetric fashion. RSCS formerly supported VMB and VMC protocols for RSCS-to-RSCS communications over BSC lines or channel-to-channel adapters. They were phased out in favor of the exclusive use of NJE protocol, since NJE supported MVS in addition to VM, and worked with both BSC lines and CTCA devices. NJE protocol is implemented on non-IBM equipment by a number of vendors, allowing peer-to-peer file transmission over Network System, Inc.'s *Hyperchannel*, and to DEC VAX systems using Joiner Associates' JNET product.

RJE (Remote Job Entry) is the protocol built into IBM's 2780, 3780, and related remote workstations. These devices usually consisted of a line printer, punched card reader, and (sometimes) a keyboard and small display. They were used, in most cases, to submit batch jobs to remote OS/360, DOS, or MVS systems.

RJE protocol is widely emulated by personal computers, workstations, minicomputers, and by mainframe programs like RSCS. There are probably more computers emulating 2780 and 3780 terminals than were ever built. RSCS supports RJE protocol both as a host and as a remote station; that is, it can assume either the master or slave role in the unequal conversation that a 3780 terminal has with a host.

`MRJE` (Multileaving Remote Job Entry) is similar to RJE protocol, except that it allows concurrent, multileaved transmission of data to different devices at the same time. For example, an MRJE station might have three printers, a card reader, and a card punch, and one communications link to a host computer. An MRJE station can simultaneously read from the card reader to the communications line, and from the communications line to each of the output devices. Data is buffered in workstation storage before being transmitted or written (the chief difference between RJE and MRJE terminals is that MRJE requires "dumb terminals" smart enough to have some computer storage and an intelligent buffering program.

MRJE is also referred to as *HASP protocol*, since it was popularized by the OS/360 HASP component's remote job entry facilities. Like RJE protocol, MRJE is emulated by a wide variety of computer systems. As with RJE, RSCS can take either side of an MRJE communication.

RSCS supports leased line and dial-up connections for each of these protocols. Leased lines are usually "conditioned" and therefore more reliable and capable of higher data transfer rates. Dialed lines use whatever voice-grade lines the local and long distance telephone carriers happen to select at the moment a call is completed, and are therefore less reliable. Dialed links are far less expensive when only intermittent file transfers are needed, and are charged by connect time, distance and time of day like normal telephone conversations. The tariff structure for dedicated circuits is considerably more complex, and usually includes a monthly fee independent of how much the circuit is used.

When leased lines are used, the networked machines have a dedicated telephone circuit between them, and usually keep it connected (active for transmission) at all times. When dial-up links are used, one system places a telephone call to the remote system. RSCS uses the *autodial* feature of 3705-family communications controllers to initiate a call to a specified telephone number, and uses the *autoanswer* feature to answer dialed calls. RSCS issues an `ENABLE` channel command to allow communications; this raises the *data terminal ready* (DTR) signal on the modem connected to the link. A special `WRITE` command can be used to initiate a dial sequence; the data in the write buffer contains the telephone number.

RSCS also supports a simple *3270P* protocol to print files on 3270-family printers. This is the most common method VM systems use to print on distributed printers. RSCS makes it easy for VM users to print on their own printers, instead of printing at a centralized site and having printouts delivered. Many companies use inexpensive ASCII printers connected to a protocol converter to emulate a 3287 printer. RSCS now also directly supports ASCII printers to make protocol conversion unnecessary.

For SNA networks, RSCS supports *SNANJE*, *SNARJE*, and *SNA3270P* connections. These are equivalent to NJE, RJE, and 3270P links, except that dedicated communications lines are not needed. RSCS uses its VTAM interface to transmit and receive data from the SNA network, which provides the data transport. This lets RSCS share the same network resources and monitoring facilities as other SNA applications, and relieves RSCS of the responsibility of performing its own line transmission and error handling.

TCP/IP line drivers have been developed at universities, making it easy to transparently extend the scope of RSCS transmission to Internet-style networks. In some cases, this is used to allow RSCS nodes to communicate with one another via an Internet gateway; it is also used to make it easier for IBM mainframe systems to interact with non-IBM systems on a network.

RSCS organization and control

RSCS consists of a master task, a line driver task for each active remote link, a spool task to read and write spool files, and a command processing task. Originally, RSCS used its own multithreading supervisor to create a multitasking environment for itself. RSCS IPLed from disk and provided all of its own program services. RSCS borrowed a certain amount of code from CMS to allow it to read configuration files from minidisks, but basically it was a totally independent operating system, relying only on CP services for I/O access.

RSCS Versions 2 and 3 support SNA links, operate in a GCS group, and communicate with VTAM via the standard VTAM application interface. This let IBM discard the multitasking supervisor built into the original RSCS, and use the same multitasking, I/O, interrupt processing, and storage management primitives available to all GCS applications. RSCS is loaded from a program library as a task, and creates subtasks for each active line driver. RSCS Version 2 introduced reentrant line-drivers: multiple active links using the same protocol share the same line driver code in virtual storage, and read/write data resides in dynamically acquired storage.

RSCS uses a simple control file, called `RSCS CONFIG`, to describe the remote links it can connect to, and indirectly accessed destinations behind them. The LINK statement specifies the node name, password, time-zone, link address or SNA application name, telephone number (for dial links), protocol, and other attributes of each directly connected link. The ROUTE statement identifies indirectly accessed nodes and specifies the node identifier of a node that can be used as an intermediate path to it.

RSCS provides operator commands that let authorized userids control RSCS operation. The configuration file identifies operator userids, and their host nodes, if commands from remote systems are permitted. Operators can start or stop links via START, STOP, and DRAIN commands (DRAIN stops a link when the currently transmitting files are sent; STOP stops a link immediately), create or remove links at any time through the RSCS DEFINE and DELETE commands, and change indirect routing through the ROUTE command.

Operators can also display the queue of files awaiting transmission and the progress of the file currently being processed, purge files, hold or release files for processing, and change their position in transmission queues. General users can also be allowed to issue operator commands for individual links. This can be used to let users control the order at which printouts arrive at their own printers, or to cancel printouts they realize they don't want.

RSCS developments

RSCS is a flexible and low-overhead mechanism for many purposes. IBM continues to enhance RSCS function by providing new line drivers and improving performance.

RSCS also increasingly finds itself a home in *Electronic Data Interchange* (EDI) applications between different companies. RSCS provides highly secure network access for a wide variety of computer types. Almost every computer vendor supports one of the previously mentioned protocols, making it possible for companies to use RSCS as a universal file transmission vehicle.

RSCS also has an important advantage over networking products like MVS's JES subsystems: files are not themselves executable, as jobs streams submitted to JES are. Companies can use RSCS to safely receive files from unsecured locations without having to provide them with "job card" information that would let them submit arbitrary (and possibly dangerous) MVS jobs. It is very easy to write applications that wait for a file to arrive from RSCS, load it to disk, and validate and process it, making RSCS an inexpensive applications enabler for distributed applications.

System Network Architecture (SNA)

System Network Architecture (SNA) is IBM's proprietary networking architecture, almost universally used in corporate mainframe data centers using IBM equipment. SNA is a layered architecture, similar to the OSI seven-layer network architecture. SNA provides deterministic, robust delivery of data between application and device, or between application and application. SNA isolates applications from details of line control and physical addressing of networked terminals, and provides network management, diagnostic, and monitoring functions.

A key function of SNA is the ability for any terminal in an SNA network, or collection of interconnected SNA networks, to sign on to or be acquired by any application known to the network. An important part of SNA is its ability to push much of the burden of handling physical resources, such as line polling, error recovery, message blocking and deblocking, and character set translation, from the CPU to front-end processors. For example, SNA supports communication between network nodes separated by intermediate nodes, but uses front-end processors to transmit messages to their destinations without requiring the services of CPUs at the intermediate locations.

Brief overview of SNA concepts

SNA includes a bewildering, complex set of entities and attributes, and a language and notation uniquely its own. SNA's complexity, and its hierarchical, host-oriented world view are often cited as its largest defects. Only a tiny fraction of SNA's architecture is needed for this book's purposes.

SNA defines resources called *Physical Units* (PU), and *Logical Units* (LU), and protocols that let them talk to one another. A Logical Unit can be thought of as an active agent or program that uses the physical unit for actual data transmission. LUs reside at different *nodes* in a network. Nodes may be computer systems or intelligent peripherals. LUs come in different types, designated by a number: an LU1 or LU2 node is a relatively unintelligent peripheral device, while LU6.2 is a protocol that allows programs to communication with one another one a message by message basis. APPC/VM, VM's application interface to SNA LU6.2, is discussed in "Advanced Program-to-Program Communication/VM (APPC/VM)" on page 372.

LUs establish *sessions* with one another, with the assistance of their associated PUs and "higher authorities" that negotiate authorization, message routing, buffer sizes, priorities, and a variety of other *session bind* characteristics. LUs may have multiple *parallel sessions* between one another, up to a predefined *session limit*. Sessions are independent of one another and may be in different processing states. LUs may be in session with one another even if intermediate nodes exist between them: no single point to point connections are necessary. Data is transmitted over *routes* defined to SNA under the control of intelligent front-end processors. SNA can route traffic to different or multiple routes if a communications line fails or is overloaded.

The *Virtual Telecommunication Access Method* (VTAM) is the key mainframe component for SNA. VTAM manages both physical resources like front-end controllers and applications, and routes data between host applications and the LUs in session with it. Other mainframe components of SNA include *NetView*, which provides network monitoring and control.

SNA provides a number of physical advantages over BSC remote devices: it uses a more robust line protocol, *Synchronous Data Link Control* (SDLC), with better error handling, and better performance at high line utilizations and over satellite links. SDLC supports higher line speeds than BSC, such as T1 links, which transmit data at 1.544 million bits per second. SNA also supports IBM's Token Ring LAN architecture, and makes it available for host-to-host, host-to-workstation, and host-to-terminal communication.

SNA and VTAM are far too complicated to be fully described here, and too large to have been implemented within CP. In fact, VTAM is several times the size of CP in lines of source code and bytes of object code.[3] Putting SNA support directly in CP would have been a considerable violation of the principle of maintaining CP as a small, consistent kernel.

VM VTAM

IBM implements SNA functions for VM via service virtual machines. A VTAM service machine (VSM) passes terminal data between CP and the SNA network. VM/VTAM consists of two components: the VTAM task performs network I/O to front-end processors and converses with VTAM applications, and is essentially the same VTAM code that runs in MVS, and the *VTAM SNA Console Services* (VSCS) task, which is the gateway between VTAM and CP.

VSCS is a VTAM application, and uses the standard VTAM application interface to get and put network data. VSCS also maintains an IUCV connection with the *Console Communications Service* (*CCS) IUCV CP system service interface to route inbound traffic and status to CP. VSCS issues an IUCV SEND to *CCS when data arrives from the network, and *CCS issues an IUCV SEND to VSCS when CP has data to send to SNA connected devices, such as an SNA-connected 3270 or printer.

VSCS connects to *CCS when it initializes. The maximum number of users logged on through SNA is controlled by the `OPTION MAXCONN` statement in the VSCS userid's directory entry.

Group Control System (GCS)

When IBM introduced VM VTAM, it ported VTAM from MVS to VM reusing as much original VTAM code as possible. This reduced the time and effort needed for the implementation, ensured compatibility, and provided a common code base for future development. In its original form, VTAM is an MVS application that makes heavy use of MVS system functions, some of which, like multitasking, are not provided by CMS.

Instead of implementing these MVS functions in CMS, a task that would have introduced significant complexity and risked incompatibility with existing CMS applications, IBM created a new VM component, the *Group Control*

---

[3] When SNA support was added to VM, a SHARE button soon appeared depicting a massive elephant labeled "SNA" sitting on and squashing a VM bear.

System (GCS), which includes precisely the set of MVS-like functions, combined with a subset of CMS functions, needed to run VTAM. Most significantly, GCS supports the MVS style of multitasking provided by the ATTACH assembly language macro, as well as MVS program linkage, error trapping, and timer management macros. ATTACH causes both MVS and GCS to create a *task*, a body of code with an independent path of execution from its parent task.

GCS also introduced a new concept for cooperating virtual machines: the GCS *group*. A group consists of virtual machines that IPL the same GCS saved system, and have access to the same shared read-only and read-write storage. Access to shared storage is made safe by only letting pre-authorized users alter it. Authorized users use locking and message passing protocols to safely share read-write data and communicate with one another. The storage shared by a GCS group emulates the MVS *Common Storage Area* (CSA), a globally visible storage area used as a mailbox for data passed between MVS applications. In the case of VTAM, MVS and GCS uses the CSA to pass buffers between the network and VTAM applications. GCS storage is illustrated in Fig. 14.4.

Members of a GCS group include the virtual machines that run VTAM, VSCS, NetView, RSCS, Advanced Function Printing, and any other application that makes use of VTAM services. VSCS and VTAM can reside in the same virtual machine, or they can reside in different members of the same GCS group. There is slightly reduced CPU overhead for passing messages between VSCS and VTAM if they share the same virtual machine, since GCS inter-virtual machine synchronization is not needed. Using separate virtual machines makes additional virtual storage available to both tasks and lets them execute in parallel on separate real CPU processors when VM is running on a multiprocessor CPU.

GCS relies on a *recovery machine* which is notified by CP whenever a member enters the group by IPLing the GCS system, or leaves it by logging off, crashing, or IPLing a different system. The recovery machine must en-

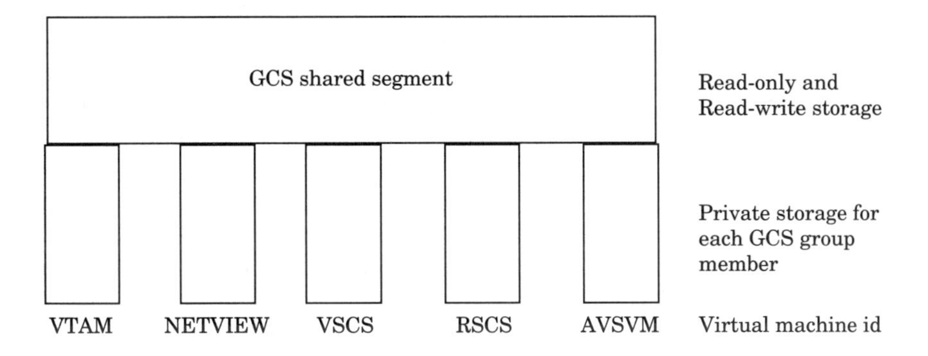

Fig. 14.4 Group Control System storage.

ter the group first. When subsequent users enter or exit from the group, CP sends the recovery machine a message from the *SIGNAL IUCV system service. GCS uses this notification to clean up after exiting virtual machines by freeing locked real storage and taking storage dumps for debugging.

When entering a GCS group, a virtual machine connects to *SIGNAL, and is assigned a 16-bit identifier number. The virtual machine specifies an 8-byte data area to be broadcast via IUCV SEND to existing members of the group. Option bits on the CONNECT parameter list specify if the virtual machine wants to receive notification via IUCV SEND when virtual machines enter or leave the group. The GCS recovery machine uses these bits to determine when a new member has entered the group. When a virtual machine crashes or logs off, the connection to *SIGNAL is severed, and CP sends a notification message to the recovery machine.

*SIGNAL can also be used to send short messages to one another without setting up IUCV connections between one another. This greatly simplifies programming and reduces the number of IUCV links CP would have to maintain. A GCS group with *N* virtual machines would otherwise need *N**(*N*-1)/2 IUCV links to provide full any-to-any communication (each of *N* userids would need *N*-1 connections to other users, divided in half since we would otherwise count each connection twice.)

To signal other members of a GCS group, as is done for communication with VM/VTAM, a virtual machine issues a send to *SIGNAL containing 8 message bytes, the signal ID of the virtual machine to send the signal to, or a flag indicating that the message should be broadcast to all members of the group. *SIGNAL issues an IUCV SEND to each of the specified virtual machines. For example, a VTAM application can place data in a buffer in CSA and issue a *SIGNAL message to the VTAM service machine for processing.

Networked Resource Sharing

The *Transparent Services Access Facility* (TSAF) lets multiple VM systems share access to global resources. Resources can be shared among distributed VM systems combined to form a *TSAF collection*. A resource is a program running in a virtual machine that acts as a server for client programs. Typical resources are SQL/DS databases for distributed relational database access, and SFS filepool servers for distributed filesystems.

Connections between different VM systems are managed by TSAF service virtual machines that communicate with one another over BSC lines, CTCA links, or VTAM paths when AVS is used. Up to 8 VM systems may participate in a single TSAF collection.

Virtual machines in a collection can define *local* and *global resources*. Global resources can be accessed by virtual machines anywhere in the collection, and local resources can only be accessed on the VM systems on which they are defined. TSAF uses *APPC/VM* (Advanced Program-to-program Communication/VM), described in "Advanced Program-to-program Communication/VM (APPC/VM)" on page 372, to carry messages between client and server on a peer-to-peer, message-by-message basis.

Messages between clients and resources on different VM systems are routed to the local VM's TSAF virtual machine, which forwards it to the TSAF virtual machine on the VM system for which it is intended. Neither client nor server applications need concern themselves with the location of their communications partners.

Resources declare themselves to the TSAF collection by using the *IDENT system service, described in "CP System Services" on page 372. CP tells the TSAF service machine when a virtual machine defines or revokes a logical resource. If the resource is global the TSAF server notifies other TSAF virtual machines in the collection.

Networked Resource Sharing with AVS

APPC/VM VTAM SERVICES (AVS) converts TSAF's APPC/VM messages to and from SNA's LU6.2 protocol, and lets TSAF resources be accessed by VM and non-VM systems anywhere in an SNA network. AVS runs in a service virtual machine which executes in the same GCS group as VTAM.

This makes it much easier to provide VM connectivity over large, geographically distributed networks. An SNA network might include VM systems in New York, San Francisco, and Wichita: a VM/CMS application in Wichita would be able to access files and databases in the other VM locations. *Coordinated Resource Recovery* (CRR) lets applications perform *two-phase commit* of distributed data. A transaction's changes are either *committed* or *rolled back*. CRR makes it possible for distributed systems to commit a change only if it is possible to (and desired) in each of the locations in which the data resides. Transaction changes are logged in CRR servers, SFS servers used solely for CRR synchronization.

AVS also lets APPC/VM applications communicate directly with SNA LU6.2 applications anywhere in the network. APPC/VM programs can use AVS to communicate with CICS transactions, MVS batch jobs, AS/400 and OS/2 programs, and any other LU6.2-compatible application.

In Fig. 14.5, a TSAF collection composed of VM systems 1 and 2 is linked via AVS to VM system 3 and to non-VM hosts and workstations with LU6.2 protocol applications.

AVS usually runs in a virtual machine named AVSVM, a member of the GCS group running VTAM. The AVSVM directory entry includes the statement `OPTION COMSRV`, indicating that it is a communications server for resource names defined on other hosts.

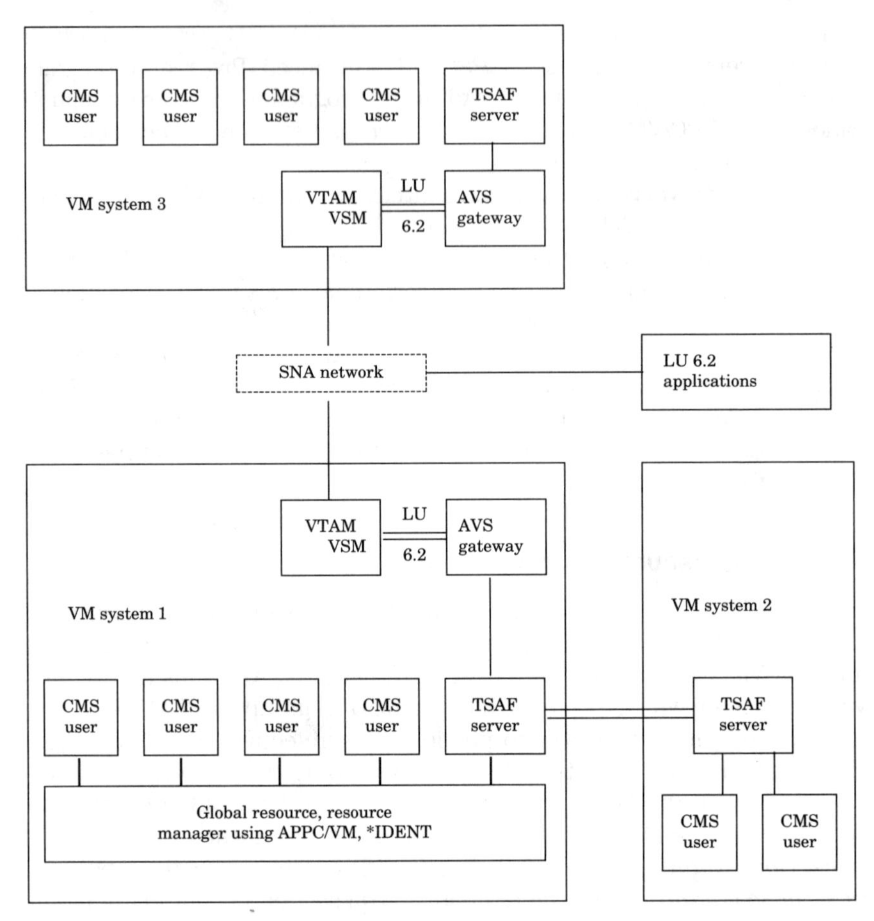

Fig. 14.5 TSAF collection and AVS link to SNA.

VTAM specification files define AVS as an application via the `VBUILD` and `APPL` statements. The following VTAM statements describe an AVS *gateway* logical unit:

```
AVSVM24  VBUILD TYPE=APPL
AVSGTWAY APPL  APPC=YES,      Use APPC protocol
DSESLIM=100,                  Session limit of 100 concurrent sess.
DMINWNL=50,                   Minimum of 50 contention losers
DMINWNR=50,                   Minimum of 50 contention winners
MODETAB=AGWTAB,               Mode table states other characteristics
PARSESS=YES,                  Allow parallel sessions
AUTOSES=50,
AUTHEXIT=YES,
SECACPT=CONV,AUTH=(ACQ)
```

The DSESLIM parameter specifies the maximum number of concurrent sessions. DMINWNL and DMINWNR parameters specify the number of *contention winners* and *contention losers* in the 100 maximum sessions between the gateway LU and its partners. Contention occurs when logical units attempt to allocate a conversation on the same session at the same time. The contention winner gains control of the session and its resources, and can grant its use to the contention user when it requests it. These are concerns for the LU itself, in this case AVS, not for application programs.

Commands in the AGWPROF GCS file on the AVS server's 191 disk activate gateways, and optionally override the contention values in the VTAM definition:

```
/* Start our standard links */
'AGW ACTIVATE GATEWAY AVSGTWAY GLOBAL'
/* Change Number Of Sessions (CNOS): Total, winners, losers */
'AGW CNOS AVSGTWAY VMSERVB AGW2AGW2 100 50 50'
```

TCP/IP

TCP/IP is a functionally rich and increasingly important communications architecture. Originally used in the academic and government communities linked by the *Internet*, the worldwide network of interconnected networks, TCP/IP has come to be the standard communications method for workstations and "open systems." VM has supported TCP/IP since 1987, and can act as a full partner in a TCP/IP network. Only recently has there been support for TCP/IP in MVS.

TCP/IP concepts

TCP/IP is based on two protocols: *Transmission Control Protocol* (TCP), a high-level connection-oriented protocol, and *Internet Protocol* (IP), a low-level protocol that transmits packets called *datagrams* between network locations.

IP addressing allows communication between loosely connected networks, owned and operated by different organizations. IP addresses are composed of four octet (8 bit) numbers separated by periods, for example: 128.0.1.65. The left-most octets identify which network a host resides on, and the rightmost octets identify the host within the network. In TCP/IP, the word *host* applies to both workstations and mainframes; it indicates any programmable node in the network. The actual bit arrangement depends on whether network addressing has been ordered in a particular network to accommodate a small number of networks and a large number of hosts, or a large number of networks with a small number of hosts on each one. *Gateway* hosts pass data between hosts in different networks.

Programmers can program at the IP level using the *User Datagram Protocol* (UDP). IP lets applications send and receive packets to and from individual hosts in a network, as well as allowing *broadcast* (transmit to all hosts in a network) and *multicast* (transmit to a subset of hosts in a network). IP packets are not guaranteed to arrive at a destination, or to arrive in the same order in which they were sent. IP traffic can be sent over X.25, Ethernet, and IEEE 802.5 Token Ring connections, as well as (in IBM implementations) SNA networks.

TCP ensures reliable delivery of packets over a possibly unreliable medium, and adds a variety of useful applications. TCP imposes error retry for failed packet transmissions, and blocks and deblocks application messages into packets transmitted by IP. If packets are received out of order, TCP correctly reassembles them before delivering their contents to the network application. TCP also provides name resolution by associating character names with 4-octet IP addresses. An Internet mailing address usually contains an individual's userid at his or her host, a host name, and the name of the network domain the host resides in, separated by periods.

The domain name indicates the type of institution that owns the host system, for example, `.edu` indicates an educational institution, and `.com` indicates a commercial institution. If I had a userid at Podunk University, it might be called *jsavit@podunk.edu*.

TCP/IP implementation under VM

VM leads the IBM mainframe product line in providing TCP/IP functions and interoperability with open systems. VM TCP/IP consists of software libraries and commands for applications and users, and a family of service virtual machines that interface with physical network resources, and act as server processes to handle user requests. The primary TCP/IP service machine, usually named TCPIP, performs the actual communications I/O with the IP-based network. Complete source code is provided with VM TCP/IP, and consists of programs written in VS Pascal, C/370, and System/370 assembly language.

Physical connection to a TCP/IP network is usually provided by an IBM 3172 or 8232 communications unit. Both devices are channel-attached, modified personal computers that drive LAN interface cards for each of the supported protocols. Other vendors, such as Network Systems, Inc. and Fibronics Inc. provide alternative devices.

TCP/IP applications and protocols

In addition to network protocols, TCP/IP provides a collection of network applications. Not all TCP/IP implementations provide all TCP/IP applications, however the VM implementation provides a large number of the popular TCP/IP applications, and unique ones as well.

- SMTP—Simple Mail Transfer Protocol. SMTP provides an easy method for transferring mail files between systems. SMTP mail files can be processed by a version of the CMS NOTE command provided with TCP/IP, and by OfficeVision/VM's Extended Mail add-on product. Probably the most popular method of interfacing with SMTP is the RICEMAIL package written by Richard Schafer of Rice University. RICEMAIL is widely used in academic sites connected to BITNET or the Internet.
- FTP—File Transfer Protocol. FTP lets users signon to a remote host and either *get* (copy a file from the remote system to the local one) or *put* (copy a file from local to remote) files. FTP is implemented by a virtual machine called FTPSERV, which links to the minidisk being read or written to and communicates with the TCP/IP server machine. Multiple FTPSERV virtual machines can be used for additional throughput.

  FTP lets users specify a variety of functions, including security authorization checking and character set conversion. A simplified interface is provided by TFTP (Trivial FTP), implemented in UDP, but it lacks FTP features.
- Telnet—lets users logon to remote computers. It is similar to VTAM or PVM terminal access to remote systems. The Telnet program interacts with the Telnet program running in the target host. The Telnet programs negotiate session parameters to determine what degree of terminal emulation is provided. Most Telnet implementations implement the popular DEC VT100 terminal, and quite a few provide 3270 emulation, using a version of Telnet called *tn3270*. The IBM mainframe implementation only supports a lowest common denominator teletype device, largely because IBM hosts don't provide the full-duplex terminal I/O needed for ASCII hosts. If the host being communicated with is also a VM system, TCP/IP provides full 3270 emulation, and is almost identical to using the PASSTHRU command with PVM.
- REXEC—Remote Execution. TCP/IP allows a user to send a command to a remote host using the closely related REXEC and RSH (remote shell) protocols. VM provides this function via the REXECD (Remote Execution Daemon) virtual machine. REXEC requires users to specify a userid and password. REXEC AUTOLOGs the virtual machine specified by the user, and passes it the command string to execute.
- NFS—Network File System. NFS is a distributed file system protocol designed by Sun Microsystems, Inc. that lets systems "mount" a remote file system and treat its files as if they are local system disk files. Originally for SunOS, Sun's version of UNIX, it is now available on a variety of oper-

ating systems. NFS servers provide remote file systems for NFS client users.

VM's implementation provides the NFS server function via a service machine called VMNFS and makes minidisk files visible to remote users. VM does not provide NFS client support, so CMS users cannot treat a UNIX system's disk files as CMS files.

- LPR—Line Printer Server. VM provides an LPSERVE virtual machine that prints files sent from TCP/IP applications to channel attached, RSCS, or Advanced Function Printing printers.
- RPC—Remote Procedure Call. RPC is a program interface that lets C programs on a TCP/IP host issue C procedure calls that execute on a remote system. TCP/IP provides "glue functions" to transport the procedure call to the remote system, and an External Data Representation (XDR) interface to map different computer's data representations to and from a common format.

  VM TCP/IP supports RPC, XDR, and a related variant: the Hewlett-Packard/Apollo Network Computing System (NCS), which provides an object oriented framework for creating distributed applications. VM implements a subset of NCS, with a pair of service machines to locate local and global NCS objects for client applications.
- Kerberos—a security authentication protocol originated at the Massachusetts Institute of Technology (MIT). Kerberos lets TCP/IP applications provide added user authentication and security checking.
- X window programming interface—a windowing system developed at MIT and universally used on UNIX workstations. VM TCP/IP provides the X Windows application programmer interface, based on the OSF (Open System Foundation) Motif graphical user interface.
- Domain Name Server—provides a mapping between Internet addresses and host names. Names may be stored in a simple CMS file of sites and addresses, or can be stored in an SQL/DS name server database. Destinations are updated while the network is running by asking remote name servers for site information.
- Route Daemon—provides a continually updated table of the routes available between a host and other hosts in the network.
- SNMP—Simple Network Management Protocol. TCP/IP provides network monitoring and diagnostics through the SNMP protocol. SNMP lets hosts run *agent* processes that can be polled for status by *monitor* processes. In VM, IBM uses NetView, IBM's standard network monitoring product, as the monitor portion, and an SNMP virtual machine as the data collecting agent.

- NDB—Network DataBase. IBM's TCP/IP Version 2 Release 2 adds a networked database facility that lets a workstation client program issue SQL/DS database calls to a VM system. A NDBSERVE server machine runs on VM and responds to SQL requests from client programs running on workstations. As client programs interact with NDBSERVE, it assumes the identity and database access rights associated with the VM userid and password provided by the client process. Source code for both client and server processes is provided, making it possible to customize them for different client computer types and differing application needs.

In addition, TCP/IP contains a number of miscellaneous commands for network control and administration. One of the most common commands is `PING`, which allows you to send a message to an IP address to see if there is a good connection between your host and it. Another command is `NETSTAT`, which lets an administer determine the state of each of the TCP/IP applications and resources.

TCP/IP ports and sockets

Programs that wish to communicate with one another associate themselves with *port* numbers. Common services, like Telnet and FTP, use a set of "well known port" numbers. For example, FTP uses port numbers 20 and 21 to transmit control and data information, and Telnet uses port 23. When Telnet on one host communicates with Telnet on another host, it connects to port 23 at the remote host node. Sites can use the socket interface to write their own applications that allocate ports and communicate over them. One of the well-known port applications is `PORTMAP`, which lets RPC applications look up the port numbers of applications they need to connect to.

The socket interface is one of the program interfaces made available by TCP/IP. With it, a TCP/IP application can write message-passing servers similar to a VM-only VMCF or IUCV server. The socket interface provides subroutine calls creating program-to-program communication with a remote application. Socket applications can use TCP for reliable connection-oriented service, or send independent packets via UDP, or use raw access to the IP protocol.

Socket calls include *open()* and *bind()* to initiate a conversation and allocate a port number; *listen()* to wait for a partner to request a connection; *connect()* and *accept()* to create a connection; *read()* and *write()* to transmit data; and *close()* to terminate a connection.

Under VM, IBM provides socket language bindings for C, Pascal, and APL2. Arthur Ecock, of the City University of New York, wrote and distributes a REXX interface called RXSOCKET. These tools can be used to build powerful applications that interact on a real time basis with workstations.

SNA support in TCP/IP

The mainframe implementation of TCP/IP also supports SNA as a transport mechanism. A TCP/IP service machine named SNALINK runs in a GCS group with VTAM, and passes TCP/IP traffic over an SNA network to partner TCP/IP systems on different hosts. This lets VM systems use either IP or SNA as their backbone networks. In the commercial marketplace, which uses SNA very heavily, it lets institutions use in-place SNA networks for TCP/IP traffic between sites.

Workstation and Personal Computer Synergy

IBM intends to position mainframes as "super servers" and data repositories, servicing hundreds and thousands of workstations. IBM has designated VM as the primary mainframe platform for what it calls "workstation synergy," that is, peer-to-peer cooperation between mainframes and workstations in heterogeneous computing environments.

IBM provides a variety of "synergy" products for inter-platform cooperative processing, in addition to their 3270 emulation, TCP/IP, and LU6.2 facilities, and products provided by other vendors. There is some overlap between the following products, but each is oriented towards providing a different type of interoperability and connectivity between VM systems and workstations of every variety.

Clearly, IBM recognizes that it is not alone in the world, and is increasingly working to make sure that its systems cooperate with other vendors' products, instead of (as in the past) insisting that they conform to IBM.

3270 emulation with personal computers

A wide variety of products let personal computers emulate 3270 terminals in the MS-DOS, Microsoft Windows, OS/2, Apple Macintosh and UNIX environments. This is an increasingly attractive alternative to so-called "dumb terminals." For many users, the price difference between a personal computer and a less-expensive 3270 is small enough to be justified by the flexibility provided by placing a computer on the desktop, even after including the cost of emulation hardware and software.

Personal computer usually emulate 3270 terminals in one of two ways, in addition to the previously mentioned dialup access. In the simpler method, a 3270 terminal emulation card is installed in the PC, and combines with PC software to emulate a single 3270 terminal. The coaxial cable formerly plugged into the 3270 simply plugs into the back of the emulation card. The other common method uses an adapter card to emulate a 3174 or 3274 cluster controller, and is usually used in PC LAN configurations. The advantage of this method is that individual coaxial cables are no longer needed for each personal computer. Otherwise, each PC on a LAN would require both a LAN cable and the coaxial cable for host access. Since cabling costs are a significant expense, this represents a substantial savings over individual 3270 emulation cards.

Personal computer emulation programs add flexibility, and make it possible to provide useful interaction between mainframe and personal computers. Almost all emulators provide upload and download capabilities to transfer files between host and personal computer. Most also provide a "hotkey" or mouse method to switch between the 3270 emulator program and personal computer applications. Some emulators allow multiple host 3270 sessions to be in progress at the same time; a hotkey is used to switch between host sessions. Products that run under a windowing environment (Apple Macintosh, Microsoft Windows, OS/2, X Windows, and so on) usually provide "cut and paste" features that allow data to be copied between a host session to a personal computer application.

Terminal emulation with personal computers is not unequivocably an improvement over real 3270 terminals. The higher cost of a personal computer makes them unattractive in applications not requiring personal computing capabilities, and support and compatibility issues can create difficulties. A surprising number of emulators have had spotty histories emulating 3270 data streams or cooperating with other programs resident on the PC. Emulation products vary in their ability to mimic a 3270. Features like 3270 graphics data streams, the APL2 character set, reverse video and blinking, are not widely supported by emulation programs, sometimes forcing users to keep 3270 terminals.

Keyboard mapping is almost always a problem: it seems that every terminal emulation program uses a different keyboard layout to simulate the 3270 keyboard. This started with early PCs, which had only 10 function keys, while 3270s typically have at least 12. Later PC keyboards provide additional function keys, but don't provide direct equivalents for the 3270 CLEAR, ERASE EOF, PAn keys, and so on. Instead, a variety of (often clumsy) key assignments are used for 3270 keys. For example, one popular vendor uses PC ALT-1 and ALT-2 keys for 3270's PA1 and PA2, while another vendor uses CNTRL-J and CNTRL-K. I have used different emulators that simulate the 3270 CLEAR key with the PC's PAUSE, CNTRL-HOME, and F2 keyboard combinations.

This is a distinct disadvantage for a touch typist, especially one who switches between PC and 3270 or between different PC emulators depending on where he or she is logged on. Additionally, nobody (including IBM) has managed to match the outstanding keyboard arrangement and tactile sensation of the original 3270 keyboard. In many cases, the best 3270 terminal is still a 3270.

Enhanced Connectivity Facilities (ECF)

IBM's Enhanced Connectivity Facilities (ECF) provides application communication between VM and personal computers. ECF uses a protocol for host to personal computer communication called the *Server Requestor Programming Interface* (SRPI). A communications manager running under VM maintains a dialogue with a communications layer program on a PC-DOS computer, which provides SRPI application calls to PC programs running under it. Communications takes place over a 3270 emulator card connected to a 3174 or 3274 communications controller. The controller may operate in either CUT mode or DFT mode.

ECF is started on VM by entering the `CMSSERV` command from the PC 3270 emulation session using IBM's 3270 workstation emulation programs for personal computers. Hotkeys can be used to switch between the VM mainframe and personal computer sessions.

Workstation Lan File Services/VM (WLFS/VM)

Workstation Lan File Services/VM (WLFS/VM) is a client-server program product from IBM that lets VM work as a LAN file server for PC-DOS, OS/2, and UNIX systems. Workstation and personal computer users access their data exactly as if it were stored on a standard LAN file server, and can use tree-structured directories, and long file names. They also can access CMS files stored in minidisks. Files stored in WLFS/VM can be backed up by WDSF/VM or DFDSM, described below.

Personal computer and workstation systems are connected to VM via either an OS/2 LAN server or TCP/IP. When used with TCP/IP, WLFS/VM replaces the NFS server supplied with VM TCP/IP. When an OS/2 LAN server is used, WLFS can use a PS/2 370 card to directly attach a PS/2 server to a mainframe channel.

Data Facility Distributed Storage Manager (DFDSM)

Data Facility Distributed Storage Manager (DFDSM) and *Workstation Data Save* (WDSF/VM) are IBM program products that let VM act as a file backup and archival server for PC-DOS, OS/2, and UNIX systems. DFDSM is the compatible successor product to WDSF/VM, introduced in late 1992. Both products backup unattended personal computers and workstations and provide automated and centralized backup facilities, thus reducing the number of support staff needed for workstation environments and ensuring that backups are taken. They also reduce the need to provide large amounts of disk storage for each workstation, since data can be migrated to inexpensive tape media and retrieved on request.

WDSF/VM includes a service virtual machine on the VM system, and client processes on each of the workstations connected to it. Under OS/2 and UNIX, a process remains resident to automatically initiate backup and migration events at prescheduled times; a TSR ("terminate and stay resident") routine provides this function for PC-DOS computers. WDSF/VM can be instructed to perform incremental backups (back up files changed since the last backup) or backups by file identifier (back up a subset or all the files on a disk volume).

Fullscreen, panel-driven interfaces on both VM and the workstation let administrators and users specify data retension periods and migration rules. Users can browse catalogs of backed up and archived disk contents, and start a backup, restore, archive or retrieve operation. DFDSM includes WDSF/VM's functions, and additionally includes the *Distributed FileManager* that provides distributed file access for OS/2 Version 2 systems.

The physical connection between VM and a workstation can be 3270 emulation using a 3270 adapter card, or either a Token Ring or Ethernet LAN connected via TCP/IP. WDSF/VM also supports NetBIOS connected workstations via the 8232 LAN channel station, combined with the *VM/Pass-Through PC Connect Facility* gateway add-on to VM/Pass-Through. Supported client systems include PC-DOS, OS/2 Extended Addition, AIX, SunOS, and Macintosh.

LAN Resource Extension and Services (LANRES/VM)

LANRES/VM (LAN Resource Extension and Services) provides server functions for personal computers by acting as a Novell Netware 386 file and print server. With LANRES/VM, files on CMS minidisks can be used for networked disk drives (in other words, a user's E: drive can be a 3390). A CMS file with 512 byte records maps directly into PC-style disk sectors, and is directly accessed just like sectors in a Netware hard disk. LANRES/VM provides print access to networked RSCS and Advanced Function Printer (AFP) printers.

Additionally, LANRES/VM makes it possible to provide centralized Netware administration and software distribution. Software can be distributed from a single mainframe copy to multiple file servers in different locations, and administrators can manage users and resources from a single point of control and auditing as well. LANRES/VM can be connected to personal computers by IPX or TCP/IP protocols, via channel attached servers or via servers connected to a host by VM PWSCS (described below).

VM Programmable Workstation Communication Service (VM PWSCS)

VM Programmable Workstation Communication Service (VM PWSCS) lets mainframe and workstation applications interact with one another on a real time basis, even if they are based on different communication protocols. VM

PWSCS allows transport of APPC data streams over SNA, TCP/IP and Novell networks, to and from a variety of workstation and personal computer models.

Applications can be written using the SAA Common Programming Interface for Communications (CPI-C) whether intended for applications running SNA LU6.2 on a mainframe, AS/400 or OS/2 computer, or TCP/IP or Novell protocols on an OS/2, MS-DOS, AIX, or other UNIX system. PWSCS lets programs written with the CPI-C protocol suite interact with almost any type of computer.

VM/ESA's Inter-System Facility for Communications (ISFC) lets PWSCS applications transmit data at extremely high rates. A LAN-connected workstation can be connected to a System/370 or System/390 channel and act as a gateway between LAN and host. The direct channel attachment allows data transfer rates as high as 6 megabytes per second, and the ISFC support in VM/ESA CP eliminates the CPU overhead of performing I/O from a service virtual machine. The combination allows extremely high performance connections between mainframe and workstation systems.

Chapter

15

Program-to-Program Communication

Real and virtual personal computers avoid interference between users and applications, compared to multiuser systems in which separate applications have read/write access to a common pool of storage. Separation into real or virtual machines also makes it more difficult to share changing data, since each user process exists in its own address space.

The lack of shared read-write storage between users made message passing protocols a natural way to implement data sharing in VM. VM/ESA dataspaces now provide a controlled method for sharing changing data in main storage, but most applications still use message passing methods.

Client-Server Orientation

VM applications tend to work by passing messages back and forth between *client* and *server* virtual machines, instead of sharing a common pool of storage. Typically, the server stores data or provides some kind of computing or communication function, and client programs send request messages to ask for services. The server receives the request message from the client, performs the requested data retrieval or service, and replies with the requested information or acknowledgement.

Many VM applications, such as SQL/DS, Shared File System, OfficeVision /VM, TCP/IP, and FOCUS, are based on a client-server paradigm. In recent years, the client-server model has been rediscovered for distributed systems environments, and is now a "hot" new buzzword. VM fits very comfortably with the client server style of computing, having used it since its inception. Originally, VM clients and servers had to be on the same CPU; the extension of client-server to span different systems and different computer types is very natural for VM applications.

Methods for Program-to-Program Communication

VM has evolved several protocols programs can use to exchange messages. Newer protocols increasingly allow separation of client and server processes, and decouple them from network or device addresses imbedded in the application.

The methods available for program-to-program communication include:

- Spool File Transmission
- Virtual Machine Communication Facility (VMCF)
- Inter-User Communication Vehicle (IUCV)
- Advanced Program-to-Program Communication/VM (APPC/VM)

These methods provide increasing generality and independence from hardware idiosyncrasies, as discussed below.

Basic Client and Server Structures

Most client-server applications, in VM and elsewhere, have similar structures. Most servers use program logic like that shown in the pseudocode in Fig. 15.1, although different systems use different protocols to communicate with clients. Additionally, some servers are single-threaded (can only process one task at a time), while others perform their own multiprogramming or rely on host operating system functions to create multiple tasks.

Typical server actions include validating the request (determining that the requestor is in fact allowed to issue the request), logging access, journaling changes via audit trails, scheduling multiple requests, and responding to administrator and operator commands.

Simple virtual machine servers can easily be written in VM using this structure, using the communication protocols described below. With pretty

```
Initialize   /* typically includes system calls to enable messages */
do forever
  wait for a message event from a client
  select action routine based on event type
end
```

Fig. 15.1 Basic flow of control in a server virtual machine.

```
Connect to server
do while running
  create a request message
  send it to server machine
  wait for response
  use results
end
```

Fig. 15.2 Basic flow of control in a client virtual machine.

straightforward programming, a non-preempting single task server can be written in REXX or a higher level language. With additional effort, IBM's *Server Tasking Environment/VM* (STE/VM) can be used to create a multitasking server written in assembly language or C.

Many existing commercially used server products use custom written schedulers to provide multitasking in the absence of CMS multitasking. VM/Pass-Through and SQL/DS perform their own multithreaded execution to allow multiple requests to proceed at the same time. VTAM and RSCS use GCS, which provides the MVS multitasking program interface, to allow concurrent execution of multiple tasks.

Most clients use a structure similar to Fig. 15.2. Requests for service are packaged in messages and sent to the server. The client may continue processing or wait for the server response. When viewed in time sequence, the conversation between client and server looks like the transactions in Fig. 15.3.

Communication via Spool

Before discussing the formal inter-user interfaces provided by VM, it's worth spending time on a ubiquitous but informal method of message passing and data sharing between users, and between servers and their clients: files transmitted via the VM spool from one user's virtual punch to another user's virtual reader.

Communicating by spool files is "low tech" and easy to implement. The WAKEUP command, part of the *CMS Utilities Feature* of VM/ESA, and similar commands from a variety of sources, make it easy for a REXX EXEC to wait until a reader file arrives. When the EXEC wakes up, it can determine who sent the reader file, and either process it by loading it to disk and using its contents, or reject it and either purge it or transfer it back to the submitter.

Figure 15.4 illustrates a REXX loop that uses WAKEUP to wait for reader files. This code adds a little more function by waking up on an hourly basis, which could be used to perform periodic housekeeping, or if an interrupt is received from the console. WAKEUP provides a return code, placed in the REXX *rc* variable that indicates the reason it woke up. In this example, the EXEC simply exits if a console or unexpected event occurs. A production server should have more sophisticated error handling than that!

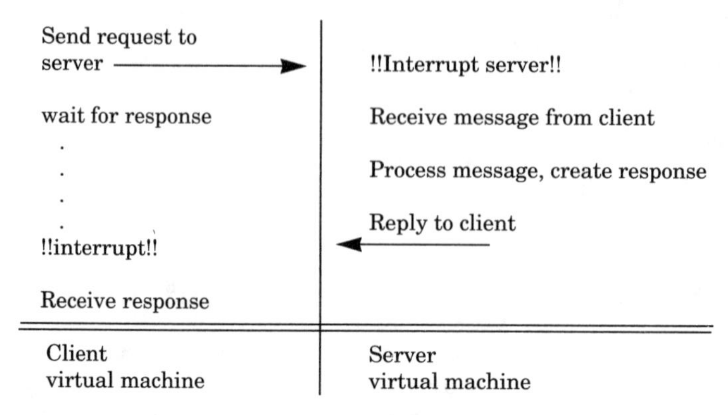

Fig. 15.3 Flow of events between generic client and server.

When a file arrives on the reader, the EXEC calls a procedure named `Reader`, shown in Fig. 15.5. In this sample EXEC fragment, a reader file is loaded to disk and then processed by a FORTRAN program. The program creates an output file that is sent back to the requestor. WAKEUP immediately exits with return code 4 if a reader file is present on the reader, not just when a file arrives, so "Reader" will be entered again if multiple files are waiting for processing.

As mentioned before, a production EXEC would perform more error checking (to handle, for example, a "disk full" situation), and might even verify that the requesting userid is one of a list of authorized users. Nonetheless, this is a representative example (abstracted from running code) of how to code a complete server based on reader files and WAKEUP.

Spool communication has several advantages over other methods. It is easily programmed, and spool data is persistent since a spool file remains on the spool until it is explicitly purged. Unlike other methods, a client can send requests to a server even if the server is not logged on. When the server is started, it can read its input reader queue and process the messages enqueued for it.

Spool files cannot be used for purposes with high message rates. Spool files reside on disk, and significant resources are expended to create spool files, and then open them for input, read them, and purge them. Spool files are a reasonable way of handling requests or messages with an arrival rate of "several per minute," instead of "several per second." In other words, they are an excellent way to process batch-like requests.

Virtual Machine Communication Facility (VMCF)

The first formal inter-user communications method provided for VM was the Virtual Machine Communication Facility (VMCF), introduced to VM in the mid-1970s in VM/370 Release 3. The purpose of VMCF was to provide an efficient method for user-to-user message passing that could be used in CMS applications. VMCF is still used, although it has been largely superceded by the IUCV and APPC/VM facilities discussed later in this chapter.

The virtual machine sending a message is referred to as the *source*, and the virtual machine receiving the message is called the *sink* machine. Data is transmitted directly from the source's virtual storage to the sink's virtual storage, using buffer addresses they each supply in VMCF SEND and RECV requests.

DIAGNOSE 68 instructions tell CP to send or receive a buffer of data, or to perform a number of control functions. Requests are encoded in the VMCPARM (VMCF parameter list) pointed to by *Rx* in the DIAGNOSE instruction.

VMCF interface between CP and virtual machines

When a message arrives, CP passes the virtual machine an external interrupt with interruption code X'4001' A VMCF application must intercept external interrupts to gain control of the virtual machine when a VMCF

```
/* Wait for reader files from users and process them */
address COMMAND
/* Notify MONITORS, a nickname in our nickname file listing */
/* userids, that we're up and running */
'EXEC TELL MONITORS' userid() 'is up and running'
Do forever
  /* Wakeup if hour elapses or reader file arrives */
  'WAKEUP AT +01:00 (RDR'
  Select
   /* Timer */
   when rc = 2 then say "Nothing ever happens here. I'm bored!"
   /* Reader event */
   when rc = 4 then call Reader
   /* Console interrupt */
   when rc = 6 then do
     say 'Stopping because you hit ENTER!'
     exit
    end
   otherwise do
     'EXEC TELL MONITORS' userid() 'received unexpected code:' rc
     'EXEC TELL MONITORS' userid() 'giving up — please FIX!'
     exit
    end
  end /* of select */
End /* of do forever */
Exit
```

Fig. 15.4 Server main loop.

```
READER:
  /* Use CMS Pipelines to query the reader queue, throw away */
  /* the header line, and obtain the origin userid and spoolid */
  /* if the first file in the list */
  'PIPE CP QUERY RDR ALL * | drop 1 | take 1 | var rdrline'
  parse var rdrline who spoolid .
  'EXEC RECEIVE' spoolid 'PROGRAM INPUT A (REPLACE NOPROMPT'
  if rc <> 0 then do
    'EXEC TELL MONITORS 'Hey! rc='rc 'from RECEIVE!!!'
    exit          /* Give up after asking for help */
   end
  /* Associate Fortran file units with input and output file */
  'FILEDEF 05 DISK PROGRAM INPUT A'
  'FILEDEF 07 DISK PROGRAM OUTPUT A'
  /* Run the analysis */
  'MYPROG'
  /* Send the results back to the requestor */
  'EXEC SENDFILE PROGRAM OUTPUT A' who
  return
```

Fig. 15.5 Receive and reply to reader file.

message arrives. In CMS, this can be done by using the HNDEXT ("HaNDle EXTernal" interrupt) macro to specify an interrupt-handler routine.

CP places information about a pending VMCF event in a message header area before signaling a VMCF interrupt to a virtual machine. The message area must be previously declared by the application before enabling VMCF processing. Message headers use a control block format called the VMCMHDR (message communication header).

VMCF functions

VMCF provides the following functions: AUTHORIZE, SEND, SENDX, SEND/RECV, RECEIVE, REPLY, CANCEL, QUIESCE, and RESUME, each of which is discussed in the following sections. For each function, DIAGNOSE 68 is coded with Rx containing the address of the VMCPARM control block. The contents of Ry are ignored.

A VMCPARM contains the following fields:

- VMCPFLG1—a flag bytes with options
- VMCPFUNC—the VMCF function being invoked
- VMCPMID—the message id number
- VMCPUSER—the userid of the virtual machine being communicated with
- VMCPVADA—the address of the virtual storage buffer to be used as the origin or destination of VMCF data

- VMCPLENA—the length of the buffer
- VMCPVADB—for SEND/RECV protocol, the address in the source virtual machine of a buffer to receive the response from the sink machine
- VMCPLENB—the length of the response buffer
- VMCPUSE—the user doubleword, which contains source machine data presented to a sink machine when a VMCF interrupt is received, without having to issue a RECEIVE command

The contents of the VMCMHDR are essentially copied from the VMCPARM of the virtual machine causing the interrupt; field names are renamed to begin with "VMCM" instead of "VMCP." The VMCMHDR has room for an optional message buffer used in the SENDX protocol, located at the end of both control blocks.

The AUTHORIZE function enables a virtual machine for VMCF processing, and must be executed before any other VMCF function is requested. AUTHORIZE uses the VMCPFLG1 field in the VMCPARM to specify processing options for a VMCF application. The address and length of the external interrupt buffer, VMCMHDR, is specified in VMCPVADA and VMCPLENA.

AUTHORIZE can be coded with a "SPECIFIC" option, in which a target virtual machine is specified as the sole userid with which VMCF communication will be performed. Other options specify whether the virtual machine is willing to accept *priority* messages, which are queued before unprocessed nonpriority messages, and whether or not the CP SMSG command can be used to send messages to this userid, in addition to DIAGNOSE 68.

The declaration of the VMCMHDR is critical because CP places information in this buffer whenever a VMCF message arrives. The VMCF external interrupt handler must inspect the contents of this buffer to determine which actions to take. In some cases, as explained below, the entire contents of the message from a source virtual machine are contained in the external interrupt buffer.

VMCF UNAUTHORIZE is executed when an application wishes to terminate VMCF processing. QUIESCE should be used first to process messages already queued; otherwise, pending messages are discarded.

VMCF SEND sends a message or buffer from a source virtual machine to a target. The length and address of the buffer is specified in the VMCMPARM pointed to by the RX register, as well as the virtual machine name, a message id number, and flag information.

The message id number identifies individual messages sent to a sink machine, and need only be unique among the messages not yet received or rejected by the sink; the same message id can be reused with other users. In practice, virtual machines that only allow one outstanding message to another virtual machine (for example, because their application logic requires

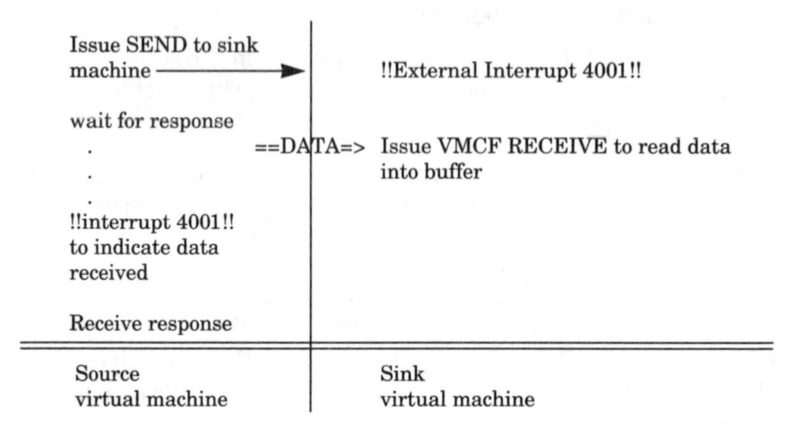

Fig. 15.6 Flow of events in VMCF SEND protocol.

an answer to each sent message) simply initialize the VMCPARM message id field to zeros, and ignore it.

Up to eight bytes of data can be included in the *VMCF user doubleword* placed in the sink virtual machine's VMCMHDR. If the message fits in the user doubleword, no additional data need be transmitted (a send buffer can be specified with a length of zero bytes).

If the sink machine permits it, a flag can be turned on in the VMCPARM to indicate that this is a priority message. Priority messages are enqueued first-in, first-out behind unprocessed priority messages already enqueued on the virtual machine, but in front of all nonpriority messages waiting to be received.

The sink virtual machine receives an external interrupt when a SEND is issued. VMCMHDR contents indicate that it has a pending VMCF message sent to it. When the sink issues VMCF RECEIVE, the source virtual machine receives an external interrupt that tells it that the data was received and its send buffer can be reused for other messages. Note that the SEND and the RECEIVE are completely asynchronous. The RECEIVE may not occur until quite some time after the SEND was issued. The flow of execution and data is illustrated in Fig. 15.6.

`VMCF SENDX` is a simplified version of SEND used for one-way transfer of data with a predeclared buffer size and location in the sink machine. When SENDX is used, the source buffer is copied directly into the VMCMHDR buffer of the sink. SENDX is more efficient than SEND, because the sink virtual machine need not execute a VMCF RECEIVE function. Many service machines, such as VM Pass-Through, respond to SENDX in the form of the CP SMSG (special message) command. An SMSG is entered much like the CP MSG command. Instead of displaying text on the terminal of the target virtual machine, CP transforms the message into a VMCF SENDX. The sending virtual machine doesn't have to authorize itself for VMCF; all VMCF details are handled implicitly by CP.

SENDX applications can easily be programmed in REXX by using the SMSG command to send an SENDX, and WAKEUP to receive it. If WAKEUP is coded with the SMSG option, it authorizes for VMCF messages and receives SENDX messages. When an SMSG is received, the sending userid and the message are placed in the stack, and WAKEUP exits with return code 1. Figure 15.7 shows statements changed and added to the EXEC in Fig. 15.4 that let it process SMSGs in addition to the previously handled event types.

`VMCF SEND/RECV` provides bidirectional data transmission; it is typically used when a client asks a server to provide some information, for example, perform a database lookup. Even if no explicit result information is needed, a client often needs at least status information to let it know if the request was successful.

When a sink machine receives a SEND/RECV message, VMCMHDR flags indicate that a SEND/RECV was issued. The sink issues a RECEIVE to read the data into its storage, and then, after creating a response buffer, issues a REPLY to send the results back to the sink. The flow of data and control is illustrated in Fig. 15.8.

SEND/RECV protocol can be simulated by SEND protocol by having the server and client take turns initiating SEND transactions with one another (the first SEND sends the request from client to server; the second SEND is the response from server to client). SEND/RECV reduces both the num-

```
Do forever
  /* Wakeup if hour elapses or reader file arrives */
 'WAKEUP AT +01:00 (RDR SMSG'
  Select
   /* SMSG */
   when rc = 1 then do
      parse pull smsg_source  /* get id of SMSG sender */
      parse pull smsg_text    /* get text from SMSG  */
      parse var smsg_text verb arguments
      select
        when verb = 'STOP'   then call Stop_the_server
        when verb = 'LOAD'   then call Load_new_input
        when verb = 'READ'   then call Client_reads_data
        when verb = 'WRITE' then call Client_writes_data
        otherwise /* unrecognised command */
           'CP SMSG'smsg_source 'Oh yeah? Same to you too!'
      end
     end
  ...other statements as specified before...
  end
```

Fig. 15.7 A combined reader and SMSG/SENDX server using WAKEUP.

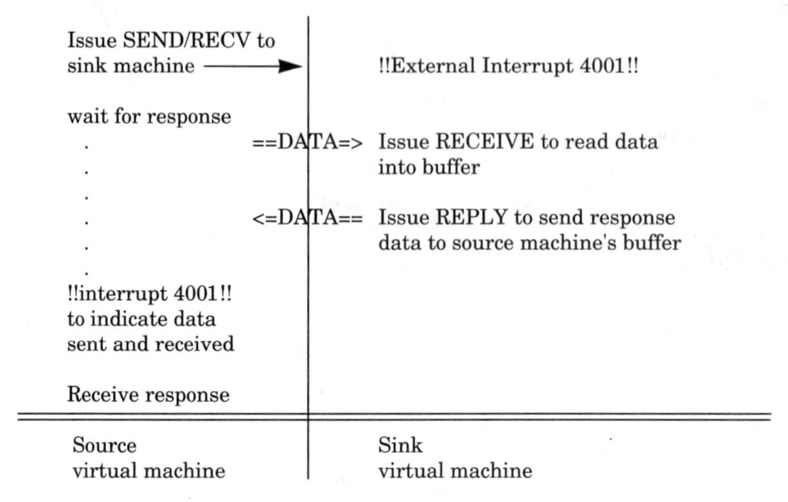

Fig. 15.8 Flow of events in VMCF SEND/RECV protocol.

ber of external interrupts CP has to reflect to the virtual machines, and the number of VMCF requests they have to make.

`VMCF RECEIVE` (obviously) receives a pending VMCF message into storage. When a RECEIVE is issued, CP copies data from source virtual machine storage into sink virtual storage.

Information about the message to be received is obtained from the VMCMHDR data stored when the VMCF external interrupt was presented by CP. This includes the source virtual machine's userid and the message id number. The first fields of a VMCMHDR are identical to the beginning of a VMCPARM, so they can be copied over the sink machine's VMCPARM and used directly in a RECEIVE command. The VMCMHDR field that identify the source userid and message number are in the VMCPARM used to receive that message. RECEIVE can receive messages out of the order in which they were sent, when multiple messages are pending, by putting the associated userids and message ids in the VMCPARM used in the RECEIVE call.

`VMCF REJECT` rejects a SEND or SENDX message. It is coded like a RECEIVE, except for the difference in function code. The source virtual machine receives an external interrupt, with VMCMHDR values indicating that the message was rejected.

`VMCF REPLY` replies to a SEND/RECV message.

`VMCF CANCEL` cancels an outgoing message from SEND, SEND/RECV, or SENDX. An error code is provided if the message has already been received by the sink.

`VMCF QUIESCE` temporarily refuses additional SEND, SENDX, or SEND /RECV messages. Messages that are already queued are processed, but subsequent messages from source machines are rejected; the source receives an error code on their attempt to send a message.

QUIESCE can be used by a server application to prevent further message traffic because it is busy ("Don't bother me now, I'm busy"), or to process pending messages before stopping execution.

`VMCF RESUME` does the opposite of QUIESCE and again allows other virtual machines to initiate messages to you. IDENTIFY should be used to let client virtual machines know that they can send messages again.

`VMCF IDENTIFY` lets a virtual machine to announce its presence to a sink virtual machine. It's simply a way for a virtual machine to "say hello" to a communications partner. Virtual machines also use IDENTIFY after leaving QUIESCE state to inform partners that they have resumed VMCF communications.

Limitations of VMCF

VMCF is an efficient and surprisingly durable protocol for inter-user message communications. Nonetheless, it suffers from limitations which have led to it being made obsolete by IUCV and APPC/VM.

One problem is that no higher-level application program interface was ever provided by IBM, making it difficult for programmers to create VMCF applications. Publically distributed programs on VMSHARE and "tools tapes" do include assembly language subroutines that can be called from FORTRAN, PL/I, and other languages, so this lack has been remedied by public domain solutions. Interestingly enough, IBM's APL2 interpreter provides an exception to this rule although the *Global Shared Variable* processor, which lets APL2 applications *offer* and *retract* variables for sharing with other virtual machines. The implementation uses a read-write shared segment, with access synchronized (under the covers, and hidden from the APL2 programmer) via VMCF.

A more serious problem with VMCF is that a virtual machine cannot run multiple simultaneous VMCF applications. A single program can maintain conversations with multiple other userids, but only one VMCF application can be active at one time. Every VMCF application has its own VMCMHDR buffer, and there is no way to ask CP for the current VMCMHDR address before declaring a new one (and thereby obliterating the previously existing one). Moreover, there is no way for multiple applications to distinguish between their messages and messages intended for other programs.

This becomes a problem when a VMCF application invokes a CMS command that is also a VMCF application. For example, APL2, FOCUS, and ISPF all use VMCF, and all allow a user to issue CMS commands. VMCF cannot handle this situation gracefully.

VMCF has other limitations: a VMCF application either authorizes for all users or for only a specific one; there is no way to authorize for only a set of users. An unwanted user can repeatedly send messages to a server he or she should have no access to. The server can reject each message sent to it from an unwanted user, but must take an external interrupt and issue REJECT for each message.

This is part of a general lack in VMCF: the absence of flow control to let applications manage the rate at which messages are recognized, and the total number of messages allowed to be outstanding.

A system-wide restriction of VMCF for VM/ESA and VM/XA is that VMCF messages are only processed on the master processor of a multiprocessor VM system. A high rate of VMCF messages can saturate the master processor and become a bottleneck on system performance, even when other CPUs have reserve capacity. VMCF has different performance problems on VM/SP and HPO: VMCF requires the global lock, causing a multiprocessor contention problem worse than on VM/ESA. VMCF also searches for the VMBLOK of the target userid on every message.

Inter-User Communication Vehicle (IUCV)

The Inter-User Communication Vehicle (IUCV) addresses the concerns raised in the last few paragraphs, and provides valuable new functions, such as the ability for a virtual machine to maintain conversation with CP, as described in "CP System Services" on page 366. IUCV is nonetheless very similar to VMCF in many respects. If you understand one of them you're not far from understanding the other.

IUCV was introduced to VM with VM/SP Release 1, which also added support for SNA. VM implements SNA through the *Console Communication Services* (CCS) IUCV system service. Apparently, many IUCV functions were designed to support the way messages are passed between CP and the VTAM service machine responsible for communication with the SNA network.

IUCV has become a key application enabling tool for products written by IBM, other vendors, and customers. SQL/DS, and VM/Pass-Through use IUCV for communication between client and server, as do OfficeVision/VM, Advanced Function Printing, and VTAM. CMS's console services use IUCV to intercept screen traffic and create a fullscreen windowed environment. CP uses IUCV to interact with service virtual machines used as security managers, and for logging performance, accounting, and error data to disk.

IUCV protocol

IUCV messages are sent from a *source* virtual machine to a *target* (the IUCV name for what VMCF calls a *sink*). Messages are sent over *paths*, which are created when a virtual machine *connects* to another virtual machine and the target of the connect *accepts* the connection. Each path has a separate *message limit* that specifies the maximum number of messages that can be awaiting processing. Virtual machines can have multiple paths between one another, or even with themselves, with different message traffic along each path.

A path remains available until either side *severs* it; CP implicitly severs a path if either virtual machine performs a system reset or IPL, or logs off. A virtual machine may *quiesce* a path to prevent initiation of new messages, and *resume* it without affecting communications along other paths. Applications quiesce IUCV paths when they are about to shut down, in order to process pending messages but not allow new ones. Applications may also quiesce and resume paths to perform flow control: they quiesce paths during "storage full" or "busy" situations, to defer arrival of new messages until they are ready to handle them.

Messages are created when a source virtual machine issues an IUCV *send* to a target machine. The target may *receive* or *reject* the message. An IUCV message may be a 1-way or a 2-way message; for a 2-way message the target machine issues a *reply*. A 1-way message is like a VMCF SEND, and a 2-way message is like a VMCF SEND/RECV. IUCV SEND tells CP the location of the source's send buffer, and if a 2-way message, the location to put the response from the target. When the target issues a RECEIVE, CP copies data directly from source machine storage to the target's receive buffer. When the target issues a REPLY to a 2-way message, CP copies the target's reply buffer to the source's response buffer, as illustrated in Fig. 15.9.

IUCV message queues

CP maintains queues of messages pending processing by a virtual machine, anchored in link list chains originating in the VMDBK or VMBLOK of the virtual machine that will process it:

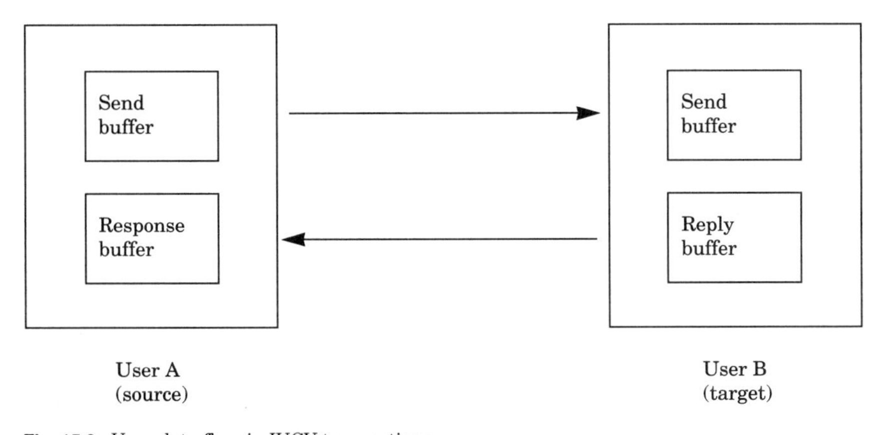

Fig. 15.9 User data flow in IUCV transactions.

1. `Send queue` contains messages sent to but not yet processed by a target machine. The IUCV SEND function places a message on the send queue of the target.
2. `Receive queue` contains messages received by the target, but not yet replied to. When the target issues a RECEIVE, CP moves the message to the receive queue.
3. Reply queue on the source virtual machine contains replies to messages.

Message queues describe each in-progress message. The actual data resides solely in virtual machine buffers. CP directly copies data between virtual machine storages when performing a RECEIVE or REPLY.

IUCV interface between CP and virtual machines

CP notifies a virtual machine that an IUCV event has occurred, such as a pending message, by passing the virtual machine an external interrupt with interruption code X'4000'. The virtual machine must also turn on the IUCV interrupt mask bit in control register 0 to enable this interrupt type. IUCV applications can process messages on an interrupt basis, or use the DESCRIBE or TESTCMPL functions to synchronously test for a pending message. Changes in connection status are always signaled via interrupts. Before reflecting a IUCV interrupt to a virtual machine, CP places information about the pending event in an buffer previously declared by the `DCLBFR` (declare buffer) function.

IUCV functions are initiated by virtual machines executing the IUCV macro, which generates a special instruction operation code. CP passes control to the IUCV service routines to interpret the IUCV function. The IUCV instruction includes a pointer to the `IPARML`, the IUCV Parameter List.

The following sections describe the IUCV functions, some of which have already been alluded to. With one exception, the IUCV macro points to the IPARML describing the requests. The functions are presented in the following order:

- Functions used to establish, manage, and end communication
- Functions used to transmit data
- Miscellaneous functions

IUCV `QUERY` asks CP to provide the amount of storage that should be reserved for the external interrupt buffer, and the maximum number of connections available to a virtual machine. This information is returned in registers 0 and 1.

An IUCV `DCLBFR` (declare buffer) function must be issued before performing additional IUCV functions. It specifies the location, specified in the

IPARML passed to CP, where CP will store interrupt information, much like the VMCF external interrupt header. DCLBFR also enables the IUCV interrupt submask.

The CONNECT function tells CP to establish a communications path with the virtual machine, system service, or resource id name specified in the IPARML. Other IPARML fields specify the maximum number of messages allowed pending over the path, and whether priority messages are allowed. The source machine can also ask that the path be initiated in quiesced mode, indicating that the target communicator cannot SEND messages to the source.

IUCV reflects an interrupt to the source machine when the target either accepts or rejects the connection. The external interrupt buffer contains the path identifier number assigned by CP. Path ids are only meaningful within a virtual machine; communications partners may be assigned different path numbers for the same path. For example, if a client service machine has no prior IUCV paths and connects to a service machine that has 100 existing paths, the client may be assigned path number 0 while the server sees the same path as path 100.

The path is established when the communications partner issues an ACCEPT. CP notifies the target machine that a user wants to connect to it by issuing an external interrupt to it, and placing the "connection pending" flag and the source userid in the IUCV buffer. As with CONNECT, flags in the IPARML specify the maximum number of messages, indicate whether or not priority messages are accepted, and request that the path be initiated in quiesced mode. If the target requests a quiesced path, it means that the userid issuing the connect cannot send messages.

The QUIESCE function is issued to temporarily prevent the initiation of new messages along an IUCV path. The communications partner is sent an external interrupt to let it know that it cannot send messages. QUIESCE should be issued before terminating a connection, to allow pending messages to be processed. RESUME allows the partner to send messages again. A path can be left in quiesced state to allow messages in only one direction.

Since a virtual machine is notified when an IUCV partner performs a QUIESCE or RESUME, these functions can be used as low-cost semaphores between virtual machines. This can be used when no other information need be transmitted, or when data is passed through previously agreed-upon locations in shared virtual storage, such as in VM dataspaces.[1]

The SEVER function terminates an IUCV path or rejects a pending connection. The partner is sent an interrupt with status indicating that the path has been severed or rejected, and should issue its own SEVER to break its half of the path. When an application is finished processing, it issues a RTRVBFR (retrieve buffer), which cancels all pending messages and existing paths.

---

[1] This method was described at SHARE 78 by Romney White of Velocity Software, Inc.

SEND transmits data along a path. The IPARML contains the address and length of the buffer to be sent to the target userid, as well as flags indicating whether this is a priority message and whether it is a 1-way or 2-way transfer. For 2-way messages, the IPARML also contains the address and length of the answer buffer to receive the reply from the target. CP returns the message identifier associated with the message; the message id can be referred to in subsequent IUCV functions.

Priority messages are enqueued on the send queue of the target after other priority messages and before nonpriority messages. The source virtual machine can also specify a target message class to associate with the message.

A target machine issues a RECEIVE after receiving a message pending interrupt from CP. The interrupt buffer contains the source userid, the path id the message was sent on, its message id, and the message class specified by the sender.

The target machine can receive the message immediately, or defer it until a convenient moment. CP reflects only a single interrupt for a pending message; pending messages remain on the target's send queue until processed or purged. The RECEIVE parameter list can select a message by specifying the path id, message class, and identifier of a pending message, or it can omit them and receive the next message on the queue.

When RECEIVE is executed, CP copies data directly from the send buffer of the source to the receive buffer of the target, paging virtual storage buffers into real memory as needed. If the buffer length specified in the RECEIVE parameter list is too small for the number of bytes being sent, data is copied until the receive buffer is filled. The residual count of untransferred data bytes is placed in the parameter list. The remaining data can be read with a subsequent RECEIVE.

A target machine can REJECT a message instead of receiving it. The message can be selected by message id, class, or path identifier. When a message is rejected, it is moved from the target's send or receive queue back to the source's reply queue, with a flag set to indicate that the message was rejected instead of received.

REPLY sends a response to a 2-way message. As with RECEIVE and REJECT, the target machine can select a message by message id, path, and class number. When REPLY is executed, CP moves the message descriptor to the reply queue of the source machine, and copies the reply buffer specified in the REPLY parameter list to the answer buffer specified earlier in the source's SEND.

PURGE removes a message sent to another virtual machine but not yet processed. If the target was aware of the message due to a DESCRIBE or interrupt, the target is notified that the message was purged via a status flag when it attempts to RECEIVE or REPLY to it. If the target had not become aware of the message, the message is purged without the target ever knowing it had been sent.

The SETMASK function enables and disables the IUCV interrupt submask, while leaving other external interrupts enabled.

Applications can use the DESCRIBE function to explicitly check for pending messages instead of intercepting "message pending" interrupts. This lets a virtual machine test for a message while disabled for interrupts. The external interrupt buffer is filled with the description of the message, just as if an interrupt had been received. Individual messages are signaled only once by either an interrupt or a DESCRIBE.

Test Message (TESTMSG) and Test Completion (TESTCMPL) explicitly check for the presence of a message on a partner's SEND or RECEIVE queue (TESTMSG), or test for completion of a sent message (TESTCMPL), analogous to how DESCRIBE is used to test for a pending message.

The flow of interactions between IUCV partners is shown in Fig. 15.10.

IUCV application interface

The IUCV application interface makes it possible to operate multiple IUCV and APPC/VM applications in the same virtual machine. For example, a user might invoke a QMF (Query Management Facility for SQL/DS databases) panel from within OfficeVision/VM. Both SQL/DS and OfficeVision use IUCV and APPC/VM to communicate with service machines, and can do so without interfering with one another.

IBM provides access to IUCV functions to assembler programmers through the IUCV, CMSIUCV, and HNDIUCV assembly language macros. The IUCV macro provides access to all of the functions just described. A typical IUCV call looks like this:

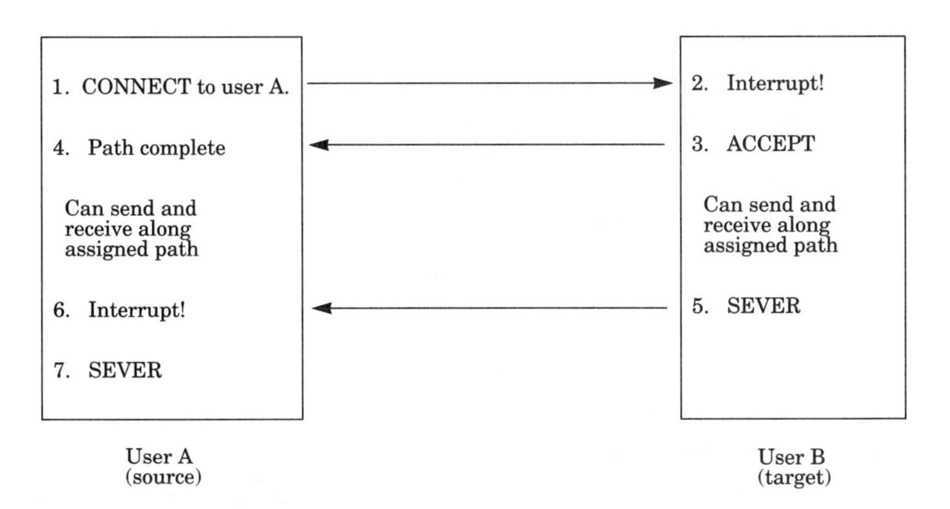

Fig. 15.10 Flow of interactions between IUCV partners.

```
IUCV RECEIVE,               Indicate function
     PRMLIST=MYIPARML,      Point to IPARML
     BUFFER=RCVBUF,         Point to receive buffer
     BUFLEN=RCVLEN,         Length of receive buffer
     MSGID=MYMSG,           MYMSG contains msg id
     PATHID=MYPATH          MYPATH contains path id
```

Applications can directly process external interrupts generated by IUCV events, but this precludes simultaneously running other IUCV or VMCF applications in the same virtual machine. Instead, programs should use HNDIUCV and CMSIUCV to let CMS handle interrupts and route messages to applications.

The HNDIUCV macro tells CMS that a program wishes to use IUCV functions. It associates the program with an 8 character symbolic name and an exit routine address to be called when an IUCV event occurs. CMS also performs an DCLBFR if no buffer is allocated. CMS routes to the user exit messages containing a user data field matching the symbolic name given to HNDIUCV. Multiple applications can have HNDIUCV exits in effect for different application names. A properly written IUCV application therefore specifies the name of the application it wants to communicate with in a target virtual machine.

The CMSIUCV macro provides CONNECT, ACCEPT, and SEVER operands to let an application create or destroy paths with its communications partners, using the same name specified in the HNDIUCV macro. CMS routes all interrupts associated with a path to the exit routine established by the program using the path. The program then uses IUCV SEND, RECEIVE, REPLY, and so on to actually transfer data. When an application terminates, it issues the HNDIUCV CLR (clear) function to tell CMS that it is finished. CMS severs any paths remaining open for the application, and issues an IUCV RTRVBFR if this was the last IUCV program in effect.

The omission of an interface for traditional compiled languages was not remedied until the arrival of the APPC/VM Common Programming Interface for Communications (CPI-C), described later in this chapter. A number of public domain programs provide IUCV functions for REXX and other languages. Among the most popular are IUCVTRAP, written by Arthur Ecock at the City University of New York, which provides a REXX interface comparable to that provided by REXXIUCV, and SVM, which provides a subroutine interface to VMCF and IUCV functions for PL/I and other languages. SVM was written by Bill Fischofer, formerly of Comsat Laboratories and now at IBM.

Directory control of IUCV functions

Access to IUCV servers is controlled by statements in the user directory. This lets installations manage access to IUCV-based servers, instead of having to program each server to continually reject undesired attempts to communicate.

The IUCV statement specifies which virtual machines or CP system services a userid can communicate with. `IUCV ALLOW` can be coded in a virtual machine's directory entry to indicate that all users are allowed to connect to it. `IUCV ANY` indicates that a user can connect to all IUCV services. The IUCV statement also can specify whether a virtual machine can connect to the *Identify* system service to identify itself as a resource. This is discussed in the sections "CP System Services" on page 366 and "Advanced Program-to-Program Communication/VM (APPC/VM)" on page 372.

The IUCV statement also specifies the maximum number of unprocessed messages that can be in stored on these links, and whether or not priority messages will be allowed. An important IUCV-related option is specified on the `OPTION MAXCONN` directory statement: it specifies the maximum number of APPC/VM or IUCV paths that can be open at one time, and defaults to 16 connections. In most cases, VM defaults are suitable for the "general user,"

```
USER JOJO
* JoJo can connect to PRICING with up to 20 open messages
 IUCV PRICING MSGLIMIT 20

USER LORETTA
* Loretta can connect to SPOT database
 IUCV SPOT

USER SQLDBA
* SPOT is a global resource
 OPTION ACCT SVMSTAT QUICKDSP MAXCONN 100 OPTION NOMDCFS
 IUCV ALLOW
 IUCV *IDENT SPOT GLOBAL

USER VMSERVU
* Let as many as 500 users connect to this server
 OPTION MAXCONN 500
* General SFS server allows all users to connect to it
 IUCV ALLOW
* SFS identifies itself as the local filepool "VMSYSU:"
 IUCV *IDENT VMSYSU LOCAL

USER VMSERVP
* Price database, identifies itself to the network as a global
* resource, using the name "Prices"
 IUCV *IDENT RESANY GLOBAL

USER DANIEL
* This user can connect to ANY other virtual machine
 IUCV ANY
```

Fig. 15.11 IUCV statements in directory.

and options need not be specified. Directory settings override values specified in application programs. IUCV statements are illustrated in Fig. 15.11.

CP system services

IUCV generalizes inter-program communication to let virtual machines communicate directly with *CP system services* exactly as they communicate with other virtual machines. This makes a number of extremely valuable services available to virtual machines, and lets virtual machines act as logical extensions of CP. One trend in VM development has been to introduce new facilities through service virtual machines that pass service requests to and from CP via IUCV messages.

CP system services are connected to by their names, just as virtual machines are. System service names begin with an asterisk, to make sure that they never conflict with a valid VM userid. The following CP system services are provided in VM/ESA:

- `*MSG`
- `*MSGALL`
- `*BLOCKIO`
- `*IDENT`
- `*MONITOR`
- `*ACCOUNT`
- `*LOGREC`
- `*SYMPTOM`
- `*RPI`
- `*SPL`
- `*SIGNAL`
- `*CCS`
- `*CRM`
- `*CONFIG`

Access to system services is controlled via the user directory IUCV statement, with the exception that *MSG, *MSGALL, and *BLOCKIO are available to all users.

A message router in CP routes IUCV traffic between virtual machines and the modules implementing system services. Each system service provides separate entry points to process CONNECT, SEND, SEVER, QUIESCE, and RESUME requests. The IUCV macro, when issued from CP, calls IUCV service routines to manage paths or transfer data between the system service and connected virtual machines.

*MSG and *MSGALL message processing

*MSG, the *Message System Service*, and *MSGALL system services let applications intercept system messages and responses that would normally be displayed on the terminal.

Messages sent to *MSG are controlled by the CP SET command. For example, the command `SET MSG IUCV` causes messages from other users to be sent to the IUCV application. Similar routing can be performed for `WNG` (warning) messages, `SMSG` messages that otherwise would be sent as `VMCF SENDX` messages, `EMSG` (error messages), `IMSG` (informational messages), `VMCONIO` (all virtual machine generated messages), and `CPCONIO` (CP responses). A virtual machine that intercepts all message types via *MSG would issue the commands in Fig. 15.12.

The message received by the IUCV program is a buffer containing the userid of the virtual machine originating the message, followed by the actual message text. CP tells the *MSG application what type of message it is sending by placing a message type code in the IUCV message class, as shown in Fig. 15.13.

WAKEUP can be used to catch IUCV messages by specifying the IUCVMSG option. When an IUCV message is received, WAKEUP exits with return code 5, and places in the CMS stack the type of message received, the userid it came from, and the actual message text. Other programs that catch *MSG events are the *starmsg* device driver in CMS Pipelines, and the public domain `MSGTRAP` command written at Wichita State University by Sam Drake, now at IBM, and `SUPERMSG` by Barry Leiba, also of IBM.

*MSGALL is an alternative to *MSG. All console output is sent to *MSGALL (after a program connects to it), unless explicitly directed to *MSG by one of the commands in Fig. 15.12.

*BLOCKIO asynchronous disk block I/O

`*BLOCKIO` (DASD block I/O system service) gives virtual machines an efficient, disk device geometry independent, asynchronous I/O interface to mini-

```
/* Prepare for *MSG processing */
'CP SET MSG IUCV'          /* Catch MSG output sent to me */
'CP SET WNG IUCV'          /* Catch WNG output sent to me */
'CP SET IMSG IUCV'         /* Catch informational messages*/
'CP SET EMSG IUCV'         /* Catch error messages */
'CP SET VMCONIO IUCV'      /* Catch virtual machine console output */
'CP SET CPCONIO IUCV'      /* Catch CP generated console output */
```

Fig. 15.12 Commands to route responses to *MSG.

Message Class	Message Type
1	MSG
2	WNG
3	CPCONIO
4	SMSG
5	VMCONIO
6	EMSG
7	IMSG
8	Secondary Console Image Facility (SCIF messages)

Fig. 15.13 *MSG message types.

disks. *BLOCKIO lets applications retrieve data by block number, rather than cylinder, track and record number. Like DIAGNOSE A4, which it predates, *BLOCKIO simplifies I/O programming in virtual machines. Unlike DIAGNOSE disk I/O, *BLOCKIO lets a virtual machine continue execution before the I/O request completes, and allows multiple overlapped I/O requests. This makes *BLOCKIO ideal for file and database service virtual machines, and in fact the first clients of *BLOCKIO were SQL/DS and SFS.

*BLOCKIO is available to all virtual machines without special authorization via a directory IUCV statement. A separate *BLOCKIO connection is needed for each minidisk it is used with. The MAXCONN option in the directory may have to be raised from the default of 16 to accommodate connections to *BLOCKIO, other system services, and virtual machines.

When an application connects to *BLOCKIO, it specifies the virtual device number of the disk on which block I/O is to be performed, the CMS block size it was formatted with, and the offset into the minidisk at which the reserved file (described in "Reserved Disk Areas and *BLOCKIO" on page XXX) begins. The offset is actually the number of disk blocks occupied by the CMS file system directory, allocation map, and other system reserved blocks. When CP accepts the connection, it places in the IUCV interrupt buffer the range of block numbers the application can read and write.

I/O to a disk is performed by issuing an IUCV SEND to its *BLOCKIO path. The SEND data includes the virtual machine I/O buffer address, the block number to be read or written, and a service request code indicating which operation should be performed:

- 1—Write
- 2—Read
- 3—Multiple requests

- 81—Write, bypassing minidisk cache
- 82—Read, bypassing minidisk cache
- 83—Multiple requests, bypassing minidisk cache.

*BLOCKIO immediately provides a return code that indicates whether or not the request was coded properly. The option to bypass minidisk cache is used for data that is referred to infrequently or is mostly written and infrequently read. This prevents it from displacing more frequently used data from high-speed minidisk cache. If minidisk caching was permitted for a read operation, the *BLOCKIO return code also indicates whether or not the data was present in minidisk cache. If it was, the return code indicates that the data has already been copied into the application's buffer. Otherwise, the application must wait until CP issues an IUCV REPLY indicating that the read completed.

An application to read or write to disk would perform the following steps:

1. Fill in the buffer address, block number, and request code.
2. IUCV SEND to *BLOCKIO.
3. If it failed, then exit with error.
4. If it completed immediately due to caching, exit normally.
5. Wait for IUCV REPLY indicating that the data was transmitted.
6. Check return codes, exit normally if no error occurred.

The multiple request formats let the application initiate a string of reads and writes in a single IUCV SEND. The parameter list sent in the IUCV SEND includes the number of blocks to be transferred, and points to a table containing, for each block:

- function code (read or write)
- disk block number
- buffer address in storage

When the operation completes, *BLOCKIO returns an success/failure result indicator for each block. An error reading or writing one block has no effect on other blocks in the same multiple block request.

CP data recording system services

`*MONITOR`, `*ACCOUNT`, `*LOGREC`, `*SYMPTOM`, and `*CONFIG` system services are used to funnel data collected by CP to virtual machines for logging or processing. This type of system service originated in VM/XA, and provides an architectured and extensible method for letting virtual machines receive data from CP. The different services and data they collect are as follows:

- *MONITOR—performance monitoring data
- *ACCOUNT—system accounting data
- *LOGREC—hardware error logs
- *SYMPTOM—software error symptoms
- *CONFIG—dynamic device configuration changes in ESCON hardware

IBM provides a RETRIEVE program to write *ACCOUNT, *LOGREC, and *SYMPTOM data to disk, and a MONWRITE program for *MONITOR data, although installation and vendor-written programs can provide the same function. A virtual machine can connect to each of these system services; CP then issues IUCV SEND commands when it has data to transmit.

As mentioned in "Monitor Data Collection" on page 366, CP uses the *MONITOR system service to notify the collector virtual machine when data is available in the monitor shared segment, rather than as the method for actually transmitting the data. In VM/ESA, multiple virtual machines can collect to *MONITOR and receive notification of performance data.

*CONFIG is a new system service for ESCON dynamic device reconfiguration. A dynamic device change generates an ES/9000 machine check. CP intercepts the interrupt and sends a message to the userid connected to *CONFIG. This is an interesting reversal of the traditional virtualization of real hardware features: VM/ESA reflects similar machine checks to XA and ESA-mode virtual machines when their I/O configurations change. CMS uses this to detect that a minidisk was detached. This facility is now available on real computers, showing that virtual machines can be used to test facilities to be added to real ones.

Access Control Interface system service *RPI

CP uses *RPI to pass authorization requests to an external security manager (ESM). CP issues an IUCV 2-way SEND to the ESM when a user requests access to a function protected by ACI. The ESM consults its' rules database and issues an IUCV REPLY to tell CP to determine whether the request should be granted or denied. Typically, the ESM also logs the access attempt, whether permitted or not, to a log file for subsequent auditing.

The *RPI interface was introduced by IBM with VM/SP Release 3 for their *Resource Access Control Facility* (RACF), but is also used by other vendors' products, such as System Center, Inc.'s *VMSECURE*. ESM products replace "stub" modules that CP calls at decision points (e.g., at the point where a LINK command is validated) with their own modules. Stub modules return to the caller with a return code indicating that CP should perform its default action, for example, using the directory LINK or LOGON password to validate a link. The modules replacing the stubs issue the IUCV calls to the ESM. In some cases, for efficiency sake, rules may be hard-coded in the CP modules. For example, read-links to the public CMS minidisks may be granted to all users without consulting the ESM database. The following CP modules are involved with access control:

- `HCPRPI` performs the IUCV communication between CP and the ESM.
- `HCPRPW` is called when a LOGON, AUTOLOG, or XAUTOLOG command is entered and needs validation.
- `HCPRPD` implements DIAGNOSE A0. which let virtual machines interface with the external security manager.

Communication of the request type and the decision taken is performed by passing an `ACIPARMS` control block between CP and the ESM. ACIPARMS describes the type of command or operation being performed by the virtual machine. The ESM replies with an ACIPARMS value with an ACICODE return code indicating how the request should be processed: a request can be permitted or denied, or its authorization be deferred to CP's default rules. The ESM can also ask CP to logoff the requestor.

System spool system service (*SPL)

`*SPL` lets CP communicate with virtual machines that act as a logical extension of the CP real printer services. A *SPL application connects to *SPL specifying the name of a *logical printer*. Users can direct print files to logical printers using the commands they would use for a printer directly driven by CP. *SPL was introduced by IBM to support *Advanced Function Printing* (AFP), which provide font and form management control for locally and network attached laser printers.

The AFP *Spool File Conversion Machine* (SFCM) connects to *SPL to receive IUCV messages from CP when a print file is closed and queued for printing. SFCM converts print output from the form it is stored in the spool into a format usable by *Printer Driver Machines* (PDMS).

*SPL recognizes IUCV SEND requests for the following types of action:

- Select and open print file for processing.
- Close a previously opened file.
- Read spool file descriptive information and contents associated with a spool file.
- Read XAB (External Attribute Buffers) containing font and form information associated with a print file. XAB information is associated with a file via DIAGNOSE code B4.

CP sends an IUCV REPLY down the *SPL connection to answer each of these requests. Additionally, CP can originate IUCV SENDs to route operator commands for the printer (drain, flush, query, and start), to notify the SPL application that a file has arrived for processing, and to tell the application to purge the file it is currently processing.

Console Communication Services (*CCS)

Console Communication Services (*CCS) provides bidirectional communication for terminal traffic between CP and virtual machines. CCS was introduced with VM/SP Release 1 to allow VM systems to participate in SNA networks; as discussed in "VM VTAM" on page 332. *CCS is also used by TCP/IP, which uses it to implement the Telnet application for remote logon.

Signal system service (*SIGNAL)

`*SIGNAL` is used by GCS virtual machines to coordinate their activities, and especially to be signaled when virtual machines enter and leave a GCS group, as discussed in "Group Control System (GCS)" on page 332.

TSAF and APPC/VM system services, *IDENT AND *CRM

`*IDENT` and `*CRM` are used by TSAF and APPC/VM to control association of resources with virtual machines. Resource manager virtual machines, such as SQL/DS, SFS servers, and APPC/VM applications, connect to *IDENT, the *Identify* system service, to declare their presence within a TSAF collection or SNA network, or to revoke ownership of the resource. *IDENT authorization is controlled in the user directory IUCV statement; a userid can be allowed to control or revoke specific resources, or to manage any resource identifier.

*CRM, the *Configuration Resource Manager* system service, is used by TSAF to coordinate association of globally known names across a TSAF collection. When a resource manager invokes *IDENT to associate itself with a global resource, CP issues an IUCV SEND to the userid connected to *CRM. This userid, running TSAF, communicates with other TSAF virtual machines to inform them of the resource manager that just declared itself. The table of resource identifiers is maintained in a hash-accessed table in CP based on information supplied by *CRM and *IDENT.

Once a virtual machine is identified as a resource manager, CP routes APPC/VM connections to its resource name to it as "connection pending" messages. The virtual machine can then accept the connection and communicate with a client process that may be on a remote system.

Advanced Program-to-Program Communication/VM (APPC/VM)

APPC/VM is a generalization of IUCV for cross-system communication. APPC/VM programs can communicate with other APPC/VM programs within a TSAF *collection* of VM systems linked together via communications lines, or use an SNA network to communicate with both APPC/VM and non-VM programs using the SNA LU6.2 protocol. VM's *APPC/VM VTAM Services* (AVS) component is a *gateway* application that converts APPC/VM messages, actually a specialized form of IUCV message, to and from LU6.2 data streams transmitted over an SNA network.

APPC/VM applications include SFS, SQL/DS, and OfficeVision. SFS and SQL/DS use APPC/VM to let files and databases be transparently accessed from remote systems. OfficeVision uses APPC/VM to let multiple VM systems share access to a calendar database.

SNA's LU6.2 concepts

Probably the hardest problem in understanding APPC/VM and LU6.2 is relating the vocabulary and concepts used by VM and SNA to one another. Many concepts overlap, but not exactly, but very little of the vocabulary does.

LU6.2 protocol is SNA's equivalent of the program-to-program communication methods in VM systems. An LU6.2 program at a node in an SNA network establishes *sessions* with LU6.2 programs at other nodes, using lower-level SNA services for physical transport, message flow and pacing, routing and retry, and other services. Application programs ask the LU to establish *conversations* with applications residing at a different LU. Conversations are allocated one of the sessions available between the LUs.

An application using LU6.2 protocol is called a *transaction program* or a *resource*, and may be referred to by its *Transaction Program Name* (TPN) or *resource name*. If a transaction program is not executing at the remote LU when a conversation is started, support services at the remote LU's node may start the application up. Pools of service machines can be defined for a resource. CP automatically AUTOLOGs an available service machine from the pool when a client wants to invoke the resource.

APPC/VM resource types

In VMCF and IUCV, applications connect to a virtual machine userid or a system service name. In APPC/VM, applications connect to a *resource name*, which represents a logical resource that may be defined by a program residing in a virtual machine on the same VM system, a different VM system connected by the network, or a network-connected machine running any operating system.

Communications directories map resource names into the LU6.2 LU name and TP name of the network node and application that define a resource. Communications directories are normal CMS NAMES files. SCOMDIR NAMES can be on the S-disk to provide a list of resource mappings available to all users; individual users can have personal user UCOMDIR NAMES files. A communications directory shown in Fig. 15.14 contains definitions that link two VM systems together to let them share access to a remote SFS filepool and several application program servers.

Communication directories can identify their owners using the userid and password of a userid defined at the remote system. This is necessary to handle duplicate userids: two systems might have userids named JONES; the "visitor" at a system can be assigned an alternate userid (say JONES2), and identify him or herself by that userid in the communications directory. The communications directory also defines the security requirements needed for an application: NONE, which is suitable for applications open to all users, SAME, which uses the security rights owned by the invoker, and PGM, determined by the program's authority rights and checking.

CP uses the *IDENT and *CRM system services to resolve the resource name into its network location and the identity of its actual server. There are three type of resources:

- *Local Resource*—a resource known only to the local system. A local resource name can exist on each system in a collection.
- *Global Resource*—a resource known to all TSAF virtual machines in the collection. A global resource can exist on only one system in a TSAF collection. When an application connects to a global resource by its name, TSAF directs it to the system containing the resource.
- *System Resource*—a resource which can exist on each system in a collection, which is globally accessible through the AVS virtual machine, but which is not known to the TSAF virtual machine.

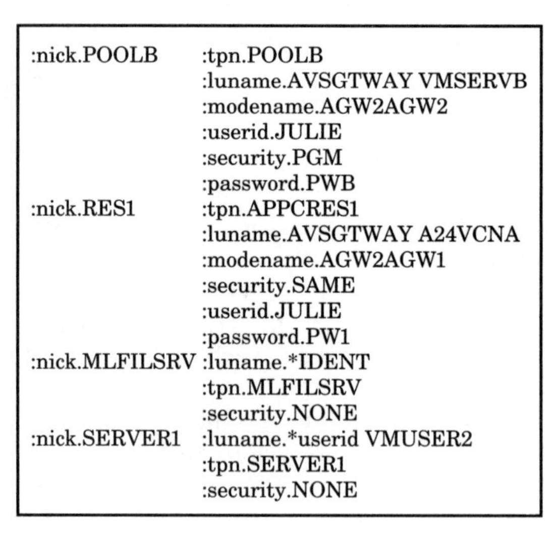

```
:nick.POOLB     :tpn.POOLB
                :luname.AVSGTWAY VMSERVB
                :modename.AGW2AGW2
                :userid.JULIE
                :security.PGM
                :password.PWB
:nick.RES1      :tpn.APPCRES1
                :luname.AVSGTWAY A24VCNA
                :modename.AGW2AGW1
                :security.SAME
                :userid.JULIE
                :password.PW1
:nick.MLFILSRV  :luname.*IDENT
                :tpn.MLFILSRV
                :security.NONE
:nick.SERVER1   :luname.*userid VMUSER2
                :tpn.SERVER1
                :security.NONE
```

Fig. 15.14 Communications directory.

Additionally, the gateway LU running in an AVS virtual machine is also a global resource visible to all hosts in a network.

An APPC/VM resource announces its presence to the local system or global environment by connecting to *IDENT. When *IDENT completes the resource association and updates the resource tables, it reflects an IUCV "connection complete" message back to the APPC/VM resource program. Users connecting to the resource specify the resource name and are routed to it via TSAF.

APPC/VM programming interfaces

APPC/VM programs are coded using either of two programming interfaces: a low level assembly language interface using the CMSIUCV, HNDIUCV, IUCV, and APPCVM macros, and a portable, high level interface using the *Common Programming Interface for Communications* (CPI-C) verbs and conventions. CPI-C is a formally defined and central component of IBM's *Systems Application Architecture* (SAA). APPC/VM programs are therefore compatible with the communication protocols used with other SAA platforms. These systems include AS/400, MVS/ESA Version 4.2 and later, MVS/ESA CICS Version 2.1 and later, AIX/ESA, and AIX/6000 on RISC/6000 workstations.

With APPC/VM, IBM finally announced a high-level language interface to inter-program communications. CMS now includes `CMSSAA TXTLIB`, which contains subroutines callable from programs written in FORTRAN, PL/I, C, COBOL, RPG, Pascal, and the CSP (Cross System Product) application generator. Additionally, REXX programs can issue APPC program calls by prefacing the subroutine name with `ADDRESS CPICOMM`, for example:

```
address CPICOMM 'CMACP .......' /* Accept a connection */
```

Among the many verbs available for CPI communications are:

- CMINIT—initialize communication with a partner.
- CMALLC—allocate a conversation.
- CMACP—accept a conversation.
- CMSEND—send a message.
- CMCFMD—request a confirmation. This forces the buffer from a CMSEND to be sent to the partner, if it hasn't been transmitted previously, and asks the partner to acknowledge that the message was received.
- CMRCV—receive a message.
- CMECS—end a conversation.
- CMDEAL—deallocate the conversation resources.

The above verbs are SAA standard functions. VM adds unique verbs for APPC/VM, including XCIDRM, which lets an application identify itself as a resource manager, and XCWOE, which lets an application wait for a variety of events at the same time. This is used by applications that participate in APPC/VM conversations, but also respond to console and reader events. In most part, the APPC/VM verb set is analogous to the IUCV command set.

One key difference between APPC/VM and predecessor methods is that it is a *half duplex* method. At any one time, only one of the partners in a two-way conversation can be sending data. One program is said to be in *send state*, while the other program is in *receive state*. Applications must remember which state they are in for each conversation they are engaging in; only a subset of the APPC/VM verbs is "legal" in each of the states (e.g., a SENDDATA cannot be issued in receive state). An APPC/VM application can be in one of the following states:

- Reset—no conversation is in effect.
- Connect—a source program has initiated a CONNECT operation, and it hasn't yet been accepted, or a target program has just received a connection-pending interrupt.
- Send—the program can send data.
- Receive—the program is prepared to receive data.
- Confirm—a program's partner has asked it to respond (confirm).
- Sever—the conversation with the partner program is being terminated. This is also referred to as *deallocate* state, since the conversation is being deallocated.

Half-duplex communication is a significant restriction compared to IUCV and VMCF, both of which let programs send messages to one another whenever the need arises. Programmers experienced with IUCV and VMCF often find this APPC/VM restriction a nuisance. IUCV and VMCF have no problem exchanging data in either direction between a pair of communications partners.

However, APPC/VM and SNA's LU6.2 are designed for remote transmission links, unlike IUCV and VMCF which only operate within a CPU. Half-duplex communication helps decouple timing from the protocol, and let the implementation control pacing, buffering, optimization of bandwidth, and message acknowledgement. Full duplex messages must be delivered as soon as they are sent. Half duplex messages can be briefly postponed to allow "piggybacking" of additional messages in the same transferred block of data.

APPC/VM assembly language interface

APPC/VM is accessed using the APPCVM and IUCV macros. The low-level APPC/VM verb set has several operations in common with IUCV, invoked by

IUCV or CMSIUCV macros just as in pure IUCV applications. DCLBFR, CONNECT, DESCRIBE, TESTMSG, TESTCMPL, SEVER, and RTRVBFR perform essentially the same functions as with IUCV. For example, the IUCV DCLBFR function is used to create a standard IUCV external interrupt buffer to receive interrupt information.

The APPCVM macro adds verbs called SENDDATA, SENDCNF, SENDCNFD, SENDERR, and SENDREQ, and significantly changes the meaning of RECEIVE. The APPCVM macro uses the same IPARML structure as IUCV. Except for the half-duplex protocol, APPC/VM programming at the assembler level looks much like IUCV programming. Most programmers, however, will use the higher-level language interface.

Chapter

16

CP DIAGNOSE Functions

CP provides a rich suite of program services for applications residing in virtual machines. CP can be thought of as providing a "better machine" by providing a virtual computer with useful facilities not installed in real 370 and 390 computers. Some facilities let virtual machines repay the favor to CP by letting virtual machines act as logical extensions to CP.

As mentioned in "DIAGNOSE Instructions in the Virtual Machine" on page 46, CP provides many program services via the `DIAGNOSE` instruction. DIAGNOSE calls are used much like SVC calls in other IBM operating systems. Since DIAGNOSE calls are processed by the CP "hypervisor" controlling multiple operating systems, they are also referred to as "hypervisor" calls. In 370-mode VM systems, DIAGNOSEs are interpreted in a module named DMKHVC (HyperVisor Call); in VM/ESA they are handled in HCPHVC.

DIAGNOSE services can be invoked directly from assembler programs or CSL calls, and are invoked by CMS system routines. Many DIAGNOSE functions can also be directly invoked by REXX programs.

DIAGNOSE Instruction Format

DIAGNOSE is a four-byte long instruction with the following format:

83	Rx Ry	B	DDD

where

`83` is the hexadecimal instruction opcode byte for DIAGNOSE

RX and RY are 4-bit fields designating registers used to contain parameter values or addresses passed between the virtual machine and CP routines called from DIAGNOSE. For some DIAGNOSE codes, Rx and Ry specify pairs of registers, and registers Rx+1 and Ry+1 are also used to pass parameters. Unfortunately, there is no general convention for the register assignments, so programmers must look up the calling conventions for each DIAGNOSE function.

B is a base register. Register zero should be used for compatibility with VM/SP and HPO. If any other register is used, the contents of the register are added to the value specified for DDD to produce the DIAGNOSE function code.

DDD is the DIAGNOSE function code.

DIAGNOSE function codes are evenly divisible by 4: values between 0 and hexadecimal 'FC' are used by IBM, as are values from hexadecimal 200 and up. The range X'100'to X'1FC' is available for user installations. Many VM sites, and some vendor products, add special functions to CP and use this interface to make them available to virtual machines.

There is no particular order to the DIAGNOSE definitions: DIAGNOSE functions were added to VM in many VM releases, so some newer DIAGNOSE codes have higher numeric values. When the range between X'00' and X'FC' was used up, IBM skipped over the X'100' to X'1FC' range to prevent conflicts for installations with local DIAGNOSEs.

Using DIAGNOSE in Assembly Language

DIAGNOSE functions are invoked by setting up parameter registers and executing the DIAGNOSE instruction. IBM assemblers do not provide a mnemonic instruction for DIAGNOSE. Assembly language programmers either hard code the hexadecimal representation of the instruction, or use a macro call to generate it. For convenience, CMS provides a DIAG macro that expands into a DIAGNOSE. The Rx, Ry, and DIAGNOSE function codes are specified in the DIAG call, as illustrated in Fig. 16.2.

CP provides the result of a DIAGNOSE code as the PSW condition code, which can be tested by a conditional branch, and as a return code returned in a register. The return code is usually placed in Rx or Ry, and sometimes in a specially designated register like register 15.

Storage address values passed to DIAGNOSE must be "second-level" virtual addresses, also called "guest real" addresses; that is, virtual addresses created by the host CP that appear "real" to the virtual machine operating system. This is only a consideration when issuing DIAGNOSE instructions from virtual storage operating systems like DOS/VSE or MVS, which create a third level of storage addressing. MVS or DOS/VSE applications using DIAGNOSE must place operands in storage that is allocated "virtual=real" from the guest system perspective, or page-fix their third level addresses and use the LRA (Load Real Address) instruction to get their second level addresses.

If a DIAGNOSE call is done incorrectly, CP returns error indication by reflecting a program exception to the virtual machine. Usually an *addressing exception* indicates use of an address outside the bounds of the virtual machine's storage, a *protection exception* is signaled if the DIAGNOSE call specifies an output area in virtual storage that is read-only, and a *specification exception* is signaled for violating other requirements (for example, specifying a DIAGNOSE code that is not evenly divisible by 4).

Using DIAGNOSE in REXX

The CMS REXX language provides *diag* and *diagrc* function calls for executing a subset of the DIAGNOSE functions. These function calls associate their parameters with the Rx and Ry registers, so the REXX programmer need not be concerned with the assembly language description of the DIAGNOSE interface.

Both functions return unconverted binary results provided by DIAGNOSE; REXX conversion functions are used to convert the data into standard REXX formats. The results can be used in an expression, assigned to a variable, or processed by a *parse value* statement. If invoked by a *call* statement instead of a function call, the result is discarded. The difference between *diag* and *diagrc* is that *diagrc* prefaces the result data with a character string containing the PSW condition code and DIAGNOSE return code. The prefix is a 16 character long string; characters 1 through 9 contain the DIAGNOSE return code, and character 11 contains the PSW condition code (an integer from 0 to 3).

The REXX interface only supports a subset of the DIAGNOSE commands. The DIAGNOSEs that can be used are hexadecimal codes 0, 8, C, 14, 24, 5C, 60, 64, 8C, CC, F8, and 210.

DIAGNOSE Processing in CP

DIAGNOSE is a privileged instruction: a virtual machine executing a DIAGNOSE instruction under VM/SP or HPO produces a privileged operation exception, which causes a PSW swap to CP's program check handler module, DMKPRG. DMKPRG then branches to DMKHVC ("HyperVisor Call"), the DIAGNOSE processor. In VM/ESA, DIAGNOSE causes a SIE intercept. CP regains control and calls HCPHVC, the ESA equivalent of DMKHVC.

In both cases CP uses a branch table, indexed by the DIAGNOSE function code, to select the routine for each DIAGNOSE function. While the DIAGNOSE is being processed, the virtual machine is marked as being in *simulation wait*, and cannot be dispatched until DIAGNOSE processing completes.

Execution might be delayed if a page of virtual storage must be brought into main storage from disk, or if the DIAGNOSE requests an I/O operation.

When the DIAGNOSE routine completes, CP updates virtual machine registers, virtual PSW, and storage locations as specified for each DIAGNOSE function, ends simulation wait, and then returns to the dispatcher. The dispatcher then can continue running the virtual machine, unless a higher priority CP task or virtual machine has also become ready-to-run.

DIAGNOSE Functions

The following are DIAGNOSE functions available in current VM versions, their official names, and their calling sequences, and purposes. Additional details on DIAGNOSE specifications can be found in the *CP Programming Services* manual for each release of VM.

DIAGNOSE code 0: store extended identification

DIAGNOSE 0 provides identification information to the calling virtual machine. Rx points to a result buffer, and Ry contains the buffer's length. Information from DIAGNOSE 0 includes the following:

- The name of the version of CP (for example, "VM/ESA").
- Version code of the real CPU, returned by the STIDP instruction
- The virtual machine's userid.
- CP's program product bit map, which indicates the version of CP and features installed in it. For example, "APSS" support for Advanced Function Printing (AFP) was added to VM/XA SP after it was released, so knowing that VM/XA SP was installed wouldn't be sufficient to determine if APSS

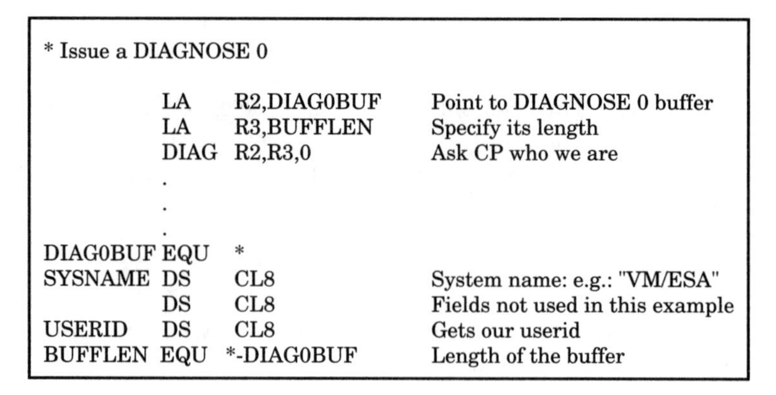

```
* Issue a DIAGNOSE 0

          LA    R2,DIAG0BUF        Point to DIAGNOSE 0 buffer
          LA    R3,BUFFLEN         Specify its length
          DIAG  R2,R3,0            Ask CP who we are
          .
          .
          .
DIAG0BUF EQU   *
SYSNAME  DS    CL8                 System name: e.g.: "VM/ESA"
         DS    CL8                 Fields not used in this example
USERID   DS    CL8                 Gets our userid
BUFFLEN  EQU   *-DIAG0BUF          Length of the buffer
```

Fig. 16.1 DIAGNOSE 0 call from REXX.

```
x = diag(00)
VM_version = substr(x,1,8)        /* eg: VM/ESA */
My_userid  = substr(x,17,8)       /* eg: JEFF   */
```

Fig. 16.2 DIAGNOSE 0 call from assembler.

was available. Bit settings for each version of VM are documented in the IBM manual *CP Programming Services*.

- Time zone differential: the number of seconds between the local time zone and Greenwich Mean Time. This value can be used to adjust CPU clock values for the local time zone. A negative number indicates a time zone west of GMT (for example, the United States), a positive number indicates a time zone east of GMT.
- Version number, containing the CP release, version and service level numbers.

When VM runs under VM, DIAGNOSE 0 returns information for "higher level" VM systems. For example, if VM/SP is running under VM/ESA, the output buffer will first contain information about VM/SP and then VM/ESA. DIAGNOSE 0 output occupies 40 bytes and up to 200 bytes of information can be returned by DIAGNOSE 0, enough to describe five levels of executing VM under VM. Ry is decremented by the number of bytes of data returned. If the specified buffer length is less than 40 bytes, only the number of bytes specified are stored by CP.

DIAGNOSE 0 is used by CMS to determine the VM userid, and by various CMS commands to determine which features are installed in CP. This is especially important for CMS 7, which runs both in VM/ESA ESA feature and 370 feature, and thus runs in both ESA and 370 host environments. DIAGNOSE 0 coding is shown in REXX in Fig. 16.1, and in assembly language in Fig. 16.2.

DIAGNOSE code 4: examine real storage

DIAGNOSE 4 is used by class C or E virtual machines to read the contents of real storage. Class C and E therefore must be assigned only to "trusted" virtual machines, since it could be used to "snoop" on sensitive information. Normally, DIAGNOSE 4 is used by monitoring products that inspect CP data areas for performance or diagnostic information.

Rx points to a table of 4-byte real storage addresses. Ry contains the number of entries, and Ry+1 points to a table to receive the contents of storage at those addresses. DIAGNOSE 4 places the value of storage pointed to by each word in Rx's table in the corresponding word in the table pointed to by Ry+1.

The tables pointed to by Rx and Ry+1 must be in the same page of virtual storage in the virtual machine. IBM recommends that this page be resident at the time of the DIAGNOSE instruction to avoid having performance monitoring software alter performance statistics by inspecting them. This can be arranged by issuing the DIAGNOSE instruction from the same page as the tables, or by "touching" one of the table elements immediately before issuing the DIAGNOSE.

For performance sake, it is good practice to fetch as many real storage values as possible in the same DIAGNOSE 4 call. Programs issuing DIAGNOSE 4 must be prepared for changes to real storage values. For example, CP might add or delete elements in a linked list while a DIAGNOSE 4 application is traversing the list.

DIAGNOSE code 8: virtual console function

DIAGNOSE 8 is used to issue CP commands from a virtual machine. For example, CMS uses DIAGNOSE 8 to issue CP commands entered from the command line (if `#CP` is not specified to escape directly to CP) or from EXECs and other programs.

Input to DIAGNOSE 8 is specified in a buffer. Command response may be displayed on the virtual machine console or stored in an output buffer. Registers for DIAGNOSE 8 are set up as follows:

- Rx contains the virtual storage address of the command string. Multiple CP commands can be specified in the same DIAGNOSE call by separating them with the hexadecimal character X'15'.
- Rx+1 contains the virtual storage address of the output buffer for command response messages.
- Ry contains option flags and the length of the command string. The option flags are in the high order byte, and the length is in the lower order 3 bytes of Ry. The options are as follows:
  - X'80'—reject passwords entered on the same line as a LINK, AU TOLOG or XAUTOLOG command.
  - X'40'—returns the command response in the buffer pointed to by Rx+1, instead of on the console.
  - X'20'—indicates that CP should tell the virtual machine when a password is needed for LINK, AUTOLOG or XAUTOLOG, so the virtual machine can prompt the user for it.
- Ry+1 contains the length of the output buffer.

On output, Ry contains the return code from the CP command. CP also returns a condition code indicating whether the DIAGNOSE itself was successful (that is, the output fits in the specified buffer).

DIAGNOSE 8 is the fastest way for REXX programs to issue CP com-

```
/* save current EMSG value */
parse value diag(8,'QUERY SET') with . 'EMSG' emsg_value .
/* turn off EMSG while calling "noisy" program that generates */
/* error message we know are uninteresting                    */
Call diag(8,'SET EMSG OFF')
Call Noisy
/* Restore original EMSG value so we don't cause side-effect   */
if emsg_value <> 'OFF' then Call diag(8,'SET EMSG' emsg_value)

/* Determine if we're in an 31-bit capable virtual machine
  This includes userids in XA, ESA, or XC (eXtended Configuration)
  modes. */
parse value diag(8,'QUERY SET') with . 'MACHINE' Mode ',' .
if Pos(space(Mode),'XA ESA XC')<>0
then say 'We can use 31-bit addressing and other XA stuff
```

Fig. 16.3 DIAGNOSE 8 calls from REXX.

mands and obtain their responses, and can be used as an alternative to the CMS `EXECIO` command and CMS Pipelines (both of which ultimately issue DIAGNOSE 8 anyway). For example, a REXX program can use DIAGNOSE 8 to determine the current `EMSG` setting before turning it off, as shown in Fig. 16.3. This example also shows how to obtain the current machine architecture setting.

The diag(8) function has an optional third parameter, the size of the buffer REXX uses for the output from the CP command. The default buffer size is 4,096 bytes, and must be increased if the command response is larger. For example, the buffer must be enlarged if `diag(8,'QUERY NAMES')` is issued on a system with many logged on users. The proper technique is to determine the buffer size in advance, as illustrated in Fig. 16.4.

DIAGNOSE code C: pseudo-timer

DIAGNOSE C provides a convenient way to obtain the current date and time in displayable format, as well as the amount of CPU time consumed by the virtual machine. Rx points to a buffer to receive the time information. Ry is not used. The data returned by DIAGNOSE C is as follows:

- month, day and year in EBCDIC, formatted as "mm/dd/yy" (8 characters)
- time of day in hours, minutes and seconds, in EBCDIC and formatted as "hh:mm:ss" (8 characters)
- virtual CPU time (VTIME) consumed by the user in microseconds, stored in an 8 byte binary number
- total CPU time (TTIME) consumed by the user in microseconds, stored in an 8 byte binary number

```
/* Get number of users logged on */
parse value diag(8,'QUERY USERS') with N_users .
/* need about 25 bytes per user (based on command output format)
   plus a fudge factor in case users log on right this instant */
query_name_output = diag(8, 'QUERY NAMES' ,25*N_users+100)

/* Get information about each queued reader file */
parse value diag(8, 'QUERY FILES') with N_files .
if N_files = 'NO' then exit        /* we have no reader files: exit */
/* Each entry in 'query reader' all display occupies 80 bytes */
/* Add one more line for header line, plus extra in case a few more */
/* files arrive between the QUERY FILES command and the next line */
query_rdr_all=diag(8,'QUERY Reader ALL' ,80*(N_files+10))
```

Fig. 16.4 DIAGNOSE 8 buffer estimates.

Virtual CPU time is the time that the virtual machine was itself executing. Total CPU is VTIME plus time spent in CP servicing the virtual machine (for example, spent performing DIAGNOSE functions). CMS uses DIAGNOSE C in a number of places. For example, if CMS is printing long format "Ready;" messages, CMS uses DIAGNOSE C to obtain the virtual and total CPU times and time of day.

DIAGNOSE C can be used by REXX programs to obtain timing information with a high level of accuracy, as shown in Fig. 16.5.

DIAGNOSE code 10: release pages

DIAGNOSE 10 tells CP that the virtual machine no longer needs the contents of a range of virtual storage pages. If the pages are resident, CP releases their real storage page frames. If the pages have been paged out to expanded storage or disk, CP releases the page slots they occupy there. The next time the virtual machine refers to a released page, CP provides an empty page frame containing binary zeros.

Rx and Ry contain the page-aligned addresses of the beginning and end pages to release. The DIAGNOSE call is in error if either address is not on a page boundary (the address must be evenly divisible by 4,096; in hexadecimal notation, the last three digits are zeros), Ry contains a value less than Rx, or either address is higher than the highest virtual storage address.

DIAGNOSE 10 is how CMS applications release storage they have referred to, and is very important to VM system performance. For example, arrays in a Fortran program or file contents in an XEDIT session might reside in several megabytes of virtual storage, and occupy hundreds or thousands of pages of real storage. By releasing these pages when the program or XEDIT session ends, CMS frees real storage for other users and for other virtual storage addresses in the same virtual machine. If CMS did not do this, pages would remain resident in real storage until they had been unreferenced long enough to be migrated to auxiliary storage. This would dramatically increase paging and contention for main storage.

CMS storage management issues DIAGNOSE 10 when an application releases a block of storage containing complete pages. This can be turned off under special circumstances by issuing the command `SET RELPAGE OFF` (set "release page" option off). This is only a good idea when an application is known to repeatedly and rapidly acquire and free the same storage many times in succession. In this case, there is no savings in real storage, and turning off CMS's page release processing eliminates the overhead of releasing and reacquiring real storage. Under VM/ESA 1.1 and later, DIAGNOSE 214 provides an enhanced form of page release, discussed later, that handles this situation as well.

DIAGNOSE code 14: input spool file manipulation

DIAGNOSE 14 provides multiple functions for reading and controlling input spool files. Input spool files can be read by issuing `SIO` or `SSCH` native I/O instructions to the virtual reader. DIAGNOSE 14 provides an additional, synchronous I/O interface to spool I/O. DIAGNOSE 14 is more efficient, and also provides functions for backspacing, selecting and otherwise controlling spool files.

An important feature of DIAGNOSE 14 is that it returns the actual 4K byte spool file buffer used by CP, while SIO and SSCH I/O reads the record level (typically, card image) contents of the records stored in the buffer. DIAGNOSE 14 increases efficiency because multiple records are made available in a single call to CP.

DIAGNOSE 14 also lets the application see additional information, since the spool file buffer contains both spool file data and the channel commands used to write it. CP TAG information is stored as if created by a "no operation" channel command; print file output is stored along with the

```
/* Provide accurate timing of a specified command */
parse arg command_to_do        /* get target command string */
numeric digits 20              /* allow arithmetic on big numbers */
before_CPU = diag('C')         /* Prior time information */
command_to_do                  /* issue target command */
after_CPU = diag('C')          /* time information after command */
/* Convert the TTIME values and get their difference */
before_ttime= c2d(substr(before_CPU,25,8))
after_ttime  = c2d(substr(after_CPU, 25,8))
delta_ttime  = after_ttime - before_ttime
say 'CPU time used in microseconds =' delta_ttime
```

Fig. 16.5 DIAGNOSE C call from REXX.

printer orders that control page positioning ("skip to top of page," "advance two lines and then write").

Rx and Ry are data registers whose contents depend on the subfunction used. The subfunction code is placed in Ry+1. Ry and Ry+1 must be an even/odd register pair. The subfunctions are as follows:

- `CODE X'0000'`—read next spool file buffer. Rx contains the address of a 4K byte buffer, and Ry has the device number of the input address. This function is used by RSCS to read files from multiple reader devices. CMS only directly supports one reader device, but applications can use additional ones if they perform their own input.
- `CODE X'0004'`—read next print spool file block. This function selects the next reader spool file in 'print' format, that is, originating from a virtual console or printer device.
- `CODE X'0008'`—read next punch spool file block. this function selects the next reader spool file in 'punch' format, that is, originating from a virtual punch.
- `CODE X'000C'`—order a file to the front of a queue. This function moves the spool file whose file number is contained in Rx to the front of the reader queue.
- `CODE X'0010'`—repeat active file. The copy count in Rx is given to the active (in use) file. This allows the file to be read the specified number of times before CP purges it.
- `CODE X'0014'`—restarts the active file at the beginning.
- `CODE X'0018'`—backspace active file one record.
- `CODE X'001C'`—read next MONITOR spool file block (VM/SP, HPO only). This is like subfunctions 0004 and 0008, except it applies to CP MONITOR data, which is stored in spool files in VM/SP and HPO.
- `CODE X'0020'`—read next MONITOR spool record (VM/SP, HPO only). Like function code 0000, except only MONITOR files are read.
- `CODE X'0024'`—read the last spool file buffer of the active file.
- `CODE X'0FFE'`—select the next file not previously selected. If Ry is 0, the next file not yet selected by DIAGNOSE 14 is selected, and description is placed in a buffer pointed to by Rx. If Ry is 1, then the 'already selected' bit is turned off for all spool files in the userid's reader queue, and the first file is selected.
- `CODE X'0FFF'`—retrieve next file descriptor following the spool file identified by the file number in Ry, or from the beginning of the reader queue if Ry is zero.

DIAGNOSE 14 is used by a number of CMS commands that process reader files, such as the NETDATA module invoked by the RECEIVE command. DIAGNOSE 14 is also used by RSCS, which spends a considerable portion of its time manipulating spool files on multiple reader devices.

DIAGNOSE 14 functions are invoked from REXX by using symbolic names for the subfunctions, instead of their numbers. Typical subfunction names are RNSB (Read Next Spool Buffer), and RNPUSFB (Read Next PUnch Spool File Block).

DIAGNOSE code 18: standard DASD I/O

DIAGNOSE 18 is used for CMS disk I/O in VM/SP and HPO. VM/ESA supports DIAGNOSE 18 for virtual machines running in 370 mode.

Rx contains the device number of the disk to which I/O is performed. Ry contains a channel address word (CAW) in System/370 format. The CAW's left-most 3 bits contain the protect key of the storage to be used for the virtual storage operands of the I/O operation, and the right-most 24 bits contain the virtual address of the first channel command in the I/O operation. The I/O operation may perform multiple chained reads or writes, provided they all access the same DASD cylinder. Register 15 must contain the number of reads or writes in the channel program.

On completion of the I/O operation, CP sets a PSW return code and a numeric return code in register 15. CP returns error indications for attempting I/O to a nonexistent disk, for trying to write to a read-only minidisk, for trying to seek beyond the extent of a minidisk, and for a number of other programming errors or physical I/O errors.

DIAGNOSE 18 is superceded by DIAG A4 under VM/XA and VM/ESA, but is supported for compatibility purposes for virtual machines running in 370 mode. Applications that perform DIAGNOSE I/O and want to use the "best" interface for the version of CP in use can use DIAGNOSE 0 to determine which CP they are running under, and then use either DIAGNOSE 18 or DIAGNOSE A4.

DIAGNOSE code 1C: clear error recording cylinders (VM/SP, HPO)

In VM/SP and HPO, but not in VM/XA and VM/ESA, the log of hardware error incidents is kept in specially reserved disk cylinders. DIAGNOSE 1C allows a class F userid to clear the error cylinders. This is normally done from the `EREP` utility after producing the hardware error report.

DIAGNOSE code 20: 370 synchronous I/O

DIAGNOSE 20 provides synchronous I/O to tape, DASD, and dedicated (attached) printers and other unit record devices. Like DIAGNOSE 18, DIAGNOSE 20 is the interface provided under VM/SP and HPO, and supported under VM/ESA for compatibility reasons, which provides the preferred DIAGNOSE A8. Rx contains the virtual device address, and Ry contains the CAW, as in DIAGNOSE 18.

DIAGNOSE code 24: device type and features

DIAGNOSE 24 provides lets an application identify device characteristics for a specified device. Rx contains the device address or the value –1. If –1 is specified, CP returns the device address of the virtual machine console in Rx.

On output, Rx contains the device address in the lower order 2 bytes, and contains terminal flags (for terminal devices) in the upper byte that indicate whether APL translation is in effect. Ry contains the following information for the virtual device:

- Device Class—a 1-byte number that specifies the class of the device: CLASDASD for DASD devices, CLASTAPE for tape devices, and so on.
- Device Type—a 1-byte number specifying the model of the device within its class. For example, whether a disk is a 3380 or 3390 model.
- Device Statistics—a 1-byte flag with bits indicating if the associated device is busy, not ready, or a dedicated device. 604
- Device Flags—device attribute flags. On DASD devices, for examples, the flags indicate if the device is read-only, a temporary disk, and whether or not the device supports reserve-release commands.

Register Ry+1 contains information about the real device associated with the virtual device. The device class and type have the same meanings as for the virtual device; bytes describing real device features and device model numbers are also provided. For 3270 family terminals, the model number indicates the number of screen rows and columns installed in the display:

- Model 2: 24 lines by 80 columns
- Model 3: 32 lines by 80 columns
- Model 4: 43 lines by 80 columns
- Model 5: 24 lines by 132 columns

The REXX code in Fig. 16.6 displays console information (implied by specifying -1 for the device number), and determines if CMS is executing in a disconnected session.

DIAGNOSE code 28: dynamic channel program modification

DIAGNOSE 28 is used by communications software to change channel programs on a communications line while the channel program is executing.

```
/* Tell me about my console */
diag24info = C2X(diag(24,-1)); /* get info on logon terminal */
devbyte = substr(diag24info,11,2)
Select
  when devbyte = '04' then devtype = '3277'
  when devbyte = '01' then devtype = '3278 or 3279'
  otherwise devtype = 'Unknown'
end
devmdl = substr(diag24info,13,2)
say 'Device Type and Features'
say ' (Ry)    ' substr(diag24info,1,8)
say ' (Ry+1)' substr(diag24info,9,8) 'and is a' devtype'-'devmdl
say ' (Rx)    ' substr(diag24info,17,8) 'is the virtual console address'
if word(diagrc(24,-1),2) <> 0
then say 'This is a disconnected virtual machine'
```

Fig. 16.6 DIAGNOSE 24 used to determine virtual console information.

This lets applications exploit the programmability of the 370/390 channel interface to reduce CPU load to drive terminal networks.

Some communications protocols *poll* a line for activity (data becoming available), and then issue a read or selection command to the activated terminal device. A channel program can poll a group of terminals by testing each one, and then loop to the top of the poll sequence if none of the terminals have requested service.

This can be done without any CPU intervention (a process called `AUTOPOLL`) by using a Transfer in Channel (`TIC`) command, the equivalent of a BRANCH or GOTO command for channels, to branch to the top of the channel program. When a user generates an *attention interrupt* on a terminal (by pressing Enter, a program function (PF) or program access (PA) key) the channel can signal a Program Controlled Interrupt (`PCI`) to the CPU. The application can then break the channel program loop and cause it to issue a READ command to the terminal.

DIAGNOSE 28 can alter the running channel program flow of control by changing a No-operation (NOP) channel command to a TIC, or vice-versa, or alter the address contained in a TIC CCW. Rx contains the address of the TIC or NOP command modified in the virtual machine, and Ry contains the virtual device address of the communications line.

CP translates the changed channel command into real storage addresses, and applies the change to the channel command executing on the real hardware. If the change was successful, the channel program flow of control is changed as specified by the application. Otherwise an error indication is returned to the DIAGNOSE issuer via register 15. For example, the channel program could have already completed if the application did not respond quickly enough to the PCI.

DIAGNOSE code 2C: return DASD start of LOGREC (VM/SP, HPO)

DIAGNOSE 2C lets a class C, E, or F userid obtain the disk origin of the error records referred to under DIAGNOSE 1C. This is done from within VM/SP and HPO EREP to locate the data to be formatted and printed.

DIAGNOSE code 30: read on page of LOGREC data (VM/SP, HPO)

DIAGNOSE 30 reads a single 4K page of error data from the error cylinders. Rx contains the disk address to read, and Ry points to a buffer in the virtual machine.

DIAGNOSE code 34: read system dump spool file

DIAGNOSE 34 lets class C and E userids read a dump file produced by a CP abend (abnormal end). Rx contains the address of a page aligned page-length buffer to receive data from spool, and Ry contains the device address of the reader.

DIAGNOSE code 38: read system symbol table (VM/SP, HPO)

VM/SP and HPO contain a 4K-long symbol table consisting of 12-byte entries: the 8-byte external entry point name of a CP subroutine or data area, and its 4-byte address in real storage. DIAGNOSE 38 copies this page to virtual storage, where applications can look up the real storage locations of key CP data items. This is used by monitoring programs like IBM's Real Time Monitor.

Rx points to the page buffer to receive the symbol page. The application then searches the table for the entries it is looking for.

DIAGNOSE code 3C: CP directory update

DIAGNOSE 3C lets a class A, B, or C userid activate a CP object directory, described in "Source and Object Directories" on page 101. DIAGNOSE 3C is usually issued by the DIRECTXA command. Rx contains the first 4 characters of the directory DASD volume's label. Ry contains the remaining characters and the device address of the volume. For example, if the directory is being written to volume VMSRES on device address 0123, the registers contain:

Rx =	V	M	S	R

Ry =	E	S	01	23

DIAGNOSE code 40: clean up after IPL by device

DIAGNOSE 40 is used internally by CP itself when virtual machines IPL from a virtual device instead of a named saved system like CMS. DIAGNOSE

40 cannot be used by a virtual machine application, because CP checks to ensure that it is executed only from the virtual machine IPL simulator, described earlier in "Virtual IPL" on page 139.

DIAGNOSE 40 provides two subcodes: one subcode is used if the initial CCWs would overwrite CP's IPL simulator while it is executing. DIAGNOSE 40 relocates the simulator into an unused virtual storage address. The other subcode is used to clean up after IPL completes. DIAGNOSE 40 restores the original contents of storage overlaid by the IPL simulator and passes virtual machine control to the loaded operating system.

DIAGNOSE code 44: voluntary time-slice end

DIAGNOSE 44 is used by multi-CPU guest operating systems when they enter a spin-loop to acquire a serially reusable resource or main storage lock. The different virtual CPUs of multiprocessor guests execute independently of one of another on the real CPUs of the VM system; operating systems use the same methods for synchronizing resource access as when running natively.

DIAGNOSE 44 tells CP to worsen the execution priority of the CPU executing the DIAGNOSE. For example, if the dual-processor MVS/ESA guest system illustrated in Fig. 16.7 issues DIAGNOSE 44 from CPU 0, CP worsens the priority virtual CPU 0 is dispatched with to allow CPU 1 to process in front of it. DIAGNOSE 44 reduces unproductive CPU consumption when a process running on a different virtual CPU owns a lock, by helping the other CPU run first and finish its use of the locked resource.

DIAGNOSE 44 is issued by VM systems from VM/XA SP and later, and from MVS releases starting with MVS/SP 2.1.1.

DIAGNOSE code 48: second-level SVC 76 (VM/SP, HPO)

SVC 76 writes hardware error reports to a log file. VM/SP and HPO use DIAGNOSE 48 to tell a first level VM/SP or HPO to record hardware errors on its log. Otherwise, SVC 76 is reflected back to the virtual machine and errors cannot be reported centrally. DIAGNOSE 48 is a "no operation" under VM/XA and VM/ESA, as the same function is provided directly by CP.

DIAGNOSE code 4C: generate accounting records

DIAGNOSE 4C creates accounting records, and can be issued by virtual machines with `OPTION ACCOUNT` in the directory. DIAGNOSE 4C is used by virtual machines that provide services to multiple VM users, and lets installations charge for services provided by service virtual machines. IBM products that create accounting data include SQL/DS, SFS, RSCS, and PVM.

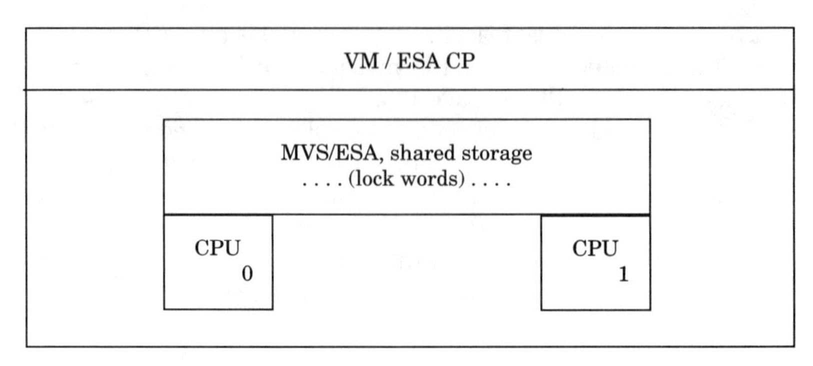

Fig. 16.7 DIAGNOSE 44.

Rx contains the address of either a 24-byte parameter list identifying the user to which resources are being charged, or a buffer containing arbitrary data to be placed in the accounting file. Ry contains one of the following function codes:

- `0000`—Rx points to a parameter list containing a userid.
- `0004`—Rx points to a parameter list containing a userid and account number.
- `000C`—Rx points to a parameter list containing a userid and distribution code.
- `000C`—Rx points to a parameter list containing a userid account number, and distribution code.
- `0010`—Rx points to a buffer of up to 70 bytes of data to be placed in the accounting file. Ry+1 contains the length.

DIAGNOSE code 50: save 370X control program image (VM/SP,HPO)

DIAGNOSE 50 allows a privilege class A, B, or C userid in VM/SP or HPO to create a loadable network control program for a 3704 or 3705 communications controller. DIAGNOSE 50 is used by the SAVENCP utility program.

DIAGNOSE code 54: control function of PA2 KEY

The normal VM function of the PA2 key (Program Access 2) on a 3270-family display device is to clear the screen's output area. DIAGNOSE 54 causes PA2 to send an external interrupt signal to the virtual machine instead. The virtual machine application can then handle the screen as it chooses.

The contents of Rx determine PA2's setting: if non-zero, a PA2 key generates an external interrupt, a zero value reverts the session to standard VM behavior. APL2 uses DIAGNOSE 54 when the APL2 session manager is not in use. The session manager takes complete control of the screen via DIAGNOSE 58, and therefore controls the PA2 key directly. Without the session manager, the screen is under CP control, and APL2 uses DIAGNOSE 54 to pass PA2 interrupts to it. PA2 is used to correct APL2 expressions. The CP setting TERMINAL APL ON must be in effect for DIAGNOSE 54 to have any effect.

DIAGNOSE code 58: 3270 virtual console interface

DIAGNOSE 58 is used for line-mode and fullscreen I/O to 3270 display devices. This is normally used for a user's logon terminal, but can also be used for a 3270 terminal DIALed or ATTACHed to a virtual machine. DIAGNOSE 58 lets applications fully or partially control the appearance of the screen, and lets applications perform fullscreen 3270 I/O on devices defined as virtual 3215 (line-mode) teletypewriters.

Rx contains the channel address word for the channel program to execute, and Ry contains the device number. Channel commands are in the following format:

- opcode—a code specifying the operation performed
- dataddr—address of an input or output buffer
- flags—370/390 channel command flags
- ctl—a control byte for DIAGNOSE 58 options
- length—the length of the data to write or maximum length to read

DIAGNOSE 58 uses the following codes in line-mode:

- `X'19'` writes data starting at a specified line on the screen. If the high order bit of CTL is set to 1, CP clears the screen before writing. The remaining bits specify the display line to start writing the data. The special CTL X'FF' value tells CP to just clear the screen. X'FE' puts the screen in standard line-mode format by clearing the screen and writing 3270 attribute characters to separate input, output, and status areas, and positions the cursor in the beginning of the input area.
- `X'49'` writes data starting at the next available display line.

The display is placed in fullscreen mode by performing an ERASE/WRITE or ERASE/WRITE ALTERNATE command. The following codes are used in fullscreen mode, and require knowledge of 3270 datastreams and device characteristics:

- `X'29'` writes a 3270 datastream. The type of write operation depends on the CTL field:

  - `X'80'` performs an ERASE/WRITE command. The display screen is erased (cleared) and placed in the default 24 rows by 80 columns character arrangement.
  - `X'C0'` and `X'40'` perform ERASE/WRITE ALTERNATE. This is similar to ERASE/WRITE, except that alternate screen coordinates are used, as described in the section on DIAGNOSE 24. For example, a 3279 model 3 is formatted for 32 rows by 80 columns.
  - `X'20'` performs a WRITE STRUCTURED FIELD operation.
  - Other values cause a WRITE operation.
- `X'2A'` reads from the 3270 display. The type of read also depends on the CTL field. `X'80'` performs a *Read Modified* operation. Only modified display fields are transmitted from the terminal to the host. This is the most efficient mode of operation for terminals connected to VM via a network. Other values result in a *Read Buffer* operation. The entire display contents are transmitted to the host.

Unlike DIAGNOSE I/O commands mentioned earlier, the virtual machine is responsible for performing its own error checking and handling, just as if a native start-I/O instruction were used.

DIAGNOSE code 5C: error message editing

DIAGNOSE 5C formats messages according to the current `EMSG` setting. CMS uses DIAGNOSE 5C to determine whether error messages should be displayed with or without the DMS *xxxnnnns* header (where *xxx* is the module name suffix, *nnnn* is the message number, and *s* indicates the message severity), or simply ignored.

Rx contains the address of the message to be edited, complete with message header. Ry contains a subfunction code that specifies how the message header length is determined. After the DIAGNOSE, the Rx and Ry contain the address and length of the message portion to be displayed. If EMSG is set to TEXT, for example, Rx will point to the text portion of the message, and Ry will contain its length. If EMSG is OFF, then Ry is set to 0.

DIAGNOSE code 60: determine virtual machine storage size

DIAGNOSE 60 returns the virtual machine storage size in bytes. After the DIAGNOSE, Rx contains the current storage value. In REXX, DIAG(60) can be used as an alternative to the *storage()* function.

DIAGNOSE code 64: finding, loading, and purging a named saved segment

DIAGNOSE 64 manipulates named saved segments (also called Discontiguous Shared Segments). Different function codes load, locate, or purge a saved segment. Most CMS applications should use the `SEGMENT` command (which uses DIAGNOSE 64) to avoid conflicts with CMS saved segment management.

Rx points to the name of the saved segment. Ry contains one of the following function subcodes:

- `0 - LOADSHR`—load a shared copy of the saved segment. The virtual storage contents of the segment become addressable to the virtual machine, even if they are outside the private address range of the virtual machine. Any saved segment that overlaps the newly loaded saved segment is purged. After the DIAGNOSE, Rx and Ry contain the starting and ending addresses of the segment.
- `4 - LOADNSHR`—load a nonshared copy of the saved segment.
- `8 - PURGESEG`—purges the saved segment from the virtual machine's address space.

```
/* NAMESYS fcn NSSname — locate,load or purge a Named Saved System */
parse upper arg fcn NSSname . '(' opts
Select
 when abbrev('LS',fcn)        then subcode = 'S' /* accepts 'L' */
 when abbrev('LN',fcn)        then subcode = 'L'
 when abbrev('PURGE',fcn) then subcode = 'P'
 when abbrev('FIND',fcn)      then subcode = 'F'
 Otherwise do
   Say "Unknown function ' "fcn" ' "; exit 24
   end
end
result = diagrc(64,'F',NSSname); where = substr(result,17,4)
parse var result retcode .
if retcode <> 0 then do
  Say 'Error' retcode 'locating' NSSname
  Exit retcode
  end
x = 'Start' c2x(substr(result,17,4))', end' c2x(substr(result,21,4))
Select
  when subcode = 'F' then say x
  when subcode = 'P' then result = diagrc(64,'P',NSSname)
  otherwise do
   if diag(60) > where then do
     Say 'Virtual machine size overlaps' NSSname': use SEGMENT'
     exit 24
     end
   result = diagrc(64,subcode,NSSname)
  end
end
```

Fig. 16.8 DIAGNOSE 64 REXX example.

- `12 - FINDSEG`—places the starting and ending addresses of the specified segment in Rx and Ry.
- `16 - LOADONLY`—loads a segment in shared mode, only if it does not overlap a previously loaded segment.
- `20 - SEGEXT`—returns extended segment information in a buffer pointed to by Rx. SEGEXT lets an application find information about skeleton saved segments (defined via the DEFSEG command, and not yet saved), segment spaces, and members of segment spaces.

The EXEC in Fig. 16.8 can be used to locate, load, or purge a saved segment, although the SEGMENT command should be used for real applications.

DIAGNOSE code 68: Virtual Machine Communication Facility (VMCF)

DIAGNOSE 68 performs virtual machine to virtual machine communication via the VMCF protocol, and is discussed in "Virtual Machine Communication Facility (VMCF)" on page 350.

DIAGNOSE code 6C: special DIAGNOSE for shadow table maintenance

DIAGNOSE 6C is used by MVS/370 to tell CP the virtual address of a page table entry mapping MVS page 0. This enables the *low address protect* facility MVS uses to protect itself from wild stores into low memory.

DIAGNOSE code 70: time of day (TOD) clock accounting interface

DIAGNOSE 70 lets virtual machines efficiently obtain accurate timing information, and is used by multiuser servers, such as SQL/DS and SFS, to determine the amount of CPU time spent servicing a client.

Rx points to a 16-byte communication area. Every time the virtual machine is dispatched, CP places the virtual CPU time (VTIME) consumed up to that point in the first eight bytes of the buffer, and places the most current time of day (TOD) clock in the second eight bytes. Time values are stored in System/370 and 390 clock format, which provides sub-microsecond resolution.

To get timing information, an application saves a copy of the TOD clock in the communication area, and issues a STCK instruction to obtain the current TOD value. The difference between the current TOD and the saved TOD is the VTIME consumed since the saved clock value (which was current the last time the virtual machine was dispatched). The difference in VTIME can also be added to the VTIME saved in the communications area to obtain the total CPU time consumed. If the communication area TOD clock has changed, the virtual machine has been stopped and redispatched, and the difference in VTIME must be recalculated.

IBM recommends that the communication area be located in page 0 of virtual machine storage. Both page 0 and the communication area must be in real storage when the virtual machine is run, so putting the buffer in page 0 saves a real storage page frame.

DIAGNOSE code 74: saving and loading image library file

IBM 3800-family laser printers keep font and forms overlay definitions in *image libraries*. DIAGNOSE 74 lets class A, B, C, or E virtual machines create or read CP image libraries.

Rx and Rx+1 contain the 8-character image library name. Ry contains the page-aligned buffer address of the image library loaded into virtual storage. Ry+1 contains a subfunction code in the upper byte (0 to load, and 4 to save), and the length of the buffer.

DIAGNOSE code 78: MSS communication (VM/SP,HPO)

The 3850 Mass Storage System (MSS) was a large-capacity direct access device that provided IBM systems “virtual disk drives” by emulating large numbers of 3330 volumes on a small amount of real 3330 disk space. In essence, the MSS provided virtual storage for disk resident data. Data was stored on tape cartridges and *staged* to real disk on an as-needed basis. Tape cartridges were stored in storage cells and retrieved automatically by a robotic arm.

Much of VM’s support code for the MSS was implemented by an OS/VS1 or MVS guest, rather than CP. DIAGNOSE 78 was used by the MSS communication program running in the guest, to identify itself to CP and to pass commands and status information between the MSS controller and CP.

The MSS was made obsolete by higher-density disk drives (especially the 3380) and is no longer supported.

DIAGNOSE code 7C: Logical Device Support Facility (LDSF)

DIAGNOSE 7C is the program interface for the Logical Device Support Facility (LDSF). LDEV hosts use DIAGNOSE 7C to create, destroy, write to, and read from logical terminals.

When CP has data to write to the device, or status information to send to an LDEV host, it generates an external interrupt to the virtual machine with interrupt code X'2402'. Locations X'80' through X'83' in the virtual machine receive the logical device number, flag information, and a reason code explaining why CP generated the interrupt. When the application writes to the device, it uses the DIAGNOSE 7C “Present” function.

DIAGNOSE 7C has the following subfunctions, specified by a code placed in Ry:

- `1 - Initiate`—create a logical device. CP creates a logical devices with the 3270 model type and features described in Rx+1, and displays the system VM logo on it. Rx can be used to specify a specific logical device number.
- `2 - Accept`—accepts data from the logical terminal. Accept is issued after receiving a X'2402' external interrupt with a reason code indicating that CP issued a write. Accept is issued with Rx containing the logical device number, Rx+1 pointing to the buffer to receive the screen contents, and Ry+1 containing the buffer length.
- `3 - Present`—the application presents data to CP, in essence, simulating the 3270 keyboard. Rx+1 and Ry+1 can describe a buffer, as with Accept, or Rx+1 can point to a list of length and address pairs. The latter form allows multiple noncontiguous buffers to be presented in a single DIAGNOSE call, and is indicated by complementing the contents or Rx+1.
- `4 - Terminate`—terminates a specified logical terminal.
- `5 - Terminate All`—terminates all logical devices created by the logical device host.
- `6 - Status`—lets the application present "ending status" to CP after performing an Accept. This is used with logical 328x printers.

DIAGNOSE code 80: MSSFCALL

DIAGNOSE 80 lets virtual machines interact with the *Monitoring and Service Support Facility* (MSSF) of 308x, 3090, and ES/9000 systems. Privilege class C or E users use DIAGNOSE 80 to read or write an *I/O Configuration Data Set* (IOCDS), the I/O device configuration file used by the CPU complex itself.

Interestingly enough, DIAGNOSE 80 cause VM/SP and HPO to issue a *real* DIAGNOSE 80 instruction to communicate with the MSSF on the real CPU.

DIAGNOSE code 84: directory update-in-place

DIAGNOSE 84 is used by directory managers, which must have privilege class B, to replace data stored in a user's object directory entry. Since DIAGNOSE 84 alters the directory, including passwords, it must be restricted to trusted userids. The User Class Restructure (UCR) facility of VM can be used to reassign DIAGNOSE 28 from class B (which is often given to system operators) to a unique privilege class.

Directory changes made through DIAGNOSE 84 are more efficient than rewriting the entire directory and issuing DIAGNOSE 3C, but can only used to overwrite disk-resident control blocks in place. DIAGNOSE 84 cannot be used to add or delete users, or to add or delete devices assigned to an existing user.

Rx points to a parameter list, and Ry contains the length of the list. The parameter list consists of a fixed 24-byte field containing the userid being updated, its password, and the name of the field being replaced. If the password is left blank, the syntax of the request is checked, otherwise it is compared to the password of the user being updated. Directory manager userids with `OPTION D84NOPAS` can update users without knowing their passwords.

The fixed area is followed by variable data containing replacement data for the updated field. Data that can be changed for a userid include the following:

- logon and minidisk passwords
- default and maximum virtual storage sizes
- privilege classes
- logical line editing characters
- account and distribution codes
- system or device to be IPLed at logon
- SCREEN color options
- CPU architecture: 370, XA, ESA, or XC, and number of virtual CPUs
- expanded storage allocation
- share or priority settings

DIAGNOSE code 8C: access 3270 display device information

DIAGNOSE 8C allows applications to obtain model-dependent information about 3270-family terminals. For example, DIAGNOSE 8C can determine whether the specified 3270 terminal has extended highlighting (hardware-provided reverse video and blinking)

Rx points to an output data buffer, Ry contains the buffer length. Rx+1 contains the 3270 device's virtual device number, or -1 for the logon console. DIAGNOSE 8C is illustrated in Fig. 16.9.

DIAGNOSE code 90: read symbol table

DIAGNOSE 90 is the VM/XA and VM/ESA replacement for DIAGNOSE 38. Instead of reading the entire symbol table into a page-size buffer (which restricted HPO symbol tables to a single page in length) and then searching

```
/* DIAG8C EXEC */
diag8cinfo = C2X(DIAG('8C'))
flag8c = substr(diag8cinfo,1,2)
say 'Device Dependent Information'
say ' ' flag8c 'indicates'
xflag8c = X2C(flag8c)
if bittst('01'x,xflag8c) then say '    14 bit addressing'
if bittst('20'x,xflag8c) then say '    Program Symbol Sets available'
if bittst('40'x,xflag8c) then say '    extended highlighting'
if bittst('80'x,xflag8c) then say '    extended color'
say ' ' substr(diag8cinfo,3,2) 'is the number of partitions (hex)'
say ' ' x2d(substr(diag8cinfo,5,4)) 'is the number of columns'
say ' ' x2d(substr(diag8cinfo,9,4)) 'is the number of rows'
exit

bittst: procedure
arg mask, target
return C2D(BITAND(mask,target)) > 0
```

Fig. 16.9 DIAG 8C used to get terminal information.

for the needed symbol, DIAGNOSE 90 returns the address of a specific symbol table entry. Symbols returned by DIAGNOSE 90 may be either resident in CP storage or pageable; DIAGNOSE 38 symbol table entries could only be resident.

Rx contains the length of the symbol name, and Ry contains the address of the symbol. On exit, Ry contains the address of the symbol in real storage (for resident symbols) or in CP's virtual address space (for pageable symbols). The PSW condition code is 0 for resident symbols, 1 for pageable symbols, and 2 for unknown symbols.

DIAGNOSE code 94: VMDUMP

DIAGNOSE 94 is similar to the CP VMDUMP command: it dumps specified user virtual machine addresses into a spool file that can be loaded to disk and interpreted by a dump debugging program like IBM's *Dump Viewing Facility*, which is distributed with VM, or VM Systems Group's *KPROBE* debugger. DIAGNOSE 94 can also create *symptom records* that describe the dump. Symptom records are placed in the dump, and are also sent in real-time to a virtual machine connected to the *SYMPTOM CP system service.

Rx contains the address of a parameter list, and Ry its length. The parameter list contains text similar to the operands specified for the VMDUMP CP command.

DIAGNOSE code 98: real I/O

DIAGNOSE 98 lets userids with the DIAG98 directory option perform "real I/O" operations to buffers in real storage. DIAGNOSE 98 is used to improve the CPU time needed to service critical I/O-intensive virtual machines. DIAGNOSE 98's main use is to provide higher performance for VTAM.

DIAGNOSE 98 lets an application lock and unlock pages in real storage so that they are not paged out or moved, and to issue I/O operations using their real storage addresses. This bypasses channel command translation performed for normal I/O operations, and significantly reduces CPU instruction path lengths for I/O operations. It also bypasses checking CP performs, so an incorrectly coded program could potentially overlay any storage location that has a different storage protection key than key 0. DIAGNOSE 98 should therefore only be used for debugged and "trusted" applications.

On entry to DIAGNOSE 98, Rx contains a subfunction code. The contents of Ry and register contents after the DIAGNOSE depend on the subfunction code:

- `0 - lock a page`—Ry contains the address of the virtual storage page to be locked into real memory. After DIAGNOSE 98, Ry+1 contains the real storage address assigned to the page.
- `4 - unlock a page`—Ry contains the virtual storage address of the page to be unlocked.
- `8 - SIOF real I/O`—starts a 370-style SIOF instruction using a channel program located in a locked page. Ry contains the device address, and the System/370 channel address word (CAW) in virtual storage location 48 points to the channel program. After the DIAGNOSE 98, Ry+1 contains the SIOF condition code.
- `12 - SSCH real I/O`—starts an XA-style SSCH instruction using a channel program located in a locked page. R1 contains the virtual devices subchannel identifier (SID), and Ry contains the address of the XA mode *Output Request Block* (ORB).

DIAGNOSE code A0: obtain ACI groupname

DIAGNOSE A0 is used to determine the *Access Control Interface* (ACI) groupname associated with a userid, or to determine if the CP ACI interface is in use.

The function performed is specified by a subcode number placed in Ry: 0 to request the "obtain ACI" function, and 8 to check for the ACI interface. For subcode 0, Rx points to an 16-byte parameter list: the first 8 bytes con-

```
          LA    R4,ACIBUFF          Point to DIAGNOSE A0 buffer
          SLR   R5,R5               Specify 'obtain ACI' function
          DIAG  R4,R5,X'00A0'       Ask CP for the ACI group
          CLC   ACIGROUP,=CL8'SYSTEMS' Belongs to system programmer ACI?
          BNE   REJECT              No...reject the request!
          ...
          ...
ACIBUFF   EQU   *
USERID    DS    CL8                 Client userid
ACIGROUP  DS    CL8                 Client's ACI group
```

Fig. 16.10 DIAGNOSE A0 example.

tain the userid to be checked. On exit from DIAGNOSE A0, the second 8 bytes contain the user's ACI group.

A user is associated with an ACI group via the user directory statement ACIGROUP. The ACI group is a convenient way of categorizing users. For example, a service machine can accept or reject a request from a userid based on whether the user belongs to a specified ACI group, as illustrated in Fig. 16.10.

DIAGNOSE code A4: synchronous standard I/O for CMS DASD

DIAGNOSE A4 is used for CMS disk I/O under VM/ESA and VM/XA, replacing VM/SP's DIAGNOSE 18. DIAGNOSE A4 supports XA, ESA, or XC-mode virtual machines as well as 370-mode machines.

Communication with DIAGNOSE A4 is done through the synchronous block I/O parameter list, HCPSBIOP. On entry to DIAGNOSE A4, Rx contains the address of the HCPSBIOP for the I/O operation. The parameter list contains the disk's device number, the type of request (READ or WRITE), and the block size of the disk (which must be a valid CMS block size: 512, 1024, 2048, or 4096).

The parameter list also contains the address of a list of paired disk block numbers and buffer addresses. Block numbers are assigned from the beginning of the minidisk when the disk is FORMATed, starting with block 0. CP creates the channel commands to read or write each block. This relieves CMS of having to create channel programs, and CP of having to translate and verify them.

DIAGNOSE code A8: synchronous I/O for all devices

DIAGNOSE A8 is the ESA replacement for DIAGNOSE 20, as DIAGNOSE A4 is the replacement for DIAGNOSE 18. DIAGNOSE A8 allows I/O to all devices, except for consoles, 3270 devices, and channel-to-channel adapters.

The HCPSBIOP control block is used to describe the I/O request, as with DIAGNOSE A4, except that it now contains the address of the channel program to be sent to the device.

DIAGNOSE code B0: get protected application re-IPL data

Virtual machines under the control of the `OPTION CONCEAL` directory option use DIAGNOSE B0 to determine the reason for an automatic CMS reIPL. CP automatically reIPLs CMS when a CMS session crashes for an OPTION CONCEAL user. This protects end users from having to reIPL CMS for themselves. DIAGNOSE B0 lets a CMS application determine the reason for the CMS crash and reIPL.

Rx points to a storage buffer, and Ry contains its length. On exit from DIAGNOSE B0, the buffer contains a code indicating the reason for the reIPL. Reasons include a soft CP ABEND (a CP system crash that CP was able to recover from), a virtual machine disabled wait state or program check loop, or a CPU hardware failure.

DIAGNOSE code B4: virtual printer external attribute buffer manipulation

DIAGNOSE B4 is use to associate external attribute buffer (XAB) information with a virtual printer. When the spool file is closed, both its contents and its XAB information are written to spool. XAB information is used by *Advanced Function Printing* (AFP) and by *SPL system service virtual machines. CP neither creates nor uses XAB data. Instead, the userid creating the file and the agent printing it use XAB data to describe the format of a document.

DIAGNOSE code B8: spool file external attribute buffer manipulation

DIAGNOSE B8 allows an application in a virtual machine to create, inspect, or remove an external attribute buffer (XAB) associated with a spool file.

DIAGNOSE code BC: open spool file

DIAGNOSE BC opens a spool file on the userid's reader queue, and returns information about the opened file. Rx and Rx+1 specify the address and length of a buffer to receive the file information, and Ry contains the device address of the virtual reader device.

Information returned by DIAGNOSE BC is the same as the output from the `QUERY READER ALL` command, and includes the files spool file id number, its class, type, number of copies, filename, filetype, creation timestamp, the originating userid, distribution code, forms and FCB specifications, and 3800 laser printer attributes.

DIAGNOSE code C4: handle class override data for UCR file

DIAGNOSE C4 is used by class B userids running the OVERRIDE command, to create a *User Class Restructure* (UCR) override file. This assigns CP commands and DIAGNOSE commands from the IBM default privilege classes A to G to the privilege classes A to Z and 1 to 6. For example, DIAGNOSE 04 can be reassigned from privilege classes C and E to a new privilege class 4, to provide better control over which users can issue it.

DIAGNOSE code C8: set language

DIAGNOSE C8 is used to tell CP which language to use for messages. Rx and Rx+1 contain the 5-character language identifier left-adjusted in the Rx, Rx+1 register pair. Ry's upper byte must contain a zero-value function code (presumably, IBM will add other function codes later). In REXX, the language is passed as the second parameter to DIAGNOSE, for example, `DIAG('C8','AMENG')` to select American-style English.

DIAGNOSE code CC: set message repository

DIAGNOSE CC saves a CP message repository; normally this is invoked via the `LANGGEN` command. Rx, Rx+1, and Ry are set as with DIAGNOSE C8, and Ry+1 contains the page aligned address of the message repository in virtual storage. CP copies the message repository from virtual storage to CP storage and saves it in a system data spool file.

DIAGNOSE code D0: volume serial support

DIAGNOSE D0 is provided for the pragmatic purpose of allowing CP to report which tape volumes have read or write errors. Normally, CP is unaware of the volume serial (VOLSER) labels of tape volumes attached to a virtual machine. Label support is the responsibility of the virtual machine operating system (including CMS).

CP performs all hardware and media error reporting, so applications can use DIAGNOSE D0 to tell CP the volsers of their tapes. CP then records the volsers of volumes experiencing temporary or permanent media errors. Data center staff use the resulting error reports to select tapes which should have their contents copied to new volumes.

Rx contains the address of the 6-character volser, and Ry contains the tape drive's virtual devices number.

DIAGNOSE code D4: set alternate userid

DIAGNOSE D4 lets privilege class B userids associate server virtual machine processing with the client it is doing for. DIAGNOSE D4 can be issued by a "scheduler" virtual machine that controls a set of "worker" or "slave" virtual machines, and passes client requests to a worker for processing.

After DIAGNOSE D4 is issued, spool files created by the worker have the client's userid as the originating userid instead of the worker's name. More importantly, attempts to LINK to a disk (or issue other commands that invoke the access control facility) are validated using the access rights of the client, not the worker. This is important for "CMS batch" worker machines.

Rx points to a control block containing the server or worker virtual machine userid in its first 8 bytes, followed by either the client's userid, to enable the alternate userid, or binary zeros to turn it off.

DIAGNOSE code D8: read spool file control blocks on system spool file queues

DIAGNOSE D8 is used by class D (spooling operator) privilege class userids to process the spool file control blocks on the system reader, printer, or punch queues. Files can be specified by user, or all files control blocks can be retrieved.

DIAGNOSE D8 is used to collect statistics about all spool files, and is issued by spool file manager products such as V/SPOOL from VM Systems Group and VMSPOOL from System Center, Inc.

DIAGNOSE code DC: declare/delete buffer for application data

DIAGNOSE DC lets users with the directory statement `OPTION APPLMON` define a virtual storage buffer containing data to be collected by the CP monitoring facility. Prior to APPLMON and DIAGNOSE DC, CP only recorded its own performance and configuration data. With DIAGNOSE DC, an application can define a buffer whose contents will be sampled on a periodic basis and included in system monitor data. The first client of DIAGNOSE DC is the Shared File System.

Rx points to a virtual storage parameter list that includes the buffer address and length, the address of a product identification string (placed in monitor records to identify which product created which data), and a subcode indicating whether interval recording should be started or stopped.

DIAGNOSE code E0: system trace file interface

DIAGNOSE E0 opens, reads and closes system trace files created by the TRSOURCE and TRSAVE commands. It is used by the TRACERED ("trace read") system programmer command. System trace data is used to debug system problems by recording CP data areas and module flow.

Rx points to the 4-character spool file id to process, Rx+1 contains the read buffer address, and Ry contains the subfunction code for open, read, and close functions.

DIAGNOSE code E4: return minidisk real device information

DIAGNOSE E4 lets users with the directory statement `OPTION DEVINFO` or `OPTION DEVMAINT` obtain real device information about a minidisk, or define a full-pack minidisk over a specified DASD volume. DIAGNOSE E4 functions are normally used for DASD hardware maintenance.

DIAGNOSE code EC: query guest trace status

DIAGNOSE EC is used to determine whether TRSOURCE data is being collected for a virtual machine.

DIAGNOSE code F0: VM/CSE interface to communication

This DIAGNOSE is used by VM systems participating in a *Cross System Extension* (CSE) complex. DIAGNOSE F0 lets the caller obtain a list of systems included in the complex, synchronize systems, and send and receive data to partner systems via a CSE server machine.

DIAGNOSE code F8: spool file origin information

DIAGNOSE F8 specifies or obtains the origin of a spool file. It is used by applications that want to make sure that they only process reader files from specific locations. This increases application security by preventing erroneous processing of "spoofed" spool files that pretend to be from trusted users.

Ry points to a control block described by the DF8PARM COPY file distributed with VM. DF8PARM contains the system node (the system's name) and the userid associated (on output) with a particular virtual device, or (on input) with a named spool file.

Rx contains one of two subfunction codes: X'00' specifies the node and userid to be associated with all spool files created on a specific virtual punch or printer device. This function requires that the user have `OPTION SETORIG`. Subfunction X'01' can be used by any virtual machine, and returns the originating system node and userid for the specified file.

DIAGNOSE code FC: channel path reconfiguration

DIAGNOSE FC is used by VM/ESA guests that support ESCON dynamic path reconfiguration. The guest system passes a reconfiguration request control block to hardware, pointed to by Rx, to CP, which passes it to System/390 hardware.

DIAGNOSE code 210: return disk device information

DIAGNOSE 210 is a replacement for DIAGNOSE 24; IBM encourages the use of DIAGNOSE 210 for new applications. DIAGNOSE 210 is passed the address of a control block in Rx: on input this contains the virtual device address of the device being queried, and the length of the control block. On output, the control block contains, in addition to the information provided by DIAGNOSE 24, feature and descriptive information about the device and its control unit. For disk drives, this includes the number of disk cylinders, the number of tracks per cylinder, sectors per track, track capacity, and other addressing information.

DIAGNOSE code 214: pending page release (VM/ESA)

DIAGNOSE 214, introduced with VM/ESA 1.1, lets virtual machines release storage and reacquire it with less overhead than DIAGNOSE 10. Instead of immediately placing real storage pages on the available list as DIAGNOSE 10 does, DIAGNOSE 214 lets virtual machines establish or cancel lists of pages that may be released. Pages pending release are not taken from the virtual machine until CP's available list replenishment requires them. Until that time the virtual machine can cancel the list of pages, in essence retracting its prior hint to CP.

Rx and Rx+1 are passed the low and high addresses of a range of virtual storage pages. The low-order byte of Rx+1 contains a function code:

- 0 - Establish Pending Release: designate a range of addresses that may be released. Expanded storage or disk locations containing these virtual locations are immediately released, since their contents will be obsolete even if the pending release is cancelled.
- 1 - Cancel Pending Release: cancel the prior page release call for the storage locations pointed to by Rx and Rx+1.
- 2 - Cancel All Pending Release: cancel all prior page releases.
- 3 - Cancel Pending Release and Validate: the contents of released pages are set to zero, and their protect keys are set to the key contained in Ry.

DIAGNOSE code 23C: address space services (VM/ESA)

DIAGNOSE 23C, new with VM/ESA, lets an XC-mode virtual machine manipulate dataspaces, subject to directory authorization. Rx points to a parameter control block, and Ry contains a function code. Function codes create and destroy spaces, query their attributes, and permit other users to access them. DIAGNOSE 23C is generated by the `ADRSPACE` macro.

DIAGNOSE code 240: access list services (VM/ESA)

DIAGNOSE 240 is generated by the `ALSERV` macro, and lets an XC-mode virtual machine under VM/ESA manipulate Access List Entries (ALEs). Rx points to a parameter block, and Ry contains a function code indicating whether an ALE is being created or removed.

DIAGNOSE code 244: minidisk extent mapping services (VM/ESA)

DIAGNOSE 244 is generated by the VM/ESA MAPMDISK macro, and lets XC-mode virtual machines establish a relationship between a VM dataspace and minidisk 4K blocks.

DIAGNOSE code 248: copy to primary address space (VM/ESA)

DIAGNOSE 248 lets 370, XA, and ESA-mode virtual machines make use of VM dataspaces. XC-mode virtual machines can directly work with dataspaces by referring to storage operands via access registers, but other architectures can only work with their primary address spaces. Rx contains the address of a page in a dataspace to be copied to the primary address space, and Rx+1 contains the ALET that names the dataspace. Ry contains the address of a page in the primary address, and Ry+1 contains the number of pages to be copied to it from the location pointed to by Ry. Rx and Ry must specify even-odd register pairs.

DIAGNOSE code 258: page reference services (VM/ESA)

DIAGNOSE 258 is generated by the VM/ESA `REFPAGE` and `PFAULT` macros, and lets XC-mode virtual machines describe an expected pattern of storage references, and set up page fault handlers. CP uses page reference information to page in data areas before they are needed, reducing page fault delays, and to write to secondary storage pages that it knows will not be needed for a long period of time, making more real storage available.

The PFAULT function lets a multitasking application specify an exit address to be invoked when a page fault occurs. The application can let other tasks continue execution while CP resolves a page fault. This function is similar to the VM/VS handshaking present in VM since the mid-1970s.

Rx points to a parameter control block describing a pattern of references or a list of pages, and Ry contains a function code.

DIAGNOSE code 260: access certain virtual machine information (VM/ESA)

This is a new DIAGNOSE code that IBM will probably use for multiple functions. At this writing, the only subfunction (specified in Ry) is function 0, which returns the highest addressable byte of virtual storage in Rx. This is different from the value returned by DIAGNOSE 60, since it includes the virtual storage associated with named saved systems, while DIAGNOSE 60 returns only the virtual machine's private storage size.

Chapter

17

Guest Machines

An important VM workload is supporting "guest" virtual machines running MVS, ESA, DOS/VSE, AIX, MUSIC/SP, VS1, or VM itself. Many sites use VM for parallel production, testing, or development of different operating systems on the same physical computer. The operating systems are called "guests" because they run under the VM "host" Control Program.

Hardware-based *partitioning* with some VM-like features is now available for a number of CPU models, making it possible to use a CPU complex for multiple system images without VM. This can be used for testing or for production. Hardware partitioning is compared to VM in a section of this chapter.

Guest System Applications

Guest systems are useful for a variety of applications, and can improve flexibility, reliability and quality, and reduce costs in a number of creative ways.

Converting from one operating system to another

Computer sites sometimes convert from one operating system to another, a complex maneuver that must be accomplished without error on a predetermined schedule. A conversion from DOS/VSE to MVS/ESA might take several months (or longer) while applications are converted and tested.

Conversions are often incremental, in order to control the risk and scope of conversion problems experienced at any one time, and applications are moved to the new system one at a time. This requires that both old and new environments be operated at the same time.

VM lets both new and old systems be executed in parallel, on the same computer hardware, until the older system is completely phased out. This eliminates the need to purchase an additional computer system for the conversion or risk an "all at once" conversion.

Operating multiple independent workloads on the same system

Sometimes a data center needs to process multiple unrelated workloads. This occurs, for example, when several data centers are consolidated for cost reduction, or when companies outsource their data centers to a service bureau.

Instead of obtaining separate physical computer systems for each client workload, the service provider can run several workloads on the same CPU as VM guests, and with reduced cost.

Merging multiple systems to a larger single CPU often reduces both hardware and software costs. Each of the systems being consolidated might run on a lightly loaded CPU, with resulting hardware and software license costs. This is especially attractive if the different workloads have different "peak load" times, perhaps due to serving different time zones. VM lets multiple systems share the same hardware and software, and exploit economies of scale.

Testing new system versions

VM provides a safe and convenient method of testing operating system code and configurations. A new system can be tested for reliability and compatibility during normal production use of the computer, and VM debugging commands can be used to assist problem determination.

VM has been essential for IBM's own operating system development. For example, MVS was developed using CP/67 systems modified to create System/370 (instead of System/360) virtual machines, since there weren't enough virtual storage 370 systems for MVS developers to test on. Later, MVS/XA was developed using an early version of VM/XA. VM was modified to provide XA-mode virtual machines on pre-XA 370 hardware. When real XA-mode machines became available in the IBM labs, VM was the first operating system to run on them. MVS/XA ran under VM/XA until it was ready to be IPLed on real hardware.

Most sites, however, use VM to "burn in" new versions of system software before placing them in production with live workloads.

Traditionally, sites without VM modify and exercise system software during weekend or late night "test shots." These are invariably scheduled for the least disruption to the production workload, and thus the largest disruption to system programmer lives. The trend towards "around-the-clock" service makes it increasingly difficult to schedule adequate test times.

System programmer productivity at such sites can be extremely low. It takes a long time to reproduce problems and test corrections, or stress test new system versions, when testing is only conducted during infrequent and short test periods. An alternative used at some large non-VM sites is to provide a dedicated test CPU for system programmers. The expense of a test CPU places it out of reach for many companies.

Sites with VM do most testing in second-level environments. Fixes can be applied and tested, and entire new versions of an operating system can be installed and stressed in second-level test guests. This can be done during normal working hours, and without obtaining an additional CPU for each operating system being tested. While this doesn't eliminate dedicated test time, it sharply reduces the number of times test shots are necessary. The increased time for testing leads to improved quality, since testing is less rushed and can be more comprehensive.

Second-level testing works for every IBM operating system. VM system programmers tend to use it with the greatest regularity, because they are most familiar with VM, because less effort and resources are required for a test VM environment than for other operating systems, and because they are guaranteed to have a VM system to test on.

Parallel/test environments

A difficult task in operating a data center is ensuring that test and production environments are adequately insulated from one another. Without proper controls, it is all too possible for a program being tested to run against production files and databases, causing loss or destruction of data. An MVS or VSE application programmer could accidentally submit an update job using the name of a production database instead of a test copy.

Prudence, auditors, and in some cases, legal requirements, make some data centers operate separate test and production facilities to prevent this type of mishap. VM can be used to create walls between production and test systems, as shown in Fig. 17.1. By placing the test environment in a VM guest, application testing can proceed, just as with operating system testing, without need for a dedicated computer system. Each guest system has its own disk devices, and has no way of affecting or even browsing the disks assigned to other guests, unless explicitly authorized by VM system administrators.

Training computer operations staff

Many procedures for operating computer systems are disruptive, for example, starting or stopping the system, loading new network software, starting or terminating applications, and so on. This makes it difficult to validate operational procedures and train operators to use them. Inadequate prepara-

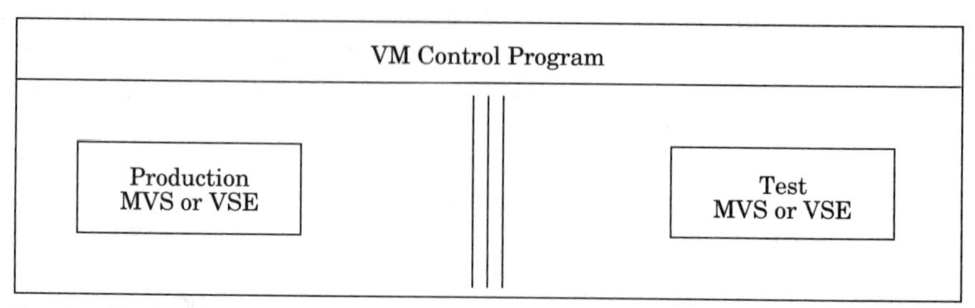

Fig. 17.1 Firewall between production and test.

tion leads to disasters if procedures turn out to be incorrectly documented, or operators are insufficiently trained to execute them.

The traditional non-VM way to exercise procedures and operators is to run off-hours test periods. This is extremely difficult for complicated system environments such as an MVS/ESA complex. Bringing a real MVS/ESA system up and down might require bring it in and out of the GRS (Global Resource Serialization) ring or performing a JES3 DSI (Dynamic System Interchange) to reassign the JES3 global processor. Doing this might require taking an entire multi-CPU data center for test time, instead of just a single CPU. Since most data centers operate continuously, the training periods may have to be repeated for multiple shifts of operators, causing a scheduling nightmare.

VM makes it possible to define test environments in which these procedures can be exercised safely at any time. This lets a data center train the operations staff working on all shifts.

Programmable operator testing

Considerations that apply to procedures performed by human operators apply equally when automated operator software is used, whether it be VM's Programmable Operator (PROP) and NetView from IBM, or packages from other vendors, such as Legent's Automate/MVS and Automate/VM, or System Center Inc's VMOPERATOR. Untested automated operator procedures can be extremely dangerous: software can issue the wrong system commands many times per second. Procedures for handling system startup and shutdown, or other exceptional conditions, simply can't be tested in the normal system environment without disruption.

Software verification

A specialized problem occurs for software vendors, or any company in which a central site prepares software for distribution to other locations. Quite frequently, centrally developed software fails to work at a new location because the developers assume that the target location is configured in a particular manner, or has access to specific products or libraries available at the development site.

Second-level test systems can eliminate these problems by providing a "clean" system environment separate from the development facility, even if on the same physical CPU. When a new version of the software is ready for shipment, the installation process and product can be tested second-level in order to make sure that all software prerequisites have been properly identified.

Disaster recovery

Most companies depend on their computer systems for survival, and many plan in advance for disasters that make the computing center unusable (fire, flood, bomb, extended power grid outage) by making arrangements for off-site data center recovery. A number of vendors provide disaster site services: Comdisco, IBM, and Sunguard among them. Some companies and universities make reciprocal recovery agreements, where the failing site moves its work to the surviving location.

In some cases, only key applications are moved to the disaster site. This is difficult to achieve, since the disaster site operating system must be identical to the original site, even down to the level of file names and up-to-date security authorizations. This degree of compatibility is difficult to achieve among multiple data centers operated by a single company, and is even harder when backup facilities are provided by a disaster service.

Instead, disaster plans are usually implemented by moving entire system images to the disaster site. VM lets the failed system run at the disaster site using an I/O configuration, CPU architecture, number of CPUs, and sometimes even the same CPU serial number, as when running at the original location.

Virtual Machine Facilities for Guests

In addition to the basic capability of providing multiple software system images on the same hardware, VM provides capabilities not available on real computer systems.

Virtual machines can be set up with little consideration for the physical hardware VM is running on. Guest systems can run in a variety of hardware environments on a single computer system. VM separates guest systems from the physical I/O configuration by *virtualizing* its I/O operations. This has two main benefits:

1. *Device address independence.* Guest system device addresses are completely independent of the actual device numbers installed on the

real computer system. This is essential when testing operating systems that will run at a data center different than the test site, or for testing "I/O gens" in advance of a hardware change. Similarly, guest systems need not change their I/O definitions if VM's real hardware configuration is changed.

2. *Device simulation.* VM can simulate certain devices purely in software. This is used by all VM users, since a typical CMS userid has virtual reader, printer and punch devices, and is equally useful for testing varying I/O configurations. Virtual unit record devices can also be used for sending job streams to a batch guest system, and retrieving job output from it.

VM also simulates or extends a number of CPU features:

- *Number of CPUs.* VM lets a guest system have more or fewer CPUs than are installed on the real hardware. This can be used to run systems like DOS/VSE, which only run on uniprocessors, when the real system is a multiprocessor. It also lets production guests on a multiprocessor system consume more than one CPU engine's computing power.

  Multiprocessor testing is important for systems like VM/ESA and MVS/ESA. Routines that fail to properly serialize logical resources through locking or enqueuing mechanisms may appear correct on single-CPU test machines, but fail when run on multiple-CPU systems. When more than one processor is available, processes running on the different engines may simultaneously update the same variables in storage if they haven't been properly protected. VM allows multi-processor testing, even on single-engine systems.

  VM/ESA and VM/XA virtual machines can be defined with up to 64 processors, far more than the maximum of 8 processors available on any currently delivered 370/390 or compatible CPU.

- *Main storage.* Virtual machines can be defined with more or less storage than is available on the real computer system. This can be used for developing software on a less expensive platform than one it will use in production, or ensure that it performs adequately on smaller real storage sizes than the one used at the development site.

- *Expanded storage.* VM cannot simulate expanded storage for guests on processors that have none, but it lets an arbitrary number of guests share sections of expanded storage on processors that do. VM allocates contiguous megabytes of expanded storage to guests when they logon, if XSTORE statements are placed in their directory entries, or if requested via the ATTACH XSTORE command.

- *Vector Facility.* IBM 3090s and ES/9000s provide optional vector facilities that perform multiple floating point operations in a single clock cycle.

As with expanded storage, VM does not simulate vector facilities on processors that have none, but an arbitrary number of guest systems or CMS users can share a limited number of vector facilities on the real CPU. Multiprocessor guests can be defined to have more vector facilities than are present on the real CPU.

- *CPU serial number.* Virtual machines can be defined with different CPU serial numbers (also called a `CPUID`) than the real computer system. This is useful for guests with serial number dependent code. The `STIDP` (Store Processor ID) instruction is a privileged instruction, so VM intercepts and simulates it.

  For example, DOS/VSE systems use CPU serial numbers to identify different systems sharing DASD in read/write mode. Under VM, each VSE guest with shared access to a minidisk is given a different CPUID to simulate the CPUIDs multiple DOS/VSE systems would have on separate CPUs.

  Virtual CPU serial numbers can also be used in disaster recovery situations when production systems are run at an alternate site, to make the alternate site identical to the original location.

- *Clock setting.* VM lets guest operating systems set their own clock values, making it possible to run systems that think they are in different time zones and dates. This lets, for example, a VM system in New York run separate production MVS systems for users in London and Tokyo. The users of each guest MVS see their local times, rather than the local time in New York.

  The ability to run guests with different dates than the local date will become increasingly useful as the end of the century nears, and all date routines using a two-digit year need to be discovered and corrected. As the end of the century nears, guest systems will probably run under VM with next-century dates to see which routines "fall apart."

Virtual CPU emulation is illustrated in Fig. 17.2. in which guest systems on a 4-CPU ES/9000 model 820 with one Vector Facility have virtual storage sizes and vector facilities that exceed the values installed on the real CPU, as well has having different architectures.

Operating Second-Level

Second-level operation is similar to real system operation, except that the guest system logs onto a VM system, and CP commands are used in place of hardware procedures for performing IPL, SYSTEM RESET, SYSTEM RESTART, and so on. It is useful to have the guest IPL CMS and run a PROFILE EXEC that automates its initialization. Once the guest operating system is IPLed it behaves much as it does when executing natively.

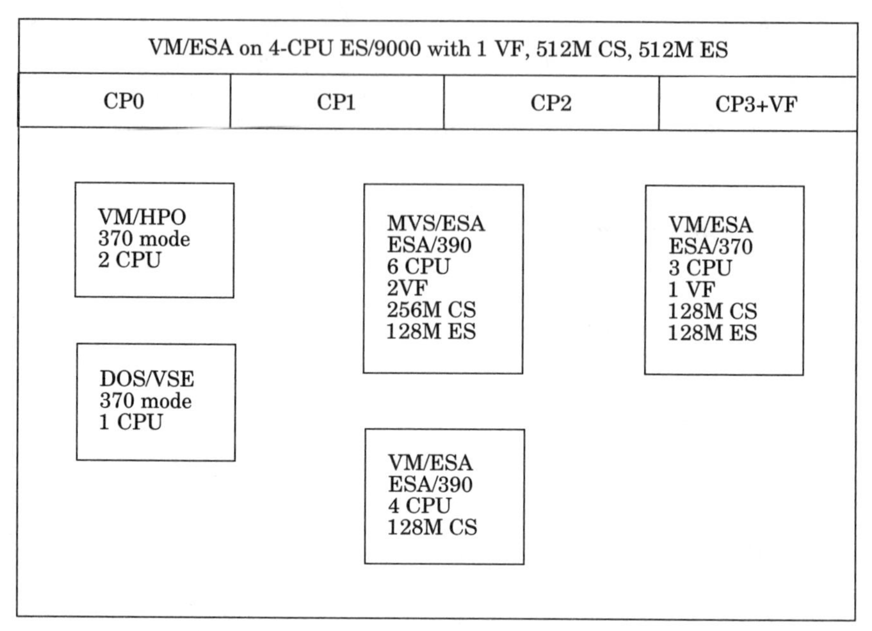

Fig. 17.2 Different CPU architectures on one CPU complex.

Attention is needed to handle assignment of resources: for example issuing a VARY ON command from the guest system console after a device is attached or defined to the virtual machine, and issuing VARY OFF before a device is detached. Additionally, a CP CLOSE command may be needed to close print files sent to a spooled printer device. This is done automatically when DOS/VSE runs under VM. For other guests it may be more convenient to print indirectly through a dedicated printer or VTAM printer acquired by the guest.

DOS/VSE Guests

The combination of DOS/VSE and VM is extremely successful. Approximately half of all DOS/VSE sites are said to run under VM. VM provides a better timesharing and program development environment than the ones available with DOS, and has better resource administration algorithms. Many sites use VM to let multiple test and production DOS/VSE systems run on the same processor. Comments about DOS/VSE applied equally to OS/VS1, the simple version of OS/VS (VS1 has been almost completely replaced by MVS).

DOS/VSE runs very well in virtual machines, and DOS/VSE can be made aware of VM via systems generation options. When its “VM options” are in effect, it cooperates with CP for better performance. VSE should always be defined with the VM option when guest operation is planned.

VM/VS handshaking

DOS/VSE uses VM/VS handshaking, described earlier in Chapter 8, to communicate with VM when a page fault occurs. CP reflects an external interrupt to VSE to notify it that the running task has taken a page fault; VSE places the task in page-wait and dispatches another ready-to-run task. When CP resolves the page fault, VSE is again notified, and VSE lets the task execute again.

DOS/VSE guests can be generated to operate in non-paging mode. In non-paging mode, it no longer acts as a virtual storage operating system. This reduces CPU overhead because the guest no longer performs redundant virtual storage management, issues fewer privileged operations, and CP no longer handles address mapping to a third-level storage.

Non-paging mode also eliminates the double CCW translation normally present when a virtual operating system itself executes in virtual storage. When non-paging mode is in effect, DOS application CCWs contain "real" addresses from the point of view of the guest system and are not translated.

DOS/VSE virtual addressing extended mode

DOS/VSE, and its successor VSE/ESA, can be generated for Virtual Addressing Extended (VAE), which increases the address space available to DOS applications. VAE cannot be used in non-paging mode, and is expensive when DOS/VSE runs in a virtual=virtual machine.

VAE is used when a single large VSE system is needed, for example, to support a large CICS teleprocessing application. Without VAE, DOS/VSE's limited address space size may require installations to split their DOS/VSE work into separate guests. VAE's enlarged address space can be used to merge multiple DOS/VSE guests into a single guest. The single guest may perform better than multiple handshaking guests, especially if the separate guests had to use disk files for data sharing.

MVS Guests

The most challenging guest to run efficiently is MVS. MVS is a very large resource consumer, and does not have a handshaking facility like DOS/VSE or VS1 to let it cooperate with CP.

Just as MVS systems running native require large amounts of real storage, MVS guests tend to have large virtual storage working sets, due to the complexity and size of the MVS operating system itself. Each MVS job, system task, or TSO user has an address space. Common storage areas are shared with other jobs, but a unique private area is provided for each user, as shown in Fig. 17.3.

In VM/SP and HPO, CP storage for segment and page tables can be saved

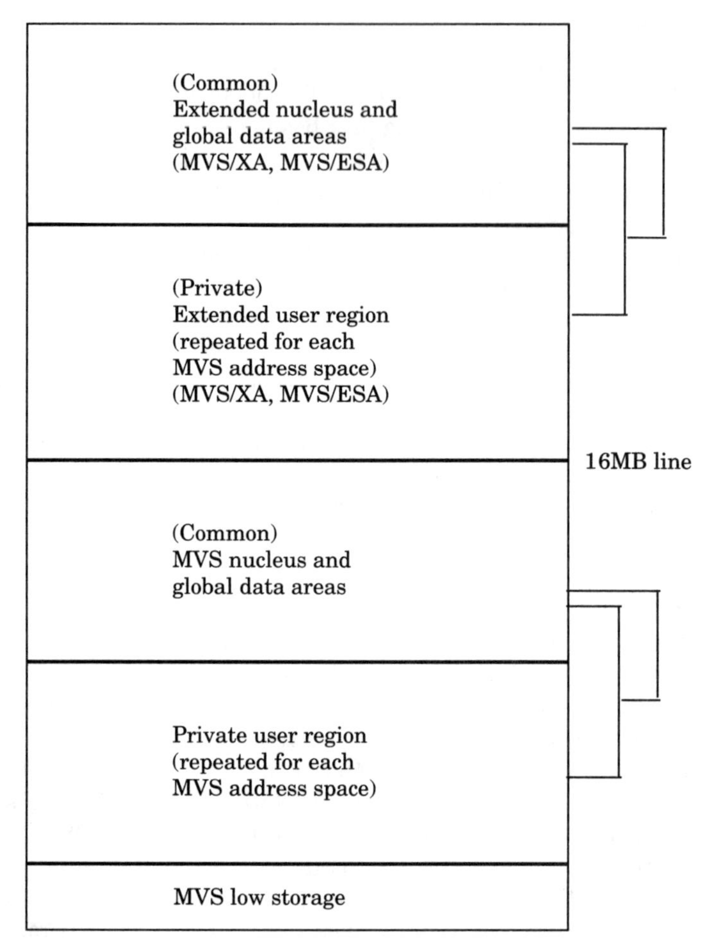

Fig. 17.3 MVS address space structure.

by telling CP the extents of the common areas. The `SET STBYPASS` command is used for this purpose for V=V MVS/370 guests; its parameters specify the ranges of the common address components.

CP remembers MVS's segment table origins so it can use previously translated mappings between first- and third-level storage. MVS switches between address spaces by changing the segment table origin register (STO, or control register 1) as it processes different applications. If CP recognizes the address in the STO register, it can use a previously created shadow table. Otherwise, CP builds one by resolving page faults.

Under VM/ESA, SIE is aware of third-level storage, and handles the correspondence between first and third-level storage automatically.

Virtual=real and virtual=fixed MVS

V=R and V=F storage dramatically improves guest system performance. They let CP bypass CCW translation, and for VM/ESA and VM/XA systems, use ES/9000 or 3090 microcode to directly implement guest I/O operations without CP simulation. It is almost essential to run a production MVS system as V=R or V=F. MVS guests under current VM systems can execute with almost-native performance.

The virtual machine must have OPTION V=R or V=F in its directory entry, and must IPL a device address, not a saved system, as shown below:

```
USER MVSSYS
OPTION V=R
IPL 129
CONSOLE 020 3270
DEDICATE 150 150
DEDICATE 151 151
```

Trends for Supporting Production Guest Systems

IBM has provided a variety of methods for providing optimal performance and reliability for production guest systems. The trend has been to increasingly coordinate CP software with microcoded features to provide enhanced guest operation. These methods have evolved over the years from VM's original implementation, to the point where current VM systems can run production guests with only negligible overhead.

The original VM/370 systems were unable to run guest operating systems efficiently. Code paths in CP were too long to emulate frequently executed privileged operations without noticeable performance degradation. This folklore about "VM overhead" for guest systems even came to confuse people about CMS interactive performance. While early VM was obviously an effective tool for testing operating systems, it was certainly not effective for running production OS/VS guests.

Providing adequate guest performance was the hardest technical challenge facing VM. Methods used to solve this have profoundly influenced VM development, and are used in other operating systems from IBM and other sources.

Reducing the cost of virtualization

IBM began to address these problems in the mid-1970's by providing VMA, described in "VMA and ECPS Microcode Assists in System/370" on page 341, beginning a trend of providing microcoded enhancements to CPUs to make VM run faster. This established the important principle that microcoded enhancements to System/370 could provide remarkable performance improvements with relatively little effort. In most environments, guest performance was doubled simply by adding VMA. ECPS, described earlier, and

SPMODE and PMA operation, discussed below, are cases of microcode developed for performance or functional improvement.

At about the same time, programmers at IBM and user sites wrote enhancements to CP to shorten high-frequency code paths, and to introduce special-case algorithms for formerly expensive operations. For example, shadow-table maintenance code was introduced by Robert Fischer at Texas Instruments, and widely distributed. "Fast-path" code to simulate privileged operations and redispatch the guest that issued it was developed at a number of sites.

Finally, with VM/XA, IBM completely generalized the function of virtual execution. Interpretive execution makes possible the multiprocessor guests and I/O assisted operation available under VM/XA and VM/ESA.

Host-guest cooperation

OS/360 had been shoehorned to fit into the early 360 storage sizes, so it very frequently saved transient data on disk. VM improved OS/360 performance by running it in large virtual machines and having OS refer to data in virtual storage instead of disk.

Users enhanced OS/360 to let it retrieve temporary information (typically, descriptions of currently executing and queued jobs) from storage instead of writing it to disk, just to read it shortly afterwards. If the data was still retained in main storage, the expense of writing out and reading the data back was avoided altogether.

Performance was improved even if data had been paged out. CP had shorter path lengths than OS/360 and DOS for doing I/O, and its 4K block size was larger than the small blocks the guest systems too frequently used. Consequently, CP could page data in from its paging devices more cheaply than the guest could read it from its own disks. Later, as main storage became less expensive and therefore available in larger quantities, buffering data in addressable storage became increasingly more effective. This was one of the first experiences of using virtual storage as a higher-performance alternative to application disk I/O.

Explicit interaction between CP host and guest was provided by *handshaking*. Guest-host handshaking was proven in the field by VM customers. OS/360 and VM were enhanced by Dewayne Hendricks (then of Southern Illinois University) to include handshaking similar to that eventually built by IBM into the official product.

DOS and OS/360 could be made to execute faster in virtual machines than they were able to execute on real systems. This demonstrated that an operating system could be made sensitive to executing as a guest with little effort, and with significant payback in performance and operational flexibility. Handshaking code made its way into DOS/VS and VS1, so they also executed efficiently under VM.

A special form of handshaking was devised by Robert Cowles of Cornell University, to let an OS/360 guest interact with the CP scheduler. Most guest systems run multiprogramming environment with both low and high priority work, and are also given favored CP scheduler status. A low priority compute-intensive guest application could absorb high-priority CPU service provided by CP to the detriment of CMS interactive users. By absorbing the guest's quota of high-priority service, it can also ruin the performance of high-priority guest applications.

The OS dispatcher was enhanced to tell CP the importance of the work about to be dispatched. Low priority guest batch work ran at lower priority than interactive CMS users and did not subtract from the high-priority CPU service to be provided by CP. High priority guest work (such as servicing communications lines or TSO users) ran at high priority.

Unfortunately, the MVS development organization never permitted handshaking software of either variety to be added to MVS, although conceptually it would not have been difficult. Years passed before IBM's VM, MVS, and hardware developers cooperated to provide near-native performance MVS guests.

SPMODE and PMA

Single Processor Mode (SPMODE) is a feature in HPO for MVS/370 guests running on dual-CPU System/370 systems. It causes VM to run in single-processor mode on a dual-processor, while MVS runs on the non-VM processor.

MVS then runs as an MP system, and the non-VM side of the processor runs in true supervisor state without simulation overhead. Since the guest runs "native" on the non-IPL processor, its "SYGENNed" I/O configuration must match the real hardware, and virtual devices must be defined to only be accessible from the VM-owned processor.

Preferred Machine Assist (PMA) is an extension to SPMODE for 3081 and 3083 CPUs running HPO. PMA microcode enhancements let an MVS guest run in supervisor state, even as a VM guest. PMA is in effect when a V=R user IPLs by device address using the `PMA` option, for example `IPL 360 PMA`. PMA guests run in supervisor state, and therefore experience no overhead executing privileged instructions. Even I/O instructions proceed without CP intervention, if executed for a device on a channel unknown to CP.

PMA microcode knows which I/O channels are defined in CP's DMKRIO (real I/O configuration). When MVS executes an I/O operation against one of CP's channel, PMA causes a privileged operation exception to invoke CP's I/O simulation. If the channel is not known to CP, PMA processes the I/O operations without software simulation. Guest devices should be placed on dedicated channels, and these channels omitted from DMKRIO. If an I/O interrupt comes back from one of MVS's devices while CP is running, PMA queues the interrupt until the next time CP dispatches MVS. Similar filtering for VM's devices is in effect when MVS is running.

PMA lets an MVS/SP (370-mode) system run with almost native speed. PMA requires a 308x or 3090 processor, and both HPO and MVS/SP. A benefit of PMA is "nondisruptive transition": if the HPO system crashes, the PMA guest can continue operation without VM. However, the MVS guest must be shutdown to reIPL VM and resume normal operations.

VM/ESA and VM/XA Preferred Guests

VM/ESA and VM/XA generalize PMA operation by letting a preferred guest execute on one or more CPU engines using any of 370, XA, or ESA modes. The I/O assist feature of ES/9000 and most 3090 models lets hardware completely emulate virtual machine I/O to dedicated or attached devices, thus sharply reducing the CP overhead needed to run guests.

VM/ESA and VM/XA can also dedicate real CPUs to V=R or V=F guests for their exclusive use, as shown for CPU 0 in the example below:

```
USER MVSPROD
OPTION V=R
MACHINE ESA 3
* Virtual CPU 0 gets a dedicated real CPU
CPU 0 BASE DEDICATE
CPU 1 NODEDICATE
CPU 2 NODEDICATE
IPL 900
...
...
```

A dedicated CPU is used only by the owning guest system. When the guest logs on, CP assigns a real CPU to the dedicated virtual CPU. All but one of the real CPUs in a system can be dedicated to guests; at least one is needed for CP and nondedicated guest use.

Dedicated CPUs guarantee guest access to the CPU, and reduce overhead by eliminating TLB and cache displacement when other users run. Unlike PMA, dedicated CPU guests need not run the same CPU architecture or I/O configuration as the host system. SIE intercepts occur only if the guest system requires a CP host service.

A dedicated CPU is wasted when the guest is idle, so it should only be used for guest systems that are expected to fully utilize the CPU. The `DEDICATE` and `UNDEDICATE` commands can be used to assign or remove a dedicated CPU from a virtual machine.

V=R Guest Recovery

VM/ESA does not support PMA's nondisruptive transition. The guest machine may not be running the same CPU architecture (it may be a 370 guest on ESA hardware) or I/O configuration as the host hardware, and therefore needs VM to run. However, the guest system can continue operation after a VM abnormal termination and restart (sometimes referred to as a "bounce"). Guest operations are suspended while the VM system is taking its storage dump and restarting itself. When VM finishes its restart process, it lets the V=R guest resume execution. To the guest, it looks as if its CPUs were placed in manual "stopped" state for the duration of the VM crash and restart.

Only DEDICATE and ATTACH devices remain connected to the guest after a restart. Devices supported by VM software simulation must be redefined when VM resumes. Consequently, guest DASD should be attached rather than minidisks, and the guest system console should be an attached 3270 console instead of a DIALed terminal or the logon terminal. The virtual CPUs themselves need not be dedicated to the guest.

The guest should be AUTOLOGed for the greatest flexibility. During normal startup, the guest can IPL a non-shared copy of CMS (since V=R userids cannot IPL saved systems). The PROFILE EXEC can DISABLE and ATTACH the guest system console, and then IPL the guest system residence volume, as shown in Fig. 17.4.

After a restart, the PROFILE EXEC is not reexecuted, since the guest continues running MVS. Commands to reestablish virtual devices can be issued from a separate userid if it is defined as the secondary console (SCIF) for the guest. For example, AUTOLOG1 is logged on by VM after every IPL or restart. If it is the SCIF console for an MVS guest named MVSGUEST, it can issue commands, as shown in Fig. 17.5.

ESA Exploitation for ESCON and Sysplex

System/390, announced in September 1990, included several important architectural enhancements. The new ESCON serial channel architecture and the *Sysplex timer* let several host systems more consistently share resources. For example, a device taken "offline" for service can be made of-

```
/* Define console and then IPL the guest system */
'CP DISABLE 100'              /* Take CP logo off our console */
'CP SLEEP 1 SEC'              /* Give it a chance to happen */
'CP ATTACH 100 *'             /* Grab it. It will survive a VM restart */
'CP DEFINE 3088 500 VTAM'     /* define a virtual CTCA to VTAM */
                              /* It will be GONE after a restart */
'CP SLEEP 1 SEC'              /* Give it a chance to happen */
'CP COUPLE 500 VTAM 500'      /* Connect our CTCA to VTAM */
'CP IPL 360 CLEAR'            /* Now IPL our SYSRES pack */
```

Fig. 17.4 Guest system PROFILE EXEC for autologged guest.

```
/* The system has just been IPLed or restarted after a crash */
'CP QUERY MVSGUEST'    /* Is MVS already up? */
if rc=0 then do        /* Yes: this must be a restart */
   /* redefine all devices lost during the restart */
   'CP SEND CP MVSGUEST DEFINE 3088 500 VTAM'
   'CP SLEEP 1 SEC' /* Wait long enough for DEFINE to complete */
   'CP SEND CP MVSGUEST COUPLE 500 VTAM 500'
  end
else 'CP XAUTOLOG MVSGUEST' /* A normal IPL: let the guest PROFILE */
                            /* do all the work */
```

Fig. 17.5 AUTOLOG1 PROFILE EXEC with statements for guest recovery.

fline to all systems at once; all hosts in a *Sysplex complex* are polled to ensure that none of them are actually using the device. Similar cooperation is now available for dynamically reconfigurable hardware: this is an important consideration for around-the-clock system operation. Previously, service had to be interrupted to add new disk drives and other devices.

VM supports ESCON channels, and also provides software emulation that completely emulates a Sysplex environment. Sites planning for conversion to Sysplex can run multiple MVS/ESA systems under VM, and test Sysplex without acquiring Sysplex timer hardware.

Comparison with Hardware Partitioning

For many years, the only way to create multiple system images was to obtain additional computer systems or run them in virtual machines. In recent years, hardware vendors have produced computers that allow multiple system images on the same system without VM. Amdahl pioneered this capability when it introduced the *Multiple Domain Facility* for its 5890 processors. IBM followed suit with *Logical Partitioning* (LPAR), made available by the *Processor Resource/Systems Manager* (PR/SM) feature of its 3090 models; a similar capability is now available on Hitachi systems. PR/SM is a standard feature of ES/9000 systems. To all external indications, PR/SM is in fact a VM kernel running a subset of a normal VM system. In effect, this part of VM has been moved into 3090 and ES/9000 microcode.

Some analysts have seen the availability of MDF and PR/SM as making VM unnecessary for guest system environments, especially since the announcement of ES/9000. MDF is only available on Amdahl CPUs, which are only a small percentage of IBM mainframe compatible CPUs in the field, and PR/SM on 3090 CPUs is only available to large IBM sites. By making PR/SM standard on all ES/9000 systems from its smallest rack-mounted to its largest raised-floor complexes, IBM has made hardware partitioning available to the entire 370/390 marketplace.

MDF and PR/SM will undoubtably let some guest-only VM sites eliminate

VM in favor of hardware partitioning, but significant differences in functionality and resource requirements keep VM the most attractive option for partitioning a computer system into multiple system images. VM/ESA enhances this capability by running every 370/390 architecture operating system provided by IBM on the same System 390 hardware.

Functional capabilities

A key difference between hardware and software-based systems is the flexibility they provide. Software is generally more flexible and adaptable than hardware with similar responsibilities. This is true when MDF and PR/SM are compared to VM.

Hardware partitioning provides none of the "VM-only" facilities listed in "Virtual machine facilities for guests" on page 415. This makes it inflexible: only a very small number of domains or partitions can be created in MDF or PR/SM, and each of them is restricted to using a subset of the physical resources installed on the real processor, and using the actual installed device numbers. With VM, an arbitrary number of pageable guests can be defined in addition to a limited number of high-performance guests.

Hardware partitioning lacks the tracing and debugging commands available under VM. Even taking a storage dump can only be performed via the services of the system being tested, or a standalone dump program. The former may not be possible, since it requires the guest system be functional. Standalone dumps crash the system being debugged.

This is an important issue for production guest environments, as well as for test systems. Under VM, a system programmer can issue a VMDUMP command when a guest experiences trouble, and let the guest continue operation. In native environments, a dump may be impossible without altering or terminating the failing system. If the problem is experienced during "prime" production hours, but is not critical enough to justify an outage, the dump may not be taken at all.

Debugging of the type easily performed under VM via TRACE, DISPLAY, and STORE can only be done without VM at the CPU hardware console, instead of at a guest system's console, and is extremely limited in function. Only one console is available for this purpose at any one moment, and it must be one of the processor's builtin consoles in the computer room. Since it would be too easy for the tester to accidentally disrupt a domain or partition belonging to someone else (like the CPU's production workload), this facility is essentially unusable for testing.

Resource requirements

Hardware partitioning via MDF and PR/SM have resource requirements that make them impractical for some applications.

Each partition must be allocated a fixed allotment of real and expanded storage. Procedures for reassigning storage are possible for some operating systems, but require manual intervention at the operator's console. VM provides similar storage assignment for virtual=real and virtual=fixed high-performance guests, but also assigns real storage to pageable guests on an as-needed basis.

One obvious advantage is that real storage can be overcommitted under VM, which is impossible in hardware partitioning. When the guest system is DOS/VSE, as most VM guest systems are, pageable execution is very effective, making the fixed storage assignment necessary under hardware partitioning expensive and unattractive.

Partitioned systems require dedicated channel paths to I/O devices because a channel path can be assigned to only one domain or partition at a time. VM granularity is at the device level, and certain devices, such as disk devices, can easily be shared. In hardware-partitioned environments, control unit channel adapters must be assigned to different partitions, and additional control units may be required to provide equivalent pathing.

The absence of virtual devices when using hardware partitioning means that additional devices must be purchased. Each domain or partition requires its own 3174 or 3274 control unit for operator's consoles. Instead of using virtual 3088s to connect test systems, a real 3088 may have to be purchased to provide network, GRS, or JES3 connectivity.

Summary

Guest operating systems under VM enhance the effectiveness of System /370 and 390 systems by providing a unique capability for system sharing not available with other architectures.

VM is very effective for production guest environments. VM provides flexible sharing of computer resources, especially for pageable guests, possible with any other available technology. For production guests, current IBM processors and VM versions provide near-native performance when operating under VM.

VM can also be used to test both operating systems and applications in controlled, non-interfering environments without risk to production applications. System test under VM provides longer and more thorough system testing, and allows testing in more varied configurations than possible with other methods.

Chapter

18

Summary

This book describes VM from several perspectives, starting with fundamental properties, discussing details of how they work, moving to the applications areas in which they are applied, and finally describing program and communication services VM provides applications. This chapter summarizes some of the key concepts discussed in the book, and shows how they shaped VM and other systems.

VM'S Key Concepts

The most obvious concept in VM is the virtual machine style of computing. This is a durable and extensible way to provide computing services. IBM has repeatedly and compatibly extended the virtual machine concept for efficiency and increased function.

For example, synthetic I/O instructions provided by DIAGNOSE and *BLOCKIO relieve virtual machines of details of hardware characteristics, and reduce effort needed to virtualize I/O operations. Other operations provide virtual machine features unlike those in real machines, such as inter-virtual machine communication, or the ability to create logical terminals. These capabilities were added without disruption to existing virtual machines, providing a continuous improvement in compatible function not provided in any other computing environment.

Virtual machines lead naturally to virtualization of other physical computer facilities: virtual storage, device-independent I/O operations, virtual disks, and other abstractions. The "data in storage" capabilities in current MVS systems, and the remote file systems available in VM, UNIX, and personal computers are consequences of letting logical resources be separated from the physical media used to implement them, as in a virtual machine.

The virtual machine concept has been adopted by other systems. For example, Microsoft Windows refers to its applications as running in virtual machines. The attractions of separable, noninterfering virtual machines, with architecturally defined interfaces to the real machine and each other, are increasingly compelling reasons for new operating systems to be designed with virtual machines.

VM simulates aspects of real computers in virtual ones, by performing hardware functions in software. This inspired creation of microcoded routines to provide software functions in hardware. Although the original intention was to improve performance, the ability to implement functions in either software or hardware has proven to be a valuable way to extend both real and virtual computer systems. Microcoded assists on real machines are analogous to DIAGNOSE functions available to virtual machines.

Virtual machines also encourage structuring operating systems into micro-kernels instead of large monolithic systems. If a carefully selected set of functions, including an efficient process dispatcher and message passing protocol, is placed in the kernel, then traditional operating system functions can be moved into user processes. This reduces the size of the operating system, making it easier to write, understand and debug. Operating systems with system functions in user processes are inherently more reliable than monolithic ones, since less code runs in the kernel without hardware protection from programming errors.

If processes implementing system functions are insulated from one another, as in virtual machines, then the resulting system is also more secure. VM shows that operating systems that partition users into virtual machines, and place security decisions in virtual machines as well, are extremely hard for intruders to penetrate.

Additionally, micro-kernel systems make it easier to configure operating environments with different replaceable parts. A security manager that exists independently of the rest of the operating system, for example, can be replaced with a new one as needed. In addition to CP, operating systems like *Mach* use the micro-kernel model to increase flexibility and reliability.

Micro-kernel systems require a robust and general interface for communication between separate parts. This, and the need to foster communication and data sharing between virtual machines, encouraged VM's development of increasingly general message passing protocols. VM interprocess communication protocols have evolved to connection-oriented, system-independent ways of connecting communicating processes and reliably transmitting data between them. VM lets virtual machines communicate on a peer basis with applications on other VM systems, MVS and other SNA hosts, Netware, and TCP/IP networks. VM is the first IBM system to provide this degree of universal connectivity.

VM's influence is clearly seen in LU6.2 and TCP/IP socket programming. Facilities like IUCV provide in software exactly what is furnished by a local area network: a high-bandwidth, reliable transport mechanism for transporting messages between processes.

Inter-process communication is the underlying structure beneath the increasingly important client-server style of computing. VM has used client-server computing since its origin, since it is the obvious way to structure applications that reside in separate machines, whether they are real or virtual ones.

Client-server computing is now available for personal computers and workstations, and is the fastest growing style of computing. VM participates naturally in this world. VM applications can easily be written to use universal protocols like APPC/VM and TCP/IP sockets in addition to VM-only protocols.

No other platform allows such easy access to inter-process and client-server interaction, usually at the CMS command or REXX level, or supports as many types of networking protocols. VM/CMS is unique in being able to communicate in RJE/NJE, Novell, LU6.2 and TCP/IP styles. VM/CMS enjoys more connectivity options, and makes them more programmable, than any other environment.

VM leads IBM's other environments in support of "open system" interoperability. "Workstation Synergy" enhancements, such as Internet-style communication via TCP/IP, LANRES/VM, and PWSF/VM continue to emerge on VM.

Another VM innovation, now expected of all modern systems, is conversational access to computer systems used as business tools by end-users. VM pioneered the idea that interactive computer systems could be an effective tool for end-users, not just programmers.

Systems accessed by end-users require an easily learned and retained command set. It must be possible for the casual or infrequent user to be productive without having to invest a great deal of effort in learning a computer system's idiosyncrasies. It is essential that the computer system protects the user from mistakes.

CMS has high ease of use, even without graphical interfaces. It often amazes me how people without computer training not only use CMS for their business, but actually build their own applications. The sensible CMS command language, its reasonable defaults, and its tolerance for incorrect usage remain exceptional. The continual invention of productivity tools like REXX and CMS Pipelines indicates how well VM is suited for end-user computing. Other systems with cryptic command languages, or ones that let you erase all your files with a single-character typing error, are simply not as good for end-users.

Systems for end-users also must produce short and consistent response times at a relatively low cost. Here, VM is the clear innovator: studies showing the economic benefits of sub-second response times were performed on

VM in the mid-1970s. At the time, standard response times for other interactive systems were measured in seconds instead of fractions of a second.

VM was designed to deliver short response times, and retains this traditional characteristic. IBM tracks the path lengths of key system functions, and expends considerable effort to ensure they don't balloon with new releases. VM/ESA shows that systems providing significant new function can be much *more* efficient than their predecessors.

Modern VM algorithms are flexible enough to be effective on both small and large platforms; other systems are not. VM fits without pinching on small platforms like 9370s or the P/370, yet can run on a high-end ES/9000 and take full advantage of the large system's capabilities. No other operating system has such a range of compatible performance.

"Large systems effect" reduces the effectiveness of operating systems being scaled up from simple to complex environments. Increased sophistication is needed in process scheduling, I/O, and memory management to support thousands of processes and arrays of I/O devices. It takes special consideration for lock management, serialization, and multiprocessor cache interference to effectively manage multiple CPUs. Linear running time algorithms, fine when 20 processes or users are on a system, break down when the same system has 2000.

VM has already been through the seasoning needed to avoid large system effect, for example, it no longer uses "order-of-*N*" algorithms for critical functions. The elegant generalized hash methods introduced with VM/XA are an example of this. VM can drive multi-CPU complexes under real workloads, with increases in usable computing power proportional to the number of CPU processors in a multiprocessor.

Other operating systems either do not fit well on small CPUs, such as MVS, or lack the resource management needed to work well on large complex systems, such as UNIX. VM works well on all sizes of computing system.

Conclusions

VM introduced system concepts that influence all computing systems, and continues to provide valuable services for programmers and end-users, and to users of guest operating systems. VM is one of the most flexible computing environments in existence, and continues to be used in new and innovative ways.

Glossary

ABEND Stands for "ABnormal END." Occurs when an application fails by violating an operating system or hardware rule, such as dividing by zero.

absolute storage Storage addressed without virtual storage translation or hardware prefixing.

ACCESS CMS command to make the files in a minidisk or directory usable.

ACI Access Control Interface, VM security mechanism to categorize users and grant or deny access to data or system functions.

ADT Active Disk Table, control block that describes an accessed minidisk.

address A number that is the location of a data item in a storage medium, usually the address of a location in computer main storage.

address space A range of addresses available to an application for programs and data.

AFP Advanced Function Printing, used to print documents with control over graphics and fonts.

AIX Advanced Interactive Executive, IBM's version of UNIX for mainframes, RS/6000, and PS/2 computers.

AMODE Addressing mode, determines whether a program runs with 24-bit addresses or 31-bit addresses under VM/ESA and VM/XA.

APL A Programming Language, a high-level language that lets programmers manipulate many data objects in a single expression. APL2 is IBM's current version of APL.

APPC Advanced Program-to-Program Communication, a protocol that lets programs communicate with one another on a message-by-message basis.

ASP OS/360 job and spooling system, predecessor of JES3.

ATTACH CP operator command that assigns a device to a user or to the entire VM system.

ATTN CP command that generates an "attention interrupt" to a virtual machine console.

AUTOLOG Command that logs on a virtual machine without a console.

AUTOLOG1 Virtual machine automatically logged on without a console at VM startup. It is used to AUTOLOG other virtual machines and perform startup chores.

AVS APPC/VM VTAM Services, program interface that converts APPC/VM protocol conversations into SNA traffic for communication with programs on a network-connected computer.

BITNET U.S. academic network, "Because It's Time"-net

***BLOCKIO** CP system service that lets programs perform asynchronous disk I/O by block number.

block paging Reading or writing a group of pages with a single I/O operation, instead of singly. Used in VM/ESA, VM/XA, and HPO.

cache A high-speed memory buffer that operates faster than a computer's normal main storage.

CSL Callable Subroutine Library, a library of programs that can be called from all VM languages to perform file and command operations in a language independent manner.

channel A special-purpose computer used to perform input/output operations.

CAW Channel Address Word, location in memory used in System/370 to contain the address of a channel program.

CCW Channel Command Word, an individual command in a channel program, e.g.: READ or WRITE a buffer.

CSW Channel Status Word, a word in storage in which the System/370 computers store status information describing the success or failure of an I/O operation.

CTC, CTCA Channel-to-Channel Adapter, a fast point-to-point communications line, used for inter-system communication between operating systems running on different real or virtual CPUs.

CTSS Compatible Time-Sharing System, early timesharing system that is the ancestor of all interactive computing systems.

cylinder The disk areas that can be accessed without moving the disk's read/write arms.

***CCS** Console Communications Service, protocol that provides bidirectional communication for terminal traffic between CP and virtual machines.

CDF Conventional Disk Format, CMS disk format used in early versions of CMS.

CISC Complex Instruction Set Computers, which provide individual instructions that perform complex operations. See RISC.

CMS Conversational Monitor System: the VM component used for interactive computing by end users.

CMSBATCH Batch job interface for CMS applications.

console Terminal used by an operator to manage a real or virtual machine.

CORTABLE VM/SP, HPO control block describing real storage.

CP Control Program. The VM component that manages the real computer hardware and creates virtual machines for users.

CP/67 Control Program/67. The virtual machine based interactive system from which current VM systems have evolved.

CPEBK Control block describing a CP internal task in VM/XA and VM/ESA.

CPEXBLOK Control block describing a CP internal task in VM/SP and HPO.

CPFMTXA VM/XA and VM/ESA program for formatting a disk drive's contents for paging and spooling.

CPFORMAT VM/SP, HPO equivalent of CPFMTXA.

CPI-C Callable Program Interface for Communications, subroutine interface for APPC/VM applications.

CPU Central Processing Unit. This term once precisely meant the instruction processing portion of a computer system. With multiprocessor computers, which have more than one instruction processing unit, this can mean either an individual unit, or (due to tradition) the entire computer system.

CRR Coordinate Resource Recovery, a protocol that lets applications commit or rollback changes to a database or file, in cooperation with other programs that may be connected to it via a network. Implements the policy. See "two-phase commit."

Count Key Data (CKD) IBM's standard disk architecture.

DASD Direct Access Storage Device, IBM's word for disks.

datagram An encoded message sent in Internet Protocol.

dataset MVS word for a file.

dataspace An auxiliary address space used in VM/ESA for data.

DCSS DisContiguous Saved Segment, a segment of storage locations that can be connected to a virtual machine to provide shared access to programs and data.

DDR Disk Dump Restore, VM utility for copying disk volumes, and making tape backups.

DEDICATE VM directory entry to assign a device to a virtual machine. Also, an option on the directory CPU statement to indicate that a CPU engine in a multiprocessor is assigned to a virtual machine.

DEFAULTS CMS command to list and set program defaults for common commands.

DEFSEG Define segment command to create a DCSS.

DEFSYS Define system command to create a named, saved system.

DETACH CP command that removes a device from a virtual machine.

DEVINFO, DEVMAINT Directory options that let a virtual machine execute diagnostic commands to real devices.

DFDSM Data Facility Distributed Storage Manager, lets VM systems provide file backup and archival server for PC-DOS, OS/2, and UNIX systems. Successor to WDSF/VM.

DFSMS Data Facility System Managed Storage, an IBM set of program products and methods for providing system control over data residency, backup, migration, and archival.

DFW DASD Fast Write, 3390 disk feature that caches writes to disks.

DIAGNOSE Instruction used to pass service requests from a virtual machine to CP.

directory Several meanings: the VM user directory contains the attributes of all virtual machines registered in a VM system. A directory is also a file space in a tree structured file system, such as provided by SFS, UNIX, or MS-DOS.

DIRECT, DIRECTXA Programs system administrators use to create a VM user directory.

DIRMAINT Directory Maintenance Program Product, IBM tool to simplify directory administration.

disconnect Several usages: disconnect a virtual machine from a terminal; disconnect a device I/O operation from a channel for efficiency.

dispatcher Part of an operating system that selects users for execution and gives them time slices of activity.

DLCS Definition Language for Command Syntax, files that define the syntax used to invoke a command separate from the command source code. A part of National Language Support.

DMK Prefix used by VM/SP and HPO versions of CP.

DMKBOX VM/SP and HPO module used to define the VM logo.

DMKCPE VM/SP and HPO module marks the end of the pageable nucleus.

DMKFRE, DMKFRET VM/SP and HPO entry points for acquiring and releasing blocks of storage.

DMKHVC VM/SP and HPO module implementing the DIAGNOSE instruction.

DMKIOS VM/SP and HPO I/O supervisor.

DMKPRG VM/SP and HPO program check handler module.

DMKRIO VM/SP and HPO Real I/O control block definition module.

DMKSNT VM/SP and HPO System Name Table, contains definitions of all DCSSes.

DMKSVC VM/SP and HPO module that handles SVC interrupts.

DMKSYS VM/SP and HPO system generation module, specifies the system name, page areas, and other options.

DMKVMI VM/SP and HPO module that handles IPL simulation.

DMS Prefix used for CMS modules and messages.

DMSCSL Front-end subroutine to invoke CSL functions.

DMSNGP CMS module for defining system options.

DOS/VSE Disk Operating System/Virtual Storage Extended: IBM operating system for small to medium-size 370 family computers.

doubleword 8-byte data item aligned on an address divisible by 8.

DPA Dynamic Pageable Area, pool of storage available for virtual machine and CP pageable storage.

DRAIN Operator command to stop a printer or punch when it has finished printing the current file.

DVF Dump Viewing Facility, VM component for reading storage dumps produced by VMDUMP command or system failures.

EARN European Academic Research Network.

EBCDIC Extended Binary Coded Decimal Interchange Code

ECF Extended Connectivity Facility, PC connectivity product

ECKD Extended Count Key Data, disk architecture used on newer IBM disk devices.

ECPS Extended Control Program Support: microcoded assist for the VM/SP and HPO control program.

EDF Extended Disk Facility, the disk arrangement used by the current CMS file system.

EDGAR A popular full-screen editor used in CMS before XEDIT

eligible list Lists of virtual machines not being given service, in order to prevent overcommittment of real storage.

ENDCMD A command attribute that invokes a module loaded as a nucleus extension at the end of each CMS command.

EPLIST Extended parameter list passed to CMS commands

ESA Enterprise System Architecture, the enhanced System/370 Extended Architecture used on current IBM mainframes.

ESCON The new channel architecture IBM introduced with ES/9000.

ETS Elapsed Time Slice, the period VM/ESA and VM/XA let an application compete for service before imposing a queue-drop.

EXEC Command shell language.

EXECIO CMS command that performs file I/O and other functions for EXEC procedures written in EXEC 2 or REXX.

EXECLOAD CMS command to load an EXEC or XEDIT macro into storage, so it can be executed repeatedly without being reloaded from disk.

EXECOS CMS command to execute an OS simulation program and then clean up the OS simulation environment by closing files and releasing storage.

EXEC 2 older EXEC language largely superceded by REXX.

FBA Fixed Block Architecture, disk architecture used on smaller IBM computers.

FIFO First In, First Out. A classic queueing order, also used when queueing lines onto the CMS program stack.

FILELIST Command to list collections of files

Filemode Part of a CMS file identifier that specifies the disk or directory a file resides in.

filename Part of a CMS file identifier.

filetype Part of a CMS file identifier that specifies the type of a file.

FINIS CMS command and internal function that closes disk files.

firmware Control logic built into a computer system, and implemented via microcode.

FORCE Operator command that forcibly logs off a VM user.

FRAMETBL VM/ESA, VM/XA control block describing real storage.

FREEMAIN OS macro to release a block of main storage.

FSCB, FSCLOSE, FSERASE, FSOPEN, FSPOINT, FSREAD, FSSTATE, FSWRITE CMS macros used to access disk files. The FSCB is the File System Control Block, the other macros use FSCBs to open, close, read, write and position files.

FST File Status Table, control block describes a CMS file's attributes.

FTP File Transfer Protocol, a component of TCP/IP that lets files be copied between networked computers.

FTPSERV Service virtual machine used to implement FTP

FULLSCREEN CMS, also called CMS Windows or CMS Session Services, the full-screen windowing interface in CMS.

fullword An integer occupying 4 bytes in memory.

GDDM Graphical Data Display Manager: IBM's graphics application package for mainframes.

GENCMD CMS command converts a DLCS file into a TEXT file that can be loaded into memory and used by applications.

Genmod CMS command saves a program image into a MODULE file.

GENMSG CMS command converts a message repository file into a TEXT file that can be loaded into storage.

GETMAIN OS macro to acquire a block of main storage.

gigabyte Approximately one billion bytes.

gigaflops One billion floating point operations per second.

Global CMS command specifies program libraries.

GLOBALV CMS command defines global variables that can be created, set, and referred to by multiple EXECs.

GML Generalized Markup Language, a text formatting specification language used to produce documents.

halfword An integer occupying 2 bytes in memory.

handshaking Process by which CP and virtual machines interact with one another for better performance. Usually refers to page fault handshaking.

HASP OS/360 job and spooling system, predecessor of JES2.

HCP Prefix used for VM/XA and VM/ESA CP component.

HCPBOX VM/XA and VM/ESA module used to define the VM logo.

HCPCALL VM/XA and VM/ESA macro for calling a subroutine.

HCPCPE VM/XA and VM/ESA module marks the end of the pageable nucleus.

HCPFRE VM/XA and VM/ESA entry points for acquiring and releasing blocks of storage.

HCPGETST VM/XA and VM/ESA macro for acquiring blocks of storage.

HCPHVC VM/XA and VM/ESA module implementing the DIAGNOSE instruction.

HCPIOS VM/XA and VM/ESA I/O supervisor.

HCPLNK VM/XA, VM/ESA module that performs the LINK command.

HCPMDLAT VM/XA, VM/ESA macro the defines module attributes.

HCPRELST VM/XA and VM/ESA macro for releasing blocks of storage.

HCPRIO VM/XA and VM/ESA Real I/O control block definition module.

HCPRPD, HCPRPI, HCPRPW VM/XA, VM/ESA modules used in the Access Control Interface.

HCPRUN VM/XA and VM/ESA module that actually runs a user by executing the SIE instruction.

HCPSBIOP VM/XA and VM/ESA synchronous block I/O parameter list for DIAGNOSE A4.

HCPSVC VM/XA and VM/ESA module that handles SVC interrupts.

HCPSYS VM/XA and VM/ESA system generation module, specifies the system name, page areas, and other options.

HCPVMI VM/XA and VM/ESA module that handles IPL simulation.

hexadecimal Base sixteen number system. hiperspaces—MVS/ESA feature for buffering data in expanded storage.

HNDEXT CMS macro that lets applications intercept external interrupts.

HNDINT, HNDIO CMS macros that let applications intercept I/O interrupts.

HNDIUCV CMS macro that lets applications intercept IUCV interrupts.

HNDSVC CMS macro that lets applications intercept SVC interrupts.

HOLDING 3270 status area indicator that the screen is full and contains an alarm message, and more data is waiting to be displayed.

HPO VM/SP's High Performance Option.

HSA Hardware Storage Area, main storage used by the CPU itself, and not by software.

HT Halt Typing immediate command.

HX Halt eXecution immediate command.

hypervisor An operating system, like CP, that runs other operating systems underneath it.

IBG Interblock gap, a gap of unused disk or tape media between blocks of data.

ICCF DOS/VSE interactive system.

ICU Integrated Control Unit, I/O adapters on some System/370 or 390 models used instead of separate control units.

IML Initial Microprogram Load, hardware operation to load microcode into a programmable device.

IMMCMD CMS command and assembler macro to let applications create immediate commands.

IMPCP Implied CP option, controls whether CMS passes unrecognized commands to CP if it doesn't recognize them.

IMPEX Implied EXEC option, controls whether CMS first searches for EXEC files before searching for MODULEs.

IMS Information Management System, an MVS database and teleprocessing system.

IMSG informational message, a CP option that controls whether status messages are displayed.

Interrupt An event that interrupts the normal order of instruction processing.

IOASSIST ES/9000 and 3090 feature that lets VM/XA and VM/ESA preferred guests perform I/O operations without CP emulation overhead.

IOBLOK VM/SP, HPO control block describing an I/O operation.

IOCDS I/O Control Data Set, disk file used by hardware to describe I/O configurations.

IOCP I/O Configuration Program, software program to create an IOCDS.

IORBK VM/XA and VM/ESA control block describing an I/O operation.

IP Internet Protocol, the underlying protocol of TCP/IP.

IPARML IUCV parameter list.

IPL Initial Program Load, load and operating system into memory.

ISF Inter-System Facility, an optional feature of VM to join several VM systems into a single processing image.

ISFC Inter-System Facility for Communications, lets workstations communicate with VM applications at extremely high data transfer rates

ISPF Interactive System Productivity Facility, dialog manager and editor system. Available under both CMS and TSO.

ISQL Interactive SQL, full-screen application tool for interacting with a SQL/DS database.

IUCV Inter User Communication Vehicle, VM message passing protocol.

JES2 Job Entry Subsystem 2, MVS subsystem for job and printout handling, descended from HASP.

JES3 Job Entry Subsystem 2, MVS subsystem for job and printout handling, descended from ASP.

Katakana Character set used for Japanese characters.

Kerberos TCP/IP security interface for distributed applications.

kernel Most fundamental, low-level portion of an operating system.

LAN Local Area Network.

LDEV Logical device, a software created emulation of a 3270.

LDSF Logical Device Support Facility, lets programs create logical devices.

LEXX the Live Parsing Editor.

LIFO Last In, First Out. A classic queueing order, also used when pushing lines onto the CMS program stack.

LOGOFF End a VM session.

LOGON Begin a VM session (sign-on to VM).

LPAR Hardware Logical Partitioning, available on ES/9000 and 3090s.

LRU Least Recently Used, algorithm for selecting storage locations to displace in cache and virtual memory systems.

LU Logical Unit, an SNA program or device.

luname The 8-character name associated with an LU.

LUW Logical Unit of Work, a unit of processing whose results can be committed or rolled back.

LU1, LU2, LU6.2 SNA protocols.

Mach An operating system for workstations that uses a micro-kernel architecture to re-implement many of the UNIX program interfaces.

MACLIB A library of program statements.

MACLIST Command to list MACLIB contents.

macro A pseudo-instruction that expands into a predefined set of programming statements.

MAKEBUF CMS command to create a program stack buffer.

MAXCONN VM directory entry option specifying the maximum number of IUCV connections a user may have open.

MDC Minidisk Cache, a VM/XA and VM/ESA feature that buffers disk contents in expanded storage.

MDF Multiple Domain Feature, Amdahl hardware option to run multiple operating systems on one computer.

megabyte Approximately one million bytes of data.

MFD Master File Directory, describes files on a minidisk.

microcode Programs imbedded in the computer, to implement the view of the computing system visible to its applications.

MIN Minimum cost algorithm, the optimal cost, but generally unimplementable virtual storage replacement algorithm.

minidisk A contiguous band of disk space assigned to an individual VM userid.

MIPS Millions of Instructions Per Second, a crude estimate of computer performance.

module A program unit.

MPVM Multiple session feature of VM/Pass-Through.

MRJE Multileaving Remote Job Entry, RSCS line driver.

MSSF Monitoring and Service Support Facility, hardware interface for maintenance functions.

multicast A TCP/IP message sent to multiple destinations.

MULTICS An early, influential operating system.

multiplexor A channel (or any device, actually), that processes multiple stream of data or requests in an interleaved manner.

MPG Multiple Preferred Guest facility of VM/XA and VM/ESA.

multiprocessor A computer system with more than one instruction processing "CPU."

multiprogramming Running more than one application on the same computer system.

multitasking Often used interchangeably with multiprogramming, however, is application use of independently executing processes.

MUSIC An operating system used for interactive computing, usually in academic environments.

MVS. Multiple Virtual Storage—IBM's other major operating system.

NAMEDEF CMS command to associate a logical name with an SFS file or directory.

NAMEFIND CMS command to look up entries in a nickname file.

NAMES CMS full-screen command to add to or edit nickname files.

NCS Hewlett-Packard's Network Computing System, an object oriented framework for creating distributed applications supported under VM's TCP/IP.

NCP Network Control Program, the software running in a 3745 (or related) communications front-end processor.

NDB TCP/IP's Network DataBase facility, lets a workstation client program issues SQL/DS database calls.

NetBIOS Novell LAN protocol, also supported by LANRES/VM.

NETDATA CMS command and data format that for transmitting files between CMS users. The protocol is also used by the TSO command XMIT.

NetView IBM's standard network monitoring product

NFS Network File System, a distributed file system protocol supported by VM TCP/IP.

NJE Network Job Entry protocol used by RSCS, JES2, and JES3.

NLS National Language Support, VM facility for displaying messages in multiple languages.

NOTE CMS command to send a mail file to another user.

NOTEBOOK CMS file that stores mail messages.

NSS Named Saved System, a sharable virtual storage location used to provide efficient access to commonly used software.

NUCEXT CMS command and macro to create a nucleus extension.

nucleus Most fundamental, low-level portion of an operating system, equivalent to kernel.

nucleus extension CMS facility to provide a logical extension to the CMS nucleus.

OCO Object Code Only, IBM's controversial policy to ship some software without source code.

OfficeVision IBM's automated office product suite, which provides, mail, calendar, document processing, and scheduling capabilities.

opcode The portion of a machine instruction that specifies which instruction it is.

ORB Output Request Block, XA-architecture control block for specifying an I/O operation.

OS/360 Operating System/360: the batch operating system from which MVS descended.

page frame 4,096 byte block of main storage.

page 4,096 byte unit of data, which may reside in a page frame or in auxiliary storage.

PARSECMD CMS command to parse command syntax according to a DLCS file.

pathlength The number of CPU instructions needed to implement a function.

PA1 Program Access 1, 3270 key, normally used to place a user in CP READ status.

PA2 Program Access 2, 3270 key, normally used to clear the 3270 screen.

PCI Program Controlled Interrupt, a channel command option to interrupt the host after a channel command completes, while the rest of the channel program continues.

PEEK CMS command to browse a reader file, and then log it to disk or discard it.

Program Function Key PF keys on 3270 terminals.

PING TCP/IP command to test the connection to a remote host.

Pipeline CMS Pipelines product, provides a superset of the UNIX pipe capability.

PLDV Processor Local Dispatch Vector, VM/XA and VM/ESA per-CPU dispatch list.

PLIST Tokenized parameter list for CMS commands.

PMA Preferred Machine Assist: HPO feature for a high performance MVS guest.

PMX Programmable Operator/NetView Message Exchange, lets the VM Programmable Operator interact with NetView.

POR Power On Reset, maintenance function performed to load a CPU's IOCDS into storage.

PORTMAP TCP/IP application to let programs look up the port numbers of programs they wish to communicate with.

Prefix Page The first 4,096 bytes of storage, used as a scratch pad for per-CPU processing, and contains architecturally specified data areas.

privilege classes Letters or numeric digits associated with a VM userid that specify which commands and DIAGNOSE functions it can issue.

privop Privileged operation, a supervisor state instruction that requires emulation for a virtual machine.

PROFS Prior name for OfficeVision/VM.

PROP VM's Programable Operator, used to automate responses to system messages.

PR/SM, LPAR Processor Resource/System Manager, logical partitioning: a method of using a single 3090 to run multiple environments without VM.

PSA VM/SP, HPO name for the prefix page.

PSW Program Status Word, describes the current state of the program running on the CPU.

push REXX instruction to LIFO stack a line into the program stack.

PVM Common name for VM/Pass-through.

PVMG VM/Pass-through Gateway into an SNA network.

PWSCS Programmable Workstation Communication Service, VM product that lets mainframe and workstation applications interact with one another on a real time basis, even if they are based on different communication protocols.

push REXX instruction to FIFO stack a line into the program stack.

QMF Query Management Facility, an end-user tool for formulating SQL/DS queries.

QUICKDSP Virtual machine option to prevent being placed in an eligible list.

Q0, Q1, Q2, Q3 VM dispatcher queues.

RACF Resource Access Control Facility, IBM security product for VM and MVS.

RCHBLOK, RCUBLOK, RDEVBLOK Control blocks describing real channels, control units and devices in VM/SP and HPO.

RDEV Control block describing a real device in VM/XA and VM/ESA.

RDRLIST CMS command to browse the set of files on a virtual reader.

READCARD CMS command to read a file from the virtual reader to disk.

reader Queue of input files, in simulated card reader format.

RECEIVE CMS command to read a file from the virtual reader. More general than READCARD.

reconnect logon to a VM session that was disconnected from a terminal.

REXEC Remote Execution facility in TCP/IP, implemented by the REXECD service virtual machine.

REXX The SAA Procedures Language, developed by Michael Cowlishaw and first implemented on CMS.

RISC Reduced Instruction Set Computers, use instructions that perform very fundamental operations in a single operation. See CISC

RJE Remote Job Entry, RSCS line driver.

RLDSAVE Option on CMS LOAD and INCLUDE commands to produce relocatable program images (programs that can be loaded into different storage locations at different times).

RMODE Residency mode, XA and ESA program attribute specifying whether a program may be loaded above the 16MB address line.

ROCF Remote Operator Console Facility) lets VM/Pass-through simulate a remote CPU's hardware console for distributed 4300 processors.

RPS Rotational Position Sensing, disk hardware feature that lets the disk drive disconnect the channel during rotational delay, and request its attention when the data approaches the read/write head.

RSCS Remote Spooling Communication Subsystem: VM product for job and file transmission between systems.

SAA IBM's System Application Architecture, a way of programming to provide consistency among IBM's multiple types of computing system.

SAD System Activity Display, hardware display of system utilization.

SAVEFD CMS command to save a minidisk's file directory in shared storage.

SAVESYS CP command to save virtual storage constants in a named saved system.

Scheduler Part of an operating system that decides which users to run.

SCIF Secondary Console Image Facility, VM facility that lets a single operator control multiple virtual machines.

SCOMDIR System Communication directory, used in APPC/VM to relate application names to their network addresses, and to provide additional information needed to establish connections.

SDF System Data File, VM/XA and VM/ESA spool file used to store named saved systems, trace data, class restructure data, and other system information.

SDLC Synchronous Data Link Control, communication line protocol used in SNA.

sed UNIX stream editor.

seek Position a disk's read/write head by moving it to a specific radius from the center of the disk volume.

semaphores An inter-process signalling mechanism.

SENTRIES CMS command to determine the number of lines in the CMS stack.

SFBLOK VM/SP, HPO Spool File Control Block, describes a spool file.

SFS CMS's Shared File System, which provides tree-structured file directories, remote file access, and per-file data update and access control.

SHARE Several meanings: the proportional amount of system resources allocated to a VM/XA or VM/ESA user, and SHARE Inc., the largest IBM user group.

SIE Start Interpretive Execution: Extended Architecture method of running a virtual machine user.

SIGP Signal Processor, instruction used for inter-CPU signalling in a multiprocessor.

SIO, SIOF System/370 I/O instructions.

SLEEP CP command to cause a virtual machine to "sleep" for a specified time, used for self-imposed wait periods.

SMART (RTM) IBM's Real Time Monitor.

SMS System Managed Storage, IBM's product suite and methodology for managing data in a comprehensive manner.

SMSG Special Message, CP command to send a line of data to a virtual machine running a VMCF application.

SMTP Simple Mail Transfer Protocol, TCP/IP mail protocol.

SNA System Network Architecture: IBM's network architecture.

SNALINK TCP/IP gateway to an SNA network.

SNANJE RSCS line driver to MVS or VM hosts connected via an SNA network.

SNARJE RSCS line driver to simple workstations connected via an SNA network.

SNA3270P RSCS line driver to 3270-family printers connected via an SNA network.

SNMP TCP/IP's Simple Network Management Protocol, used for network monitoring.

SPFBK VM/XA, VM/ESA Spool File Block, describes a spool file.

Spool Temporary disk storage area for print files and files transmitted between users.

SQL/DS Structured Query Language/Data System. IBM's relational database system for VM.

SRM System Resource Manager, CP scheduler component.

SRPI Server Requestor Program Interface for client-server applications.

SSCH Start Subchannel, XA and ESA I/O instruction.

subchannel Physical path between CPU complex and device.

SVC Supervisor Call instruction, used to request operating system functions.

SVM Service Virtual Machine.

SVMSTAT Directory option that identifies a virtual machine as an SVM for measurement purposes.

swapping HPO's name for block paging.

swap set The fixed size group of pages transferred in an HPO swap.

Sysplex A complex of coordinated System/390 systems sharing devices and a common timer.

SYSPROF System profile, an EXEC that runs whenever a CMS session starts.

SYSRES System residence device, disk volume containing the operating system.

TCP/IP Transmission Control Protocol/Internet Protocol, a popular networking protocol used on the world-wide Internet.

teletype An archaic terminal

Telnet TCP/IP component that lets users logon to remote computers.

TIC Transfer In Channel command in channel programs.

timesharing Interactive use of a computer shared by multiple users.

TIO Test I/O, a System/370 I/O instruction.

TLB Translation Lookaside Buffer.

tn3270 A variety of Telnet that provides 3270 emulation via a TCP/IP network.

TRACE CP debugging command that traces program execution.

TRQBK VM/SP and HPO Timer Request Block.

TRSAVE, TRSOURCE VM/XA and VM/ESA system trace data collection commands.

TSAF Transparent Services Access Facility lets VM systems share data, program, and communication resources.

SSCH Start Subchannel, XA and ESA I/O instruction.

TSCH Test Subchannel, XA and ESA I/O instruction.

TSO Time Sharing Option: an MVS subsystem used for interactive computing.

two-phase commit Used in CRR applications to commit a change only if all partners in a distributed application agree to the change and are able to perform it.

TXTLIB CMS object code program library.

UCOMDIR User Communication directory, used in APPC/VM to relate application names to their network addresses, and to provide additional information needed to establish connections.

UCR User Class Restructure, lets VM administrators assign different meanings to CP privilege classes.

UDP User Datagram Protocol, a low-level communications protocol available to TCP/IP programmers.

UNIX A widely used multiprogramming, multitasking operating system, available on many computer types.

VAE Virtual Addressing Extended, a DOS/VSE execution mode that lets DOS/VSE refer to more than 16MB of storage.

VARY Make a device, CPU, or channel "online" (available) to the system, or place it in "offline" status for service.

VAX A minicomputer made by Digital Equipment Corporation.

Vector Facility An ES/9000 and 3090 hardware feature for parallel floating point arithmetic.

V=R, V=F Virtual=Real and Virtual=Fixed: performance options for guest systems.

virtualization Emulation of a hardware capability in software or microcode.

VLSI Very Large Scale Integration, of electronic circuits.

VM Virtual Machine.

VMA Virtual Machine Assist: microcoded assist for VM/SP and HPO.

VMBLOK VM/SP and HPO control block describing a virtual machine

VMCF Virtual Machine Communication Facility, an inter-virtual machine message passing protocol.

VMDBK VM/XA and VM/ESA control block describing a virtual machine.

VMDUMP CP debugging command that produces a storage dump.

VMFBUILD Maintenance command used to build a CP or CMS nucleus.

VMMAP Virtual Machine Monitor Analysis Program: IBM's program for VM/SP and HPO monitor data analysis.

VM/Pass-Through VM product that provides networked terminal access and multiple session access to systems.

VMPRF Virtual Machine Performance Recording Facility: IBM's program for VM/XA monitor data analysis.

VMSHARE The SHARE-affiliated bulletin board used by many VM system programmers from around the world.

VSCS VTAM SNA Console Services, VM VTAM interface to CP.

VSE IBM operating system for small and medium-sized mainframes.

VS1 A smaller version of MVS with fewer functions and lower resource requirements. No longer widely used.

VTAM Virtual Telecommunication and Access Method: mainframe software component for communicating with SNA networks.

WDSF See DFDSM.

WLFS Workstation LAN File Services/VM, a client-server program product from IBM that lets VM work as a LAN file server for PC-DOS, OS/2, and UNIX systems.

XAMAP, XAMON Velocity Software products for performance analysis.

XEDIT The CMS text editor.

XAUTOLOG Command that logs on a virtual machine without a console.

XMITMSG National Language Support command for displaying messages.

370-mode The traditional System/370 architecture, with 24-bit addressing for an address space of up to 16 megabytes.

370-XA mode 370 Extended Architecture, with 31-bit addressing for an address space of up to 2 gigabytes.

Bibliography

IBM Systems Journal, Vol 28, No. 1, 1989

This issue of the *Systems Journal* contains two articles describing VM/XA-SP2 performance—VM/XA SP2 Minidisk Cache, and VM/XA storage management. These articles describe the design and performance of VM/XA's administration of main and auxiliary storage, and its use of 3090 Expanded Storage as a cache for CMS disk I/O. The articles are equally relevant for VM/ESA. In the same issue are: Large systems and Enterprise Systems Architecture, Enterprise Systems Architecture/370: An architecture for multiple virtual space access and authorization, Concepts of Enterprise Systems Architecture/370, and Storage Hierarchies. Although the articles are MVS-oriented, they represent IBM's thoughts on how large systems should be structured for growth and performance.

IBM Mainframes: Architecture and Design. N. S. Prasad. McGraw-Hill, 1989. (ISBN-0-02-949592-X)

This easily read description of System/370 and 370-XA architecture, includes description of CPU details, and of channel, control unit, and device interactions.

VM and the VM Community: Past, Present, and Future. Melinda Varian, Proceedings of SHARE 73, August, 1989, pp. 779-844.

VM Inter User Communication Vehicle, Part III, James McMaster, Technical Support, November 1990, pp. 32-34.

XEDIT User's Guide, James C. McMaster, McGraw-Hill, 1992.

The REXX Handbook. Gabriel Goldberg and Phil Smith III, editors, McGraw-Hill 1992. (ISBN 0-07-023682-8)

The REXX Language: a Practical Approach. M.F. Cowlishaw. Prentice-Hall, 1985 and 1990. (ISBN 0-13-708651-5)

Modern Programming Using REXX. Bob O'Hara and Dave Gomberg. Prentice-Hall, 1985 and 1988. (ISBN 0-13-579329-5)

Programming in REXX. Charles Daney. McGraw-Hill, 1992

IBM manuals

The titles and manual numbers cited here are the VM/ESA versions. Other VM versions have related manuals.

End user manuals

VM/ESA Introduction, GC24-5441

VM/ESA CMS Primer, SC24-5458

VM/ESA CMS User's Guide, SC24-5460

VM/ESA CMS Command Reference, SC24-5461

VM/ESA XEDIT User's Guide, SC24-5463

VM/ESA XEDIT Command and Macro Reference, SC24-5464

VM/ESA CP Command and Utility Reference, SC24-5519

VM/ESA CMS Utilities Feature, SC24-5535

Application programmer manuals

VM/ESA CMS Application Development Guide, SC24-5450

VM/ESA CMS Application Development Reference, SC24-5451

VM/ESA CMS Application Development Guide for Assembler, SC24-5452

VM/ESA CMS Application Development Reference for Assembler, SC24-5453

VM/ESA CMS Application Migration Guide, SC24-5454

VM/ESA Procedures Language VM/REXX User's Guide, SC24-5465

VM/ESA Procedures Language VM/REXX Reference, SC24-5466

CMS Pipelines

CMS Pipelines Tutorial, GG66-3158, J. Hartmann, L. Kraines, and J. Lynn, J. Gobeille, editors February 1990

CMS Pipelines Users Guide, SL26-0018

CMS Pipelines Toolsmith's Guide and Filter Programming Reference, SL26-0018

Internals and diagnostics manuals

VM/ESA CP Programming Services, SC24-5520

VM/ESA CMS Diagnosis Reference, LY24-5244

VM/ESA CMS Data Areas and Control Blocks, LY24-5245

VM/ESA Features Summary, LY24-5252

VM/ESA Diagnosis Guide, LY24-5250

VM/ESA CP Diagnosis Reference, LY24-5251

System administration

VM/ESA CMS Planning and Administration Guide, SC24-5445

VM/ESA CMS Administration Reference, SC24-5446

VM/ESA Connectivity Planning, Administration, and Operation, SC24-5448

VM/ESA Service Introduction and Reference, SC24-5444

VM/ESA DFSMS/VM Function Level 210 Overview, GC26-4703

VM/ESA DFSMS/VM Function Level 210 User's Guide, SC26-4705

VM External Security Manager Interface Macro Reference, SC24-5554

System installation and maintenance

VM/ESA Installation, SC24-5526

VM/ESA CP Planning and Administration, SC24-5521

VM/ESA Conversion Notebook, SC24-5525

VM/ESA Features Summary, LY24-5252

Communications programming

VM/ESA Programmer's Guide to the Server-Requester Programming Interface for VM, SC24-5455

VM Personal Workstation Communication Facility, GC24-5558

VM Programmable Workstation Communication Services Licensed Programming Specifications, GC24-5584

VM Programmable Workstation Communication Services Managing VM PWSCS, GC24-5585

VM Programmable Workstation Communication Services Programming VM PWSCS, GC24-5586

VM Programmable Workstation Communication Services, GC24-5558

VM Programmable Workstation Communication Services, GC24-5558

VM Programmable Workstation Communication Services, GC24-5558

VM Programmable Workstation Communication Services, GC24-5558

Workstation Data Save Facility/VM General Information, GH24-5232, January 1991.

Workstation Data Save Facility/VM Programmers Reference, SH24-5238, January 1991.

Workstation Data Save Facility/VM Administrators Guide, SH24-5234, January 1991.

LANRES/VM General Information, GC24-5618, January 1991.

LANRES/VM Planning and Installation, SC24-5619, January 1991.

LANRES/VM Administration, SC24-5620, January 1991.

VM/ESA Group Control System Reference for ESA, SC24-5531

TCP/IP Tutorial and Technical Overview, Frederic Debulois, GG24-3376, September 1991.

TCP/IP Version 2 for VM Installation and Interoperability, GG24-3624, March 1991.

Operating VM

VM/ESA Running Guest Operating Systems, SC24-5522

VM/ESA System Operation, SC24-5528

VM/ESA Virtual Machine Operation, SC24-5523

Advanced Function Printing PSF/VM Release 3.0 Installation and Use Guide, November 1989, GG24-3474.

System application architecture

Systems Application Architecture Common Programming Interface Communications Reference, October 1988, SC26-4399.

Systems Application Architecture Overview, October 1988, SC26-4331.

Systems Application Architecture Panel Design and User Interaction, October 1988, SC26-4351.

Systems Application Architecture: Writing Applications: A Design Guide, October 1988, SC26-4362.

Hardware features

IBM 3990 Storage Control ESCON Features Presentation Guide, GG24-3803, December 1991. Daniel Asselin, et al.

Extended Count Key Data and Nonsynchronous DASD I/O, GG24-3571, December 1991. Daniel Asselin, et al.

IBM 3310 Direct Access Storage Reference Manual, GA26-1660, November 1979.

IBM 3380 Direct Access Storage Description and User's Guide, GA26-1664, December 1981.

IBM 3830 Storage Control Model 2 Reference Manual, GA26-1617, November 1983.

VM/XA System Product Multiple Preferred Guest Guidelines, GG24-3285.

PR/SM: A Comparison of LPAR and VM/XA SP MPG, GG66-3112.

Index

ABOUT THE AUTHOR

Jeff Savit is Vice President and Manager of the VM Systems Programming Group with Merrill Lynch, where he and a staff of systems programmers are responsible for mission-critical applications supporting the company's trading activities. He is the author of VM AND CMS: PERFORMANCE AND FINE-TUNING (McGraw-Hill, 1991) and a contributor to the VM/ESA SYSTEMS HANDBOOK (McGraw-Hill, 1993).